Guiding Learning

READINGS IN EDUCATIONAL PSYCHOLOGY

Guiding Learning

READINGS IN EDUCATIONAL PSYCHOLOGY

Marvin D. Glock, EDITOR

John Wiley & Sons, Inc., NEW YORK LONDON SYDNEY TORONTO

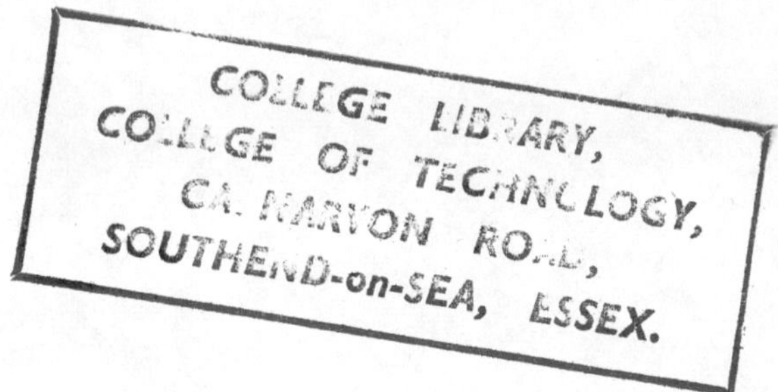

Library of Congress Catalogue Card Number: 71-142714

Cloth: ISBN 0-471-30830-7 Paper: ISBN 0-471-30831-5

Printed in the United States of America

10 9 8 7 6 5 4 3 2 1

To Carol and Sandra

Preface

This volume is designed to aid the student in the study of the various issues in educational psychology and their relation to the total teaching-learning process. A series of topics has been presented in a sequence that should provide help in integrating and relating their substance to the teaching task. These readings form the basic text for my course in educational psychology. The theme of this course is borrowed from the writings of Coladarci,[1] who maintains that the effective teacher formulates defensible hypotheses as a basis for teaching acts. The selections in this volume, augmented by additional readings, provide my students with suggestions for varied decisions that will be necessary for them to make as teachers.

The selections are, however, also useful as supplementary readings with a basic text. Texts of educational psychology by necessity tend to be synoptic, and are essentially amplified outlines attempting to survey the substance of this wide subject-matter area. Because this volume presents extended discussions of the issues of educational psychology by experts in the field, it should enhance the value of any text. Only a few of the ar-

[1] A. P. Coladarci, "The Teacher as a Hypothesis-maker," *California Journal for Instructional Improvement*, 2, 1959, 3-6.

ticles were published before 1960; as much as is possible in one volume, the forefront of thought in educational psychology is included.

The book consists of six parts and eighteen chapters. Each part and each selection is preceded with an introduction that not only points up the issues, but also integrates the various selections into a cohesive whole. References for additional reading are added in appropriate places. Some examples of the topics covered will be outlined here.

In Part One, excerpts from writings about schools, teaching, and learning were selected from the popular literature. These authors also emphasize issues, but they impart an urgency and concern clothed in pessimism that make the succeeding discussions relevant and useful. The student may wish to read the references excerpted in Part One in their entirety.

Part Two presents the integrating theme of the volume, the teacher as a decision maker. Readings that follow give him the basis for making defensible hypotheses. Acceptable goals must be selected and stated.

There is disagreement on the feasibility of behaviorally stated goals. In Chapter 3, Gagné discusses opposing points of view. In formulating and pursuing objectives there is the issue of an individual's right to determine his own destiny. Skinner and Rogers present opposing arguments here.

As he strives to attain his goals, a teacher will find that his decisions and his strategies are affected by his personal characteristics. In Chapter 4 the authors argue for the study and consideration of these traits. But learning is affected by more than the teacher's personality; the manner in which he structures his subject matter becomes a component of teaching effectiveness. Jerome Bruner called the professional world's attention to this component of subject matter. Little has been done empirically to give the teacher guidance in dealing with structure. The selections in this volume do emphasize some of the problems. Objectives, the teacher's characteristics, and the structure of the learning task all modify the guiding of learning.

There are various approaches to teaching. Chapter 6 presents an analysis of classroom verbal behavior, oral and written. A selection also appears on the merit of discovery learning compared to learning by other procedures.

No discussion of classroom teaching could afford to omit a consideration of classroom control. There is no adequate theory of discipline at present, but Ladd proposes some basic underpinnings borrowed from varied disciplines and industry. A good classroom climate is the sine qua non of effective teaching.

Historically, teachers have used various tools as aids. Certainly the blackboard is an important one. However, in this technological age we have more sophisticated help such as TV, tape recorders, and computer-assisted instruction. Bright and Atkinson outline possibilities and describe available hardware in Chapter 7. But there are arguments against the uncontrolled use of technology. Questions are raised by Mumford.

Teaching implies learning, and individuals who learn have varying characteristics and capacities. Readings on growth are included to emphasize that varied maturity produces individual differences that affect learning. There are many dimensions of individual differences that modify the input of the teacher; only a few can be presented. Some cognitive and affective traits are discussed in Chapter 9 of Part Three. Characteristics related to the Psychomotor domain could not be included here for lack of space.

Part Four emphasizes the change of behavior in the cognitive, affective, and psychomotor domains. (Part Three, on the other hand, presents information about characteristics of pupils in these domains that interact with teaching.) The importance of motivation is recognized. Likewise, if learning is to generalize and become useful, it must be retained and provision made for transfer. Readings by Reynolds and Glaser and by Ellis discuss aspects of retention and transfer.

We have now come full circle to the point of determining whether our teaching objectives have been realized. In Chapter 15 of Part Five there are readings that will aid the teacher in the measurement of specific objectives and in reporting student achievement. The issues in the chapter are two: the use of tests with the disadvantaged child, and defensible methods of marking and reporting. Because specific problems are incurred in testing minority groups, Fishman's suggestions are included here.

Since there has been public concern about the use and misuse of tests, it seemed advisable to bring out the bases of these concerns. Anastasi and Ebel do this with clarity and forthrightness in Chapter 16.

Recently, considerable attention has been given to criterion-referenced tests, in which a pupil's performance is compared with some performance standard. For example, we may want to determine whether he can read seventh-grade-level narrative material with understanding. This type of measurement is in contrast to norm-referenced tests, in which a pupil's performance is compared to that of others. In Chapter 17, Glaser argues that the criterion-referenced type will be most effective with instructional technology. Tyler describes the national assessment program and also explains how this type of measurement is employed.

Particular attention should be given to the free materials listed at the end of Part Five. Test-publishing companies and nonprofit organizations such as the Educational Testing Service have excellent materials available.

Part Six can be viewed as an epilogue. The authors suggest possible directions for progress in educational psychology. Rather than including selections on method and content of educational psychology at the beginning of my course, I include them after students have had an opportunity to study the thinking of the leaders in the field. Then they have a background to appreciate the different viewpoints as they are summarized and focused on the over-all substance of educational psychology. Because of the student's limited background at first, discussions such as these do not serve well as advance organizers. He is in a much better position to react intelligently and knowledgeably about the issues at the end of the course.

Criteria for Selecting Papers

Several criteria were adhered to in selecting the papers for this book:

1. It was necessary for the subject of each paper to fit into the organizational plan for presenting the chosen topics of educational psychology.
2. The paper had to be substantive.
3. Papers were required to have clear implications for learning. The focus of the entire book is on the improvement of learning.
4. Whenever possible, recent papers concerning important issues and written by authors recognized for their significant contributions to the field were selected.
5. A number of papers were chosen to illustrate research methodology in educational psychology.
6. Other criteria having been met, a careful attempt was made to select papers that were interesting and had clarity of style.

Marvin D. Glock
Ithaca, New York, 1970

Acknowledgments

I express appreciation to the authors and publishers for permission to reprint the papers in this volume.

These articles represent a portion of those assigned to students in the editor's educational psychology course. Students' critical comments were most helpful in the selection of these specific papers. I especially thank these students for their helpful suggestions. I am also appreciative of the suggestions of Dr. Conrad Reichert and Beverly Lederman.

Finally, I thank my wife, who assumed responsibility for the arduous task of typing and assembling the manuscript.

M. D. G.

Contents

Guiding Learning

READINGS IN EDUCATIONAL PSYCHOLOGY

PART I

Learning in Our Schools

Part One consists of a number of quotes from a series of descriptive books at what goes on in our schools. The authors of these volumes were either teachers or observers who had spent extended periods of time in the classroom. Their comments focus on many of the issues presented in the articles in this volume.

A course in educational psychology should not be devoted to methods; nevertheless, teachers must see the relevance of the literature in the field if it is to have an impact on their behavior. It must give them a basis for formulating teaching hypotheses.

Philip Jackson describes the various climates of the classroom. Both he and John Holt delineate the problems of motivating pupils in the school setting. Here, attendance is compulsory and masses of humanity are crowded together in a small space for long periods of time.

Kaufmann and Holt emphasize the importance of a child's involvement in learning; it is important that they help to make decisions about what and how they will learn. Children want to learn when it satisfies their needs.

Jackson suggests that a teacher must have certain qualities in order to function in the classroom. Often affective rather than cognitive characteristics are the more important in enabling him to cope with an energetic and unpredictable group of youngsters. But Kohl emphasizes that affective characteristics alone cannot replace the need for a teacher to have a thorough understanding of the organization and structure of his subject matter. No longer can he teach by rote; relationships among facts, principles, and concepts are too important.

The teacher is further challenged because of the many individual differences among children. Kaufmann and Kohl mention only a few of these varied characteristics; there are many. Holt emphasizes the importance of a child's self-concept. The expectations that a child has of his ability to a large degree determine his achievement. Furthermore, the teacher plays an important role in developing and changing a child's feelings about himself. Concern is expressed about teachers' expectations of children. Many teachers appear to prize docility, conformity, and the giving of expected answers. They appear to be overly content-centered, rather than child-centered.

A number of writers fear that evaluation isn't being used to pupils' advantage. Children don't fail before they come to school. Why should there be so many failures in school? They fail not only in their subject matter, but even more unfortunately as developing persons. The chief purpose of evaluation is to aid teaching and learning. All too often its focus is on passing and failing. Many children cannot, therefore, perceive it as a helpful process.

Popular books about education tend to be very critical. Nevertheless, the reader who completes the volumes from which these passages were excerpted, should gain a healthy respect for the power and potential of our schools to help children grow. The authors' distress is caused by their impatience with the slow progress of schools in utilizing their potential.

CHAPTER 1

Pupils, Teachers, and Classrooms

"School is a place where tests are failed and passed, where amusing things happen, where new insights are stumbled upon, and skills acquired. But it is also a place in which people sit, and listen, and wait, and raise their hands, and pass out paper, and stand in line, and sharpen pencils. School is where we encounter both friends and foes, where imagination is unleashed and misunderstanding brought to ground. But it is also a place in which yawns are stifled and initials scratched on desktops, where milk money is collected and recess lines are formed. Both aspects of school life, the celebrated and the unnoticed, are familiar to all of us, but the latter, if only because of its characteristic neglect, seems to deserve more attention than it has received to date from those who are interested in education."[1]

". . . aside from sleeping, and perhaps playing, there is no other activity that occupies as much of the child's time as that involved in attending school. Apart from the bedroom (where he has his eyes closed most of the time) there is no single enclosure in which he spends a longer time than

[1] Philip Jackson, *Life in Classrooms.* New York: Holt, Rinehart & Winston, 1968, p. 4.

he does in the classroom. From the age of six onward he is a more familiar sight to his teacher than to his father, and possibly even to his mother."[2]

"There is an important fact about a student's life that teachers and parents often prefer not to talk about, at least not in front of students. This is the fact that young people have to be in school, whether they want to be or not. In this regard students have something in common with the members of two other of our social institutions that have involuntary attendance: prisons and mental hospitals. The analogy, though dramatic, is not intended to be shocking, and certainly there is no comparison between the unpleasantness of life for inmates of our prisons and mental institutions, on the one hand, and the daily travails of a first or second grader, on the other. Yet the school child, like the incarcerated adult, is, in a sense, a prisoner. He too must come to grips with the inevitability of his experience. He too must develop strategies for dealing with the conflict that frequently arises between his natural desires and interests on the one hand and institutional expectations on the other."[3]

For some children school is a happy place where they feel secure and accepted. Thomas Wolfe praised his teacher, Mrs. Roberts, for memorable and happy school days.

"During the years Mrs. Roberts taught me she exercised an influence that is inestimable on almost every particular of my life and thought. With the other boys of my age I know she did the same. We turned instinctively to this lady for her advice and direction and we trusted it unfalteringly. I think that kind of relation is one of the profoundest experiences of anyone's life—I put the relation of a fine teacher to a student just below the relation of a mother to her son and I don't think I could say more than this."[4]

But other children find school to be a prison. They discover no interest in the classroom. The experiences seem to have little value for them.

"Imagine yourself thirteen summers young in a world that stretched as far as the eye could see, but no further: a world of boring visits to ancient aunts and Sunday drives and triple features plus serials and two cartoons of baseball in the streets and zoos and jawbreakers and Indian gum and penmanship and firecrackers and Tarzan and the Scarecrow. It's morning. Off to the grey prison, school, and the heavy books, the

[2] Ibid., p. 5.

[3] Ibid., p. 9.

[4] Thomas Wolfe, "A Letter of Gratitude and Indebtedness." In Claude M. Fuess and Emory S. Basford (Eds.), *Unseen Harvests*. New York: MacMillan, 1947, p. 438.

ceramic women with their fiery eyes, and the clockhands that never moved. One o'clock. A century later, two o'clock. Two centuries later, three o'clock. Saved by the bell!"[5]

"Thus teachers feel, as I once did, that their interests and their students' are fundamentally the same. I used to feel that I was guiding and helping my students on a journey that they wanted to take but could not take without my help. I knew the way looked hard, but I assumed they could see the goal almost as clearly as I and that they were almost as eager to reach it. It seemed very important to give students this feeling of being on a journey to a worthwhile destination. I see now that most of my talk to this end was wasted breath. Maybe I thought the students were in my class because they were eager to learn what I was trying to teach, but they knew better. They were in school because they had to be, and in my class either because they had to be, or because otherwise they would have had to be in another class, which might even be worse."[6]

"We need to ask more often of everything we do in school, 'Where are we trying to get, and is this thing we are doing helping us to get there?' Do we do something because we want to help the children and can see that what we are doing is helping them? Or do we do it because it is inexpensive or convenient for school, teachers, administrators? Or because everyone else does it? We must beware of making a virtue of necessity, and cooking up high-sounding educational reasons for doing what is done really for reasons of administrative economy or convenience. The still greater danger is that, having started to do something for good enough reasons, we may go on doing it stubbornly and blindly, as I did that day, unable or unwilling to see that we are doing more harm than good."[7]

"School should be a place where children learn what they most want to know, instead of what we think they ought to know. The child who wants to know something remembers it and uses it once he has it; the child who learns something to please or appease someone else forgets it when the need for pleasing or the danger of not appeasing is past. This is why children quickly forget all but a small part of what they learn in school. It is of no use or interest to them; they do not want, or expect, or even intend to remember it. The only difference between bad and good students in this respect is that bad students forget right away, while the good students are careful to wait until after the exam. If for no other

[5] Charles Beaumont, *Remember? Remember?* New York: Macmillan, 1963, p. 49.

[6] John Holt, *How Children Fail*, New York: Pitman Publishing Corporation, 1964, p. 23.

[7] Holt, *How Children Fail*, op. cit., p. 23.

reason, we could well afford to throw out most of what we teach in school because the children throw out almost all of it anyway."[8]

But determining what children are to learn and how is only the first step. These carefully selected and formulated objectives must be achieved within a climate unmatched anywhere in our society. Teachers and pupils must live and work together for a large part of their waking hours.

"There is a social intimacy in school that is unmatched elsewhere in our society. Buses and movie theaters may be more crowded than classrooms, but people rarely stay in such densely populated settings for extended periods of time and, while there, they usually are not expected to concentrate on work or to interact with each other. Even factory workers are not clustered as close together as students in a standard classroom. Indeed, imagine what would happen if a factory the size of a typical elementary school contained three or four hundred adult workers. In all likelihood the unions would not allow it. Only in schools do thirty or more people spend several hours each day literally side by side. Once we leave the classroom we seldom again are required to have contact with so many people for so long a time."[9]

However, children do learn in this kind of climate if the teacher makes it possible for them to learn.

"What is essential is to realize that children learn independently, not in bunches; that they learn out of interest and curiosity, not to please or appease the adults in power; and that they ought to be in control of their own learning, deciding for themselves what they want to learn and how they want to learn it."[10]

"There is a premium on conformity, and on silence. Enthusiasm is frowned upon, since it is likely to be noisy. . . . Yesterday, for example, we were discussing 'The fault, dear Brutus, lies not in our stars/ But in ourselves that we are underlings.' I had been trying to relate Julius Caesar to their own experiences. Is this true? I asked. Are we really masters of our fate? Is there such a thing as luck? A small boy in the first row, waving his hand frantically: 'Oh, call on me, please, please call on me!' was propelled by the momentum of his exuberant arm smack out of his seat and fell on the floor. Wild laughter. Enter McHabe. That after-

[8] Holt, *How Children Fail*, op. cit., p. 175.

[9] Jackson, p. 8.

[10] John Holt, *How Children Learn*, New York: Pitman Publishing Corporation, 1967, p. 185.

noon, in my letter-box, it had come to his attention that my 'control of the class lacked control.'

But I had made that little boy think. I started something in him that emerged as an idea. I got him excited by a concept. And that's a lot!"[11]

What are the characteristics of a teacher that enable him to work in a crowded room whose occupants are required to be there and to learn things not of their choosing?

"The personal qualities enabling teachers to withstand the demands of classroom life have never been adequately described. But among those qualities is surely the ability to tolerate the enormous amount of ambiguity, unpredictability, and occasional chaos created each hour by 25 or 30 not-so-willing learners. What is here called the conceptual simplicity evident in teachers' language may be related to that ability. If teachers sought a more thorough understanding of their world, insisted on greater rationality in their actions, were completely open-minded in their consideration of pedagogical choices, and profound in their view of the human condition, they might well receive greater applause from intellectuals, but it is doubtful that they would perform with greater efficiency in the classroom. On the contrary, it is quite possible that such paragons of virtue, if they could be found to exist, would actually have a deuce of a time coping in any sustained way with a class of third graders or a play-yard full of nursery school tots."[12]

Of course, what effect a teacher has on learning is also dependent on the structuring of the substance of what is being taught.

"The need for elementary teachers who are serious-thinking adults, who explore and learn while they teach, who know that to teach young children mathematics, history, or literature isn't to empty these subjects of content or complexity but to reduce and present them in forms which are accurate, honest, and open to development and discovery, and, therefore, require subtle understanding and careful work, cannot be exaggerated. The time has passed when the school-marm, equipped to teach the three R's by rote and impose morality by authority, has something useful and important to give children."[13]

[11] Bel Kaufman, *Up The Down Staircase,* Englewood Cliffs, New Jersey: Prentice-Hall, Inc., 1964, pp. 67–77.

[12] Jackson, op. cit., p. 149.

[13] Herbert Kohl, *Thirty-Six Children,* New York: New American Library, 1968, p. 54.

Whatever a teacher may do in guiding learning, it will be modified by the varied characteristics of his pupils. Children differ in many ways and do not learn equally well from a given teaching approach.

"So far most of them are still a field of faces, rippling with every wind, but a few are beginning to emerge.

"There is Lou Martin, the class comedian, whose forte is facial expressions. No one can look more crestfallen over unprepared homework: hand clasped to brow, knees buckling, shoulder sagging with remorse, he is a penitent to end all penitents . . . I'm beginning to learn some of their names and to help them—if they would let me. But I am still the Alien and the Foe; I have not passed the test, whatever it is.

"I'm a foe to Eddie Williams because my skin is white; to Joe Ferone because I am a teacher; to Carrie Paine because I am attractive.

"Eddie uses the grievance of his color to browbeat the world.

"Joe is flunking every subject, though he is very bright. He has become a bone of contention between McHabe and me because I believed in his innocence in the stolen wallet incident. I trust him, and he-he keeps watching me, ready to spring at the first false move I make.

"Carrie is a sullen, cruelly homely girl, hiding and hating behind a wall of fat.

"Harry Kagan is a politician and apple-polisher. He is running for G.O. president, and I'm afraid he'll be elected.

"Linda Rosen is an over-ripe under-achiever, bursting with hormones.

"And pretty Alice Blake, pale with love, lost in a dream of True Romances, is vulnerable and committed as one can be only at 16.

"She feels deeply, I'm sure, but can translate her feelings only into the cheap cliches she's been brought up on.

"Then there is Rusty, the woman-hater.

"And a quiet defeated-looking Puerto Rican boy, whose name I can't even remember.

"These children have been nourished on sorry scraps, on shabby facsimiles, and there is no one—not at home, not in school—who has not shortchanged them.

"You know, I've just realized there is not even a name for them in the English language. 'Teen-agers,' 'Youngsters,' 'Students,' 'Kids,' Young adults,' 'Children'—these are inappropriate, offensive, stilted, patronizing or inaccurate. On paper they are our 'Pupil-load'; on lecture platform they are our 'Youngsters'—but what is their proper name?

"The frightening thing is their unquestioning acceptance of whatever is taught to them by anyone in front of the room. This has nothing to do with rebellion against authority; they rebel, all right, and loudly. But it doesn't occur to them to think."[14]

Mr. Kohl talks about the individual differences—a white teacher facing a sea of black faces on that first day of school.

"My alarm clock rang at seven-thirty, but I was up and dressed at seven. It was only a fifteen-minute bus ride from my apartment on 90th Street and Madison Avenue to the school on 119th Street and Madison.

"There had been an orientation session the day before. I remembered the principal's words. 'In times like these, this is the most exciting place to be, in the midst of ferment and creative activity. Never has teaching offered such opportunities . . . we are together here in a difficult situation. They are not the easiest children, yet the rewards are so great—a smile, loving concern, what an inspiration, a felicitous experience.'

"I remembered my barren classroom, no books, a battered piano, broken windows and desks, falling plaster, and an oppressive darkness.

"I was handed a roll book with thirty-six names and thirty-six cumulative record cards, years of judgments already passed upon the children, their official personalities. I read through the names, twenty girls and sixteen boys, the 6-1 class, though I was supposed to be teaching the fifth grade and had planned for it all summer. Then I locked the record cards away in the closet. The children would tell me who they were. Each child, each new school year, is potentially many things, only one of which the cumulative record card documents. It is amazing how 'emotional' problems can disappear, how the dullest child can be transformed into the keenest and the brightest into the most ordinary when the prefabricated judgments of other teachers are forgotten.

The children entered at nine and filled up the seats. They were silent and stared at me. It was a shock to see thirty-six black faces before me. No preparation helped. It is one thing to be liberal and talk, another to face something and learn that you're afraid.

"The children sat quietly, expectant. Everything must go well; we must like each other."[15]

Children vary in so many ways. One of the greatest differences lies in their cognitive styles.

"The poor thinker dashes madly after an answer; the good thinker takes his time and looks at the problem. Is the difference merely a matter of a skill in thought, a technique which, with ingenuity and luck, we might

[14] Kaufman, op. cit., pp. 75–76.

[15] Kohl, op. cit., p. 13.

teach and train into children? I'm afraid not. The good thinker can take his time because he can tolerate uncertainty, he can stand not knowing. The poor thinker can't stand not knowing; it drives him crazy."[16]

Another important characteristic that varies among children is their self-image. Pupils with negative self-concepts can't learn because to learn would be inconsistent with the manner in which they view themselves.

"Incompetence has one other advantage. Not only does it reduce what others expect and demand of you, it reduces what you expect or even hope for yourself. When you set out to fail, one thing is certain—you can't be disappointed. As the old saying goes, you can't fall out of bed when you sleep on the floor."[17]

The extent to which a pupil is motivated also affects his learning. On page 415 of this volume, White discusses the competence motive. This is the basis for motivation that teachers would hope to achieve.

"If children could do more of the kind of work I have described and suggested, they would get, not just knowledge, but skill. This is important to a child. To be able to do something well, to get visible results, gives him a sense of his own being and worth which he can never get from regular schoolwork, from teacher-pleasing, no matter how good he is at it. There is too little opportunity for this in school. In my own high-priced and high-powered education, there was virtually none; until I was about thirty, the only things I ever made were some model airplanes, and those out of school, and only when I was nine and ten. This was, and is, a mistake. Maria Montessori showed, among other things, that children could make, and like to make, movements that are careful and precise, as well as movements that are exuberant. Some of the time, at least, children like to be careful, when it is the work or the situation, and not some grownup, that demands it. We should give them many more opportunities and ways to use and develop skill and precision."[18]

Children should learn knowledge, understanding, thinking, and problem solving in school. But sometimes the teacher gets in the way of this learning.

"In the midst of all this, there came a vivid example of the kind of thing we say in school that makes no sense, that only bewilders and confuses the thoughtful child who tries to make sense out of it. The teacher,

[16] Holt, *How Children Fail*, op cit., p. 47.
[17] Holt, *How Children Fail*, op. cit., p. 59.
[18] Holt, *How Children Learn*, op. cit., p. 146.

whose specialty, by the way, was English, had told these children that a verb is a word of action—which is not always true. One of the words she asked was 'dream.' She was thinking of the noun, and apparently did not remember that 'dream' can as easily be a verb. One little boy, making a pure guess, said it was a verb. Here the teacher to be helpful, contributed one of those 'explanations' that are so much more hindrance than help. She said, 'But a verb has to have action; can you give me a sentence, using "dream," that has action?' The child thought a bit, and said, 'I had a dream about the Trojan War.' Now it's pretty hard to get much more action than that. But the teacher told him he was wrong, and he sat silent, with an utterly baffled and frightened expression on his face. She was so busy thinking about what she wanted him to say, she was so obsessed with that right answer hidden in her mind, that she could not think about what he was really saying and thinking, could not see that his reasoning was logical and correct, and that the mistake was not his, but hers."[19]

When a child feels that he must give the answer a teacher wants or please the teacher in other ways, it precludes his development.

"The really able thinkers in our class turn out to be, without exception, children who don't feel so strongly the need to please grownups. Some of them are good students, some not so good; but good or not, they don't work to please us, but to please themselves."[20]

Although it may appear that all of the teacher's concerns for learning lie in the cognitive domain–concept development, improving problem-solving abilities, and the like—the teacher is very interested in pupils attitudes, values, interests, and personal-social adjustment. These components lie in the affective domain. Not only do educational objectives include goals to change and develop these components, but also, the teacher realizes that they interact with the cognitive domain. Prejudices, bias, lack of interest, deep anxieties, and a negative self-concept all interfere with the learning of concepts and the development of thinking.

"Teachers and schools tend to mistake good behavior for good character. What they prize above all else is docility, suggestibility; the child who will do what he is told; or even better, the child who will do what is wanted without even having to be told. They value most in children what children least value in themselves. Small wonder that their effort to build character is such a failure; they don't know it when they see it."[21]

[19] Holt, *How Children Fail*, op. cit., p. 16.
[20] Holt, *How Children Fail*, op. cit., p. 18.
[21] Holt, *How Children Fail*, op. cit., p. 136.

"For we like children who are a little afraid of us, docile, deferential children, though not, of course, if they are so obviously afraid that they threaten our image of ourselves as kind, lovable people whom there is no reason to fear. We find ideal the kind of "good" children who are just enough afraid of us to do everything we want, without making us feel that fear of us is what is making them do it."[22]

Perhaps no role of the teacher is more important than evaluation. Did he attain his objectives? What teaching strategies appear to be effective? Where should he concentrate more effort? How do his measurement techniques affect children's learning? Does he have confidence in his measurement?

"His IQ is 133; his marks last term: 65, 20, F, 94, 45. The 94 is in Social Studies. The 20 is in English. I marvel: why 20. Why not 18? or 33? or 92? Is it based on his thinking, feeling, punctuation, absence, self-expression, memory, insolence? And where on the precentile curve does he fit? Or a girl like Alice? Or a boy like Eddie? What mark does Eddie get for the way the white world has treated him? Or Alice O for the fantasies the movies have fed her? Or I—or even I?

"On the left of the blue line are Attitude Ratings for Citizenship, Co-operation, Cleanliness, Leadership Potential—to be marked from 1 to 5. Ferone's average is 1 1/2. Getting along with Peers = Good; Getting along with Teachers = Poor.

"Next to that—'Disciplined on the following dates,' and a long list, ending with 'Obscene language in auditorium.'

"On the right of the blue line are the CC's—Capsule Characterizations. At the end of each term, each teacher enters a succinct phrase for each student.

" 'Should try harder' is the favorite.

"I glance through other PRC's.

" 'fine boy'

" 'fine boy'

" 'should try harder'

" 'fine boy'

"This is the defeated looking Puerto Rican boy whose name no one remembers and who signs himself: Me. (He wishes himself a happy birthday in my Suggestion Box.) I make sure of his name: José Rodriguez.

"The CC's are followed by the PPP's—Pupil Personality Profiles—devised by Miss Friedenberg—a self-appointed Freud. They are based on her interviews with the kids, and are phrased in pseudo-analyse. Ferone

[22] Holt, *How Children Fail*, op. cit., p. 168.

'should channel his libidino-aggressive impulses into socially acceptable attitudes.' Vivian Paine 'suffers from malfunctioning of the ego due to compulsive obesity.' Lou Martin 'exhibits inverted hostility in manic behavior-patterns.' Eddie Williams 'must curb tendency to paranoia due to socioeconomic environmental factors.' Rusty, the woman-hater 'shows signs of latent homosexuality induced by a narcissistic mother and permissive masturbatory practices.' Alice Blake 'is well balanced and integrated.'

"Occasionally, among the inanities in the PRC's, are sudden entries of teachers with insight and a desire to help; entries of afterschool conferences with kids, home visits, extra tutoring, honest attempts to deal with their problems. But they are rare.

"Right now, I feel, is the most critical time in the children's lives—their last chance to turn into what they will eventually be. And so many are lost to us forever! Statistics on dropouts are staggering. What has become of those kinds, and where are they now."[23]

"Evaluations, by definition, connote value. Accordingly, each can be described, at least ideally, according to the kind and degree of value it connotes. Some are positive, others are negative. Some are very positive or negative, others are less so. In the classroom, as everyone knows, both positive and negative assessments are made and are communicated to students. Teachers scold as well as praise, classmates compliment as well as criticize.

"The question of whether smiles are more frequent than frowns, and compliments more abundant than criticisms, depends in part, of course, on the particular classroom under discussion. Some teachers are just not the smiling type, others find it difficult to suppress their grins. The answer also varies dramatically from one student to the next. Some youngsters receive many more negative sanctions than do others, and the same is true with respect to rewards. Conditions also vary for the sexes. From the early grades onward boys are more likely than are girls to violate institutional regulations and, thus, to receive an unequal share of control messages from the teacher. All of these inequalities make it difficult to describe with great accuracy the evaluative setting as it is experienced by any particular child. All that can be said with assurance is that the classroom environment of most students contains some mixture of praise and reproof."[24]

Evaluation of pupils does not have to result in feelings of inadequacy and failure.

[23] Kaufman, op. cit., pp. 138–139.
[24] Jackson, op. cit., p. 24.

"Very few children come to school failures, none come labeled failures; it is school and school alone which pins the label of failure on children. Most of them have a success identity, regardless of their homes or environments. In school they expect to achieve recognition and, with the faith of the young, they hope also to gain the love and respect of their teachers and classmates. The shattering of this optimistic outlook is the most serious problem of the schools."[25]

"What made the child so successful and so optimistic prior to entering school? He was successful because he used his brain to solve problems relevant to his life; he was optimistic because he had a lot of fun. He discovered that, although reality may be harsh, he could find ways to cope with it, ways that for the most part were successful. Most important, however, even when he failed, he was not labeled a failure; one way or another, harshly or lovingly, he was shown a better way."[26]

How valid is an evaluation procedure that allows the following to happen?

"But only in very rare instances is compliance the only strategy a student uses to make his way in the evaluative environment of the classroom. Another course of action engaged in by most students at least some of the time is to behave in ways that disguise the failure to comply: in short, to cheat. It may seem unduly severe to label as 'cheating' all the little maneuvers that students engage in to cloak aspects of their behavior that might be displeasing to the teacher or their fellow students. Perhaps the term should be reserved to describe the seemingly more serious behavior of trying to falsify performance on a test. But this restriction bestows greater significance than is warranted to test situations and implies that similar behavior in other settings is harmless or hardly worthy of notice.

"Yet why should a student who copies an answer from his neighbor's test paper be considered guilty of more serious misbehavior than the student who attempts to misinform by raising his hand when the teacher asks how many have completed their homework assignment? Why is cheating on a test considered a greater breach of educational etiquette than is faking interest during a social studies discussion or sneaking a peek at a comic book during arithmetic class? The answer, presumably, is the performance on tests counts for more, in that it is preserved as a lasting mark on the student's record. And that answer might justify the differences in our attitudes toward these various practices. But it should

[25] Glasser, W. *Schools Without Failure.* New York: Harper & Row, 1968, p. 26.
[26] Glasser, op. cit., p. 29.

not permit us to overlook the fact that copying an answer on a test, feigning interest during a discussion, giving a false answer to a teacher's query, and discussing forbidden activities are all of a piece. Each represents an effort to avoid censure or to win unwarranted praise. Such efforts are far more common in the classroom than our focus on cheating in test situations would have us believe. Learning how to make it in school invloves, in part, learning how to falsify our behavior."[27]

Your study of measurement and evaluation in educational psychology should give you more confidence in the use of objective measures to improve classroom learning than most teachers appear to have.

"Thus, the interview excerpts give the impression that the outstanding elementary teacher does not often turn to objective measures of school achievement for evidence of his effectiveness and as a source of professional satisfaction. Rather, the question of how well he is doing seems to be answered by the continual flow of information from the students during the teaching session. Spontaneous expressions of interest and enthusiasm are among the most highly valued indicators of good teaching, although the quality of the students' contributions to daily sessions is also mentioned frequently.

"The attitude of these teachers toward testing and their reliance on fleeting behavioral cues combine to create a seeming paradox: present-oriented teachers in future-oriented institutions. Or is this as paradoxical as it first seems? Does the teacher's focus on today necessarily conflict with the school's focus on tomorrow? The answer, it would seem, is 'No, not necessarily.' Apparently teachers can and do give tests and keep an eye on long-range goals while concentrating on the immediate signs of student involvement and enthusiasm. Yet the fact that such a dual focus is possible suggests that it might become a source of discomfort for the teacher under certain circumstances. Our interview material reveals some signs of this discomfort even among teachers who have achieved an enviable reputation in their school systems."[28]

Lest these quotations leave the feeling that nothing worthwhile is going on in our schools, let us hasten to add that schools are in general doing more exciting things today than ever before. Unfortunately, the critics of the school have been much more vocal in the popular press and they have the advantage of far more dramatic substance to discuss than is true of the careful, tedious experimentation to improve learning. Hopefully, the reader of this volume, along with his course in educational

[27] Jackson, op. cit., pp. 26–27.
[28] Jackson, op. cit., p. 26.

psychology, will experience an expansion of his vision and a development of bases for the formulation of defensible hypotheses to be tested by new teaching strategies. The quiet resolution of new approaches to teaching and learning in our schools will in the long run be the dramatic but positive story in the history of education.

"Dear Syl,

"Look at the cherub who is delivering this note. Look closely. Did you ever see a lovelier smile? A prouder bearing? She has just made the Honor Society. Last year she was ready to quit school.

"Walk through the halls. Listen at the classroom doors. In one—a lesson on the nature of Greek tragedy. In another—a drill on who and whom. In another—a hum of voices intoning French declensions. In another—committee reports on slum clearance. In another—silence: a math quiz.

"Whatever the waste, stupidity, ineptitude, whatever the problems and frustrations of teachers and pupils, something very exciting is going on. In each of the classrooms, on each of the floors, all at the same time, education is going on. In some form or other, for all its abuses, young people are exposed to education.

"That's how I manage to stand up.

"And that's why you're standing, too.

"Let's meet at 3. If you're swamped with work, let's at least walk to the subway together.

Bea"[29]

[29] Kaufman, op cit., pp. 300–301.

PART II

The Role of the Teacher

Part Two is composed of six chapters. Each deals with a different function or role of a central character in the classroom—the teacher. What is the sphere of activities of this individual? How do his personality characteristics affect pupil learning? How can he most effectively and efficiently set learning goals? To what extent should the learning situation be structured and guided by him for maximal learning and attainment of goals? What effect does and will educational technology have on the role of the teacher as we traditionally know it? The chapters in Part Two address themselves to these important issues on the forefront in educational psychology today.

Chapter 2 presents two points of view of the teacher as he generally effects changes of behavior in students. Frederick McDonald offers a cybernetic model of teacher-pupil interaction in which the teacher is seen as a processor and evaluator of decisions. McDonald believes that the teacher's function of hypothesis-generating and subsequent testing is central to the performance of the teaching role. Nathan Gage, on the other hand, recognizes the teaching process as overwhelming and believes that one must narrow one's focus before arriving at any theory of teaching. His focus is the function of the teacher as one who engenders comprehension. Accordingly, the teacher manipulates the learner's environment in harmony with the laws of logic and cognition so that the learner can comprehend the material presented. Nevertheless, the teacher must also play the role of the decision-maker.

It is true that overall educational objectives are determined by state and local authorities. Nevertheless, the teacher must make the most crucial decisions concerning goals to be attained in classroom learning. The nature of goal statements, goal emphasis, and the evidence to be accepted as representing goal attainment is within the province of the teacher. Furthermore, there are certain subtle outcomes of classroom learning that are difficult to prescribe by external forces. In the first selection of Chapter 3, Krathwohl emphasizes the breadth as well as depth of the important objectives in the cognitive and affective domains. Gagné deals particularly with the issues involved in stating educational goals and answers the arguments of those who oppose stating objectives in behavorial terminology. He maintains that the more precisely, in terms of actual performance, a goal is defined the more likely will be the attainment of that goal. Flanagan defends the idea of specificity of goals by presenting data from Project Talent, a survey of the achievement of secondary-school pupils. Evaluations of this kind provide a diagnostic approach to the formulation of objectives. A fitting final selection in this chapter presents philosophical differences in educational goals as they relate to the personal decisions of individual pupils. Rogers and Skinner defend their different points of view in this regard.

While there are many things that may be manipulated by the teacher to maximize learning, there are some other extremely subtle aspects of the classroom environment affecting learning that may not be so easily managed—teacher personality, for example. In Chapter 4 Gage emphasizes the importance of teacher characteristics for effective pupil learning. He cites research to support this conclusion. Washburne and Heil report research on the effect of specific aspects of teacher personality as they interact with pupil individual differences. Although numerous researchers have been very pessimistic[1] about findings from studies on teacher characteristics, John Carroll[2] lauds the promising results of this particular research study. He suggests that other researchers may have failed to ask the right questions.

Still another concern of the teacher is the adequacy of the structure of the subject he teaches. Bruner[3] emphasizes that non-specific transfer, the transfer of principles and attitudes, is dependent on the structure of the subject matter. Pupils must be taught structure rather than simply facts and techniques if their education is to be generalizable and, therefore, useful.

Lowe introduces the topic of the structure of subject matter as it relates to teaching and learning. Schwab continues the discussion by outlining a method of teaching subject matter, through utilizing the "structure of a discipline": In revealing his thoughts, he distinguishes what he terms the conceptual from the syntactical structure of the discipline. Conceptual structure refers to our specific focus on the truth we seek. The syntactical structure refers to those operations that differentiate truth from falsehood.

Chapter 6 contains a number of readings that describe what the teacher does as he guides the learner. Verbal behavior is stressed because studies

[1] J. W. Getzels, and P. W. Jackson, "The Teacher's Personality and Characteristics." In N. L. Gage (Ed.), *Handbook of Research in Teaching.* Chicago: Rand McNally & Co., 1963, pp. 506–582.

[2] J. B. Carroll, "The Place of Educational Psychology in the Study of Education." In J. Walton & J. L. Keuthe (Eds.), *The Discipline of Education.* Madison: The University of Wisconsin Press, 1963, pp. 105–119.

[3] J. Bruner, *The Process of Education.* Cambridge: Harvard University Press, 1961, p. 17.

show that two thirds of the time someone is talking in the classroom. Also, in the typical classroom the teacher is talking two thirds of this time. In the Flanders article, the various kinds of teacher talk are delineated: accepting feelings, praising, accepting ideas, questioning, lecturing, giving directions, and criticizing. Shulman offers a compromise solution to the proponents and opponents of the discovery method. Page shows the importance of giving feedback to pupils in grading their papers. Ladd demonstrates the possibility that the teacher can capitalize on control techniques developed from other disciplines and industry to provide the kind of pupil control needed for a good learning environment.

A delineation of the roles of the teacher would not be complete without a discussion of how he can employ technology for more effective learning. Louis Bright discusses variations of technology, including both television and programmed learning. Atkinson demonstrates the manner in which reading may be taught by computer-assisted instruction (CAI). Lewis Mumford makes it very clear that the school has problems to face in using the new technology. The contribution of these new devices and techniques is not all positive.

CHAPTER 2

The Teacher as a Decision-Maker

2.1 A Model of the Decision-Making Process

Frederick J. McDonald

Each teacher has some theory of learning that determines what he does in the classroom. He may not have articulated it, but you need only observe him in the classroom to note that he punishes when demands are not met, or he searches for an opportunity to praise all pupils. Another may believe that the most effective learning occurs when the pupils respect the teacher; to earn this respect one must be stern. In this article, the author discusses the decision-making process as it relates to his theory of teaching and learning.

Figure 1, a cybernetic model of human behavior, represents the decision-making process. The word "cybernetic" derives from a Greek word meaning "steersman." In this model, then, feedback provides the kind of control that a steersman gives to a ship. The navigator, to pursue this analogy briefly, has a plan, charted as a course. The ship is set on this compass course, and the navigator controls its movement in relation to the plan by using the steersman's feedback information about the ship's position. Human behavior is an analogous process. A person controls the

SOURCE. Frederick J. McDonald, *Educational Psychology*, Second Edition. Belmont, California: Wadsworth Publishing Company, Inc., 1965. Reprinted by permission of the publisher.

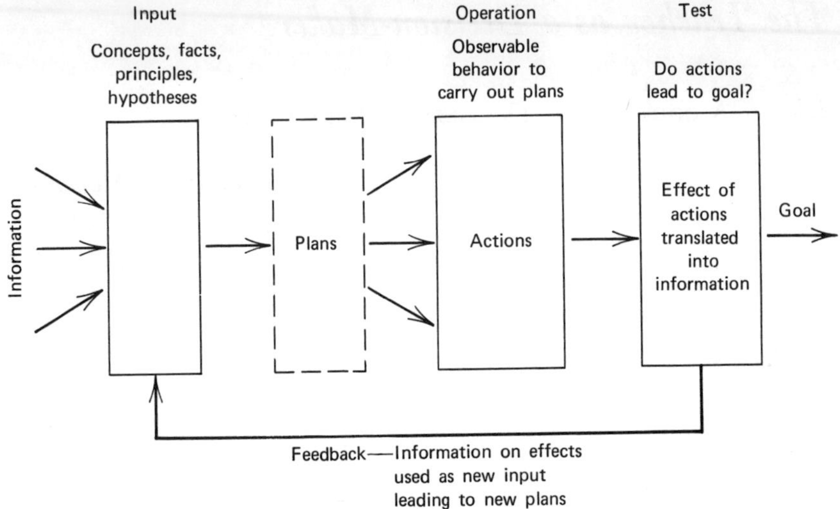

FIGURE 1. A model of the decision-making process.

enactment of a plan by utilizing feedback information from the effects of his actions. The decisions that form the plan serve as a set of instructions; and these instructions order the behavior sequence in relation to a goal to be achieved.

This conception, of course, is only a model—a simplification and an abstraction, to be used for descriptive and explanatory purposes. This model assumes that teaching behavior is goal directed—the goal, broadly stated, being some change in student behavior. The input information is the material the teacher uses to construct the plan or strategy. The operations sequence is the plan in action, manifested in the observable behavior of the teacher. Feedback is information received by the planner on the effects of the plan.

This model conceives of the teacher as active, as a constructor of events, as responsive to information he is continually receiving from the effects of his actions. He is not a passive recipient of stimuli. Neither is he a digital computer capable only of enacting a fixed program. He can modify his own programs, and he can control the feedback process—that is, he can select both the amount and kind of feedback he will use.

Uses of the Decision-Making Model

Why has this model been introduced? Each teacher has some theory of human behavior, some conception of how humans learn, and some notion of the functions and purposes of a teacher. Naturally, the way a teacher views the world of teaching will shape his teaching strategies. The author once knew a teacher who viewed every class as a setting for an uprising and every student as a potential plotter. He interpreted any deviation from rigid attention as a sign of insurrection. Almost all his teaching strategies were designed to control attention; the feedback of importance to him was any sign of inattention. A happier example is represented by the teacher who uses test information on student ability to modify the difficulty level of a learning session.

A model is offered as a way of presenting a theory of teaching. This model may or may not fit with your conceptions of what teaching is. It is introduced here because we want to look at teaching and learning as decision-making behavior and because we want to use psychological knowledge as a way of improving these decisions. The advantages of using this model are worth noting.

A model of any phenomenon focuses our attention on selected aspects of that phenomenon. This model of teaching behavior directs attention to the modifiability of teaching behavior, and to the effects of teaching behavior on student behavior.

Modifiability is to be studied by considering what information a teacher uses in constructing and changing his teaching strategies: that is, how does the teacher conceptualize teaching and student behavior; what principles does he use to interpret and to describe these behaviors; what are his value judgments and his probability estimates of the consequences of his decisions?

We also want to study teaching strategies objectively. If plans are deliberate constructions, then we should be able to describe the factors that need to be considered in developing teaching strategies. If a teacher has a theory of learning, we should be able to evaluate that theory and to see its relation to decision making.

This book invites you to engage in a critical analysis of teaching strategies. A course in educational psychology introduces you to the study of human learning. The ideas and information you will acquire may be used to construct teaching strategies. This knowledge will not be given in the form of nostrums, simple rules of the game, or psychological patent medicine. In the following section an important aspect of the model presented will be discussed.

Decisions and Hypotheses

Decisions are hypothetical; that is, assuming a certain set of conditions, they predict certain effects. They state a relation between the set of conditions and an effect. You decide to start your automobile; that is, you predict that if you turn the key to connect the ignition circuit, an electric current will be set up that will fire an explosive mixture in the cylinders, which in turn will move a mechanical system that will rotate the wheels. This sequence of events occurs if a set of conditions prevails: no breaks in the electric circuit, gasoline in engine, the mechanical parts properly connected. Change any of these conditions and the automobile either will not start or will not move when started.

This example may seem trivial until we recall how much knowledge was necessary to construct a system of such high reliability. The system has been so contrived that the decision to start an automobile depends on personal considerations, not on technical ones. I decide only whether I want to use the system. Only rarely do I have to think about the system itself.

Teaching plans are similar systems in principle. They too are constructions designed to achieve specific effects. But admittedly they rarely have the high reliability of the ignition system of an automobile. Why not? In the first place, our knowledge of human learning is neither so extensive nor so precise as our knowledge of the electrochemical and mechanical systems of an automobile. Second, our knowledge of teaching plans as instructional systems is comparably deficient. However, if perfectly reliable knowledge were needed to act, mankind would be immobilized. Considerable knowledge is available, and our problem is to learn to use it to produce more knowledge.

The response of many individuals is to fall back on "tried-and-true" methods, usually something a teacher has found "works for me." Although this reaction may provide a feeling of security, it hardly does justice to the complexity of the problems a teacher faces. This approach strips teaching of its challenge and depreciates the curiosity that it may both excite and satisfy.

The model of teaching behavior used here implies that decisions and sets of decisions formulated as plans be treated as hypotheses.

Decisions as Hypotheses About Learning

Each of the decisions that a teacher makes in formulating and enacting a teaching plan is a hypothesis about learning. Although the teacher may not formulate his plans in hypothetical language, what he does may be stated in propositions something like this: "If I introduce these words into the vocabulary lesson, then the pupils will have more words available to read Scott's *The Lady of the Lake.*" A general teaching strategy is also a hypothesis. Language teachers, for example, believe that students should, as soon as possible, speak in the language being learned. They are hypothesizing that extensive practice in hearing and speaking the language will enable students to use the language without having to translate consciously as they speak. These hypotheses, simple or complex, are predictions about the behavior that will result from certain kinds of learning experiences. In principle, such hypotheses have varying degrees of probable validity.

Coladarci points up the essential characteristics of this kind of thinking:

"Intelligent hypotheses are not chosen randomly nor are they found fullblown. An intelligent hypothesizer thinks along the lines of the following model: '*On the basis of what I know now* about individual differences and the reading process, I hypothesize that this kind of grouping-for-reading will lead to the kind of pupil-progress in reading that I would like to bring about.' "[1]

An example will make clear how a teacher's choices can shape what a child will learn. A fourth-grade teacher was introducing a unit on "Pioneer Life." He asked the students what they wanted to study about "Pioneer Life" and what kinds of questions they should raise concerning the subject. As the discussion proceeded, the children suggested the usual categories for studying a history unit—namely, the pioneer's food, shelter, and clothing. One child mentioned that he had seen a Western movie in which a man accused of horse stealing was immediately hanged. This comment on the movie evoked considerable interest in the group, and one of the children asked why the man was hanged right away. The teacher dismissed this question as irrelevant to a discussion of pioneer life. The decision not to utilize this question in effect set the stage for the kinds of things that the pupils would talk about. Had the teacher chosen to capitalize upon this question, topics concerning pioneer conceptions of justice and due process of law, the function of law-enforcing bodies, and the validity of citizens' arrests could have been developed. These topics did not emerge in the ensuing discussion, nor were they included as relevant points in the outline of topics to be studied under the heading of "Pioneer Life." The teacher's decision at this point, then, determined the character of what the children could learn.

Would this teacher have profited by thinking about his decisions, by examining the hypotheses he held about the effects of his teaching? For example, did this teacher predict that his students would understand pioneer conceptions of justice? It seems unlikely that they would when questions about these ideas are quickly dismissed. Had he tested to see what the students were learning about these conceptions, the result might

[1] A. P. Coladarci, "The Relevancy of Educational Psychology," *Educational Leadership*, 18 (1956), 489–492. See also A. P. Coladarci, "The Teacher as a Hypothesis-Maker," *California Journal for Instructional Improvement*, 2 (1959), 3–6.

have prompted him to modify his teaching strategy. He would also have learned that the hypotheses which supported his original decisions were probably invalid.

The first step in learning to view teaching behavior as hypotheses being tested in action is to see the effects of teachers' decisions on learning. Prescott has described this relation as follows:

"These accumulating decisions create the conditions under which the pupils live and learn at school. For example, they determine the freedom or restriction of movement, of speech, of access to materials, of spontaneous inquiries or comments, of choice of experiences. They profoundly influence the kinds of relationships the children are able to establish and maintain with adults in the school and with each other in the classroom, on the playground, and everywhere about the school. These decisions often determine the actual learning experiences to which the children are exposed, the content upon which attention is focused, and the food for mental, social, and spiritual growth that is offered each child. They determine the aspects of life and the world with which the pupils are brought into contact, and they evoke or fail to evoke the various steps of the reasoning process, and encourage or discourage curiosity and imagination. They promote certain codes of conduct and imply the validity of certain attitudes and values for living in our times and in our society. These judgments permit some adjustment processes and mechanisms to operate and discourage others. They emphasize certain meanings as valid and condemn others as untrue and unacceptable."[2]

The second step is to see the hypothetical character of these decisions, to examine one's conceptions of the learning process as they influence the formulation of these hypotheses. The third step is to learn to test these hypotheses, to utilize the feedback process to reshape teaching plans.

[2] D. A. Prescott, *The Child in the Educative Process.* (New York: McGraw-Hill Book Company, 1957), pp. 6–7.

2.2 Toward a Cognitive Theory of Teaching

N. L. Gage

Dr. Gage believes that to improve classroom learning we must develop a theory of teaching. He suggests that just as there are a number of different kinds of learning, so teaching is not a unitary phenomenon. He mentions various ways in which teaching may be analyzed, and, finally, focuses on the specific role of the teacher in engendering comprehension in the academic disciplines. This article presents clearly the breadth of a teacher's concerns and by implication the many decisions he must make to attain his objectives.

Let me begin with the assertion that, before we can undertake to develop theories of teaching, we need to analyze the concept of teaching. "Teaching" is a misleadingly generic term that simply covers too much. It falsely suggests a single, unitary phenomenon that can fruitfully be made the subject of theory development.

Learning theory, in my opinion, has long been hung up on a similar fallacy. Because the same term, "learning," has been applied to an enormous range of phenomena, psychologists have been misled into believing

SOURCE. N. L. Gage, "Toward a Cognitive Theory of Teaching," *Teachers College Record*, LXV, 5 (1964), pp. 408–412. Reprinted by permission of the author and *Teachers College Record*.

that a single theory can be developed to explain the whole gamut. Animal learning in puzzle boxes and Skinner boxes, human learning of meaningless paired associates, and the learning of school subjects in classrooms have all been termed "learning." And because all these activities have been given the same name, some psychologists have attempted to account for all of them by a single, general, unified theory.

I shall support my references to this enterprise as a fallacy in learning theory by merely quoting Tolman, who said in 1949,

"I wish to suggest that our familiar theoretical disputes about learning may *perhaps* . . . be resolved, if we can agree that there are really a number of different kinds of learning. For it may then turn out that the theory and laws appropriate to one kind may well be different from those appropriate to other kinds (5, p. 144).

What Tolman saw as a saving possibility in learning theory is what I see as an absolute necessity at the present early beginnings of our concern with theories of teaching. We must guard against what I see as inevitably futile attempts to develop a single theory that will embrace all the phenomena that go under the single name of teaching.

Toward Analysis

If so, then the concept of teaching must be analyzed into processes or elements that might properly constitute the subject of theories. What kinds of analyses can be made? I want to offer some illustrative analyses about whose fruitfulness I have as yet almost no conviction but which do indicate what I have in mind.

First, teaching can be analyzed according to *types of teacher activity*. Rather than use my own examples, let me draw upon those listed in a recent paper by Sorenson and Husek (3). In developing an instrument for assessing teacher role expectations, they identified the following six role dimensions: information-giver, disciplinarian, adviser, counselor, motivator, and referrer. Their set omits such other dimensions as explainer, demonstrator, housekeeper, record-keeper, curriculum planner, and evaluator. My point is simply that teaching consists of many kinds of activity and that it is unreasonable to expect a single theory to explain all of them.

A second way to analyze teaching goes according to the *types of educational objectives*, the things to be learned. One well known categorization of objectives puts them into the cognitive, affective, and psychomotor domains. Tolman (5) classified the things to be learned—or the connections or relations that get learned—into six types, which he named cathexes, equivalence beliefs, field expectancies, field-cognition modes, drive discriminations, and motor patterns. No matter how we do it, we must recognize that teachers teach different things, different not only from one course to another, but even within a single class session; the same theory of teaching should not be expected to apply to all things taught.

A third way to analyze teaching might proceed on the basis of the *different families of learning theory* that now seem useful. My own favorite way of classifying these families refers to them as conditioning, identification, and cognitive theories. Each of these can be stood on its head to suggest a corresponding view of the teaching process. At the moment, I see such views not as competing but as complementary. Hence, again, I see them as providing alternative ways of analyzing the phenomena called teaching.

My fourth and last illustration of an analysis of teaching draws upon *components of the learning process* as formulated by any of the learning theories. The well known paradigm developed by Neal Miller (2) sets up four components of learning: drive, cue, response, and reward. Corresponding components of teaching would be "motivating," "cue-providing," "response-eliciting," and "rewarding." It may well be that we shall have to develop separate theories for each of such components of the teaching process.

Thus far, I have argued that teaching as such is too broad, vague, and unwieldy to provide the proper subject of attempts at theory development. And I have then offered some examples of ways in which it can perhaps be broken down into components that will support valid attempts at theory development. I have considered all this necessary as an introduction to my main concern in this paper, which is an attempt to outline a special—as against a general—theory that applies to just the kind of delimited concern that I am advocating.

Engendering Comprehension

Here I want to offer a point of view, a program, concerning aspects of research on teaching that I consider important, neglected, and promising. I have in mind the promotion of theory and research on engendering comprehension in the academic disciplines. This is a much narrower concern than all of teaching. I mean to omit from this focus such matters as motivating students, evaluating their achievement, promoting their mental health, increasing their store of information, improving their motor skills, developing their effectiveness as group members, and so on. Even within the realm of school subjects, my concern omits such matters as handwriting, spelling, woodshop, and physical education. I propose to focus, in short, on one relatively specific, although still immensely broad, aspect of all teaching: the teacher's role in engendering comprehension of concepts and principles as they are found in such so-called academic subjects as

English, mathematics, science, and social studies. In doing so, I intend no value judgment either about school subjects or about other aspects of the learning process even within a single academic discipline. I grant that motivation, mental health, social relationships, and the like are important even in the acquisition of comprehension in the academic disciplines. But for the moment, I choose to regard them as merely subservient to the present focus, to the moment of truth in any classroom when the teacher has the attention of his well-motivated, emotionally and socially secure, and otherwise fully ready students, and faces the task of producing in them a comprehension of some concept or principle in the academic discipline with which he is concerned. What should he do? What *must* he do, if his behavior is to have the desired effect on the comprehension of his youngsters? How can the behavior of one person, a teacher, have an effect on another person's comprehension of a concept or principle? Here, at last, is the question to which I wish to address myself.

My answer, in very general terms, is that the teacher will manipulate the learner's environment, in accordance with the laws of logic and cognition, in the same way that he can influence another person's perceptions by manipulating the environment in accordance with the laws of perception. The latter kinds of laws are familiar to all of us; they refer to such matters as the constancies of perceived size and shape, the determiners of figure and ground, grouping and patterning, proximity, similarity, continuity, and closure. We can to a great extent compel others to perceive what we want them to perceive by controlling the patterning and structure of stimuli in their environment. We are compelled to see motion in stationary objects when lights go on and off in certain temporal and spatial patterns, *i.e.*, we are compelled to see the phi phenomenon or moving pictures by the manipulator of our visual environment. We are compelled to see the Big Dipper by someone who points it out to us because he calls our attention to it and gives us a set for a certain perception of this particular pattern of stars.

Cognition in the Classroom

The teacher, by the same token, can compel us to comprehend concepts and principles, depending on whether the stimuli or ideas themselves exist in certain patterns, whether they have certain relationships to one another, and, of course, on whether the pupil has certain cognitive capacities, sets, and the like.

Such an approach to the function of the teacher in engendering comprehension must rest on the assumption that what is to be learned does have a logical structure and organization, analogous to the structuring of dots and lines in the classical discussions of visual perception. It is because of this necessary assumption that I have restricted this discussion to the teaching of comprehension in the academic disciplines, which I define as those bodies of knowledge that have well formulated, clearly articulated, logical structures of powerful concepts and principles.

There happens to be a movement within educational psychology at present that is concerned with exactly the aspect of teaching to which I am restricting this discussion. I am referring to the efforts now being made to develop principles of programing instructional materials. For various reasons, at least some of which seem to be merely incidental and irrelevant, these efforts are currently being made on the basis of a stimulus-response, conditioning, or reinforcement paradigm of the learning process. Yet it seems to me that, at the heart of the programed instruction movement, where principles of programing are being developed, there lies not a reinforcement psychology but a cognitive psychology of which its users often seem to be obvious. Consider the following statement from a discussion of the Ruleg (rule-example) system of programing:

> "The third step is to arrange the ru index cards in an approximate order for program presentation. . . . Ordering may be according to a continuum of complexity . . . , chronology . . . , spatiality . . . , or dependence on other ru's. Interdependent relationships among rules should be carefully considered, because the understanding of one rule may depend upon the mastery of some other rules (*4*, p. 72)."

Later, in describing another way of systematizing the program's task, the same authors discuss outlining the material to be taught and state that the major headings should be "ordered in some *rational* sequence" (*4*, p. 74, my italics).

It is not only in the broad structuring of the subject that cognitive properties of instruction are invoked. Within the frames, or small units, of a program, the programers are also advised to give heed to laws of cognition. Thus, we are told that, in all good frames, "the response is evoked in the presence of a *meaningful* context which is new to the student" (*4*, p. 87, my italics). In discussing prompts, or stimuli in a frame intended to make it more effective in evoking the desired response, the authors say they provide "context" (*4*, p. 89). Presumably, a prompt depends for its effectiveness on such perception-relevant or cognition-relevant properties as its similarity to, proximity to, contrast, or continuity with the other stimuli in the frame and the response to be evoked by the frame. Formal prompts work because of their mere visual or auditory similarity, while thematic prompts depend on their similarity in meaning to the desired response. Without saying so, the authors refer to perceptual and cognitive properties of stimuli throughout their discussion of the many different kinds of prompts that they describe and illustrate.

Finally, it would be easy to identify references to ideas about perception and cognition in the programer's treatments of sequences of frames and general program characteristics. Such ideas as that of the "generalization sequence," aimed at broadening the range of stimuli to which a given response will be made, are described as including statements describing the "common properties" of the stimulus class involved. The notion of common property is a perceptual or logical one, and principles of perception and cognition enter into the determination and communication of a common property in a class of stimuli.

From Programs to Teachers

My purpose in identifying what seems to me to be a saturation of the programed instruction movement with cognitive psychology is not the invidious one of detracting from the power and relevance of reinforcement approaches to teaching. For some aspects of teaching, reinforcement models seem pertinent indeed. For other aspects of teaching, however, and particularly for understanding and improving the work of live teachers in promoting comprehension within the academic disciplines, we need to focus just as sharply on the cognitive aspects of teacher behavior as the students of programing principles have focused, however unwittingly, on the cognitive aspects of their programs. This kind of concern has been most notable by its absence in the research on teaching conducted by psychologists. Such research has often been concerned with who talks to whom and how much in the classroom. Or it has dealt with the teacher's warmth, permissiveness, or authoritarianism. Or it has dealt with the amount of organization and systematization that a teacher displayed in his preparation for and conduct of classroom work. But only rarely, it seems to me, have we been concerned with the actual intellectual content, the cognitive organization, and the logical validity of what teachers say to their pupils and of what the pupils say to their teacher and to one another. When we examine a textbook, of course, these aspects of its content and organization come to the fore. We pay close attention to the logic of its arguments and the aptness and compelling power of the data and examples that the authors adduce. I am saying that we ought to look in the same way at what teachers do in the classroom. The laws of logic and the principles of cognition, analogous to the principles of perception, give us a convenient point of entry into such an enterprise. If teaching gets studied in this way, it may eventually be possible to formulate a cognitive theory of teaching that will yield us the power we need to understand, predict, and improve the ability of teachers to engender comprehension in the academic disciplines. And that ability is not the least important or intriguing of the components of the complex of phenomena that we call teaching.

I have attempted two things: First, I have tried to demonstrate that the phenomenon called teaching is too broad and complex to support any attempt at a single, general theory that will embrace all of it. The concept of teaching needs to be analyzed, and I have offered examples of such analyses according to teacher functions, teaching objectives, families of learning theory, and components of the learning process. A valid theory of teaching had better be concerned with only a specific component resulting from such analyses.

Second, focusing on one part of teaching, the teacher's function of engendering comprehension in the academic disciplines, I have tried to indicate what cognitive theory has to offer toward a theory of teaching. Using analogies from perception and drawing upon recent efforts to develop principles for programing instructional materials, I have indicated the kinds of properties of teaching that would be the concern of such a theory of teaching. Finally, I have concluded by urging more research on teaching deal with cognitive variables, in contrast to the effective, social, and motor variables to which it has in recent decades been almost exclusively devoted.

References

1. Gage, N. L. Theories of teaching. In E. R. Hilgard (Chmn.) Theories of learning and education. *Yearb. Natl. Soc. Stud. Educ.*, 1964, *63* (in press).
2. Miller, N. E., & Dollard, J. *Social learning and imitation.* New Haven: Yale Univer. Press, 1941.
3. Sorenson, G., & Husek, T. Development of a measure of teacher role expectations. *Amer. Psychologist,* 1963, *18,* 389 (Abst.).
4. Taber, J. I., Glaser, R., *et al. A guide to the preparation of programed instructional material.* Pittsburgh: Dept. Psychol., Univer. Pittsburgh, 1962 (Mimeo.).
5. Tolman, E. C. There is more than one kind of learning. *Psychol. Rev.*, 1949, *56,* 144–155.

Selected Readings

Broudy, H. S. Historic exemplars of teaching method. In N. S. Gage (Ed.), *Handbook of research on teaching.* Chicago: Rand McNally and Co., 1963, pp. 1–43.

Bruner, J. Needed: a theory of instruction. *Educational Leadership,* 1963, **20,** 523–532.

Bruner, J. S. *Toward a theory of instruction.* Cambridge, Mass.: Belknap Press, 1966.

Carroll, J. B. A model of school learning. *Teachers College Record,* 1963, **64,** 723–733.

Clayton, T. E. *Teaching and learning: a psychological perspective.* Englewood Cliffs, N. J.: Prentice-Hall, Inc., 1965, pp. 13–20.

DeCecco, J. P. *The psychology of learning and instruction: educational psychology.* Englewood Cliffs, N. J.: Prentice-Hall, Inc., 1968, pp. 5–29.

Gage, N. L. Theories of teaching. In E. R. Hilgard (Ed.), *Theories of learning and instruction,* Part I, 63rd Yrbk. of the National Society for the Study of Education. Chicago: University of Chicago Press, 1964, pp. 268–85.

Scheffler, I. Philosophical models of teaching. *Harvard Educational Review,* 1965, **35,** 131–143.

CHAPTER 3

Delineating Goals to Be Attained In Classroom Learning

3.1 The Taxonomy of Educational Objectives

David R. Krathwohl

The author discusses the reason why we need a taxonomy of educational objectives. He then outlines the taxonomies for the cognitive and affective domains (there has been no widely accepted taxonomy for the psychomotor domain developed to date), providing test items for the various categories as illustrations. The paper is concluded with a discussion of the suggested uses of the taxonomies.

When teachers say they want their students to "really understand" the principle of acceleration, what do they mean? Is it that the student recall a formula about acceleration? Should he be able to understand an article written about it? Should he be able to apply the formula to a new situation? Should he be able to think up new situations to which the formula is relevant? Any or all these are possible interpretations of the term "really understand." Do you think two teachers, both of whom agreed that they wanted their students to "really understand this principle," would independently select the same aspects from among those just mentioned? It

SOURCE. David R. Krathwohl, "The Taxonomy of Educational Objectives—Its Use in Curriculum Building." In C. Lindvall, (Ed.), *Defining Educational Objectives*, University of Pittsburgh Press, 1964, pp. 19–36. Reprinted by permission of University of Pittsburgh Press.

seems unlikely. Yet, rarely do our curriculum meetings get this specific. But only as one becomes this specific can one decide which among the possible learning experiences to use in the classroom. Usually it is not until the curriculum is translated into learning experiences that this becomes apparent.

The state of communication with respect to a term like "really understand" is nothing compared to the confusion that surrounds objectives dealing with attitudes, interests and appreciation. When we say that we want a child to "appreciate" art, do we mean that he should be aware of artwork? Should he be willing to give it some attention when it is around? Do we mean that he should seek it out—go to the museum on his own, for instance? Do we mean that he should regard artwork as having positive values? Should he experience an emotional kick or thrill when he sees artwork? Should he be able to evaluate it and to know why and how it is effective? Should he be able to compare its esthetic impact with that of other art forms?

We could extend this list, but it is enough to suggest that the term "appreciation" covers a wide variety of meanings. And worse—not all of these are distinct from the terms "attitude" and "interest." Thus, if appreciation has the meaning that we want him to like artwork well enough to seek it out, how would we distinguish such behavior from an interest in art—or are interests and appreciations, as we use these words, the same thing?

If the student *values* art, does he have a favorable *attitude* toward it? Are our appreciation objectives the same as, overlapping with, or in some respects distinct from our attitude objectives? Most of us would argue that there are distinctions in the way we use the terms "appreciation," "attitude" and "interest." It is, however, much less certain that when we use these terms in our discussions of curriculum that we are using them in ways that do not differ from one person to another person. When we delve deep enough to determine which meaning we are using, we get into lengthy discussions—and many of our meetings turn out to be just that.

These kinds of problems which exist for curriculum builders are equally serious for those who have the responsibility of evaluating the success of the teacher in meeting the curriculum's objectives. For them there is the problem of very specific communication between curriculum builder and evaluator. In addition, if there are any similarities among different curriculum, similarities that can be meaningfully and precisely communicated, one could compare programs, trade evaluation instruments, and compare the effectiveness of learning devices, materials and curricular organizations. It was with this in mind that a group of college and university examiners, under the leadership of Dr. Benjamin S. Bloom, attempted to devise some means which would permit greater precision of communication with respect to educational objectives. The taxonomy is this means.

What is a taxonomy? You've undoubtedly heard of the biological taxonomies which permit classification into the categories of phyllum, class, order, family, genius, species and variety. Ours is also a classification scheme, but the objectives being classified are not plants or animals but educational objectives, and the categories are terms descriptive of the kinds of behavior that we seek from students in educational institutions.

The taxonomy is based on the assumption that the educational program can be conceived as an attempt to change the behavior of students with respect to some subject matter. When we describe the behavior and the subject matter, we construct an educational objective. For instance: the student should be able to recall the major features of Chinese culture; he should be able to recognize form and pattern in literary and artworks. The two parts of the objective, the subject matter and what is to be done with respect to the subject matter by the student, are both categorizable. It is, however, the latter, what is to be *done* with the subject matter, which constitutes the categories of the taxonomy. The categorization of subject matter we leave to the librarian.

The taxonomy is divided into three domains: cognitive, affective, and psychomotor. The cognitive includes those objectives having to do with thanking, knowing, and problem solving. The affective includes those objectives dealing with attitudes, values, interests and appreciation. The psychomotor covers objectives having to do with manual and motor skills and has yet to be developed. Our Handbook (1) on the cognitive domain has been published for some time, and has been developed in thc most detail. The affective domain, on the other hand, is going through its second and, we hope, final draft. Let us look at the cognitive study first.

Similar to the distinctions most teachers make, this domain is divided into the acquisition of knowledge, and the development of those skills and abilities necessary to use knowledge. Under the heading "Knowledge," which is the first major category of the cognitive domain, one finds a series of sub-categories, each describing the recall of a different category of knowledge. Each of the other subheadings is accompanied by a definition of the behavior classified there and by illustrative objectives taken from the educational literature. In addition, there is a summary of the kinds of test items that may be used to test for each category, a discussion of the problems which beset the individual attempting to evaluate behavior in the category, and a large number of examples of test items—mainly multiple choice, but some essay type. These illustrate how items may be built to measure each of the categories.

The classification scheme is hierarchical in nature, that is, each category is assumed to involve behavior which is more complex and abstract than the previous category. Thus the categories are arranged from simple to more complex behavior, and from concrete to more abstract behavior.

Perhaps the idea of the continuum is most easily gained from looking at the major headings of the cognitive domain, which include knowledge, comprehension (ability to restate knowledge in new words), application (understanding it well enough to apply it), analysis (understanding it well enough to break it apart into its parts and make the relations among ideas explicit), synthesis (the ability to produce wholes from parts, to produce a plan of operation, to derive a set of abstracts relations) and evaluation (be able to judge the value of material for given purposes). An objective may include many elementary behaviors, but it is properly classified at the highest level of behavior involved.

There are a number of subheads which lend a specificity and precision to the main headings and help to further define them.

Basically the taxonomy is an educational-logical-psychological classification system. The terms in this order reflect the emphasis given to the organizating principles upon which it is built. It makes educational distinctions in the sense that the boundaries between categories reflect the decisions that teachers make among student behaviors in their development of curriculums, and in choosing learning situations. It is a logical system in the sense that its terms are defined precisely and are used consistently. In addition, each category permits logical subdivisions which can be clearly defined and further subdivided as necessary and useful. Finally the taxonomy seems to be consistent with our present understanding of psychological phenomena, though it does not rest on any single theory.

The scheme is intended to be purely descriptive so that every type of educational goal can be represented. It does not indicate the value or quality of one class as compared to another. It is impartial with respect to views of education. One of the tests of the taxonomy has been that of inclusiveness—could one classify all kinds of educational objectives (if stated as student behaviors) in the framework. In general we have been satisfied that it has met this test.

The Cognitive Domain

The categories of the cognitive domain and some illustrative objectives follow (1, p. 201):

Knowledge

1.00 Knowledge

Knowledge, as defined here, involves the recall of specifics and universals, the recall of methods and processes, or the recall of a pattern, structure or setting. For measurement purposes, the recall situation involves little more than bringing to mind the appropriate material. Although some alteration of the material may be required, this is a relatively minor part of the task. The knowledge objectives emphasize most the psychological processes of remembering. The process of relating is also involved in that a knowledge test situation requires the organization and reorganization of a problem such that it will furnish the appropriate signals and cues for the information and knowledge the individual possesses. To use an analogy, if one thinks of the mind as a file, the problem in a knowledge test situation is that of finding in the problem or task the appropriate signals, cues and clues which will most effectively bring out whatever knowledge is filed or stored.

1.10 *Knowledge of Specifics.* The recall of specific and isolable bits of information. The emphasis is on symbols with concrete referents. This material, which is at a very low level of abstraction, may be thought of as the elements from which more complex and abstract forms of knowledge are built.

1.11 *Knowledge of Terminology.* Knowledge of the referents for specific symbols (verbal and nonverbal). This may include knowledge of the most generally accepted symbol referent, knowledge of the variety symbols which may be used for a single referent, or knowledge of the referent most appropriate to a given use of a symbol.

*To define technical terms by giving their attributes, properties or relations.

*Familiarity with a large number of words in their common range of meanings.

1.12 *Knowledge of Specific Facts.* Knowledge of dates, events, persons, places, etc. This may include very precise and specific information such as the specific date or exact magnitude of a phenomenon. It may also include approximate or relative information such as an approximate time period or the general order of magnitude of a phenomenon.

*The recall of major facts about particular cultures.

*The possession of a minimum knowledge about the organisms studied in the laboratory.

1.20 *Knowledge of Ways and Means of Dealing with Specifics.* Knowledge of the ways of organizing studying, judging and criticizing. This includes the methods of inquiry, the chronological sequences and the standards of judgment within a field as well as the patterns of orga-

* Illustrative educational objectives from the literature.

nization through which the areas of the fields themselves are determined and internally organized. This knowledge is at an intermediate level of abstraction between specific knowledge on the one hand and knowledge of universals on the other. It does not so much demand the activity of the student in using the materials as it does a more passive awareness of their nature.

1.21 ***Knowledge of Conventions.*** Knowledge of characteristic ways of treating and presenting ideas and phenomena. For purposes of communication and consistency, workers in a field employ usages, styles, practices and forms which best suit their purposes and/or which appear to suit best the phenomena with which they deal. It should be recognized that although these forms and conventions are likely to be set up on arbitrary, accidental, or authoritative bases, they are retained because of the general agreement or concurrence of individuals concerned with the subject, phenomena or problem.

*Familarity with the forms and conventions of the major types of works, e.g. verse, plays, scientific papers, etc.

*To make pupils conscious of correct form and usage in speech and writing.

1.22 ***Knowledge of Trends and Sequences.*** Knowledge of the processes, directions, and movement of phenomena with respect to time.

*Understanding of the continuity and development of American culture as exemplified in American life.

*Knowledge of the basic trends underlying the development of public assistance programs.

1.23 ***Knowledge of Classifications and Categories.*** Knowledge of the classes, sets, divisions and arrangements which are regarded as fundamental for a given subject field, purpose, argument or problem.

*To recognize the area encompassed by various kinds of problems or materials.

*Becoming familiar with a range of t[illegible].

1.24 ***Knowledge of Criteria.*** Knowled[illegible] by which facts, principles, opinions and conduct are tes[illegible].

*Familiarity with criteria for judgment appropriate to the type of work and the purpose for which it is read.

*Knowledge of criteria for the evaluation of recreational activities.

* Illustrative educational objectives from the literature.

1.25 ***Knowledge of Methodology.*** Knowledge of the methods of inquiry, techniques and procedures employed in a particular subject field as well as those employed in investigating particular problems and phenomena. The emphasis here is on the individual's knowledge of the method rather than his ability to use the method.

*Knowledge of scientific methods for evaluating health concepts.

*The student shall know the methods of attack relevant to the kinds of problems of concern to the social sciences.

1.30 ***Knowledge of the Universals and Abstractions in a Field.*** Knowledge of the major schemes and patterns by which phenomena and ideas are organized. These are the large structures, theories and generalizations which dominate a subject field or which are quite generally used in studying phenomena or solving problems. These are at the highest levels of abstraction and complexity.

1.31 ***Knowledge of Principles and Generalizations.*** Knowledge of particular abstractions which summarize observations of phenomena. These are the abstractions which are of value in explaining, describing, predicting or in determining the most appropriate and relevant action or direction to be taken.

*Knowledge of the important principles by which our experience with biological phenomena is summarized.

*The recall of major generalizations about particular cultures.

1.32 ***Knowledge of Theories and Structures.*** Knowledge of the *body* of principles and generalizations together with their interrelations which present a clear, rounded and systematic view of a complex phenomenon, problem or field. These are the most abstract formulations, and they can be used to show the interrelation and organization of a great range of specifics.

*The recall of major theories about particular cultures.

*Knowledge of a relatively complete formulation of the theory of evolution.

Intellectual Skills and Abilities

Abilities and skills refer to organized modes of operation and generalized techniques for dealing with materials and problems. The materials and problems may be of such a nature that little or no specialized and technical information is required. Such information as is required

* Illustrative educational objectives from the literature.

can be assumed to be part of the individual's general fund of knowledge. Other problems may require specialized and technical information at a rather high level such that specific knowledge and skill in dealing with the problem and the materials are required. The ability and skill objectives emphasize the mental processes of organizing and reorganizing material to achieve a particular purpose. The materials may be given or remembered.

2.00 Comprehension

This represents the lowest level of understanding. It refers to a type of understanding or apprehension such that the individual knows what is being communicated and can make use of the material or idea being communicated without necessarily relating it to other material or seeing its fullest implications.

2.10 *Translation.* Comprehension as evidenced by the care and accuracy with which the communication is paraphrased or rendered from one language or form of communication to another. Translation is judged on the basis of faithfulness and accuracy, that is, on the extent to which the material in the original communication is preserved although the form of the communication has been altered.

*The ability to understand non-literal statements (metaphor, symbolism, irony, exaggeration).

*Skill in translating mathematical verbal material into symbolic statements and vice versa.

2.20 *Interpretation.* The explanation or summarization of a communication. Whereas translation involves an objective part-for-part rendering of a communication, interpretation involves a reordering, reaarangement or a new view of the material.

*The ability to grasp the thought of the work as a whole at any desired level of generality.

*The ability to interpret various types of social data.

2.30 *Extralopation.* The extension of trends or tendencies beyond the given data to determine implications, consequences, corollaries, effects, etc., which are in accordance with the condition described in the original communication.

*The ability to deal with the conclusions of a work in terms of the immediate inference made from the explicit statements.

*Skill in predicting continuation of trends.

* Illustrative educational objectives from the literature.

3.00 Application

The use of abstractions in particular and concrete situations. The abstractions may be in the form of general ideas, rules of procedures, or generalized methods. The abstractions may also be technical principles, ideas and theories which must be remembered and applied.

*Application to the phenomena discussed in one part of the scientific terms or concepts used in other papers.

*The ability to predict the probable effect of a change in a factor on a biological situation previously at equilibrium.

4.00 Analysis

The breakdown of a communication into its constitutent elements or parts such that the relative hierarchy of ideas is made clear and/or the relations between the ideas expressed are made explicit. Such analyses are intended to clarify the communication, to indicate how the communication is organized, and the way in which it manages to convey its effects, as well as its basis and arrangement.

4.10 *Analysis of Elements.* Identification of the elements included in a communication.

*The ability to recognize unstated assumptions.

*Skill in distinguishing facts from hypotheses.

4.20 *Analysis of Relationships.* The connections and interactions between elements and parts of a communication.

*The ability to check the consistency of hypotheses with given information and assumptions.

*Skill in comprehending the interrelationships among the ideas in a passage.

4.30. *Analysis of Organizational Principles.* The organization, systematic arrangement and structure which holds the communication together. This includes the "explicit" as well as "implicit" structure. It includes the bases, necessary arrangement and the mechanics which made the communication a unit.

*The ability to recognize form and pattern in literary or artistic works as a means of understanding their meaning.

*Ability to recognize the general techniques used in persuasive materials, such as advertising, propaganda, etc.

* Illustrative educational objectives from the literature.

5.00 Synthesis

The putting together of elements and parts so as to form a whole. This involves the process of working with pieces, parts, elements, etc., and arranging and combining them in such a way as to constitute a pattern or structure not clearly there before.

5.10 ***Production of a Unique Communication.*** The development of a communication in which the writer or speaker attempts to convey ideas, feelings and/or experiences to others.

*Skill in writing, using an excellent organization of ideas and statements.

*Ability to tell a personal experience effectively.

5.20 ***Production of a Plan, or Proposed Set of Operations.*** The development of a plan of work or the proposal of a plan of operations. The plan should satisfy requirements of the task which may be given to the student or which he may develop for himself.

*Ability to propose ways of testing hypotheses.

*Ability to plan a unit of instruction for a particular teaching situation.

5.30 ***Derivation of a Set of Abstract Relations.*** The development of a set of abstract relations either to classify or explain particular data or phenomena, or the deduction of propositions and relations from a set of basic propositions or symbolic representations.

*Ability to formulate appropriate hypotheses based upon an analysis of factors involved, and to modify such hypotheses in the light of new factors and considerations.

*Ability to make mathematical discoveries and generalizations.

6.00 Evaluation

Judgments about the value of material and methods for given purposes. Quantitative and qualitative judgments about the extent to which material and methods satisfy criteria. Use of a standard of appraisal. The criteria may be those determined by the student or those which are given to him.

6.10 ***Judgments in Terms of Internal Evidence.*** Evaluation of the accuracy of a communication from such evidence as logical accuracy, consistency and other internal criteria.

* Illustrative educational objectives from the literature.

*Judging by internal standards, the ability to assess general probability of accuracy in reporting facts from the care given to exactness of statement, documentation, proof, etc.

*The ability to indicate logical fallacies in arguments.

6.20 ***Judgments in Terms of External Criteria.*** Evaluation of material with reference to selected or remembered criteria.

*The comparison of major theories, generalizations and facts about particular cultures.

*Judging by external standards, the ability to compare a work with the highest known standards in its field—especially with other works of recognized excellence.

The Affective Domain

The cognitive domain was developed first since it was expected to be the most useful of the three domains. Work on the affective domain was begun immediately but has proceeded much more slowly (4). It presented some special problems. For example, the hierarchical structure has been most difficult to find in the affective part of the taxonomy. We found the principles of simple to complex and concrete to abstract were not sufficient for developing the affective domain. Something additional was needed.

We hoped that in seeking the unique characteristics of the affective domain we would discover the additional principles needed to structure an affective continuum. Analysis of affective objectives showed the following characteristics which the continuum should embody: the emotional quality which is an important distinguishing feature of an affective response at certain levels of the continuum, the increasing automaticity as one progresses up the continuum, the increasing willingness to attend to a specified stimulus or stimulus type as one ascends the continuum, and the developing integration of a value pattern at the upper levels of the continuum.

We had at first hoped that somehow we could derive a structure by attaching certain meanings to the terms "attitude," "value," "appreciation" and "interest." But the multitude of meanings which these terms encompassed, as we observed their use in educational objectives, showed that this was impossible. After trying a number of schemes and organizing principles, the one which appeared best to account for the affective phenomena and which best described the process of learning and growth in the affective field was the process of internalization.

* Illustrative educational objectives from the literature.

The term internalization is perhaps best defined by the descriptions of the categories of the affective domain. Generally speaking, however, it refers to the inner growth that occurs as the individual becomes aware of and then adopts the attitudes, principles, codes and sanctions that become a part of him in forming value judgments and in guiding his conduct. It has many elements in common with the term socialization. At its lowest level we have:

1.0 Receiving (Attending)

At this level we are concerned that the learner be sensitized to the existence of certain phenomena and stimuli—that is, that he be willing to receive or to attend to them. To the uninitiated, Bach is repetitive and boring. To those who know what to listen for, his music is intricate and complex; but even the unsophisticated can understand that in some of his works he has written "rounds" if they are made aware of it. The teacher who makes the student aware of such a characteristic in Bach's work is accomplishing the lowest level of behavior in this category.

1.1 ***Awareness.*** Though it is the bottom rung of the affective domain, "Awareness" is almost a cognitive behavior. But unlike "Knowledge," the lowest level of the cognitive domain, we are not so much concerned with a memory of, or ability to recall, an item or fact as we are that, given an appropriate opportunity, the learner will merely be conscious of something; that he takes into account a situation, phenomenon, object or state of affairs.

*Develops awareness of esthetic factors in dress, furnishings, architecture, city design and the like.

*Observes with increasing differentiation the sights and sounds of the city.

1.2 ***Willingness to Receive.*** In this category we have come a step up the ladder, but are still dealing with apparently cognitive behavior. At a minimum level, we are describing the behavior of being willing to tolerate a given stimulus, not to avoid it. Like "awareness" it involves neutrality or suspended judgment toward the stimulus. This is a frequently used category of teachers of the arts since we are prone to reject and avoid some of the newer art forms .

*Develops a tolerance for a variety of types of music.

*Accepts differences of race and culture, among one's acquaintances.

1.3 ***Controlled or Selected Attention.*** At a somewhat higher level we are concerned with a new phenomenon, the differentiation of a given

* Illustrative educational objectives from the literature.

stimulus into figure and ground at a conscious or perhaps semi-conscious level, the differentiation of aspects of a stimulus which are perceived as clearly marked off from adjacent impressions. The perception is still without tension or assessment, and the student may not know the technical terms or symbols with which to correctly or precisely describe it to others.

*Listens to music with some discrimination as to its mood and meaning and with some recognition of the contributions of various musical elements and instruments to the total effect.

*Listens for rhythm in poetry or prose read aloud.

2.0 *Responding*

At this level we are concerned with responses which go beyond merely attending to the phenomenon. The student is sufficiently motivated that he is not just "willing to attend" but perhaps it is correct to say that he is actively attending. As a first stage in a "learning by doing" process, the student is committing himself in some small measure to the phenomena involved. This is a very low level of commitment, and we would not at this level say that this was "a value of his" or that he had "such and such an attitude." These terms belong to the next higher level that we will describe. But we could say that he is doing something with or about the phenomena beside merely perceiving it as was true at the level previously described—of "selected or controlled attention." An example of such "responding" would be the compliance with rules of good health or safety, or obedience to rules of conduct.

The category of "responding" has been subdivided into three subcategories to describe the continuum of responding as the learner becomes more fully committed to the practice and phenomena of the objective. The lowest stage is illustrated in the preceding paragraph and is named "acquiescence in responding." As the name implies, there is the element of compliance or obedience at this level which distinguishes it from the next level, that of "willingness to respond." Finally, at a still higher level of internalization, there is found a "satisfaction in response" not reached at the previous level of willingness or assent to respond. When there is an emotional response of pleasure, zest, or enjoyment, we have reached this third level.

2.1 *Acquiescence in Responding.*

*Willingness to comply with health regulations.

*Observes traffic rules on foot and on a bicycle at intersections and elsewhere.

* Illustrative educational objectives from the literature.

2.2 *Willingness to Respond*

*Engages, on his own, in a variety of constructive hobbies and recreational activities.

*Keeps still when the occasion or the situation calls for silence. (Situation must be clearly defined.)

*Contributes to group discussion by asking thought-provoking questions.

2.3 *Satisfaction in Response*

*Finds pleasure in reading for recreation.

*Enjoys listening to a variety of human voices, with wide variations in pitch, voice quality and regional accents.

3.0 Valuing

This is the only category headed by a term which is in common use among the expressions of objectives by teachers. Further, it is employed in its usual sense—namely, that a thing, phenomenon or behavior has worth. This abstract concept of worth is not so much the result of the individual's own valuing or assessment as it is a social product that has been slowly internalized or accepted and come to be used by the student as his own criterion of worth.

Behavior categorized at this level is sufficiently consistent and stable that it has come to have the characteristics of a belief or an attitude. The learner displays this behavior with sufficient consistency in appropriate situations that he comes to be perceived as holding a value. At the lowest level of valuing, he is at least willing to permit himself to be so perceived, and at the higher level, he may behave so as to actively further this impression.

3.1 *Acceptance of a Value*

*A sense of responsibility for listening to and participating in a discussion.

3.2 *Preference for a Value*

*Draws reticent members of a group into conversation.

*Interest in enabling other persons to attain satisfaction of basic common needs.

*Willingness to work for improvement of health regulations.

* Illustrative educational objectives from the literature.

3.3 *Commitment*

*Firm loyalty to the various groups in which one holds membership.

*Practices religion actively in his personal and family living.

*Faith in the power of reason and in the methods of experiment and discussion.

4.0 Organization

As the learner successively internalizes values, he encounters situations for which more than one value is relevant. Thus necessity arises for (a) organizing the values into a system, (b) determining the interrelationships among them, (c) finding which will be the dominant and pervasive ones.

4.1 *Conceptualization of a Value*

*Desire to evaluate the thing appreciated.

*Finding and crystallizing the basic assumptions which underlie codes of ethics and are the basis of faith.

4.2 *Organization of a Value System*

*Weigh alternative social policies and practices against the standards of the public welfare rather than the advantage of specialized and narrow interest groups.

5.0 Characterization by a Value or Value Concept

At this level of internalization the values already have a place in the individual's value hierarchy, are organized into some kind of internally consistent system, have controlled the behavior of the individual for a sufficient time so that he has adapted to behaving this way, and an evocation of the behavior is no longer regularly accompanied by emotion or affect.

The individual consistently acts in accord with the values he has internalized at this level, and our concern is to indicate two things—(a) the generalization of this control to so much of the individual's behavior that he is described and characterized as a person by these pervasive controlling tendencies, (b) the integration of these beliefs, ideas and attitudes into a total philosophy or world view. These two aspects constitute the subcategories.

* Illustrative educational objectives from the literature.

5.1 *Generalized Set*

*Readiness to revise judgments and to change behavior in the light of evidence.

*Acceptance of objectivity and systematic planning as basic methods in arriving at satisfying choices.

5.2 *Characterization.*

*Develop for regulation of one's personal and civic life a code of behavior based on ethical principles consistent with democratic ideals.

*Develop a consistent philosophy of life.

*Develop a conscience.

Use of the Taxonomy

You now know what the taxonomy is. Of what value is it? Earlier in discussing some of the problems of curriculum construction we hinted at some of its potential uses.

As you now realize, it focuses on the student's behavior as it is expressed in educational objectives. While objectives are by no means foreign to the elementary and secondary school, not all objectives specify these goals in terms of student behavior. Often they are in terms of teacher behavior—on the assumption that student behavior changes follow certain teacher actions—surely not an airtight assumption! We have found that stating objectives as student behavior puts the focus where it belongs, on the change to be made in the student. It leaves the way open to experimentation with different teacher behaviors to attain most effectively and efficiently the desired goal. Stated this way, the taxonomy provides a basis for working with objectives with a specificity and a precision that is not generally typical of such statements. Further, this specificity and precision in the description of a student behavior makes it much easier to choose the kinds of learning experiences that are appropriate to developing the desired behavior and to building evalution instruments.

No longer is a teacher faced with an objective like this: "The student should understand the taxonomy of educational objectives." Rather the teacher now specifies whether this would be at the lowest level of Comprehension where he would at least expect the student to be able to translate the term "taxonomy" into something like "a classification system of educational goals," or perhaps at a deeper level of understanding, classified as Interpretation, where the student could restate the ideas of

* Illustrative educational objectives from the literature.

the taxonomy in his own words. In short, you should find the taxonomy a relatively concise model for the analysis of education objectives.

In building a curriculum you have undoubtedly paused to consider, "Are there things left out—behaviors I'd have included if I'd thought of them?" The taxonomy, like the period table of elements or a "check-off" shopping list, provides the panorama of objectives. Comparing the range of the present curriculum with the range of possible outcomes may suggest additional goals that might be included. Further, the illustrative objectives may suggest wordings that might be adapted to the area you are exploring.

Frequently when we are searching for ideas in building a curriculum we turn to the work of others who have preceded us. Where both your work and that of others are built in terms of the taxonomy categories, comparison is markedly facilitated. Translation of objectives into the taxonomy framework can provide a basis for precise comparison. Further, where similarities exist, it becomes possible to trade experiences regarding the values of certain learning experiences with confidence that there is a firm basis for comparison and that the other person's experience will be truly relevant.

It is perhaps also important to note the implication of the hierarchical nature of the taxonomy for curriculum building. If our analysis of the cognitive and affective areas is correct, then a hierarchy of objectives dealing with the same subject matter concepts suggests a readiness relationship that exists between those objectives lower in the hierarchy and those higher in it. While we regularly give some attention to this kind of sequential relation for objectives in the cognitive domain, it is less a prominent feature of the affective—a point to which we shall return.

How might the taxonomy be useful in better evaluating teaching? For one thing, teachers rarely analyze standardized tests. They have the feeling that these were put together by experts who know more than they do and, though they may feel a vague discontent with the test, too often they do not analyze the content of these tests against their objectives to determine how well they match. Here again, by using the taxonomy as a translating framework one can compare the test with the teacher's goals. In its simplest form this may be a determination of the proportion of items in each of the major taxonomy categories. This alone is often enough information to help a teacher determine a test's relevance. Such an analysis is particularly useful where one test must be selected from several considered for adoption. For instance, the taxonomy could be used as a common framework for comparing the Iowa Tests of Basic Skills with the revised Stanford Achievement Test.

A similar analysis of the items of the tests the teacher constructs himself checked against his own objectives may be revealing of over- or under-emphasis on particular objectives.

As has already been indicated, the *Handbook's* sample items and discussions of how to build test items at each of the taxonomy levels may be quite helpful to a teacher. But above and beyond this, the teacher will find the taxonomy is a key to increasing numbers of item collections. Dressel and Nelson (2) have published an 805 page folio of test items in science keyed to the taxonomy and subject matter. A teacher can use such a folio to select the items needed for a test, modifying them to fit the class level.

A related use of the taxonomy is its role in facilitating evaluation of a school's educational experiments. The most frequent type of school experimentation is the comparison of teaching methods, devices or curricula. In all of these comparisons, use of the taxonomy facilitates better communications and comparisons between experiments and between experimenters and adds to the precision of the operational definitions of the variables involved. Thus some television experimentation has resorted to taxonomic classifications to determine the instructor's competence in teaching abilities and skills as well as in conveying knowledge via this medium.

The emphasis in programmed learning on a complete and detailed analysis of the behaviors to be taught immediately suggests a possible role for the taxonomy. Recent literature on programming (3, 5) has recognized the taxonomy as a tool for the analysis of curriculums as the first step in programming. Because of its hierarchical structure, analysis by means of the taxonomy assists programming in still another way. The level of categorization aids in placing the material in the program sequence and in planning the over-all sequential development of the skill or ability.

So far, we have been discussing largely those uses of the taxonomy which stem from the cognitive domain. Curricula trends seem to show a move away from emphasis in the affective area. Indeed, schools have been attacked because of their concern with these kinds of objectives. But even though teachers continue to think affective goals are important, in comparison with the emphasis on cognitive objectives, there is little direct attack on these goals. There are occasional sociometric tests, group work, and some class elections, but the bulk of learning in this area is incidental learning. Partly this is a matter of confusion about what goals we are seeking. Partly this is a matter of not knowing how best to seek the goals even if the confusion were resolved.

The analytic framework which the taxonomy brings to the affective area should aid in the clarification of what goals are being sought. Guidance and counseling personnel using instruments dealing with the affective domain may find it useful to categorize the measures yielded by their instruments and, to the extent possible, compare this information with that needed by the teachers to reach their goals. The qualification "to the extent possible" is necessary because the taxonomy does not provide categories for all behavior, but only that which is desirable behavior, such as would be sought in a school curriculum. Psychological tests frequently include measures of undesirable behavior. In general, however, it is hoped that the affective domain categories will prove a useful framework for clarification of terminology and relating counselor data to teacher goals.

Along these same lines, an analysis of existing instruments demonstrates that the bulk of our measurement is concentrated at the very top levels—at the most complex behaviors. Use of this framework to analyze the Edwards Personnel Preference Schedule or the California Test of Personality, for instance, shows no measures of the lower levels of the affective area. This suggests that increased concentration on measurement instruments for the lower levels of the affective area might be helpful.

If our analysis of the affective domain is correct, we have a developmental picture of the way in which these goals are reached, from simple receiving and responding through characterization. It makes clear the beginnings of complex objectives such as appreciations, interests and attitudes. It focuses the teachers attention on the development of these simple behaviors which are the building blocks out of which the more complex objectives grow—simple behaviors which rarely are now deliberately taught.

You can, no doubt, now think of additional implications of the taxonomy for your school situation. This material may be enough to help you "understand" the taxonomy a little better. By "understand" we mean that you have some knowledge of the taxonomy, that you have been able to comprehend what it is about—that is, be able to describe it in your own words. Hopefully, you are at least at the level of application and can see some possible uses. Perhaps in the discussion of this material at the Conference it will be time for some evaluation to see how well my objectives were achieved.

References

1. Benjamin S. Bloom (Ed.), Max. D. Englehart, Edward J. Furst, Walker H. Hill, David R. Krathwohl. *A Taxonomy of Educational Objectives: Handbook I, the Cognitive Domain.* New York: Longmans, Green and Co., 1956. 207 p.

2. Paul Dressel and Clarence Nelson. *Questions and Problems in Science—* Test Folio No. 1. Princeton, N.J.: Cooperative Test Service, Educational Testing Service, 1956. 805 p.
3. Edmond Fry. *Teaching Machine and Programmed Instruction.* New York: McGraw Hill, 1963. 206 p.
4. David R. Krathwohl, Benjamin S. Bloom, Bertram Masia. *A Taxonomy of Educational Objectives, Handbook II, The Affective Domain.* New York: David MacKay & Co., Inc. To be published the first of 1964.
5. Robert F. Mager. *Preparing Objectives for Programmed Instruction.* San Francisco: Fearon Press, 1962. 62 p.

3.2 Educational Objectives and Human Performance

Robert M. Gagné

Utilizing the taxonomies is but the first step for the teacher in formulating his objectives. Objectives must be stated so that the teacher has clarified how he wants to change the behavior of his pupils—what he wants them to be able to do if his objectives have been reached. Gagné admits that there are critics of his ideas, but he answers each argument that they present. He defends the use of behavioral objectives with illustrations from the classroom.

There is something that seems incongruous in the two topics of my title—educational objectives and human performance. The combining of these ideas seems to be analogous to certain other strange concatenations, like sunspots and the stock market, or like soybean prices and the length of ladies' skirts. It will be my task, therefore, to reduce this incongruity—to explore the relations between these two topics. Why or how do educational objectives have anything to do with human performance, and vice versa?

The phrase "educational objectives" means different things to different

SOURCE. Robert M. Gagné, "Educational Objectives and Human Performance." In J. D. Krumboltz (Ed.), *Learning and the Educational Process.* (Chicago: Rand McNally & Co., 1965), pp. 1–24. Reprinted by permission of Rand McNally & Co.

people. The boy in the fourth grade may say: "Why do I have to study mathematics?" He may be asking a very fundamental question, and it is difficult to know what answer will satisfy him. Shall we say to him:

1. You need it in order to learn more mathematics, or to learn science?
2. You need it in order to balance your checkbook when you grow up?
3. You need it in order to be successful in almost any job?
4. You need it in order to become an informed and responsible citizen?
5. You need to appreciate the beauty of numbers?
6. You need it in order to think logically in solving problems?

Any or all of these answers might occur to a thoughtful adult. And if the student then asks: "How do you know?" it is apparent that a response could be given with somewhat differing degrees of confidence, depending upon the choice of a first answer. It is not difficult to demonstrate that trigonometry enters into the solving of problems about velocities of physical particles; it is surely more difficult to show the beauty of number relationships to someone who hasn't experienced them. Some educational objectives, in other words, are much more nearly immediate than others. Some pertain to longer time periods of the individual's life than do others, and some relate to more comprehensive aspects of his human existence than do others. The first step toward seeking relationships between human performance and educational objectives, then, may be to restrict the scope of the problem somewhat.

The Broad Goals of Education

The broad goals of education have been formulated by a number of distinguished national groups and commissions (National Education Association, 1964; Rockefeller Brothers Fund, 1958) as well as by outstanding scholars of the educational scene (Gardner, 1960). It will not be possible to deal with these extensively in the present context—only with a relatively small component of them. Suffice it to say here that there is a relatively high amount of agreement about these broad goals. It appears that there are three major emphases, which I summarize here in my own words.

1. Education has the purpose of making it possible for the individual to participate in and to share with other people a variety of aesthetic experiences.
2. A second major goal is the development of responsible citizenship.
3. The development of individual talents to the end of achieving satisfaction in a life work or vocation is a third goal.

However these three goals may be expressed, and my expression of them is surely not the best, it is difficult to disagree with them. They do in fact seem to represent goals of education with which a vast majority of informed people in the United States would agree.

To the student or practitioner of education, the questions raised by these statements of goals are difficult ones indeed. How do we know that what is being done in the education of the young gets us as far toward these goals as possible? How does one know that a particular content or a particular educational method will be optimally effective in reaching these ultimate objectives? The answer has at least two different parts to it. First, we need to understand and to specify to the best of our ability what is meant by "participating in aesthetic experiences," and what is meant by "responsible citizenship," and what is meant by "satisfying vocational activity." In other words, we need to be able to inform ourselves how we can tell when these things *have been achieved* by individuals. And second, we need to analyze, or break down into smaller components and stages, the progression toward these goals. We need to be able to see what it is about what the student can achieve in the eleventh grade which will relate to what he does as a voter, or as a father, or as a productive scientist.

Having acknowledged the problems posed by these broad goals, I can now state that it is not my intention to deal with them further here. Instead, I shall restrict my attention to the third and most frequently mentioned educational objective, pertaining to the acquiring of intellectual competence which will ultimately fulfill a vocational aim. I am interested in discussing mainly the objectives of instruction which attempt to provide the individual with ever increasing power to deal with and master his environment—the kind of instruction which we think of as including such subjects as English and mathematics and languages and science. This should not be taken to mean that I consider these the only important parts of the curriculum—far from it. But one has to start somewhere. Furthermore, I shall be concerned, as you will shortly see, with the problem of how to analyze or break down broadly stated objectives into smaller pieces, so that they can be dealt with more readily.

Human Performance

What about the other phrase in my title, *human performance*? What is that, and what does it have to do with educational objectives? Performance may be defined in several ways. The definition I wish to use here is an observable human accomplishment." "Behavior" is what brings performance about, but performance, as defined in this context, is the *outcome* of behavior. We can observe an individual close a door; that is a performance, and the proof of it is the outcome—the door is closed. Or, we can observe an individual solving a mathematical problem; the performance is the solution.

The fundamental reason why human performance is related to education is that it must be used to define what happens, or what is supposed to happen, in the educational process. Education is for learning, we say. Yet it is of great importance to keep in mind just what learning means, and how we know when it has taken place. We *infer* that learning has occurred when there is a difference in *performance* of the student from time X to time $X + 1$ (which difference for other reasons we cannot attribute to growth). On one day we observe that Johnny cannot add two-place numbers; on a subsequent day he can. There is a change in his performance, and we say he has learned. On one day a student cannot tell us where or what Ghana is; on the next day he can. Again, the change in his performance is what provides evidence of learning.

Occasionally, educational language appears to depart from this principle. For example, there is the phrase "learning experience." I should not want to deny that there may be such a thing. But one cannot tell whether learning has occurred until a difference in performance is observed. It will not suffice for the student to report he has learned something, or for the teacher to report that a learning situation has been provided. I have heard several separate reports recently from educational experimenters who undertook to give a test *before* the lesson as opposed to afterwards, just to see what would happen. Besides a certain amount of teacher shock, what happened was that half the students were able to complete the test nearly perfectly *before* instruction had begun! For this group of students, if the lesson had been given without the test, would there have been a "learning experience"? At any rate, if one compared their performance before and after, it would be quite clear that there had been no learning. Human performance is the fundamental class of data one must have in order to infer learning. It is, therefore, of equally basic importance to education.

Issues in Defining Objectives by Human Performance

Since observable human performances form the basis on which the inference of learning is made, it would seem to be a corollary that these same performances should constitute the objectives of education. If one could specify all the performances he expected of a high-school graduate, for example, this would serve two purposes: it would tell us what the student is able to do at the end of high school, and it would also tell us what he is able to do before he goes to college. The first could be used to compare with what he could do when he entered high school, and thus provide an idea of how much learning has occurred; the second could provide a base line for the changes in performance we hope will occur during his college attendance. It is indeed difficult to see how one can assess learning without such "before and after" observations of human performance.

Yet the defining of educational objectives in terms of human performance is not a universally accepted practice. There are two quite different sorts of objections raised to such a procedure.

Accomplishment Versus Direction of Change

First, there is the argument that objectives should state what is to be *attempted,* not what is to be *accomplished.* In line with this idea, one sometimes finds objectives stated in some such way as this:

> The student should acquire a developing awareness of the magnitude of the solar system and the universe; or
>
> The child should become increasingly confident in extemporaneous oral expression.

It is difficult to know what to say about such statements except that they are weasle-worded. Why is it not possible to say exactly what one wants the student to do in showing his awareness of solar system magnitudes? Why is it not possible to state what kind of extemporaneous oral expression one expects the child to perform? The answer may be, of course, that the latter kind of objectives can indeed be stated, but not all students will attain them. Unfortunately, this is probably true under present circumstances. It would be good, though, if we could amend the statement to read: "Not all students will attain them *with the same speed.*" Then they would still remain objectives which any intelligent person could identify, rather than descriptions which if not deliberately hedging are at least ambiguous.

Long-Range Unanticipated Outcomes Versus Intermediate Specified Events

A second kind of objection to clearly stated objectives is a much more serious one. It runs like this: "I can't be sure exactly what the student should be able to do at the end of some period of instruction. In fact, I am not interested in this. What I am interested in is how he will perform five or ten or even twenty years hence. If he studies science, this should mean that he will make wise decisions about science as an adult. If he studies English, this should mean that he will make wise choices of literature as an adult." In other words, the tenor of this objection is that it is not possible to state immediate objectives of instruction because some of them cannot be anticipated. How does one know what a student will be able to do following some unit of instruction when he might just do something which even the curriculum designer has not thought of yet? Better keep one's eye on far-reaching or long-term objectives, and say what one hopes he will do when he gets to college, or even when he finishes college.

I have said that this kind of objection is the more serious, and the reason is that it is held with such emotional vigor by some influential people. This is the only reason I can see that it is more serious, because actually it is intellectually insupportable. If one is actually interested in performances which will appear ten years hence, there is nothing wrong with that. Two courses of action are then available. The first is to perform some longitudinal studies to determine what differential factors are in the current educational backgrounds of people who behave desirably and people who behave undesirably at some future time. Alternatively, one could experimentally introduce certain differences in the education of groups of present students, and follow them up after five or ten years to see what kinds of decisions they make. Both of these techniques are of course well known to behavioral scientists, and successful studies have been and are being done to find answers such as these.

But such studies take time, and some curriculum designers are naturally impatient to get on with the job of "improving" education. It is then up to them to make some reasonable guesses about *what kinds of capabilities learned now* will have the desirable effects wished for ten years hence. It is of course necessary to recognize that these *are* hypotheses. But that is no reason not to state them explicitly and in terms which meet the criteria of ordinary operational definitions. What would we think of a biologist who behaved this way toward the growth of plants? Suppose he said: "I am really only interested in the flowering of this plant, which may happen ten weeks from now. In the meantime, I think it would be wrong, possibly even dangerous, to say what I think the necessary stages which precede this flowering may be. I will say that the plant must be watered properly and exposed to sunlight, but beyond that I will not go. It is really the future flowering I am interested in—the events between now and then are entirely up to the plant." What ridiculous behavior this would be for a scientist to display! Is there a way of justifying similar behavior when it is said with reference to the intellectual development of a human being? I think not.

If we must make hypotheses concerning the precursors or determinants of some ultimate performances in advanced stages of education, or in adult life, by all means let us do so. But there is no reason not to make these hypotheses explicit. In fact I should call it presumptuous not to do so. What can I make of such a statement as that which informs me that my son is going to study astronomy in the seventh grade? Is it because thereby one of his college requirements will be met? What in fact will he be able to do after he has studied astronomy? It is not that I am playing the carping parent when I ask these questions. These are serious questions, because I really do not know what hypotheses are guiding such instruction. If these were made explicit, if they were in fact stated in terms of human performance, it *might* become apparent whether my son needs to study astronomy in the seventh grade, as opposed, perhaps, to something else.

And what about the idea that there may really be some unanticipated outcome from studying astronomy, or probability, or geography, at some particular age and in a way which encourages problem solving? Well, of course there may. I shall be just as pleased as anyone if this is the case. But I return to an earlier point—unless it can be demonstrated that learning has occurred, the expectation of some *other* outcome seems slim indeed. And if one expects that learning is going to occur then this means there must be a demonstrable change in performance. There may be some other unexpected kind of change, but there *has* to be some particular kind of change that can be specified. And that brings us back to human performance, since that is where the observable change will appear. There would seem to be no valid reason why such performances cannot be described.

Reasons for Describing Educational Objectives

By this time, or perhaps long before this, the question may have occurred to you, "Why describe educational objectives, anyhow? Why bother?"

The fundamental reason is one that I have already given and it is primarily aimed at those who are trying to understand education, to study it as a process, or to improve its quality. Nowadays, let it be noted such persons are not only "professional educators"; they are university professors of physics and chemistry and mathematics and English; they are experimental and educational psychologists and sociologists; and they are also many intelligent public-spirited citizens whose profession does not lie directly in the educational realm. What these individuals need to understand is perhaps the most fundamental fact about *learning,* namely, its definition. Learning is a change in capability which is inferred from differences in an individual's performance from one time to a later time. Learning has some mystery about it, for many people. But the most important fact about it is embodied in this definition, which relates it integrally to human performance.

There are, however, other reasons for defining educational objectives, which have some practical implications for education itself. Perhaps no one has written more sensibly and persuasively on this subject than has Tyler (1949; 1950). In a relatively recent paper (1964), he describes some reasons which I shall mention here in my own words:

1. Definitions of objectives are necessary to guide the behavior of the teacher. While many teachers are able to recognize educational goals and translate them into effective conditions for learning, some teachers have not carried their thinking beyond the stage of selecting the content to be presented. The danger here is that the teacher will not recognize effective ways of reaching the necessary objectives if in fact he has not formulated these objectives for himself.
2. Defining objectives for the student is an inadequately exploited educational technique. Tyler reports that unless students know what the objectives are they are likely to resort to memorization and mechanical completion of exercises in textbooks or workbooks, rather than carrying out relevant sorts of learning activities. When one tells the student what he is expected to do after he learns, this is not "giving him the answer." Rather it is providing him with a goal which he himself can use to organize his own learning activities. Of relevance here is a study of Mager and McCann (1961), who found that when a group of engineers were told the objectives of their learning they succeeded in reaching them in much less time than under other instructional conditions.
3. Another purpose of defining objectives has often been emphasized by Tyler and others: unless the objectives are known, it is impossible to know what the student's capabilities are at any given moment. This reason for objectives has often been stated in terms of the requirements for measurement, or "testing." But "testing" is also sometimes an emotional word, and it may therefore be thought that this is an unpersuasive reason for defining objectives. Whatever emotionally toned arguments there may be about "testing," one thing is perfectly clear. It is impossible to carry on the enterprise of education without assessing each student's attainments. Quite possibly, students need to be assessed much more frequently and perhaps less elaborately than they have been up to now. But it makes no sense to undertake to *teach* something which the student either knows already or, alternatively, which he cannot possibly learn because he does not have the prerequisite knowledge. We must know what the student is capable of doing at any given moment in his educational progress. And this means we must have statements of objectives which define what we except him to be able to do.

There are, then, several important reasons for seeking to define educational objectives in terms of human performances. These objectives are used to tell us whether the inference of learning can be made. They are used as specifications of the kinds of questions to ask the student in assessing his current capabilities. They become important guides for the teacher's behavior in selecting appropriate instruction. And they could probably be used to greater advantage than they are at present in informing the student of goals to be achieved.

The Process of Defining Objectives

How does one go about defining objectives in terms of human performance? There are, after all, many action words, verbs, in the English language, and these can be used to contruct a great variety of descriptive sentences. How can one decide what the components of a good description are?

First of all, it is evident that a description of human performance must contain a good "strong" verb, a verb referring to observable human action. This point has been elaborated in a delightful book by Mager (1962). As a first approximation, or as an approximate way of speaking, it seems reasonable to try a statement of an objective in some such terms as "understands probability." The trouble is, however, that this may mean several different things, and not just one thing. Does it mean that the student can "state a verbal definition of probability"? Does it mean he can "predict the probability of a hit for a batter with a batting average of .240"? Does it mean he can "compute the probability of tossing a penny to obtain nine heads in a row"? Or perhaps all of these? Actually, the answer to people who insist on using such verbs as "understand" in statements of objectives is very simple. It consists of another question: How would you be able to tell that the student understands? The answer to this second question has a high probability of containing a verb referring to observable human action.

How detailed or specific does an acceptable definition of an objective need to be? One degree of nonspecificity is represented by such a statement as "solves problems in algebra." But this is not very helpful because it doesn't tell us what kinds of problems, and there are, after all, many possible kinds. Another degree of specificity is suggested by the statement "computes the normality of a chemical solution." Still more specific would be a statement like "identifies nouns or noun-phrases in English prose sentences." Each of these statements describes performance with a verb which implies that objective observation is possible. Yet they obviously differ considerably in their degree of specificity, in the fineness of detail they contain. They therefore suggest the question of how finely performance should be described.

Here is one of the striking parallels with the work of investigators who have been trying to find the right level of description for human performances in jobs. These peoples too have long been plagued with the same kind of question. For example, one can describe the job of policeman, if one so chooses, as "enforcing the law." Yet it would be immediately recognized that such a statement is in one way or another highly inadequate in conveying to another person what a policeman does. Accordingly, researchers in this field have generally agreed that one must describe performance in somewhat greater detail. In these terms, a policeman's job is considered to be composed of *tasks,* such as "checks the locked condition of doors on his beat"; "disperses sidewalk crowds"; "provides information on locations of major traffic arteries"; and so forth. As a part of a job, a task may be defined as the smallest component of performance which has a distinct and independent purpose. Describing a policeman's job in any greater detail (e.g., "puts left foot in front of right foot") would be meaningless because the purposes of such detailed performances are not evident. The task is, then, an extremely useful unit of description, which can be rather readily identified for any job, old or new.

It seems to me that the problem of describing educational objectives is a very similar one. Again we are up against the problem of how detailed to make a description. If the statement is too broad, like "writes English compositions," we are dissatisfied because we recognize a great lack of information. On the other hand, if a statement is too detailed, like "identifies the infinitive forms of irregular French verbs," we are unlikely to see its purpose; we are inclined to say, "What does anyone want to do *that* for?" What is needed, apparently, is a level of description that is comparable to the *task.* In other words, it must be the *smallest unit of performance which can be identified as having a distinct and independent purpose.* "Punctuating sentences" is a performance that has a distinct purpose. "Differentiating the varieties of 'stop' marks" does not have a clear purpose; it is therefore too detailed as a statement of an educational objective.

Here I must refer again to Tyler's recent statement regarding this problem of level of specificity of definitions of objectives (Tyler, 1964). The most useful degree of specificity, he says, is at the level of generality of behavior that one is seeking to help the student acquire. One of the main indications of this is that the description identify a performance which can be valued in and of itself as being of effective use in the individual's life. This view, I think, corresponds closely to the one I have tried to state in somewhat different terms. Tyler is emphasizing two points about a useful level of description for behavioral objectives: (1) they should express a *purpose* which makes sense within the larger context of the person's life goals; (2) this purpose should be *distinguishable* from others. Tyler's criterion would lead us to seek statements of objectives such as "reads a French newspaper," rather than "reads French"; "solves problems requiring the use of sine, cosine, and tangent," rather than "understands trigonometry"; "makes a quantitative description of dispersion of errors in observations," rather than "knows statistics."

Analysis of Human Performances

If educational objectives are stated as tasks, and the level of greater generality is avoided, we can expect communication about education, its goals and its procedures, to be most effective. There will be little remaining obscurity about what is to be learned. And as I have previously stated, this can probably have salutary effects on the process of education itself insofar as clarity of purpose is conveyed to both teacher and student. In addition, the improvement in communication to educational administrators within school systems, and to parents and the larger public as well, is another highly desirable outcome to be expected.

For the person who wishes to study the process of education, to analyze it, to perform research upon it for the purpose of understanding it, statements of educational objectives as human performances are an absolutely essential starting point. For one thing, they help to keep in sharp focus the fact that learning of the individual student is the central purpose of education, and that all other questions, such as those of homogeneous groupings, guidance services, class scheduling, library facilities, and the other practical questions of school administration, are simply contributors to that central purpose. In addition, objective statements of performance provide the empirically observable foundations to which all speculations, hypotheses, and innovative hunches about educational improvement must be referred. The number of differences of opinion about educational procedures which can be rather simply resolved if both parties agree to base their arguments on performance objectives is surprising, even startling.

It is also true that for the individual who wants to do certain kinds of research in education, statements of performance objectives are *merely* a starting point. Having achieved good objective statements of human performance, one must go farther than this. There must be, for purposes of investigation, an *analysis* of these objectives. The entities with which one must deal in educational research are even finer, more detailed, performances. A number of problems illustrate this need for further analysis:

1. In *designing a curriculum,* it becomes very evident that certain objectives depend on other ones. In other words, there are such things as subordinate objectives; there are performances which are

prerequisite to other performances. If one states an objective as "reading prose material composed of the 1000 most frequent English words," for example, it is immediately evident that the child must learn some other things first. He cannot simply plunge into a book written in basic English before he has mastered other performances such as recognizing words, sounding phonemes, and recognizing printed letters. Similarly, a student of physics cannot meet the objective of "computing the resultants of forces" unless he has previously acquired the performance of "determining the lengths of sides of triangles using trigonometric relationships." Practically all educational objectives have prerequisites, and such an analysis of objectives must be done if an effective sequence of instruction is to be designed. Some of my own work with colleagues in the University of Maryland Mathematics Project (Gagné, 1963; Gagné & Bassler, 1963; Gagné, Mayor, Garstens, & Paradise, 1962) demonstrates this point with reference to some topics of junior-high mathematics. When one conducts such an analysis, he begins with a task, a statement of an objective having a distinct purpose. But the statements of performances which result from the analysis are considerably more detailed than this. Their purposes can usually not be understood by themselves, but only as prerequisites to the more generally stated objective with which the analysis was begun.

2. Closely related to this reason for breaking down educational objectives into finer units is the need for *assessing student progress*. If it is true that there are really prerequisites in continuous learning (and not just the ones suspected of being phony that often appear in college catalogs), then the need to test whether a student has met these prerequisites before going on should be an important educational procedure. It appears doubtful if this function of assessing student performance on prerequisites is being done very carefully and systematically in most schools today. To do it properly, it is necessary not only to state objectives but also to analyze them. Tests which are based on such detailed performance statements can be truly diagnostic of the progress of students within the framework of a curriculum.
3. One of the most important reasons for analyzing objectives is to determine some important facts about the *conditions for learning* them. Statements of objectives do not in themselves provide all the information that is needed to make it clear how they need to be taught, even though they do perform the very important function of communicating in unambiguous terms what the accomplishments that follow learning are to be. To clarify what is needed for learn-

ing, the original objective must be broken down into more specific statements of performance. Suppose, for example, one has decided upon the objective of "constructing utterances in German which are understandable to a German-speaking person." The statement itself gives few clues to how this performance is going to be learned. Does one learn to do this by acquiring German words and German grammar? Should a learner learn to say the words first, then acquire their meanings, and finally learn the structural features of the language? How much can he learn by listening to a recorded German speaker? All of these questions are of course familiar to teachers of foreign languages. They are faced and solved in a variety of ways in American schools. But they obviously demand an analysis of the objective for their answer, if one is concerned with the proper conditions for efficient learning.

The Consequences of Analyzing Objectives

Here, then, are three important reasons for making a more detailed analysis of educational objectives stated in terms of human performance. They are, as I have said, primarily important to the individual who wishes to understand the educational process by the use of analytic and experimental methods. They do not contribute to an immediate purpose of communicating facts or ideas about education, but to a more long-term purpose of explaining how the process of education works.

Reduction of Complexity

If one persists in analyzing educational objectives into finer units, what are the consequences? Doesn't one end up with large masses of detail that become difficult to grasp and to do anything with? In some sense, this is true. If one is determined to analyze human performances, he must be prepared to deal with great numbers of individual facts. The fundamental reason for this, of course, is that human performance *is* complex; the variety of unitary actions that can be performed by human beings, in a variety of settings, is tremendous. Dealing with the "fine grain" of human performance is perhaps something for which a modern computer could be used, although I am not aware that that particular usage has been previously suggested.

However, in another sense, the analysis of objective statements of human tasks (or objectives) does *not* have the consequence of making things more complicated, varied, and difficult to deal with. Instead, a marvelous possibility becomes evident: all of this tremendous variety of human performance begins to fit together into categories, which can then be dealt with and thought about as *classes of events,* rather than as separate and distinct ones. The advantages of thinking about performance events as classes are the same as those which occur in other scientific disciplines. The biologist is able to study the properties of skin and muscle and bone and blood in some common ways because they are composed of a class of entities called *cells;* the chemist is able to deal with a great variety of acids, bases, and salts in solution because they form a class of *electrolytes.* In quite a similar way, it is possible to identify classes of human performance and to use them as tools in thinking about the previously mentioned problems of curriculum design, of student assessment, and of the conditions for efficient learning.

It is at this point that those who are concerned with analysis of tasks, or objectives, must, I think, make contact with psychology. For here is the science which attempts to formulate the fundamental principles of behavior that make a set of classes possible. Those who began with task statements for jobs and human work arrived at this conclusion as they continued their analysis of human performances (Gagné, 1962; Miller, 1962a; Miller, 1962b). There are many reasons to think that the analysis of educational objectives will similarly draw upon the principles of psychology to derive useful classes of performance which can serve the purposes already mentioned.

The basic principle which appears to be of use in deriving classes of human performance may be called the *principle of stimulus processing.* This is the principle that the stimulus inputs to the human organism undergo a limited number of kinds of transformations into outputs, or human performances. If one examines human behavior in an analytic fashion, as psychologists have been doing for many years, it becomes evident that there are several different kinds of these stimulus-performance transformations. Without necessarily knowing their exact sites or mechanisms, it is nevertheless possible to distinguish them from each other. These different kinds of transformations of stimuli into human action form a class of events which may be collectively called varieties of stimulus processing; in other words, varieties of behavior.

Categories of Behavior

If one employs the principle of stimulus processing to differentiate classes of human behavior, he arrives at not a great many classes—more than one or two, but probably fewer than twelve. In other words, rather than there being a tremendous variety of entities to be considered, there are only relatively few classes of behavior, and these can serve many purposes of reasoning about the variables which produce human performance. I have described these more extensively elsewhere (Gagné, 1964a, Gagné, 1964b), but it will be possible to state them briefly here, using as examples the kinds of performances familiar to the education scene. Six classes of behavior which are of some importance to education are these, beginning with the simplest:

1. A simple *connection*. The young child learns to say "mama" when his mother gives the stimulus "mama." Not different in principle is the American adult learning to pronounce the German word *ich* in response to some appropriate stimulus.
2. A *chain* or *sequence*. The child is able to draw a square. Or he may recite verbatim and in sequence the names of the letters in the alphabet or the names of the numerals from one to ten. Verbal associations, such as those involved in translating a foreign word, may be an important subcategory.
3. *Identification*. The student may learn to distinguish among stimuli of different physical appearance. A young child having a set of leaves on his desk may learn to distinguish them by means of the verbal labels "elm," "maple," "oak," "poplar," and so forth. A student of astronomy learns to identify certain stars and certain constellations. He distinguishes them, one from the other, by giving them different names, or perhaps by pointing to them.
4. A *concept*. A great many performances established by school learning involve the use of concepts, which are *classes* of objects or events. Early instruction in mathematics, for example, consists in teaching such concepts as the numbers one, two, three, and four, the concept of set and member of set, the concepts of joining and separation, and so on. A student of biology learns to use the concept "cell"; a student of chemistry the concept "gas"; a student of physics the concept "force."
5. A *principle*. A principle is a chain of concepts; in its simplest form, if A, then B. Many such principles are typically called "facts," such as "Water boils at 212° F," or "Birds fly south in the winter," or "The atomic weight of oxygen is 16." Obviously, a great many subordinate performances of school learning belong to this class.
6. A *higher-order principle*, or *general principle*. A higher-order principle results from the combination of two or more simpler ones. These are the generalizations that enable the student to think about an ever broadening set of new problems. They may, and hopefully do, result from problem-solving behavior on the part of the student. As performances, they make possible the solving of novel problems by application of the principle to new situations. A student may be able, for example, to apply Newton's second law to a specific problem involving an automobile rolling downhill. Or a student of

English may be able to select some metaphoric language to express an idea in a composition.

Each of these classes of performance may readily be identified in the things that a student is able to do after he has learned something. They represent, in a sense, the unitary steps in accomplishment that he takes on the road to the attainment of each more generally stated educational objective.

The Implications of Behavior Categories

Each of these stimulus-processing categories, or "behavior categories," carries some definite implications for certain important procedures of education.

First, the establishment of each of these categories of performance requires a different set of conditions for learning, and thus makes a difference in the method of instruction used to bring it about. It is not possible for me to discuss these differences in learning conditions extensively here, as I have done elsewhere (Gagné, 1965). But surely it is quite evident that the conditions one has to arrange in order to bring about the correct pronunciation of an umlauted "u" are quite different from the conditions one must set up when the learner is to be engaged in learning to use the proper order of words in a German sentence. Similarly, it is evident that learning to identify a triangle requires considerably different conditions for learning than does learning to formulate a definition of a triangle ("three line segments joining three points which are not on the same straight line"). One of the most important implications resulting from the *analysis* of performance objectives, then, is that the researcher, and the designer of instructional methods, are able to deal with classes of behavior which are quite independent of specific content, but which demand a common set of procedures for the arrangement of conditions of instruction.

Second, each of these performance classes implies something different with respect to the sequencing of instruction within a topic to be learned. For example, a principle cannot be learned unless the concepts which make it up have previously been mastered. The child who is expected to learn to perform according to the principle "The sum of three and five is eight" must have previously acquired the concepts "sum," "three," "five," and "eight." Learning a principle, in other words, requires some prerequisite performances. The same is true for the other behavior categories. Establishing the proper sequences within the topics of a course of study is a matter of considerable importance to the effectiveness of education.

Third, the classes of performance which are analyzed out of educational objectives suggest the possibility of "diagnostic" assessments of student progress along the way to a more comprehensive goal. This idea appears to be related to the differentiation of types of tests described in *Taxonomy of Educational Objectives*, by Bloom and his colleagues (1956). These investigators distinguished the testing categories of knowledge, comprehension, application, analysis, synthesis, and evaluation and suggested that these may be arranged in a hierarchical order. Although there is not a one-to-one correspondence of these categories with those I have outlined, there are definable relationships between them, and the similarity of the basic idea is apparent. Classes of performance which represent different kinds of behavior—different kinds of stimulus processing—must be differentially tested. Each requires a different kind of test item to reflect what is being measured. Each in turn has a different meaning for student progress, depending upon the sequence of instruction that is being followed to reach the educational objective.

A Summary View of Educational Objectives

Let me now summarize some of the major points of what I have tried to say.

For those goals of education which ultimately pertain to productive occupational goals, and probably for others as well, clear statements of educational objectives can have some very important and desirable effects. Primary among these is unambiguous communication among educators, students, parents, and the public. Clear statements require definitions which refer to human performances, since the fundamental events which are the focus of interest are those of learning, and learning means a change in human performance. The advantages of clear communication to educational change and improvement are many. They include not only an increase in general understanding and support for innovations, but also more direct and immediate uses in the educational process itself in affecting the techniques of teachers and the goals and motivations of students.

Those who question the desirability of defining objectives in performance terms seem to have advanced no valid arguments to support such a position. There is no conflict between statements phrased in terms of performance and the use of more abstract nouns like "comprehension," "understanding," or "appreciation." It is simply a matter of answering the further question: "How shall I be able to tell when 'understanding' has occurred?" There is also no conflict with the idea that some of the outcomes of education must surely be projected into the future, or that some may be unanticipated. Again there is a further question to be answered, which is something like this: "What are the changes in present performance without which such long-term or unexpected outcomes could not occur?" Each of these questions leads one back to a dependence on statements about human performance as expressions of educational objectives.

Clear statements of objectives need to represent some particular level of specificity. I have suggested that this level is what researchers in another related field have called the "task" level, defined as the smallest unit of performance having a distinct and independent purpose. For greatest communicability, educational objectives need to have some evident relation to useful life activities.

For many purposes of educational research, such performance statements provide an essential starting point, but only a starting point. Further analysis is necessary into finer and more detailed entities of performance. Order can be brought into this mass of detail with the use of the principle of stimulus processing, by means of which one is enabled to classify the great variety of performances in which human beings engage. The employment of such a classification of behavior makes possible the drawing of systematic implications for three important aspects of the educational process; the definition of conditions for effective learning, the design of proper sequences of instruction, and the assessment of student progress. All of these rest upon the basic relationship between educational objectives and human performance.

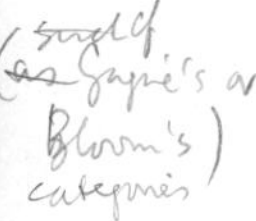

References

Bloom, B. S. (Ed.), Engelhart, M. D., Furst, E. J., Hill, W. H., & Krathwohl, D. R. *Taxonomy of educational objectives:* Book 1. *Cognitive domain.* New York: Longmans, Green, 1956.

Gagné, R. M. *The conditions of learning.* New York: Holt, Rinehart & Winston, 1965.

Gagné, R. M. Human functions in systems. In R. M. Gagné (Ed.). *Psychological principles in system development.* New York: Holt, Rinehart & Winston, 1962.

Gagné, R. M. Learning and proficiency in mathematics. *Math. Teacher,* 1963, **56**, 620–626.

Gagné, R. M. Problem solving. In A. W. Melton (Ed.), *Categories of human learning.* New York: Academic Press, 1964. (a)

Gagné, R. M. The implications of instructional objectives for learning. In C. M. Lindvall (Ed.), *Defining educational objectives.* Pittsburgh: Univer. of Pittsburgh Press, 1964. (b)

Gagné, R. M., & Bassler, O. C. A study of retention of some topics of elementary non-metric geometry. *J. educ. Psychol.*, 1963, **54**, 123–131.

Gagné, R. M., Mayor, J. R., Garstens, H. L., & Paradise, N. E. Factors in acquiring knowledge of a mathematical task. *Psychol. Monogr.*, 1962, **76** (Whole No. 526).

Gardner, J. W. National goals in education. In *Goals for Americans.* The Report of the President's Commission on National Goals. Englewood Cliffs, N.J.: Prentice-Hall, 1960.

Mager, R. F. *Preparing objectives for programmed instruction.* San Francisco: Fearon, 1962.

Mager, R. F., & McCann, J. *Learner-controlled instruction.* Palo Alto, Calif.: Varian Associates, 1961.

National Education Association, Project on Instruction. *Schools for the sixties.* New York: McGraw-Hill, 1964.

Rockefeller Brothers Fund. *The pursuit of excellence: Education and the future of America.* Panel Report V of the Special Studies Project. Garden City, N.Y.: Doubleday, 1958.

Tyler, R. W. Achievement testing and curriculum construction. In E. G. Williamson (Ed.), *Trends in student personnel work.* Minneapolis: Univer. of Minnesota Press, 1949.

Tyler, R. W. The functions of measurement in improving instruction. In E. F. Lindquist (Ed.), *Educational measurement.* Washington, D. C.: American Council on Education, 1950.

Tyler, R. W. Some persistent questions on the defining of objectives. In C. M. Lindvall (Ed.), *Defining educational objectives.* Pittsburgh: Univer. of Pittsburgh Press, 1964.

3.3 Implications of Recent Research for Improving Secondary Education[1]

John C. Flanagan

The author was the director of Project Talent, a survey of American secondary school pupils. The findings of this project gave us a basis for determining the extent to which educational objectives have been reached. Examples of comparative achievement on the basis of such variables as sex, type of school, and environment are discussed. Flanagan believes that objectives should be formulated with an understanding of the wide differences among individuals and the possibilities for greater achievement by the employment of technology for individualized instruction. Furthermore, the author believes that objectives should be tailored to the talents of the individual. Progress must be determined by giving consideration to special procedures for measuring the attainment of objectives.

SOURCE. John C. Flanagan, "The Implications of Recent Research for the Improvement of Secondary Education," *American Educational Research Journal*, I, 1 (1964), pp. 1–9. Reprinted by permission of the author and the American Educational Research Association.

[1] Invited Address for Division 15 (Educational Psychology) of the American Psychological Association, presented August 29, 1963, at the Sheraton Hotel, Philadelphia, Pennsylvania.

Education at the secondary-school level has been one of our most stable institutions during the past fifty years. During this period the percentages of young Americans entering the ninth grade and graduating from high school have risen to 90 and 65, respectively. However, there has been little change in the program of studies to which these students have been exposed. There have been strong influences for change, especially in recent years; and there are many signs that radical changes can be expected in the next ten years. If such changes are to represent progress and improvements in secondary education and not mere change and innovation, they must be based on systematic research and evaluation.

There has been relatively little research in the field of secondary education. The studies of Edward L. Thorndike about fifty years ago did much to remove scientific support from the doctrine of mental discipline as a basis for many of the courses and methods being used in secondary education. As a result, modern languages were substituted for the study of Latin and Greek. At about the same time a different type of factor, federal support for vocational education at the secondary-school level, became a strong force in shaping the secondary-school program.

This discussion of recent research and its implications for secondary education will focus on current status, findings, and conclusions in each of three aspects of education:

1. Objectives, curricula, and the content of the instructional program.
2. Methods, technology, and the development of procedures for efficient learning.
3. Measurement, evaluation, and guidance of the individual student so that he may set and work toward realistic educational and occupational goals.

The objectives and content of programs of instruction undoubtedly comprise the most important of these three aspects of secondary education. Efficient instructional methods and precise measurement of results cannot compensate for inadequate attention to objectives and content. It is unfortunate that this is the area in which there has been the least research. Individual textbook authors, educational publishers, and numerous *ad hoc* committees of teachers and scholars have given serious thought to these matters. Rarely, however, have they engaged in the systematic collection and evaluation of data which might provide a sound basis for their decisions and choices.

College-preparatory courses continue to include the same subjects that were required fifty years ago, except, perhaps, for Latin and Greek. Recently, committees of university scholars in the fields of science and mathematics undertook the revision of secondary-school courses in their fields. They found that much of the information being taught in mathematics and science was out of date. They have attempted to bring into these courses an approach and an appreciation of methods more appropriate to present-day activities in these fields. However, these committees have not usually applied research methods to the study of objectives and content.

Vocational-education courses in many instances have changed little over the past decades in spite of the technological revolution in industry. Except for a few questionnaires and interviews collecting impressions from former students and their employers, the vocational-education program has not been studied objectively in terms of the needs of business and industry.

Since decisions regarding educational objectives and course content depend on value systems, it is unlikely that various local school authorities can be expected to agree on the relative importance of each of the goals and topics. It *is* true that more data can be expected to result in more intelligent decisions regarding objectives. If the specific nature of the student learning that can be expected from each of various defined educational experiences is known, choices of instructional materials for educational programs can be made in terms of the desired types of learning.

A number of findings from a recent survey of a representative sample of American students in the ninth, tenth, eleventh, and twelfth grades appear relevant to the problems of objectives and contents. This study, called Project TALENT, involved the testing of 440,000 students, using a comprehensive set of tests and questionnaires. One finding was that high-school girls in the twelfth grade knew very little more about mathematics and the physical sciences than girls in the ninth grade. This poses a real question for educational planners. Should the women in this country continue to grow up in relative ignorance of science, with little appreciation of the power and value of mathematical and scientific developments?

Another finding from Project TALENT is the lack of progress made by the students in vocational schools in the tool subjects of reading, writing, and mathematics. The students in the twelfth grade are only slightly more advanced in these fields than students in the ninth grade. It appears likely that these basic skills will be of increasing importance for skilled workers in industry because of the growing need for learning new methods of operation and new information to adapt to new equipment and procedures.

Project TALENT findings indicate that although the students from small rural schools did about as well as those from large city schools on subjects such as English, history, and the first two years of secondary-school mathematics, they were markedly inferior in advanced mathematics and sciences. It appears that unless this situation is remedied a significant segment of the population with potential talent will be seriously handicapped, if not eliminated, from further training in science and mathematics.

Project TALENT has provided a large amount of other information regarding the levels of achievement now reached by our high-school students with respect to a variety of educational objectives. Through follow-up studies planned for 1, 5, 10, and 20 years after high-school graduation, much additional data should be forthcoming. These follow-ups will be helpful in establishing the relative importance for civic and occupational activities of the various objectives in secondary education programs.

Data of many other types and from many other sources are needed to provide a sound basis for choosing educational objectives. For example, objectives for college-preparatory students should be based on a systematic study of the types of college programs that they are likely to enter. This study should include necessary knowledge, skills, habits, and attitudes.

Probably the two most effective ways to study college programs are by making a comprehensive task analysis of a sample of learning activities and by collecting a large representative sample of college situations that reveal especially effective or ineffective preparation at the secondary-school level.

The analysis of learning activities should include the study of sample paragraphs from textbooks, lectures, and reference materials. Similarly, typical assignments should be analyzed to study the prerequisites necessary for satisfactory and for superior completion. To obtain a large representative sample of college situations that reveal especially effective or ineffective preparation, the critical-incident technique may be used. Students and instructors should be asked for specific examples of situations in which a student performed unusually well or poorly because of a particular aspect of his secondary-school training. It would be necessary to collect such data for a number of courses in each of a variety of fields of study.

Similar systematic studies of the preparation of graduates of vocational schools for effective performance on the job should be carried out. One badly neglected area consists of the study of the effectiveness of the school's program to prepare students for adult life as revealed by the same type of analyses of adult activities and situations. It is proposed that the studies mentioned above be carried out initially to establish a reasonably sound basis for formulating educational objectives. Following these steps, more precise information could be obtained regarding objectives and content for the secondary-school program by devising new formulations of objectives and conducting controlled experiments to evaluate them against later performance. These experiments would make it possible to discover new and more effective types of preparation rather than relying entirely on information as to which of the present practices produced the best results.

In summarizing this discussion of the objectives and contents of secondary education, it can be said that recent efforts of scientists and scholars have made some progress in removing out-of-date content from courses in their fields. Each group has made a number of judgments as to appropriate objectives and content. These judgments have not been based on research evidence, nor have they been evaluated. It is clear that research data now available suggest some of the directions that revisions of objectives and content should take. A systematic research approach is essential if these decisions are to be based on more than hunches and educated guesses.

Let us look next at methods, technology, and the development of procedures for efficient learning. There has been much research on these problems. The findings suggest many improvements with respect to current methods of instruction. The psychological study of intellectual processes has given us some basic data regarding the learning process. Even in a simple problem like acquiring specific items of information, such as the English meaning of words in a foreign language, recent studies indicate that current methods are much less efficient than they could be. Substantial increases have been obtained in the number of foreign words "learned per minute" by using a simple linkage rule.

Another set of research findings refers to the importance of structure. Many specific items of information can be much more readily learned and remembered if they are related to concepts and principles of which they are examples. That is, if items are examples of a structure system they need not be memorized, because any item can be reproduced by anyone knowing the nature of the system.

A well-known but seriously neglected body of psychological knowledge relates to forgetting and retention. It has been well established that information that has been learned must be reviewed and integrated with new information if it is to be retained. The principles governing review for various types of information are not fully known, but much of what is known about effective methods of review is ignored in typical secondary-education programs. For example, foreign languages, mathematics and science are given as isolated course units and then dropped without regard for much-needed, systematically scheduled reviews. There is no application of these subjects to later courses in other fields. Only at the college-preparatory schools in which the students are preparing for external examinations is any thought given to review and retention of courses that have been completed, and for which "Carnegie Units" are duly entered on the student's record card.

Another area in which there is a large amount of well-established knowledge is transfer and generalization. Educational psychologists have learned a great deal about the kinds of presentation which are most likely to be generalized or transferred to new situations. Many psychologists believe that the burden of establishing generalizations should be placed with the student, and that he should be encouraged and stimulated to develop his own set of principles as part of his experience in learning how to learn. Certainly these new approaches to improving the student's ability to generalize should be given a trial, and evaluated in the school situation.

A topic which has attracted recent attention is creativity. A large amount of evidence has been obtained indicating that teachers and school procedures are combining to frustrate and discourage any creative tendencies shown by students. Recent studies have shown that beginning in the intermediate grades of the elementary school, teachers and fellow students alike regard the original, imaginative, and curious student as a "smart alec" and a trouble-maker (Torrance, 1959). Certainly, substantial changes will need to be made in our present secondary-school programs if we are to nurture and develop originality, imagination, and ingenuity in our students.

Another topic of fundamental importance in secondary education is motivation to learn. Recent studies in the field of industrial psychology have shown that the basic motivating factors leading men to work long hours under unsatisfactory conditions are not factors related to the context of the job, such as good pay, job security, a good supervisor, or good working conditions. (Herzberg, Mausner, and Snyderman, 1959). The effective motivators are more closely related to the contents of the job. They are based on feelings of accomplishment, achievement, and growth or advancement with respect to valued objectives. The same factors are very likely to be the most effective motivators of students. To develop these feelings, the student must have well-defined educational objectives and must be provided with some means for measuring his personal development and progress toward these objectives.

In recent years the greatest impact on educational methods has been made by technological developments. The use of motion pictures, television, sound tapes, teaching machines, and programed texts has opened up many new possibilities for instructional programs. There have been many studies comparing the new media of instruction with more conventional procedures. These have been valuable in demonstrating the promise of the new technologies. There needs to be much more research on the problems of determining how these new media can contribute most effectively to the total educational program. One recent study found that programing, combined with standard teaching procedures, substantially and significantly increased the amount of learning compared to the standard teaching procedures (Goldbeck *and others,* 1962).

The development of procedures for efficient learning has lagged behind research on methods and technologies. The very large individual differences in students at the secondary-school level have been known for a long time. The Project TALENT survey indicated that 25 to 30 per cent of ninth-grade students in the high schools of the United States already know more about many educational subjects than the average twelfth-grade student. Similarly, the top 5 per cent of the students in a grade can learn the English meanings of twice as many foreign words as the average student can in the same period of time. These findings suggest the need for adapting the instructional program to the individual. Clearly, to provide the same educational activities and experiences for all of the students in a grade cannot be wasteful. Procedures must be developed which will take each student from his present level of information and skill to the next higher level at his optimal rate of learning. Focusing learning activities on the individual rather than on the class has long been advocated by educators. New developments in methods and technology now make this possible.

The present structure of secondary education with its one- and two-year courses is not at all well suited to meet the educational needs of the individual student. Each individual's instructional program should be based on his broad educational and vocational objectives. It should provide for review of materials already learned, integration of ideas from one field to facilitate learning of another, and the continuous development of a better understanding and appreciation of all fields of knowledge. Another benefit that could be realized in an individualized program of instruction is the coordination of out-of-school learning through hobbies and recreational activities with the in-school program. The results of the Project TALENT Information Test suggest that for many students almost as much is learned out of school as in it.

The teacher can be a crucial factor in a student's educational program. However, at the secondary-school level, the teacher's role has frequently become merely that of a lecturer and clerk. By eliminating much, if not all, of this activity through new methods and media, the teacher should be freed to get better acquainted with each student, thereby providing opportunities for individual tutoring and special assistance.

To take full advantage of the recent findings regarding methods and media, a comprehensive new program should be developed for secondary-school students. In the development of this program each segment should be evaluated in terms of its effectiveness in preparing students to reach their objectives. By designing the instructional program in terms of established research findings and systematically testing all materials in terms of the performance of the students, effective instructional programs can be developed. The importance of testing the effectiveness of new procedures is illustrated by the study of a televised science demonstration. On the basis of tryout and testing of students, the filmed demonstration was revised. The study showed that a comparison with the original film indicated that students learned about 50 per cent more from the revised film than they did from the original film (Gropper, Lumsdaine, and Shipman, 1961).

As indicated above, the measurement, evaluation, and guidance of each student is essential to an effective instructional program. At the present time, measures of the individual's talents, interests, and personal characteristics are not effectively used to assist students in educational and vocational planning. Studies such as Project TALENT have demonstrated that not only do students differ very greatly in general ability to learn verbal materials from books, but also with respect to their pattern of talents for many activities such as mathematical reasoning, mechanical comprehension, clerical ability, creativity, memory, and inspection of objects.

To assist the student in appropriately interpreting his scores on various tests of aptitude, interest, and other characteristics, it is necessary to have a comprehensive picture of his family background, hobbies, reading habits, activities, and plans. There is a considerable amount of data available indicating the aptitude and other personal requirements for various educational and occupational activities. However, most attention has been given to a relatively small number of the more popular courses and jobs. Several hundred others need further study. Project TALENT hopes to carry out follow-up studies necessary to identify the aptitude patterns required for effective work in a large number of additional activities.

About half of the twelfth-grade boys in the Project TALENT sample in 1960 did not go on to college. An indication of the aptitude patterns that are likely to characterize various jobs entered by students just out of high school is provided by the results of a follow-up of these students one year after they left high school. The test scores of boys engaged in electrical and electronic work, for example, are substantially above the average of the scores for all twelfth-grade boys, including those going on to college, on the tests of mechanical reasoning, visualization in two and three dimensions, and creativity. They are somewhat above the mean in reading comprehension, abstract reasoning, arithmetic reasoning, mathematics, and object inspection. They are below the average of twelfth-grade boys on the English test and on the clerical checking test.

By contrast, the boys who have gone into bookkeeping and other computational jobs are well above the average for twelfth-grade boys on the tests of English, reading comprehension, clerical checking, and arithmetic computation. They are also somewhat above average on the tests of abstract reasoning, arithmetic reasoning, and mathematics. They are below average on mechanical reasoning and visualization in two dimensions. The group of boys who went into sales activities tends to be close to average on most tests. They were a little above average on arithmetic computation. The boys who entered farming and agricultural activities immediately after high school are about average or a little above on mechanical reasoning and the two visualization tests, and generally below average on all other tests. They are especially low in English and reading comprehension.

One other group deserving special comment consists of the boys who, after leaving high school, went into unskilled labor jobs. This group is somewhat below average on all tests except the clerical checking and object inspection tests, on which they were about average. They are especially low on the tests of English and mathematics.

The groups entering these various jobs uniformly expressed preferences for these types of activities on the *Interest Inventory*. They indicated much participation in the types of activities closely related to the jobs they entered. On sections of the *General Information Test*, they show a greater amount of information about the topics relating to jobs they subsequently entered than to other kinds of jobs.

It appears that as additional follow-up data are obtained it should be possible to describe the special aptitude and interest patterns of each of a very large number of jobs. These data can provide a sound background for individual plans and choices.

On the basis of a relatively comprehensive picture of his talents and other assets, and the degree of correspondence of these with those of successful participants in various courses and fields of work, a secondary-school pupil should be given the opportunity to work out his educational and occupational plans with a panel of advisors. At least one of the panel members should have had counseling-and-guidance training; the responsibility for choices would be placed with the student, but the burden of interpreting and advising him of the evidence of his potential for such choices would rest on his panel of advisors.

It has been found that many students in high schools set unrealistic objectives for themselves. The Project TALENT survey showed that more than 62 per cent of the twelfth-grade boys selected occupations that require a college degree. Since it is known that only a few more than a quarter of these students will graduate from college, there is an implication that many of them make unrealistic choices.

It is proposed that a plan of the objectives to be achieved during his four years of secondary-school training be worked out by each beginning ninth-grade student with the help of his panel of advisors. These objectives and the student's progress with respect to each of them should be reviewed every two months. On the basis of the progress made, and any new evidence available, the objectives should be revised as necessary.

If the student's objectives and the measures of progress with respect to his objectives are to be effective, they must be given in terms that have direct meaning to him. Recent work on Project TALENT has provided some meaningful scores for certain types of measures. For example, the scores on the reading-comprehension tests can be interpreted in terms of the magazines and authors that the student is able to read and understand. Slightly less than half of the twelfth-grade students, for example, understand the subtler points in typical paragraphs from the stories of Sinclair Lewis, Jules Verne, and Rudyard Kipling. They also fail to grasp many of the points in typical articles in such magazines as the *Saturday Evening Post, Reader's Digest, McCall's,* and *Time.* Similarly, vocabulary in English and foreign languages can be given in terms of the number of words for which the meanings are known. There is a need for developing this type of meaningful interpretation for the other measures of the various objectives of secondary education so that the student understands clearly the nature of his progress in various fields and the practical need for attaining higher levels of competency in them.

In conclusion, the field of secondary education today presents an opportunity for substantial and important improvement. Whether one looks at objectives and the content of instructional programs; methods and technology; or measurement, evaluation, and guidance, it is clear that a comprehensive development program based on present knowledge could improve greatly on present educational activities in our secondary schools. In all of these areas there are also critical research needs. The area of greatest need and of least current knowledge is that of educational objectives and the contents of the educational program. Research is required to develop a sound, factual basis for describing objectives.

Each objective should be defined in terms of specific procedures to be used in evaluating the student's progress with respect to it. It is time that educational psychologists take an active part not only in the theoretical and laboratory aspects of secondary education but in practical applied work aimed directly at improving the total educational program in secondary schools.

References

Flanagan, J. C. and others. *The Talents of American Youth. 1. Design for a Study of American Youth.* Boston: Houghton Mifflin, 1962.

Goldbeck, Robert A., and others. *Integrating Programmed Instruction With Conventional Classroom Teaching.* San Mateo, California: American Institute for Research, 1962.

Gropper, George L.; Lumsdaine, Arthur A.; and Shipmen, Virginia I. C. *Studies in Televised Instruction: Report No. 1—Improvement of Televised Instruction Based on Student Responses to Achievement Tests.* Pittsburgh: American Institute for Research, March 1961.

Herzberg, Frederick I.; Mausner, Bernard; and Snyderman, Barbara B. *The Motivation to Work.* New York: John Wiley & Sons, Inc., 1959.

Torrance, E. Paul, and others. *Explorations in Creative Thinking in the Early School Years:* I-XII. Minneapolis: Bureau of Educational Research, University of Minnesota, 1959.

Each objective should be defined in terms of specific procedures to be used in evaluating the student's progress with respect to it. It is true that educational psychologists take an active part not only in the theoretical and laboratory aspects of [illegible]

3.4 Some Issues Concerning the Control of Human Behavior: A Symposium

Carl R. Rogers and B. F. Skinner

Typically, the teacher's concerns are focused on goals of achievement in subject matter—learning to read, solving quadratic equations, performing well with laboratory experiments, etc. At times, goals in the affective domains are articulated—the development of specific attitudes, values, or interests, for example. However, the authors of this paper make it clear that consciously or unconsciously a teacher shapes behavior in terms of the process of learning and coping with the environments as well as its products. Rogers believes that the powerful external controls available to the teacher should be used to develop internal control by the individual. Professor Skinner is very critical of a number of Dr. Roger's arguments. Their discussion is crucial for a teacher considering his overall objectives.

I [Skinner]

Science is steadily increasing our power to influence, change, mold—in a word, control—human behavior. It has extended our "understand-

SOURCE. Carl R. Rogers and B. F. Skinner, "Some Issues Concerning the Control of Human Behavior: A Symposium," *Science*, **CXXIV**, 3231 (1956), pp. 1057–1066. Reprinted by permission of the authors and the American Association for the Advancement of Science.

ing" (whatever that may be) so that we deal more successfully with people in nonscientific ways, but it has also identified conditions or variables which can be used to predict and control behavior in a new, and increasingly rigorous, technology. The broad disciplines of government and economics offer examples of this, but there is special cogency in those contributions of anthropology, sociology, and psychology which deal with individual behavior. Carl Rogers has listed some of the achievements to date in a recent paper (*1*). Those of his examples which show or imply the control of the single organism are primarily due, as we should expect, to psychology. It is the experimental study of behavior which carries us beyond awkward or inaccessible "principles," "factors," and so on, to variables which can be directly manipulated.

It is also, and for more or less the same reasons, the conception of human behavior emerging from an experimental analysis which most directly challenges traditional views. Psychologists themselves often do not seem to be aware of how far they have moved in this direction. But the change is not passing unnoticed by others. Until only recently it was customary to deny the possibility of a rigorous science of human behavior by arguing, either that a lawful science was impossible because man was a free agent, or that merely statistical predictions would always leave room for personal freedom. But those who used to take this line have become most vociferous in expressing their alarm at the way these obstacles are being surmounted.

Now, the control of human behavior has always been unpopular. Any undisguised effort to control usually arouses emotional reactions. We hesitate to admit, even to ourselves, that we are engaged in control, and we may refuse to control, even when this would be helpful, for fear of criticism. Those who have explicitly avowed an interest in control have been roughly treated by history. Machiavelli is the great prototype. As Macaulay said of him, "Out of his surname they coined an epithet for a knave and out of his Christian name a synonym for the devil." There were obvious reasons. The control that Machiavelli analyzed and recommended, like most political control, used techniques that were aversive to the controllee. The threats and punishments of the bully, like those of the government operating on the same plan, are not designed—whatever their success—to endear themselves to those who are controlled. Even when the techniques themselves are not aversive, control is usually exercised for the selfish purposes of the controller and, hence, has indirectly punishing effects upon others.

Man's natural inclination to revolt against selfish control has been exploited to good purpose in what we call the philosophy and literature of democracy. The doctrine of the rights of man has been effective in arousing individuals to concerted action against governmental and religious tyranny. The literature which has had this effect has greatly extended the number of terms in our language which express reactions to the control of men. But the ubiquity and ease of expression of this attitude spells trouble for any science which may give birth to a powerful technology of behavior. Intelligent men and women, dominated by the humanistic philosophy of the past two centuries, cannot view with equanimity what Andrew Hacker has called "the specter of predictable man" (2). Even the statistical or actuarial prediction of human events, such as the number of fatalities to be expected on a holiday weekend, strikes many people as uncanny and evil, while the prediction and control of individual behavior is regarded as little less than the work of the devil. I am not so much concerned here with the political or economic consequences for psychology, although research following certain channels may well suffer harmful effects. We ourselves, as intelligent men and women, and as exponents of Western thought, share these attitudes. They have already interfered with the free exercise of a scientific analysis, and their influence threatens to assume more serious proportions.

Three broad areas of human behavior supply good examples. The first of these—*personal control*—may be taken to include person-to-person relationships in the family, among friends, in social and work groups, and in counseling and psychotherapy. Other fields are *education* and *government.* A few examples from each will show how nonscientific preconceptions are affecting our current thinking about human behavior.

Personal Control

People living together in groups come to control one another with a technique which is not inappropriately called "ethical." When an individual behaves in a fashion acceptable to the group, he receives admiration, approval, affection, and many other reinforcements which increase the likelihood that he will continue to behave in that fashion. When his behavior is not acceptable, he is criticized, censured, blamed, or otherwise punished. In the first case the group calls him "good"; in the second, "bad." This practice is so thoroughly ingrained in our culture that we often fail to see that it is a technique of control. Yet we are almost always engaged in such control, even though the reinforcements and punishments are often subtle.

The practice of admiration is an important part of a culture, because behavior which is otherwise inclined to be weak can be set up and maintained with its help. The individual is especially likely to be praised, admired, or loved when he acts for the group in the face of great danger, for example, or sacrifices himself or his possessions, or submits to prolonged hardship, or suffers martyrdom. These actions are not admirable in any absolute sense, but they require admiration if they are to be strong. Similarly, we admire people who behave in original or exceptional ways, not because such behavior is itself admirable, but because we do not know how to encourage original or exceptional behavior in any other way. The group acclaims independent, unaided behavior in part because it is easier to reinforce than to help.

As long as this technique of control is misunderstood, we cannot judge correctly an environment in which there is less need for heroism, hardship, or independent action. We are likely to argue that such an environment is itself less admirable or produces less admirable people. In the old days, for example, young scholars often lived in undesirable quarters, ate unappetizing or inadequate food, performed unprofitable tasks for a living or to pay for necessary books and materials or publication. Older scholars and other members of the group offered compensating reinforcement in the form of approval and admiration for these sacrifices. When the modern graduate student receives a generous scholarship, enjoys good living conditions, and has his research and publication subsidized, the grounds for evaluation seem to be pulled from under us. Such a student no longer *needs* admiration to carry him over a series of obstacles (no matter how much he may need it for other reasons), and, in missing certain familiar objects of admiration, we are likely to conclude that such *conditions* are less admirable. Obstacles to scholarly work may serve as a useful measure of motivation—and we may go wrong unless some substitute is found—but we can scarcely defend a deliberate harassment of the student for this purpose. The productivity of any set of conditions can be evaluated only when we have freed ourselves of the attitudes which have been generated in us as members of an ethical group.

A similar difficulty arises from our use of punishment in the form of censure or blame. The concept of responsibility and the related concepts of foreknowledge and choice are used to justify techniques of control using punishment. Was So-and-So aware of the probable consequences of his action, and was the action deliberate? If so, we are justified in punishing him. But what does this mean? It appears to be a question concerning the efficacy of the contingent relations between behavior and punishing consequences. We punish behavior because it is objectionable to us or the group, but in a minor refinement of rather recent origin we have come to withhold punishment when it cannot be expected to have any effect. If the objectionable consequences of an act were accidental and not likely to occur again, there is no point in punishing. We say that the individual was not "aware of the consequences of his action" or that the consequences were not "intentional." If the action could not have been avoided—if the individual "had no choice"—punishment is also withheld, as it is if the individual is incapable of being changed by punishment because he is of "unsound mind." In all these cases—different as they are—the individual is held "not responsible" and goes unpunished.

Just as we say that it is "not fair" to punish a man for something he could not help doing, so we call it "unfair" when one is rewarded beyond his due or for something he could not help doing. In other words, we also object to wasting *reinforcers* where they are not needed or will do no good. We make the same point with the words *just* and *right*. Thus we have no right to punish the irresponsible, and a man has no right to reinforcers he does not earn or deserve. But concepts of choice, responsibility, justice, and so on, provide a most inadequate analysis of efficient reinforcing and punishing contingencies because they carry a heavy semantic cargo of a quite different sort, which obscures any attempt to clarify controlling practices or to improve techniques. In particular, they fail to prepare us for techniques based on other than aversive techniques of control. Most people would object to forcing prisoners to serve as subjects of dangerous medical experiments, but few object when they are induced to serve by the offer of return privileges—even when the reinforcing effect of these privileges has been created by forcible deprivation. In the traditional scheme the right to refuse guarantees the individual against coercion or an unfair bargain. But to what extent *can* a prisoner refuse under such circumstances?

We need not go so far afield to make the point. We can observe, our own attitude toward personal freedom in the way we resent any interference with what we want to do. Suppose we want to buy a car of a particular sort. Then we may object, for example, if our wife urges us to buy a less expensive model and to put the difference into a new refrigerator. Or we may resent it if our neighbor questions our need for such a car or our ability to pay for it. We would certainly resent it if it were illegal to buy such a car (remember Prohibition); and if we find we cannot actually afford it, we may resent governmental control of the price through tariffs and taxes. We resent it if we discover that we cannot get the car because the manufacturer is holding the model in deliberately short supply in order to push a model we do not want. In all this we assert our democratic right to buy the car of our choice. We are well prepared to do so and to resent any restriction on our freedom.

But why do we not ask *why* it is the car of our choice and resent the forces which made it so? Perhaps our favorite toy as a child was a car, of a very different model, but nevertheless bearing the name of the car we now want. Perhaps our favorite TV program is sponsored by the manufacturer of that car. Perhaps we have seen pictures of many beautiful or prestigeful persons driving it—in pleasant or glamorous places. Perhaps the car has been designed with respect to our motivational patterns: the device on the hood is a phallic symbol; or the horsepower has been stepped up to please our competitive spirit in enabling us to pass other cars swiftly (or, as the advertisements say, "safely"). The concept of freedom that has emerged as part of the cultural practice of our group makes little or no provision for recognizing or dealing with these kinds of control. Concepts like "responsibility" and "rights" are scarcely applicable. We are prepared to deal with coercive measures, but we have no traditional recourse with respect to other measures which in the long run (and especially with the help of science) may be much more powerful and dangerous.

Education

The techniques of education were once frankly aversive. The teacher was usually older and stronger than its pupils and was able to "make them learn." This meant that they were not actually taught but were surrounded by a threatening world from which they could escape only by learning. Usually they were left to their own resources in discovering how to do so. Claude Coleman has published a grimly amusing reminder of these older practices (3). He tells of a schoolteacher who published a careful account of his services during 51 years of teaching, during which he administered: ". . . 911,527 blows with a cane; 124,010 with a rod; 20,989 with a ruler; 136,715 with the hand; 10,295 over the mouth; 7,905 boxes on the ear; [and] 1,115,800 slaps on the head. . . ."

Progressive education was a humanitarian effort to substitute positive reinforcement for such aversive measures, but in the search for useful human values in the classroom it has never fully replaced the variables it abandoned. Viewed as a branch of behavioral technology, education remains relatively inefficient. We supplement it, and rationalize it, by admiring the pupil who learns *for himself*; and we often attribute the learning process, or knowledge itself, to something *inside* the individual. We admire behavior which seems to have inner sources. Thus we admire one who *recites* a poem more than one who simply *reads* it. We admire one who *knows* the answer more than one who *knows where to look it up*. We admire the *writer* rather than the *reader*. We admire the arithmetician who can do a problem in his head rather than with a slide rule or calculating machine, or in "original" ways rather than by a strict application of rules. In general we feel that any aid or "crutch"—except those aids to which we are now thoroughly accustomed—reduces the credit due. In Plato's *Phaedus,* Thamus, the king, attacks the invention of the alphabet on similar grounds! He is afraid "it will produce forgetfulness in the minds of those who learn to use it, because they will not practice their memories. . . ." In other words, he holds it more admirable to remember than to use a memorandum. He also objects that pupils "will read many things without instruction. . . [and] will therefore seem to know many things when they are for the most part ignorant." In the same vein we are today sometimes contemptuous of book learning, but, as educators, we can scarcely afford to adopt this view without reservation.

By admiring the student for knowledge and blaming him for ignorance, we escape some of the responsibility of teaching him. We resist any analysis of the educational process which threatens the notion of inner wisdom or questions the contention that the fault of ignorance lies with the student. More powerful techniques which bring about the same changes in behavior by manipulating *external* variables are decried as brain-washing or thought control. We are quite unprepared to judge *effective* educational measures. As long as only a few pupils learn much of what is taught, we do not worry about uniformity or regimentation. We do not fear the feeble technique; but we should view with dismay a system under which every student learned everything listed in a syllabus—although such a condition is far from unthinkable. Similarly, we do not fear a system which is so defective that the student must *work* for an education; but we are loath to give credit for anything learned without effort—although this could well be taken as an ideal result—and we flatly refuse to give credit if the student already knows what a school teaches.

A world in which people are wise and good without trying, without "having to be," without "choosing to be," could conceivably be a far better world for everyone. In such a world we should not have to "give anyone credit"—we should not need to admire anyone—for being wise and good. From our present point of view we cannot believe that such a world would be admirable. We do not even permit ourselves to imagine what it would be like.

Government

Government has always been the special field of aversive control. The state is frequently defined in terms of the power to punish, and jurisprudence leans heavily upon the associated notion of personal responsibility. Yet it is becoming increasingly difficult to reconcile current practice and theory with these earlier views. In criminology, for example, there is a strong tendency to drop the notion of responsibility in favor of some such alternative as capacity or controllability. But no matter how strongly the facts, or even practical expedience, support such a change, it is difficult to make the change in a legal system designed on a different plan. When governments resort to other techniques (for example, positive reinforcement), the concept of responsibility is no longer relevant and the theory of government is no longer applicable.

The conflict is illustrated by two decisions of the Supreme Court in the 1930's which dealt with, and disagreed on, the definition of control or coercion (*4*, p. 233). The Agricultural Adjustment Act proposed that the Secretary of Agriculture make "rental or benefit payments" to those farmers who agreed to reduce production. The government agreed that the Act would be unconstitutional if the farmer had been *compelled* to reduce production but was not, since he was merely *invited* to do so. Justice Roberts (*4*) expressed the contrary majority view of the court that "The power to confer or withhold unlimited benefits is the power to coerce or destroy." This recognition of positive reinforcement was withdrawn a few years later in another case in which Justice Cardozo (*4*, p. 244) wrote "To hold that motive or temptation is equivalent to coercion is to plunge the law in endless difficulties." We may agree with him, without implying that the proposition is therefore wrong. Sooner or later the law must be prepared to deal with all possible techniques of governmental control.

The uneasiness with which we view government (in the broadest possible sense) when it does not use punishment is shown by the reception of my utopian novel, *Walden Two* (*4a*). This was essentially a proposal to apply a behavioral technology to the construction of a workable, effective, and productive pattern of government. It was greeted with wrathful violence. *Life* magazine called it "a travesty on the good life," and "a menace . . . a triumph of mortmain or the dead hand not envisaged since the days of Sparta . . . a slur upon a name, a corruption of an impulse." Joseph Wood Krutch devoted a substantial part of his book, *The Measure of Man* (*5*), to attacking my views and those of the protagonist, Frazier, in the same vein, and Morris Viteles has recently criticized the book in a similar manner in *Science (6)*. Perhaps the reaction is best expressed in a quotation from *The Quest for Utopia* by Negley and Patrick (*7*):

"Halfway through this contemporary utopia, the reader may feel sure, as we did, that this is a beautifully ironic satire on what has been called 'behavioral engineering.' The longer one stays in this better world of the psychologist, however, the plainer it becomes that the inspiration is not satiric, but messianic. This is indeed the behaviorally engineered society, and while it was to be expected that sooner or later the principle of psychological conditioning would be made the basis of a serious construction of utopia—Brown anticipated it in *Limanora*—yet not even the effective satire of Huxley is adequate preparation for the shocking horror of the idea when positively presented. Of all the dictatorships espoused by utopists, this is the most profound, and incipient dictators might well find in this utopia a guidebook of political practice."

One would scarcely guess that the authors are talking about a world in which there is food, clothing, and shelter for all, where everyone chooses his own work and works on the average only 4 hours a day, where music and the arts flourish, where personal relationships develop under the most favorable circumstances, where education prepares every child for the social and intellectual life which lies before him, where—in short—people are truly happy, productive, creative, and forward-looking. What is wrong with it? Only one thing: someone "planned it that way." If these critics had come upon a society in some remote corner of the world which boasted similar advantages, they would undoubtedly have hailed it as providing a pattern we all might well follow—provided that it was clearly the result of a natural process of cultural evolution. Any evidence that intelligence had been used in arriving at this version of the good life would, in their eyes, be a serious flaw. No matter if the planner of *Walden Two* diverts none of the proceeds of the community to his own use, no matter if he has no current control or is, indeed, unknown to most of the other members of the community (he planned that, too), somewhere back of it all he occupies the position of prime mover. And this, to the child of the democratic tradition, spoils it all.

The dangers inherent in the control of human behavior are very real. The possibility of the misuse of scientific knowledge must always be faced. We cannot escape by denying the power of a science of behavior or arresting its development. It is no help to cling to familiar philosophies of human behavior simply because they are more reassuring. As I have pointed out elsewhere. (8), the new techniques emerging from a science of behavior must be subject to the explicit countercontrol which has already been applied to earlier and cruder forms. Brute force and deception, for example, are now fairly generally suppressed by ethical practices and by explicit governmental and religious agencies. A similar countercontrol of scientific knowledge in the interests of the group is a feasible and promising possibility. Although we cannot say how devious the course of its evolution may be, a cultural pattern of control and countercontrol will presumably emerge which will be most widely supported because it is most widely reinforcing.

If we cannot foresee all the details of this (as we obviously cannot), it is important to remember that this is true of the critics of science as well. The dire consequences of new techniques of control, the hidden menace in original cultural designs—these need some proof. It is only another example of my present point that the need for proof is so often overlooked. Man has got himself into some pretty fixes, and it is easy to believe that he will do so again. But there is a more optimistic possibility. The slow growth of the methods of science, now for the first time being applied to human affairs, *may* mean a new and exciting phase of human life to which historical analogies will not apply and in which earlier political slogans will not be appropriate. If we are to use the knowledge that a science of behavior is now making available with any hope of success, we must look at human nature as it is brought into focus through the methods of science rather than as it has been presented to us in a series of historical accidents.

If the advent of a powerful science of behavior causes trouble, it will not be because science itself is inimical to human welfare but because older conceptions have not yielded easily or gracefully. We expect resistance to new techniques of control from those who have heavy investments in the old, but we have no reason to help them preserve a series of principles that are not ends in themselves but rather outmoded means to an end. What is needed is a new conception of human behavior which is compatible with the implications of a scientific analysis. All men control and are controlled. The question of government in the broadest possible sense is not how freedom is to be preserved but what kinds of control are to be used and to what ends. Control must be analyzed and considered in its proper proportions. No one, I am sure, wishes to develop new master-slave relationships or bend the will of the people to despotic rulers in new ways. These are patterns of control appropriate to a world without science. They may well be the first to go when the experimental analysis of behavior comes into its own in the design of cultural practices.

II [Rogers]

There are, I believe, a number of matters in connection with this important topic on which the authors of this article, and probably a large majority of psychologists, are in agreement. These matters then are not issues as far as we are concerned, and I should like to mention them briefly in order to put them to one side.

Points of Agreement

I am sure we agree that men—as individuals and as societies—have always endeavored to understand, predict, influence, and control human behavior—their own behavior and that of others.

I believe we agree that the behavioral sciences are making and will continue to make increasingly rapid progress in the understanding of behavior, and that as a consequence the capacity to predict and to control behavior is developing with equal rapidity.

I believe we agree to deny these advances, or to claim that man's behavior cannot be a field of science, is unrealistic. Even this is not an issue for us, we should recognize that many intelligent men still hold strongly to the view that the actions of men are free in some sense such that scientific knowledge of man's behavior is impossible. Thus Reinhold Niebuhr, the noted theologian, heaps scorn on the concept of psychology as a science of man's behavior and even says, "In any event, no scientiffc investigation of past behavior can become the basis of productions of future behavior" (*9*). So, while this is not an issue for psychologists, we should at least notice in passing that it is an issue for many people.

I believe we are in agreement that the tremendous potential power of a science which permits the prediction and control of behavior may be misused, and that the possibility of such misuse constitutes a serious threat.

Consequently Skinner and I are in agreement that the whole question of the scientific control of human behavior is a matter with which psychologists and the general public should concern themselves. As Robert Oppenheimer told the American Psychological Association last year (*10*) the problems that psychologists will pose for society by their growing ability to control behavior will be much more grave than the problems posed by the ability of physicists to control the reactions of matter. I am not sure whether psychologists generally recognize this. My impression is that by and large they hold a laissez-faire attitude. Obviously Skinner and I do not hold this laissez-faire view, or we would not have written this article.

Points at Discussion

With these several points of basic and important agreement, are there then any issues that remain on which there are differences? I believe there are. They can be stated very briefly: Who will be controlled? Who will exercise control? What type of control will be exercised? Most important of all, toward what end or what purpose, or in the pursuit of what value, will control be exercised?

It is on questions of this sort that there exist ambiguities, misunderstandings, and probably deep differences. These differences exist among psychologists, among members of the general public in this country, and among various world cultures. Without any hope of achieving a final resolution of these questions, we can, I believe, put these issues in clearer form.

Some Meanings

To avoid ambiguity and faulty communication, I would like to clarify the meanings of some of the terms we are using.

Behavioral science is a term that might be defined from several angles but in the context of this discussion it refers primarily to knowledge that the existence of certain describable conditions in the human being and/or in his environment is followed by certain describable consequences in his actions.

Prediction means the prior identification of behaviors which then occur. Because it is important in some things I wish to say later, I would point out that one may predict a highly specific behavior, such as an eye blink, or one may predict a class of behaviors. One might correctly predict "avoidant behavior," for example, without being able to specify whether the individual will run away or simply close his eyes.

The word *control* is a very slippery one, which can be used with any one of several meanings. I would like to specify three that seem most important for our present purposes. *Control* may mean: (i) The setting of conditions by *B* for *A*, *A* having no voice in the matter, such that certain predictable behaviors then occur in *A*. I refer to this as external control. (ii) The setting of conditions by *B* for *A*, *A* giving some degree of consent to these conditions, such that certain predictable behaviors then occur in *A*. I refer to this as the influence of *B* on *A*. (iii) The setting of conditions by *A* such that certain predictable behaviors then occur in himself. I refer to this as internal control. It will be noted that Skinner lumps together the first two meanings, external control and influence, under the concept of control. I find this confusing.

Usual Concept of Control of Human Behavior

With the underbrush thus cleared away (I hope), let us review very briefly the various elements that are involved in the usual concepts of the control of human behavior as mediated by the behavioral sciences. I am drawing here on the previous writings of Skinner, on his present statements, on the writings of others who have considered in either friendly or antagonistic fashion the meanings that would be involved in such control. I have not excluded the science fiction writers, as reported recently by Vandenburg (*11*), since they often show an awareness of the issues involved, even though the methods described are as yet fictional. These then are the elements that seem common to these different concepts of the application of science to human behavior.

1. There must first be some sort of decision about goals. Usually desirable goals are assumed, but sometimes, as in George Orwell's book *1984,* the goal that is selected is an aggrandizement of individual power with which most of us would disagree. In a recent paper Skinner suggests that one possible set of goals to be assigned to the behavioral technology is this: "Let men be happy, informed, skillful, well-behaved and productive" (*12*). In the first draft of his part of this article, which he was kind enough to show me, he did not mention such definite goals as these, but desired "improved" educational practices, "wiser" use of knowledge in government, and the like. In the final version of his article he avoids even these value-laden terms, and his implicit goal is the very general one that scientific control of behavior is desirable, because it would perhaps bring "a far better world for everyone."

   Thus the first step in thinking about the control of human behavior is the choice of goals, whether specific or general. It is necessary to come to terms in some way with the issue, "For what purpose?"
2. A second element is that, whether the end selected is highly specific or is a very general one such as wanting "a better world," we proceed by the methods of science to discover the means to these ends. We continue through further experimentation and investigation to discover more effective means. The method of science is self-correcting in thus arriving at increasingly effective ways of achieving the purpose we have in mind.
3. The third aspect of such control is that as the conditions or methods are discovered by which to reach the goal, some person or some group establishes these conditions and uses these methods, having in one way or another obtained the power to do so.
4. The fourth element is the exposure of individuals to the prescribed conditions, and this leads, with a high degree of probability, to behavior which is in line with the goals desired. Individuals are now happy, if that has been the goal, or well-behaved, or submissive, or whatever it has been decided to make them.
5. The fifth element is that if the process I have described is put in motion then there is a continuing social organization which will continue to produce the types of behavior that have been valued.

Some Flaws

Are there any flaws in this way of viewing the control of human behavior? I believe there are. In fact the only element in this description with which I find myself in agreement is the second. It seems to me quite incontrovertibly true that the scientific method is an excellent way to discover the means by which to achieve our goals. Beyond that, I feel many sharp differences, which I will try to spell out.

I believe that in Skinner's presentation here and in his previous writings, there is a serious underestimation of the problem of power. To hope that the power which is being made available by the behavioral sciences will be exercised by the scientists, or by a benevolent group, seems to me a hope little supported by either recent or distant history. It seems far more likely that behavioral scientists, holding their present attitudes, will be in the position of the German rocket scientists specializing in guided missiles. First they worked devotedly for Hitler to destroy the U.S.S.R. and the United States. Now, depending on who captured them, they work devotedly for the U.S.S.R. in the interest of destroying the United States, or devotedly for the United States in the interest of destroying the U.S.S.R. If behavioral scientists are concerned solely with advancing their science, it seems most probable that they will serve the purposes of whatever individual or group has the power.

But the major flaw I see in this review of what is involved in the scientific control of human behavior is the denial, misunderstanding, or gross underestimation of the place of ends, goals or values in their relationship to science. This error (as it sems to me) has so many implications that I would like to devote some space to it.

Ends and Values in Relation to Science

In sharp contradiction to some views that have been advanced, I would like to propose a two-pronged thesis: (i) In any scientific endeavor —whether "pure" or applied science—there is a prior subjective choice of the purpose or value which that scientific work is perceived as serving. (ii) This subjective value choice which brings the scientific endeavor into being must always lie outside of that endeavor and can never become a part of the science involved in that endeavor.

Let me illustrate the first point from Skinner himself. It is clear that in his earlier writing (*12*) it is recognized that a prior value choice is necessary, and it is specified as the goal that men are to become happy, well-behaved, productive, and so on. I am pleased that Skinner has retreated from the goals he then chose, because to me they seem to be stultifying values. I can only feel that he was choosing these goals for others, not for himself. I would hate to see Skinner become "well-behaved," as that term would be defined for him by behavioral scientists. His recent article in the *American Psychologist* (*13*) shows that he certainly does not want to be "productive" as that value is defined by most psychologists. And the most awful fate I can imagine for him would be to have him constantly "happy." It is the fact that he is very unhappy about many things which makes me prize him.

In the first draft of his part of this article, he also included such prior value choices, saying for example, "We must decide how we are to use the knowledge which a science of human behavior is now making available." Now he has dropped all mention of such choices, and if I understand him correctly, he believes that science can proceed without them. He has suggested this view in another recent paper, stating that "We must continue to experiment in cultural design . . . testing the consequences as we go. Eventually the practices which make for the greatest biological and psychological strength of the group will presumably survive" (*8*, p. 549).

I would point out, however, that to choose to experiment is a value choice. Even to move in the direction of perfectly random experimention is a value choice. To test the consequences of an experiment is possible only if we have first made a subjective choice of a criterion value. And implicit in his statement is a valuing of biological and psychological strength. So even when trying to avoid such choice, it seems inescapable that a prior subjective value choice is necessary for any scientific endeavor, or for any application of scientific knowledge.

I wish to make it clear that I am not saying that values cannot be included as a subject of science. It is not true that sciencc deals only with certain classes of "facts" and that these classes do not include values. It is a bit more complex than that, as a simple illustration or two may make clear.

If I value knowledge of the "three R's" as a goal of education, the methods of science can give me increasingly accurate information on how this goal may be achieved. If I value problem-solving ability as a goal of education, the scientific method can give me the same kind of help.

Now, if I wish to determine whether problem-solving ability is "better" than knowledge of the three R's, then scientific method can also study those two values but *only*—and this is very important—in terms of some other value which I have subjectively chosen. I may value college success. Then I can determine whether problem-solving ability or knowledge of the three R's is most closely associated with that value. I may value personal integration or vocational success or responsible citizenship. I can determine whether problem-solving ability or knowledge of the three R's is "better" for achieving any one of these values. But the value or purpose that gives meaning to a particular scientific endeavor must always lie outside of that endeavor.

Although our concern in this symposium is largely with applied science, what I have been saying seems equally true of so-called "pure" science. In pure science the usual prior subjective value choice is the discovery of truth. But this is a subjective choice, and science can never say whether it is the best choice, save in the light of some other value. Geneticists in the U.S.S.R., for example, had to make a subjective choice of whether it was better to pursue truth or to discover facts which upheld a governmental dogma. Which choice is "better"? We could make a scientific investigation of those alternatives but only in the light of some other subjectively chosen value. If, for example, we value the survival of a culture, then we could begin to investigate with the methods of science the question of whether pursuit of truth or support of governmental dogma is most closely associated with cultural survival.

My point then is that any endeavor in science, pure or applied, is carried on in the pursuit of a purpose or value that is subjectively chosen by persons. It is important that this choice be made explicit, since the particular value which is being sought can never be tested or evaluated, confirmed or denied, by the scientific endeavor to which it gives birth. The initial purpose or value always and necessarily lies outside the scope of the scientific effort which it sets in motion.

Among other things this means that if we choose some particular goal or series of goals for human beings and then set out on a large scale to control human behavior to the end of achieving those goals, we are locked in the rigidity of our initial choice, because such a scientific endeavor can never transcend itself to select new goals. Only subjective human persons can do that. Thus if we chose as our goal the state of happiness for human beings (a goal deservedly ridiculed by Aldous Huxley in *Brave New World*), and if we involved all of society in a successful scientific program by which people became happy, we would be locked in a colossal rigidity in which no one would be free to question this goal, because our scientific operations could not transcend themselves to question their guiding purposes. And without laboring this point, I would remark that colossal rigidity, whether in dinosaurs or dictatorships, has a very poor record of evolutionary survival.

If, however, a part of our scheme is to set free some "planners" who do not have to be happy, who are not controlled, and who are therefore free to choose other values, this has several meanings. It means that the purpose we have chosen as our goal is not a sufficient and a satisfying one for human beings but must be supplemented. It also means that if it is necessary to set up an elite group which is free, then this shows all too clearly that the great majority are only the slaves—no matter by what high-sounding name we call them—of those who select the goals.

Perhaps, however, the thought is that a continuing scientific endeavor will evolve its own goals; that the initial findings will alter the directions, and subsequent findings will alter them still further, and that science somehow develops its own purpose. Although he does not clearly say so, this appears to be the pattern Skinner has in mind. It is surely a reasonable description, but it overlooks one element in this continuing development, which is that subjective personal choice enters in at every point at which the direction changes. The findings of a science, the results of an experiment, do not and never can tell us what next scientific purpose to pursue. Even in the purest of science, the scientist must decide what the findings mean and must subjectively choose what next step will be most profitable in the pursuit of his purpose. And if we are speaking of the application of scientific knowledge, then it is distressingly clear that the increasing scientific knowledge of the structure of the atom carries with it no necessary choice as to the purpose to which this knowledge will be put. This is a subjective personal choice which must be made by many individuals.

Thus I return to the proposition with which I began this section of my remarks—and which I now repeat in different words. Science has its meaning as the objective pursuit of a purpose which has been subjectively chosen by a person or persons. This purpose or value can never be investigated by the particular scientific experiment or investigation to which it has given birth and meaning. Consequently, any discussion of the control of human beings by the behavioral sciences must first and most deeply concern itself with the subjectively chosen purposes which such an application of science is intended to implement.

Is the Situation Hopeless?

The thoughtful reader may recognize that, although my remarks up to this point have introduced some modifications in the conception of the processes by which human behavior will be controlled, these remarks may have made such control seem, if anything, even more inevitable. We might sum it up this way: Behavioral science is clearly moving forward; the increasing power for control which it gives will be held by someone or some group; such an individual or group will surely choose the values or goals to be achieved; and most of us will then be increasingly controlled by means so subtle that we will not even be aware of them as controls. Thus, whether a council of wise psychologists (if this is not a contradiction in terms), or a Stalin, or a Big Brother has the power, and whether the goal is happiness, or productivity, or resolution of the Oedipus complex, or submission, or love of Big Brother, we will inevitably find ourselves moving toward the chosen goal and probably thinking that we ourselves desire it. Thus, if this line of reasoning is correct, it appears that some form of *Walden Two* or of *1984* (and at a deep philosophic level they seem indistinguishable) is coming. The fact that it would surely arrive piecemeal, rather than all at once, does not greatly change the fundamental issues. In any event, as Skinner as indicated in his writings, he would then look back upon the concepts of human freedom, the capacity for choice, the responsibility for choice, and the worth of the human individual as historical curiosities which once existed by cultural accident as values in a prescientific civilization.

I believe that any person observant of trends must regard something like the foregoing sequence as a real possibility. It is not simply a fantasy. Something of that sort may even be the most likely future. But is it an inevitable future? I want to devote the remainder of my remarks to an alternative possibility.

Alternative Set of Values

Suppose we start with a set of ends, values, purposes, quite different from the type of goals we have been considering. Suppose we do this quite openly, setting them forth as a possible value choice to be accepted or repected. Suppose we select a set of values that focuses on fluid elements of process rather than static attributes. We might then value: man as a process of becoming, as a process of achieving worth and dignity through the development of his potentialities; the individual human being as a self-actualizing process, moving on to more challenging and enriching experiences; the process by which the individual creatively adapts to an ever-new and changing world; the process by which knowledge transcends itself, as, for example, the theory of relativity transcended Newtonian physics, itself to be transcended in some future day by a new perception.

If we select values such as these we turn to our science and technology of behavior with a very different set of questions. We will want to know such things as these: Can science aid in the discovery of new modes of richly rewarding living? more meaningful and satisfying modes of interpersonal relationship? Can science inform us on how the human race can become a more intelligent participant in its own evolution—its physical, psychological and social evolution? Can science inform us on ways of releasing the creative capacity of individuals, which seem so necessary if we are to survive in this fantastically expanding atomic age? Oppenheimer has pointed out (*14*) that knowledge, which used to double in millenia or centuries, now doubles in a generation or a decade. It appears that we must discover the utmost in release of creativity if we are to be able to adapt effectively. In short, can science discover the methods by which man can most readily become a continually developing and self-transcending process, in his behavior, his thinking, his knowledge? Can science predict and release an essentially "unpredictable" freedom?

It is one of the virtues of science as a method that it is as able to advance and implement goals and purposes of this sort as it is to serve static values, such as states of being well-informed, happy, obedient. Indeed we have some evidence of this.

Small Example

I will perhaps be forgiven if I document some of the possibilities along this line by turning to psychotherapy, the field I know best.

Psychotherapy, as Meerloo (*15*) and others have pointed out, can be one of the most subtle tools for the control of *A* by *B*. The therapist can subtly mold individuals in imitation of himself. He can cause an individual to become a submissive and conforming being. When certain therapeutic principles are used in extreme fashion, we call it brainwashing, an instance of the disintegration of the personality and a reformulation of the person along lines desired by the controlling individual. So the principles of therapy can be used as an effective means of external control of human personality and behavior. Can psychotherapy be anything else?

Here I find the developments going on in client-centered psychotherapy (*16*) an exciting hint of what a behavioral science can do in achieving the kinds of values I have stated. Quite aside from being a somewhat new orientation in psychotherapy, this development has important implications regarding the relation of a behavioral science to the control of human behavior. Let me describe our experience as it relates to the issues of this discussion.

In client-centered therapy, we are deeply engaged in the prediction and influencing of behavior, or even the control of behavior. As therapists, we institute certain attitudinal conditions, and the client has relatively little voice in the establishment of these conditions. We predict that if these conditions are instituted, certain behavioral consequences will ensue in the client. Up to this point this is largely external control, no different from what Skinner has described, and no different from what I have discussed in the preceding sections of this article. But here any similarity ceases.

The conditions we have chosen to establish predict such behavioral consequences as these: that the client will become self-directing, less rigid, more open to the evidence of his senses, better organized and integrated, more similar to the ideal which he has chosen for himself. In other words, we have established by external control conditions which we predict will be followed by internal control by the individual, in pursuit of internally chosen goals. We have set the conditions which predict various classes of behaviors—self-directing behaviors, sensitivity to realities within and without, flexible adaptiveness—which are by their very nature unpredictable in their specifics. Our recent research (*17*) indicates that our predictions are to a significant degree corroborated, and our commitment to the scientific method causes us to believe that more effective means of achieving these goals may be realized.

Research exists in other fields—industry, education, group dynamics which seems to support our own findngs. I believe it may be conservatively stated that scientific progress has been made in identifying those conditions in an interpersonal relationship which, if they exist in *B*, are followed in *A* by greater maturity in behavior, less dependence on others, an increase in expressiveness as a person, an increase in variability, flexibility and effectiveness of adaptation, an increase in self-responsibility and self-direction. And, quite in contrast to the concern expressed by some, we do not find that the creatively adaptive behavior which results from such self-directed variability of expression is a "happy accident" which occurs in "chaos." Rather, the individual who is open to his experience, and self-directing, is harmonious not chaotic, ingenious rather than random, as he orders his responses imaginatively toward the achievement of his own purposes. His creative actions are no more a "happy accident" than was Einstein's development of the theory of relativity.

Thus we find ourselves in fundamental agreement with John Dewey's statement: "Science has made its way by releasing, not by suppressing, the elements of variation, of invention and innovation, of novel creation in individuals" (*18*). Progress in personal life and in group living is, we believe, made in the same way.

Possible Concept of the Control of Human Behavior

It is quite clear that the point of view I am expressing is in sharp contrast to the usual conception of the relationship of the behavioral sciences to the control of human behavior. In order to make this contrast even more blunt, I will state this possibility in paragraphs parallel to those used before.

1. It is possible for us to choose to value man as a self-actualizing process of becoming; to value creativity, and the process by which knowledge becomes self-transcending.
2. We can proceed, by the methods of science, to discover the condi-

tions which necessarily precede these processes and, through continuing experimentation, to discover better means of achieving these purposes.

3. It is possible for individuals or groups to set these conditions, with a minimum of power or control. According to present knowledge, the only authority necessary is the authority to establish certain qualities of interpersonal relationship.
4. Exposed to these conditions, present knowledge suggests that individuals become more self-responsible, making progress in self-actualization, become more flexible, and become more creatively adaptive.
5. Thus such an initial choice would inaugurate the beginnings of a social system or subsystem in which values, knowledge, adaptive skills, and even the concept of science would be continually changing and self-transcending. The emphasis would be upon man as a process of becoming.

I believe it is clear that such a view as I have been describing does not lead to any definable utopia. It would be impossible to predict its final outcome. It involves a step-by-step development, based on a continuing subjective choice of purposes, which are implemented by the behavioral sciences. It is in the direction of the "open society," as that term has been defined by Popper (*19*), where individuals carry responsibility for personal decisions. It is at the opposite pole from his concept of the closed society, of which *Walden Two* would be an example.

I trust it is also evident that the whole emphasis is on process, not on end-states of being. I am suggesting that it is by choosing to value certain qualitative elements of the process of becoming that we can find a pathway toward the open society.

The Choice

It is my hope that we have helped to clarify the range of choice which will lie before us and our children in regard to the behavioral sciences. We can choose to use our growing knowledge to enslave people in ways never dreamed of before, depersonalizing them, controlling them by means so carefully selected that they will perhaps never be aware of their loss of personhood. We can choose to utilize our scientific knowledge to make men happy, well-behaved, and productive, as Skinner earlier suggested. Or we can insure that each person learns all the syllabus which we select and set before him, as Skinner now suggests. Or at the other end of the spectrum of choice we can choose to use the behavioral sciences in ways which will free, not control; which will bring about constructive variability, not conformity; which will develop creativity, not contentment; which will facilitate each person in his self-directed process of becoming; which will aid individuals, groups, and even the concept of science to become self-transcending in freshly adaptive ways of meeting life and its problems. The choice is up to us, and, the human race being what it is, we are likely to stumble about, making at times some nearly disastrous value choices and at other times highly constructive ones.

I am aware that to some, this setting forth of a choice is unrealistic, because a choice of values is regarded as not possible. Skinner has stated: "Man's vaunted creative powers . . . his capacity to choose and our right to hold him responsible for his choice—none of these is conspicuous in this new self-portrait (provided by science). Man, we once believed, was free to express himself in art, music, and literature, to inquire into nature, to seek salvation in his own way. He could initiate action and make spontaneous and capricious changes of course. . . . But science insists that action is initiated by forces impinging upon the individual, and that caprice is only another name for behavior for which we have not yet found a cause" (*12*, pp. 52–53).

I can understand this point of view, but I believe that it avoids looking at the great paradox of behavioral science. Behavior, when it is examined scientifically, is surely best understood as determined by prior causation. This is one great fact of science. But responsible personal choice, which is the most essential element in being a person, which is the core experience in psychotherapy, which exists prior to any scientific endeavor, is an equally prominent fact in our lives. To deny the experience of responsible choice is, to me, as restricted a view as to deny the possibility of a behavioral science. That these two important elements of our experience appear to be in contradiction has perhaps the same significance as the contradiction between the wave theory and the corpuscular theory of light, both of which can be shown to be true, even though incompatible. We cannot profitably deny our subjective life, any more than we can deny the objective description of that life.

In conclusion then, it is my contention that science cannot come into being without a personal choice of the values we wish to achieve. And these values we choose to implement will forever lie outside of the science which implements them; the goals we select, the purposes we wish to follow, must always be outside of the science which achieves them. To me this has the encouraging meaning that the human person, with his capacity of subjective choice, can and will always exist, separate from and prior to any of his scientific undertakings. Unless as individuals and groups we choose to relinquish our capacity of subjective choice, we will always remain persons, not simply pawns of a self-created science.

III [Skinner]

I cannot quite agree that the practice of science *requires* a prior decision about goals or a prior choice of values. The metallurgist can study the properties of steel and the engineer can design a bridge without raising the question of whether a bridge is to be built. But such questions are certainly frequently raised and tentatively answered. Rogers wants to call the answers "subjective choices of values." To me, such an expression suggests that we have had to abandon more rigorous scientific practices in order to talk about our own behavior. In the experimental analysis of other organisms I would use other terms, and I shall try to do so here. Any list of values is a list of reinforcers—conditioned or otherwise. We are so constituted that under certain circumstances food, water, sexual contact, and so on, will make any behavior which produces them more likely to occur again. Other things may acquire this power. We do not need to say that an organism chooses to eat rather than to starve. If you answer that it is a very different thing when a man chooses to starve, I am only too happy to agree. If it were not so, we should have cleared up the question of choice long ago. An organism can be reinforced by—can be made to "choose"—almost any given state of affairs.

Rogers is concerned with choices that involve multiple and usually conflicting consequences. I have dealt with some of these elsewhere (*20*) in an analysis of self-control. Shall I eat these delicious strawberries today if I will then suffer an annoying rash tomorrow? The decision I am to make used to be assigned to the province of ethics. But we are now studying similar combinations of positive and negative consequences, as well as collateral conditions which affect the result, in the laboratory. Even a pigeon can be taught some measure of self-control! And this work helps us to understand the operation of certain formulas—among them value judgments—which folk-wisdom, religion, and psychotherapy have advanced in the interests of self-discipline. The observable effect of any statement of value is to alter the relative effectiveness of reinforcers. We may no longer enjoy the strawberries for thinking about the rash. If rashes are made sufficiently shameful, illegal, sinful, maladjusted, or unwise, we may glow with satisfaction as we push the strawberries aside in a grandiose avoidance response which would bring a smile to the lips of Murray Sidman.

People behave in ways which, as we say, conform to ethical, governmental, or religious patterns because they are reinforced for doing so. The resulting behavior may have far-reaching consequences for the survival of the pattern to which it conforms. And whether we like it or not, survival is the ultimate criterion. This is where, it seems to me, science can help—not in choosing a goal, but in enabling us to predict the survival value of cultural practices. Man has too long tried to get the kind of world he wants by glorifying some brand of immediate reinforcement. As science points up more and more of the remoter consequences, he may begin to work to strengthen behavior, not in a slavish devotion to a chosen value, but with respect to the ultimate survival of mankind. Do not ask me why I want mankind to survive. I can tell you why only in the sense in which the physiologist can tell you why I want to breathe. Once the relation between a given step and the survival of my group has been pointed out, I will take that step. And it is the business of science to point out just such relations.

The values I have occasionally recommended (and Rogers has not led me to recant) are transitional. Other things being equal, I am betting on the group whose practices make for healthy, happy, secure, productive, and creative people. And I insist that the values recommended by Rogers are transitional, too, for I can ask him the same kind of question. Man as a process of becoming—*what?* Self-actualization—for what? Inner control is no more a goal than external.

What Rogers seems to me to be proposing, both here and elsewhere (*1*), is this: Let us use our increasing power of control to create individuals who will not need and perhaps will no longer respond to control. Let us solve the problem of our power by renouncing it. At first blush this seems as implausible as a benevolent despot. Yet power has occasionally been foresworn. A nation has burned its Reichstag, rich men have given away their wealth, beautiful women have become ugly hermits in the desert, and psychotherapists have become nondirective. When this happens, I look to other possible reinforcements for a plausible explanation. A people relinquish democratic power when a tyrant promises them the earth. Rich men give away wealth to escape the accusing finger of their fellowmen. A woman destroys her beauty in the hope of salvation. And a psychotherapist relinquishes control because he can thus help his client more effectively.

The solution that Rogers is suggesting is thus understandable. But is he correctly interpreting the result? What evidence is there that a cilent ever becomes truly *self*-directing? What evidence is there that he ever makes a truly *inner* choice of ideal or goal? Even though the therapist does not do the choosing, even though he encourages "self-actualization"

—he is not out of control as long as he holds himself ready to step in when occasion demands—when, for example, the client chooses the goal of becoming a more accomplished liar or murdering his boss. But supposing the therapist does withdraw completely or is no longer necessary —what about all the other forces acting upon the client? Is the self-chosen goal independent of his early ethical and religious training? of the folk-wisdom of his group? of the opinions and attitudes of others who are important to him? Surely not. The therapeutic situation is only a small part of the world of the client. From the therapist's point of view it may appear to be possible to relinquish control. But the control passes, not to a "self," but to forces in other parts of the client's world. The solution of the therapist's problem of power cannot be *our* solution, for we must consider *all* the forces acting upon the individual.

The child who must be prodded and nagged is something less than a fully developed human being. We want to see him hurrying to his appointment, not because each step is taken in response to verbal reminders from his mother, but because certain temporal contingencies, in which dawdling has been punished and hurrying reinforced, have worked a change in his behavior. Call this a state of better organization, a greater sensitivity to reality, or what you will. The plain fact is that the child passes from a temporary verbal control exercised by his parents to control by certain inexorable features of the environment. I should suppose that something of the same sort happens in successful psychotherapy. Rogers seems to me to be saying this: Let us put an end, as quickly as possible, to any pattern of master-and-slave, to any direct obedience to command, to the submissive following of suggestions. Let the individual be free to adjust himself to more rewarding features of the world about him. In the end, let his teachers and counselors "wither away," like the Marxist state. I not only agree with this as a useful ideal, I have constructed a fanciful world to demonstrate its advantages. It saddens me to hear Rogers say that "at a deep philosophic level" *Walden Two* and George Orwell's *1984* "seem indistinguishable." They could scarcely be more unlike—at any level. The book *1984* is a picture of immediate aversive control for vicious selfish purposes. The founder of *Walden Two,* on the other hand, has built a community in which neither he nor any other person exerts any *current* control. His achievement lay in his original *plan,* and when he boasts of this ("It is enough to satisfy the thirtiest tyrant") we do not fear him but only pity him for his weakness.

Another critic of *Walden Two,* Andrew Hacker (*21*), has discussed this point in considering the bearing of mass conditioning upon the liberal notion of autonomous man. In drawing certain parallels between the Grand Inquisition passage in Dostoevsky's *Brothers Karamazov,* Huxley's *Brave New World,* and *Walden Two,* he attempts to set up a distinction to be drawn in any society betwen conditioners and conditioned. He assumes that "the conditioner can be said to be autonomous in the traditional liberal sense." But then he notes: "Of course the conditioner has been conditioned. But he has not been conditioned by the conscious manipulation of another *person.*" But how does this affect the resulting behavior? Can we not soon forget the origins of the "artificial" diamond which is identical with the real thing? Whether it is an "accidental" cultural pattern, such as is said to have produced the founder of *Walden Two,* or the engineered environment which is about to produce his successors, we are dealing with sets of conditions generating human behavior which will ultimately be measured by their contribution to the strength of the group. We look to the future, not the past, for the test of "goodness" or acceptability.

If we are worthy of our democratic heritage we shall, of course, be ready to resist any tyrannical use of science for immediate or selfish purposes. But if we value the achievements and goals of democracy we must not refuse to apply science to the design and construction of cultural patterns, even though we may then find ourselves in some sense in the position of controllers. Fear of control, generalized beyond any warrant, has led to a misinterpretation of valid practices and the blind rejection of intelligent planning for a better way of life. In terms which I trust Rogers will approve, in conquering this fear we shall become more mature and better organized and shall, thus, more fully actualize ourselves as human beings.

References

1. C. R. Rogers, *Teachers College Record* **57**, 316 (1956).
2. A. Hacker, *Antioch Rev.* **14**, 195 (1954).
3. C. Coleman, *Bull. Am. Assoc. Univ. Professors* **39**, 457 (1953).
4. P. A. Freund *et al., Constitutional Law: Cases and Other Problems,* vol. 1 (Little, Brown, Boston, 1954).

4*a*. B. F. Skinner, *Walden Two* (Macmillan, New York, 1948).

5. J. W. Krutch. *The Measure of Man* (Bobbs-Merrill, Indianapolis, 1953).
6. M. Viteles, *Science* **122**, 1167 (1955).
7. G. Negley and J. M. Patrick, *The Quest for Utopia* (Schuman, New York, 1952).

8. B. F. Skinner, *Trans. N.Y. Acad. Sci.* **17**, 547 (1955).
9. R. Niebuhr, *The Self and the Dramas of History* (Scribner, New York, 1955), p. 47.
10. R. Oppenheimer, *Am. Psychol.* **11**, 127 (1956).
11. S. G. Vandenberg, *ibid.* **11**, 339 (1956).
12. B. F. Skinner, *Am. Scholar* **25**, 47 (1955–56).
13. B. F. Skinner, *Am. Psychol.* **11**, 221 (1956).
14. R. Oppenheimer, *Roosevelt University Occasional Papers* **2** (1956).
15. J. A. M. Meerloo, *J. Nervous Mental Disease* **122**, 353 (1955).
16. C. R. Rogers, *Client-Centered Therapy* (Houghton-Mifflin, Boston, 1951).
17. C. R. Rogers and R. Dymond, Eds., *Psychotherapy and Personality Change* (Univ. of Chicago Press, Chicago, 1954).
18. J. Ratner, Ed., *Intelligence in the Modern World: John Dewey's Philosophy* (Modern Library, New York, 1939), p. 359.
19. K. R. Popper, *The Open Society and Its Enemies* (Rutledge and Kegan Paul, London, 1945).
20. B. F. Skinner, *Science and Human Behavior* (Macmillan, New York, 1953).
21. A. Hacker, *J. Politics* **17**, 590 (1955).

Selected Readings

Ahmann, J S., and Glock, M. D. *Evaluating pupil growth: principles of measurement* (4th ed.). Boston: Allyn and Bacon, Inc., 1971, Chapter 2.

Ammons, M. Objectives and outcomes. In R. L. Ebel (Ed.), *Encyclopedia of educational research* (4th ed.). London: Macmillan, 1969, pp. 908–914.

Baker, L. E. The instructional objectives exchange: assistance in goal-referenced evaluation. *Journal of Secondary Education,* 1970, **45**, 158–162.

Bloom, B. et al. (Eds.), Taxonomy of educational objectives. The classification of educational goals. *Handbook I: cognitive domain.* New York: David McKay Co., Inc., 1956.

Eisner, E. W. Educational objectives: help or hindrance. *School Review,* 1967, **75**, 250–260.

Gronlund, N. E. *Stating behavioral objectives for classroom instruction.* London: Macmillan, 1970.

Kliebard, H. M. The Tyler rationale. *School Review.* 1970, **78**, 259–272.

Krathwohl, D. R., Bloom, B. S., and Masia, B. B. Taxonomy of educational objectives. The classification of educational goals. *Handbook II: affective domain.* New York: David McKay Co., Inc., 1956.

Mager, R. F. Preparing instructional objectives. Palo Alto, California: Fearon Publishers, 1962.

Milton, D. "What it is . . . I measure I do not know." *Educational Record,* 1968, **49**, 160–165.

Popham, W. J., Eisener, E. W., Sullivan, H. J., and Tyler, L.L. Instructional objectives. *AERA Monograph Series on Curriculum Evaluation,* 1969, No. 3.

Tyler, R. W. The knowledge explosion: implications for secondary education. *Educational Forum,* 1965, **29**, 2, 145–153.

CHAPTER 4

Effects of Teacher Characteristics on Learning

4.1 Can Science Contribute to the Art of Teaching?

N. L. Gage

One of the important issues in educational psychology is whether there is any relationship between teacher characteristics and effective teaching. Gage reports the negative findings of a number of researchers and reviewers concerning this relationship. Then by means of four research examples, he makes some positive statements about this relationship. He concludes that teachers do differ reliably from each other and that these differences are related to various desirable things about teachers. Some of the teacher behaviors at the desirable end of the dimension are approving, accepting, supporting, liking, and trusting. He finds that they make use of the guided-discovery method and tend to be indirect as opposed to direct in their teaching approach (see Chapter 6, Reading 6.1). The behavior of these teachers also seems to exhibit a valid cognitive organization reflecting an intellectual grasp of their subject matter.

Can science contribute to the art of teaching? It would be nice if the answer could be a resounding "Yes," followed by a long parade of conclusive evidence and examples of richly useful findings. Unfortunately, that happy paper cannot yet be written in any honest way. Instead, I must offer a rather more complex response to the question. First, I shall define the sense in which I shall use the term "successful" and delimit the

SOURCE. N. L. Gage, "Can Science Contribute to the Art of Teaching?", *Phi Delta Kappan*, 49 (March, 1968), pp. 399–403. Reprinted by permission of the author and publisher.

setting of the kind of teaching to be discussed. Second, I am going to consider reasons for pessimism on the question of whether research on teaching has any real likelihood of yielding scientific findings that can be used to improve teaching. The third and fourth sections will be an effort to temper some of the pessimism.

Definition and Delimitation

My present definition of "successful" is one based on research on teaching. The findings of such research may or may not accord with common sense. They may or may not accord with the virtues of personality and character, or desirable behaviors, described in writings on ethics, the Boy Scout handbook, or a Dale Carnegie course. Also, a research-based characterization of successful teacher behavior will not necessarily be extremely original, or completely non-obvious. Nor will such a description of successful teacher behavior necessarily be highly systematic, since research findings at any given moment do not necessarily form a coherent scheme. As for validity, it is not inconceivable that in the long run some nonscientific insight or artistic hunch may turn out to be superior to what can now be cited on the basis of research evidence. That is, the truths propounded in the past by novelists, essayists, or skilled supervisors of teachers may eventually outstrip in scientific validity the results of research now available.

Despite the possible limitations just mentioned, we shall consider only what the research literature has to offer. This literature takes the form of reports on empirical studies of one kind or another. In these studies, various kinds of teacher behavior have been related to other variables on which some sort of educational valuation can be placed. So, by the present definition, "successful" teacher behaviors or characteristics are those that have been found through empirical research to be related to something desirable about teachers. The "something desirable" may be improved achievement by pupils of any of the various cognitive, affective, or psychomotor objectives of education. Or the "something desirable" may be a favorable evaluation of the teacher by pupils, a supervisor, a principal, or someone else whose judgment is important.

The empirical relations between the teacher behaviors and the desirable somethings may be found in two different ways. First, the relationship may be demonstrated in true experiments; if so, they may be considered to be genuine causal or functional relationships. Or they may be found only through correlational studies; if so, the inference that the teacher behavior causes the something desirable may be hazardous. Although it may be urged that conceptual, logical, or historical methods can also establish what is "successful teacher behavior," I am going to exclude such methods from the present argument, i.e., from my present definition of scientific method. That is, I shall assume that scientific knowledge as to what constitutes successful teacher behavior must be based on inference from an experiment or a correlational study that the behavior is related to something desirable.

Now let us specify the kind of setting in which the teacher behavior to be considered takes place. Various innovations being considered by educators may make the setting of teaching one that is not always the conventional classroom. In the future, the setting may change in accordance with the needs of the learners and the kinds of learning in which they are engaged. For some kinds of learning, pupils may be taught in large-group settings, such as movie and lecture halls. For other kinds, the setting will be the small-group seminar, programmed instruction, individually prescribed instruction, or independent study. In the future, these settings will, it is said, supplement and perhaps supplant today's conventional classroom.

But these different kinds of settings still lie in the future, for the most part. And my definition of successful teaching requires empirical research demonstrating a relationship between the behaviors of teachers and other desirable things. So this discussion is going to be restricted to the behavior of teachers in the conventional classroom.

Reasons for Pessimism

Let us now consider reasons for pessimism on the question, Can science contribute to the art of teaching? To begin, it should be noted that making positive statements about the results of research on successful teacher behavior is not fashionable among educational research workers. Many reviewers of research on teaching have concluded that it has yielded little of value.

Recent Summary Statements. This disparaging style in appraising research results has had a great vogue. In 1953, as a member of an AERA Committee on the Criteria of Teacher Effectiveness, I rendered the verdict that "the present condition of research on teacher effectiveness holds little promise of yielding results commensurate with the needs of American education."[1] In 1958, Orville Brim[2] concluded from his examination of reviews of the literature that there were no consistent relations between teacher characteristics and effectiveness in teaching. In 1963, in the *Handbook of Research on Teaching*, the authors of the chapter on teaching methods reported an impression that "teaching methods do not seem to make much difference" and that "there is hardly any evidence

[1] American Educational Research Association, "Committee on the Criteria of Teacher Effectiveness," *Journal of Educational Research*, 1953, p. 657.

[2] O. G. Brim, Jr., *Sociology and the Field of Education*. New York: Russell Sage Foundation, 1958, p. 32.

to favor one method over another."[3] The authors of the chapter on teacher personality and characteristics concluded that ". . . very little is known for certain . . . about the relation between teacher personality and teacher effectiveness."[4] And the authors of the chapter on social interaction in the classroom concluded that "until very recently, the approach to the analysis of teacher-pupil and pupil-pupil interaction . . . has tended to be unrewarding and sterile."[5] It would not be hard to find other summary statements to the effect that empirical research on teaching has not yielded much enlightenment about successful teaching.

Stephens' Theory of Spontaneous Schooling. Some writers hold that all research on school variables, not merely research on teacher behavior, has yielded negative results for the most part. In fact, the view that educational research yields negative findings has even been assimilated into a whole theory of the origins and process of schooling. Stephens[6] has looked at the research reports and the summaries of research and has concluded that practically nothing seems to make any difference in the effectiveness of instruction. Stephens considers this "flood of negative results" to be understandable in the light of his theory of spontaneous schooling. This theory postulates spontaneous, automatic, forces to be found in the background of the student—his maturational tendencies, various out-of-school agencies such as the home and the general community, and the reputation of the school as a place concerned about academic matters. The theory also refers to various spontaneous tendencies on the part of humans in the role of the teacher—tendencies to manipulate and communicate. These two kinds of force, the background forces and the automatic teaching forces, account for most of the learning that takes place. Hence, the changes introduced by research variables of one kind or another are inadequate to produce any major difference. Furthermore, the spontaneous powerful forces operate early in the growth process, when influences on learning have greater effects. For this reason, also, administrative factors and pedagogical refinements produce only minor differences, if any.

Stephens documented his position with references to summaries of studies of a host of specific educational variables, procedures, practices,

[3] N. E. Wallen and R. M. W. Travers, "Analysis and Investigation of Teaching Methods," in *Handbook of Research on Teaching* (N. L. Gage, ed.). Chicago: Rand McNally, 1963, p. 484.

[4] J. W. Getzels and P. W. Jackson, "The Teachers' Personality and Characteristics," in *Handbook of Research on Teaching* (N. L. Gage, ed.). Chicago: Rand McNally, 1963, p. 574.

[5] J. Withall and W. W. Lewis, "Social Interaction in the Classroom," in *Handbook of Research on Teaching* (N. L. Gage, ed.). Chicago: Rand McNally, 1963, p. 708.

[6] J. M. Stephens, *The Process of Schooling*. New York: Holt, Rinehart & Winston, 1967, p. 84.

and orientations—namely, school attendance, instructional television, independent study and correspondence courses, size of class, individual consultation and tutoring, counseling, concentration on specific students, the student's involvement, the amount of time spent in study, distraction by jobs and extracurricular activities, size of school, the qualities of teachers that can be rated by principals and supervisors, nongraded schools, team teaching, ability grouping, progressivism versus traditionalism, discussion versus lecture, group-centered versus teacher-centered approaches, the use of frequent quizzes, and programmed instruction. Studies of all these have failed to show that they make a consistent and significant difference.

Stephens considered briefly the possibility that the negative results are due to methodological errors, such as concentrating on one narrow segment of achievement, using insensitive tests, employing poor controls, exerting overcontrol that holds constant too much and thus restricts the differences, and using too stringent a criterion of statistical significance. But all in all, Stephens concluded, the negative results are only to be expected, because "in the typical comparison of two administrative devices [such as teaching methods] we have two groups that are comparable in the forces responsible for (say) 95 percent of the growth to be had and which differ only in the force that, at best, can affect only a small fraction of the growth."[7]

At any rate, according to many writers, of whom Stephens is merely the most systematic, the major generalization to be drawn from research is that variations in teaching and educational practice do not make any consistent, significant, or practical difference.

The Coleman Report. Apparent support for this view of the effects of educational variables on scholastic achievement can be found in the recent Coleman Report, *Equality of Educational Opportunity*.[8] According to that report, when the social background and attitudes of individual students and their schoolmates are held constant, achievement is only slightly related to school characteristics, such as per pupil expenditures, books in the library, and a number of other facilities and curricular measures. Conversely, the report found that family background accounted for a relatively high proportion of the variance in student achievement. Stephens seems to be vindicated by the Coleman Report.

Questioning the Pessimism

So far we have considered the reasons for pessimism about the promise

[7] *Ibid.*, p. 84.

[8] J. S. Coleman *et al.*, *Equality of Educational Opportunity*. Washington, D.C.: U.S. Department of Health, Education, and Welfare; Office of Education, 1966. Government Printing Office, Superintendent of Documents, Catalog #FS5.-238: 38001.

of empirical research on teaching, as offered by reviews of the research, by a systematic theory of schooling, and by the recent and massive Coleman Report. Let us raise questions about these lugubrious views.

In the first place, these dismal generalizations may not do complete justice to the research domains for which they have been made. Here and there, in research on teaching methods, on teacher personality and characteristics, and on social interaction in the classroom, it might have been possible to come up with more sanguine judgments about the meaning of the research findings.

The disparaging statements about the yield of past research may reflect the fact that research workers are inveterate critics. Their reflex on hearing about positive findings is to look for flaws in rationale, design, sampling, measurement, and statistical analysis. Only when such a quest for error is unsuccessful are research workers willing to grant credence to positive findings.

This attitude is, of course, all to the good. It protects against fallacies, artifacts, and wishful thinking. But it can also be carried to the point of wholesale and unwarranted rejection of what has gone before. We need more searching reviews of what research on teaching has to offer. Such reviews would piece together the evidence from a variety of approaches to a given problem and determine whether constructive suggestions concerning the practice of teaching might be warranted. The new Educational Resources Information Centers, with their improved facilities for tracking down and collating research, ought to make possible "state-of-the-art" papers based on more meticulous sifting of the literature. If so, my guess is that future conclusions about research on teaching will be less melancholy and that Stephens' theory will tend to be disproven as positive results emerge and survive.

What about the Coleman Report? Here also there are reasons for questioning the pessimism. According to Bowles and Levin, the research design of the Coleman study "was overwhelmingly biased in a direction that would dampen the importance of school characteristics."[9] For example, expenditure per pupil was measured in terms of the average expenditure within an entire school district rather than within the given school in which the pupils were located. Hence the expenditure per pupil was overstated for schools attended by lower-class students and understated for schools attended by students of higher social status.

Further, as Bowles and Levin have pointed out, the Coleman study used faulty statistical models in estimating the importance of school factors in accounting for achievement. In the report, the importance of a

[9] S. Bowles and H. M. Levin, "The Determinants of Scholastic Achievement—An Appraisal of Some Recent Evidence," *Journal of Human Resources*, 1968. (in press)

variable was estimated in terms of how much the proportion of variance in achievement explained was increased by adding that variable to the multiple regression equation. But, as Bowles and Levin have indicated, if two predictor variables are correlated, then the additional proportion of variance in achievement that each will explain is "dependent on the order in which each is entered into the regression equation . . . the shared portion of variance in achievement which could be accounted for by either X_1 or X_2 will always be attributed to that variable which is entered into the regression first. Accordingly, the explanatory value of the first variable will be overstated, and that of the second variable understated."[10] Thus when the family background characteristics are entered into the regression first and school resources are entered second, the amount of variance accounted for by the school resource variables is "consistently derogated."[11]

Despite these biases, the Coleman Report found that measures of teacher quality were significantly related to achievement, probably because teacher characteristics were measured individually and averaged for each school. Indeed, the report stated that teacher characteristics accounted for a "higher proportion of variation in student achievement than did all other aspects of the school combined, excluding the student body characteristics."[12] These teacher characteristics were family educational level, years of experience, localism (living in the area most of their lives), teacher's own educational level, score on a vocabulary test, preference for middle-class students, and proportion of teachers in the school who were white. And such factors make a bigger difference, according to the Coleman Report, for Negro than for white students, perhaps because their out-of-school environment contributes less of the spontaneous educative forces of which Stephens writes. Accordingly, the characteristics of teachers who work with culturally disadvantaged pupils become all the more important.

These findings of the Coleman Report and the Bowles-Levin analysis indicate that Stephens' view of the relative unimportance of school and teacher variables may be unwarranted. More adequate surveys of educational achievement, analyzed with more sophisticated statistical tools, may show that teacher behaviors and characteristics make a substantial difference.

Some Positive Statements

Now, having emphasized the difficulties of making positive research-based statements about successful teaching behaviors, I wish nonetheless

[10] *Ibid.*, p. 20.
[11] *Ibid.*, p. 21.
[12] J. S. Coleman *et al.*, *op. cit.*, p. 316.

to attempt such statements—to attempt what is altogether unfashionable among students of research on teaching. My procedure will be to present a series of operational definitions of teacher behaviors that seem to belong on the same dimension. These definitions will be drawn from various research procedures and measuring instruments. Then I shall cite some of the evidence on which it is possible to base the inference that these behaviors or characteristics are desirable. Finally, I shall provide a single summary term that may be used to label this dimension of behaviors and characteristics. (In part, this section is based on an earlier paper.[13] In short, I shall attempt to piece together some evidence from a variety of approaches. I do not consider my present effort to be very convincing. It is intended merely to illustrate the kind of effort that may alleviate the pessimism stemming from other reviews.

Behavior Dimension A. First, let us consider two of the well-known categories for interaction analysis developed by Flanders[14] for use by classroom observers. Category 1 is "Accepts and clarifies the feeling tone of the students in a non-threatening manner . . . ," and Category 2 is "Praises or encourages student action or behavior. Jokes that release tension not at the expense of another individual, nodding head or saying 'um hum?' or 'go on' are included." At the end of a period of observation, one determines the number of instances of behavior in these two categories.

A second example of this dimension of teacher behavior is in the responses of teachers to the Minnesota Teacher Attitude Inventory.[15] Here, the teacher responds on a five-point agree-disagree scale to such statements as "Most children are obedient." "Minor disciplinary situations should sometimes be turned into jokes," "Most pupils lack productive imagination," and "Most pupils are resourceful when left on their own."

As a third example of the same dimension, consider teachers' responses to the California F Scale.[16] Among the items are "Obedience and respect for authority are the most important virtues children should learn," "People can be divided into two distinct classes: the weak and the strong," and "Most of our social problems would be solved if we could somehow get rid of the immoral, crooked, and feeble-minded people."

13 N. L. Gage, "Desirable Behaviors of Teachers," *Urban Education,* 1965, pp. 85–95.

14 N. A. Flanders, "Teacher Influence, Pupil Attitudes, and Achievement." Minneapolis: University of Minnesota, College of Education, November 30, 1960. (Final Report, Cooperative Research Project No. 397, U.S. Office of Education.)

15 W. W. Cook, C. H. Leeds, and R. Callis, *The Minnesota Teacher Attitude Inventory.* New York: Psychological Corporation, 1951.

16 H. M. McGee, "Measurement of Authoritarianism and Its Relation to Teachers' Classroom Behavior," *Genetic Psychology Monographs,* 1955, pp. 89–146.

A fourth example can be drawn from the work of Ryans,[17] who developed a Teacher Characteristic Schedule comprised of such items as the following: "Pupils can behave themselves without constant supervision," "Most pupils are considerate of the teacher's wishes," and "Most teachers are willing to assume their share of the unpleasant tasks associated with teaching."

Now what is the basis for the proposition that certain patterns of responses to attitude statements of this kind, or behaviors of the kind tabulated in the first two of Flanders' categories, are "desirable"? The answer is that these kinds of attitudes and behaviors tend to be correlated positively with favorable assessments of the teachers by pupils and trained observers, and with pupils' scores on achievement tests. The Minnesota Teacher Attitude Inventory has fairly consistently been found to correlate positively with favorable mean ratings of the teachers by their pupils.[18] The items of Ryans' inventory correlated positively with observers' ratings of elementary school teachers on all three of his teacher behavior patterns—warm, understanding, friendly versus aloof, egocentric, and restricted; responsible, business-like, systematic versus evading, unplanned, and slipshod; and stimulating, imaginative versus dull, routine.[19] Similarly, Flanders[20] has reported consistent positive relationships between the degree to which teachers behave in accordance with these two categories and their scores on achievement tests adjusted for pupil ability. McGee[21] found that pupils' scores on the California F Scale correlated 6 with previous ratings of the teachers by trained observers on dimensions like aloof versus approachable, unresponsive versus responsive, dominative versus integrative, and harsh versus kindly. Cogan[22] found that descriptions of teachers by their students on similar items correlated positively with the amount of required and also voluntary school work done by the pupils.

In short, a substantial body of evidence justifies two conclusions: (1) Teachers differ reliably from one another on a series of measuring instruments that seem to have a great deal in common. (2) These reliable

[17] D. G. Ryans, *Characteristics of Teachers.* Washington, D.C.: American Council on Education, 1960.

[18] A. H. Yee, "Is the Minnesota Teacher Attitude Inventory Valid and Homogeneous?" *Journal of Educational Measurement*, 1967, pp. 151–61.

[19] D. G. Ryans, *op. cit.*

[20] N. A. Flanders, *op. cit.*

[21] H. M. McGee, *op. cit.*

[22] M. L. Cogan, "The Behavior of Teachers and the Productive Behavior of Their Pupils: I 'Perception' Analysis; II 'Trait' Analysis," *Journal of Experimental Education*, 1958, pp. 89–105, 107–24.

individual differences among teachers are, by and large, consistently related to various desirable things about teachers.

What term can be applied to the desirable end of this dimension of behaviors and attitudes? Teachers at this desirable end tend to behave approvingly, acceptantly, and supportively; they tend to speak well of their own pupils, pupils in general, and people in general. They tend to like and trust rather than fear other people of all kinds. How they get that way is not our concern at the moment. The point I am making is that it is not impossible to find extremely plausible similarities among the teacher behaviors measured and found desirable by a number of independent investigators working with their own methods, instruments, and concepts. Although any single term is inadequate, it seems safe to use the term "warmth." Teacher warmth, operationally defined as indicated above, seems—on the basis of abundant and varied research evidence—to be quite defensible as a desirable characteristic of teachers.

Behavior Dimension B. To identify a second dimension of teacher behavior, we begin with two more of Flanders' categories. Category 3 is "Accepts or uses ideas of student: clarifying, building, or developing ideas suggested by a student," and Category 4 is "Asks questions: asking a question about content or procedure with the intent that a student answer." In the classrooms of teachers that behave in these ways relatively often, one also finds more instances of Category 8: "Student talk-response: talk by students in response to teacher. Teacher initiates the contact or solicits student statement," and Category 9: "Student talk-initiation: talk by students which they initiate. If 'calling on' student is only to indicate who may talk next, observer must decide whether student wanted to talk. If he did, use this category."

A second example of this dimension of teacher behavior may be seen in the research on what is called "learning by discovery." This research deals with the question, "How much and what kind of guidance should the teacher provide? . . . the degree of guidance by the teacher varies from time to time along a continuum, with almost complete direction of what the pupil must do at one extreme to practically no direction at the other."[23] This dimension consists of the degree to which the teacher permits pupils to discover underlying concepts and generalization for themselves, giving them less rather than more direct guidance. The teacher at the higher level of this dimension realizes that it is not always desirable merely to tell the pupil what you want him to know and understand. Rather, it is sometimes better to ask questions, encourage the pupil

[23] L. Shulman and E. Keislar (eds.), *Learning by Discovery: A Critical Appraisal.* Chicago: Rand McNally, 1966.

to become active, seek for himself, use his own ideas, and engage in some trial and error. This kind of teaching represents a willingness to forbear giving the pupil everything he needs to know; it does not mean abandoning the pupil entirely to his own devices.

Now what is the evidence that this dimension of teacher behavior—exemplified in Flanders' categories and in teaching-by-discovery—has a significant relationship to something educationally desirable? Flanders[24] found that what he called indirectness in teachers went along with greater achievement on the part of their pupils in units on geography and geometry. Flanders (in a personal communication) has referred to some dozen studies by various investigators that have yielded positive correlations between his dimension of indirectness and measures of student achievement. Ausubel concluded from his review of the experiments on learning by discovery that the furnishing of completely explicit rules is relatively less effective than some degree of arranging for pupils to discover rules for themselves.[25]

It seems safe to say that a reasonable use of the guided discovery method, or "indirectness," in teaching is desirable. Teachers not sensitized to its desirability typically exhibit too little indirectness. As Flanders[26] put it, "our theory suggests an indirect approach; most teachers use a direct approach."

Behavior Dimension C. The third dimension of teacher behavior to be discussed is more difficult to define operationally, and its connection with desirable outcomes is, despite great plausibility, still not well established empirically. This is the kind of behavior that reflects the teacher's intellectual grasp, or "cognitive organization," of what he is trying to teach.

In one investigation, teachers were tested as to whether they understood the processes and concepts of multiplication; one item measured the teacher's understanding of the reason for moving each sub-product one digit to the left when the multiplier has more than one digit.[27] Studies by B. O. Smith and his co-workers have dealt with the degree to which the teacher's verbal behavior manifests an understanding of the logical properties of a good definition, explanation, or conditional inference.[28] Ausubel has studied the degree to which the teacher, or his in-

[24] N. A. Flanders, *op. cit.*

[25] D. P. Ausubel, *The Psychology of Meaningful Verbal Learning: An Introduction to School Learning*. New York: Grune & Stratton, 1963, p. 171.

[26] N. A. Flanders, *op. cit.*, p. 114.

[27] J. S. Orleans, *The Understanding of Arithmetic Processes and Concepts Possessed by Teachers of Arithmetic*. New York: Board of Education of the City of New York, Division of Teacher Education, Office of Research and Evaluation, 1952.

[28] M. Meux and B. O. Smith, *Logical Dimensions of Teaching Behavior*. Urbana: Bureau of Educational Research. University of Illinois, 1961. (Mimeographed)

structional material, provides a set of "organizers" for his subject matter that embodies "relevant ideational scaffolding," discriminates new material from previously learned material, and integrates it "at a level of abstraction, generality, and inclusiveness which is much higher than that of the learning material itself."[29] Other research workers express similar ideas in such terms as "cognitive structure" (Ausubel[30] and Bruner[31]), "learning structure" (Gagne[32]), and "logic tree" (Hickey and Newton[33]).

Although the general conception of this aspect of teaching behavior can be identified, operational definitions are hard to come by. Perhaps the best operational definitions of such variables must be inferred from the procedures of those who develop programmed instructional materials. These procedures call for behavioral definitions of objectives and detailed "learning structures"[34] that analyze the steps involved in achieving a "terminal behavior" into hierarchies of subtasks. Gagné illustrated such learning structures in mathematics and science; Glaser and Reynolds[35] worked out a detailed sequence of subbehaviors involved in programmed instructional materials for teaching children to tell time from a clock.

In some ways, the injunctions derived from this kind of technical work on teaching and learning have implications for curriculum development rather than for teaching as such. But the curriculum is inevitably shaped through the teacher's behavior in the classroom as well as in the materials that his pupils read. The implications of such instructional research for the behavior of the live teacher in the classroom seem clear: If curricular material should exhibit a valid cognitive organization, so should the behavior of the teacher.

What can we conclude on the question, Can science contribute to the art of teaching? As you will recall, I began by defining successful teaching behavior as that found by empirical methods to be related to something desirable about teachers, and by restricting the discussion to teacher behavior in the conventional classroom in which most of the empirical

29 D. P. Ausubel, *op. cit.*, p. 214.

30 *Ibid.*

31 J. S. Bruner, *Toward a Theory of Instruction.* Cambridge: Harvard University Press, 1966.

32 R. M. Gagné. *The Conditions of Learning.* New York: Holt, Rinehart & Winston, 1965.

33 A. E. Hickey and J. M. Newton. "The Logical Basis of Teaching: I The Effect of Sub-concept Sequence on Learning," Final Report to Office of Naval Research. Personnel and Training Branch, Contract Nonr-4215(00), January, 1964.

34 R. M. Gagné, *op. cit.*

35 R. Glaser and H. H. Reynolds, "Instructional Objectives and Programmed Instruction: A Case Study," in *Defining Educational Objectives* (C. M. Lindvall, ed.). Pittsburgh: University of Pittsburgh Press, 1964, pp. 47–76.

research on teachers' behaviors and characteristics has been done. I then reviewed some of the reasons for a pessimistic answer to the question, namely, the negative findings and even a general theory that rationalizes the findings of much of the research on teaching and other educational practices. Then I proceeded to consider some bases for questioning the pessimism, namely, the inadequacies of past analyses of the research literature and errors in statistical weighting of teacher and school variables as correlates of achievement in school. Finally, I attempted to illustrate the kind of collation of the evidence from research on teaching that may yield a better basis for more affirmative answers in the future. My examples of such collations of past research are, of course, far from adequate as evidence of anything. They merely serve at present as bases for hypotheses to be tested by the more valid research designs now available.

The field of research on teaching is today engaged in continuous and intensive analysis of its approaches and theoretical formulations (e.g., Gage & Unruh[36]). More complex research designs capable of taking more categories of significant variables into account are now being propounded (e.g., Siegel and Siegel[37]). The psychological, educational, and methodological sophistication of research workers is being raised by greatly improved predoctoral and postdoctoral training programs. And more adequate financial support is providing better organizations and facilities for educational research and development. The faith persists that educationally significant differences can be consistently produced in the future as new intellectual and material resources are brought to bear on educational problems.

[36] N. L. Gage and W. R. Unruh, "Theoretical Formulations for Research on Teaching." *Review of Educational Research,* June, 1967, pp. 358–70.

[37] L. Siegel and L. C. Siegel, "The Instructional Gestalt," in *Instruction: Some Contemporary Viewpoints,* L. Siegel (ed.). San Francisco: Chandler Publishing Co., 1967, pp. 261–90.

4.2 What Characteristics of Teachers Affect Children's Growth?

Carleton Washburne and Louis M. Heil

In this study it was found that teachers with diverse characteristics obtained varying amounts of achievement from different kinds of pupils. Furthermore, specific types of teachers affected the behavior of pupils with varying characteristics in different ways. The authors describe the categories of pupils and teachers and discuss the effects of their classroom interaction.

What measurable characteristics of a teacher have a measurable effect on the intellectual, social, and emotional growth of her pupils? Past research on this crucial question has generally yielded inconclusive results. Yet without a definitive answer we have no way of determining the value of our programs of teacher education or of directing them toward a clearly seen goal. Nor can we use anything other than subjective judgment in selecting candidates for teacher training or teachers for our schools.

After eight years of research, the last two of them subsidized by the U.S. Office of Education, the Office of Testing and Research of Brooklyn

SOURCE. Carleton Washburne and Louis M. Heil, "What Characteristics of Teachers Affect Children's Growth?", *School Review,* **LXVIII**, 4 (1960), pp. 420–428. Reprinted by permission of The University of Chicago Press.

College has data indicating that at least part of the answer to this question has been found. A two-hundred page report on the findings to date is available. (1).

Only some of the high points of the research can be covered here—the hypothesis underlying the study, the general design of the research, the nature of the instrumentation, some of the most striking conclusions, and suggestions on future studies.

Our hypothesis is that teachers who deal with children all day long throughout the year have a definite and determinable influence on the intellectual, social, and emotional growth of children and that this influence is conditioned by both the type of teacher and the kind of children with whom she is dealing. If we can categorize children and if we can distinguish among types of teachers, we should be able to determine what kinds of teachers have what kinds of effects on what kinds of children.

Our plan involved the study of children in nine public schools of Brooklyn. Three of the schools were in lower socioeconomic areas, three in upper socioeconomic areas, and three in intermediate areas. In each school the principal was asked to select two teachers in Grade 4, two in Grade 5, and two in Grade 6. Three of these teachers were to be, in his judgment, "pretty good," and three, "not so good," but the principal was not to identify which teachers came under which heading. These fifty-four teachers, plus an additional teacher, and their pupils were the subjects of the study.

We selected Grades 4, 5, and 6 because these are the last grades in which children are exposed to one teacher throughout the day and the year, yet the children in these grades have enough skill in reading and writing to be easily tested. Our hope was that one or more of the instruments selected or devised would indicate a clear-cut relation between certain measurable characteristics of the teachers and the progress made by children of various groups in academic, social, or emotional development during the year.

One major problem was threefold: to find, or construct, evaluative instruments that would measure certain aspects of the intellectual, social, and emotional growth of the children during one school year under the same teacher; to find ways of differentiating the children in different categories; and to find ways of identifying different types of teachers.

All children were given the Stanford Achievement Test early in the year and another form of the test near the end of the year. All children were also given the Ohio Social Acceptance Scale at the beginning and at the end of the year. This instrument, which might be called a measure of children's friendliness, is a sociometric test that shows the number of children in the class toward whom each child feels various degrees of friendliness and the number of children in the class who feel various degrees of friendliness toward him.

Toward the end of the school year all the children were given the Otis Group Intelligence Test, Form AS, and another instrument called "Assessing Children's Feelings." The latter instrument, devised at Brooklyn College and carefully validated during the six-year period before the experiment began, consists of a series of tape-recorded dramatic episodes, involving various relationships and drawing forth projective responses from the children in a form that can be machine scored.

On the basis of their responses to the children's feelings test the children were categorized. Each of the categories into which the children were placed has been analyzed in detail, and the description of the clusters of traits exhibited by each has been given in the full report. Here we shall refer to them in brief terms that we have found convenient: Conformers, Opposers, Waverers, Strivers.

All teachers were rated on the Teacher Observation Scale prepared at Brooklyn College. Five faculty members of the Department of Education at Brooklyn College who were accustomed to the observation of student teaching were given preliminary training in the use of the scale and, in preliminary trials working in teams, had obtained a high degree of reliability in their ratings. Individually, these observers visited each teacher six to eight times during the year and rated her behavior in the classroom on the Teacher Observation Scale.

This scale owes the idea of polar categories, for example, Democratic-Autocratic—and many of the headings to Ryans (2) and much of the material describing teacher behavior to the Cooperative Research Project (3). The teachers were rated on each of seventeen categories, described operationally in a manual, on a six-point scale.

The other three measures of most of the teachers were obtained toward the end of the year in a four-hour testing period (May, 1959). In this testing period the teachers took the Teacher Education Examination (Educational Testing Service, Princeton), the Manifold Interest Schedule, and a special role-playing type of test not reported here. Since the Manifold Interest Schedule yielded the most clear-cut results, it merits description.

The Manifold Interest Schedule consists of 420 activity statements. The teacher (or other subject) is asked to make one of three responses to each item: "Like," "Dislike," or "Indifferent." A few of the items follow:

Throwing whatever is handy when I'm angry.

Going to a dance.

Attending parties where I meet new people.

Writing a petition and collecting signatures.

Making up a play with a little group of friends.

Having people feel definite about me, either liking or disliking me.

The statements of the Manifold Interest Schedule fall under thirty categories—twelve academic and eighteen personality—with fourteen statements for each category.

The responses to the Manifold Interest Schedule are scored, category by category, by subtracting the number of dislikes from the number of likes. The thirty resulting category scores are then adjusted upward or downward depending on the extent of the subject's over-all tendency to be a "liker" or a "disliker." A statistical analysis of subject's profile of the eighteen personality categories has resulted in six recurring patterns or clusters. The teachers in our experiment tend to fall in three of these patterns, which are called "the turbulent person," "the self-controlling person," and "the fearful person." Detailed descriptions of each of these three kinds of persons are presented in the report (1).

On the negative side, we found no significant relation between teachers' scores on the Teacher Education Examination and any kind of growth on the part of their pupils. Does this mean that the teacher's knowledge of child psychology or professional education as measured by the test has no significance in her teaching? That the test is completely invalid? No such sweeping generalization is justified. All the teachers in the experiment had had the standard amount of professional training; all had been repeatedly examined on their professional knowledge before being graduated from college and certificated. All had passed the license examination to teach in the city. It is quite possible that had we included in our experiment a sizable number of teachers who had had no professional training, the Teacher Education Examination might have shown a difference between the progress of their pupils and the progress of pupils taught by trained teachers.

Our experiment does show that whatever effects the teacher's knowledge measured in the Teacher Education Examination might have are completely masked by the effects of the teacher's personality.

A second negative result was found in responses to the Teacher Observation Scale. The teachers' observed behavior, as identified in the scale and as reported by the observers, bore no general and significant relation to the children's progress. Does this mean that the teacher's behavior had nothing to do with the children's progress? Or that it is impossible to recognize a good teacher when you watch her at work?

Not at all. The same selectivity regarding the subjects referred to in connection with the results from the Teacher Education Examination applies to the Teacher Observation Scale. These teachers' classroom behavior had been such that they had passed their practice teaching while in college and had also passed their probationary years out in the schools. Students or teachers with outlandishly undesirable behavior would not, as a general rule, be teaching and hence taking part in the experiment.

But there is a more basic question. Is it not likely that in preparing the Teacher Observation Scale we had preconceived ideas of what constituted effective teaching and had prepared the scale in terms of these ideas? Is it not likely that the observers themselves, while consistent, also had presumptions of what kind of behavior was desirable from the standpoint of its effects on the children and that these presumptions contained fallacies? Perhaps in the light of our positive findings a new type of Teacher Observation Scale can be devised that will show a relationship between observed teacher behavior and children's progress.

Parenthetically, there is a positive correlation, in the order of .50, between the ratings on the Teacher Education Examination and those on the Teacher Observation Scale. Maybe the makers of the Teacher Education Examination also had preconceived ideas that were fallacious, and a new examination could be devised on sounder hypotheses.

The one striking positive result of the experiment has been clear evidence that the teacher's personality has a clear and measurable effect on the progress of her pupils academically and socially—academically in terms of progress on the Stanford Achievement Test, socially in terms of growth in friendliness and recipiency of friendliness as measured on the Ohio Social Acceptance Scale. There appears also to be a relationship between the type of teacher and her children's emotional adjustment as shown on the children's feelings test.

The results verified the major hypothesis of the study—that different kinds of teachers get varying amounts of achievement from different kinds of children. The self-controlling teacher got the most achievement from the several different kinds of children; the fearful teacher got the least achievement. The turbulent teacher got almost as much achievement as the self-controlling teacher from children classified as conformers and strivers but less than half as much achievement from children classified as opposers and waverers. Although the fearful teacher got the greatest achievement with strivers, the amount of such achievement did not differ appreciably from that obtained by the self-controlling teacher and the turbulent teacher.

In terms of growth in friendliness, the fearful teacher actually got more gain than either the turbulent teacher or the self-controlling teacher from children categorized as waverers.

Another interesting fact emerged when we analyzed the various parts of growth on the Stanford Achievement Test. By testing thousands of Brooklyn College Freshmen on the Manifold Interest Scale and watching their choice of subjects and their marks, we found that the turbulent student had a strong inclination toward science and mathematics and away from verbal subjects and tended to make good marks in science and mathematics. This inclination also appeared to exist with the teachers in our study and to have an effect on the kinds of gain in achievement demonstrated by the children. In our study we found that the turbulent teacher, who got less total achievement from children than the self-controlling teacher, got markedly more achievement from the children in science and arithmetic.

Brooklyn College students classified as fearful tend to do well in the social sciences. Fearful teachers, although at the bottom of the heap generally in terms of children's progress, are at the top for three of the four categories of children in academic progress in the social studies. The one exception is the wavering category of children from whom self-controlling teachers achieve somewhat better progress, .747 of a grade level against .704 for the fearful teacher.

One other point must be recognized. While the self-controlling teacher is definitely superior to either of the other two types in obtaining academic achievement and social acceptance, children under this type of teacher appear to be less free in the expression of their feelings and less self-reliant. They tend to be more prone to disclaim responsibility and put it back into the hands of the authority figure.

Space does not permit a full description of the three types of teachers. The terms, *turbulent, self-controlling,* and *fearful* are so inadequate that we must give a more detailed picture of each type.

The turbulent teacher appears to place little emphasis on structure and order. Thinking, conjecturing, and objectivity appear to be her center of focus. She tends to move away from people and toward ideas. She accepts and expresses her impulses. She is much more effective with conforming and striving children than with opposing and wavering children. She is more effective with those who already have an inner security and order than with those who do not. It is possible that she might be more effective with adolescents than with young children. This hypothesis needs exploration.

The self-controlling teacher focuses on structure, order, and planning and is work inclined. She is definitely empathetic and warm in her feeling toward her pupils. Her pupils show less anxiety than those of the other two types of teacher. She has strong leadership tendencies but tends to show acquiescence toward immediate superiors. She is notably sensitive to the feelings of others.

The fearful teacher is anxious, variable in her behavior. She seems unable to inject structure and order into the teaching atmosphere. She tends to induce anxiety in her pupils and to arouse defensive reactions in them. Her thinking appears to be constricted in the face of uncertainty. She has a severe conscience. In relations with others she tends to be self-protective, cautious about committing herself. She likes to have rules to guide her action and wants others as well as herself to abide by rules.

Like all pioneering studies, this one needs to be repeated by other researchers working under similar and under varying conditions. It certainly should be tried in different environments. Our data are all derived from schools in a highly urban community. The current study should be regarded as one that points the way to highly fruitful research rather than as one that gives a final answer to our basic question on the measurable characteristics of the teacher that relate directly to the development of her pupils.

As to the next step we propose to take at Brooklyn College: We have set up an interdepartmental committee consisting of two members of the psychology department, one sociologist, a clinical psychologist from our educational clinic, a psychologically oriented professor of education who has been a classroom teacher and knows the schools, and, as chairman, the director of testing and research.

This committee has been given released time to explore the type of experiences that may lead to the development in undergraduate students of the insights and the personality characteristics most effective in dealing with various categories of children. Can a turbulent-type person, as late as the college years, recognize his or her limitations in structuring and limit-setting and learn to do something about them? Can he or she learn to deal differentially with the various categories of children? Can a self-controlling type develop the capacity to give more self-reliance and power of independent thought to children without loss of the structuring that yields many positive results? Can a college give to the fearful type the sort of security that will at least mitigate the fearfulness and anxiety, or must such persons be guided out of teaching?

Can we make the educational experiences of the students such that they see directly how different types of pupils' personalities can be appropriately dealt with, through being taught differentially according to their own different personality types?

It is with such questions that our committee will wrestle. When they feel that they have devised a suitable set of experiences to yield some sort of answer to these questions, two or three sections of undergraduate students will be freed of our present prepractice-teaching professional requirements and will be trained according to the tentative plan, under carefully selected staff members. The training of such prospective teachers may occur in special sections in departments other than education as well as in the education department. Such students will be carefully pre-tested and post-tested, and later will be followed up in the schools. We do not propose to modify, at least at present, the practice-teaching and the methods course, which usually occupies the senior year, although there may well be some changes even in the methods–practice-teaching course for the experimental group of students.

It is, however, much too early to tell what kind of changes will be made in the program of these students. It should be a radical change, oriented not to the acquisition of knowledge, although the students will certainly be acquiring pertinent knowledge, but rather toward changes in basic attitudes and insights. It may be necessary to ignore license requirements (we believe the city and the state will permit this) and preconceived notions as to what sort of training, what courses, would-be teachers should have. We shall search for a means of developing in the various types of students those characteristics that the present experiment indicates are most likely to contribute effectively to children's intellectual, social, and emotional growth.

References

1. Louis M. Heil, Marion Powell, and Irwin Feifer, "Characteristics of Teacher Behavior Related to the Achievement of Children in Several Elementary Grades" (Brooklyn, New York: Brooklyn College Bookstore, Brooklyn College).
2. David G. Ryans, "A Study of Criterion Data," *Educational and Psychological Measurement,* XII (Autumn, 1952), 333–44; "The Investigation of Teacher Character," *Educational Record,* XXXIV (Otober, 1953), 371–96.
3. Cooperative Research Project, the University of Buffalo School of Education, *Studies in Professional Education,* July 15 and August 1, 1958.

Selected Readings

Gage, N. L. Desirable behaviors of teachers. *Urban Education.* 1965, 1, 85–95.

Getzels, J. W., and Jackson, P. W. The teacher's personality and characteristics. In N. L. Gage (Ed.), *Handbook of research on teaching.* Chicago: Rand McNally & Co., 1963, pp. 506–582.

Goldberg, Miriam L. Adapting teacher style to pupil differences: teachers for disadvantaged children. *Merrill-Palmer Quarterly of Behavior and Development,* 1964, **10**, 161–178.

Haas, K. The middle-class professional and the lower-class patient. *Mental Hygiene,* 1963, **47**, 408–410.

Hamachek, D. E. What research tells us about the characteristics of "good" and "bad" teachers. *Human Dynamics In Psychology and Education,* 1968.

Harvey, O. J., Prather, Misha, White, B. J., and Hoffmeister, J. K. Teachers' beliefs, classroom atmosphere and student behavior. *American Educational Research Journal,* 1968, **5**, 151–166.

Jersild, A. T. The voice of the self. *NEA Journal,* 1965, **54**, 7, 23–25.

Jersild, A. T. *When teachers face themselves.* New York: Bureau of Publications, Teachers College, Columbia University, 1955.

Kounin, J. S., and Gump, P. V. The comparative influence of punitive and nonpunitive teachers upon children's concepts of school misconduct. *Journal of Educational Psychology,* 1961, **52**, 44–49.

Kuhlen, R. Psychological needs of teachers and perceived need satisfaction opportunity in teaching. *Journal of Applied Psychology,* 1963, **47**, 56–64.

McGuigan, F. J. The experimenter: a major factor in experimental outcomes. *Psychological Bulletin,* 1963, **60**, 421–428.

Ryans, D. G. Teacher behavior; theory and research: implications for teacher education. 1963, **14**, 274–293.

Snow, R. H. Anxieties and discontents in teaching. *Phi Delta Kappan,* 1963, **44**, 318–321.

CHAPTER 5

Structuring the Learning Task

5.1 Structure and Related Ideas

William T. Lowe

In September 1959, scholars from a wide range of disciplines had a conference at Woods Hole, Massachusetts to analyze what was happening in the field of curriculum. As a result of this conference, its chairman, Harvard psychologist Jerome S. Bruner, published a very important book, The Process of Education. *(See selected readings). Perhaps no other single reference has stimulated more thought about curriculum than Bruner's little volume.*

In this reading, Professor Lowe simplifies a number of Bruner's points on structure. He also clarifies the importance of the structure of subject matter for teaching and learning. In the other chapters of his book, Dr. Lowe relates his ideas on structure to the disciplines of history, geography, sociology, anthropology, economics, and government.

Four major hypotheses were stated in *The Process of Education:* (1) All disciplines are reducible to fundamental and development ideas—that is, structure. (2) These basic ideas can be taught to almost all individuals at any age and any level of ability in some intellectually honest manner. (3) All children can develop a type of "intuitive grasp" of the nature of the disciplines that is now possessed typically only by scholars. (4) Intellectual curiosity is ample motivation for students if they are given the opportunity to think for themselves or to "discover" the structure of the disciplines; the excitement of intellectual activity or discovery is possible for everyone, and it is sufficient to motivate the student to do schoolwork. All four of these hypotheses will be briefly discussed here. The most important of the four for Bruner and for our curriculum study group is structure; consequently, it will receive most of our attention. (Actually, all four hypotheses are related and are based on structure.)

What is structure? In spite of all we have said regarding the impact of *The Process of Education,* the concept of structure is not clearly defined in the book. Bruner's later writing seems to take the reader even farther away from a precise definition.[1] He does say that the purpose of teaching is to "give a student as quickly as possible a sense of the fundamental ideas of a discipline," that "underlying principles . . . give structure to the subject," that "grasping the structure of a subject is understanding it in a way that permits many other things to be related to it meaningfully."[2] The inference then is that structure has to do with relationships among the fundamentals of a subject. Structure seems to be the fabric of fundamental ideas of a discipline and the relationships among the ideas. It is the body of ideas from a subject that must be understood if further comprehension of the field is to be obtained. This definition, of course, still leaves a lot of room for various interpretations.

Structure is now perceived to have two dimensions. The first comprehends those fundamental concepts, propositions, principles, generalizations, understandings, and ideas that are foundational to each discipline. The second includes the organization, methods if inquiry, and ways of approaching knowledge that are distinct (or partially so), those attributes that Bruner seems to have meant when he spoke of the developmental relations between concepts. In describing the first dimension we have deliberately ignored the semantic confusion that exists over the precise meanings of "concepts," "generalizations," and the other terms. It is true that the distinction between some of these are important. But for our purposes, since all of them are included in structure, commonsense meanings should suffice.

Bruner and most other writers on this subject have said that all disciplines have structure. In fact, they argue, structure sets the boundaries

[1] See, for example, Jerome S. Bruner, *On Knowing: Essays for the Left Hand* (Cambridge: Harvard University Press, 1962), and *Toward a Theory of Instruction* (Cambridge: Cambridge University Press, 1966).

[2] Jerome S. Bruner, *The Process of Education.* Cambridge: Harvard Univ. Press, 1960, pp 3, 7, 31.

or the scope of a discipline. According to this view a discipline is an identifiable category of knowledge because it has a specific and at least partially unique subject matter and an explicit, generally accepted method and approach for discovering truth. The "rockbottom," fundamental ideas —both substantive and methodological—are the structure. A discipline also includes less powerful ideas and facts which are added to the structure in a developmental fashion. These ideas may be ordered in terms of their importance from those with the greatest power to explain phenomena to those with the least.

The separation of structure into conceptual and methodological aspects is artificial; the two cannot be permanently disjoined. A concept only has validity if the student knows how it was conceived and how it relates to other concepts. Methodological ideas are empty and meaningless unless the student knows something of the product of their use. Still, it seems useful to separate the two aspects for purposes of analysis.

Each discipline, then, has concepts, principles, and methods having the power to explain what we observe and experience in a particular subject of interest. Some of these ideas are more basic than others—they have more power to explain, they are fundamental to other ideas which cannot be understood without a grasp of their foundations. Studying a field of knowledge means investigating its hierarchial structure.

It would be difficult to overemphasize the fact that the ways of looking at and working with these ideas is as crucial to the discipline as are the concepts and principles themselves. Phenix puts it this way:

"Representative ideas are . . . at one and the same time principles of growth and principles of simplification. They are principles of growth because the patterns they reveal prove to be reproductive of further insight, yielding more and more exemplifications of what they typify. They are principles of simplification because they provide a kind of map of the discipline that keeps one from getting lost in the details. This is a surprising fact, that an understanding of the very ideas that make a discipline fertile, causing knowledge in it to expand rapidly, is also the basis for simplifying the task of learning the discipline."[3]

According to the pioneers of the new curriculum, the modes of inquiry and thought processes in the various field of knowledge differ not only because they have different subject matter but because they strive for distinct kinds of explanation. For example, the natural scientist is looking for general laws, while the historian is trying to explain unique sit-

[3] Philip Phenix, *Realms of Meaning: A Philosophy of the Curriculum for General Education*. New York: McGraw Hill, 1964, p. 324.

uations of the past. They work in different kinds of "laboratories," with different kinds of data, and must use different means of gathering, verifying, and analyzing their materials. (As we will see, this fact gets us in trouble). Knowledge in all fields is a process as well as a product. Scholars in the same field must have some basic agreement on the procedures for knowing and discovering truth; otherwise they cannot even communicate, let alone build on the work of others. At the heart of each discipline must be certain criteria for determining valid and reliable truths, and as previously indicated, the ideas of a field have significance for a student only if he perceives the ways in which these ideas were uncovered and how they lead to "new" knowledge. "The right of a scholar to speak as an authority in his field rests on his acceptance of the canons of inquiry on which knowledge in it is created and validated."[4] And Bruner's objective is to make a scholar of each student in each subject to which he is exposed.

The notion of structure implies a pragmatic epistemology. Knowledge is relative. There is no absolute truth. Substantive and methodological structure changes. Much misunderstanding of Bruner and his "disciples" has resulted from the misconception that the position is founded on a belief in a single fixed structure for each discipline. Bruner himself is partly responsible for this confusion because of his failure to deal directly with the issue. He speaks at times of *the* structure, and the reader is given the impression that there exists a final truth out there, available to the man who seeks it. But, Bruner also says, "knowledge is a model *we* construct to give meaning and structure to the regularities in experience. The organizing ideas of any body of knowledge are *inventions* for rendering experience economical and corrected."[5] This statement seems to say that structure is not inherent in knowledge, but is invented by men. Bruner also speaks of the necessity of having different structures for the same discipline in order to deal with conflicting theories which cannot be proved or disproved given our present state of knowledge.

To be sure, Bruner is consistently vague on this point, even in his later writings, but some of his followers are not. Schwab and Ausubel speak of the "tentativeness," the "adequacy," and the "variety" of structures.[6] The champions of the "new curriculum" also applaud the fact that there are a good many approaches to the "new math" and at least three versions of biology that are focused on distinct structures for the field. In fact, one of the most attractive aspects of the idea of structure is that it provides a theoretical basis for dealing with change and controversy in a

[4] *Ibid.*, p. 322.
[5] Bruner, *On Knowing*, p. 120; italics mine.
[6] Elam, *Education and the Structure of Knowledge*, pp. 10, 234.

field. The student recognizes, or should recognize, that as we learn more and document or refute old theories we need to revise the old structure or develop new ones. Bruner reminds us that scholars do this continually. They discover something and then seek a way of fitting this observation into what is already known. Frequently, the process involves rejecting what they had formerly believed to be true. This is the process of structuring. It is dynamic and it is in an important sense personal, at least at first. It is the imperfect and unfinished product of men, not an everlasting verity.

There is one final element in this definition: structure as a pedagogical concept. A structure, the one held by the teacher, should be used initially to give meaning and organization to what the child learns. This structure should serve as a model and should show the power of a structure to give meaning and substance to what one learns. The child should be encouraged to internalize a structure, modifying the teacher's when this is justified. Bruner believes, for example, that Physical Sciences Study Committee (P.S.S.C.) physics encourages students to try their hand at structuring. The teacher must help the student to find a structure that works for him.

Rationale for Structure

Structure, then, is not only the fundamental ideas of a subject; it is also the internalized way of perceiving the logical relations between these ideas and the means of arriving at them. Bruner claims a number of advantages for a structured curriculum: Structure helps students learn what is important; it helps in retention; it fosters transfer of learning; and it helps reduce the gap between the work of scholars and what takes place in the classroom.

The first claim is based on the "principle of learning," which asserts that we understand more and, therefore, learn more if what we are learning is perceived to be logically organized. This idea has been around for a long time; in fact, it seems to be one of the few things that we can take for granted about human learning. We learn more if we can sense meaningful relations with what we already know and have experienced. We learn more if we can perceive an order and sequence.

The second claim—that of increased retention—is based on the same contention; that is, learning will be more durable if the learner perceives relations and organization. Bruner makes the commonplace observation in his essay "After John Dewey, What?" that isolated, disassociated information is not long remembered.[7] Facts and ideas learned in relation

[7] Bruner, *On Knowing*, p. 120.

to other and more fundamental facts and ideas help us to recall both. The process of retrieving a fact is aided by an awareness of the relation of that item to basic concepts and principles.

Of course, both these claims might be equally true of a curriculum ordered on any integrating or organizing principle. Structure is just one way to capitalize on the human need for logical order. The transfer argument, however, seems more specifically tied to the idea of structure. The point is made that the "explosion of knowledge" forces us to be even more conscious of the need to teach for transfer than in the past. We cannot teach all there is to know and much of what we do teach will be quickly obsolete unless we concentrate on fundamentals and, equally important, on methods of inquiry. These change less rapidly and provide a framework for adding and amending when the situation warrants. According to those who accept the idea of structure, the best way to help students transfer what they have learned in one context to another situation outside the classroom is to teach them the basic ideas, the relationships among the ideas, or the methods of inquiry from the various teaching fields. In this regard Bruner and others speak of the "economic," "generative," and "regenerative" power of the idea of structure.[8] These terms refer to the efficiency and developmental, or stimulating, character of studying structural ideas.

The final claim Bruner makes for structuring the curriculum is that the gap between student and scholar, between classroom practices and scholarship, will be lessened. Students will spend their time on learning the important, exciting, and yet basic ideas, the same ones being used by men on the frontiers of scholarship, rather than on acquiring that dull, grey background of details which people have traditionally thought had to be learned prior to the act of thinking. The students start by thinking about significant ideas instead of ending there.

This, then, is the nature and defense of structure, the first of Bruner's hypotheses and the one that he regarded as the most significant of the four ideas underlying the curriculum revision movement in all fields. Before we try to assess this concept, however, we will return for a moment to the other three ideas or hypotheses that Bruner cited. As I have said, these hypotheses seem to depend on structure.

Three Related Ideas

The second of the four hypotheses is concerned with readiness—anything can be taught to anybody in some intellectually respectable way. This idea was greeted with surprise and outrage when it was first ex-

[8] Bruner, *Process,* p. 25.

pounded. The argument seemed to reject the years of research by developmental psychologists. In fact, it seemed contrary to the very work cited by Bruner and done by the Geneva School, particularly by Piaget and Inhelder. But was it contradictory?

Bruner's explanation suggests not. One of the assumptions held by many professional educators is a belief that children develop in stages—the "average" child goes through fairly predictable steps in his growth. If we know these stages, then there is a golden moment to introduce a topic, a skill, or an attitude. It was believed that in the interest of efficiency it was better to wait until the child was ready—intellectually, emotionally, experientially, and physically—for the introduction of something new.

Bruner does not deny that children get more sophisticated as they mature; in fact the whole idea of structure rests on this fact. But he also thinks that young children can and do perceive significant ideas in their own way, in their "own grammar," in their own logic systems. Basic ideas and methods—the structure of a discipline—can and should be introduced early, using the language appropriate to the stage of development of the child. The leaders of the new curriculum think that readiness has been improperly used to withhold ideas from pupils. Educators have tried to fill pupils' heads with a store of facts in the belief that connections and relationships and "big ideas" must come later. But the curriculum organization we need is one that emphasizes ideas at the beginning and then returns to the ideas again and again in different and ever more sophisticated contexts—the spiral curriculum.

Bruner accepts at least in part the stages of development that have been identified by the Geneva group of psychologists. He wants to use this information to help determine the most appropriate language and context available for introducing structure. Young children, at least most of the time, have to be introduced to ideas first through action, as opposed to abstract thinking; they have to "act out" the idea or in other ways do something with it. Setting up a store to teach economic principles is a commonplace example. Later, students may be introduced to ideas through imaginery. Here, diagraming is helpful. Finally, when the child has gone through these stages, ideas can be presented through symbols, including verbal forms. Sometimes it is possible to skip a stage, but the pattern holds more often than not.

The problem is to identify the basic ideas and then place them in the language, context, stages, and "grammar" appropriate for the child. We are strongly warned of the dangers inherent in delaying this process on the grounds that students cannot comprehend the fundamentals. To document his view that students can learn significant ideas early, Bruner cites impressive but inconclusive evidence.[9] The evidence, mainly Inhelder's work, is based on research in teaching mathematics and physics. Bruner speculates that "a comparable approach can surely be taken to the teaching of social studies and literature."[10]

The third and fourth of Bruner's hypotheses are concerned with "the intuitive grasp of structure" and "discovery." Many of the leaders of the curriculum revision movement argue that the program of studies of the past has been almost exclusively organized on an analytic, formalistic basis. If thinking was desired at all in the old curriculum, then the teacher wanted analytical thinking—a formal, step-by-step, logical progression. The new curriculum ought to emphasize intuition, "the intellectual technique of arriving at plausible but tentative formulations without going through the analytical steps by which such formulations would be found to be valid or invalid conclusions."[11]

The "intuitive leap" involves insight, the apprehension of meaning suddenly and dramatically, the "ah-ha" phenomenon. The hunch, the hypothesis, and the "big picture" are placed at a premium. Again, this notion is clearly not new. The Gestalt principle was with us long before Koffka and Lewin provided language for it. Bruner's interpretation has some special twists, but these are unimportant for us here. We need only note that an underlying idea of the movement is the belief that "it [is] of first importance to establish an intuitive understanding of materials before we expose our students to more traditional and formal methods of deduction and proof."[12] The testing of hunches must come, to be sure, but later. In almost poetic style Bruner has called for more "left-handedness," dreaming, intuiting, and less "right-handedness," or formal analysis.[13] One encourages intuition by teaching structure—by raising the questions scholars are discussing at the same time providing a stimulating, open, intellectual climate. In a fascinating way Bruner sees intuition as an end and a means, a cause and an effect of teaching structure. A teacher encourages pupils to be intuitive so that they may arrive at an understanding of structural ideas, and, in turn, the acquiring of these ideas develops intuitive powers. One begins to teach on the basis of the child's natural but undeveloped powers of insight and then develops them.

This appealing idea of intuition is, of course, itself intuitive. The de-

[9] Jerome S. Bruner, "Some Theorems on Instruction Illustrated with Reference to Mathematics," *Theories of Learning and Instruction*, ed. Ernest Hilgard (Chicago: University of Chicago Press, 1964), pp. 314, 329-331, and Bruner, *Process*, pp. 40, 41.

[10] Bruner, *Process*, p. 46.

[11] *Ibid.*, p. 13.

[12] *Ibid.*, p. 59.

[13] Bruner, *On Knowing*.

ductive formal testing stage for the notion of intuition has not yet been achieved by psychologists, as Bruner knows. He admits that it is even impossible at the present time to behaviorally and precisely define intuition. Still, the appeal is there. What teacher can fail to be attracted to a position that encourages individuality, freedom, and creativity and discourages dreary formalism? Think of a school in which students are motivated to discover principles and relationships among ideas with the same drive that mature scholars have. Think of a school in which teachers themselves act on intuitive hunches and are thrilled by working with ideas. Think of a school in which the intrinsic rewards of discovering structure are all the motivation that a student needs. Imagine the sheer delight of having students engaged together in first intuitive and then analytical thinking. Of course the idea has appeal. But is it an inspired fantasy? This is quite another matter and the evidence is not yet in.

The essence of the fourth hypothesis, discovery, Bruner describes as "a matter of rearranging or transforming in such a way that [the learner] is enabled to go beyond the evidence so reassembled to new insights."[14] Once again, the "discovery" idea is clearly not new. Mauritz Johnson, Jr., documents this point in an effective and witty way in "Who Discovered Discovery?"[15] But Saint Jerome must be given credit for making the word a regular part of our jargon. if not of our teaching procedures.

According to this hypothesis, teachers must employ techniques that lead pupils to find generalizations for themselves. Of course, this process cannot be attempted in every case or we would never have any progress, but the most productive learning and retention situation is the discovery one. Phenix more modestly calls the process "guided re-discovery."[16] The terms "guided" and "rediscovery" might seem like half a loaf, stopping short of the goal, for Bruner. Massialas and Cox have called their approach "inquiry-centered."[17] This description also suggests an affinity with Bruner, but he would probably insist on the intuitive aspect of the act of learning far more than does Massialas. A curriculum could be focused on the inquiry process and be highly formalistic. One can imagine a teacher having students recite the steps in the scientific method and then go through dull drill sessions in which one problem after another would be subjected to the formal stages. The teacher would supply the data and clarify the problem, and the students would dutifully arrive at the conclusion the teacher had expected. This may be a useful exercise,

[14] *Ibid.*, pp. 82–83.
[15] *Phi Delta Kappan,* XLVIII (Nov. 1966), 120.
[16] *Realms of Meaning*, pp. 336–337.
[17] *Inquiry in Social Studies.*

but it is not discovery-teaching in Bruner's sense. Of course, it is not what Cox and Massialas want either. The terms employed by Phenix and Massialas and Cox have only been introduced here to suggest a few of the qualifications that have been added to Bruner's ideas.

How much freedom should the child have and how much guiding or directing should the teacher do? Should the students be encouraged to discover or merely rediscover? Should they be encouraged to develop their own methods of inquiry or should the young child, particularly, be required to learn to follow traditional ways? Bruner does not hedge on these questions:

"Intellectual activity anywhere is the same, whether at the frontier of knowledge or in a third-grade classroom. What a scientist does at his desk or in his laboratory, what a literary critic does in reading a poem, are of the same order as what anybody else does when he is engaged in like activities—if he is to achieve understanding. The difference is in degree, not in kind. The schoolboy learning physics *is* a physicist, and it is easier for him to learn physics behaving like a physicist than doing something else. The "something else" usually involves the task of mastering . . . a "middle language"—classroom discussions and textbooks that talk about the conclusions in a field of intellectual inquiry rather than centering upon the inquiry itself."[18]

A central purpose of the curriculum for Bruner is bridging the gap between scholarship and the classroom. The way to do this is to force the schoolboy to be a scientist, a historian, an author. He must not study scholarship alone, he must do it. He must use the methods of others, and he must develop his own. In so doing he learns how to learn. This is the essence of transfer. Methods of inquiry are more durable than facts and even generalizations.

[18] *Process,* p. 14.

5.2 The Concept of the Structure of a Discipline

Joseph J. Schwab

Jerome Bruner discusses the importance of structure in his book The Process of Education. *He states that there is a type of transfer at the heart of the educational process, namely, the learning of a general idea rather than a skill. The idea can then be used as the basis for future learning. Learning, therefore, becomes dependent on knowing the structure of subject matter. In this paper, Dr. Schwab lists and defines what he believes to be the important components of the structure of a discipline. He emphasizes that the diversity and complexity of knowledge demand that we recognize the need for different structures, each of which will be appropriate or best for a given discipline or group of disciplines.*

In 1941, my colleagues and I offered for the first time a course in the structure of the disciplines. We had devoted an entire year to developing its plan and content. But we had spent no time at all on the problem of how to teach it. The first few weeks, in consequence, were a severe trial of our students' patience. Finally, one of them cornered me.

"Tell me," she said, "what this course is about."

I did so—in twelve minutes. I was impressed by my clarity as much

SOURCE. Educational Record, **XLIII**, No. 3 (1962), pp. 197–205. Reprinted permission of American Council on Education.

as by my brevity. So, apparently, was my student. For she eyed me a moment and then said, "Thank you. Now I understand. And if the truth is that complicated, I am not interested."

The young lady was right on two of three counts. First, the concept of a structure of a discipline is concerned in a highly important sense with truth, not with truth in some vaguely poetic sense, but with answerable, material questions of the extent to which, and the sense in which, the content of a discipline is warranted and meaningful. Second, study of the structures of the disciplines is complicated—at least by contrast to the simple assumptions about truth and meaning which we have used in the past in determining the content and the organization of the school curriculum.

On the third count, however, the young lady was wrong. We cannot afford to be uninterested in the structures of the disciplines. We cannot so afford because they pose problems with which we in education must deal. The structures of the modern disciplines are complex and diverse. Only occasionally do we now find among them a highly esteemed body of knowledge which consists simply of collections of literal statements standing in one-for-one relation to corresponding facts. Instead of collections, we find organizations in which each member-statement depends on the others for its meaning. And the verifying relations of such organizations to their facts are convoluted and diverse. This complexity of modern structures means that problems of comprehension and understanding of modern knowledge now exist which we in education have barely recognized. The diversity of modern structures means that we must look, not for a simple theory of learning leading to a one best learning-teaching structure for our schools, but for a complex theory leading to a number of different structures, each appropriate or "best" for a given discipline or group of disciplines.

In brief, the structures of the disciplines are twice important to education. First, they are necessary to teachers and educators: they must be taken into account as we plan curriculum and prepare our teaching materials; otherwise, our plans are likely to miscarry and our materials, to misteach. Second, they are necessary in some part and degree *within* the curriculum, as elements of what we teach. Otherwise, there will be failure of learning or gross mislearning by our students.

Let us turn now to examination of a structure, using the sciences as the example.

Forty years ago it was possible for many scientists and most educators to nurse the illusion that science was a matter of patiently seeking the facts of nature and accurately reporting them. The conclusions of science were supposed to be nothing more than summaries of these facts.

This *was* an illusion, and it was revealed as such by events in the science of physics that began in the late 1890's. The discovery of radioactivity suddenly revealed a world within the world then thought to be the only world. The study of that world and of its relations to the world already known led to a revolution in the goals and the structures of physics. By the mid-twenties, this revolution in physics had gone so far that we were faced with the fact that some of the oldest and least questioned of our ideas could no longer be treated as literally true—or literally false. Classical space had been a homogeneous, neutral stage on which the dramas of motion and existence were acted out. The flow of classical time was always and everywhere the same. The mass and length of bodies were each elementary properties independent of other properties. Bodies occupied a definite location and a definite amount of space.

The new physics changed these notions. In its knowledge structure, space was something which could be distorted and its distortions affected bodies in it. The magnitude and position of sub-atomic particles could not be described as we describe the magnitude and position of a one-inch cube here-now.

But these new assertions did *not* come about because direct observations of space, place, time, and magnitude disclosed that our past views about them were merely mistaken. Rather, our old assertions about these matters were changed because physicists had found it fruitful to treat them in a new way—neither as self-evident truths nor as matters for immediate empirical verification. They were to be treated, instead, as principles of inquiry—conceptual structures which could be revised when necessary, in directions dictated by large complexes of theory, diverse bodies of data, and numerous criteria of progress in science.

Today, almost all parts of the subject-matter sciences proceed in this way. A fresh line of scientific research has its origin not in objective facts alone, but in a conception, a deliberate construction of the mind. On this conception, all else depends. It tells us what facts to look for in the research. It tells us what meaning to assign these facts.

A moment's thought is enough to show us how this process operates. That we propose to investigate a chosen subject is to say, of course, that we are, in large part, ignorant of it. We may have some knowledge, based on common experience or on data garnered in preliminary study. But this preliminary knowledge is only a nibbling at the edges. We barely know the superficial exterior of our subject, much less its inner character. Hence, we do not *know* with certainty what further facts to look for, what facts will tell us the significant story of the subject in hand. We can only *guess*.

In physiology, for example, we did not know, but only supposed, that the functioning of the human organism is carried out by distinct parts, that each part has a character and a fixed function in the economy of the whole. Hence, we did not *know* that the facts we ought to seek in physiological research should be facts about the structure of each organ and what happens when each organ is removed. On the contrary, the conceptions of organ and of function were developed prior to sure knowledge of these matters and where developed precisely to make such knowledge possible through research. The conceptions are guiding principles of inquiry, not its immediate fruits.

In physics, similarly, we did not *know* from the beginning that the properties of particles of matter are fundamental and determine the behavior of these particles, their relations to one another. It was not verified knowledge but a heuristic principle, needed to structure inquiry, that led us to investigate mass and charge and, later, spin.

It may, indeed, be the case that the particles of matter are social particles, that their most significant properties are not properties of their very own but properties which accrue to them from association with other particles, properties that change as the associations change. Therefore, it may be that the more significant facts to seek in physical inquiry are not facts about the properties of particles but facts about kinds of associations and the consequences of associations.

Similar alternatives exist for physiology. There are conceptions of the organism that yield, when pursued in inquiry, a more profound knowledge than that afforded by the notions of organ and function.

In short, what facts to seek in the long course of an inquiry and what meaning to assign them are decisions that are made before the fact. The scientific knowledge of any given time rests on *the* facts but on *selected* facts—and the selection rests on the conceptual principles of the inquiry.

Moreover, scientific knowledge—the knowledge won through inquiry—is not knowledge merely of the facts. It is of the facts *interpreted.* This interpretation, too, depends on the conceptual principles of the inquiry. The structure-function physiologists does not report merely the numerous changes displayed by an experimental animal from which an organ has been removed. He interprets these changes as indicative of the lost function once performed by the organ removed. It is this interpretation of the facts that is the conclusion drawn from the experiment and reported as a piece of scientific knowledge, and its meaning and validity depend on the conception of organ and function as much as they depend on the selected facts.

Here, then, is a first approximation of what is meant by the structure of a discipline. The structure of a discipline consists, in part, of the body of imposed conceptions which define the investigated subject matter of that discipline and control its inquiries.

The significance to education of these guiding conceptions becomes clearer if we repeat once more the way in which they act as guides. First, they severely restrict the range of data which the scientist seeks in inquiry. He does *not* study the whole of his subject, but only some aspect of it, an aspect which his then-current principles of inquiry lead him to treat as the significant aspect. The conclusions of that line of inquiry may be true, but most certainly they are not the whole truth about that subject matter. They are not about some aspect of nature taken in its pristine state but about something which the principles of the inquiry have made, altered, or restricted. Furthermore, what the scientist makes of these data, what he takes them to mean, is also determined not by full knowledge of their significance, but by the tentative principles of the inquiry.

Now the subject matter may be—in fact, almost always is—far richer and more complex than the limited model of it embodied in the conclusions of the restricted inquiry. Thus, the first significance to education of the structure of a discipline: we cannot, with impunity, teach the conclusions of a discipline as if they were about the whole subject matter and were the whole truth about it. For the intelligent student will discover in time—unless we have thoroughly blinded him by our teaching—that any subject behaves in ways which do not conform to what he has been told about it. His bodily illnesses, for example, are often not reducible to the malfunctioning of specific organs or the presence of a specific bacterium. His automobile does not appear to obey the "laws" of the particular science of mechanics which he was taught. Legislatures and executives do not behave as a dogmatic political science says they do.

It is the case, however, that a structure-function physiology, a Newtonian mechanics, or some particular reading of political behavior throws *some* light on the behavior of our bodies, our automobiles, or our democracy. Or it would if the body of knowledge were understood in the light of the restricted circumstances in which it is valid and known in connection with the restricted range of data which it subsumes. In short, the bodies of knowledge *would* have defensible and valuable meaning to those who learn them had they been learned, not in a context of dogma, but in a context of the conceptions and data that determine their limited meaning and confer their limited validity. This is one significance of the structure of the disciplines to education.

A second significance becomes visible if we look at a further consequence of the operation of a conceptual structure in inquiry. It renders scientific knowledge fragile and subject to change; research does not proceed indefinitely on the basis of the principles that guided its first inquiries. On the contrary, the same inquiries that accumulate limited knowledge by the aid of assumed principles of inquiry also test these principles. As the selected principles are used, two consequences ensure. Knowledge of the subject unfolds; experimental techniques are refined and invented. The new knowledge lets us envisage new, more adequate, more telling conceptions of the subject matter. The growth of technique permits us to put the new conceptions into practice as guiding principles of a renewed inquiry.

The effect of these perennial rewards of inquiry is perennial revision of scientific knowledge. With each change in conceptual system, the older knowledge gained through use of the older principles sinks into limbo. The *facts* embodied are salvaged, reordered, and reused, but the *knowledge* which formerly embodied these facts is replaced. There is, then, a continuing and pervasive revision of scientific knowledge as principles of inquiry are used, tested, and supplanted.

Furthermore, our scientific and scholarly establishment is now so large, so many men are now engaged in inquiry, that the rate of this revision is exceedingly rapid. We can expect radical reorganization of a given body of scientific knowledge, not once in the coming century but several times, at intervals of five to fifteen years. This means, of course, that our students—if they continue to receive all their learning in a dogmatic context, outside the structure of the disciplines—will confront at least once in their lives what appears to be a flat contradiction of much that they were taught about some subject. The effect of this lie-direct to teaching in the schools can only be exacerbation, to an intolerable degree, of the confusion, uncertainty, and cynicism which our young people already exhibit with respect to *expertise,* to schooling and to bodies of organized knowledge.

Our students and our nation could be protected from the consequences of such misunderstanding, if, again, our students learned what they learned not as a body of literal and irrevocable truths but as what it is: one embodiment of one attack on something less than the whole of the matter under investigation. This is a third significance of the conceptual structure of the disciplines to education.

Whereas the second significance to education arises from the existence of a process of revision, the third and fourth significances emerge from the outcomes of this process—from the advances which it has made possible. In the process of revision, improvement of principle is sought in two different directions. On the one hand, more *valid* principles are sought, principles which will embrace more and more of the richness and complexity of the subject under investigation. On the other hand, principles of wider *scope* are sought, principles which will embrace a wider and wider range of subject matters, which will reduce what were before considered as separate and different phenomena to related aspects of a common kind or source. (Thus, Newtonian mechanics united the movements of the heavenly bodies with the behavior of objects thrown and dropped by man on earth, rendering these formerly diverse phenomena but varying expressions of a common law. Similarly, the physics of the century just past found new principles that united the formerly separated phenomena of light, electricity and magnetism.)

The successful search for more *valid* principles—for more adequate models of investigated phenomena—has led to scientific knowledge of a new "shape" or character, in sharp contrast to older knowledge. Older knowledge tended toward the shape of a catalogue. Old descriptive biology, for example, was necessarily a catalogue: of the organs, tissues, or kinds of cells which made up the body. Another part of descriptive biology was a catalogue of the species, genera, classes, and so on of the living organisms that populated the earth. Even the experimental physiology of years only recently past tended toward a similarly encyclopedic character—for example, lists of parts of bodies with their functions, meticulous itemizing of hereditary units and their consequent traits. Chemistry, in similar fashion, tended to be a classificatory scheme of elements and of the more complex substances that arose from their combination.

Modern scientific inquiry, conversely, tends to look for patterns—patterns of change and patterns of relations—as their explanatory principles. When such patterns are found, they throw a new and more complex light on the items of our old catalogues. The items lose their primary significance and lose their independence. On the side of significance, an item ceases to be something which simply is, and becomes, instead, one of possibly many "somethings" that fulfill conditions required by the pattern. On the side of dependence-independence, an item ceases to be something which can be understood by itself; it becomes, instead, something which can be understood only by knowing the relations it bears to the other items that fill out the pattern or blueprint.

Thus, it was once possible to teach something about the significance of glucose to the living body by reciting a formula for it—naming the three elements which compose it, indicating the number of each—and naming it as an energy source. Today, it is necessary to talk about the basic pattern of a carbohydrate molecule, how the elements are connected to one another, what happens when connections are made or broken, and so on. This story of pattern is imbedded, in turn, in a still larger pattern—the pattern of processes by which energy is captured, stored, transferred, and utilized in the body. The educational significance of this emphasis on pattern in the sciences is more clearly indicated by the further point that, a few years ago, we could tell the story of energy sources merely by cataloguing glucose and two or three other substances as the common energy sources of the body. Today, the story must be the story of where and when and under what circumstances each of these substances functions as an energy source, and how, in a sense, they function as *interchangeable* parts to fulfill the conditions of the determining pattern.

This shift from catalogues to patterns in the disciplines means, in turn, that teaching and learning take on a new dimension. Instead of focusing on one thing or idea at a time, clarifying each and going on to the next, teaching becomes a process of focusing on points of contact and connection among things and ideas, of clarifying the effect of each thing on the others, of conveying the way in which each connection modifies the participants in the connection—in brief, the task of portraying phenomena and ideas not as things in themselves but as fulfillments of a pattern.

The successful search for principles of greater scope has led to developments of a parallel kind. As the scope of a set of principles enlarges, so does the coherence of the body of knowledge which develops from it, the interdependence of its component statements, a fifth significance. Thus, in a theory which embraces electricity and magnetism as well as light, an assertion about the nature of light borrows part of its meaning and part of its warrant from statements about electricity and magnetism. The significance of the assertion about light cannot be grasped by understanding only its terms and the light phenomena to which it applies. For these terms are defined in part by terms in other statements about other phenomena.

This kind of coherence in scientific knowledge means that our most common way of applying the old query "What knowledge is of most worth?" is no longer entirely defensible. We can no longer safely select from the conclusions of the disciplines the separate and different bits and pieces that we think would be most useful to the clients of the schools. We cannot because the separation of these bits, their removal from the structure of other statements which confer on them their meaning, alters or curtails that meaning. The statements will no longer convey the warranted and valid knowledge they convey in context, but something else or something less.

For students of some ages or of very limited learning competence, such bits and pieces may be appropriate as limited guides to limited actions, limited understanding, and a limited role in society. For many children at many ages, however, we need to face the fact that such a disintegrated content is not only a distorted image of scientific knowledge but a distorted image of the physical world it purports to represent; it will betray itself.

This means, in turn, that teaching and learning, as we have suggested above, need an added dimension. As patterns replace lists and catalogues, learning and remembering of parts remain necessary conditions of learning but cease to be sufficient conditions. A new flexibility is required, a capacity to deal with the roles of things, as well as with things as such, and to understand the relations among roles. The following crude metaphor may suggest the nature of this flexibility. Natural phenomena as now conceived by the sciences must be understood as a dynamic, a drama. The drama unfolds as the outcome of many interacting roles. Therefore, the relation of each role to others must be understood. Second, each role may be played by more than one actor; different "actors," despite their apparent diversities, must be recognized as potential players of the same role. Third, each potential player of a role modifies somewhat the role he plays and, through this effect, also modifies the roles played by other actors. Hence, the unfolding, the climax, and outcome of the drama are flexible, not one rigid pattern, but variations on a theme.

A sixth significance of conceptual principle to education is quickly told.

Different disciplines have widely different conceptual structures. Despite the passionate concern of some philosophers and some scientists for a unity of the sciences, biologists and physicists, for example, continue to ask widely different questions in their inquiries seek different kinds of data, and formulate their respective bodies of knowledge in widely different forms. It is not quite obsolete in biology, for instance, to ask what system of classes will best organize our knowledge of living things and to seek data primarily in terms of similarities and differences. The physicist, however, continues to find it most rewarding to ask what relations among what varying quantities will best organize our knowledge of the behavior of matter; consequently, he seeks data which consist primarily of measurements of such changing quantities.

Such differences among sciences are so persistent and so rewarding that it is hard to avoid the conviction that there are real and genuine differences among different bodies of phenomena, that differences in questions put and data sought are not merely the products of historical habits among the different disciplines but also reflect some stubbornnesses of the subjects. Some subject matters answer when one set of questions is put. Another answers to another set. And neither will answer the questions to which the other responds.

Among these differences of conceptual structure, there are some which deserve special attention from educators because of the confusion they create if ignored. These are the specific differences among conceptions which two or more disciplines apparently hold in common. Two large-scale examples occur to me: the concept of *time* and the concept of *class*.

Time is deeply imbedded in the conceptual structure of both physics and biology. In many respects, the concept of time is the same in both sciences. In one respect it is radically different. Time for the biologist is unavoidably vectorial and has direction from past to future, like the time of common sense. It cannot, in any sense, be considered reversible. Time, as it appears in most physical equations, in contrast, has no notion of past and future attached to it; it permits, in a certain sense, reversibility.

The concept of class is, perhaps, a more telling instance of difference for the purposes of education. The class of biology is a loose and messy affair compared to the class with which traditional logic (and much of mathematics) is concerned. The logical class consists of members which are all alike in some defining respect. The biologists' class, however, consists of members of which it can be said, at best, that most of them have most of *many* properties which, together, define the class.

The special problem posed by such differences as these is easily seen. The *logical* class, consisting of members alike in some defining respect, permits us to infer with confidence knowledge about members of the class from knowledge of the class. The *biological* class permits no such confident inference. What is true for the class may or may not be true of some member or subclass. Obviously, instruction which permitted this crucially instrumental conceptual difference to go unnoted by teachers and students would lead to all sorts of later confusion and error.

I remarked earlier that a body of concepts—commitments about the nature of a subject matter, functioning as a guide to inquiry—was *one* component of the structure of a discipline. Let us turn briefly to another which I shall call the syntactical structure of the disciplines. By the syntax of a discipline, I mean the pattern of its procedure, its method, how it goes about using its conceptions to attain its goals.

Most of us were taught a schoolbook version of a syntax under the guise of "scientific method." Though oversimple, full of error, and by no means the universal method of the sciences, it will suffice as an example. This schoolbook story (borrowed, incidentally, from an early work of Dewey) tells us that science proceeds through four steps. There is, first, the noting of data relevant to our problem. Second, there is the conceiving of a hypothesis. Third, the hypothesis is tested by determining whether consequences expected if the hypothesis were true are, in fact, found to occur. Finally, a conclusion is stated, asserting the verification or nonverification of the hypothesis.

So we are given the impression that the goal of all the sciences is a congeries of well-verified hypotheses. We are left with the impression that verification is of only one kind—the discovery that expected consequences occur in fact.

If this were all there were to the syntax of the disciplines, it would be of little importance to teaching, learning, and the curriculum. Unfortunately, this is not all there is. For different disciplines have different starting points and different goals. That is, their subject matters may be conceived in vastly different ways, so also may what they conceive to be sound knowledge or fruits of the inquiry. Consequently, the path, the syntax, the process of discovery and verification is also different.

Such differences in method of verification and discovery hold even for the similar disciplines called the sciences. They hold, *a fortiori,* between the sciences on one count, mathematics on another, and history on a third.

Among the sciences, let us contrast, once more, biology and physics. Biology, until very recently, has been the science that comes closest to fulfilling the schoolbook version of science. It has consisted, in large part, of a congeries of tested hypotheses. Its inquiries have turned from the verification of one to the verification of another with little twinge of conscience. Biologists have rarely hesitated to formulate hypotheses for different problems that differed widely from one another, that had little, indeed, of a common body of conceptions. Thus, verification for biology was largely a matter of chasing down, one by one, many and various expected consequences of many and various hypotheses.

Physics, on the other hand, has for centuries held as its goal not a congeries of almost independent hypotheses but a coherent and closely knit body of knowledge. It has sought to impose on its diverse formulations of diverse phenomena a body of conceptions which would relate them to one another and make of them one body, inferable from the conceptions which bound them together. Hence, for physics, verification has often meant something far otherwise than its meaning in biology. It has meant, in many cases, that expected consequences had been observed. In a few cases, however, the first reason for accepting a certain hypothetical had nothing to do with observed consequences. Rather, the hypothetical in question was accepted in order to save another conception, one which lay deep in the structure of physical knowledge and had ramifications extending over most of its conclusion. Thus, the "verifying" circumstance had to do with the structure of existing knowledge rather than the structure of existing things. (In one such case, the hypothetical in question—the neutrino—was verified some years later by the discovery of expected consequences, to the great relief of many physicists. In still another case—that of the parity principle—the principle itself was discarded and replaced.)

Where physics and biology differ in their goals, science and mathematics differ primarily in their starting points, that is, their subject matters. The consequent differences in their syntax are vast. Let us take algebra as our example and agree for the moment that the subject matter of algebra is number. Now, whatever number may be, one thing is certain: it does not consist of a body of material things, of events accessible to our senses. The idea of testing for the presence of materially existential consequences is meaningless in algebra. The algebraist may conceivably use something called data, but if he does, it is something vastly different from what is meant by data in a science which studies a material, sense-accessible subject matter. Yet, there can be error as well as truth in algebra, hence, some means of discovery and of test. Clearly, then, the means, the syntax of mathematics, must be vastly different from the syntax which has a material subject matter.

A similar great difference holds between most history and the sciences. Few historians would hold that their goal, like the goal of science, is discovery of general laws. They do not take as their starting points things and events which they think of as repeated instances of a *kind* of thing or event. On the contrary, most historians take as their goal the recovery or the reconstruction of some selected, time-limited or space-limited group of past and unique events. But again, there are such things as better history and worse history—the more and the less well verified. Yet, only by the wildest of equivocations can we assert that the historian discovers and verifies in the same way as does the investigator of living things, of falling bodies, or of numbers.

In brief, truth is a complicated matter. The conceptual structure of a discipline determines what we shall seek the truth about and in what terms that truth shall be couched. The syntactical structure of a discipline is concerned with the operations that distinguish the truth, the verified, and the warranted in that discipline from the unverified and unwarranted. Both of these—the conceptual and the syntactical—are different in different disciplines. The significance for education of these diverse structures lies precisely in the extent to which we want to teach what is true and have it understood.

References

AAAS Commission on Science Education. *Science—A Process Approach. Purposes, Accomplishments, Expectations. Washington, D.C.:* American Association for the Advancement of Science, 1967.

Ausubel, D. P. *Educational Psychology: A Cognitive View.* New York: Holt, Rinehart & Winston, 1968.

Battig, W. F. Paired-associate learning. In T. R. Dixon and D. L. Horton (Eds.), *Verbal Behavior and General Behavior Theory,* pp. 149–171. Englewood Cliffs, N.J.: Prentice-Hall, 1968.

Beauty, W. E., and Weir, M. W. Children's performance on the intermediate-size transposition problem as a function of two different training procedures. *Journal of Experimental Child Psychology,* 1966, **4**, 332–340.

Beilin, H., Kagan, J., and Rabinowitz, R. Effects of verbal and perceptual training on water level representation. *Child Development,* 1966, **37**, 317–330.

Caron, A. J. Far transposition of intermediate-size in preverbal children. *Journal of Experimental Child Psychology,* 1966, **3**, 296–311.

Cox, R. C., and Graham, G. T. The development of a sequentially scaled achievement test. Paper read at Annual Meeting, American Educational Research Association, Chicago, 1966.

Davis, G. A. Detrimental effects of distraction, additional response alternatives, and longer response chains in solving switch-light problems. *Journal of Experimental Psychology,* 1967, **73**, 45–55.

DiVesta, F. J., and Walls, R. T. Transfer of object-function in problem solving. *American Educational Research Journal,* 1967, **4**, 207–216.

Gagné, R. M. The acquisition of knowledge. *Psychological Review,* 1962, **69**, 355–365.

Gagné, R. M. *The Conditions of Learning.* New York: Holt, Rinehart & Winston, 1965.

Gagné, R. M. Curriculum research and the promotion of learning. In *Perspectives of Curriculum Evaluation,* AERA Monograph Series on Curriculum Evaluation, No. 1, pp. 19–38. Chicago: Rand-McNally, 1967.

Gagné, R. M. Contributions of learning to human development. *Psychological Review,* 1968, **75**, 177–191.

Gagné, R. M., and Brown, L. T. Some factors in the programming of conceptual learning. *Journal of Experimental Psychology,* 1961, **62**, 313–321.

Gagné, R. M., Major, J. R., Garstens, H. L., and Paradise, N. E. Factors in acquiring knowledge of a mathematical task. *Psychological Monographs,* 1962, **76**, No. 526.

Gagné, R. M., and Paradise, N. E. Abilities and learning sets in knowledge acquisition. *Psychological Monographs,* 1961, **75**, No. 518.

Guilford, J. P. *The Nature of Human Intelligence.* New York: McGraw-Hill, 1968.

Johnson, P. J., and White, P. M. Jr. Concept of dimensionality and reversal shift performance in children. *Journal of Experimental Child Psychology,* 1967, **5**, 223–227.

Kingsley, R. C., and Hall, V. C. Training conservation through the use of learning sets. *Child Development,* 1967, **38**, 1111–1126.

Mayzner, M. S., and Tresselt, M. E. Solving words as anagrams: An issue re-examined. *Psychonomic Science,* 1965, **3**, 363–364.

Merrill, M. D. Correction and review on successive parts in learning a hierarchical task. *Journal of Education Psychology,* 1965, **56**, 225–234.

Overing, R. L. R., and Travers, R. M. W. Effect upon transfer of variations in training conditions. *Journal of Educational Psychology,* 1965, **57**, 179–188.

Overing, R. L. R., and Travers, R. M. W. Variation in the amount of irrelevant cues in training and test conditions and the effect upon transfer. *Journal of Educational Psychology,* 1967, **58**, 62–68.

Selected Readings

Bruner, J. S. *The Process of Education.* Cambridge: Harvard University Press, 1961, pp. 17–32.

Elam, S. *Education and the structure of knowledge* (Phi Delta Kappa symposium, 1963). Chicago: Rand McNally, 1964.

Gagne, R. M. Learning hierarchies. *Educational Psychologist,* 1968, **6**, 1, 3–6, 9.

Gowin, D. B. The structure of knowledge. *Educational Theory* (To be published in the Fall of 1970). This is a somewhat difficult and sophisticated presentation of the subject.

Kliebard, H. M. Structure of the disciplines as an educational slogan. *Teachers College Record,* 1965, **66**, 598–603.

Kline, M. Intellectuals and the schools: A case history. *Harvard Educational Review,* 1966, **36**, 505–511.

Krug, M. M. Bruner's new social studies: A critique. *Social Education,* 1966, **30**, 400–406.

Martin, V., and Oliver, W. The structure of knowledge in the social sciences. In B. O. Smith (Ed.), *Education and the Structure of Knowledge.* Chicago: Rand McNally & Company, 1964, pp. 188–207.

CHAPTER 6

Guiding Learning

6.1 Intent, Action and Feedback: A Preparation for Teaching

Ned A. Flanders

In their very thorough review of the measurement of classroom behavior, Medley and Mitzel[1] *emphasize that the obvious way to study teaching is by observing what teachers do in the classroom. Generally these behaviors are recorded in the form of tallies, checks, or other marks. In this manner predefined categories can be coded to yield a variety of information such as the kind of behaviors occurring, their sequence, and their frequency. Typically researchers have concerned themselves only with antecedents and consequents of classroom happenings; they haven't observed how teachers teach and pupils learn. They suggest that observation should be used to gain insight into the nature of effective teaching. These insights would be relevant for teaching selection, training, and in-service education.*

Unfortunately most observers have preconceptions of what good and bad teaching are. Instead of determining what the effective teacher does,

SOURCE. Ned A. Flanders, "Intent, Action and Feedback: A Preparation for Teaching," *The Journal of Teacher Education,* **XIV**, 3 (1963), pp. 251–260. Reprinted by permission of *The Journal of Teacher Education.*

[1] Medley, D. M. and Mitzel, H. E. Measuring classroom behavior by systematic observation. In N. L. Gage (Ed.), *Handbook of Research on Teaching,* Rand McNally & Co., 1963, pp. 247–328.

they decide whether the teacher is behaving effectively—in the manner that they believe he should behave. Ratings used by these visitors have been based on certain dimensions thought to be related to teacher effectiveness. These measures have been unsuccessful in differentiating effective teaching. It is a myth that laymen or professional educators can judge a teacher's effectiveness by watching him.

These discouraging results, however, do not mean that effectiveness of teaching cannot be measured during the process. It is just a matter of identifying the crucial behaviors, recording them, and scoring them. There have been a few studies whose findings demonstrate that it is possible to determine varying levels of effectiveness.

Further progress with the use of direct observation was its successful application to the study of "classroom climate." Dorothy S. Thomas[2] *and her associates made a number of highly objective studies of nursery-school behavior. Instead of focusing on actions involving material objects or the self, they observed interactions between individuals. For example, one technique involved plotting the actual movements of a single child around the nursery-school floor. Medley and Mitzel believe that the most serious limitation of these studies was their overconcern with agreement among observers. Nevertheless, the premium they placed on objectivity was carried over to the work of Anderson and his coworkers. They recorded "contacts" made among nursery-school children and "contacts" of teachers with children. Their data resulted in the formation of two behavioral categories—dominative and integrative. Dominative included such behavior as matching a toy, striking a playmate, or forcing him in some way. Behaviors such as offering a companion a choice or soliciting an expression of his desires were categorized as integrative. Findings showed clearly that classrooms differed markedly in these two dimensions. There was also evidence that the dimensions were related to the teacher's personality.*

Further work in measuring teacher behavior was done by Withall.[3] *He changed the name of the* Integrative-Dominative Index *to* Social-Emotional Climate. *He developed a set of categories such as* Learner-supportive, *and* reproving or deprecating *statements by which he could classify teacher behavior. He saw his seven categories as lying along a continuum from "learner-centeredness" to "teacher-centeredness." Unlike that of previous researchers mentioned above, his technique was not designed for classroom observation, but was a method for coding type-*

[2] D. S. Thomas and associates. Some new techniques for studying behavior. *Child Development Monograph,* 1929, 1.

[3] J. Withall. Development of a technique for the measurement of socio-emotional climate in classrooms. *Journal of Experimental Education,* 17 (1949), 347–361.

written transcripts made from sound recordings. Medley and Mitzel replicated the research by using the scale when observing in the classroom.

No one has given more impetus to the objective analysis of what a teacher does in the classroom as it relates to pupil behavior and classroom climate than Professor Flanders. In this paper, he describes his procedure for tabulating, analyzing, and interpreting the verbal behavior of teachers and pupils. He then suggests how a teacher might profit from applying the Flanders Interaction Analysis Technique to a recorded tape of his own teaching. From this kind of feedback a teacher can learn to control his behavior for the improvement of classroom learning.

When Nathaniel Cantor (5) published his nine assumptions of orthodox teaching, there was little evidence to support his criticisms. Must pupils be coerced into working on tasks? In what way is the teacher responsible for pupils' acquiring knowledge? Is education a preparation for later life rather than a present, living experience? Is subject matter the same to the learner as it is to the teacher? The last decade has provided more evidence in support of Cantor's criticism than it has in defense of existing practice.

H. H. Anderson and his colleagues (1,2,3,4) first demonstrated that dominative teacher contacts create more compliance and resistance to compliance, that dominative teacher contacts with pupils spread to the pupil-to-pupil contacts even in the absence of the teacher, and that this pattern of teaching creates situations in which pupils are more easily distracted and more dependent on teacher initiative.

Flanders and Havumaki (8) demonstrated that dominative teacher influence was more persuasive in changing pupil opinions but that such shifts of opinion were not stable since inner resistance was so high.

A research team in Provo, Utah (9) believes that patterns of spontaneous teacher action can be identified and that more effective patterns can be distinguished from less effective patterns. The difference is that more dominative patterns are less effective.

Our own eight-year research program which involved the development of interaction analysis as a tool for quantifying patterns of teacher influence lends further support to Cantor. The generalizations to follow are based on all teachers observed in our different research projects. This total is only 147 teachers, representing all grade levels, six different school districts in two countries; but these teachers came from the extremes of a distribution involving several thousand teachers. The total bits of information collected by interaction analysis are well in excess of 1,250,000.

The present, average domination of teachers is best expressed as the rule of two-thirds. About two-thirds of the time spent in a classroom, someone is talking. The chances are two out of three that this person is the teacher. When the teacher talks, two-thirds of the time is spent by many expressions of opinion and fact, giving some direction and occasionally criticizing the pupils. The fact that teachers are taking too active a part for effective learning is shown by comparing superior with less effective classrooms. A superior classroom scores above average on constructive attitudes toward the teacher and the classwork. It also scores higher on achievement tests of the content to be learned, adjusted for initial ability. In studies (7) of seventh grade social studies and eighth grade mathematics, it was found that the teachers in superior classrooms spoke only slightly less, say 50 to 60 per cent of the time, but the more directive aspects of their verbal influence went down to 40 to 50 per cent. These teachers were much more flexible in the quality of their influence, sometimes very direct, but on more occasions very indirect.

To describe the classrooms which were below average in constructive pupil attitudes and in content achievement (they are positively correlated), just change the rule of two-thirds to the rule of three-fourths plus.

The foregoing evidence shows that no matter what a prospective teacher hears in an education course, he has, on the average, been exposed to living models of what teaching is and can be that are basically quite directive. After fourteen or so years he is likely to be quite dependent, expecting the instructor to tell him what to do, how to do it, when he is finished, and then tell him how well he did it. Now it is in this general context that we turn to the question of how we can develop a spirit of inquiry with regard to teaching.

Thelen (10) has described a model of personal inquiry, as well as other models, and the question is whether teacher education can or should move toward this model. He describes this model as follows (*ibid.*, p. 89):

"... (personal inquiry) is a process of interaction between the student and his natural and societal environment. In this situation the student will be aware of the process of which he is a part; during this process he will be aware of many choices among ways he might behave; he will make decisions among these ways; he will then act and see what happens; he will review the process and study it with the help of books and other people; he will speculate about it, and draw tentative conclusions from it."

Returning to the education course, the student will be aware of the learning process of *that* classroom, he will confront choices, he will make decisions among the choices, he will act and then evaluate his actions, and then he will try to make some sense out of it with the help of books, the instructor, and his peers. This is a tall order, but who knows, it may be the only route to discovery and independence for the prospective teacher.

Occasionally we hear of exciting learning experiences in which education students attain a sort of intellectual spirit of inquiry. A unit on motivation can begin with an assessment of the motivation patterns of the education students. The same assessment procedures can then be used at other grade levels, permitting comparisons and generalizations. Principles of child growth and development can be discovered by observation and learned more thoroughly, perhaps, than is possible with only lecture and reading. But this is not what is meant by inquiry.

Inquiry in teacher education means translating understanding into action as part of the teaching process. It means experimenting with one's own behavior, obtaining objective information about one's own behavior, evaluating this information in terms of the teacher's role; in short, attaining self-insight while acting like a teacher.

Procedures for obtaining self-insight have been remarkably improved during the last decade in the field of human relations training. Two characteristics of these training methods seem relevant to this discussion. First, information and insights about behavior must become available in a way that can be accepted and in a form that is understood. Second, opportunities to utilize or act out these insights must be provided. Our ability to accept information about ourselves is a complex problem, but it helps if we believe the information is objective, valid, and given in an effort to help rather than hurt. Our understanding of this information will depend a great deal on our ability to organize the information conceptually. Freedom to act at least requires freedom from threat or embarrassment.

From all of these things, a spirit of inquiry develops.

The Technique of Interaction Analysis

Interaction analysis is nothing more and nothing less than an observation technique which can be used to obtain a fairly reliable record of spontaneous verbal statements. Most teacher influence is exerted by verbal statements, and to determine their quality is to approximate total teacher influence. This technique was first developed as a research tool, but every observer we ever hired testified that the process of learning the system and using it in classrooms was more valuable than anything else he learned in his education courses. Since interaction analysis is only a technique, it probably could be applied to teacher education in a fashion that is consistent or even totally inconsistent with a philosophy of personal inquiry. How it is used in teacher preparation is obviously as important as understanding the procedure itself.

The writing of this manuscript followed the completion of a terminal contract report of a U.S. Office of Education-sponsored, in-service training program based on interaction analysis as a tool for gathering information. How we used interaction analysis is illustrated by the conditions we tried to create for the fifty-five participating teachers, most of whom represented about one-half of the faculties of two junior high schools:[1]

1. Teachers developed new (to them) concepts as tools for thinking about their behavior and the consequences of their behavior. These concepts were used to discover principles of teacher influence. Both types of concepts were necessary: those for describing actions and those for describing consequences.
2. Procedures for assessing both types of concepts in practical classroom situations were tried out. These procedures were used to test principles, to modify them, and to determine when they might be appropriately applied.
3. The training activities involved in becoming proficient in the assessment of spontaneous behavior, in and of themselves, increased the sensitivity of teachers to their own behavior and the behavior of others. Most important, teachers could compare their intentions with their actions.
4. By avoiding a discussion of right and wrong ways of teaching and emphasizing the discovery of principles of teacher influence, teachers gradually became more independent and self-directing. Our most successful participants investigated problems of their own choosing, designed their own plans, and arranged collaboration with others when this seemed advantageous.

Five filmstrips and one teacher's manual have been produced and written. These materials would have to be modified before they could be used with undergraduate students. Before asking how interaction analysis might be used in teacher preparation, we turn next to a description of the procedures.

[1] Interaction analysis as a research tool has been used ever since R. F. Bales first developed a set of categories for studying groups. Most of our research results can be found in the references at the end of this paper. Its use as a training device is more recent. Projects have taken place in New Jersey, Philadelphia, Chicago, and Minneapolis. Systematic evaluation is available in only the Minneapolis project.

The Procedure of Observation

The observer sits in a classroom in the best position to hear and see the participants. At the end of each three-second period, he decides which category best represents the communication events just completed. He writes this category number down while simultaneously assessing communication in the next period and continues at a rate of 20 to 25 observations per minute, keeping his tempo as steady as possible. His notes are merely a series of numbers written in a column, top to bottom, so that the original sequence of events is preserved. Occasionally marginal notes are used to explain the class formation or any unusual circumstances. When there is a major change in class formation, the communication pattern, or the subject under discussion, a double line is drawn and the time indicated. As soon as the total observation is completed, the observer retires to a nearby room and completes a general description of each separate activity period separated by the double lines, including the nature of the activities, the class formation, and the position of the teacher. The observer also notes any additional facts that seem pertinent to an adequate interpretation and recall of the total visit.

The ten categories that we used for interaction analysis are shown in Table 1.

The numbers that an observer writes down are tabulated in a 10 × 10 matrix as sequence pairs, that is, a separate tabulation is made for each overlapping pair of numbers. An illustration will serve to explain this procedure.

TEACHER: Class! The bell has rung. May I have your attention please! [6] During the next three seconds talking and noise diminish. [10]

TEACHER: Jimmy, we are all waiting for you. [7] Pause.

TEACHER: Now today we are going to have a very pleasant surprise, [5] and I think you will find it very exciting and interesting. [1] Have any of you heard anything about what we are going to do? [4]

PUPIL: I think we are going on a trip in the bus that's out in front. [8]

TEACHER: Oh! You've found out! How did you learn about our trip? [4]

By now the observer has written down 6, 10, 7, 5, 1, 4, 8, and 4. As the interaction proceeds, the observer will continue to write down numbers. To tabulate these observations in a 10 × 10 matrix, the first step is to make sure that the entire series begins and ends with the same number. The convention we use is to add a 10 to the beginning and end of the series unless the 10 is already present. Our series now becomes 10, 6, 10, 7, 5, 1, 4, 8, 4, and 10.

Table 1
Categories For Interaction Analysis

Teacher Talk	Indirect Influence	1. * Accepts Feeling: accepts and clarifies the feeling tone of the students in a nonthreatening manner. Feelings may be positive or negative. Predicting or recalling feelings are included.
		2. * Praises or Encourages: praises or encourages student action or behavior. Jokes that release tension, not at the expense of another individual, nodding head or saying, "um hm?" or "go on" are included.
		3. * Accepts or Uses Ideas of Student: clarifying, building or developing ideas suggested by a student. As teacher brings more of his own ideas into play, shift to category five.
		4. * Asks Questions: asking a question about content or procedure with the intent that a student answer.
	Direct Influence	5. * Lecturing: giving facts or opinions about content or procedures; expressing his own ideas, asking rhetorical questions.
		6. * Giving Directions: directions, commands, or orders with which a student is expected to comply.
		7. * Criticizing or Justifying Authority: statements intended to change student behavior from nonacceptable to acceptable pattern; bawling someone out; stating why the teacher is doing what he is doing; extreme self-reference.
Student Talk		8. * Student Talk—Response: talk by students in response to teacher. Teacher initiates the contact or solicits student statement.
		9. * Student Talk—Initiation: talk by students which they initiate. If "calling on" students is only to indicate who may talk next, observer must decide whether student wanted to talk. If he did, use this category.
		10. * Silence or Confusion: pauses, short periods of silence and periods of confusion in which communication cannot be understood by the observer.

* There is no scale implied by these numbers. Each number is classificatory; it designates a particular kind of communication event. To write these numbers down during observation is to enumerate, not to judge a position on a scale.

These numbers are tabulated in a matrix, one pair at a time. The column is indicated by the second number, the row is indicated by the first number. The first pair is 10-6; the tally is placed in row ten, column six cell. The second pair is 6-10; tally this in the row six, column ten cell. The third pair is 10-7, the fourth pair is 7-5, and so on. Each pair overlaps with the next, and the total number of observations, "N," always will be tabulated by N-1 tallies in the matrix. In this case we started a series of ten numbers, and the series produced nine tallies in the matrix.

Table 2

Category	1	2	3	4	5	6	7	8	9	10	Total
1				1							1
2											0
3											0
4								1		1	2
5	1										1
6										1	1
7					1						1
8				1							1
9											0
10						1	1				2
Total	1	0	0	2	1	1	1	1	0	2	9

Table 2 shows our completed matrix. Notice that in a correctly tabulated matrix the sums of the corresponding rows and columns are equal.

The problem of reliability is extremely complex, and a more complete discussion can be found in two terminal contract reports (6,7) one of which will be published as a research monograph in the 1963 series of the Cooperative Research Program. Education students can learn how to make quick field checks of their reliability and work toward higher reliability under the direction of an instructor.

The Interpretation of Matrices

A matrix should have at least 400 tallies, covering about twenty minutes or more of a homogeneous activity period, before attempting to make an interpretation.

Certain areas within the matrix are particularly useful for describing teacher influence. Some of these areas will now be discussed by making reference to Table 3.

Table 3
Matrix Analysis

Category	Classification		Category	1	2	3	4	5	6	7	8	9	10	Total
Accepts Feelings			1											
Praise		Indirect	2		Area E									
Student Idea		Influence	3											
Asks Questions	Teacher		4											
Lectures	Talk		5			"Content Cross"					Area I			
Gives Directions		Direct	6											
Criticism		Influence	7						Area F					
Student Response	Student Talk		8											
Student Initiation			9		Area G				Area H		Area J			
Silence			10											
			Total		Area A				Area B		Area C		Area D	
					Indirect Teacher Talk				Direct Teacher Talk		Student Talk			

The column totals of a matrix are indicated as Areas "A," "B," "C," and "D." The figures in these areas provide a general picture by answering the following questions: What proportion of the time was someone talking compared with the portion in which confusion or no talking existed? When someone was talking, what proportion of the time was used by the students? By the teacher? Of the time that the teacher talked, what proportion of his talk involved indirect influence? Direct influence?

The answers to these questions form a necessary backdrop to the interpretation of the other parts of the matrix. If student participation is about 30 or 40 per cent, we would expect to find out why it was so high by studying the matrix. If the teacher is particularly direct or indirect, we would expect certain relationships to exist with student talk and silence.

The next two areas to consider are areas "E" and "F." Evidence that categories 1, 2, and 3 were used for periods longer than three seconds can be found in the diagonal cells, 1-1, 2-2, and 3-3. The other six cells of Area E indicate various types of transitions between these three categories. Sustained praise or clarification of student ideas is especially significant because such elaboration often involves criteria for praise or reasons for accepting ideas and feelings. The elaboration of praise or student ideas must be present if the student's ideas are to be integrated with the content being discussed by the class.

Area F is a four-cell combination of giving directions (category 6) and giving criticisms or self-justification (category 7). The transition cells 6-7 and 7-6 are particularly sensitive to difficulties that the teacher may have with classroom discipline or resistance on the part of students. When criticism follows directions or direction follows criticism, this means that the students are not complying satisfactorily. Often there is a high loading on the 6-9 cell under these circumstances. Excessively high frequencies in the 6-6 cell *and* 7-7 cells indicate teacher domination and supervision of the students' activities. A high loading of tallies in the 6-6 cell alone often indicates that the teacher is merely giving lengthy directions to the class.

The next two areas to be considered are Areas G and H. Tallies in these two areas occur at the instant the student stops talking and the teacher starts. Area G indicates those instances in which the teacher responds to the termination of student talk with indirect influence. Area H indicates those instances in which the teacher responds to the termination of student talk with direct influence. An interesting comparison can be made by contrasting the proportion G to H versus the proportion A to B. If these two proportions are quite different, it indicates that the teacher tends to act differently at the instant a student stops talking compared with his overall average. Often this is a mark of flexible teacher influence.

There are interesting relationships between Area E and Area G and between Area F and Area H. For example, Area G may indicate that a teacher responds indirectly to students at the instant they terminate their talk, but an observer may wish to inspect Area E to see if this indirect response is sustained in any way. The same question with regard to direct influence can be asked of Areas F and H. Areas G and H together usually fascinate teachers. They are often interested in knowing more about their immediate response to student participation.

Area I indicates an answer to the question, What types of teacher statements trigger student participation? Usually there is a high tally loading in cells 4-8 and 4-9. This is expected because students often answer questions posed by the teacher. A high loading on 4-8 and 8-4 cells alone usually indicates classroom drill directed by the teacher. The contrast of tallies in columns 8 and 9 in this area gives a rough indication of the frequency with which students initiate their own ideas versus respond to those of the teacher.

Area I is often considered in combination with Area J. Area J indicates either lengthy student statements or sustained student-to-student communication. An above-average frequency in Area C, but not in Area J, indicates that short answers, usually in response to teacher stimulation, have occurred. One would normally expect to find frequencies in Area E positively correlated with frequencies in Area J.

We turn next to concepts and principles of teacher influence before speculating about how this technique can be applied to teacher education.

Concepts and Principles of Teacher Influence

It may be too early to determine what are the *fewest* number of concepts which, if organized into logically related principles, can be used by a teacher to plan how he will use his authority. Surely he will need concepts that refer to his authority and its use. He will need concepts to describe learning goals and pupil tasks. He will need concepts to classify the responses of students. He may also need concepts to characterize class formations and patterns of classroom communication. These concepts are at least the minimum.

Concepts That Refer to Teacher Behavior

Indirect Influence. Indirect influence is defined as actions taken by the teacher which encourage and support student participation. Accepting, clarifying, praising, and developing the ideas and feelings expressed by the pupils will support student participation. We can define indirect behavior operationally by noting the per cent of teacher statements falling into categories 1, 2, 3, and 4.

Direct Influence. This concept refers to actions taken by the teacher which restrict student participation. Expressing one's own views through lecture, giving directions, and criticizing with the expectation of compliance tend to restrict pupil participation. We can define direct behavior operationally by noting the per cent of teacher statements falling into categories 5, 6, and 7.

Other concepts which we do not have the space to discuss include: flexibility of teacher influence, dominance or sustained direct influence, and intervention.

Concepts That Refer to Learning Goals

Clear Goals. Goal perceptions are defined from the point of view of the pupil, not the teacher. "Clear goals" is a state of affairs in which the pupil knows what he is doing, the purpose, and can guess at the first few steps to be taken. It can be measured by paper-and-pencil tests, often administered at differed points in a problem-solving sequence.

Ambiguous Goals. "Ambiguous goals" describes a state of affairs in which a pupil is not sure of what he is expected to do, is not sure of the first few steps, or is unable to proceed for one reason or another. It can be measured as above.

Other concepts in this area include: attractive and unattractive clear goals, pupil tasks, task requirements, and similar concepts.

Concepts That Refer to Pupil Responses

Dependent Acts. Acts of dependence occur when a pupil not only complies with teacher influence but solicits such direction. A pupil who asks a teacher to approve of his work in order to make sure that it is satisfactory, before going on to the next logical step, is acting dependently. This type of response can be measured by observation techniques and by paper-and-pencil tests on which he indicates what kind of help he would like from the teacher.

Independent Acts. Acts of independence occur when the pupils react primarily to task requirements and are less directly concerned with teacher approval. The measurement of this concept is the same as for dependent acts.

Other concepts include: dependence proneness—a trait, compliance, conformity, counterdependence, and similar concepts.

Some Principles That Can Be Discovered

We discovered in our research (7) that, during the first few days of a two-week unit of study in seventh grade social studies and when introducing new material in eighth grade mathematics, superior teachers (as previously defined, page 252) are initially more indirect, becoming more direct as goals and associated tasks become clarified. We also suspect that these same teachers are more indirect when helping pupils diagnose difficulties, when trying to motivate pupils by arousing their interest, and in other situations in which the expression of pupil perceptions is helpful. On the other hand, the average or below average teacher did exactly the opposite.

Now the problem in teacher education is not only to create a situation in which education students could verify these relationships but could practice controlling their own behavior so as to become indirect or more direct at will. One place to begin is to have two six-man groups work on a task under the direction of a leader. One task is something like an assembly line; it has a clear end product and sharp role differentiation. The other task is much more difficult to describe and does not have clear role differentiation. Now let the class superimpose different patterns of leader influence. Let them interview the role players, collect interaction analysis data by some simplified system of categories, and discuss the results. When undergraduate students first try to classify verbal statements, it sometimes helps to use only two or three categories. In one instance, the issue was the effect of using broad questions versus narrow questions. A broad question was one to which it was hard to predict the type of answer. A narrow question was one to which it was easy to guess at the type of answer. Which type of question was more likely to increase pupil participation? The students role-played this and kept a record of broad questions, narrow questions, and the length of the response. The fact that they verified their prediction correctly for this rather superficial problem was much less important compared with the experience that they gained. They learned how to verify a prediction with empirical evidence, and some had a chance to practice control of their own behavior for professional purposes.

There is no space here to list a complete set of principles that can be investigated by systematic or intuitive data-collecting procedures. The following questions might stimulate useful learning activities. Does dependence always decrease as goals become clear? Is the final level of dependence determined by the pattern of teacher influence when goals are first formulated? Are measures of content achievement related to the pupils' attitudes toward the teacher and the schoolwork? What effects can you expect from excessive and pedantic clarification of pupil ideas and feelings? And many others.

Applications of Interaction Analysis to Teacher Education

Suppose that before education students were given their practice teaching assignment, they had been exposed to a variety of data-collecting techniques for assessing pupil perceptions, measuring achievement, and quantifying spontaneous teacher influence. Suppose, further, that these skills had been taught in a context of personal inquiry as described earlier. What effect would this have on their approach to practice teaching?

One of their suggestions might be that two students should be assigned as a team to the first assignment. While one took over the class the other could be collecting information; the next day or so, the roles could be reversed. Together they would work out a lesson plan, agree on the data to be collected, go over the results with the help of the supervising teacher who might also have the same data-collecting skills. This situation could approach the inquiry model described earlier. The practice teacher might discover that his failure to clarify the pupils' ideas restricted the development of curiosity or that his directions were too short when he was asked for further help; both of these inferences can be made from an interaction matrix with reasonable reliability and objectivity.

Later on a student may wish to take a practice teaching assignment by himself and turn to the supervising teacher for aid in feedback. In either case, the requirement is that the learner be able to compare his intentions with feedback information about his actions and analyze this information by using concepts which he found useful in his earlier courses in education.

There are some precautions that can already be stated with regard to the use of interaction analysis in such a situation.

First, no interaction analysis data should be collected unless the person observed is familiar with the entire process and knows its limitations.

Second, the questions to be answered by inspecting the matrix should be developed before the observation takes place.

Third, value judgments about good and bad teaching behavior are to be avoided. Emphasis is given to the problem being investigated so that cause-and-effect relationships can be discovered.

Fourth, a certain amount of defensive behavior is likely to be present at the initial consultation; it is something like listening to a tape recording for the first time.

Fifth, a consultation based on two observations or at least two matrices helps to eliminate value judgments or at least control them. Comparisons between the matrices are more likely to lead to principles.

Just how experiences of the type we have been discussing will fit into the present curricula is difficult to know. If activities of the sort described in this paper are valuable, are they to be superimposed on the present list of courses or is more radical surgery necessary?

Perhaps this is the point to risk a prediction, which is that teacher education will become increasingly concerned with the process of teaching itself during the next few decades. Instead of emphasizing knowledge which *we think* teachers will need in order to teach effectively, as we have in the past, we will turn more and more to an analysis of teaching acts as they occur in spontaneous classroom interaction. We are now at the point in our technology of data collecting at which procedures for analyzing and conceptualizing teaching behavior can be developed. Systems for doing this will become available regardless of whether they are similar or dissimilar to the procedures described in this paper. When this fine day arrives, the role of the education instructor will change, and the dichotomy between field and theory will disappear. The instructor's role will shift from talking about effective teaching to the rigorous challenge of demonstrating effective teaching. The process of inquiry will create problem-solving activities that will produce more independent, self-directing teachers whose first day on the job will be their worst, not their best.

These changes will be successful to the extent that the graduates of teacher education can learn to control their own behavior for the professional purpose of managing effective classroom learning. It will be the responsibility of the education instructor to help prospective teachers discover what their teaching intentions should be and then create training situations in which behavior gradually matches intentions with practice. Teaching will remain an art, but it will be studied scientifically.

References

1. Anderson, Harold H. "The Measurement of Domination and of Socially Integrative Behavior in Teachers' Contacts with Children." *Child Development* 10: 73–89; June 1939.
2. Anderson, Harold H., and Brewer, Helen M. *Studies of Teachers' Classroom Personalities,* I: *Dominative and Socially Integrative Behavior of Kindergarten Teachers.* Applied Psychology Monographs of the American Psychological Association. No. 6. Stanford, California: Stanford University Press, July 1945.
3. Anderson, Harold H., and Brewer, Joseph E. *Studies of Teachers' Classroom Personalities,* II: *Effects of Teachers' Dominative and Integrative*

Contacts on Children's Classroom Behavior. Applied Psychology Monographs of the American Psychological Association. No. 8. Stanford, California: Stanford University Press, June 1946.

4. Anderson, Harold H.; Brewer, J. E.; and Reed, M. F. *Studies of Teachers' Classroom Personalities,* III: *Follow-up Studies of the Effects of Dominative and Integrative Contacts on Children's Behavior.* Applied Psychology Monographs of the American Psychological Association. No. 11. Stanford, California: Stanford University Press, December 1946.
5. Cantor, Nathaniel. *The Teaching-Learning Process.* New York: Dryden Press, 1953. pp. 59–72.
6. Flanders, N. A. A terminal contract report on using interaction analysis for the inservice training of teachers. To be submitted to the U.S. Office of Education, N.D.E.A., Title VII. Available from the author, University of Michigan, after April 1963.
7. Flanders, N. A. *Teacher Influence, Pupil Attitudes, and Achievement.* Dittoed manuscript to be published in 1963 as a Research Monograph, Cooperative Research Program, U.S. Office of Education. Available from author, University of Michigan, 1962. 176 pp.
8. Flanders, N. A., and Havumaki, S. "Group Compliance to Dominative Teacher Influence." *Human Relations* 13:67–82.
9. Romney, G. P.; Hughes, M. M.; and others. *Progress Report of the Merit Study of the Provo City Schools.* Provo, Utah, August 1958. XIX + 226 pp. See also *Patterns of Effective Teaching: Second Progress Report of the Merit Study of the Provo City Schools.* Provo, Utah, June 1961. XII + 93 pp.
10. Thelen, H. A. *Education and the Human Quest.* New York: Harper Brothers, 1960. pp. 74–112.

6.2 Psychological Controversies in the Teaching of Science and Mathematics[1]

Lee S. Shulman

All educators are not as enthusiastic about the discovery method as is Jerome Bruner.[2] David Ausubel[3] is particularly critical and opts for reception of knowledge rather than its discovery. But knowledge must be meaningful rather than rote if it is not to be isolated from the cognitive structure.

Robert Gagné has advocated the sequencing of learning tasks and the careful guidance of learners through them (see selected readings, Chapter 5). Lee Schulman compares the viewpoints of Bruner and Gagné in this article and offers a compromise such as a middle route of guided discovery.

SOURCE. Lee S. Shulman, "Psychological Controversies in the Teaching of Science and Mathematics," *Science Teacher*, **35**, 1968, pp. 34–38, 89–90. Reprinted by permission of the National Science Teachers Association.

From *Science Teacher*, 1968, **35**: 34–38, 89–90. Reprinted with permission of the author and National Science Teachers Association.

[1] Invited paper to the American Association for the Advancement of Science. Division Q (Education), New York City. December 1967.

[2] Bruner, J. R. *The Process of Education.* Cambridge: Harvard University Press, 1961.

[3] Ausubel, D. P. Learning by discovery: rationale and mystique. *Bulletin of the National Association of Secondary School Principals*, **45**, 1961, pp. 18–58.

The popular press has discovered the discovery method of teaching. It is by now, for example, an annual ritual for the Education section of *Time* magazine to sound a peal of praise for learning by discovery (e.g., *Time,* December 8, 1967 [7]. *Time's* hosannas for discovery are by no means unique, reflecting as they do the educational establishment's general tendency to make good things seem better than they are. Since even the soundest of methods can be brought to premature mortality through an overdose of unremitting praise, it becomes periodically necessary even for advocates of discovery, such as I, to temper enthusiasm with considered judgment.

The learning by discovery controversy is a complex issue which can easily be oversimplified. A recent volume has dealt with many aspects of the issue in great detail [8]. The controversy seems to center essentially about the question of how much and what kind of guidance ought to be provided to students in the learning situation. Those favoring learning by discovery advocate the teaching of broad principles and problem-solving through minimal teacher guidance and maximal opportunity for exploration and trial-and-error on the part of the student. Those preferring guided learning emphasize the importance of carefully sequencing instructional experiences through maximum guidance and stress the importance of basic associations or facts in the service of the eventual mastering of principles and problem-solving.

Needless to say, there is considerable ambiguity over the use of the term *discovery*. One man's discovery approach can easily be confused with another's guided learning curriculum if the unwary observer is not alerted to the preferred labels ahead of time. For this reason I have decided to contrast the two positions by carefully examining the work of two men, each of whom is considered a leader of one of these general schools of thought.

Professor Jerome S. Bruner of Harvard University is undoubtedly the single person most closely identified with the learning-by-discovery position. His book, *The Process of Education* [1], captured the spirit of discovery in the new mathematics and science curricula and communicated it effectively to professionals and laymen. His thinking will be examined as representative of the advocates of discovery learning.

Professor Robert M. Gagné of the University of California is a major force in the guided learning approach. His analysis of *The Conditions of Learning* [3] is one of the finest contemporary statements of the principles of guided learning and instruction.

I recognize the potential danger inherent in any explicit attempt to polarize the positions of two eminent scholars. My purpose is to clarify the dimensions of a complex problem, not to cosign Bruner and Gagné to irrevocable extremes. Their published writings are employed merely to characterize two possible positions on the role of discovery in learning, which each has expressed eloquently at some time in the recent past.

In this paper I will discuss the manner in which Bruner and Gagné, respectively, describe the teaching of some particular topic. Using these two examples as starting points, we will then compare their positions with respect to instructional objectives, instructional styles, readiness for learning, and transfer of training. We will then examine the implications of this controversy for the process of instruction in science and mathematics and the conduct of research relevant to that process.

Instructional Example: Discovery Learning

In a number of his papers, Jerome Bruner uses an instructional example from mathematics that derives from his collaboration with the mathematics educator, Z. P. Dienes [2].

A class is composed of eight-year-old children who are there to learn some mathematics. In one of the instructional units, children are first introduced to three kinds of flat pieces of wood or "flats." The first one, they are told, is to be called either the "unknown square" or "X square." The second flat, which is rectangular, is called "1 X" or just X, since it is X long on one side and 1 long on the other. The third flat is a small square which is 1 by 1, and is called 1.

After allowing the children many opportunities simply to play with these materials and get a feel for them, Bruner gives the children a problem. He asks them, "Can you make larger squares than this X square by using as many of these flats as you want?" This is not a difficult task for most children and they readily make another square such as the one illustrated below. [At right.]

Bruner then asks them if they can describe what they have done. They might reply, "We have one square X, with two X's and a 1." He then asks them to keep a record of what they have done. He may even suggest a notational system to use. The symbol X□ could represent the square X, and a + for "and." Thus, the pieces used could be described as X□ + 2X + 1.

Another way to describe their new square, he points out, is simply to describe each side. With an X and a 1 on each side, the side can be described as X + 1 and the square as (X + 1) (X + 1) after some work with parentheses. Since these are two basic ways of describing the same square, they can be written in this way: X□ + 2X + 1 = (X + 1) (X + 1). This description, of course, far over-simplifies the procedure used.

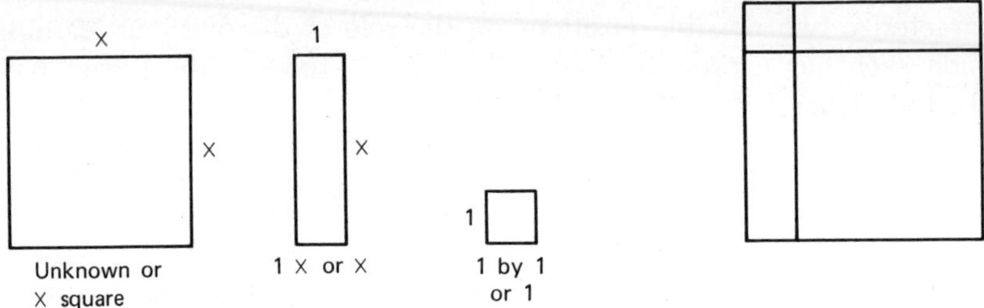

The children continue making squares and generating the notation for them. (See next diagram.)

At some point Bruner hypothesizes that they will begin to discern a pattern. While the X's are progressing at the rate of 2, 4, 6, 8, the ones are going 1, 4, 9, 16, and on the right side of the equation the pattern is 1, 2, 3, 4. Provocative or leading questions are often used Socratically to elicit this discovery. Bruner maintains that, even if the children are initially unable to break the code, they will sense that there is a pattern and try to discover it. Bruner then illustrates how the pupils transfer what they have learned to working with a balance beam. The youngsters are ostensibly learning not only something about quadratic equations, but more important, something about the discovery of mathematical regularities.

The general learning process described by Bruner occurs in the following manner: First, the child finds regularities in his manipulation of the materials that correspond with intuitive regularities he has already come to understand. Notice that what the child does for Bruner is to find some sort of match between what he is doing in the outside world and some models or templates that he already has in his mind. For Bruner, it is rarely something *outside* the learner that is discovered. Instead the discovery involves an internal reorganization of previously known ideas in order to establish a better fit between those ideas and the regularities of an encounter to which the learner has had to accommodate.

This is precisely the philosophy of education we associate with Socrates. Remember the lovely dialogue of the *Meno* by Plato, in which the young slave boy is brought to an understanding of what is involved in doubling the area of a square. Socrates maintains throughout this dialogue that he is not teaching the boy anything new; he is simply helping the boy reorganize and bring to the fore what he has always known.

Bruner almost always begins with a focus on the production and manipulation of materials. He describes the child as moving through three levels of representation. The first level is the *enactive level,* where the child manipulates materials directly. He then progresses to the *ikonic level,* where he deals with mental images of objects but does not manipulate them directly. Finally he moves to the *symbolic level,* where he is strictly manipulating symbols and no longer mental images of objects. This sequence is an outgrowth of the developmental work of Jean Piaget. The synthesis of these concepts of manipulation of actual materials as part of a developmental model and the Socratic notion of learning as internal reorganization into a learning-by-discovery approach is the unique contribution of Jerome Bruner.

The Process of Education was written in 1959, after most mathematics innovations that use discovery as a core had already begun. It is an error to say that Bruner initiated the learning-by-discovery approach. It is far more accurate to say that, more than any one man, he managed to capture its spirit, provide it with a theoretical foundation, and disseminate it. Bruner is not the discoverer of discovery; he is its prophet.

Instructional Example: Guided Learning

Robert Gagné takes a very different approach to instruction. He begins

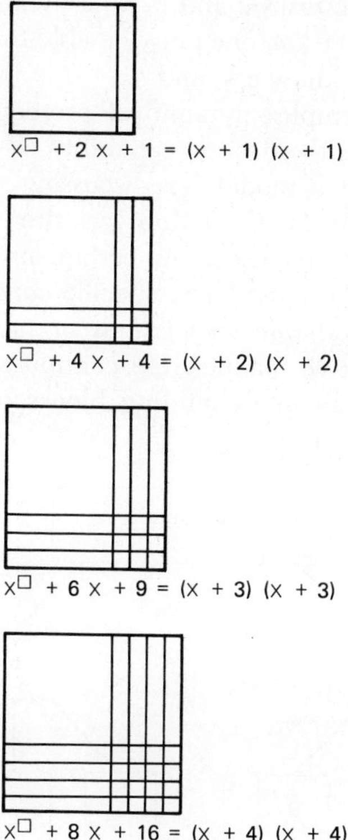

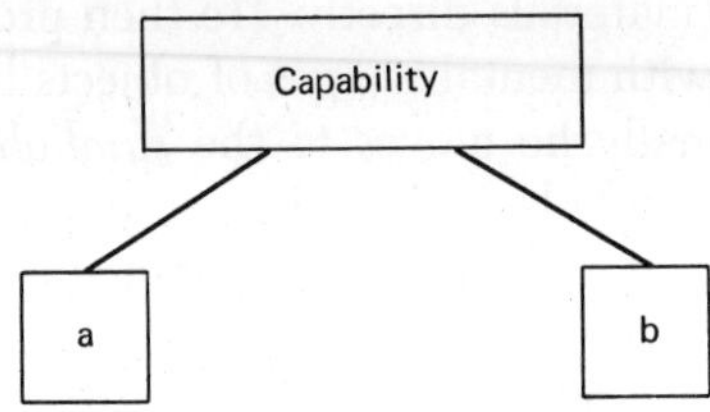

with a task analysis of the instructional objectives. He always asks the question, "What is it you want the learner to be able to do?" This *capability* he insists, must be stated *specifically* and *behaviorally*.

By capability, he means the ability to perform certain specific functions under specified conditions. A capability could be the ability to solve a number series. It might be the ability to solve some problems in non-metric geometry.

This capability can be conceived of as a terminal behavior and placed at the top of what will eventually be a complex pyramid. After analyzing the task, Gagné asks, "What would you need to know in order to do that?" Let us say that one could not complete the task unless he could first perform prerequisite tasks *a* and *b*. So a pyramid begins.
But in order to perform task *a*, one must be able to perform tasks *c* and *d* and for task *b*, one must know *e*, *f*, and *g*.
So one builds a very complex pyramid of prerequisites to prerequisites to the objective which is the desired capability.

Gagné has developed a model for discussing the different levels of such a hierarchy. If the final capability desired is a *problem-solving* capability, the learner first must know certain *principles*. But to understand those principles, he must know specific *concepts*, and prerequisite to these are particular *simple associations* or *facts* discriminated from each other in a distinctive manner. He continues the analysis until he ends up with the fundamental building blocks of learning—classically or operantly conditioned responses.

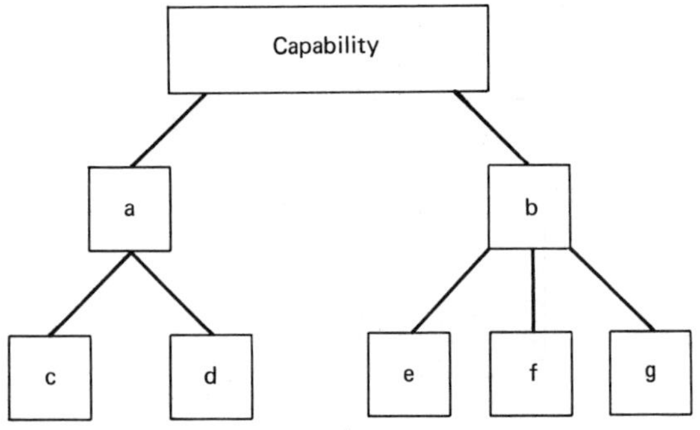

Gagné, upon completing the whole map of prerequisites, would administer pretests to determine which have already been mastered. Upon completing the diagnostic testing, the resulting pattern identifies precisely what must be taught. This model is particularly conducive to subsequent programing of materials and programed instruction. When prerequisites are established, a very tight teaching program or package develops.

Earlier, we discussed the influences on Bruner. What influenced Gagné? This approach to teaching comes essentially from a combination of the neo-behaviorist psychological tradition and the task analysis model that dominates the fields of military and industrial training. It was precisely this kind of task analysis that contributed to successful programs of pilot training in World War II. Gagné was trained in the neo-behaviorist tradition and spent the major portion of his early career as an Air Force psychologist.

Nature of Objectives

The positions of Bruner and Gagné take very different points of view with respect to the objectives of education. This is one of the major reasons why most attempts at evaluating the relative effectiveness of these two approaches have come to naught. They really cannot agree on the same set of objectives. Any attempt to ask which is better—Michigan State's football team or the Chicago White Sox—will never succeed. The criteria for success are different, and it would be absurd to have them both on the same field competing against each other.

For Gagné, or the programed-instruction position which can be derived from him, the objectives of instruction are capabilities. They are behavioral products that can be specified in operational terms. Subsequently they can be task-analyzed; then they can be taught. Gagné would subscribe to the position that psychology has been successful in suggesting ways of teaching only when objectives have been made operationally clear. When objectives are not clearly stated, the psychologist can be of little assistance. He insists on objectives clearly stated in behavioral terms. They are the cornerstones of his position.

For Bruner, the emphasis is quite different. The emphasis is not on the *products* of learning but on the *processes*. One paragraph from *Toward a Theory of Instruction* captures the spirit of educational objectives for Bruner. After discussing the mathematics example previously mentioned, he concludes,

"Finally, a theory of instruction seeks to take account of the fact that a curriculum reflects not only the nature of knowledge itself—the specific capabilities—but also the nature of the knower and of the knowledge-getting process. It is the enterprise par excellence where the line between the subject matter and the method grows necessarily indistinct. A body of knowledge, enshrined in a university faculty, and embodied in a series of authoritative volumes is the result of much prior intellectual activity. To instruct someone in these disciplines is not a matter of getting him to commit the results to mind; rather, it is to teach him to participate in the process that makes possible the establishment of knowledge. We teach a subject, not to produce little living libraries from that subject, but rather to get a student to think mathematically for himself, to consider matters as a historian does, *to take part in the process of knowledge-getting. Knowing is a process, not a product.*" [2, p. 72] (Italics mine)

Speaking to the same issue, Gagné's position is clearly different.

"Obviously, strategies are important for problem solving, regardless of the content of the problem. The suggestion from some writings is that they are of overriding importance as a goal of education. After all, should not formal instruction in the schools have the aim of teaching the student 'how to think'? If strategies were deliberately taught, would not this produce people who could then bring to bear superior problem-solving capabilities to any new situation? Although no one would disagree with the aims expressed, it is exceedingly doubtful that they can be brought about by teaching students 'strategies' or 'styles' of thinking. Even if these could be taught (and it is possible that they could), they would not provide the individual with the basic firmament of thought, which is subject-matter knowledge. Knowing a set of strategies is not all that is required for thinking; it is not even a substantial part of what is needed. *To be an effective problem solver, the individual must somehow have acquired masses of structurally organized knowledge. Such knowledge is made up of content principles, not heuristic ones.*" [3, p. 170] (Italics mine)

While for Bruner "knowing is a process, not a product," for Gagné, "knowledge is made up of content principles, not heuristic ones." Thus, though both espouse the acquisition of knowledge as the major objective of education, their definitions of *knowledge* and *knowing* are so disparate that the educational objectives sought by each scarcely overlap. The philosophical and psychological sources of these differences will be discussed later in this paper. For the moment, let it be noted that when two conflicting approaches seek such contrasting objectives, the conduct of comparative educational studies becomes extremely difficult.[4]

[4] Gagné has modified his own position somewhat since 1965. He would now tend to agree, more or less, with Bruner on the importance of processes or strategies as

Instructional Styles

Implicit in this contrast is a difference in what is meant by the very words *learning by discovery*. For Gagné, *learning* is the goal. How a behavior or capability is learned is a function of the task. It may be by discovery, by guided teaching, by practice, by drill, or by review. The focus is on *learning* and discovery is but one way to learn something. For Bruner, it is learning *by discovery*. The method of learning is the significant aspect.

For Gagné, in an instructional program the child is carefully guided. He may work with programed materials or a programed teacher (one who follows quite explicitly a step-by-step guide). The child may be quite active. He is not necessarily passive; he is doing things, he is working exercises, he is solving problems. But the sequence is determined entirely by the program. (Here the term "program" is used in a broad sense, not necessarily simply a series of frames.)

For Bruner much less system or order is necessary for the package, although such order is not precluded. In general Bruner insists on the child manipulating materials and dealing with incongruities or contrasts. He will always try to build potential or emergent incongruities into the materials. Robert Davis calls this operation "torpedoing" when it is initiated by the teacher. He teaches a child something until he is certain the child knows it. Then he provides him with a whopper of a counterexample. This is what Bruner does constantly—providing contrasts and incongruities in order to get the child, because of his discomfort, to try to resolve this disequilibrium by making some discovery (cognitive restructuring). This discovery can take the form of a new synthesis or a new distinction. Piaget, too, maintains that cognitive development is a process of successive disequilibria and equilibria. The child, confronted by a new situation, gets out of balance and must accommodate to achieve a new balance by modifying the previous cognitive structure.

Thus, for Gagné, instruction is a smoothly guided tour up a carefully constructed hierarchy of objectives; for Bruner, instruction is a rollercoaster ride of successive disequilibria and equilibria until the desired cognitive state is reached or discovered.

Readiness

The guided learning point of view, represented by Gagné, maintains

objectives of education. He has not, however, changed his position regarding the role of sequence in instruction, the nature of readiness, or any of the remaining topics in this paper. [5] The point of view concerning specific behavioral products as objectives is still espoused by many educational theorists and Gagné's earlier arguments are thus still relevant as reflections of that position.

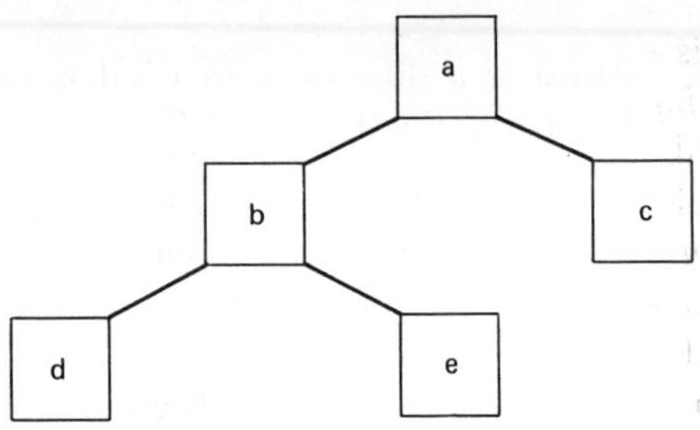

that readiness is essentially a function of the presence or absence of prerequisite learning. [*Refer to diagram above.*]

When the child is capable of *d* and *e* [*see diagram*], he is by definition ready to learn *b*. Until then he is not ready. Gagné is not concerned with genetically developmental considerations. If the child at age five does not have the concept of the conservation of liquid volume, it is not because of an unfolding in his mind; he just has not had the necessary prior experiences. Ensure that he has acquired the prerequisite behaviors, and he will be able to conserve [4].

For Piaget (and Bruner) the child is a developing organism, passing through cognitive stages that are biologically determined. These stages are more or less age-related, although in different cultures certain stages may come earlier than others. To identify whether the child is ready to learn a particular concept or principle, one analyzes the structure of that to be taught and compares it with what is already known about the cognitive structure of the child at that age. If they are consonant, it can be taught; if they are dissonant, it cannot.

Given this characterization of the two positions on readiness, to which one would you attribute the following statement? ". . . any subject can be taught effectively in some intellectually honest form to any child at any stage of development." While it sounds like Gagné, you recognize that it isn't—it's Bruner! [2, p. 33] And in this same chapter he includes an extensive discussion of Piaget's position. Essentially he is attempting to translate Piaget's theories into a psychology of instruction.

Many are puzzled by this stand, including Piaget. In a recent paper delivered in the United States, he admitted that he did not understand how Bruner could make such a statement in the light of Piaget's experiments. If Bruner meant the statement literally; i.e., *any* child can learn *any*thing, then it just is not true! There are always things a child cannot learn, especially not in an intellectually honest way. If he means it homilectically, i.e., we can take almost anything and somehow resay it, reconstruct it, restructure it so it now has a parallel at the child's level of cognitive functioning, then it may be a truism.

I believe that what Bruner is saying, and it is neither trivial nor absurd, is that our older conceptions of readiness have tended to apply Piagetian theory in the same way as some have for generations applied Rousseau's. The old thesis was, "There is the child—he is a developing organism, with invariant order, invariant schedule. Here, too, is the subject matter, equally hallowed by time and unchanging. We take the subject matter as our starting point, watch the child develop, and feed it in at appropriate times as he reaches readiness." Let's face it; that has been our general conception of readiness. We gave reading readiness tests and hesitated to teach the pupil reading until he was "ready." The notion is quite new that the reading readiness tests tell not when to begin teaching the child, but rather what has to be done to get him more ready. We used to just wait until he got ready. What Bruner is suggesting is that we must modify our conception of readiness so that it includes not only the child but the subject matter. Subject matter, too, goes through stages of readiness. The same subject matter can be represented at a manipulative or enactive level, at an ikonic level, and finally at a symbolic or formal level. The resulting model is Bruner's concept of a spiral curriculum.

Piaget himself seems quite dubious over the attempts to accelerate cognitive development that are reflected in many modern math and science curricula. On a recent trip to the United States, Piaget commented,

". . . we know that it takes nine to twelve months before babies develop the notion that an object is still there even when a screen is placed in front of it. Now kittens go through the same stages as children, all the same sub-stages, but they do it in three months—so they're six months ahead of babies. Is this an advantage or isn't it? We can certainly see our answer in one sense. The kitten is not going to go much further. The child has taken longer, but he is capable of going further, so it seems to me that the nine months probably were not for nothing.

It's probably possible to accelerate, but maximal acceleration is not desirable. There seems to be an optimal time. What this optimal time is will surely depend upon each individual and on the subject matter. We still need a great deal of research to know what the optimal time would be." [6, p. 82]

The question that has not been answered, and which Piaget whimsically calls the "American question," is the empirical experimental question: To what extent it is possible through a Gagnéan approach to accelerate what Piaget maintains is the invariant clockwork of the order? Studies being conducted in Scandinavia by Smedslund and in this country by Irving Sigel, Egon Mermelstein, and others are attempting to identify the degree to which such processes as the principle of conservation of volume can be accelerated. If I had to make a broad generalization, I would have to conclude that at this point, in general, the score for those who say you cannot accelerate is somewhat higher than the score for those who say that you can. But the question is far from resolved; we need many more inventive attempts to accelerate cognitive development than we have had thus far. There remains the question of whether such attempts at experimental acceleration are strictly of interest for psychological theory, or have important pedagogical implications as well—a question we do not have space to examine here.

Sequence of the Curriculum

The implications for the sequence of the curriculum growing from these two positions are quite different. For Gagné, the highest level of learning is problem solving; lower levels involve facts, concepts, principles, etc. Clearly, for Gagné, the appropriate sequence in learning is, in terms of the diagram below, from the bottom up. One begins with simple prerequisites and works up, pyramid fashion, to the complex capability sought.

For Bruner, the same diagram may be appropriate, but the direction of the arrow would be changed. He has a pupil begin with *problem solving*. This process is analogous to teaching someone to swim by throwing him into deep water. The theory is that he will learn the fundamentals because he needs them. The analogy is not totally misbegotten. In some of the extreme discovery approaches we lose a lot of pupils by mathematical or scientific drowning. As one goes to the extreme of this position, he runs the risk of some drownings. For Gagné, the sequence is from the simple to the complex; for Bruner one starts with the complex and plans to learn the simple components in the context of working with the complex.

It is unclear whether Bruner subscribes to his position because of his

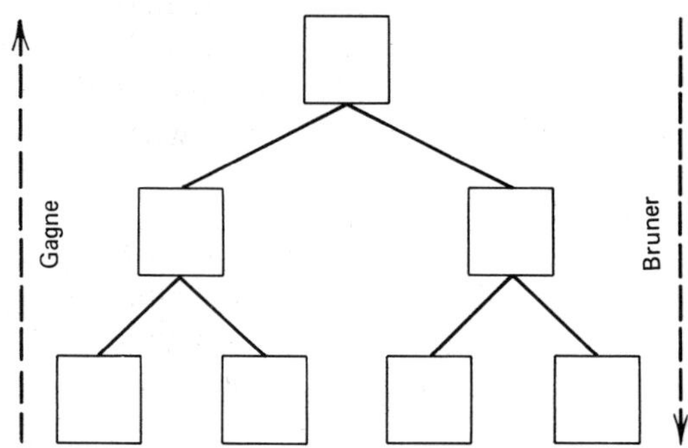

concept of the nature of learning or for strictly motivational reasons. Children may be motivated more quickly when given a problem they cannot solve, than they are when given some little things to learn on the promise that if they learn these well, three weeks from now they will be able to solve an exciting problem. Yet, Bruner clearly maintains that learning things in this fashion also improves the transferability of what is learned. It is to a consideration of the issue of transfer of training that we now turn.

Transfer of Training

To examine the psychologies of learning of these two positions in any kind of comprehensive form would require greater attention than can be devoted here, but we shall consider one concept—that of transfer of training. This is probably the central concept, or should be, in any educationally relevant psychology of learning.

Gagné considers himself a conservative on matters of transfer. He states that "transfer occurs because of the occurrence of specific identical (or highly similar) elements within developmental sequences" [4, p. 20]. To the extent that an element which has been learned, be it association, concept, or principle, can be directly employed in a new situation, transfer will occur. If the new context requires a behavior substantially different from the specific capability mastered earlier, there will be no transfer.

Bruner, on the other hand, subscribes to the broadest theories of transfer of training. Bruner believes that we can have massive transfer from one learning situation to another. Broad transfer of training occurs when one can identify in the structures of subject matters basic, fundamentally simple concepts or principles which, if learned well, can be transferred both to other subject matters within that discipline and to other disciplines as well. He gives examples such as the concept of conservation or balance. Is it not possible to teach balance of trade in economics in such a way that when ecological balance is considered, pupils see the parallel? This could then be extended to balance of power in political science, or to balancing equations.

Even more important, for Bruner, is the broad transferability of the knowledge-getting processes—strategies, heuristics, and the like—a transfer whose viability leaves Gagné with deep feelings of doubt. This is the question of whether learning by discovery leads to the ability *to* discover, that is, the development of broad inquiry competencies in students.

What does the evidence from empirical studies of this issue seem to demonstrate? The findings are not all that consistent. I would generalize them by saying that most often guided learning or expository sequences seem to be superior methods for achieving immediate learning. With regard to long-term retention, the results seem equivocal, with neither approach consistently better. Discovery learning approaches appear to be superior when the criterion of transfer of principles to new situations is employed [9]. Notably absent are studies which deal with the question of whether general techniques, strategies, and heuristics of discovery can be learned—by discovery or in any other manner—which will transfer across grossly different kinds of tasks.

Why is transfer of training superior in the discovery situation when the learning of principles is involved? There are two kinds of transfer—positive transfer and negative transfer. We call something positive transfer when mastery of task X facilitates mastery of task Y. Negative transfer occurs when mastery of task X inhibits mastery of task Y. Positive transfer is a familiar notion for us. Negative transfer can be exemplified by a piece of advice baseball coaches often give their players. They tell them not to play golf during the baseball season because the baseball swing and the golf swing involve totally different muscles and body movements. Becoming a better golf swinger interferes with the baseball swing. In psychological terms there is negative transfer between golf and baseball.

What is needed for positive transfer is to minimize all possible interference. In transfer of training, there are some ways in which the tasks transferred to are like the ones learned first, but in other ways they are different. So transfer always involves striking a balance between these conflicting potentials for both positive and negative transfer. In discovery methods, learners may transfer more easily because they learn *the immediate things less well.* They may thus learn the broad strokes of a principle, which is the aspect most critical for remote transfer, while not learning well the detailed application of that specific principle, which could interfere somewhat with successful remote transfer.

If this formulation is correct, we are never going to find a method that will both allow for tremendous specific learning of products and broad transfer, because we are dealing in a closed system in which one must make a choice. To the extent that initial learning is well done, transfer is restricted. The instructor may have to decide which is more important—an immediate specific product or broad transfer—and choose his subsequent teaching method on the basis of that decision. This is a pessimistic view, and I hope that future studies might find it flawed.

Synthesis or Selection

Need we eternally code these as two alternatives—discovery versus expository teaching—or can we, without being heretical, manage to keep both of these in our methodological repertories as mathematics and science educators?

John Dewey was always very suspicious whenever he approached a controversy between two strongly stated positions, each of which insisted that the other was totally in error. The classic example of this is in his monograph *Experience and Education,* in which he examines the controversy of traditional versus progressive education. Dewey teaches us that whenever we confront this kind of controversy, we must look for the possibility that each position is massively buttressed by a brilliant half-truth from which is extrapolated the whole cloth of an educational philosophy. That is, too often a good idea wears thin as its advocates insist that it be applied outside its appropriate domain.

As educators, we find it extremely important to identify the conditions under which each of these theories can be applied most fruitfully. First, one must examine the nature of the objectives. More than half of this controversy can be resolved not at the level of which is the better psychology, but at the level of evaluative philosophical judgments. Given one set of goals, clearly the position Gagné advocates presently has more evidence in its favor; given another set of goals, there is no question but that Bruner's position is preferable to Gagné's.

But there are other questions. The age and personality of the learner must be taken into account. All things being equal, there are some kinds of children who cannot tolerate the ambiguity of a discovery experience. We all know this; some of us prefer to hear lectures that are well organized so that we can take notes in a systematic manner. Others of us like nothing better than a free-flowing bull session; and each of us is convinced that we learn more in our preferred mode than the others learn in theirs. Individual differences in learning styles are major determinants of the kinds of approaches that work best with different children.

Yet this is something we have in general not taken into consideration at all in planning curricula—and for very good reasons. As yet, we do not have any really valid ways of measuring these styles. Once we do, we will have a powerful diagnostic tool. Subject matter, objectives, characteristics of children, and characteristics of the teacher are all involved in this educational decision. Some teachers are no more likely to conduct a discovery learning sequence than they are to go frugging at a local nightclub.

There appear to be middle routes as well. In many of the experimental studies of discovery learning, an experimental treatment labeled *guided discovery* is used. In guided discovery, the subjects are carefully directed down a particular path along which they are called upon to discover regularities and solutions on their own. They are provided with cues in a carefully programed manner, but the actual statement of the principle or problem solution is left up to them. Many of the well-planned Socratic dialogues of our fine teachers are forms of guided discovery. The teacher carefully leads the pupils into a series of traps from which they must now rescue themselves.

In the published studies, guided discovery treatments generally have done quite well both at the level of immediate learning and later transfer. Perhaps this approach allows us to put the Bruner roller-coaster of discovery on the well-laid track of a Gagné hierarchy.

Thus, the earlier question of which is better, learning by discovery or guided learning, now can be restated in more functional and pragmatic terms. Under what conditions are each of these instructional approaches, some sequence or combination of the two, or some synthesis of them, most likely to be appropriate? The answers to such questions ought to grow out of quite comprehensive principles of human learning. Where are we to find such principles?

Theories of Learning and the Science and Mathematics Curriculum

There is a growing psychology of learning that is finally becoming meaningful to curriculum construction and educational practice. Children are being studied as often as rats, and classrooms as often as mazes. Research with lower animals has been extremely useful in identifying some principles of learning that are so basic, so fundamental, so universal that they apply to any fairly well-organized blob of protoplasm. But there is a diminishing return in this approach insofar as transfer to educational practice is concerned. Today, a developing, empirically based psychology of learning for *homo sapiens* offers tremendous promise. But it can never be immediately translatable into a psychology of the teaching of mathematics or science. Mathematics and science educators must not make the mistake that the reading people have made and continue to make. The reason that the psychology of the teaching of reading has made such meager progress in the last 25 years is that the reading people have insisted on being borrowers. Something new happens in linguistics and within three years a linguistic reading series is off the press. It is an attempt to bootleg an idea from one field and put it directly into another without the necessary intervening steps of empirical testing and research.

Mathematics and science education are in grave danger of making that same error, especially with the work of Piaget and Bruner. What is needed now are well-developed empirically based psychologies of mathematics and science learning. Surely they will grow out of what is already known about the psychology of learning in general, but they must necessarily depend upon people like yourselves, your students, and your colleagues who are interested in mathematics and science conducting empirical studies of how certain specific concepts are learned under certain specific conditions with certain specific kinds of pupils. If anything is true about the field of mathematics and science education today, it is that rarely have any disciplines been so rich in theory and brilliant ideas. But we must seriously consider the admonition of Ivan Pavlov, the great Russian psychologist, who is said to have told his students the following:

"Ideas and theories are like the wings of birds; they allow man to soar and to climb to the heavens. But facts are like the atmosphere against which those wings must beat, and without which the soaring bird will surely plummet back to earth."

References

1. Bruner, Jerome S. *The Process of Education.* Harvard University Press, Cambridge, Massachusetts. 1960.
2. Bruner, Jerome S. *Toward a Theory of Instruction.* Belknap Press, Cambridge, Massachusetts. 1966.
3. Gagné, Robert M. *The Conditions of Learning.* Holt, Rinehart & Winston, New York. 1965.
4. Gagné, Robert M. Contributions of Learning to Human Development. Address of the Vice-President, Section I (Psychology), American Association for the Advancement of Science, Washington, D.C. December 1966.
5. Gagné, Robert M. Personal communication. May 1968.
6. Jennings, Frank G. "Jean Piaget: Notes on Learning." *Saturday Review,* May 20, 1967, p. 82.
7. "Pain & Progress in Discovery." *Time,* December 8, 1967, pp. 110 ff.
8. Shulman, Lee S. and Keislar, Evan R., Editors. *Learning by Discovery: A Critical Appraisal.* Rand-McNally, Chicago. 1966.
9. Worthen, Blaine R. "Discovery and Expository Task Presentation in Elementary Mathematics." *Journal of Educational Psychology Monograph Supplement* 59: 1, Part 2; February 1968.

6.3 Teacher Comments and Student Performance

Ellis Batten Page

One of a teacher's roles is to give feedback reinforcement to pupils by correcting their written work. The typical teacher spends many hours correcting papers. Some teachers make very few marks on these papers, if any, and return the work of a pupil with only a grade. Others write copious comments giving suggestions for improvement. Does the extra time spent in making these comments result in superior pupil performance? This is one of the important questions that Professor Page answers with his research.

This selection is also important because it is an example of good educational research. It was conducted in a natural classroom setting using the required assignments for data analysis; a variable, marking procedure, was experimentally manipulated; and the sample of teachers was properly selected and employed.

Each year teachers spend millions of hours marking and writing comments upon papers being returned to students, apparently in the belief

SOURCE. Excerpted from Ellis Batten Page, "Teacher Comments and Student Performances: A Seventy-Four Classroom Experiment in School Motivation," *Journal of Educational Psychology,* **49,** 1958, pp. 173–181. Reprinted by permission of the author and the American Psychological Association.

that their words will produce some result, in student performance, superior to that obtained without such words. Yet on this point solid experimental evidence, obtained under genuine classroom conditions, has been conspicuously absent. Consequently each teacher is free to do as he likes; one will comment copiously, another not at all. And each believes himself to be right.

The present experiment investigated the questions: (1) Do teacher comments cause a significant improvement in student performance? (2) If comments have an effect, which comments have more than others, and what are the conditions, in students and class, conducive to such effect? The questions are obviously important for secondary education, educational psychology, learning theory, and the pressing concern of how a teacher can most effectively spend his time.

Previous Related Work

Previous investigations of "praise" and "blame," however fruitful for the general psychologist, have for the educator been encumbered by certain weaknesses: Treatments have been administered by persons who were extraneous to the normal class situation. Tests have been of a contrived nature in order to keep students (unrealistically) ignorant of the true comparative quality of their work. Comments of praise or blame have been administered on a random basis, unlike the classroom where their administration is not at all random. Subjects have often lacked any independent measures of their performance, unlike students in the classroom. Areas of training have often been those considered so fresh that the students would have little previous history of related success or failure, an assumption impossible to make in the classroom. There have furthermore been certain statistical errors: tests of significance have been conducted as if students were totally independent of one another, when in truth they were interacting members of a small number of groups with, very probably, some group effects upon the experimental outcome.

For the educator such experimental deviations from ordinary classroom conditions have some grave implications, explored elsewhere by the present writer (5). Where the conditions are highly contrived, no matter how tight the *controls,* efforts to apply the findings to the ordinary teacher-pupil relationship are at best rather tenuous. This study was therefore intended to fill both a psychological and methodological lack by *leaving the total classroom procedures exactly what they would have been without the experiment,* except for the written comments themselves.

Method

Assigning the Subjects. Seventy-four teachers, randomly selected from among the secondary teachers of three districts, followed detailed printed instructions in conducting the experiment. By random procedures each teacher chose one class to be subject from among his available classes.[1] As one might expect, these classes represented about equally all secondary grades from seventh through twelfth, and most of the secondary subject-matter fields. They contained 2,139 individual students.

First the teacher administered whatever objective test would ordinarily come next in his course of study; it might be arithmetic, spelling, civics, or whatever. He collected and marked these tests in his usual way, so that each paper exhibited a numerical score and, on the basis of the score, the appropriate letter grade A, B, C, D, or F, each teacher following his usual policy of grade distribution. Next, the teacher placed the papers in numerical rank order, with the best paper on top. He rolled a specially marked die to assign the top paper to the *No Comment, Free Comment,* or *Specified Comment* group. He rolled again, assigning the second-best paper to one of the two remaining groups. He automatically assigned the third-best paper to the one treatment group remaining. He then repeated the process of rolling and assigning with the next three papers in the class, and so on until all students were assigned.

Administering Treatments. The teacher returned *all* test papers with the numerical score and letter grade, as earned. No Comment students received nothing else. Free Comment students received, in addition, whatever comment the teacher might feel it desirable to make. Teachers were instructed: "Write anything that occurs to you in the circumstances. There is not any 'right' or 'wrong' comment for this study. A comment is 'right' for the study if it conforms with your own feelings and practices." Specified Comment students, regardless of teacher or student differences, all received comments designated in advance for each letter grade, as follows:

A: Excellent! Keep it up.
B: Good work. Keep at it.
C: Perhaps try to do still better?
D: Let's bring this up.
F: Let's raise this grade!

Teachers were instructed to administer the comments "rapidly and automatically, trying not even to notice who the students are." This in-

[1] Certain classes, like certain teachers, would be ineligible for a priori reasons: giving no objective tests, etc.

struction was to prevent any extra attention to the Specified Comment students, in class or out, which might confound the experimental results. After the comments were written on each paper and recorded on the special sheet for the experimenter, the test papers were returned to the students in the teacher's customary way.

It is interesting to note that the student subjects were totally naïve. In other psychological experiments, while often not aware of precisely what is being tested, subjects are almost always sure that something unusual is underway. In 69 of the present classes there was no discussion by teacher or student of the comments being returned. In the remaining five the teachers gave ordinary brief instructions to "notice comments" and "profit by them," or similar remarks. In none of the classes were students reported to seem aware or suspicious that they were experimental subjects.

Criterion. Comment effects were judged by the scores achieved on the very next objective test given in the class, regardless of the nature of that test. Since the 74 testing instruments would naturally differ sharply from each other in subject matter, length, difficulty, and every other testing variable, they obviously presented some rather unusual problems. When the tests were regarded primarily as *ranking* instruments, however, some of the difficulties disappeared.

A class with 30 useful students, for example, formed just 10 levels on the basis of scores from the first test. Each level consisted of three students, with each student receiving a different treatment: No Comment, Free Comment, or Specified Comment. Students then achieved new scores on the second (criterion) test, as might be illustrated in Table

Table 1
Illustration of Ranked Data

	Part A (Raw Scores on Second Test)			Part B (Ranks-within-Levels on Second Test)		
Level	N	F	S	N	F	S
1	33	31	34	2	1	3
2	30	25	32	2	1	3
3	29	33	23	2	3	1
—	—	—	—	—	—	—
—	—	—	—	—	—	—
—	—	—	—	—	—	—
10	14	25	21	1	3	2
Sum:				19	21	20

Note. N is No Comment; F is Free Comment; S is Specified Comment.

1, Part A. On the basis of such scores, they were assigned rankings within levels, as illustrated in Table 1, Part B.

If the comments had no effects, the sums of ranks of Part B would not differ except by chance, and the two-way analysis of variance by ranks would be used to determine whether such differences exceeded chance.[2] Then the *sums* of ranks themselves could be ranked. (In Part B the rankings would be 1, 3, and 2 for Groups N, F, and S; the highest score is ranked 3 throughout the study.) And a new test, of the same type, could be made of all such rankings from the 74 experimental classrooms. Such a test was for the present design the better alternative, since it allowed for the likelihood of "Type G errors" (3, pp. 9–10) in the experimental outcome. Still a third way remained to use these rankings. The summation of each column could be divided by the number of levels in the class, and the result was *a mean rank within treatment within class.* This score proved very useful, since it fulfilled certain requirements for parametric data. . . .

Results

Comment vs. No Comment. . . . The Specified Comment group, which received automatic impersonal comments according to the letter grade received, achieved higher scores than the No Comment group. The Free Comment group, which received individualized comments from the teachers, achieved the highest scores of all. . . . Therefore it may be held that the comments had a real and beneficial effect upon the students' mastery of subject matter in the various experimental classes. . . . It was plain that comments, especially the individualized comments, had a marked effect upon student performance.

Comments and Schools. One might question whether comment effects

[2] The present study employed a new formula,

$$\chi_r^2 = \frac{6\Sigma\,(0 - E)^2}{\Sigma 0}$$

which represents a simplification of Friedman's twenty-year-old notation (2). The new form is the classic chi square,

$$\Sigma \frac{(0 - E)^2}{E}$$

multiplied by $6/k$ where k is simply the number of ranks! This conversion was discovered in connection with the present study by a collaboration of the writer with Alan Waterman and David Wiley. Proof that it is identical with the earlier and more cumbersome variation,

$$\chi_r^2 = \frac{12}{Nk(k+1)}\Sigma(R_i)^2 - 3N(k+1),$$

will be included in a future statistical article.

would vary from school to school, and even whether the school might not be the more appropriate unit of analysis. Since as it happened the study had 12 junior or senior high schools which had three or more experimental classes, these schools were arranged in a treatments-by-replications design. . . . Schools apparently had little measurable influence over treatment effect.

Comments and School Years. It was conceivable that students, with increasing age and grade-placement, might become increasingly independent of comments and other personal attentions from their teachers. . . . Rather surprisingly, no uniform trend was apparent. When the data were tested for interaction of school year and comment effect . . . school year did not exhibit a significant influence upon comment effect. . . . Apparently, . . . comments do *not* lose effectiveness as students move through school. Rather they appear fairly important, especially when individualized, at all secondary levels.

One must remember that, between the present class-groupings, there were many differences other than school year alone. Other teachers, other subject-matter fields, other class conditions could conceivably have been correlated beyond chance with school year. Such correlations would in some cases, possibly, tend to modify the *visible* school-year influence, so that illusions would be created. However possible, such a caution, at present, appears rather empty. In absence of contradictory evidence, it would seem reasonable to extrapolate the importance of comment to other years outside the secondary range. One might predict that comments would appear equally important if tested under comparable conditions in the early college years. Such a suggestion, in view of the large lecture halls and detached professors of higher education, would appear one of the more striking experimental results.

Table 2
The Influence of the School Upon the Treatment Effect

Source	Sum of Squares	*df*	Mean Square	*F*	Probability
Between Treatments: N, F, S	.172	2	.086	—[a]	—
Between Schools	.000	11	.000		
Between Classes Within Schools (pooled)	.000	24	.000		
Interaction: T × Schools	1.937	22	.088	—	—
Interaction: T × Cl. W. Sch. (pooled)	4.781	48	.099		
Total	6.890	107			

Note. Modified for mean-rank data from Edwards (1, p. 295 *et passim*).

[a] Absence of an important main treatment effect is probably caused by necessary restriction of sample for school year (*N* is 36, as compared with Total *N* of 74), and by some chance biasing.

Table 3
Sums of Mean Ranks for Different School Years

School Year	N	F	S
12	21.08	22.92	22.00
11	19.06	23.91	23.03
10	20.08	23.32	22.60
9	22.34	22.06	21.60
8	21.21	22.39	22.40
7	22.04	22.98	20.98

Note. Number of groups is 11 in each cell.

Table 4
The Influence of School Year Upon Treatment Effect

Source	Sum of Squares	*df*	Mean Square	*F*	Probability
Between Treatments: N, F, S	1.06	2	.530	5.25	<.01
Between School Years	0.00	5	.000		
Between Cl. Within Sch. Yr. (pooled)	0.00	60	.000		
Interaction: T × School Year	1.13	10	.113	1.12	(n.s.)
Interaction: T × Class (pooled)	12.11	120	.101		
Total	14.30	197			

Note. Modified for mean-rank data from Edwards (1, p. 295 *et passim*).

Comments and Letter Grades. In a questionnaire made out before the experiment, each teacher rated each student in his class with a number from 1 to 5, according to the student's *guessed responsiveness* to comments made by that teacher. Top rating, for example, was paired with the description: "Seems to respond quite unusually well to suggestions or comments made by the teacher of this class. Is quite apt to be influenced by praise, correction, etc." Bottom rating, on the other hand, implied: "Seems rather negativistic about suggestions made by the teacher. May be inclined more than most students to do the opposite from what the teacher urges." In daily practice, many teachers comment on some papers and not on others. Since teachers would presumably be more likely to comment on papers of those students they believed would respond positively, such ratings were an important experimental variable.

Whether teachers *were* able to predict responsiveness is a complicated question, not to be reported here. It was thought, however, that teachers might tend to believe their able students, their high achievers, were also their responsive students. A contingency table was therefore made, testing the relationship between *guessed responsiveness* and letter grade achieved on the first test. The results were as predicted. More "A" students were regarded as highly responsive to comments than were other letter grades; more "F" students were regarded as negativistic and unresponsive to comments than were other letter grades; and grades in between followed the same trend. The over-all C coefficient was .36, significant beyond the .001 level.[3] Plainly teachers believed that their *better* students were also their more *responsive* students.

If teachers were correct in their belief, one would expect in the present experiment greater comment effect for the better students than for the poorer ones. In fact, one might not be surprised if, among the "F" students, the No Comment group were even superior to the two comment groups.

The various letter grades achieved mean scores as shown in Table 5, and the analysis of variance resulted as shown in Table 6. There was

Table 5
Mean of Mean Ranks for Different Letter Grades

Letter Grade	N	F	S
A	1.93	2.04	2.03
B	1.91	2.11	1.98
C	1.90	2.06	2.04
D	2.05	1.99	1.96
F	1.57	2.55	1.88

Note. Each eligible class was assigned one mean rank for each cell of the table.

Table 6
The Relation Between Letter Grade and Treatment Effect

Source	Sum of Squares	*df*	Mean Square	*F*	Probability
Between Treatments: N, F, S	2.77	2	1.385	5.41	$<.01$
Between Letter Grades	0.00	4	0.000		
Bet. Blocks Within L. Gr. (pooled)	0.00	65	0.000		
Interaction: T × Letter Grades	4.88	8	.610	2.40	$.05>p>.01$
Residual (error term)	32.99	130	.254		
Total	40.64	209			

Note. Modified for mean-rank data from Lindquist (3, p. 269). Because sampling was irregular (see text) all eligible classes were randomly assigned to 14 groupings. This was done arbitrarily to prevent vacant cells.

considerable interaction between letter grade and treatment effect, but it was caused almost entirely by the remarkable effect which comments appeared to have *on the "F" students.* None of the other differences,

[3] In a 5 × 5 table, a perfect correlation expressed as C would be only about .9 (McNemar [4], p. 205).

including the partial reversal of the "D" students, exceeded chance expectation.

These data do not, however, represent the total sample previously used, since the analysis could use only those student levels in which all three students received the same letter grade on Test One.[4] Therefore many class-groups were not represented at all in certain letter grades. For example, although over 10% of all letter grades were "F," only 28 class-groups had even one level consisting entirely of "F" grades, and most of these classes had *only* one such level. Such circumstances might cause a somewhat unstable or biased estimate of effect.

Within such limitations, the experiment provided strong evidence against the teacher-myth about responsiveness and letter grades. The experimental teachers appeared plainly mistaken in their faith that their "A" students respond relatively brightly, and their "F" students only sluggishly or negatively to whatever encouragement they administer.

Summary

Seventy-four randomly selected secondary teachers, using 2,139 unknowing students in their daily classes, performed the following experiment: They administered to all students whatever objective test would occur in the usual course of instruction. After scoring and grading the test papers in their customary way, and matching the students by performance, they randomly assigned the papers to one of three treatment groups. The No Comment group received no marks beyond those for grading. The Free Comment group received whatever comments the teachers felt were appropriate for the particular students and tests concerned. The Specified Comment group received certain uniform comments designated beforehand by the experimenter for all similar letter grades, and thought to be generally "encouraging." Teachers returned tests to students without any unusual attention. Then teachers reported scores achieved on the next objective test given in the class, and these scores became the criterion of comment effect, with the following results:

1. Free Comment students achieved higher scores than Specified Comment students, and Specified Comments did better than No Comments. All differences were significant except that between Free Comments and Specified Comments.

[4] When levels consisted of both "A" and "B" students, for example, "A" students would tend to receive the higher scores on the second test, regardless of treatment; thus those Free Comment "A" students drawn from mixed levels would tend to appear (falsely) more responsive than the Free Comment "B" students drawn from mixed levels, etc. Therefore the total sample was considerably reduced for the letter-grade analysis.

2. When samplings from 12 different schools were compared, no significant differences of comment effect appeared between schools.
3. When the class-groups from six different school years (grades 7–12) were compared, no *conclusive* differences of comment effect appeared between the years, but if anything senior high was more responsive than junior high. It would appear logical to generalize the experimental results, concerning the effectiveness of comment, at least to the early college years.
4. Although teachers believed that their better students were also much more responsive to teacher comments than their poorer students, there was no experimental support for this belief.

When the average secondary teacher takes the time and trouble to write comments (believed to be "encouraging") on student papers, these apparently have a measurable and potent effect upon student effort, or attention, or attitude, or whatever it is which causes learning to improve, and this effect does not appear dependent on school building, school year, or student ability. Such a finding would seem very important for the studies of classroom learning and teaching method.

References

1. Edwards, A. *Experimental design in psychological research.* New York: Rinehart, 1950.
2. Friedman, M. The use of ranks to avoid the assumption of normality implicit in the analysis of variance. *J. Amer. statist. Ass.*, 1937, **32**, 675–701.
3. Lindquist, E. F. *Design and analysis of experiments in psychology and education.* Boston: Houghton Mifflin, 1953.
4. McNemar, Q. *Psychological statistics.* (2d ed.) New York: Wiley, 1955.
5. Page, E. B. Educational research: replicable or generalizable? *Phi Delta Kappan*, 1958, **39**, 302–304.

6.4 The Perplexities of the Problem of Keeping Order

Edward T. Ladd

In guiding learning, the social climate of the classroom determines to a great extent the effectiveness of teaching and learning. In order for thirty or more individuals to interact with each other in such close proximity and attain common goals, there must be controls. It is the teacher upon whom that responsibility for leadership falls. The nature of his control determines whether the climate will be authoritarian, laissez faire, or democratic, each with a varied impact on goal attainment.

The author of this article argues for a theory of discipline, that will provide a basis for better understanding of how to keep order in our schools. He states that "discipline problems are among the most persistent and pressing of the professional problems we face." However, he admonishes us that in our desperation we should not attempt to bring about conformity of pupils by procedures that would not be in consonance with our educational goals. Because of these goals a teacher is limited in a manner unlike that of a government official or a supervisor in industry. Furthermore, the author suggests that the teacher may also be limited

SOURCE. Edward T. Ladd, "The Perplexities of the Problem of Keeping Order," *Harvard Educational Review*, **28** (Winter 1958), pp. 19–28.

by being in control of his classes only up to a certain point. This is because the teacher has only a limited authority conferred on him. Because the teacher is a representative of society he should interpret action against him partially as a defiance of the larger order and not simply as action against him personally.

This paper is based on the assumption that the public school teacher has, besides his educational tasks, the task of keeping order, or, as Fritz Redl puts it, of "manipulating surface behavior."[1] It is an assumption on which there seems to be no disagreement, about a task which claims from practitioners in the schools, teachers, and administrators, a prodigious amount of attention. To judge by the statements of teachers, in fact, "discipline" problems are among the most persistent and pressing of the professional problems they face.[2] It seems curious, therefore, as well as unfortunate, that of the various problems of education those encountered in the fulfilling of this task are among the least studied.

In the first decades of this century the intellectual leaders of the profession may have given more help with the problem. At any rate the problem was then being given serious attention in their writings. They were making progress in the systematic description of misbehavior phenomena, the uncovering of their physiological and psychological causes, and the analysis and evaluation of the various techniques which teachers can use which tend to forestall or control overt misconduct. But by about 1930, broad study of the matter seems to have declined, and it has not yet had a revival.

It is interesting to speculate upon the reasons for this comparative dearth in recent years. Probably the general increase since the first World War of a spirit of humanitarianism, cooperativeness, and democracy has tended to make us feel guilty about concentrating on an aspect of teach-

[1] George Sheviakov and Fritz Redl, *Discipline for Today's Children and Youth* (Washington: Association for Supervision and Curriculum Development, N. E. A., 1944), p. 29.

[2] The N. E. A.'s Commission for the Defense of Democracy through Education is only the most recent and most important body to repeat this finding: according to a July 21, 1955 release by the Commission, on "a recent questionnaire sent to teacher leaders," next in order to inadequate salaries and inadequate facilities, the respondents listed as "the problem of greatest concern to teachers . . . the problem of 'increased restlessness in the classroom,' 'discipline in the classroom' and 'general school discipline.'" (For a report of the subsequent study see *N. E. A. Research Bulletin*, Vol. XXXIV, No. 2, "Teacher Opinion on Pupil Behavior, 1955–56," April, 1956.) It may be of interest to note that in Great Britain the National Union of Teachers felt called upon at the same time to conduct a study closely paralleling that of the N. E. A.

ing so frankly manipulative. But this cannot have been the only factor: other, more technical developments must have played a part. Many of the earlier writers on the subject had appeared to see no conflict between the controlling of surface behavior and the achieving of character education; they had tended, indeed, to see the two functions as being in harmony or even identical. For decades the very verb "discipline" was used to mean simultaneously "to bring a group under control" and "to train in self-control or obedience to given standards." But as educationists studied the new psychology and became more aware of the dynamics of character education, personality development, and mental health, they must have come to see the distinctness, indeed on occasion the oppositeness, of those two types of activity. So it may have been that in their zeal to focus the profession's attention on procedures more likely to further the long-range educational goal, they created a climate in which it became unfashionable—at least among the intelligentsia—to think about the short-range problem.

The fact is that under the enormous impact of modern psychology, concern with misbehavior became focussed upon its causes in the individual child and upon the possibility of using the resources of clinical psychology and social work to rehabilitate the child with problems. The important thing now was to bring school practice abreast with the exciting new discoveries about child development, adolescence, and personality disturbances, and the fight was on against the diehards who felt that keeping order or controlling surface behavior was the only or the chief problem.

In 1928 the famous Wickman study, destined to have enormous influence, by implication rapped the knuckles of the teacher who regarded defiance to authority and dishonest behavior as very serious problems, or who required that the pupil obey simply because "the school demands it."[3] It might even be possible to establish that with the rise of educational psychology the very terms "misbehavior," "disobedience," "disorder," and "discipline" went into something of an eclipse.

Another group of persons in the field of education continued, however, to concern themselves with "discipline." These persons, though, shared the increasing sophistication of the profession and were no longer satisfied to work on the level of collections of insights, techniques, or rules of thumb. Their search for more fundamental theoretical formulations, on the basis of which to make better recommendations, led them into another field, that of educational philosophy. Dewey, then at or nearing the zenith of his influence on the intellectual leaders of American education, had

[3] E. K. Wickman, *Children's Behavior and Teacher's Attitudes* (New York: Commonwealth Fund, 1923). See especially Chapter IX.

provided a theoretical approach useful for distinguishing between subservience or conformity on the one hand and true "discipline," the long-range goal, on the other, by defining discipline in a way in which we today might define self-discipline or maturity.[4] Thus formulated, "discipline" certainly appeared a worthy state of affairs for teachers to concern themselves with and strive to bring about. Those who were influenced by this philosophical definition tended, however, by an easy jump in reasoning, to draw from it certain unwarranted conclusions: (1) that this was the *only* type of "discipline" worth attempting to achieve; (2) that it was in fact achievable in school; and (3) that the road to its achievement was simply to challenge pupils' attention with a meaningful curriculum and interesting teaching. For the many whose thinking went along these lines the problem of keeping order began to look like a mere distraction. To concern oneself with it was to lose sight of what was really important. The one proper solution of "discipline" problems in school must lie solely along the lines of curriculum revision and/or improved teaching.

The concerns which psychology and philosophy aroused, the one for *personality development* and *mental health,* the other for *interest,* were not irrelevant to the problem of manipulating surface behavior: indeed they made great contributions to our understanding of it, one indirectly, the other directly. But it remains true that specific study of the practical business of keeping order nearly dried up.[5] Since the problem continued to exist, consideration of it likewise continued, but largely on the level of prejudice and rule of thumb as expounded in teachers' rooms—especially to neophytes. (Perhaps the commonest single admonition given to the

[4] "A person who is trained to consider his actions, to undertake them deliberately, is in so far forth disciplined," he wrote. "Add to this ability a power to endure in an intelligently chosen course in face of distraction, confusion, and difficulty, and you have the essence of discipline." John Dewey, *Democracy and Education* (New York: Macmillan Company, 1916), p. 151. It is noteworthy that, although he did not dwell on it, Dewey did describe the use of manipulative techniques, even of force, as quite legitimate in situations where actions a more modern psychology to the teacher's task of keeping order was Norma E. Cutts and Nicholas Moseley, *Practical School Discipline and Mental Health* (Boston: Houghton Mifflin Company, 1941).

[5] However, Ralph W. Pringle in his *The Psychology of High School Discipline* (Boston: D. C. Heath and Company, 1931) presented a very thoughtful analysis of misbehavior, followed by an extensive discussion of practice in "pupil control." The first part of his book drew on a psychology which now seems woefully limited; the letter, more practical, part is still very pertinent. He also allied himself with the school which held that the teacher should "govern through the use of the subject materials so managed as to meet the interests and needs of his individual pupils" (see p. 185). A much more successful—and exceptional—study, relating might be dangerous, discommoding, or obnoxious. See *ibid.*, pp. 32–33.

latter has been to "forget all those theories they taught you.") The more respectable techniques have over and over again been set down in mimeographed and printed bulletins and lists of suggestions, but few of them seem to have proved very helpful. The author of a methods book, seeking to help, will give us a chapter on "democratic discipline" or "social control," but is likely to be dissatisfied with it—and his readers more so. Apparently methods courses usually skirt the matter entirely. Teachers and student teachers continue to complain of lack of guidance, and try to solve the problem empirically, most of them, it must be said, with a real degree of success, if not satisfaction.[6] Meanwhile, very gradually, the problem seems to get worse.

The recent years having been so lean, it might be suggested that we look back for help to the books and ideas of the previous decades. Even if today we cannot accept the premise which seems to have underlain so much of what was written then, the premise that whatever produces good order is likely to produce good character education, we might still apply whatever insights are to be found in them with respect to the function of keeping order itself. But here we must agree with our philosophers: those earlier studies failed to put the problem in a general setting and give us a comprehensive body of theory regarding it, so today they make little appeal.[7] Compilations of insights and tricks of the trade are useful no doubt, but never so much to the user as to the compiler, and by their very nature they have never more than parochial relevance.

Wanted: A Body of Theory

We are stalled, it would seem, on dead center. Why are we stalled? Perhaps it is somehow the very down-to-earth nature of the attention paid to the problem in recent years that keeps us from making progress. Perhaps the fact that the thinkers in our field left the problem aside to concern themselves primarily with the other important aspects of "discipline" which we have mentioned has left us still lacking an adequate theoretical framework, an adequate systematic body of concepts and generalizations we might bring to bear on the business of keeping order. It might be such a body of theory which alone in any given situation,

[6] It is interesting that practices actually used for the purpose of keeping order tend to be similar regardless of whether the teachers are classified as "modern" or as "traditional." See the findings of Max Weiner, "The Relationship of Concepts of School Discipline to Practice" (unpublished Ph.D. dissertation, Yale University Graduate School, 1957).

[7] Again we must call attention to an exception. Willard Waller's brilliant *Sociology of Teaching* (New York: John Wiley and Son, 1932), in passages dealing with the teacher's leadership and pupil behavior, gives us a number of concepts and principles which can profitably be applied in a wide variety of situations.

could give the teacher or supervisor a handle with which to take hold of the elements involved, in the same way that the concept of "readiness" provided a handle with which to take hold of some of the problems of beginning readers.[8]

Concepts and generalizations dealing with interest and motivation would certainly be a part of such a body of theory, since interest is directly related to conduct and since our aim is enlightened self-interest. But it would be unrealistic to expect the individualization of teaching to reach the point where every pupil would always be sufficiently interested in the business at hand to refrain from creating disturbance. Hence by itself theory dealing with interest and motivation is not enough. Our formulations in the field of personality psychology also belong in the hopper,[9] if only because we wish to provide for healthy personality development. But the teacher working with a classroom group is limited in the amount of character education he or she can give to individual members of a class, to say nothing of the speed and effectiveness with which he can provide it. Ideas about more short-range procedures are needed. Even if we accept the advice of the psychologist and provide in our program for the identification, diagnosis, and referral of those pupils whose misbehavior derives from serious personal problems, we shall find that their presence was only a part of the trouble. So if we are to understand and deal with the misbehavior of pupils in general, including average or normal pupils, we shall have to supplement interest theory and psychological theory with other formulations or concepts. And if we are to think through the problem as a whole we must relate all of this into a body or bodies of theory by means of which we can analyze and classify all the relevant phenomena and make widely applicable generalizations about their relationships.

Such a body of theory can never tell us what we should do to keep order, not only because establishing the relevance of generalizations for given situations is a problem in its own right, but more importantly because a body of scientific theory by its very nature says nothing about "should" (ethical) questions. Nor could it by itself give us any new information which we do not already have. But it would suggest ways of looking at misbehavior and help us to get better answers to such questions as "What is likely to result in this school if we do this, or that?" or "What can we say to this teacher that might make him more able to handle this

[8] The author has attempted elsewhere to sketch a few elements of a theory of misbehavior in our schools in general; see his "Discipline in Secondary Schools: Some Hypotheses," *Teacher Education Quarterly*, Vol. XIII, No. 3 (Spring, 1956).

[9] Notable under this heading is the too little known contribution of Fritz Redl and David Wineman. See their *Controls From Within* (Glencoe: Free Press, 1952).

class?" It should give us cues as to the more relevant phenomena to study; a number of concepts with the aid of which we can take hold of situations and think more efficiently about what we observe; thus the basis for making better predictions about how this or that factor will influence a situation; and thus, finally, some of the premises we need if we are to reason our way to recommendations for more effective action.

Lest there be any misunderstanding, let us, before proceeding, restate in somewhat greater detail the problem with which we are here concerned. We are concerned not primarily with understanding how individuals learn to be self-disciplined, nor with understanding how teachers can promote such learning—important though those matters are. We are here concerned to find a theory or theories through which we can better understand the special problem of keeping order in public schools.

Let us remind ourselves that in the public schools attendance is compulsory for most age levels concerned, and that in most cases the individual pupil does not even have any say about the particular group to which he is assigned for a given period in the day. Secondly, public school teachers wield bits of the sovereign authority and are in greater or lesser degree responsible—through administrators and other public officials—to the citizenry. Thus, whether they like it or not, they have commensurate prior responsibility to persons not in the classroom but outside. Now, whether or not all of us approve of the situation, the fact is that practically all schools in America today, public and private, are conducted for the purpose—among other purposes—of teaching pupils certain things determined for them by adults. This means that if teachers are to do at all what they are hired to do, classes can never be entirely self-governing, and teachers cannot be, in the original, technical sense of the term, entirely "democratic." (The teacher who asks the pupils what they would like to do, structuring things so that they will end up doing something that will result in the predetermined learning, is ingenious, and probably kind and helpful, but not technically "democratic.")

Bearing this in mind, we can restate our problem more precisely. It is to build a body of theory which will help us to understand the procedures by which an individual appointed by exercise of the sovereign power of the state to a responsible position in a governmental educational institution (a public school teacher) can effectively influence the overt behavior of a number of minors, children or adolescents, in most cases ordered into his custody by exercise, again, of the sovereign power (a class of public school pupils) to such an extent and in such a fashion that they conform to certain rules and customs, and that it becomes possible for them individually to learn certain more or less prescribed things. And to this end we are of course also concerned to understand the forces which are at work tending respectively to promote and to block this type of influence.

It is our custom in the field of education, when we face a difficult problem, to seek light on it in one of the academic disciplines which has concerned itself with the kinds of factor which mesh in the problems. A cursory glance at the formulation we have just arrived at will suggest immediately some areas of study likely to be relevant. We find ourselves concerned with the exercise of sovereign power of the state, which points to the study of governmental authority and institutions, political science. We are concerned with phenomena of small-group life and leadership, which suggests that the study of small groups, known widely as group dynamics, may have something to offer.[10] But since there is another much-studied type of social institution in which a supervisory staff attempts to get certain kinds of work accomplished by large numbers of people, namely industry, we might also turn our attention to the theoretical contribution of industrial sociology. An effort to look briefly at the first of these three areas of study will conclude this article, and a look at the other two will be taken in a subsequent paper. Our purpose will be limited to trying to find out whether these fields may not have theoretical contributions to offer of which we can make use.

Only one further word of caution. Whatever we may learn from work done anywhere else than in public schools, let us not make the mistake of transferring it uncritically to our own situation. Order, the carrying out of specific directives, and productivity of a formal sort are not our main concerns but are essentially means to the furtherance of genuine and lasting education. Thus of all the possible procedures that might be used to bring pupils to conform to rules and to perform certain tasks—to return to our formulation—we should, if possible, make actual use of only those whose nature is such that they will also tend in the long run to promote, or at least not to subvert, the achievement of educational goals. Most of us nowadays include among our goals for our pupils a great deal. We include, to be sure, the ability and willingness to accept certain outside restraints. But we also include the ability and willingness to reject others, and the ability and willingness to distinguish between those which are acceptable and those which are not. We include, further, the goals of initiative, self-reliance, independence, and even mental health. Now many

[10] "Small group research is not identified in an exclusive sense with any of the existing disciplines. It is a method of approaching problems which are primary concerns of each of the major fields of the behavioral sciences." A. Paul Hare, Edward F. Borgatta, and Robert F. Bales, editors, *Small Groups: Studies in Social Interaction* (New York: Alfred A. Knopf, 1955), p. vii.

of these learnings are of such a nature that achieving them often requires a teacher in fact to use his authority over his pupils hardly at all, or to use it in paradoxical ways, such as requiring them to exercise freedom and prescribing for them the task of making important decisions for themselves. Thus the fact that the public school teacher is required above all to achieve the ultimate goal of education limits greatly the kinds of order-keeping procedure appropriate for his use, in a way that does not hold true for the ordinary government official, the industrial supervisor, or perhaps even the recreation official. Other important characteristics of the public school teacher's job which make for similarities and differences between that job and other institutional assignments of which studies have been made, have been mentioned above.

The Possibility of Borrowing from Political Theory

We shall attempt here no real excursion into the diverse and changing field of political science, but shall restrict ourselves almost entirely to brief references to a few ideas put forward by one writer in the field, Carl Friedrich, and some comments as to their suggestiveness for a theory of keeping order in school.

According to Friedrich, any sizeable group of human beings performing "definite functions which the community at large considers worth while", tends to organize itself according to a pattern which is in some respects essentially the same as that approached by any other such group.[11] This pattern is characterized by three general principles relating to ways in which members of the organization must behave, those of (1) objectivity, (2) precision and consistency, and (3) discretion. Three other characteristics have to do with the relationships between the members of the organization: those of (1) centralization, (2) differentiation of functions, and (3) qualification for office. In so far as one of these six characteristics is missing, consequences to the organization will arise, consequences which Friedrich specifies, which, he says in effect, can be predicted, and which will jeopardize the organization and/or its performance of its functions. Thus when a member of such an organization lacks "the capacity and inclination to think in terms of objective needs, in terms, that is, of what the particular job in hand requires", he will be unsuccessful at the job. And when he too readily makes exceptions to rules, "particularly to rules which have been made with regard to other rules over

[11] Carl J. Friedrich, *Constitutional Government and Democracy: Theory and Practice in Europe and America* (Boston: Ginn and Company, rev. ed., 1950), p. 44. Chapter II of this work has provided the basis for most of the present discussion.

which he has no control, he is likely to throw the whole organization into confusion."[12]

These remarks, obviously relevant to the public school, are those of a political scientist drawing up generalizations about—of all things—bureaucracy. The public school teacher may be surprised to learn that, whatever else he is, intellectual leader, professional person, psychologist, or parent-surrogate, he is also, according to Friedrich and other theorists of bureaucracy, a bureaucrat. He holds an office, he is in authority, he issues commands, "he is subject to an impersonal order to which his actions are oriented."[13] Needless to say, his commands, like those given him, have some of the force of law. In view of this, it is significant that public school teachers do not view themselves particularly as members of a bureaucracy. When asked, "As a public school teacher to whom do you consider yourself responsible?" they give preference to such answers as "To myself," "To my students," and the like, over such an answer as "To the school administration."[14]

Nevertheless, since, according to its makers, the theory of bureaucracy in general is completely applicable to the public schools, it might be helpful for the teacher—and others—to conceive of his job of maintaining order as one part of a bureaucratic assignment. Deductions from the bureaucratic principles quoted above, such as that to do this job of keeping order effectively the teacher will be well-nigh required to conduct himself with objectivity and precision, seem to fit in well with what has been observed empirically to be the case. But to classify the schools as bureaucracies involves a great deal more. Another generalization, according to which it is inherent in the very nature of government service that it should have—to some degree—a "semimilitary, authoritarian nature," may be still harder for us to swallow. However, the generalization makes no pretense of telling us what characteristics it would be nice for the public school to have, but merely asserts that a degree of authoritarianism is

[12] *Ibid.*, p. 54. "It is, of course, easy and only too common . . . to fall into the opposite error of refusing to adjust the rule, even when its application is evidently unreasonable." *Ibid.*

[13] Max Weber, "The Essentials of Bureaucratic Organization: An Ideal-Type Construction," in Robert K. Merton, *et al.*, editors, *Reader in Bureaucracy* (Glencoe: Free Press, 1952), p. 19. While Weber does not in this passage mention the public school teacher as such, his remarks obviously include him—all the more obviously, when one remembers that in Prussia, where he was writing, the role of the teacher as a bureaucrat was accepted as a matter of course. Actually both Friedrich and Weber so define bureaucracy as to include private as well as public schools, so that practically all of what follows in this section applies to both types of institution.

[14] Chandler Washburne, "The Teacher in the Authority System," *Journal of Educational Sociology*, Vol. 30, No. 9 (May, 1957), p. 391.

a characteristic which it must have. Were we, for the sake of further study, to adopt the political scientist's view of the matter, we should then confront such questions as that of the degree of rigor of authoritarianism most suitable for order-keeping—while being simultaneously, of course, consistent with education—and that of the effects upon the achievement of our objectives of an authoritarianism applied in this respect or activity or in that. Friedrich writes that "the rigor of the discipline" in any hierarchy "should be studied by the political scientist in relation to the purpose for which the administrative setup has come into existence," suggesting that in ordinary government service effectiveness is likely to be greater if discipline is fairly relaxed. Perhaps the principle of the relation between purposes to be achieved and circumstances on the one hand and appropriate degrees of discipline on the other offers another piece of a framework through which to look at our problem.

Finally, before leaving the field of political science we might mention one other concept, that of the "sphere of authority." Max Weber has pointed out[15] that once obedience is owed to the typical person in authority not as an individual but as a representative of an impersonal order, "there is an obligation to obedience only within the sphere of the rationally delimited authority which, in terms of the order, has been conferred upon him." There seems to be here a suggestion that the teacher's responsibility may be appropriately defined as a responsibility not for complete control of his classes, but for control with respect to certain matters or only up to certain points, the radical suggestion, in other words, that teachers should not always be backed up, and a suggestion, on the other hand, that disobedience to a teacher's legitimate commands should never be interpreted as simply an action taken against him, but always as a defiance of the larger order. The distinctions, already proposed once by Willard Waller,[16] may likewise prove to have some use.

[15] Max Weber, *op. cit.*, p. 19.

[16] See Willard Waller, *op. cit.*, pp. 189–204.

6.5 The Problem of Keeping Order: Theoretical Help from Two New Fields

Edward T. Ladd

In the preceding article, Dr. Ladd expressed concern that there was no suitable body of theory for effective study of keeping order in our schools. He suggested the possibility of relying on political theory. In this article, he borrows concepts from the fields of industrial sociology and small group theory and explores their relevance for building a theory on keeping order in the schools. The author does not offer a bag of tricks to aid the teacher. Rather, he seeks to find concepts and principles of a generalizable nature that can be applied to the complex problem of keeping order.

Research and theory on small groups, or "group dynamics," have very evident implications for understanding the group behavior of boys and girls, and educationists, as is well-known, have been making good use of them. In spite of the fact that a great deal of the work in this field is based upon study of voluntary and largely self-governing social work groups, adult groups, and therapy groups, it is still possible that it may help us

SOURCE. Edward T. Ladd, "The Problem of Keeping Order: Theoretical Help from Two New Fields," *Harvard Educational Review*, **28** (Spring 1958), pp. 136–149.

to understand the basic problems of misbehavior and control in the public school classroom. For obvious reasons the work which students of group dynamics have done in industry and in certain parts of the armed forces, where "undemocratic" aspects of the school situation are paralleled, may prove to be especially provocative.[1] Our purpose here will be to try to find out whether this new field of work has a contribution to make to a projected theory of order-keeping in schools.

Group Structure and Leadership

One of the simplest concepts to be developed in this field is that of group structure. In any given group the things regularly done by group members as such, rather than as individuals, can be classified: perhaps meetings are called to order; perhaps information is frequently secured; perhaps from time to time ways of doing things are suggested; perhaps efforts are frequently exerted to keep peace between two individuals; perhaps someone does the cooking; and so on. As given individuals come to perform behaviors of certain types with some degree of regularity they are said to be coming to fill roles, and, by the same token, to be acquiring certain appropriate statuses. The system of roles and statuses which prevails in any given group can be called its structure.

It has already been widely demonstrated that classroom groups have structure of this sort.[2] It appears further that the level of pupil-teacher rapport is related both to the teacher's perception of this structure and to the teacher's adaptation of his behavior in a fashion such as to give greater support to pupils of higher status in the group (1, 12). The suggestion is obvious that greater understanding of behavior and misbehavior phenomena might be achieved through any of a variety of sorts of studies of them, carefully focussed and using the conceptual framework of group structure.

We shall turn our attention, however, to one especially relevant aspect of group structure theory, namely that concerned with the role or roles of group leaders. Students of small groups have shifted strongly away from the view of leadership as a trait possessed in greater or lesser degree

[1] The most complete and useful publications in this field are two volumes of readings: Dorwin Cartwright and Alvin Zander, (Eds.) *Group Dynamics: Research and Theory* (2) and A. Paul Hare, Edgar F. Borgatta, and Robert F. Bales, (Eds.) *Small Groups: Studies in Social Interaction* (5). The present study draws heavily on the theoretical sections of these volumes, especially, in the first, the various introductory passages written by the editors and the contributions of Ralph M. Stogdill (ch. 4) and of Stanley Shacter *et al.* (ch. 27); and, in the second, the contributions of Eliot D. Chapple and Carleton S. Coon (pp. 54–57), of Raymond B. Cattell (pp. 107–120), and of Cecil A. Gibb (pp. 87–94). See also (6).

[2] For examples see (3).

by the leader, toward the general view that leadership is an aspect of group structure, that it is situational, that a person is a leader in so far as, and only in so far as, his behavior in a given group in a given situation modifies the properties of the group or helps the group to achieve its objectives, that is, fills roles of significance to the group, or serves "group functions." (For our purposes the latter definition can be broadened to include what might be called negative group leadership, behavior which inhibits the achievement of the group's objectives.) According to this approach the same person may have great leadership power in one situation and very little in another. At the same time, of course, there may well be persons whose characteristic behavior is such that they can be expected to have great leadership power in far more situations than do others.

The fact that many, though not all, students in this field tend to follow Pigors in drawing a strong distinction between "leadership" and "headship," between the leader who is an accepted member of the group he leads and the head who is not really a group member, but is imposed upon the group from without, might suggest that the situational theory of leadership is not necessarily relevant to the order-keeping role of the public school teacher. Cannot the teacher maintain order, (or could he not at least in theory), by the use of headship techniques, whatever they might be, rather than by exciting leadership? Upon analysis this does not seem to be a realistic possibility, at least if we assume that a head can influence the behavior of his wards only through a manipulation of their emotionally-colored experiences, that is, through rewards and promises, punishments and threats. The fact is that the American public school teacher today has at his disposal a very limited repertory of unpleasantnesses with which to punish or threaten pupils. Adult disapproval and detention, while often effective, are mild enough to be so in only the less difficult situations. Docking of grades, extra home-work, disciplinary non-promotion, and corporal punishment, whether effective or not, are out of favor for educational reasons which seem generally good. And suspension and expulsion are drastic enough to be little invoked, especially now that the schools have accepted the principle of lowering the drop-out rate and giving elementary and secondary education to all. Nor do we commonly find in present-day America a stern super-ego built up within pupils themselves, to which the teacher can appeal so as to make life uncomfortable for them, in the manner followed so successfully in earlier generations and still followed in other societies today. Thus it would seem unlikely that many teachers can find negative means by which alone to make their hardship of their classes effective, and it would seem reasonable to conclude that teachers will achieve effectiveness only in so far as they behave in a fashion somewhat appealing or rewarding to their pupils. But to say this is to say, among other things, that the effective teacher will in some degree be helping pupils achieve what are ultimately the latter's own goals.

Conceivably a teacher could make his appeal to, and exert his influence upon, his pupils individually, not as a group, in which case the fact of his helping them achieve their own goals would still not mean that he was a group leader. But this possibility again realism forces us to deny. In almost any kind of school room situation the pupils are a relatively homogeneous group, at least in respect to age, and think of themselves as "we"; most of the teacher's remarks are aimed at, if not actually addressed to, the class as a whole; rules of behavior are applied to the class as a whole; and many of the experiences, achievements, and frustrations of pupils are viewed as shared.[3] Thus inevitably the teacher faces not only a collection of individuals but also a group. And this is true even when, because of the presence of disaffected pupils or isolates, the membership of the group does not exactly coincide with the membership of the class. Thus, disregarding entirely the implications of the public school teacher's educational roles, we find that his role as a keeper of order in a classroom makes him properly classifiable as a group leader —by even the narrower definitions of that term.[4]

What then, may be the relevance to the keeping of order, of modern situation-oriented theory regarding group leadership? First, we often tend to think of teachers as either having or not having the ability to keep order. At the same time many teachers are successful in keeping order in some classes and unsuccessful in others. Usually we in the field tend to deal with the unpleasant problem of analysis which this fact presents by rating classes on a simple linear scale of "difficulty" and rating teachers on a corresponding linear scale of leadership skill. Up to a point this

[3] Helen Hall Jennings has presented a fascinating contrast between a fairly typical elementary school class, a sociogram of which indicated normal differentiation, suggesting that it was in the full sense a group, and another class, whose members had been allowed practically no interaction, and a sociogram of which suggested that it was merely a collection of individuals. The description she gives of the conditions under which the latter class operated shows them to have been very atypical. See (3, pp. 73–82).

[4] Although Gibb, following Pigors, says that "any person may be called a leader 'during the time when and in so far as, his will, feeling, and insight direct and control others in the pursuit of a cause which he presents,' " he somewhat surprisingly denies flatly that his discussion of leadership applies to "group situations . . . organized for professional tuition," in which, he says, "leadership . . . tends to disappear," to be replaced by domination or headship. He admits, though, that leadership and headship may co-exist in a group. See (5, pp. 93–94).

approach works, and it is certainly a useful, first-line administrative formulation. For completely effective handling of behavior problems, however, it is obviously inadequate. It is not uncommon for a teacher to be very ineffective as a leader under one set of circumstances but very effective with the same class under another.[5] Alternatively in some situations "democratic" teachers, in the sense of Lewin, Lippitt, and White, are those most effective and most liked, whereas in others—even if only a minority—rigid autocrats alone seem to be effective and liked.

The more situational ("group function") concept of leadership seems to suggest that a teacher's success or failure in maintaining classroom order might be viewed as a function not of inherent personality attributes, but of the way certain characteristics of the given class dovetail with the given teacher's perception of the status he is assigned in that class and the role it requires him to play in it, and his emotional readiness and skill for playing it. If this is so, general prescriptions as to what specific kind of person teachers should be or try to be, or as to what specific things they should do or not do to keep order are unlikely to be of much help. Much more promising would be study of, or at least the development of sensitivity to, the particular group's motivations and views of teachers and of authority in general. Thus a teacher's or student teacher's failure to keep order emerges less as a reflection of general personal inadequacy, in the face of which feelings of guilt or depression might be appropriate, and more as a product of the individual's failure to gauge the particular situation and adopt and play the role appropriate to it. Thus, if we adopt the concept of situational relativism, we can still expect certain personalities to have, in Gibb's phrase, more capacity than others to contribute to the achievement of a given group's aspirations, and can recognize that individuals do vary in leadership potential, but we acquire, it would seem, a more effective way of defining, accepting, and dealing with differences in effectiveness.

This newer concept of leadership suggests also new ways of interpreting the puzzling fact that teachers having a variety of types of personality and using a variety of styles of leadership are highly effective in keeping order, a fact for which we have never had a quite satisfactory explanation.

Another common situation to which the concept seems relevant is that of the teacher who is distressed or resentful because pupils fail to respect his position, doing his will simply because he is the teacher. Perhaps

[5] This is convincingly, if dramatically, exemplified by the fictional case of Rick Dadier in Evan Hunter's *The Blackboard Jungle* (7), where differences in the teacher's effectiveness with the same class are portrayed as having been striking even before the class was altered through the ejection of the worst trouble-maker.

under the circumstances given there is good reason to expect the pupils not to be orderly, unless, among all the other things he may do, he serves group functions and helps the class achieve goals it wants to achieve.

Finally, this way of looking at leadership suggests that in a given classroom group the teacher is probably only one of a number of leaders present; it certainly suggests that there is no need for him to be the only leader. Thus the suggestion arises, too, that behavior problems may be more likely to arise when a teacher concerned has not recognized, and does not deal with, the distribution of leadership functions actually in effect. Furthermore, the possibility of a variety of distributions of leadership functions raises the question whether there may not be a relation between the pattern of distribution and the achievement of order. It would be valuable to explore the question whether effectiveness in maintaining order is related to teachers' use of their position as sovereigns in the classroom to achieve certain kinds of distribution of leadership functions among members of their groups, including themselves, of course, among the members. Some teachers seem to find it possible and useful to vary their styles of leadership as they carry out their various roles, a procedure which Waller recommended as an aid in securing obedience. It would be interesting, therefore, to study whether teachers effective in maintaining order behave noticeably differently in performing any given role from the way they do in performing others.

Group Cohesiveness

Apart from the concepts of structure and leadership there are others related to group culture which seem to be relevant for our purposes. The concept of group cohesiveness, for example, includes the assertion that in the case of a given group there are forces impelling members toward it and forces impelling them away from it, in other words, forces making participation in the group respectively more and less attractive. Even if pupils may not physically abandon their class group, psychologically they may move far away from it—just as they may on the contrary become deeply involved in it. The forced physical proximity of the members of a classroom group does, of course, make the study of its cohesiveness or lack of cohesiveness more difficult.

Personal attraction to other pupils, personal attraction to the teacher, and attraction to the learning and other activities to be undertaken by the group as a whole—whether for their own sake or for their future usefulness—all of these might make for cohesiveness of a classroom group and, vice versa, for their opposites. Shared dislike of the teacher or the school program could also make a class cohesive. Pupils' membership in other cliques or groups whose standards, activities, or purposes conflict with those of the class group, might of course jeopardize the latter's cohesiveness. There is thus the possibility that sub-group formation may either increase or decrease the cohesiveness of the class as a whole. Nonetheless, if, as we are told, members of cohesive groups communicate better, show more sense of purpose, change each others' ideas more, enforce group norms more effectively, compete among themselves less, but, perhaps surprisingly, express more intra-group aggression and, under some conditions are more, but under others less, productive, then it is relevant for the student of behavior and misbehavior to consider the degree and basis of the cohesiveness prevailing in the group with which he is concerned. In recent years we have put much emphasis upon the educational value of social interaction among pupils and have widely stressed the principle of building a well-knit classroom group. We have sometimes, indeed, advised the beginning teacher to start off the school year by asking his pupils as a group to formulate and adopt a set of rules of good behavior. We have, in fact, been asking teachers to foster group cohesiveness. It may be that we have done this with too little consideration of the full implications for the problem of maintaining order. It would seem that the teacher who faces a collection of pupils unimpressed by, or hostile to, adult authority, and prone to disobey school rules, and who inadvertently or intentionally influences them to become a more closely-knit group can expect disorder to be increased by induction, unless, of course, other factors enter in simultaneously to reduce the amount of hostility or otherwise exert an influence toward order. Thus in really difficult situations the maxim "divide and conquer" seems to have good theoretical foundation. To be sure, in many situations educators must decide to jeopardize or sacrifice order for the sake of educational gains; yet there are many situations, probably more, where greater order is a prerequisite for the making of those very desired gains. Perhaps a study of the degree of cohesiveness of a given class group and the bases for attraction to it would provide a basis for predicting the nature of the effects to be expected from actions which would increase or decrease the group's cohesiveness or solidify or alter the bases for attraction to it.

It must be stressed that it is just as possible for group induction to work positively as it is for it to work negatively, and that increases, therefore, in the attractiveness which a well-behaved, well-knit group has for a given potential miscreant can be expected to increase the chances of his behaving well. This is a principle no doubt being already widely exploited by effective teachers.

The Equilibrium of Groups

We have touched by implication upon the seemingly useful concepts of group culture, group goals, norms, frames of reference, and the like. But another related concept seems to have particular relevance for our problem, that of the equilibrium of groups. It has been observed that states of equilibrium are characteristic not only of individuals, but also of groups of individuals. That is, if a small force is impressed upon the life of a group, a change or adjustment takes place within it, but upon removal of the force the group returns to approximately its previous state. This suggests that a teacher interested in affecting the patterns of group behavior in a class must impress upon the class either one or more constant small forces or one or more one-shot large forces, or may perhaps impress upon it a combination of the two. It suggests, also, that small forces sporadically exerted, such, perhaps, as admonitions, threats, and suggestions, will not by themselves affect in the long run the behavior of the group.

There are many teachers whose exercise of leadership appears to be a constant one, whose influence on their classes to behave in certain fashions appears to be continuous. There are others who appear to pay no attention to the problem of behavior. And in each category there are, even where the pupil groups are similar, some teachers who are very effective in keeping order and some teachers who are very ineffective in that respect. The concept of equilibrium of groups suggests that the appearances may be deceptive: perhaps the forces which the ineffective teachers exert are in fact so small or so temporary as to be doomed to be without permanent result, whereas those exerted by the effective teachers are for reasons of size or permanence sufficient to bring about the desired changes. It may be that the effectiveness of certain teachers working with difficult groups will prove to be related to their use of a combination of constant small forces, glances, smiles, gestures, locomotion about the room, together with a number of one-shot large forces, such as reseating of pupils, rearrangement of classroom furniture, selection of textbooks, establishment of reward and penalty systems, and so on and on. Furthermore, the effective teacher may be found to work the middle ground, using sporadic middle-sized forces to gain temporary results, temporary classroom sub-groupings, interruptions for standing up and stretching, and the like. It is probably unnecessary to caution that forces cannot be neatly categorized a priori into small and large, but that their size will be relative to the given situation and the way it is perceived by the pupils concerned.

Another contribution of the concept of equilibrium may be that of providing one framework through which to describe the variety of phenomena observed when new teachers take over classes, and the immediacy of, or delay in, their achievement of order or encountering of disorder.

Industrial Sociology

Let us turn our attention now to the other field of study from which we hope to draw parts of what might become a body of theory relating to the keeping of order. The field of industrial sociology, including in its bailiwick industrial relations and personnel management, is one in which a host of studies has blossomed, especially since the publication nineteen years ago of the classic report on the twelve-year research conducted at the Western Electric Hawthorne plant (13). It is a field on which up to now educationists have drawn relatively little, and practically not at all in the consideration of problems of discipline or misbehavior.

Perhaps we should first consider in a little more detail the relevance of the field to the matters which concern us. Of the many differences between industrial plants and schools a few are especially significant for our purpose.[6] Membership in the work force of a plant is not, of course, compulsory, although, especially in a time of work shortage, there are strong pressures giving it something of that character. The parallelism between plant and school seems strong only in so far as the latter's population is over the compulsory school attendance age. Normally the plant has a powerful system of rewards and punishments with which to influence workers' behavior, in contrast to an almost nonexistent system in the school. At the same time workers are like pupils in having at their disposal many subtle ways of influencing, in return, their superiors. Perhaps most important, and possibly most easily overlooked, the work goal of the plant is outside the person of the worker and independent of his psychic state, whereas the work goal of the school, learning, is inside the person of the pupil and entirely bound up with his psychic state. This means, translated into practical terms, that where a supervisor in a plant or office might keep order and get the work done without regard to—or even at the expense of—the emotional security or personal growth of his workers, a teacher or school administrator who used the same procedures to the end of keeping order might well find that he was being untrue to the chief function he is expected to fill. One of the contributions of the psychological emphasis of the past three decades has been the insight that many important kinds of learning are highly delicate and may be seriously upset by the offering of artificial rewards, by punishment, or by the creation of insecurity or anxiety.

In spite of these striking differences there are important enough sim-

[6] For one summary statement of the differences between the two types of institution see (10, pp. 609–645).

ilarities between the school, in its current form, and the plant to justify the hope that we may find help from this quarter in our search for theory. Each of these institutions brings people together by the hundreds, dividing them into two classes, management (teachers and administrators) and workers (pupils), with the first class prescribing more or less closely certain jobs to be done, and undertaking to get the second to do them. Even the atmosphere of the industrial plant, to judge by this section of a paragraph intended to portray the *differences* between school and plant, may strike teachers as not unfamiliar:

"Most factory girls adjust quickly to the routines; and if the work group is friendly, they do not mind the simple repetitious jobs. They rarely express anxiety about getting ahead or complain about the monotony of the work. To them it is only a temporary interlude until they 'get their man.' The boys . . . react quite differently. They often have a hard time settling down to the work; they like to play around; they soon get tired of doing the same thing all day long, and their attention wanders. As soon as they learn one job, they become impatient to get on to something else; they begin to complain about monotony and wonder about getting ahead. In many cases, they have so much difficulty in making this adjustment that they do poor work and quit (4, p. 242)."

All the similarities between plant and school suggest that theory developed about the one may well be relevant to the other.

We should also mention the fact that for at least three reasons research possibilities in industrial sociology are unusually rich. Considerable funds have been made available over the years for research in the field, extensive and detailed records are frequently kept of the matters under study, and variations in the amount and quality of work done in a given situation and the amount and intensity of unrest or disorder can often be established with considerable precision.

Let us look briefly at a few of the formulations which sociologists have found helpful in interpreting factors related to productivity (which we can compare with learning) or to unrest (misbehavior). Although not startling, they may be suggestive.

Human Relations and Morale

It is by now a fundamental principle of the field that an industrial plant is a "social" as well as an "economic" institution, and that this duality has implications for the work of the supervisory staff. Roethlisberger and Dickson, in the Hawthorne report referred to above, went so far as to list as one of the two major functions of management, that of "maintaining the equilibrium of the social organization so that individuals through contributing their services to this common purpose obtain personal satisfactions that make them willing to co-operate" (13, p. 569). They went on to say that if this function is not effectively performed by management the business enterprise cannot be expected to survive. So long as the public wants them to continue, public schools will not go out of business. But the suggestion is clear that disintegration of a school's educational business might be the inevitable consequence of the school's not undertaking to offer adequate "personal satisfactions" to its pupils and teachers. Would it help us to understand our problem if we were to regard education, that is, the bringing about of learning, as only one of two major functions and were to study systematically the relation between, on the one hand, the way our schools are constituted and, on the other, the extent to which they do or do not give pupils personal satisfactions?

The systematic study of the relation between the goals of management and the personal satisfactions gained by workers launched the "human relations" movement in industry; a movement which has become a powerful force in the field, though an ambiguous one, since it has meant very different things to different men. Considering the human factor has taken the form of unscrupulous manipulation, of active participation in decision-making on the part of the workers to be affected by the given decision, and even of what in schools would be termed guidance counseling or psychological help. There has been considerable debate about the relevance of human relations practices to production, but prevailing opinion seems to find these various practices and the underlying concepts highly useful so long as unwarranted assumptions about relationships are avoided. Simon has said that worker participation in decision-making is likely to be effective—from the employer's point of view—where there is "substantial parallelism of interests," that is, "in so far as the parties perceive themselves as working toward common goals" (14, pp. 111–112). By implication he raises the question to what extent such a community of goals can be properly assumed. In education we have experimented a good deal recently, with greater or lesser success, with some of the same techniques of human relations, especially that of participation in decision-making, "teacher-pupil planning." Perhaps we would be more able to understand the good and bad effects our experiments have had on behavior, as well as learning, and the reasons for these effects, were we to concern ourselves also with the question of the community of goals—or lack thereof—between pupils and teachers. Even where we dedicate our whole educational effort ostensibly to a meeting of pupils' needs, it is overhasty to assume the parallelism of interests which would mean that participation in decision-making or, for that matter (as we have seen), building group cohesiveness will further rather than subvert our achievement of order. These are questions to which research in industrial sociology gives us no answers, but about which it seems to suggest that we in education should be more cautious and more research-minded.

The distinction which industrial sociologists draw between employees' morale on the one hand and their interest in their work on the other does not seem offhand to offer very much of a contribution but may upon analysis prove well worth borrowing. Certainly in education we tend to see the two phenomena as one. Those of us who are very much concerned with curriculum and teaching method know that effective learning presupposes interest, and that interests absorb attention and energy. We tend, therefore, to focus our efforts on making the curriculum and method interesting, and often tend, similarly, to expect that success in that respect will automatically bring high morale and good behavior. Others of us, involved in administration, may be more inclined to see problems of learning and of misbehavior as problems of morale, and hence to stress school spirit, strong activity programs, and the like. Both groups seem to assume that interest and high morale are practically equivalent. The discovery in industry that morale and interest in getting the work done can vary independently of one another suggests that in the schools, too, we might find it useful to think of these phenomena separately and to keep the distinction in mind as we study them and their determinants. Can the concept of non-interest-related morale factors explain situations where there is high interest in studies yet bad behavior? Can the distinction explain why in a school with apparently high morale a given class misbehaves badly?[7]

The Informal Organization

Another suggestive concept is that of the existence in every plant of both a formal and an informal organization. The informal organization, whose bonds and dividing lines are the attitudes and feelings of the members of the plant, is the system whereby individuals or groups of individuals are unofficially related to one another, communicate with one another, and so on. For a plant it is, of course, very significant what relation there is between its formal and its informal organizations; whether, for example, the one is substantially congruent with, supports, indeed makes possible the other, or is, in a sense, subversive of it. The most obvious aspect of the informal organization is the "informal work group,"

[7] According to Dale Yoder such factors as the nature of the machinery for receiving suggestions, the nature of the rest pauses, and the extent of the counseling services offered, among others, have proved in industry to be related to the quality of morale irrespective of the level of interest workers have in the work itself. See (15, ch. 17).

and it has been well established that the qualities of the life of this group are very significant for productivity and morale. "Atomistic and impersonal relations of workers to their fellows," it was found in studies conducted during World War II, make for absenteeism and turn-over (11, p. 385). Although in recent years there has been a distinct swing away from the view that the cohesiveness and morale of the work group is the one factor most closely associated with the quality of workers' performance, it is still generally accepted in the field that the concept of the informal work group is a useful and relevant one.

In the study of the informal work team the fields of industrial sociology and group dynamics overlap, with the consequence that the major theoretical contributions to be derived from the former are those already mentioned in our discussion of the latter. Thus in industrial sociology we have the relevant concepts of group norms, performance ceilings—and floors—set and enforced by the group, and the "rate buster," whom the group takes steps to bring back into line. These are specific forms of group ideology and induction, whose relevance for the keeping of order in the classroom group we have already touched on.

Likewise, the larger concept of the informal organization of the plant as a whole, with its distinction between the informal and formal organizations, seems to be suggestive for a study of the degree to which the school does or does not succeed in keeping in good order. Not only within a faculty but also among pupils the unofficial channels of communication and influence and the unofficial status differentials may tend to promote or subvert good order.[8] The possibility comes to mind that the institution of student government vested with serious administrative prerogatives—which would certainly bring informal and formal organizations of a school closer together—might in some instances formalize and make more effective existing tendencies of students to misbehave, but might in other instances provide a means of making more effective a general disposition on their part to be orderly.

Quite a different possibility suggested by the distinction between the two types of organization is the possibility that the groups of twenty-five to thirty pupils into which schools are usually formally organized may be of such a size that the arising of a non-congruent informal orga-

[8] Earl S. Johnson, referring directly to work in industrial sociology, argues that in nearly every classroom there exists an "unofficial" social organization, "sanctioned neither by teacher nor school authorities." This "social countersystem," he asserts, is in a power conflict with the official system organized and conducted by the teacher, though the teacher, he says, is constantly obliged to attempt to bring the two systems together. According to Johnson, "the code of the countersystem has much to do with the origin of discipline cases" and with the effectiveness of teachers' attempts to deal with them. See (9, pp. 17, 22n).

nization becomes, for good or ill, almost inevitable. Some light might be cast on this possibility by experimentation with the use, for certain purposes, of other formal organizational patterns, something like a committee or squad system, perhaps.[9]

Industrial sociologists have often found executive and supervisory staffs frustrated by, and resentful of, the "stupidity" or sheer "perversity" of workers. To those in authority it has often seemed illogical and inexplicable that workers would not, for example, respond to an incentive plan which was obviously so designed as to allow them opportunities for greater earnings. Studies have shown, however, that this "perversity" can usually be understood in terms of a *workers'* "logic" or "ideology," a system of ideas, beliefs, values, and feelings on the workers' part, which may or may not have objective bases. Thus, an important influence on work behavior is reported to be "the general suspicion which workers have of the motives of management," regardless of the existence or nonexistence in a given situation of a specific factual basis for that suspicion (4, p. 181).

From, among other things, the fact observed by the writer that at teachers' meetings applause tends to be loudest when the speaker denounces the bad manners and undisciplined behavior of the young, it would appear that many of us may still feel frustrated by the inexplicably "perverse" behavior of those whom we are expected to keep in order and to teach! Can our understanding of pupil misbehavior be improved through the adoption of such a concept as that of a *pupils'* logic or ideology? Many experienced teachers seem to take it for granted that pupils will adopt and perpetuate certain stereotypes. The suggestion here seems to be of the existence not of stereotyping alone, but of a whole system of beliefs and attitudes apparently irrelevant to the realities of the situation, yet having serious effects on behavior or misbehavior. The case comes to mind of hostile Southern Negro children who are openly at war with the staff of the Northern school to which they have transferred.[10] Situations such as this have often been described in terms of

[9] The concomitant problems of span of control and of centralization and decentralization open up a whole new area for future investigation in public school organization. Judging from industry, the nature of the authority structure and the kind of supervisory relations prevailing between persons at various levels in the school hierarchy on the one hand and pupils on the other would appear to be highly relevant to the question of order. Administratively-minded persons often view misbehavior as resulting from inadequate regulations—including those dealing with sanctions; perhaps it could more profitably be explored as having some relation to overall organizational framework.

[10] The same type of phenomenon seems to be exemplified by a new pupil of the author's acquaintance whose behavior toward the faculty seemed most uncooperative,

"pupil morale," as though they could be plotted on a linear scale. The concept of a pupils' ideology suggests the need for a qualitative study of what is presumably a substantive system of beliefs and attitudes held by pupils. And it suggests that dealing with the pupils concerned may require a major task of reëducation, focussed not on the issue of morale in general, nor on the issues of good or bad conduct, or rewards or punishments, but on the pupils'—and perhaps also the teachers'—perception of the total nature of the situation in which the pupils find themselves.

Conclusion

It was our original suspicion that the problem of keeping order cannot be solved by reliance upon the bag of tricks or the born teachers alone, nor upon interesting teaching or a challenging curriculum. That suspicion seems to be confirmed by findings we have noted along the way. At the same time we seem to have found a number of concepts which give promise of a broader theoretical approach to the matter; for example, the concepts of group structure, of status, of role, of equilibrium of groups, of informal organization, of degrees of community of goals, and of pupil morale and ideology. Our analysis seems, indeed, to suggest, that in the absence of simple luck, the degree of the teacher's success in keeping order may well reflect the extent to which these concepts are present, consciously or unconsciously, in his mind. The teacher who declared to the writer, "I don't believe the school *is* a social institution: it is an intellectual institution," could be expected, in so far as his conceptions actually agreed with the first part of his statement, to be a failure in keeping order. Teachers *are* group leaders, good or bad, willy-nilly.

Our analysis has not lead us to useful, specific tips for practice; indeed it casts doubt upon their being many such. It does suggest, however, that it will be useful for teachers to look at the group behavior of their pupils not only in its educational aspect but in its bureaucratic aspect as well. It suggests, too, that it would help teachers or prospective teachers to observe and study systematically the group-leadership features of work in the classroom—drawing, perhaps, on the two fields that we have found to be relevant—and to practice the group-leadership roles they are likely to have to play.

But our analysis seems to raise more questions than it answers. What means are available to teachers for studying their classes as groups? Are there personality qualities in teachers which foster or impede their recog-

but who never misbehaved overtly: it appeared that from previous experience he had come to believe that life was most likely to be pleasant if teachers were simply circumvented and avoided; this ideology was of rather limited appropriateness in the school to which the boy had transferred.

nition that the school is a social institution, or determine their degree of willingness to play certain roles? What kinds of pupil culture do, in fact, prevail, and how are they related to the characteristics of the teacher, the type of school, the type of pupil, or perhaps even the particular subject under study? How far can the group culture be influenced by various changes in school policy and practice? In further study of questions such as these may lie the possibility of our eventually being able to offer an embattled teacher substantial help.

References

1. Bogen, I. Pupil-teacher rapport and the teacher's awareness of status structures within the group. *J. educ. Sociol.*, 1954, **28**, 104–114.
2. Cartwright, D., & Zander, A. (Eds.) *Group dynamics: research and theory.* Evanston, Ill.: Row, Peterson, 1953.
3. Cunningham, Ruth, *et al. Understanding group behavior of boys and girls.* New York: Bureau of Publ., Teach. Coll., Columbia Univer., 1951.
4. Gardner, B. B., & Moore, D. G. *Human relations in industry.* (Rev. ed.) Chicago: Richard D. Irwin, 1950.
5. Hare, A. P., Borgatta, E. F., & Bales, R. F. (Eds.) *Small groups: studies in social interaction.* New York: Alfred A. Knopf, 1955.
6. Homans, G. C. *The human group.* New York: Harcourt, Brace, 1950.
7. Hunter, E. *The blackboard jungle.* New York: Simon & Schuster, 1954.
8. Jennings, Helen Hall. *Sociometry in group relations.* Washington, D. C.: Amer. Council on Educ., 1948.
9. Johnson, E. S. *Theory and practice in the social studies.* New York: Macmillan, 1956.
10. Miller, D. C., & Form, W. H. *Industrial sociology.* New York: Harper, 1951.
11. Moore, W. E. Industrial sociology: status and prospects. *Amer. sociol. Rev.*, 1948, **13**, 382–391.
12. Polansky, Lucy. Group social climate and the teacher's supportiveness of group status systems. *J. educ. Sociol.*, 1954, **28**, 115–123.
13. Roethlisberger, F. J., & Dickson, W. J. *Management and the worker.* Cambridge: Harvard University Press, 1939.
14. Simon, H. A. Authority. In C. M. Arensberg *et al.* (Eds.), *Research in industrial human relations: a critical appraisal.* New York: Harper, 1957. Pp. 103–118.
15. Yoder, D. *Personnel management and industrial relations.* New York: Prentice-Hall, 1946.

Selected Readings

Ausubel, D. P. A new look at classroom discipline. *Phi Delta Kappan,* 1961, **43**, 25–30.

Ausubel, D. P. Learning by discovery: Rationale and mystique, *Bulletin of the National Associations Secondary School Principals,* 1961, **45**, 18–58.

Ausubel, D. P. A subsumption theory of meaningful verbal learning and retention. *The Journal of General Psychology,* 1962, **66**, 213–224.

Ausubel, D. P. The use of advance organizers in the learning and retention of meaningful verbal material. *Journal of Educational Psychology,* 1960, **51**, 267–272.

Bruner, J. S. The act of discovery. *Harvard Educational Review,* 1961, **31**, 21–32.

Canning, R. R. Does an honor system reduce classroom cheating? An experimental answer. *Journal of Experimental Education,* 1956, 291–96.

Combs, A. W. Fostering self-direction. *Educational Leadership,* 1966, **23**, 373–376.

Flanders, N. A., and Morrison, Betty M. Changes in pupil attitudes during the school year. *Journal of Educational Psychology,* 1968, **50**, 334–338.

Gronlund, N. E. Sociometry and improved social relations in the classroom. *Sociometry in the Classroom,* 1959.

Kersh, B. Y., and Wittrock, M. C. Learning by discovery: An interpretation of recent research. *Journal of Teacher Education,* 1962, **13**, 461–468.

Ryans, D. Teacher behavior theory and research: Implications for teacher education. *The Journal of Teacher Education,* 1963, **14**, 274–293.

Skinner, B. F. Why teachers fail. *Saturday Review,* 1965, **42**, 80–81, 98 ff.

Solomon, R. L. Punishment. *American Psychologist,* 1964, **19**, 239–253.

Sorenson, A. G., Husek, T. R., and Yu, Constance. The roles teachers occupy. *Journal of Educational Psychology,* 1963, **54**, 287–294.

Staats, A. W. Treatment of nonreading in a culturally deprived juvenile delinquent: An application of reinforcement principles. *Child Development,* 1965, **36**, 925–942.

Symonds, P. M. Classroom discipline. *Teachers College Record,* 1949, **51**, 147–58.

Withall, J. Mental health-teacher education research project. *The Journal of Teacher Education,* 1963, **14**, 318–325.

CHAPTER 7

Using Educational Technology

7.1 The Place of Technology in Educational Change[1]

R. Louis Bright

The author believes that with an increasing enrollment and concern for individual differences, the only answer to our educational problems is the use of individualized instruction through technology. Educational technology has already proved its value. Now the author emphasizes the need to employ specialists in our schools who have the competencies to utilize the full potentialities of technology. The teacher's role will change, providing time for him to make a greater contribution to learning than ever before.

One thing is certain: Educational research needs to be future oriented, if it is to help us develop the kind of teaching and learning we need in the years ahead. While research may be extremely efficient in analyzing mistakes of the past and reasonably useful in solving problems of the present—or trying to—its best service to education is in the direction of

SOURCE. R. Louis Bright, "The Place of Technology in Educational Change," *Audio-visual Instruction*, **XII**, 4 (1967), pp. 340–343. Reprinted by permission of the National Education Association.

[1] Adapted from an address given by Dr. Bright on June 22, 1966, at the Summer Conference on Curriculum Change, Institute for Curriculum Improvement, Gainesville, Florida.

developing new knowledge and new techniques that can make tomorrow's education do the job it needs to do for tomorrow's young people and adults.

This kind of research poses challenges far beyond any that have been faced in traditional educational research in the past. The swiftness with which changes are coming about—in society and in technology—demand that we get on with the task with all deliberate speed. To get some idea just how critical this need is, it is well to remember that children starting school this fall will be preparing to begin active participation as adults about 1980.

Systematic educational reforms take time. The longer we dillydally in getting on with the job, the more students will get through the pipeline with education that is not all that it can and should be. If it takes 10 years to devise and implement significant changes in curriculum techniques—and I might remind you that we have been working under the present traditional curriculum for generations—then it will be between 1980 and 1990 before the benefits of curriculum change will be felt by any large proportion of our graduates.

What Will Be the Task of Tomorrow's Schools?

In any kind of planning for curriculum change, one of the first questions to be asked is: What kind of curriculum will prepare the student for the kinds of problems and opportunities he will face when he leaves the protective sanctuary of formal education?

To answer that question, we have to make some careful predictions about what will be important in the 1980 to 1990 period and beyond. How is society then going to differ from society today? Obviously, we'll have continued technological advance, but what does this mean? There probably will be marked increase in division of labor, bringing with it much greater personal interaction among people on the job. Furthermore, labor forecasts suggest that the majority of new job openings will be in the service industries.

While the swift progress of technology demands a high level of technical competence, it also demands adaptability to constant change and mastery of problem-solving techniques which enable individuals to learn and do more than they have been taught. Many routine tasks will be eliminated by automation, and a shorter work week will leave more time for personal recreation and self-fulfillment. As population grows and transportation and communication improve, the "shrinking world" concept will be accompanied by increasing contacts with people in other countries and increasing concern about them. In this kind of world, the individual will need a new measure of intellectual maturity to cope with careers shaped by the pace of change; but he will spend less time at the office or the machine so that he will also have to have a whole new dimension of interests and abilities for his leisure time and for his responsibilities within an increasingly complex society.

During the past 10 years, educational developments have been moving in the direction of accommodating these kinds of changing needs of society. Perhaps they have not been moving fast enough or systematically enough, but they have been moving. The major theme of these developments has been individualization of instruction. I think this trend will continue and accelerate as we develop better techniques for improving not only what the student learns but the way he learns it.

Much research on individualized instruction is already underway, and some schools have implemented large sections of their programs on an individualized basis. It is my prediction that within another 10 years almost the entire academic portion of instruction will be on an individualized basis in most schools. I also predict that programed instruction, instructional TV, computerized instruction, and use of other new media increasingly will be important factors in providing education of the scope and depth our young people need. How else can we provide the necessary sustenance for increasing enrollments, characterized by a multiplicity of threads of interest, wide variation in learning styles and rates of progress, and great diversity of motivations and goals?

There are a great many questions still to be answered. The farther we get into individualized instruction, the more we have to face the fact that things just don't fit into the existing structure any more. Actually, I think modern curriculum developments—by concentrating primarily on texts, supplementary films, and other items that do fit into the existing curriculum—are ducking some of the most important questions we need to answer. One serious gap in our present efforts is the determination of the teacher's function in the kind of learning the newer educational technology will bring about. Closely related to this are questions about how to administer the school, how to schedule students, what kind of buildings and equipment are needed. I shall come back to these, particularly the teacher's role, after we have looked in some detail at what we know about the management and potential of emerging educational technology.

How Can Educational Technology Help the Schools of the Future?

Although we are not yet sure which of the new media is most appropriate for what, it is imperative that curriculum development projects make use of what we do know about the use of media. For example, experiments have shown that students learn as much subject matter from instructional TV as they do in live or conventional classrooms.

Results with programed instruction are spotty, but I should like to give you one example that shows something of its potential. A group of the nation's top economists determined the objectives of a college economics course and drew up programed instruction materials, which were carefully evaluated and revised. These were tried in a controlled experiment in which one group used the programed text without a teacher, one group used the standard text without a teacher, and one group was in a conventional class with a professor who had taught the course during the two previous sessions. At the end of the year, when a test made up by an independent group of prominent economists was administered, the group using the programed instructional materials was far ahead of the others. The group which used the standard text alone—without the teacher—placed second, and the group which had the conventional class came in third.

The experiment was tried with the same kinds of controlled groups in two other universities. In both cases, the group using the programed text came out far ahead. In these cases, the professors did nose out the textbook by itself but not to a statistically significant extent. What I am saying here is that, when the new technology is involved, somebody should take a serious look at the role of the teacher.

Now, what can educational technology do? And what can it not do? The answer to both of these questions will help to determine the teacher's role. Enough of the basic techniques are understood to enable us to make extremely effective programs. But we haven't done so; we aren't doing as well as we know how to do. In spite of the fact that instructional TV has been with us for 15 years, there are few examples of what I would call really effective programs—programs that produce the effects instructional TV is capable of. I think there are two reasons why it hasn't made better advances. First of all, nobody has put the necessary funds into its development; and secondly, there has not been the interdisciplinary teamwork necessary to develop TV's full capability as an instructional tool.

Let me digress for a moment and talk about what is required for excellence in instructional television. It takes a combination of four kinds of competencies—not necessarily in the order I shall name them. First, there needs to be a subject-matter expert; but it isn't enough simply to have him standing in front of a blackboard with a piece of chalk or to use an occasional close-up of a talking face on a screen. On the team, there also needs to be a Walt Disney type of producer or director, who knows the full capability of the media, the trick effects that can be helpful, and what should be done to make the material interesting and entertaining.

Third, the team needs a programed instruction expert. Unfortunately, during the last decade, the mass media experts and the programed instruction or individual-education experts have been divided into rival camps. Actually, programed instruction techniques have a great deal to offer in mass media. One of the basic postulates of programed instruction is that, if a student doesn't learn, it is the fault of the course and not of the student. If a particular course does not produce the behavioral change in a student that was intended, the course is revised until it does produce this change. This kind of feedback and revision probably accounts for the results in the economics course we discussed earlier. Programed instruction itself is not necessarily superior to other types of teaching, but adequate feedback and revision can make it superior to the one-shot kind of teaching that does not have this kind of refinement.

In the case of mass media, as in programed instruction, the need for revision is determined by breaking down overall objectives into smaller ones to see if the student, or any significant number of students, did not get a particular concept. The number of students involved in this kind of refinement may be quite small, but the ultimate production should be far more effective than the original. The refinement is costly, but it is worth the trouble. So far as I have been able to determine from about 20 different groups that have been doing first-class programed instruction work, they seem to be almost unanimous in estimating that revision accounts for about 60 percent of the cost of an effective program. Obviously, the competence of a programed instruction expert is useful on a team seeking to develop and refine an effective instructional television program.

Fourth, and by no means last in importance, the team needs to include a teacher or, if you want to use a fancier title, a cognitive psychologist. This is the person who is familiar with the learning characteristics of the particular target population for which the program is being developed and who knows what the teacher can use and how.

To the best of my knowledge, no instructional TV program has been produced with this kind of teamwork. More often than not, what is called an interdisciplinary team turns out upon closer observation to be a nationally known psychologist, a graduate student or two, and a local photographer. For real effectiveness, the team must include first-class people in all the disciplines so that they share mutual respect for each other's competence from the very beginning of the project. It isn't enough for the subject-matter specialist to decide what the curriculum objectives should be: call in the motion picture man to help him put it on film, then ask the programed instruction man what he thinks of the results, and finally invites teachers to use it with their students.

The team of experts needs to work together from the very first day. It is costly, but if the results are really effective it may be a bargain in the long run. The best figure I have been able to get for a really good job of instructional television is a cost of about $10,000 for the amount of materials a student will go through in one hour. The real cost, of course, depends upon the number of students who benefit by it. Historically, the National Science Foundation has had the most comprehensive program in support of curriculum development, but neither NSF nor the Office of Education has had the support of the magnitude needed for effective and large-scale curriculum development for the newer media, nor do we have such funds for the present fiscal year. However, the Office does have these funds in the budget for subsequent years, and I hope enough hurdles have been cleared to assure support for really major new types of curriculum development beginning in fiscal 1968.

While we're talking about costs, it might be well to take a quick look at the computerized classroom, which is one technique for programed or individualized instruction. Parenthetically, we might mention that, if you have a school of 4,000 students each going at his own speed, you'll need a computer to keep track of what's going on.

Most people don't realize that one function of the computer, while letting everyone go at his own individualized rate, is to keep everyone together in the sense of touching the same bases or learning the same basic materials and concepts. For example, when a student takes his turn at the computer, he checks in by typing his name, and the computer automatically connects him with the portion of the program for which he is ready. As soon as he finishes the assignment, the computer automatically moves him to the next segment of the program or releases him for another subject. By the time the student comes to class the next day, the teacher has a print-out from the computer indicating which students in the class did indeed go through which segments of material and pass tests on it. The print-out also indicates any particular sections that were troublesome to students in general or to individual students in particular, thus giving automatic feedback for revision of the course where appropriate. This kind of diagnostic assistance is a new experience for the teacher. She knows when everybody in the class has done the assignments, what concepts the students have learned, and how to group students for discussion.

All of this can be done in several subjects. In most of the experiments to date, a spread of about four-to-one has been found in the rate of learning in a typical class. This means that one student in a given course may be spending about four times as long at the computer console as another in a given course, but the rate of learning of a particular student may differ widely among the various courses. In any case, the students can have individualized instruction and still be held responsible for a certain level of mastery. This kind of instructional equipment obviously has great potential, but its development will require a great deal of teamwork and financial support. Furthermore, its use will drastically revolutionize much that goes on in the schools.

Now, let's get back to our discussion of what educational technology in general can do and what it cannot. With competent interdisciplinary teams, the various media available through educational technology can teach essentially all of the academic courses now in our curriculum. Not only can they teach facts; they can teach logic and they can teach concepts. But they can't do everything. They do not teach the student to formulate ideas or to express his ideas clearly and defend them against the criticism of his peers. They do not teach him to speak confidently before a group or to learn that when you talk to different groups, you express things in different ways. They do not teach him to use color in what he writes or what he says. They do not develop the student's creative ability. These are things that are really going to be important in the society of 1980 and 1990.

What Will Be the Role of Tomorrow's Teachers?

As I see it, the real promise of educational technology is that it can do enough of the routine teaching tasks well to leave the teacher time to concentrate on helping students develop their creative and communicative abilities. When the newer media are used to the maximum, the teacher should never need to stand in front of a class presenting information. The mere presentation of information, refined by feedback and revision sequences, can be done by the media. This can leave the teacher free to lead discussion groups where students express their ideas and ask questions. I don't think, for example, that a mathematics student really learns a great deal by watching a professor present an elegant proof that he spent eight hours developing the previous night. The student could learn far more by watching him develop the proof or by trying to do it himself with assistance from the teacher or even from a computer.

As a basis for our discussion of the role of tomorrow's teachers, let's look for a moment at what goes on in a school that already uses a great many of the new approaches to individualized instruction. At the Oak Leaf Elementary School, which is an experimental school in conjunction with our Research and Development Center at the University of Pittsburgh, every student has his own course independent of everyone else. The student works through perhaps 15 pages of an assignment, takes a posttest, brings it to a teaching aid for checking, and then takes it to the teacher. If he has demonstrated sufficient competence to advance to another unit, he may be sent to a file for his next assignment. If he is not ready to move on to another assignment, the teacher recommends exercises to help him master the particular points that gave him trouble. The entire day is not taken up in this way, of course. There are discussion groups and other class activities. For the most part, however, reading, arithmetic, and the conventional academic type of learning are on an individualized basis.

There are typically about 50 students in a classroom, each one working on his particular assignments. Whenever a student seeks help, the teacher may be faced with a question in second-grade arithmetic, or fourth-grade history, or some other level of some other subject. At one point last year, two sixth-grade students were studying introductory calculus. The point is that a student's question may be on any unit of any subject in the entire elementary school curriculum and beyond. This is a new experience for the teacher. It simply underlines the need to take a fresh look at what the teacher's role is going to be and the kind of preparation needed for that role.

I can visualize three—possibly four—new and different roles for the classroom teacher of the future. In a classroom where perhaps 50 students are studying individualized material on their own, one role of the teacher is to overcome the deficiencies in the material. No material is ever perfect for all students, and this is certainly a critical function that the teacher must continue to fill.

Another role of the teacher is to determine what happens when a student presents tests or other evidences of his achievement. This is a diagnostic function. For complete records of the individual student's performance, including his learning patterns, the teacher can select what materials will be appropriate as a next step in the learning experience.

A third function, of course, is that of leading discussion groups, where the objective is to improve student communication with others—and not necessarily with others of the same age. I might remind you that the school is the only social institution where people have been grouped by age, and then only since about 1830. Presumably, in the school of tomorrow where student discussion will be in groups with like accomplishment in the particular subjects, there could easily be three to five years of age difference—perhaps more—in such a group.

A fourth possible role of the teacher might be as a producer of curriculum materials, including supplementary materials, for use in an individualized system. How extensively this would be a function of the classroom teacher, or how much this function would be taken over by a central interdisciplinary committee, would probably depend upon the type of situation—for example, whether such materials are for more or less general use or to satisfy the one-in-a-lifetime needs of a particular student.

The next question is: Does the same person perform all of these functions? Or are they performed by different people with different training backgrounds? This brings up a whole cluster of unanswered questions about school administration. For example, how do you schedule students in a completely individualized system? The Oak Leaf School does not use a computer, but it's obvious that a computerized classroom would have similar problems. In fact, the trend toward individualized instruction—regardless of the media used—is already having a powerful effect, not only upon curriculum changes but upon changes in teacher education as well.

Conclusion

We might sum up this discussion with these observations: First, there can be no doubt that educational changes must be made to keep pace with changing needs in our society. Such changes should be deliberate and systematic. Future-oriented research is our best means for assuring that these changes are objective and sound. Second, at the same time technological advances and social complexities demand curriculum change, the newer media offer us important tools for providing a scope, depth, and diversity of learning never before possible in our schools. The challenge is to adapt the media to serve education, and not the other way around. And third, with these tools, our teachers will no longer spend their time passing along preinterpreted information or supervising lockstep drills. Their new role will be to help individuals learn how to learn so that, once their formal schooling is complete, they can go on learning more than they have been taught.

Perhaps the chief value of the emerging educational technology is that, properly researched and developed, it has the potential for giving the teacher time for the really important things, the things that cannot be done by a book or by a machine.

7.2 Computerized Instruction and the Learning Process[1]

Richard C. Atkinson

Professor Atkinson of Stanford University, gives us an inside look at the hardware and materials (software) used in computer assisted instruction (CAI) for the teaching of reading. He describes the tasks in the program and the required behavior of the pupil as he completes these tasks. The author emphasizes that CAI provides the facilities for research that will relate learning theory to instructional problems.

In recent years there has been a tremendous number of articles and news releases dealing with computer-assisted instruction, or as it has been abbreviated, CAI. One might conjecture that this proliferation is an indicant of rapid progress in the field. Unfortunately, I doubt that it is. A few of the reports about CAI are based on substantial experience and research, but the majority are vague speculations and conjectures with little if any data or real experience to back them up. I do not want

SOURCE. Abridged from Richard C. Atkinson, "Computerized Instruction and the Learning Process," *American Psychologist,* **XXIII**, 4 (1968), pp. 225–231 and 235–239, by permission of the author and the American Psychological Association.

[1] Invited address presented at the meeting of the Division of Educational Psychology, American Psychological Association, Washington, D. C., September 1967.

to denigrate the role of speculation and conjecture in a newly developing area like CAI. However, of late it seems to have produced little more than a repetition of ideas that were exciting in the 1950s but, in the absence of new research, are simply well-worn clichés in the late 1960s.

These remarks should not be misinterpreted. Important and significant research on CAI is being carried on in many laboratories around the country, but certainly not as much as one is led to believe by the attendant publicity. The problem for someone trying to evaluate developments in the field is to distinguish between those reports that are based on fact and those that are disguised forms of science fiction. In my paper, I shall try to stay very close to data and actual experience. My claims will be less grand than many that have been made for CAI, but they will be based on a substantial research effort.

In 1964 Patrick Suppes and I initiated a project under a grant from the Office of Education to develop and implement a CAI program in initial reading and mathematics. Because of our particular research interests, Suppes has taken responsibility for the mathematics curriculum and I have been responsible for the initial reading program. At the beginning of the project, two major hurdles had to be overcome. There was no lesson material in either mathematics or reading suitable for CAI, and an integrated CAI system had not yet been designed and produced by a single manufacturer. The development of the curricula and the development of the system have been carried out as a parallel effort over the last 3 years with each having a decided influence on the other.

Today I would like to report on the progress of the reading program with particular reference to the past school year when for the first time a sizable group of students received a major portion of their daily reading instruction under computer control. The first year's operation must be considered essentially as an extended debugging of both the computer system and the curriculum materials. Nevertheless, some interesting comments can be made on the basis of this experience regarding both the feasibility of CAI and the impact of such instruction on the overall learning process.

Before describing the Stanford Project, a few general remarks may help place it in perspective. Three levels of CAI can be defined. Discrimination between levels is based not on hardware considerations, but principally on the complexity and sophistication of the student-system interaction. An advanced student-system interaction may be achieved with a simple teletype terminal, and the most primitive interaction may require some highly sophisticated computer programming and elaborate student terminal devices.

At the simplest interactional level are those systems that present a fixed, linear sequence of problems. Student errors may be corrected in a variety of ways, but no real-time decisions are made for modifying the flow of instructional material as a function of the student's response history. Such systems have been termed "drill-and-practice" systems and at Stanford University are exemplified by a series of fourth-, fifth-, and sixth-grade programs in arithmetic and language arts that are designed to supplement classroom instruction. These particular programs are being used in several different areas of California and also in Kentucky and Mississippi, all under control of one central computer located at Stanford University. Currently as many as 2,000 students are being run per day; it requires little imagination to see how such a system could be extended to cover the entire country. Unfortunately, I do not have time to discuss these drill-and-practice programs in this paper, but there are several recent reports describing the research (Fishman, Keller, & Atkinson, 1968; Suppes, 1966; Suppes, Jerman, & Groen, 1966).

At the other extreme of our scale characterizing student-system interactions are "dialogue" programs. Such programs are under investigation at several universities and industrial concerns, but to date progress has been extremely limited. The goal of the dialogue approach is to provide the richest possible student-system interaction where the student is free to construct natural-language responses, ask questions in an unrestricted mode, and in general exercise almost complete control over the sequence of learning events.

"Tutorial" programs lie between the above extremes of student-system interaction. Tutorial programs have the capability of real-time decision making and instructional branching contingent on a single response or on some subset of the student's response history. Such programs allow students to follow separate and diverse paths through the curriculum based on their particular performance records. The probability is high in a tutorial program that no two students will encounter exactly the same sequence of lesson materials. However, student responses are greatly restricted since they must be chosen from a prescribed set of responses, or constructed in such a manner that a relatively simple text analysis will be sufficient for their evaluation. The CAI Reading Program is tutorial in nature, and it is this level of student-interaction that will be discussed today.

The Stanford CAI System

The Stanford Tutorial System was developed under a contract between the University and the IBM Corporation. Subsequent developments by IBM of the basic system have led to what has been designated the IBM-1500 Instructional System which should soon be commercially available.

The basic system consists of a central process computer with accompanying disc-storage units, proctor stations, and an interphase to 16 student terminals. The central process computer acts as an intermediary between each student and his particular course material which is stored in one of the disc-storage units. A student terminal consists of a picture projector, a cathode ray tube (CRT), a light pen, a modified typewriter keyboard, and an audio system which can play prerecorded messages (see Figure 1).

The CRT is essentially a television screen on which alpha-numeric characters and a limited set of graphics (i.e., simple line drawings) can be generated under computer control. The film projector is a rear-view projection device which permits us to display still pictures in black and

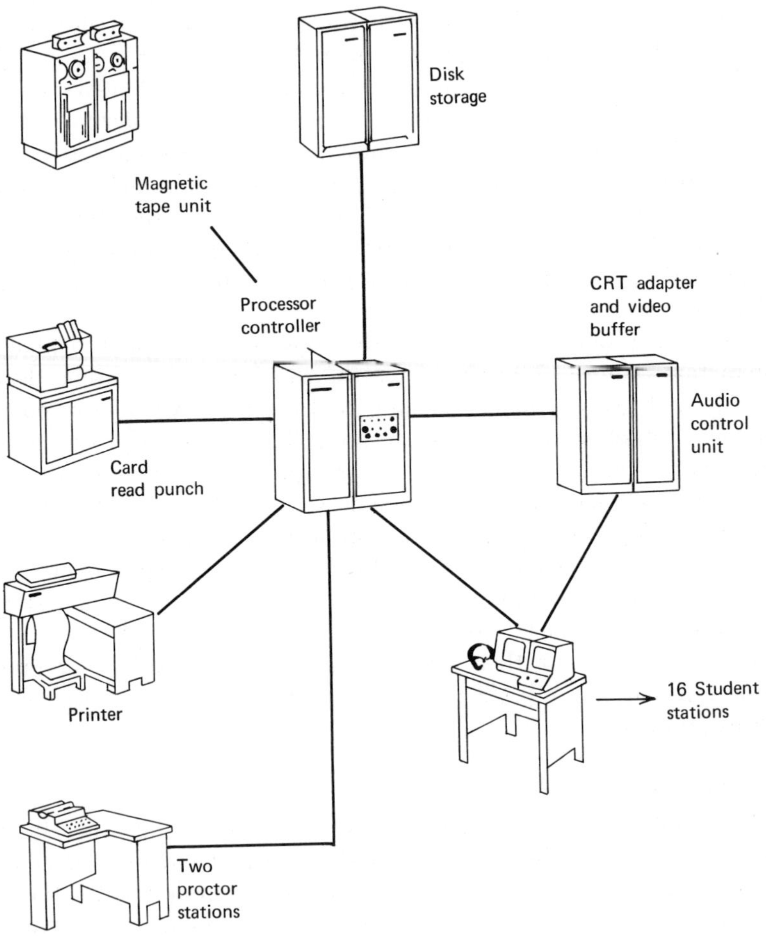

FIGURE 1. System configuration for Stanford CAI System.

white or color. Each film strip is stored in a self-threading cartridge and contains over 1,000 images which may be accessed very quickly under computer control. The student receives audio messages via a high-speed device capable of selecting any number of messages varying in length from a few seconds to over 15 minutes. The audio messages are stored in tape cartridges which contain approximately 2 hours of messages and, like the film cartridge, may be changed very quickly. To gain the student's attention, an arrow can be placed at any point on the CRT and moved in synchronization with an audio message to emphasize given words or phrases, much like the "bouncing ball" in a singing cartoon.

The major response device used in the reading program is the light pen, which is simply a light-sensitive probe. When the light pen is placed on the CRT, coordinates of the position touched are sensed as a response and recorded by the computer. Responses may also be entered into the system through the typewriter keyboard. However, only limited use has been made of this response mode in the reading program. This is not to minimize the value of keyboard responses, but rather to admit that we have not as yet addressed ourselves to the problem of teaching first-grade children to handle a typewriter keyboard.

The CAI System controls the flow of information and the input of student responses according to the instructional logic built into the curriculum materials. The sequence of events is roughly as follows: The computer assembles the necessary commands for a given instructional sequence from a disc-storage unit. The commands involve directions to the terminal device to display a given sequence of symbols on the CRT, to present a particular image on the film projector, and to play a specific audio message. After the appropriate visual and auditory materials have been presented, a "ready" signal indicates to the student that a response is expected. Once a response has been entered, it is evaluated and, on the basis of this evaluation and the student's past history, the computer makes a decision as to what materials will subsequently be presented. The time-sharing nature of the system allows us to handle 16 students simultaneously and to cycle through these evaluative steps so rapidly that from a student's viewpoint it appears that he is getting immediate attention from the computer whenever he inputs a response.

The CAI Reading Curriculum

The flexibility offered by this computer system is of value only if the curriculum materials make sense both in terms of the logical organization of the subject matter and the psychology of the learning processes involved. Time does not permit a detailed discussion of the rationale behind the curriculum that we have developed. Let me simply say that our approach to initial reading can be characterized as applied psycholinguistics. Hypotheses about the reading process and the nature of learning to read have been formulated on the basis of linguistic information, observations of language use, and an analysis of the function of the written code. These hypotheses have been tested in a series of pilot studies structured to simulate actual teaching situations. On the basis of these experimental findings, the hypotheses have been modified, retested, and ultimately incorporated into the curriculum as principles dictating the format and flow of the instructional sequence. Of course, this statement is somewhat of an idealization, since very little curriculum material can be said to have been the perfect end product of rigorous empirical evaluation. We would claim, however, that the fundamental tenets of the Stanford reading program have been formulated and modified on the basis of considerable empirical evidence. It seems probable that these will be further modified as more data accumulate.

The introduction of new words from one level of the curriculum to the next is dictated by a number of principles (Rodgers, 1967). These principles are specified in terms of a basic unit that we have called the vocalic center group (VCG). The VCG in English is defined as a vowel nucleus with zero to three preceding and zero to four following consonants. The sequencing of new vocabulary is determined by the length of the VCG units, and the regularity of the orthographic and phonological correspondences. Typical of the principles are the following:

1. VCG sets containing single consonant elements are introduced before those containing consonant clusters (*tap* and *rap* before *trap*).
2. VCG sets containing initial consonant clusters are introduced before those containing final consonant clusters (*stop* before *post*).
3. VCG sets containing check (short) vowels are introduced before those containing letter name (long) vowels (*met* and *mat* before *meat* or *mate*).
4. Single VCG sequences are introduced before multiple VCG sequences (*mat* before *matter, stut* before *stutter*).

More detailed rules are required to determine the order for introducing specific vowels and consonants within a VCG pattern, and for introducing specific VCG patterns in polysyllabic words. These rules frequently represented a compromise between linguistic factors, pattern productivity, item frequency, and textual "usefulness," in that order of significance.

The instructional materials are divided into eight levels each composed of about 32 lessons.[2] The lessons are designed so that the average

[2] For a detailed account of the curriculum materials see Wilson and Atkinson (1967) and Rodgers (1967). See also Atkinson and Hansen (1966) and Hansen and Rodgers (1965).

student will complete one in approximately 30 minutes, but this can vary greatly with the fast student finishing much sooner and the slow student sometimes taking 2 hours or more if he hits most of the remedial material. Within a lesson, the various instructional tasks can be divided into three broad areas: (*a*) decoding skills, (*b*) comprehension skills, (*c*) games and other motivational devices. Decoding skills involve such tasks as letter and letter-string identification, word list learning, phonic drills, and related types of activities. Comprehension involves such tasks as having the computer read to the child or having the child himself read sentences, paragraphs or complete stories about which he is then asked a series of questions. The questions deal with the direct recall of facts, generalization about main ideas in the story, and inferential questions which require the child to relate information presented in the story to his own experience. Finally, many different types of games are sequenced into the lessons primarily to encourage continued attention to the materials. The games are similar to those played in the classroom and are structured to evaluate the developing reading skills of the child.

Matrix Construction. To illustrate the instructional materials focusing on decoding skills let me describe a task that we have called matrix "construction." This task provides practice in learning to associate orthographically similar sequences with appropriate rhyme and alliteration patterns. Rhyming patterns are presented in the columns of the matrix, and alliteration patterns are presented in the rows of the matrix as indicated in Figure 4.

The matrix is constructed one cell at a time. The initial consonant of a CVC word is termed the initial unit, and the vowel and the final consonant are termed the final unit. The intersection of an initial unit row and a final unit column determines the entry in any cell.

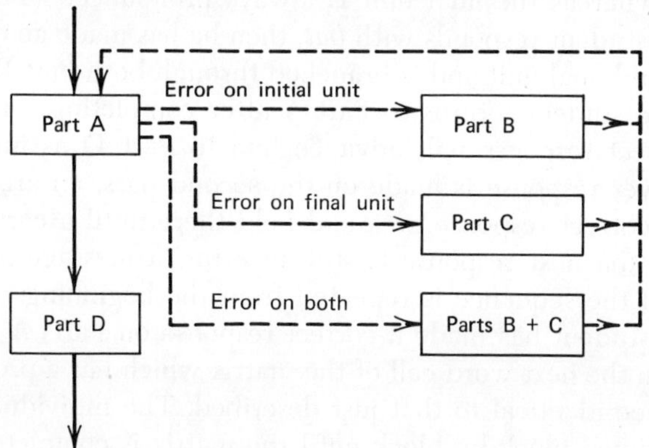

FIGURE 2. Flow chart for the construction of a cell in the matrix construction task.

The problem format for the construction of each cell is divided into four parts: Parts A and D are standard instructional sections and Parts B and C are remedial sections. The flow diagram in Figure 2 indicates that remedial Parts B and C are branches from Part A and may be presented independently or in combination.

To see how this goes, let us consider the example illustrated in Figure 3. The student first sees on the CRT the empty cell with its associated initial and final units and an array of response choices. He hears the audio message indicated by response request 1 (RR 1) in Part A of Figure 3. If the student makes the correct response (CA) (i.e., touches *ran* with his light pen), he proceeds to Part D where he sees the word written in the cell and receives one additional practice trial.

In the initial presentation in Part A, the array of multiple-choice responses is designed to identify three possible types of errors:

1. The initial unit is correct, but the final unit is not.
2. The final unit is correct, but the initial unit is not.
3. Neither the initial unit nor the final unit is correctly identified.

If, in Part A, the student responds with *fan* he is branched to remedial Part B where attention is focused on the initial unit of the cell. If a correct response is made in Part B, the student is returned to Part A for a second attempt. If an incorrect response (WA) is made in Part B, an arrow is displayed on the CRT to indicate the correct response, which the student is then asked to touch.

If, in Part A, the student responds with *rat,* he is branched to remedial Part C where additional instruction is given on the final unit of the cell. The procedure in Part C is similar to Part B. However, it should be noted that in the remedial instruction the initial letter is never pronounced (Part B), whereas the final unit is always pronounced (Part C). If, in Part A, the student responds with *bat,* then he has made an error on both the initial and final unit and is branched through both Part B and Part C.

When the student returns to Part A after completing a remedial section, a correct response will advance him to Part D as indicated. If a wrong answer response is made on the second pass, an arrow is placed beside the correct response area and held there until a correct response is made. If the next response is still an error, a message is sent to the proctor and the sequence is repeated from the beginning.

When a student has made a correct response on Parts A and D, he is advanced to the next word cell of the matrix which has a problem format and sequence identical to that just described. The individual cell building is continued block by block until the matrix is complete. The upper left-hand panel of Figure 4 indicates the CRT display for adding the next

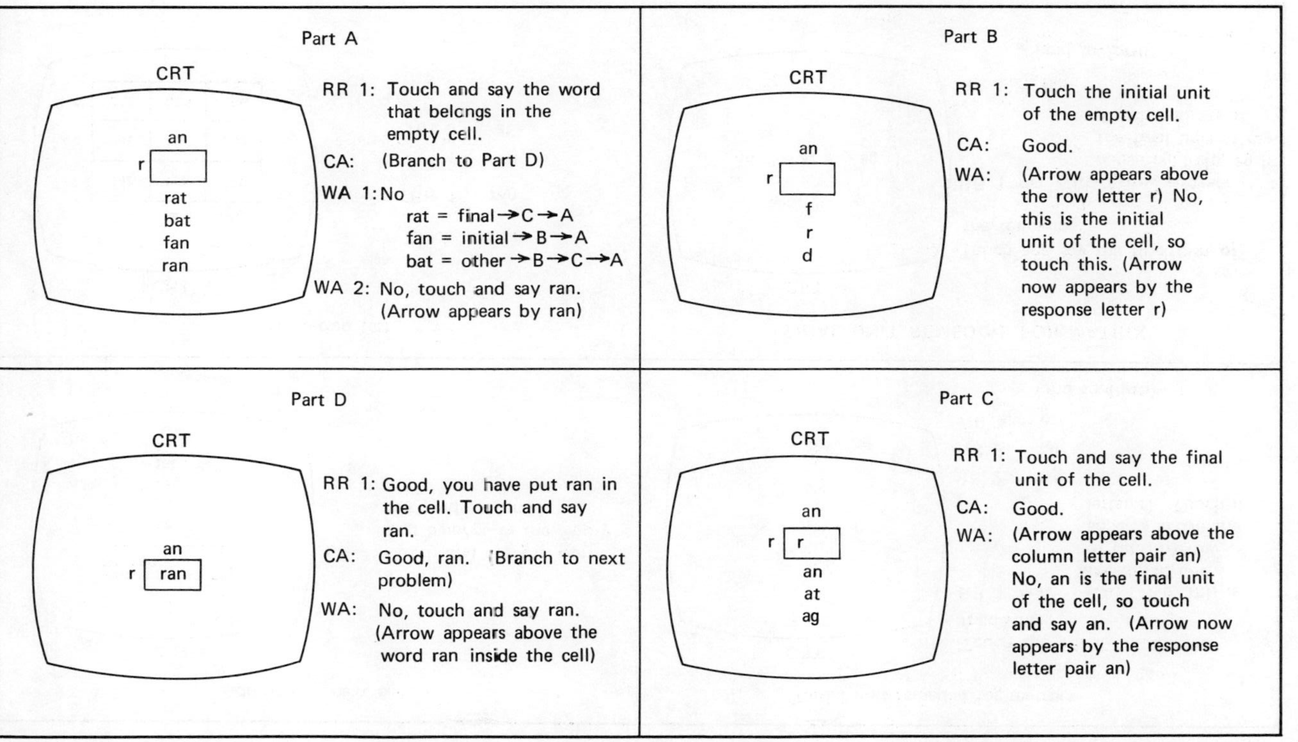

FIGURE 3. First cell of the matrix construction task.

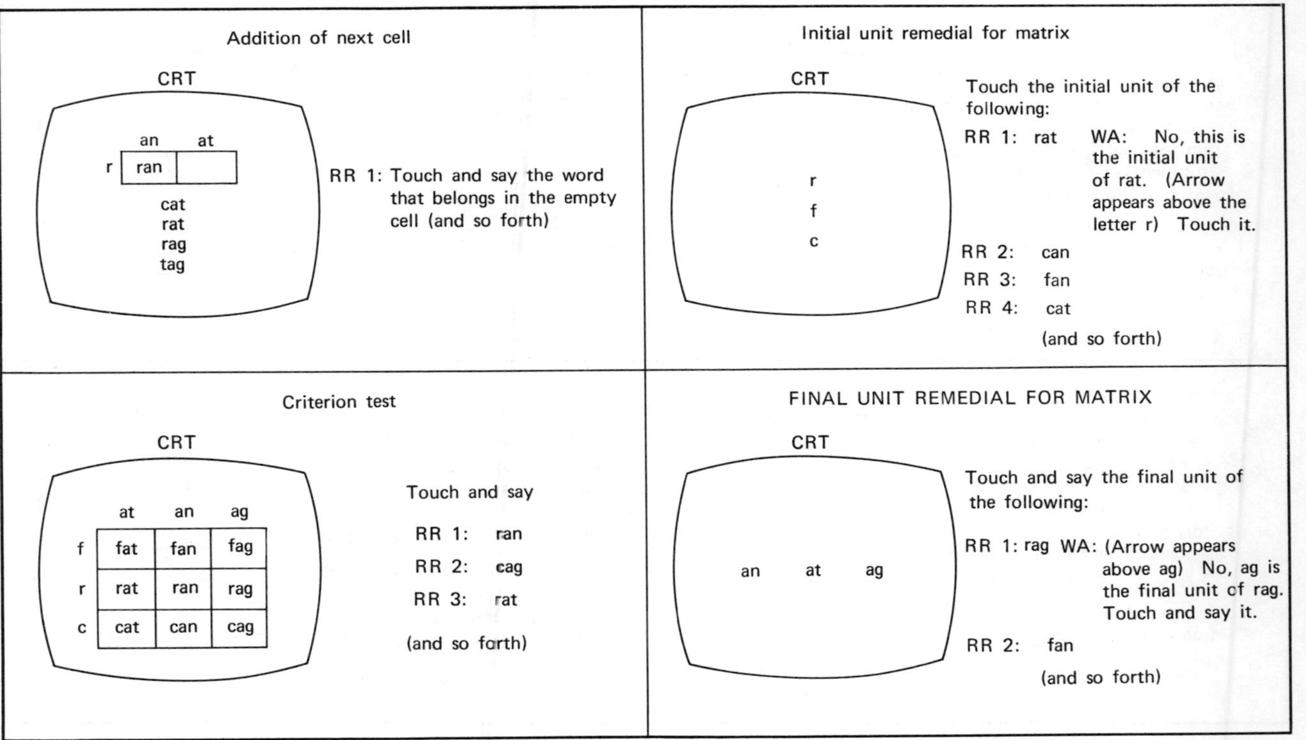

FIGURE 4. Continuation of matrix construction task.

cell in our example. The order in which row and column cells are added is essentially random.

When the matrix is complete, the entries are reordered and a criterion test is given over all cell entries. The test involves displaying the full matrix with complete cell entries as indicated in the lower left-hand panel of Figure 4. Randomized requests are made to the student to identify cell entries. Since the first pass through the full matrix is viewed as a criterion test, no reinforcement is given. Errors are categorized as initial, final, and other; if the percentage of total errors on the criterion test exceeds a predetermined value, then remedial exercises are provided of the type shown in the two right-hand panels of Figure 4. If all the errors are recorded in one category (initial or final), only the remedial material appropriate to that category is presented. If the errors are distributed over both categories, then both types of remedial material are presented. After working through one or both of the remedial sections, the student is branched back for a second pass through the criterion matrix. The second pass is a teaching trial as opposed to the initial test cycle; the student proceeds with the standard correction and optimization routines.

An analysis of performance on the matrix is still incomplete, but some preliminary results are available. On the initial pass (Part A) our students were correct about 45% of the time; however, when an error did occur, 21% of the time it involved only the final unit, 53% of the time only the initial unit, and 26% of the time both initial and final units. The pattern of performances changed markedly on the first pass through the criterion test. Here the subject was correct about 65% of the time; when an error occurred, 32% of the time it involved only the final unit, 33% of the time only the initial unit, and 35% of the time both units. Thus performance showed a significant improvement from Part A to the criterion test; equally important, initial errors were more than twice as frequent as final errors in Part A, but were virtually equal on the criterion test.

The matrix exercise is a good example of the material used in the curriculum to teaching decoding skills. We now consider two examples ("form class" and "inquiries") of tasks that are designed to teach comprehension skills.

Form Class. Comprehension of a sentence involves an understanding of English syntax. One behavioral manifestation of a child's syntactic sophistication is his ability to group words into appropriate form classes. This task provides lesson materials that teach the form-class characteristics of the words just presented in the matrix section of a lesson. The following type of problem is presented to the student (the material in the box is displayed on the CRT and below are audio messages; the child answers by appropriately placing his light pen on the CRT):

	tan	
	fat	
Dan saw the		**hat.**
	man	
	run	

Only one of the words in the column will make sense in the sentence.

Touch and say the word that belongs in the sentence.

CA: Yes, Dan saw the tan hat. Do the next one.

WA: No, tan is the word that makes sense. Dan saw the tan hat. Touch and say tan. (An arrow then appears above tan.)

The sentence is composed of words that are in the reading vocabulary of the student (i.e., they have been presented in previous or current lessons). The response set includes a word which is of the correct form class but is semantically inappropriate, two words that are of the wrong form class, and the correct word. A controlled variety of sentence types is employed, and the answer sets are distributed over all syntactic slots within each sentence type. Responses are categorized in rather broad terms as *nouns, verbs, modifiers,* and *other.* The response data can be examined for systematic errors over a large number of items. Examples of the kinds of questions that can be asked are: (a) Are errors for various form classes in various sentence positions similarly distributed? (*b*) How are response latencies affected by the syntactic and serial position of the response set within the sentence? Answers to these and other questions should provide information that will permit more systematic study of the relationship of sentence structure to reading instruction.

Inquiries. Individual words in sentences may constitute unique and conversationally correct answers to questions. These questions take the interrogative "Who . . . ? What . . . ? How . . . ?" etc. The ability to select the word in a sentence that uniquely answers one of these questions demonstrates one form of reading comprehension. The inquiry exercises constitute an assessment of this reading comprehension ability. In the following example, the sentence "John hit the ball" is displayed on the CRT accompanied by these audio messages:

Touch and say the word that answers the question.

RR 1 Who hit the ball?

CA: Yes, the word "John" tells us who hit the ball.

WA: No, John tells us who hit the ball. Touch and say John. (An arrow then appears on the CRT above John.)

RR 2 What did John hit?

CA: Yes, the word "ball" tells us what John hit.
WA: No, ball tells us what John hit. Touch and say ball. (An arrow then appears above ball.)

As in the form-class section, each sentence is composed of words from the student's reading vocabulary. A wide variety of sentence structures is utilized, beginning with simple subject-verb-object sentences and progressing to structures of increasing complexity. Data from this task bear on several hypotheses about comprehension. If comprehension is equated with a correct response to an inquiry question, then the following statements are verified by our data: (*a*) Items for which the correct answer is in the medial position of the sentence are more difficult to comprehend than items in the initial or final positions; final position items are easier to comprehend than items in the initial position. (*b*) Items for which the correct answer is an adjective are more difficult to comprehend than items in which the correct answer is a noun or verb; similarly nouns are more difficult than verbs. (*c*) Longer sentences, measured by word length, are more difficult to comprehend than shorter sentences.

These are only a few examples of the types of tasks used in the reading curriculum, but they indicate the nature of the student-system interaction. What is not illustrated by these examples is the potential for long-term optimization policies based on an extended response history from the subject. We shall return to this topic later.

Some Results from the First Year of Operation

The Stanford CAI Project is being conducted at the Brentwood School in the Ravenswood School District (East Palo Alto, California). There were several reasons for selecting this school. It had sufficient population to provide a sample of well over 100 first-grade students. The students were primarily from "culturally disadvantaged" homes. And the past performance of the school's principal and faculty had demonstrated a willingness to undertake educational innovations.

Computerized instruction began in November of 1966 with half of the first-grade students taking reading via CAI and the other half, which functioned as a control group, being taught reading by a teacher in the classroom. The children in the control group were not left out of the project, for they took mathematics from the CAI system instead. The full analysis of the student data is a tremendous task which is still underway. However, a few general results have already been tabulated that provide some measure of the program's success.

Within the lesson material there is a central core of problems which we have termed main-line problems. These are problems over which each student must exhibit mastery in one form or another. Main-line problems may be branched around by successfully passing certain screening tests, or they may be met and successfully solved; they may be met with incorrect responses, in which case the student is branched to remedial material. The first year of the project ended with a difference between the fastest and slowest student of over 4,000 main-line problems completed. The cumulative response curves for the fastest, median, and slowest students are given in Figure 5. Also of interest is the rate of progress during the course of the year. Figure 6 presents the cumulative number of problems completed per hour on a month-by-month basis again for the fastest, median, and slowest student. It is interesting to note that the rate measure was essentially constant over time for increase for the fast student.

From the standpoint of both the total number of problems completed during the year and rate of progress, it appears that the CAI curriculum

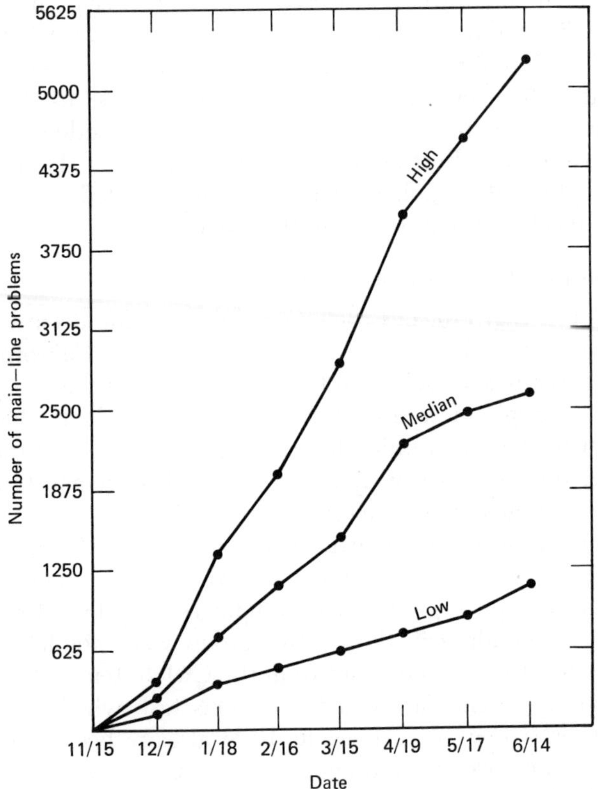

FIGURE 5. Cumulative number of main-line problems for fastest, median, and slowest student.

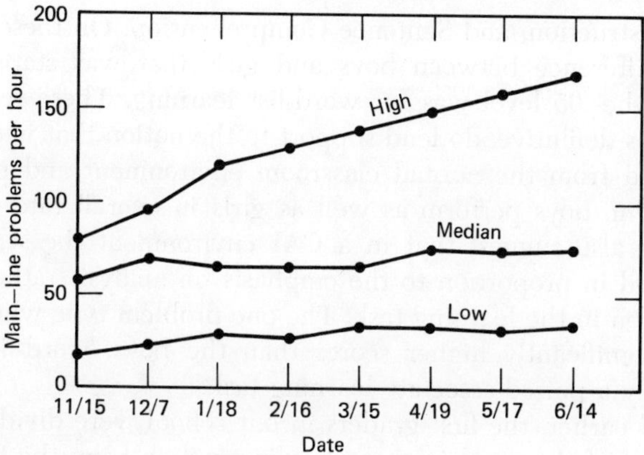

FIGURE 6. Cumulative rate of progress for fastest, median, and slowest student.

is responsive to individual differences. The differences noted above must not be confused with a variation in rate of response. The difference in response rate among students was very small. The average response rate was approximately four per minute and was not correlated with a student's rate of progress through the curriculum. The differences in total number of main-line problems completed can be accounted for by the amount of remedial material, the optimization routines, and the number of accelerations for the different students.

It has been a common finding that girls generally acquire reading skills more rapidly than boys. The sex differences in reading performance have been attributed, at least in part, to the social organization of the classroom and to the value and reward structures of the predominantly female primary grade teachers. It has also been argued on developmental grounds that first-grade girls are more facile in visual memorization than boys of the same age, and that this facility aids the girls in the sight-word method of vocabulary acquisition commonly used in basal readers. If these two arguments are correct, then one would expect that placing students in a CAI environment and using a curriculum which emphasizes analytic skills, as opposed to rote memorization, would minimize sex differences in reading. In order to test this hypothesis, the rate of progress scores were statistically evaluated for sex effects. The result, which was rather surprising, is that there was no difference between male and female students in rate of progress through the CAI curriculum.

Sex differences however might be a factor in accuracy of performance. To test this notion the final accuracy scores on four standard problem types were examined. The four problem types, which are representative of the entire curriculum, were Letter Identification, Word List Learning,

Matrix Construction, and Sentence Comprehension. On these four tasks, the only difference between boys and girls that was statistically significant at the .05 level was for word-list learning. These results, while by no means definitive, do lend support to the notion that when students are removed from the normal classroom environment and placed on a CAI program, boys perform as well as girls in overall rate of progress. The results also suggest that in a CAI environment the sex difference is minimized in proportion to the emphasis on analysis rather than rote memorization in the learning task. The one problem type where the girls achieved significantly higher scores than the boys, word-list learning, is essentially a paired-associate learning task.

As noted earlier, the first graders in our school were divided into two groups. Half of them received reading instruction from the CAI system; the other half did not (they received mathematics instruction instead). Both groups were tested extensively using conventional instruments before the project began and again near the end of the school year. The two groups were not significantly different at the start of the year. Table 1

Table 1
Posttest Results for Experimental and Control Groups

Test	Experimental	Control	p Value
California Achievement Test			
Vocabulary	45.91	38.10	<.01
Comprehension	41.45	40.62	—
Total	45.63	39.61	<.01
Hartley Reading Test			
Form class	11.22	9.00	<.05
Vocabulary	19.38	17.05	<.01
Phonetic discrimination	30.88	25.15	<.01
Pronunciation			
Nonsense word	6.03	2.30	<.01
Word	9.95	5.95	<.01
Recognition			
Nonsense word	18.43	15.25	<.01
Word	19.61	16.60	<.01

presents the results for some of the tests that were administered at the end of the year. As inspection of the table will show, the group that received reading instruction via CAI performed significantly better on all of the posttests except for the comprehension subtest of the California Achievement Test. These results are most encouraging. Further, it should be noted that at least some of the factors that might result in a "Hawthorne phenomenon" are not present here; the "control" group was exposed to CAI experience in their mathematics instruction. While that may leave room for some effects in their reading, it does remove the chief objection, since these students also had reason to feel that special attention was being given to them. It is of interest to note that the average Stanford-Binet IQ score for these students (both experimental and control) is 89.[3]

Owing to systems and hardware difficulties, our program was not in full operation until late in November of 1966. Initially, students were given a relatively brief period of time per day on the terminals. This period was increased to 20 minutes after the first 6 weeks; in the last month we allowed students to stay on the terminal 30 to 35 minutes. We wished to find out how well first-grade students would adapt to such long periods of time. They adapt quite well, and next year we plan to use 30-minute periods for all students throughout the year. This may seem like a long session for a first-grader, but our observations suggest that their span of attention is well over a half hour if the instructional sequence is truly responsive to their response inputs. This year's students had a relatively small number of total hours on the system. We hope that by beginning in the early fall and using half-hour periods, we will be able to give each student at least 80 to 90 hours on the terminals next year.

I do not have time to discuss the social-psychological effects of introducing CAI into an actual school setting. However, systematic observations have been made by a trained clinical psychologist, and a report is being prepared. To preview this report, it is fair to say that the students, teachers, and parents were quite favorable to the program.

Nor will time permit a detailed account of the various optimization routines used in the reading curriculum. But since this topic is a major focus of our research effort, it requires some discussion here. As noted earlier, the curriculum incorporates an array of screening and sequencing procedures designed to optimize learning. These optimization schemes vary in terms of the range of curriculum included, and it has been convenient to classify them as either short- or long-term procedures. Short-term procedures refer to decision rules that are applicable to specific problem formats and utilize the very recent response history of a subject to determine what instructional materials to present next. Long-term optimization procedures are applicable to diverse units of the curriculum and utilize a summarized form of the subject's complete response record to specify his future path through major instructional units.

As an example of a short-term optimization procedure, consider one

[3] More details on these and other analyses may be found in Atkinson (1967) and Wilson and Atkinson (1967).

that follows directly from a learning theoretic analysis of the reading task involved (Groen & Atkinson, 1966). Suppose that a list of m words is to be taught to the child, and it has been decided that instruction is to be carried out using the picture-to-word format described earlier. In essence, this problem format involves a series of discrete trials, where on each trial a picture illustrating the word being taught is presented on the projector screen and three words (including the word illustrated) are presented on the CRT. The student makes a response from among these words, and the trial is terminated by telling him the correct answer. If x trials are allocated for this type of instruction (where x is much larger than m), how should they be used to maximize the amount of learning that will take place? Should the m items be presented an equal number of times and distributed randomly over the x trials, or are there other strategies that take account of idiosyncratic features of a given subject's response record? If it is assumed that the learning process for this task is adequately described by the one-element model of stimulus sampling theory, and there is evidence that this is the case, then the optimal presentation strategy can be prescribed. The optimal strategy is initiated by presenting the m items in any order on the first m trials, and a continuation of this strategy is optimal over the remaining $x - m$ trials if, and only if, it conforms to the following rules.

1. For every item, set the count at 0 at the beginning of trial $m + 1$.
2. Present an item at a given trial if, and only if, its count is *least* among the counts for all items at the beginning of the trial.
3. If several items are eligible under Rule 2, select from these the item that has the smallest number of presentations; if several items are still eligible, select with equal probability from this set.
4. Following a trial, increase the count for presented item by 1 if the subject's response was correct, but set it at 0 if the response was incorrect.

Even though these decision rules are fairly simple, they would be difficult to implement without the aid of a computer. Data from this year's experiment establish that the above strategy is better than one that presents the items equally often in a fixed order.

This is only one example of the type of short-term optimization strategies that are used in the reading curriculum. Some of the other schemes are more complex, involving the application of dynamic programming principles (Groen & Atkinson, 1966), and use information not only about the response history but also the speed of responding. In some cases the optimization schemes can be derived directly from mathematical models of the learning process, whereas others are not tied to theoretical analyses but are based on intuitive considerations that seem promising.[4]

Even if short-term optimization strategies can be devised which are effective, a total reading curriculum that is optimal still has not been achieved. It is, of course, possible to optimize performance on each unit of the curriculm while, at the same time, sequencing through the units in an order that is not particularly efficient for learning. The most significant aspect of curriculum development is with regard to long-term optimization procedures, where the subject's total response history can be used to determine the best order for branching through major instructional units and also the proper balance between drill and tutorial activities. It seems clear that no theory of instruction is likely to use all the information we have on a student to make instructional decisions from one moment to the next. Even for the most sophisticated long-term schemes, only a sample of the subject's history is going to be useful. In general, the problem of deciding on an appropriate sample of the history is similar to the problem of finding an observable statistic that provides a good estimate of a population parameter. The observable history sample may be regarded as an estimate of the student's state of learning. A desirable property for such a history sample would be for it to summarize all information concerning the current learning state of the student so that no elaboration of the history would provide additional information. In the theory of statistical inference, a statistic with an analogous property is called a sufficient statistic. Hence, it seems appropriate to call an observable sample history with this property a "sufficient history."

In the present version of the reading curriculum, several long-term optimization procedures have been introduced with appropriate sufficient histories. As yet, the theoretical rationale for these procedures has not been thoroughly worked out, and not enough data have been collected to evaluate their effectiveness. However, an analysis of long-term optimization problems, and what data we do have, has been instructive and has suggested a number of experiments that need to be carried out this year. It is my hope that such analyses, combined with the potential for educational research under the highly controlled conditions offered by CAI, will lay the groundwork for a theory of instruction that is useful to the educator. Such a theory of instruction will have to be based on a model of the learning process that has broad generality and yet yields detailed predictions when applied to specific tasks.

[4] The learning models and optimization methods that underlie much of the reading curriculum are discussed in Atkinson and Shiffrin (1968), Groen and Atkinson (1966), Rodgers (1967), and Wilson and Atkinson (1967).

In my view, the development of a viable theory of instruction and the corresponding learning theory will be an interactive enterprise, with advances in each area influencing the concepts and data base in the other. For too long, psychologists studying learning have shown little interest in instructional problems, whereas educators have made only primitive and superficial applications of learning theory. Both fields would have advanced more rapidly if an appropriate interchange of ideas and problems had existed. It is my hope that prospects for CAI, as both a tool for research and a mode of instruction, will act as a catalyst for a rapid evolution of new concepts in learning theory as well as a corresponding theory of instruction.

References

Atkinson, R. C., & Hansen, D. N. Computer-assisted instruction in initial reading: The Stanford Project. *Reading Research Quarterly,* 1966, **2**, 5–25.

Atkinson, R. C., & Shiffrin, R. M. Human memory: A proposed system and its control processes. In K. W. Spence & J. T. Spence (Eds.), *The psychology of learning and motivation: Advances in research and theory.* Vol. 2. New York: Academic Press, 1968, in press.

Fishman, E. J., Keller, L., & Atkinson, R. C. Massed vs. distributed practice in computerized spelling drills. *Journal of Educational Psychology,* 1968, **59**, in press.

Groen, G. J., & Atkinson, R. C. Models for optimizing the learning process. *Psychological Bulletin,* 1966, **66**, 309–320.

Hansen, D. N., & Rodgers, T. S. An exploration of psycholinguistic units in initial reading. Technical Report 74, 1965, Stanford University, Institute for Mathematical Studies in the Social Sciences.

Rodgers, T. S. Linguistic considerations in the design of the Stanford computer-based curriculum in initial reading. Technical Report 111, 1967, Stanford University, Institute for Mathematical Studies in the Social Sciences.

Suppes, P. The uses of computers in education. *Scientific American,* 1966, **215**, 206–221.

Suppes, P., Jerman, M., & Groen, G. J. Arithmetic drills and review on a computer-based teletype. *Arithmetic Teacher,* 1966, April, 303–308.

Wilson, H. A., & Atkinson, R. C. Computer-based instruction in initial reading: A progress report on the Stanford project. Technical Report 119, 1967, Stanford University, Institute for Mathematical Studies in the Social Sciences. In H. Levin & J. Williams, Eds., *Basic Studies in reading.* New York: Harper & Row, Publishers, 1970.

7.3 The Automation of Knowledge

Lewis Mumford

"Many of us have now come to regard automation as the climax stage of human culture." "The proper name for automation is organized impotence." "Today our fundamental irreducible unit is not the atom, but the human personality." Mumford feels that man has given himself over to automation to the extent that he no longer holds the central position as actor and director in the historic drama. If the question of human autonomy is not handled swiftly, he feels that we shall soon find that the last word in automation is Automatic Man!

This article is based on an address presented by Mr. Mumford at the Opening General Session of the Nineteenth National Conference on Higher Education, sponsored by the Association for Higher Education, Chicago, April 19, 1964. Author of over 20 books, among them the National Book Award winner, *The City in History*, and recently senior fellow at the Center for Advanced Studies, Wesleyan University, Mr. Mumford offers a challenge to educators which has special relevance to readers of AVCR. Convinced that the last word in automation is "Automatic Man," that our society's eagerness to automate leads to the loss of human personality, Mr. Mumford exhorts educators to the task of making "the genuine goods derived from the automation of knowledge subservient to the superior, history-laden functions and purposes of human culture." Reader response to this article will be welcomed for possible publication in a future issue of AVCR.

SOURCE. Lewis Mumford, "The Automation of Knowledge," *AV Communication Review*, **12**, 3 (Fall 1964).

The problems I purpose to bring to your attention first shaped themselves in the course of preparing a book on which I have long been at work, as a historian of technology, on the human origins of mechanization. In tracing the machine back to its earliest manifestations in the great human machines that built the pyramids and canals and irrigation works of the Bronze Age, I found that these wonderful feats were coupled to—and repeatedly nullified by—the equally destructive and irrational activities of the military machines that came into existence at the same time.

Even at the earliest stage, beneath the imposing façade of mechanical order that made it possible to build the Great Pyramid of Gezeh with almost a watchmaker's accuracy, I discovered all sorts of demonic compulsions and infantile ambitions, which I recognized as very similar to those that have erupted again in our own age under a similar magnification of human power and technical adroitness.

Without my exploration of this historic background, I should not have found it possible, perhaps, to come to grips with present-day forces, which have turned so many of our achievements in science and technics into monumental absurdities. But, in our time, I detected a peculiar factor that had no parallel in the Pyramid Age: the automation of knowledge. The institutions that have promoted this special kind of automation are now the main power plants and the control centers of the grand system of mechanized production and depersonalized consumption and machine-fed leisure that characterizes our Western way of life. Nowhere has this become more evident than in our recent educational programs.

Those who have been instrumental in the automation of knowledge, from Francis Bacon onward, have from the beginning coupled this method with the economy of abundance that mankind for so many ages had vainly dreamed of achieving: an economy under which, as Aristotle said, the shuttle would weave by itself, the lyre would play by itself, and loaves of bread would spring out of the oven untouched by human hands. The dreams of such an economy, with its promise of wealth and freedom for all, date back to the earliest urban civilizations; and it was then that other dreams that have now been realized—the dream of human flight, of instantaneous communication, of total control over the physical environment—were first expressed as heavenly marvels in art and fable. Our age has seen those dreams come true. Powers that only the gods of the Bronze Age possessed are now our daily commonplaces. So perhaps it is no wonder that the leading exponents of automation, inflamed by their success and still prompted by ancient fantasies of godlike omnipotence and omniscience, now seek to extend automation to every other human activity.

But as often happens when fairy stories come true, we are at last beginning to discover that there was a concealed catch in the original promise. The scientific ideology that made possible these colossal benefits, we now find, cannot be easily attached to other valid and purposeful human ends. In order to enjoy all these abundant goods, one must strictly conform to the dominant system, faithfully consuming all that it produces, meekly accepting its quantitative scale of values, never once demanding the most essential of all human goods, an ever more meaningful life, for that is precisely what automation, by its very nature and on its own strict premises, is utterly impotent to produce. This is not so strange an outcome as it might at first seem, for when we examine the basic ideology of modern science, as formulated in the seventeenth century, we find that the very words *human, history, value, purpose,* and *end* were excluded as extraneous to, indeed undesirable for, any method of quantitative measurement and statistical prediction.

This situation, if I read it aright, constitutes the basic problem of education today. Shall we extend the processes of automation into every department of our lives and, in order to achieve this dubious result, proceed more rapidly than ever with the automation of knowledge; or shall we bring back, as essential to the further development of life, the complex organic components, above all the full human personality, that we have too peremptorily repressed and rejected? Shall we, in other words, restore man to his central position as the actor and director in a historic drama; or shall we banish him into the wings, first as a mere agent of an automatic control system, but eventually as a desperately bored supernumerary with no more active responsibility than a union stagehand in a modern drama that doesn't use scenery? Unless we tackle this question swiftly, we shall soon find that the last word in automation is Automatic Man.

Before going any further with this problem, let me first challenge the notion that automation is in any sense a final good, so beneficial in every aspect that the process must be hastened and extended relentlessly into every field. If the human organism had developed solely on that principle, the reflexes and the autonomic nervous system would have absorbed all the functions of the brain, and man would have been left without a thought in his head. Organic and human modes of behavior are infinitely more complex than automatic systems; and what makes them so is the margin of choice, the freedom to commit and correct errors, to explore unfrequented paths, to incorporate unpredictable accidents with self-defined purposes, to anticipate the unexpected and to "plan the impossible"—all traits that no efficient, automatic system can countenance. In human organisms the whole personality may intervene at any moment to change the tempo or alter the basic pattern.

Already most of us have witnessed the often comical embarrassment of automation, as currently employed in industry, education, and government today; too well we know its sad inability to function in situations that do not conform to its own rigid code of operation. But despite these limitations most people still regard the whole process of automation as a highly desirable one, or, if not actually desirable, then inevitable and inescapable.

Most of our fellow citizens, unless they are threatened with the loss of their jobs, are not ready to question the inevitability of eventual total automation. Not only do they look forward—as all reasonable men should—to the transference of much burdensome, servile labor to the machine, but they are equally eager to turn as many other human functions as possible over to machines, fascinated, indeed abjectly hypnotized, by their superior accuracy, their fantastic rapidity, their staggering productivity.

In other words, many of us have now come to regard automation as the climax stage of human culture. For the sake of achieving this climax, our leaders are eagerly turning over to our great mechanical collectives—industrial, financial, military, and not least educational—the remaining functions of life, wiping out, with no sense of the colossal loss, all natural richness and diversity, all ecological complexity, all independent human selectivity and purposefulness, though these are the basic conditions of human creativity in every department—not least, of course, in science and technology.

While the pace of mechanization and automation has accelerated during the past half century now that the method itself has been perfected, we have still to achieve a dispassionate evaluation of the results. Yet these results were accurately anticipated a full century ago by the English satirist Samuel Butler who as a young sheep rancher in New Zealand found himself with plenty of time to ruminate profitably, as no incipient Ph.D. would dare to ruminate today, on the Future of Man. Already Butler plainly saw, in a letter now printed in his notebooks, that mechanical life was displacing organic life: that because people then were already feeding their life into automatic systems, machines were taking on more of the attributes of living organisms, becoming self-operating, self-regulating, and self-directing; while man, on the other hand, was adapting himself with absurd docility, to the limitations of the machine. In short, man and the machine were merely exchanging roles. The new machine was man—but only a fractional man—writ large. The new man was the machine—or what was left over from the machine—writ small.

But what has proved quite as bad, we have now found out, is that as our system of automation becomes more perfect, the less possible it is to intervene in the process, to alter its pace, to change its direction, to limit its further extension, or to reorient its goal. Automation has a colossal qualitative defect that springs directly from its quantitative virtues: it increases probability and decreases possibility. Though the individual component of an automatic system may be programed like a punch card on a motor car assembly line to deal with variety, the system itself is so fixed and rigid that it seems little more than a neat, mechanical model of a compulsion neurosis. This system can operate in fact with only one set of goals, purely quantitative goals unrelated to organic capacity or human need—faster and faster, further and further, bigger and bigger, more and more.

When our translation of organic and human aptitudes into their system-controlled mechanical counterparts has fully taken place, man will have lost the full use of even his physical organs. There are areas in this country today where people have already lost the free use of their legs; in many California cities pedestrians are arrested on sight as suspicious characters by the police. The next step will be to imprison anyone who uses his own voice to sing instead of turning on his transistor radio; even the possibility of indulging in autonomous daydreams has already been largely taken over by centrally directed TV and radio stations whose final advance will be to extend their operations to sleep.

Why this massive translation of all organic aptitudes into mechanical counterfeits should be hailed as an improvement, I have yet to discover. Many people, for example, express pride over the fact that we have devised computers intelligent enough to play chess; but what will happen to human pride, or to the game of chess for that matter, when computers become so intelligent that they will deign to play only with other computers? If man's own life is indeed so utterly worthless, what new value does it acquire by being turned over to a machine? And if the "Brave New World" we have put together with the aid of science is, by definition, a world without values, on what strange logical principle can we assign value to science or automation? When you empty out the proper life of man, all that's left is emptiness.

My purpose is to challenge, as scientifically outdated as well as humanly inadequate, the whole constellation of mechanical ideas that now dominate our civilization, beginning with the automation of knowledge. The notion of concentrating on power, profit, and productivity alone and of seeking to establish total control over both man and his environment dates back to the Pyramid Age when the center of this original pyramid of power, the Pharaoh, was sustained by the official religion in the paranoid delusion that he was a god. This gross delusion lay behind the effective political and technical regimentation that made possible the construction of the great pyramids, those monuments of technological perfection and human futility; and the irrational nature of that drive, irrational in the sense that it ignored the complex ecological cooperations favorable to human development, has not been altered today, now that Nobel Prize winners have reconstructed the ancient pyramids in the form of space rockets, designed to reach the same heaven by a new route. But so completely has automation taken over today that even the personality of the divine King, who was necessary to the older system, has been eliminated. Only the paranoid ambitions and the docile conformities now remain.

In challenging these moribund conceptions, I shall suggest that our present system of higher education, focused almost exclusively on the unlimited mass production of scientific truths, is utterly incapable of dealing with the most pressing problem of our age: namely that of coping with the larger system of automation of which it is a part. Our task, I shall urge, is rather to restore to man, as the central agent and creator, the wide span of capabilities and potentialities he voluntarily surrendered or suppressed when he took it upon himself to develop the machine and consigned to automations the absolute powers once exercised by divine kings. On my reading, the mischief we now confront began when the scientific leaders of Western thought dismissed as unworthy of their attention that immense fund of accumulated human experience which was embodied in language, religion, art, literature, morals, folklore, and in the annals of human history as a whole. Without that foundation, it is impossible to create fully dimensioned human beings.

This deliberate reaction of that large realm of human life which cannot be explored, except peripherally, by the scientific method was made with open eyes, in so many declared words, when the Royal Society was founded in London in 1660; but the ground for this rejection had already been stated by René Descartes in his "Discourse on Method." By turning the subjective contributions of man over to theology and poetry, the scientist said, in effect, that for him the inner world of man and the rich fabrications of human culture no longer mattered. At the time scientists had excellent practical reasons for making such a temporary simplification and clarification: this was a first step toward fabricating the exact knowledge needed to interpret physical phenomena and control mechanical operations. But how can we still cling to this naïve limitation today, in a period during which man's inward realm, with all its creative and destructive possibilities, has been opened up and audaciously explored by Freud, Jung, and their followers? To do this is to forget how far science itself has traveled since the seventeenth century.

When the procedures of science were originally laid down, both Bacon and Descartes correctly anticipated that the new method would in time transform every aspect of human life. That prophecy and hope have been more than fulfilled. But what no one foresaw was that the ultimate effect of using an underdimensioned mechanical model, capable of effecting the mass production of both goods and knowledge, ultimately would be to introduce the process of automation into every province of existence. Still less did they suppose that the Advancement of Learning might lead to the Regression of Man. Certainly no one guessed that our vast gains in physical power would be accompanied by human impotence and frustration or that these conditions in turn would be unconsciously compensated for by massive increases in demoniac disorder, rabid violence, and psychic disintegration.

Yet all these things have been happening before our eyes, and it is fatuous to keep on thinking that there is no connection between our mechanical triumphs and our equally colossal human failures. Perhaps the most sinister aspect of our thoroughgoing increasingly compulsive automation is one that I will not explore here: the fact that this underdimensioned system of thought requires for its smooth operation equally underdimensioned men. The new operators of this system, the elite, now constitute a recognizable ideal type, that of Bureaucratic or Organization Man whose future dominance was predicted by the German sociologist Max Weber more than a generation ago. Such ideal types are now coming out of our great megalopolises of learning in large quantities as on an assembly line, cut to a uniform pattern and directly feeding into the great mechanical collectives, military or industrial, that will eagerly employ them.

As the facilities of our educational institutions expand—with their nuclear reactors, their cybernetic apparatus, their computers, their TV sets and tape recorders and learning machines, their machine-marked *yes* or *no* examination papers—the human contents necessarily shrink, for the very presence of the human personality disturbs this complex mechanism which operates increasingly as a single unit and can be managed efficiently only by remote control under centralized direction.

The only values recognized by automation are those necessary for the operation and continued expansion of the system itself. The minds that are now completely conditioned to these processing mechanisms are incapable of imagining any alternatives. Having opted for automation, they are committed to wiping out human autonomy. Not merely are the operators of our new mechanical cosmos ill at ease in the real world of cooperating organisms and self-directing personalities, but they often show active hostility toward the world of the living—if only as a neurotic tactic of self-defense.

Here, at the core of automation, lies its principal weakness, once the system becomes universal. Its exponents see no way of overcoming its deficiencies, except by a further extension of automation. Thus a large-scale automation of compulsory leisure is now in process in order to find profit-making substitutes for the pleasures of vanished work which once brought an immediate human reward. The fact is that this system as a whole, if I may use the academic slang of the day, has no "feedback" and therefore no method of evaluating its deleterious results or correcting its mistaken postulates. The give-and-take that has always existed between man and the rest of his environment and the constant dialogue that is so necessary both for self-knowledge and social cooperation have no place in an automatic regimen.

When Job's life miscarried, he was able, at least in imagination, to confront God and criticise his ways. But the suppression of personality is so complete in an automated economy that the reputed heads of our great organizations are as incapable or intervening in their operations as the lowliest file clerk. As for anyone's confronting them in person, our automatic agencies are as obscure and inaccessible as the authorities that Franz Kafka pictures in that accurate anticipatory nightmare, *The Trial.* Humanly speaking, the proper name for automation is organized impotence; and the archetypal hero of our time is no other than Eichmann, the correct functionary, the perfect bureaucrat, proud to the end that he never allowed a moral scruple or a human sentiment to keep him from carrying out the orders that came from above.

Now the radical defects could not possibly have been anticipated by those who first put together the abstract elements of automation; and though they are largely the result of the original ideological shortcomings of seventeenth century science, they have been doubled by now, being mated to much more ancient bureaucratic and military absolutisms. By attempting to eliminate the disturbing human factor, by reducing all experience to supposedly ultimate atomic components describable in terms of mass and motion, science discarded mankind's cumulative knowledge of history and biography, gave primacy to "physical" phenomena, and paid attention only to discrete passing events. The typical vice of this ideology, accordingly, is to overvalue the contemporary, the dynamic, and the novel and to neglect stability, continuity, and the cumulative time-seasoned values of both collective history and individual human experience. The scientific intelligence, however magnified by its capacity to handle abstractions, is only a partial expression of the fully dimensioned personality, not a substitute for it. Wisdom comes only from whole men who move freely over every domain proper to man, bringing past and future to bear upon the otherwise disoriented and directionless present, starving on a surfeit of undigested knowledge.

As a result of this one-sided, so-called objectivity, decisions of critical importance to the human race are being taken today on the basis of 10-year-old knowledge, confidently applied by highly disciplined specialists who too often display the shortcomings of 10-year-old minds, for they regard as a peculiar scientific merit their deliberate practice of cutting their minds off from 10,000 years of human experience and culture. Overproud of their one-generation acquisitions, they point to the fact that there are now more scientists alive than in the whole history of the world before our generation. Strangely, they seem to lack any suspicion that the vast quantity of exact knowledge now at our disposal is no guarantee whatever of our having sufficient emotional sensitiveness and moral insight to make good use of it; if anything, the exact contrary already has proved true. The current belief in mechanical quantification without constant human qualification makes a mockery of the whole educational process.

Fortunately, the original ideological framework of seventeenth century science has long been under fire. A whole generation ago Alfred North Whitehead, in his *Science and the Modern World*, published his fundamental critique of its logical naïveté and its metaphysical absurdity. Especially in advanced physics today, and perhaps still more in biology, the sacred mechanical model that for so long set the fashion for all human activities has turned out to be too crude to be present organic realities, except for limited practical applications. Physicists have finally acknowledged that even matter and energy have a history: if one stays with the chemical elements 3 billion years, one finds that some of them may become alive.

So if I feel free to speak disparagingly of the still current ideological background for the automation of knowledge, it is with the assurance that the more alert scientific minds of our generation have themselves led the way. Today our fundamental irreducible unit is not the atom, but the human personality, in all its biological complexity and cultural multiformity. And it is now plain that only by restoring the human personality to the center of our scheme of thought can mechanization and automation be brought back into the service of life. Until this happens in education, there is not a single advance in science, from the release of nuclear energy to the isolation of DNA in genetic inheritance, that may not, because of our literally absentminded automatism in applying it, bring on disastrous consequences to the human race. These consequences would have no parallel in previous history, since in both cases they would be irreversible and irretrievable. For that possible miscarriage, our educational institutions would have to take no small share of the blame.

In calling attention to the need for deliberately controlling and correcting the automation of knowledge by addressing education to larger and more central human purposes I must, I realize, cause a certain discomfort, perhaps acute pain, in many minds. Certainly I share much of this discomfort, for there are no easy answers to the problems I am raising. Who supposes that a method of thought which has been expanding its operations for three centuries, and which has in many areas produced such humanly valuable results, can be corrected and reoriented overnight?

We cannot reintroduce the historic components that have long been missing without slowing down the pace of automation. Merely to overcome the inertia of the present system may well require something like a breakdown before we shall be able to resume full control and go forward in a quite different direction, subordinating the improvement of mechanisms to the development and perfection of men. But it is high time that we recognized our situation and made a fresh start on sounder premises; and it is in the realm of higher education that, if anywhere, this change is due to begin.

In presenting this analysis, I have been sustained by the memory that I am but following in the footsteps of Henry Adams. To the credit of that great historian, he recognized half a century ago the major dangers we now confront and called the attention of his fellow historians to the seemingly automatic acceleration of extrahuman energies, by wind power, water power, coal, and electricity, which had been taking place since the thirteenth century. In a letter addressed to the teachers of history in 1910—yes, as early as 1910!—Adams foresaw that, with the discovery of radioactivity, energies on a cosmic scale would soon be available to man and that unless they were brought under human control, they would bring about the debasement of morality and the disintegration of civilization. Desperately, he urged his academic colleagues to interpret these coming events and prepare the ground for the huge political and educational transformations necessary to handle them.

I need hardly tell you how the scholarly world—even that free, sympathetic spirit, William James—reacted to this call: it was Henry Adams they thought should be placed under control, not the inordinate energies he pointed to, not this humanly defective system of thought, not this strange subjective compulsion to expand all the external instruments of power at whatever extravagant cost to living organisms and autonomous human personalities. Since the commitment to automation has grown stronger since Adams' day, I can hardly hope for a more eager response to this paper. So perhaps I would do well to remind you that Adams' predictions actually came true precisely within the time span he indicated; and it is now possible for me to back up his analysis with further evidence from the history of science itself.

The critical decision that transformed the paranoid Bronze Age fantasies of exercising unlimited control over nature and man took place through the organization of scientific discovery three and a half centuries ago. This process has recently been dated and explained, stage by stage, by a historian of science, Derek Price, in a series of Yale lectures, now in a paperback, entitled *Science Since Babylon.* By the middle of the seventeenth century the experimental method and the mathematico-physical logic of scientific thought had been formulated. The new science sought to reduce all the complexities of human experience to purely physical events which could be handled in small, isolated, controllable packets, open to exact measurement and experimental proof. On this basis scientists could increase the total body of objective knowledge by the mere addition of separate items without any need, as in organic systems, to fabricate an intelligible, over-all pattern or to unite the pieces in an effective social and moral order responsive to human needs, deliberately directed toward human development. Thus, well before the automatic machines of the nineteenth century had been invented, science had perfected in its own realm a system of subdivided labor, operating with standardized and replaceable parts, along with a progressive automation of the process of scientific discovery: the main keys to mass production in any field.

If, as scientists correctly thought, knowledge was power, then the surest way to increase external power was to increase the quantity of exact knowledge. The means for effecting this increase, Price points out, was a new mode of multiplying and communicating scientific knowledge by means of a small standard unit, the scientific paper, whereby reports on isolated observations and experiments could be promptly circulated in scientific journals. This practical device proved the effective starting point for the automation of knowledge. By now its productivity rivals anything that has been achieved in any other department of mass production. Beginning with a single journal in 1665, Price tells us that there were 100 at the beginning of the nineteenth century, 1,000 by the middle, and 10,000 by 1900. We are already on the way to achieve 100,000 journals in another century.

Here we face the great paradox of automation, put once and for all in Goethe's fable of the Sorcerer's Apprentice. Our civilization has cleverly found a magic formula for putting the academic brooms and pails of water to work by themselves, in ever-increasing quantities, at an ever-increasing speed. But we have lost the great Magician's formula for halting this process when it ceases to serve a direct human purpose, and, as a result, we are already, like the apprentice, beginning to drown in the flood. The moral is: Unless you have the power to stop an automatic process, you had better not start it. To spare ourselves humiliation over our failure to control automation, we now pretend that the automaton's purpose is our own.

In even a restricted segment of knowledge, let us say the virus diseases of the gastrointestinal tract in elderly earthworms, it is difficult for a conscientious scholar to keep his head above water. To cope with this tidal wave of knowledge our colleagues have resorted to further mechanical agents that only aggravate the original condition, because they deal only with the results of the process, not with the causes. They have created a hundred journals devoted only to abstracts of papers; and now a further abstract of all these abstracts in desperation has been proposed. At this ultimate point all that will be left of the original scientific paper will be a little vague noise, at most a title and a date, to indicate that someone has done something somewhere—heaven knows why.

For the last half century, the same process of large-scale automation has been imitated by the humanities, as a kind of status symbol, to underwrite budget requests in competition with the physical and social sciences and to provide a quantitative measure for professional promotions. So don't imagine that in their present state, the humanities, which have also been automated and depersonalized, can provide any effective means of controlling this flood or of turning it to human advantage. Whatever Sir Charles Snow may think, the two cultures are now one: both indifferent to the central concerns of man, both academically committed to automation.

Even as late as a generation ago, there was still a large margin for free activity and independent thinking within our higher education. But today, most of our institutions of higher learning are as thoroughly automated as a modern steel plant or a telephone system: the mass production of scholarly papers, discoveries, inventions, patents, students, Ph.D.'s, professors, and publicity goes on at a comparable rate; and only those who identify themselves with the goals of automation, however humanly irrelevant, are in line for promotion, for big research grants, for the political power and the financial rewards allotted to those who "go with" the system.

Now do not, I beg of you, misinterpret this factual description as mischievous satire on my part; still less must you take it as an attack either on science, scholarship, or the many exquisite present feats of electronic and cybernetic technology. No one but an idiot would belittle the immense practical benefits and the exhilarating prospects for the human spirit that science, in all its more rational moments, has opened up. All I am saying is that the automation of automation is now a demonstrable irrationality; and I suggest that this inherent defect must eventually become apparent to anyone sufficiently detached from this system—or its often excessive pecuniary rewards—to make an objective judgment.

This irrationality has been neatly summarized, with humorous exactitude, by Derek Price; for he has calculated that at the present rate of acceleration in science alone, within a couple of centuries there will be dozens of hypothetic scientists for every man, woman, child, and dog on the planet. Fortunately, ecology teaches us, under such conditions of overcrowding and stress, most of the population will have died off before it reaches this point.

In other words, if we cling to our present premises and our present methods, the whole scheme is bound to break down; and this failure is easily predictable because it will be brought on not necessarily by human rebellion, but by its own unqualified mechanical success. Does not this foreseeable outcome, already so close to fulfillment in many fields, suggest to you that there is some fundamental flaw in the whole present scheme of automating knowledge? Is it not time to work actively to preserve human autonomy in the few remaining provinces that have not yet been completely conquered and to proceed from that firm rallying point to reclaim the rich human territory that has been abjectly surrendered to automation? There are still surviving scholars in every field—people like Carl Sauer in geography, Leo Szilard[1] in physics, C. H. Waddington in biology, to serve as exemplars for postautomatic thinking and living.

The example of the noble scientist who has just died, Rachel Carson, has set us a classic standard for fully humanized thought, in which an acute scientific intelligence, stirred by deep human emotion, leads to alert moral and practical judgments that serve as a basis for effective action. Such a complete use, in thought itself, of the total human personality is not within the province of either computers or computer-minds: since it is a product of life, it requires time and experience of life for such a mind as Rachel Carson's to ripen. But the final product outweighs in significance and value far greater quantities of depersonalized research. To slow down the automation of knowledge, the best formula would be: Produce more minds like those of Michael Polanyi and Rachel Carson.

[1] Leo Szilard died on May 30, 1964.

Insofar as our colleges and universities are now expanding their physical plants in order to engage more effectively in the mass production of scientists, technicians, and engineers on the present obsolete model—I repeat, *on the present obsolete model*—they are but hastening the moment when the whole system will collapse of its own aimless and insensate productivity, even if more ominous irrational factors, such as the catastrophic misuse of nuclear energy, do not halt the automation of knowledge at a much earlier point. Are you sure then that your duty as responsible educators is to push on as fast as possible toward this culminating absurdity, this ironic "final solution"?

Perhaps I should leave the problems I have put before you with this final question. But it would be unwise if I did not, before closing, anticipate the all-but-automatic response some may be tempted to make: for the easiest way of dismissing this whole argument, even if you are troubled by it a little, would be to ask me: "*Do you suppose we can set the hands of the clock back?*" The figure of the mechanical clock, that first great triumph of automatism, is indeed wonderfully appropriate here. But it is strange that those who use it do not see that it demolishes their defense and supports the position I have taken. I have nothing against clocks. But who would harbor a clock whose hands could not be turned back—that is, a clock that could not be regulated when it went too fast in accordance with an independent standard of time? In the case of the clock, that independent standard is the daily revolution of the earth: in the case of all human institutions, including automation, our standard derives from the nature and history of man and his fathomless creative potentialities for further development.

Our task today is to make the genuine goods derived from the automation of knowledge subservient to the superior, history-laden functions and purposes of human culture. And we may well require as many centuries to develop an adequate ideology capable of uniting physical processes and organic functions with human purposes—the cosmos without and the microcosm within—as our predecessors did to produce the present sterile, underdimensioned world of the machine. There is no easy way out. No multiplication of existing facilities, no shifting of budgets from the sciences to the humanities, no interdisciplinary regrouping can possibly suffice. We must settle down to the long process of rethinking our basic premises and refabricating our whole ideological and cultural structure. But there is one thing that those of us who wield authority in education can do here and now: *We can stop saying "Yes"—so automatically!—to the automation of knowledge.*

Selected Readings

Allen, J. E. Jr., Technology and educational renewal. *Education,* 1969, **90**, 1–6.

Atkinson, R. C. and Wilson, H. A. (Eds.) *Computer-assisted instruction A book of readings.* New York: Academic Press, 1969.

Bundy, R. P. Computer-assisted instruction—where are we? *Phi Delta Kappan,* 1968, **49**, 424–429.

Coulson, J. E. Automation, electronic computers, and education. *Phi Delta Kappan,* 1966, **47**, 340–344.

Dick, W. The development and current status of computer-based instruction. *American Educational Research Journal,* 1965, **2**, 41–54.

Feldman, D. H., and Sears, P. S. Effects of computer assisted instruction on children's behavior. *Educational Technology.* 1970, **10**, 11–15.

Gagné, R. M. Educational technology as technique. *Educational Technology,* 1968, **8**, 5–13.

Hilgard, E. R. Issues within learning theory and programmed learning. *Psychology in the Schools,* 1964, **1**, 129–139.

Markle, Susan M. Individualizing programed instruction: The programer. *Teachers College Record,* 1964, **66**, 219–228.

Resnick, L. B. Programed instruction and the teaching of complex intellectual skills: Problems and prospects. *Harvard Educational Review,* 439–471.

Suppes, P. Modern learning theory and the elementary school curriculum. *American Educational Research Journal.* 1964, **1**, 79–93.

Suppes, P. Computer technology and the future of education. *Phi Delta Kappan,* 1968, **49**, 8, 420–423.

Thelen, H. A. Programed instruction: Insight vs. conditioning. *Education,* 1963, **83**, 416–420.

Thelen, H. A. Programed materials today: Critique and proposal. *Elementary School Journal,* 1963, 189–196.

Trow, W. C. Teacher and television. *Psychology in the Schools,* 1967, **4**, 246–254.

Wittich, W. A. Educational television. *Educational Perspectives,* 1962, **1**, 11–13.

PART III

Individual Differences

Part Three is confined to a discussion of individual differences in the cognitive and affective domains. Readings on characteristics such as manual dexterity, perceptual and spatial aptitude, and mechanical reasoning ability were not included because of space requirements. Certainly they are important for learning in the psychomotor domain.

In Part Two we discussed the many roles of the teacher that are so important in helping children to learn. But the input desired by the teacher is processed by children with different aptitudes, interests, attitudes, and values. Intended changes often do not come about or are modified. If there are thirty pupils in a class, it is possible that the teacher's explanations, solutions, or directions may be interpreted in thirty different ways. Teachers who have a knowledge of individual differences adjust teaching to these differences, often with excellent results.

Growth and development determine readiness characteristics for learning. In Chapter 8, the papers provide a continuous picture of development from early childhood through adolescence. The emphasis in Tuddenham's paper is on cognitive growth. His discussion of Piaget's work emphasizes how growth promotes differences in pupil's ability to learn. Dr. Eisenberg shows how affective development is a crucial factor in the adolescent stage. Wolfle, in Chapter 9, makes a plea for recognizing varied talent. Guilford's paper in this volume is a summary of his progress since his 1959 statement to members of the American Psychological Association. At that time he reported on his structure of the intellect, which he presented by a model of some one hundred twenty different abilities. Various kinds of instruments, developed to measure some of these abilities, were discussed. His aim is to assess the intellect with instruments that sample multiple talent; individuals with varied abilities will be identified along with their potential for contributions to society.

In 1928 E. K. Wickman discovered that there was a difference of opinion between teachers and mental-health workers in their evaluation of the seriousness of behavioral problems. Other investigators have reported a diminishing of this discrepancy since that time, but some differences continue. In the research of Tolar et al., although the design was improved over previous studies, differences were also found between teachers and psychologists in regard to the evaluation of certain affective characteristics. This reading was included to emphasize the importance of a teacher's valid perception of individual differences.

Other affective characteristics that determine achievement are alienation, anxiety, reflection-impulsivity, and self-concept. These individual differences among learners are all subject to change. Research evidence indicates that each of these characteristics can be modified to effect increased achievement.

CHAPTER 8

Growth: Its Relationship to Teaching and Learning

8.1 Jean Piaget and the World of the Child

Read D. Tuddenham

Jean Piaget is currently Professor of psychology at the University of Geneva and at the Sorbonne. For forty years he has been engaged in a program of research and theory building that portends a lasting influence on education.

The writings of Piaget are difficult to understand. Dr. Tuddenham has given us a clear and concise summary of how Piaget believes the child acquires a coherent organization of the world about him. Important individual differences in readiness for learning are determined by the child's progress within this growth pattern.

To throw Piaget's contributions into sharper focus, let us digress briefly to consider the epistemological problem, one of the great imponderables which have engaged men's attention at least since the golden age of Greek philosophy. Now philosophers often ask questions in ways which admit of no final answer. They thus get a great deal of mileage out of them, and the same controversies keep recurring, century after century. For our purpose we need go no further back than the views of

SOURCE. Abridged from Read D. Tuddenham, "Jean Piaget and the World of the Child," *American Psychologist*, XXI, 3 (1966), pp. 209–217, by permission of the author and the American Psychological Association.

the British associationists of the seventeenth and eighteenth centuries.

The epistemological problem has to do with the nature of reality and of our knowledge of it. It probably never occurs to the naive man in the street to question the objective reality and existence of the things of the physical world—tables, chairs, people, books, etc.—which we see all about us. So uncritical an attitude does not characterize philosophers, though different ones have taken opposite sides of the question, sides to which we give the general labels "empiricism" and "idealism."

John Locke (1947) was an empiricist. Writing near the end of the seventeenth century, he rejected the idealist doctrine offered by Descartes and tracing back through the scholastics to Plato, that the mind comes furnished a priori, with a considerable array of innate ideas. Instead he sponsored the view, then much less familiar than it is now, that *all* knowledge is derived from experience. In Book II of his great *Essay Concerning Human Understanding,* he writes,

"Let us then suppose the mind to be, as we say, white paper, void of all characters, without any ideas; how comes it to be furnished? Whence comes it by that vast store, which the busy and boundless fancy of man has painted on it with an almost endless variety? Whence has it all the materials of reason and knowledge? To this I answer one word, from experience: in that all our knowledge is founded, and from that ultimately derives itself [p. 26]."

And again in Book IV,

"Since the mind in all its thoughts and reasonings hath no other immediate object but its own ideas, which it alone does or can contemplate, it is evident that our knowledge is only conversant about them [p. 252]."

From this it would seem to follow that we cannot know of the existence of other people, or of the physical world; for these, if they exist, are not merely ideas. Each one of us, so far as knowledge is concerned, is shut up in himself and cut off from contact with the world.

Now Locke usually shrank back from drawing the implications of his theories when they seemed to run counter to his own common sense. George Berkeley, Bishop of Cloyne, is best known in California for our city of Berkeley which was named for him, although he might not recognize his own name as we pronounce it. In philosophy, he was an immediate successor of Locke and set out to resolve Locke's inconsistencies. Boldly pushing Locke's views to their logical consequence, he found himself in the position of denying the very existence of matter, i.e., the external world, and affirming that only the mind is ultimately real. He asserted that material objects exist only through being perceived. Bertrand Russell (1945) puts the matter very clearly.

"To the objection that, for example, a tree would cease to exist if no one was looking at it, he replied that God always perceives everything; if there were no God, what we take to be material objects would have a jerky life, suddenly leaping into being when we look at them; but as it is, owing to God's perceptions, trees, rocks, and stones have an existence as continuous as common sense supposes. This, in Berkeley's opinion, is a weighty argument for the existence of God [p. 647]."

Berkeley's idealist view seems intuitively false to at least some philosophers, and to most people who are not philosophers, but it is hard to refute. Berkeley's finding himself in the idealist camp by merely seeking to embrace the implications of the empiricist position shows how slippery some of the central questions of philosophy can become when phrased in traditional forms. Obviously such questions as, "Is there an external reality?" or even merely, "What is knowledge?" can lead only to speculative controversy. If the epistemological problem is formulated in more restricted terms of *how* is knowledge acquired, rather than *what* is knowledge, it may become susceptible of scientific experimental attack.

Returning to Piaget, it is clear that his genius has lain in his resourcefulness in investigating the more manageable question, "How does knowledge develop and change?" As you can see, Piaget's epistemology is at once empirical—even experimental—and developmental in orientation. Leaving aside the question of whether the world is real, he has observed and recorded the activities of the child from earliest infancy to adolescence in acquiring the strategies for coping with it.

On the traditional epistemological issue, Piaget is hard to classify. Some have considered him an idealist, some an empiricist, and both sides can marshal quotations in support. Bärbel Inhelder (1962, p. 20) writes amusingly about this. It seems that after considerable contact in a seminar, Konrad Lorenz remarked, "All along I have thought that Piaget was one of those tiresome empiricists, and only now after studying his work on the genesis of the categories of thought, have I come to realize that he is not so far removed from Kant." On the other hand, some Russian colleagues who believed Piaget to be an idealist because he did not admit that knowledge of the external world is simply a reflection of the objects in it, posed to him the following leading question: "Do you think an object exists prior to any knowledge of it?" Piaget replied, "As a psychologist, I have no idea; I only know an object to the extent that I act upon it; I can affirm nothing about it prior to such an action." Then one of the Russians said, "For us an object is part of the world. Can *the external world* exist independently of and prior to our knowledge of it?" To this, Piaget replied, "The instruments of our knowledge form part of our organism, which in turn forms part of the external world." Later, Piaget overheard them talking and agreeing, "Piaget is *not* an idealist."

Perhaps the difficulty of locating Piaget unequivocally on the empiricist-idealist continuum illustrates a central problem for the student of his work. His ideas are highly original. The terms he has coined for his central theoretical constructs are not merely unfamiliar. They seem vigorously to resist translation into other people's conceptual categories. There is no help for it, if one would understand his theories, but to try to assimilate Piaget in his own terms.

I shall try in the next few minutes to communicate a little of his theory of cognitive development which you may or may not choose to accept. In either case, his empirical findings are an enormously important body of data for students of very different theoretical positions.

Let us turn first to Piaget's theory of cognitive development. Here a confusing situation arises for the English-speaking student. Piaget's five important books of the early 1920s were translated fairly promptly into English in the first flurry of interest in his work. These volumes—*Language and Thought of the Child, Judgment and Reasoning in the Child, The Child's Conception of Physical Causality,* and *The Moral Judgment of the Child*—are widely available. It is their contents—the famous inquiries about what makes clouds move, the origins of dreams, the basis of rules for games, and a host of other such topics—which come to mind for many people when Piaget is mentioned.

Now these works were gradually superseded in Piaget's theoretical formulations, but the point has not been sufficiently appreciated. In this country, there was a decline of interest in Piaget during what Koch (1959) has called the "Age of Theory" in American psychology—roughly from the early '30s to the end of the war—a tough-minded period dominated by the rules of "hypothetico-deduction" and "operational definition" and animated by belief in the imminence of a precisely quantitative behavior theory. Piaget's work was not easily reconciled with the fashions of the period, and little was translated. Now the tide has turned, and at least a portion of Piaget's recent work is available in English, not to mention several excellent "explanations" of him by Wolff (1960), Wohlwill (1960), Hunt (1961), and especially Flavell's comprehensive volume of 1963. However, the essential continuity of development of Piaget's ideas is obscured by the discontinuity of translation. So different are the recent works from the old ones, that to read them one must master a new vocabulary and a new theoretical formulation, and this time the task is made more difficult by the heavy emphasis upon propositions of symbolic logic to explicate the developmental stages of reasoning.

To the early Piaget belonged the painstaking compilation of the forms of verbal expression according to age level from 3 years to 10 years: the demonstration that children's "explanations" of phenomena pass through *stages,* from early animistic, through magical and artificialist forms, to rational thought, and that at each level, the child constructs a systematic "cosmology" according to the modes of reasoning available to him at that stage. The empirical bases for these findings were the children's verbalizations as elicited by the *méthode clinique,* with its inherent risks of misinterpretation of what the child is trying to express. Piaget was severely and perhaps unjustly criticized on this account, for he was sharply aware of the problem. As he put it (1929),

"It is so hard not to talk too much when questioning a child, especially for a pedagogue! It is so hard not to suggest! And above all, it is so hard to find the middle course between systematization due to preconceived ideas, and incoherence due to the absence of any directing hypothesis! . . . In short, it is no simple task, and the material it yields needs to be subjected to the strictest criticism [p. 8]."

In retrospect, Piaget (1952a) recognizes that his method in those years was much too exclusively verbal.

"I well knew that thought proceeds from action, but believed then that language directly reflects the act, and that to understand the logic of the child one has to look for it in the domain of verbal interactions. It was only by studying the patterns of intelligent behavior of *the first two years* that I learned that for a complete understanding of the genesis of intellectual operations, manipulation and experience with objects had first to be considered [p. 247]."

As Piaget notes, the shift from reliance on verbalization to observation and experiment is most important for genetic epistemology because it permits one to study infants as well as the later stages of growth, and by more or less comparable methods.

The cognitive theory starts from the central postulate that motor action is the source from which mental operations emerge. The *action* of the organism is central to the acquisitions of the operations (i.e., ideas, or strategies), which we acquire for coping with the world. In the Hegelian dialectical form which his lectures often assume, Piaget contrasts his emphasis upon the active interplay of organism and environment, both with the environmentalist view in which experience or conditioning is impressed upon a passive organism, and with the nativist view that intellectual capabilities exist preformed and merely unfold in the course of development.

Motor action is *adaptive*, and so are the cognitive activities which more and more replace overt motor behavior. Piaget's biological orientation is seen in his assertion that intelligence is an adaptation, and only one aspect of biological adaptation. Intelligence is an organizing activity which extends the biological organization. With respect to intelligence, a subject to which Piaget has given much attention, it should be noted that his interest is in the typical, not in the range of variation. For him, the word "intelligence" lacks the mental-testing connotations with which it is usually invested in English, and corresponds rather to "intellect" or to intellectual activity or adaptation.

"Life is a continuous creation of increasingly complex forms, and a progressive balancing of these forms with the environment [Piaget, 1952b, p. 3]."

"Intellectual adaptation is the progressive differentiation and integration of inborn reflex mechanisms under the impact of experience. The differentiation of inborn reflex structures and their functions give rise to the mental operations by which man conceives of objects, space, time, and causality, and of the logical relationships which constitute the basis of scientific thought [Wolff, 1960, p. 9].

Another central postulate is that intellectual operations acquired by interaction between organism and environment are acquired in a *lawful sequence*. It should be emphasized again that Piaget's concern is with elucidating the sequence, *not* with establishing exact age norms for its stages. It should also be noted that Piaget has set out to write the ontogenetic history of cognition—*not* a complete account of personality development. What lies outside the cognitive domain is rigorously excluded.

The innate equipment consists of reflexes present at birth. A few reflexes, e.g., yawning or sneezing, are relatively fixed and unmodifiable by experience, though some, like the Babinski, change with maturation. The majority of reflexes, for example, grasping, *require* stimulation for their stabilization, are modified as a result of experience, and constitute the basic behavioral units from which more complex forms of behavior emerge. Most important, the feedback from the activation of a reflex alters all subsequent performance of that reflex. Thus, behavior is simultaneously determined by: first, the inborn structure; second, past activations, i.e., experience, and third, the particular present situation.

Now corresponding to each innate reflex there is assumed to exist in the mind a reflex *schema,* which will not become a stable structure unless repeatedly activated by external stimulation. The concept of schema is stimulation. The concept of schema is difficult. It is described as a flexible mental structure, the primary unit of mental organization. It is too invested with motor connotations to translate as "idea"; and being initially innate, it can hardly be a memory trace. Yet it covers both, and when fully developed bears some resemblance to Tolman's sign Gestalt.

When a reflex responds to a suitable external stimulus, the total sensory perception *and* motor activity are incorporated into the schema of that reflex, and change it; so that when the reflex is again stimulated, the schema has been modified. The stimulus is never again experienced in quite the same way, nor is the response quite the same. Thus the schema is invoked to account for the modification of response, *and* for the alteration of perception in the course of learning. In other words, the organism experiences and reacts to the environment always in terms of an existing organization. All experiences of a particular kind are molded into the already present schema, and in turn alter it according to the reality conditions. Hence, experiences are not recorded as isolated stimulus-response connections, or engrams impressed on a passive brain field, but are integrated into a constantly changing structure.

For the dual aspects of learning, Piaget has used the terms *assimilation* and *accommodation.* He points out first that there exists a fundamental coordination or tuning of the organism to its environment. We have eyes and skin receptors preadapted for the photic and thermal radiation found on earth, ears for sensing rapid waves of pressure in earth's atmosphere, and so forth. There exists, moreover, a fundamental tendency of organisms to take in substances and stimulations for which there already exist the appropriate internal structures and organization. This taking in is called *assimilation.* At a biological level, it refers to the physical incorporation of suitable nutrients into organic structure. At a primitive psychological level, it refers to the incorporation of the sensory and motor components of a behavioral act into the reflex schema they have activated. At more complex levels, assimilation refers to the tendency of the mental apparatus to incorporate ideas into a complex system of thought schemata.

Parallel to assimilation is the function of *accommodation,* i.e., the process by which a schema *changes* so as to adapt better to the assimilated reality. At the biological level, accommodation refers to modification of the organism in response to stimulation, e.g., skin tanning in response to sunlight, or muscle growth in response to exercise. At the lowest psychological level, it refers to the gradual adaptation of the reflexes to new stimulus conditions—what others have called conditioning or stimulus generalization. At higher levels it refers to the coordination of thought patterns to one another and to external reality.

While assimilation and accommodation seem not too far from conventional learning theory, the concept of *aliment* is more unfamiliar. Whatever can be assimilated to a schema is aliment for that schema. Now the aliment is not the *object* which seems from the point of view of the observer to activate behavior, but rather those properties of the object which are assimilated and accommodated to. For example, a nursing bottle filled with milk may be organic aliment for the metabolism, sucking aliment for the reflex sucking schema, and visual aliment for the visual schema. And if the idea strikes you as bizarre that a reflex requires to be fed, as it were, by appropriate stimulation, consider Riesen's (1947) report on the degeneration of the visual apparatus in chimpanzees reared in the dark—or the more familiar degeneration of unstimulated muscles when polio destroys the motor pathways.

Why the careful distinction between an object and its properties? Because for the infant the object does not exist! The idea of an object grows gradually out of the coordination of several schemata—that which is perceived by several sensorial avenues *becomes* the object. At first, the infant has not even awareness of the boundaries of his own body. Objects in the perceptual field—including his own hands and feet—are responded to according to the infant's limited reflexive repertoire. He sucks in response to oral stimulation, grasps in response to palmar stimulation, but makes no attempt to grasp the nursing bottle which he competently sucks, or to follow visually the bottle he can clutch if placed in his hand. Only gradually, by a process called generalizing assimilation, do stimuli which were initially specific aliment for one schema become aliment for other schemata. In parallel accommodation, a schema becomes attuned to more complex inputs, and tends to become coordinated with other schemata which are simultaneously activated. When this happens, things previously known tactilely by being grasped can be recognized by sight alone. Similarly, grasping attempts of increasing accuracy can be directed toward sources of visual stimulation. In such a fashion does the baby come to populate the world with objects, one of which is his own body, which supplies him at once with visual, tactile and kinesthetic stimuli—and when he cries, with auditory ones.

However, the infant still does not attach the concept of permanence to objects. "Out of sight" is quite literally "out of mind." One of Piaget's most interesting experiments—and one which can be repeated by any parent of an infant—concerns the growth of the idea of permanent objects. If you catch a young baby's attention with a small toy, and then hide it, he will make little response. When somewhat older, he will show diffuse motor behavior. If now he once happens to touch it, he will gradually learn to search more efficiently where the object is hidden. However, if the object is hidden in a different place, in full sight of the baby, he will search not where he saw it hidden, but where previously he had touched it. It is an intellectual achievement of some magnitude when the very young child learns to coordinate the space of things seen with the space of things touched, and seeks to touch an object where hitherto he has only seen it.

We can conclude our rapid survey of Piaget's basic concepts with a brief reference to *equilibrium.* Bruner (1959) otherwise most sympathetic, regards the notion of equilibrium as excess baggage, contributing to Piaget a comforting sense of continuity with biology, but offering little else. Perhaps the idea of disequilibrium is more easily described. A schema is in disequilibrium if adaptation (i.e., assimilation and accommodation) to the stimulus is incomplete.

It seems to me that the ideas of equilibrium and disequilibrium constitute most of Piaget's theory of motivation, which is a rather underelaborated part of his psychological system. The organism has a basic need to continue contact with an object as long as adaptation to it is incomplete—or, as Piaget would say, as long as the corresponding schema is in disequilibrium. The need for commerce with an object persists until the child's behavior has been wholly adapted to whatever novelty it presents, that is to say, it persists until the child has acquired mastery. Once accommodation is complete and assimilation is total, the schema is said to be "in equilibrium," and there is no further adaptation. There is, in short, no learning without a problem.

Further, two *schemata* are in disequilibrium until they have mutually accommodated and assimilated, and thereby been integrated into a new superordinate mental structure. This tendency to integrate schemata into more and more complex wholes is assumed by Piaget to be a native propensity of the mind, and as fundamental as the tendency toward equilibrium in physical systems. To put the matter in less cosmic terms, the person strives continually for more and more comprehensive mastery of his world. At each *stage,* however, he is concerned with those things which lie just beyond his intellectual grasp—far enough away to present a novelty to be assimilated, but not so far but what accommodation is possible. Phenomena too simple—i.e., already in equilibrium—and phenomena too complex for present adaptation are ignored in favor of those in the critical range. Anyone who has ever watched the persistence, and resistance to satiation, of a baby intent on mastering a developmental task—for example, learning to walk—will agree with Piaget as to the strength of the motivation, whether or not he accepts Piaget's thermodynamic metaphor.

What then are the general *stages* of intellectual development, and how may they be characterized? Piaget's stages are one of the best known aspects of his work, but he has not been altogether consistent either in the number of them or in the names assigned. Moreover, the stages are linked to particular chronological ages only rather loosely, and Piaget has himself offered data to show that the age at which a particular stage is reached differs for different content domains. For example, conservation (i.e., invariance under transformation) of a plastic object, such as a lump of clay, is acquired first with respect to mass, a year or so later with respect to weight, and a couple of years after that with respect to volume. Moreover, the Geneva group are concerned to demonstrate the invariance of the *sequence* of stages, not the age at which a given stage is achieved. In Martinique the children are 4 years retarded compared to those in Montreal (Laurendeau & Pinard, 1963), and certain Brazilian Indians appear never to achieve the last stage—but the sequence is everywhere the same.

When Piaget visited Berkeley, he deplored the preoccupation of American psychologists with accelerating a child's progress through the successive stages, and commented on recent work of Gruber, who found that kittens achieve awareness of the permanence of objects in 3 months, the human baby only in 9 months; but the important fact is that the cat never acquires the power to think in terms of formal logic, and the human being may!

The more recent books from Geneva usually divide development into four stages: the sensorimotor, from birth to 2 or 3 years; the preoperational stage, from around 2 to around 7 years; the stage of concrete operations, from roughly 7 years to 11 or 12; and finally the stage of formal operations. Each stage in turn has substages—no less than six for the sensorimotor period alone—which we shall not have time to describe today.

The sensorimotor period as a whole (i.e., from birth up to age 2) carries the child from inborn reflexes to acquired behavior patterns. It leads the child from a body-centered (i.e., self-centered) world to an object-centered one. During this period the various sensory spaces, of vision, touch, and the rest, are coordinated into a single space and objects evolve from their separate sensory properties into *things* with multiple properties, permanence, and spatial relationships to other objects. Altogether this stage comprises a most important set of intellectual achievements.

The preoperational stage (2 years to around 7 years) covers the important period when language is acquired. This permits the child to deal symbolically with the world instead of directly through motor activity, though his problem solving tends to be "action ridden." The child is himself still the focus of his own world, and space and time are centered on him. Time is only "before now," "now," and "not yet"; and space moves as the child moves. When he is taken for an evening walk, the moon follows *him.* Traces of this attitude are present even in adults, who often locate places and things in terms of distance and direction from themselves, rather than in terms of objective spatial relationships. By a process of "decentering," the child during this stage learns gradually to conceive of a time scale and of a spatial world which exist independent of himself. In dealing with physical objects and quantities, the child pays attention to one aspect to the neglect of other aspects. He concludes, for example, that there is more water in a glass graduate than in a beaker—though he has just seen it poured from the one vessel into the other—because in the graduate the column of water is taller, and the child neglects the reduction in diameter.

The stage of concrete operations has its beginnings as early as age 6 or 7. Now the child grows less dependent upon his own perceptions and motor actions and shows a capacity for reasoning, though still at a very concrete level. Among his "logical" acquisitions are classifying, ordering in series, and numbering. Asked to put a handful of sticks in order by length, he need no longer make all the pair comparisons but can pick out the longest, then the longest one left, and so forth, until the series is complete. When shown that Stick A is longer than Stick B, and Stick B is longer than Stick C, he can infer without actual demonstration that A is longer than C.

Here at Berkeley, my students and I have been developing test materials based on Piaget experiments, and intended to measure the abilities of children in the primary grades, i.e., at the transition point from the perceptual attitude of the preoperational stage to the reasoning attitude of the stage of concrete operations. Thus far, fifteen tests have been developed and administered to more than 300 school children. Although we abandoned the *méthode clinique* for a strictly standardized psychometric approach, we have observed precisely the same types of behavior which Piaget had previously reported.

The last of Piaget's major stages of intellectual development begins usually somewhere around 11 or 12 years and matures a couple of years later. He calls it the stage of formal operations. Now the child can deal with abstract relationships instead of with things, with the form of an argument while ignoring its content. For the first time he can intellectually manipulate the merely hypothetical, and systematically evaluate a lengthy set of alternatives. He learns to handle the logical relationships of Identity (I), Negation (N), Reciprocity (R), and Correlation (C), which permit him to deal with problems of proportionality, probability, permutations, and combinations.

I have just referred to the INRC logical group whose acquisition marks the last stage of intellectual growth. In Piaget's writings over the years, the characteristics of each stage and the differences between them have increasingly been formulated in the notation of symbolic logic—a circumstance which does not increase the comprehensibility of his latest books for nonmathematicians.

Nevertheless, this transition to the language of formal logic is of profound importance for Piaget's theory because it provides a set of explicit, mathematical models for cognitive structure, and serves as a vehicle to describe in a unified way the findings of experiments very different in content. The unity and economy of the logical theory as contrasted with his earlier multiplicity of explanatory terms—egocentrism, syncretism, animism, realism, etc.—is obvious. However, Piaget's critics have sometimes found the mathematical formulation strained, and have accused Piaget of distorting intellectual development to force it into the categories of formal logic.

Piaget's point of view may have been misunderstood. As he phrases it (1957),

"The aim is . . . to study the application of logical techniques to the psychological facts themselves. . . . The question whether the structures and operations of logic correspond to anything in our actual thought, and whether the latter conforms to logical laws, is still an open one. . . . On the other hand, the algebra of logic can help us to specify psychological structures, and put into calculus form those operations and structures central to our thought processes. . . . The psychologist welcomes the qualitative character of logic since its facilitates the analyses of the actual structures underlying intellectual operations, as contrasted with the quantitative treatment of their behavioral outcome. Most 'tests' of intelligence measure the latter, but our real problem is to discover the actual operational mechanisms which govern such behavior, and not simply to measure it [pp. xvii–xviii]."

Many psychologists who acknowledge the brilliant originality of many of Piaget's experiments, and the enormous importance of his empirical contribution taken as a whole, continue nevertheless to reject the formal, mathematical theory which lies closest to Piaget's heart. Yet one of the most impressive parts of Piaget's discussions here in Berkeley concerned the isomorphism between his stages and the most basic structure of mathematics itself.

Piaget points out that if one considers not the content, but the architecture, as it were, of the various branches of mathematics, one discovers first a level where the prototype structure is the group and the type of reversibility is inversion or negation. Next comes a level where structures of order, such as the lattice, are typical, and reversibility is not inversion but reciprocity. Last comes the level of topology with key concepts of neighborhood, boundary, etc. Now the first of these three levels is the oldest, one part of it, Euclidean geometry, going back to the Greeks. The second level, typified by projective geometry, dates from the late seventeenth century; and the last, or topological, level is a product only of the nineteenth century. Taken in sequence, each level is more general, i.e., involves *fewer* axioms than the preceding, and the entire sequence might theoretically be expected to have developed in the opposite order. Now the curious part is that the sequence of acquisition of mental operations by children follows not the historical sequence, but the theoretical sequence. Small children of 3 years of age, who for example are quite unable even to copy a simple geometrical figure such as a square, have no difficulty differentiating between a closed figure like a circle and an open one like a cross, and they can easily follow instructions in putting a second circle, however imperfectly drawn, inside, or outside; or even half in and half out of the experimenter's circle. Further evidence of young children's grasp of topological principles is seen in their sure knowledge of the forms into which a sphere, such as a balloon, can be deformed—i.e., sausagelike, flat sided, or dimpled figures, etc.—and those forms such as the torus or doughnut, which cannot be obtained by deformation of a sphere. Later, with the shift from the preoperational stage to the stage of concrete operations at age 6 or 7, the child learns to handle relations of order—seriation, transitivity, reciprocal relationships, and the rest to which I have already referred. Only with the approach of adolescence does he spontaneously utilize the propositional algebraic structures which are the oldest development in the history of mathematics.

What finally are the implications of Piaget's work for fields other than psychology and mathematics? Certainly they have a major bearing upon education.

If Piaget is correct—and much work now substantiates his empirical findings at least in broad outline—methods of education will be most effective when they are attuned to the patterns of thought which are natural to a child of the age concerned. It may not be true that you can teach a child *anything* if your approach is correct, but it does look as if you can teach him a great deal more than anyone might have guessed. Of course, teachers long before Piaget recognized intuitively that a child learned better when problems were approached at a concrete rather than at an abstract level. But there is more to it than that. Bruner, at Harvard, and others in this country are attempting to find ways to introduce children to some of the abstract ideas of mathematics—for example, the algebraic concept of squaring a number—by concrete, geometric models. They hope thus possibly to accelerate a child's progress—a goal which Piaget has his reservations about. Perhaps the most dramatic evidence of a revolution which owes a great deal of its impetus to Piaget is the new elementary school mathematics, in which children even in the lower grades are being taught, and learning, and actually enjoying learning basic arithmetical and geometrical ideas introduced via set theory, which most of their parents have never heard of.

I could not better conclude this appreciation of Piaget than by quoting from William James (1890) who wrote 75 years ago in his famous *Principles of Psychology* as follows: "To the infant, sounds, sights, touches and pains form probably one unanalyzed bloom of confusion [p. 496]." We can now go beyond the philosopher's speculations and describe in some detail how the unanalyzed "bloom of confusion" of the infant becomes the world of the child—in which not only objects, but time, space, causality and the rest acquire a coherent organization. And we owe this achievement in large measure to the analyses of Jean Piaget.

References

Bruner, J. S. Inhelder and Piaget's *The growth of logical thinking.* I. A psychologist's viewpoint. *British Journal of Psychology,* 1959, **50**, 363–370.

Flavell, J. H. Historical and bibliographic note. In W. Kessen & Clementina Kuhlman (Eds.), Thought in the young child. *Monographs of the Society for Research in Child Development,* 1962, **27**(2, Whole No. 83).

Flavell, J. H. *The developmental psychology of Jean Piaget.* Princeton, N.J.: Van Nostrand, 1963.

Hunt, J. McV. *Intelligence and experience.* New York: Ronald Press, 1961.

Inhelder, Barbel. Some aspects of Piaget's genetic approach to cognition. In W. Kessen & Clementina Kuhlman (Eds.), Thought in the young child. *Monographs of the Society for Research in Child Development,* 1962, **27** (2, Whole No. 83).

James, W. *The principles of psychology.* New York: Holt, 1890.

Koch, S. (Ed.) *Psychology: A study of a science.* Vol. 3. *Formulations of the person and the social context.* New York: McGraw-Hill, 1959.

Laurendeau, Monique, & Pinard, A. *Causal thinking in the child, a genetic and experimental approach.* New York: International Universities Press, 1963.

Locke, J. *An essay concerning human understanding.* London: Dent, 1947.

Piaget, J. *The child's conception of the world.* New York: Harcourt, Brace, 1929.

Piaget, J. Autobiography. In E. G. Boring (Ed.), *A history of psychology in autobiography.* Vol. 4. Worcester, Mass.: Clark Univer. Press, 1952. (a)

Piaget, J. *The origins of intelligence in children.* (2nd ed.) New York: International Universities Press, 1952. (b)

Piaget, J. *Logic and psychology.* New York: Basic Books, 1957.

Riesen, A. H. The development of visual perception in man and chimpanzee. *Science,* 1947, **106**, 107–108.

Russell, B. *A history of western philosophy.* New York: Simon & Schuster, 1945.

Wohlwill, J. F. Developmental studies of perception. *Psychological Bulletin,* 1960, **57**, 249–288.

Wohlwill, J. F. From perception to inference: A dimension of cognitive development. In W. Kessen and Clementina Kuhlman (Eds.), Thought in the young child. *Monographs of the Society for Research in Child Development,* 1962, **27**(2, Whole No. 83).

Wolff, P. H. The developmental psychologies of Jean Piaget and psychoanalysis. *Psychological Issues,* 1960, **2**(1, Whole No. 5).

8.2 A Developmental Approach to Adolescence

Leon Eisenberg

Psychological and social factors operate within wide limits determined by biological factors to determine the onset, termination, and achievement progress of adolescence. Needs of adolescents are, therefore, of an individual nature. If they are carefully assessed, teachers can better design instruction to accelerate and increase the level of attainment. Dr. Eisenberg discusses the place of adolescent involvement in the issues of our time and its relationship to the development of the individual.

Adolescence may be defined as a critical period of human development manifested at the biological, psychological, and social levels of integration, of variable onset and duration but marking the end of childhood and setting the foundation for maturity. Biologically, its onset is signaled by the acceleration of physiological growth and the beginnings of secondary sexual development, its termination by the fusion of the epiphyses of the bones and the completion of sexual maturation. Psychologically, it is marked by an acceleration of cognitive growth and of personality formation, both of which continue to be subject to further evolution,

SOURCE. Leon Eisenberg, "A Developmental Approach to Adolescence," *Children*, XII, 4 (1965), pp. 131–135. Reprinted by permission of the author.

though at a less marked rate, in subsequent stages of adulthood. Socially, it is a period of intensified preparation for the assumption of an adult role, and its termination is signaled when the individual is accorded full adult prerogatives, the timing and nature of which vary widely from society to society.

Adolescence is a "critical period" in development in being both a time of rapid and profound change in the organism and a time providing the necessary—but not sufficient—conditions for full maturation in adulthood. Optimal development in adolescence depends on successful accomplishment of the developmental tasks in infancy and childhood. Thus, clinical experience has indicated that adolescence is likely to be particularly stormy, prolonged, and sometimes poorly resolved if it follows a childhood marked by severe deficits.

Whether or not appropriate "experiential supplements" during adolescence can lead to successful negotiation of this period despite pathology in earlier life is not known. The heuristic hypothesis is to assume that repair can occur and that the task of the physician is to search for ways of encouraging optimal growth during the adolescence of a previously damaged child.

Although a rich, fulfilling adolescence provides the best groundwork for a successful adulthood, such an outcome is not automatic; it depends, in turn, on the provision of opportunities during adulthood for the creative exercise of the abilities achieved in adolescence.

The structural groundwork for adolescent development is laid by physical maturation. This developmental sequence is not preformed or automatic but depends upon an interaction between biological capacity and environmental stimulation. Just as growth requires adequate nutrition—being subject to delay or even cessation in the presence of starvation and to acceleration in the presence of optimal intake—so psychological maturation is dependent upon "psychological nutrition," that is, sequential opportunities for cognitive and social stimulation so timed that they promote further mental development.

Interdependent Developments

Thus, adolescence is simultaneously a biological, a social, and a psychological phenomenon. Development at each of these levels of integration proceeds not independently but with significant interaction, with events at any one level able to impede or to accelerate developments at each of the others.

For example, although the time at which the hypothalamic-pituitary axis initiates the biological sequence of adolescent growth is a function of individual heredity, it may, in a given individual, be delayed or advanced by environmental factors. Thus, the ultimate height attained by adolescents in economically developing countries has shown striking gains as nutrition has improved. Similarly, the time of menarche has shown a trend toward acceleration in countries in which increasingly better health of the children has been achieved. These physiological trends are the result of industrial and social organization.

Or again, biological maturation provides the increasing muscular strength and dexterity which permit the adolescent to participate successfully in the activities of his social group, thus acquiring a psychological sense of adequacy. At the same time, positive psychological motivation is a prerequisite for task perseverance and the search for variety of experience, which provide the conditions necessary for full muscular development through exercise.

Developments at the biological and psychological levels occur in a social framework, which may promote or retard them. Thus, unscientific notions about diet prevalent in a specific culture may lead to inadequate nutritional intake, and social prejudices against minority group members may deprive them of experiences necessary for full development.

The importance of such reciprocal influences is underscored by the fact that each society is dependent upon its adolescents as its future adults. Failure to provide them with the conditions necessary for optimal development will severely handicap the growth potential of that society.

Biological adolescence has fairly precise signs of its onset and termination, such as growth acceleration, sexual development, and epiphyseal fusion, but there is remarkable variation in the timing of their appearance in different individuals. Onset in normal children may occur as early as age 7 or 8 or as late as 17 or 18; termination as early as 15 or 16 or as late as 24 or 25. The timing seems to be a function both of internal factors, such as sex and inheritance, and external factors, such as nutrition or illness. In other words, the biological factors set wide limits for the onset, termination, and achievements of adolescence, the potential limits being subject to modification by environmental influences, among which both psychological and social factors play a role.

Social Preparation

Adolescence as a social phenomenon, though restricted in range by biological considerations, is a function of cultural norms. In general, the more sophisticated the society is in its technology, the more prolonged is adolescence, since the complexity of the preparation required for the assumption of adult roles depends upon the demands the society sets. In the United States, for example, the long period of study required for specialized occupational roles delays the age of self-support, the opportunity for marriage, and the age of creative contribution to society—all attributes of the adult role.

In many cultures, the onset of adolescence is clearly signaled by puberty rites, usually in the form of tests of strength and courage, the completion of which entitles the individual to recognition as a young adult. In technologically advanced societies, such clear signification of the end of childhood is absent and the requirements for adulthood less clearly defined: the individual must, therefore, undergo a more prolonged and, at times, confused struggle to attain adult status.

Each culture provides experience specifically designated as part of the training of the adolescent, such as schooling and apprenticeship; other experiences such as dating and courtship, which are for the most part limited to adolescence but are not formally organized; and other non-age-related opportunities for personal development which may be particularly meaningful for the adolescent, such as opportunities to participate in cultural and political life.

Deliberate social planning based on a scientific analysis of adolescents' needs has been relatively neglected, the forms and structures society provides having evolved empirically. Only within school systems has such planning been explicit, but even there with little careful research. Yet careful assessment of the needs of adolescents at all levels of developmental integration could lead to the design and provision of external conditions that would greatly accelerate the rate, and markedly increase the ultimate level, of the development of the human adolescent's full potentialities.

The Idealism of Adolescence

At a psychological level, the most striking attainment during adolescence is the ability to conceptualize at an abstract level. The further evolution of what Piaget calls the "concrete operations" of childhood[1] through interaction with increasingly more demanding intellectual tasks, provided both by formal schooling and informal social experience, leads to the ability to "think about thinking" and to analyze problems at a high level of generalization. It is here that the *Anlage* of scientific thought and creativity is to be found. This evolution of intellectual function requires appropriate environmental stimulation.

The adolescent's capacity for abstract thought accounts for his increasing concern with, on the one hand, national and international problems and, on the other, with the basic meanings and values of human

[1] Flavell, J. H.: The developmental psychology of Jean Piaget. Van Nostrand, New York. 1963.

existence. This "idealism" of adolescence is, of course, shaped by the cultural envelope which surrounds the individual, but its very existence leads to questioning, to examination of basic premises, and to dissatisfaction with the imperfections in the world adults have created. Its cultivation may be regarded as one of the most important tasks of society.

Fostering and strengthening this "suprapersonal" psychological trait in adolescents may lead to the creation of adults who will in turn enhance the society that bred them. The lack of adequate opportunity for its positive expression will warp the adolescent's normal development and lead to a generation of self-preoccupied adults who will fail to meet the challenge of history.

Personal Identity

A second and related psychological theme of adolescence is the search for a sense of personal identity, to employ the terminology of Erikson.[2] No longer a child and not yet an adult, the adolescent is busily engaged in determining who he is and what he is to become.

In this effort, he examines his parents from a more critical perspective and leans more to peer groups for his sense of belonging. If his relations with his parents have been soundly constructed during earlier years, and if they meet his doubts and criticisms with sympathetic understanding, this temporary unsettling of his prior role as a child leads to a resynthesis of his relations with them on a firm and lasting basis, one marked by reciprocal respect and by personal independence without abandonment of filial loyalty. Where the parent-child relationship has been one of excessive dependence or excessive hostility, the turmoil of adolescence may be prolonged and lead either to failure of emancipation or to rejection of family ties and a lasting sense of isolation.

Sexual Role

A third key developmental task consists of the further evolution of sexual identity and role-appropriate behavior. Learning the social role of one's sex is firmly rooted in childhood—in culturally differentiated role assignments, in emulation of the like-sexed parent, and in peer interactions. These experiences provide a constant feedback, both by comparison of the self with others and by praise or blame from them, which informs the child as to what sex he is and what kind of behavior expectations this entails. These preliminary psychological structures are challenged by the adolescent's consciousness of his development of adult sexual characteristics and his experience of a bewildering array of new

[2] Erikson, E. H.: Identity and the life cycle. *In* Psychological issues, monograph 1. International Universities Press, New York. 1959.

physical sensations, both of which lead to an upsurge of interest in physical sex and a psychological sensitization to a new aspect of interpersonal relationships. The forces in the social field then determine the further steps in his sexual development.

Comparative studies indicate that, as the evolutionary scale is ascended, sexual behavior is less dependent upon hormones and more upon learning. In man, the role of hormones is limited to priming the organism for biological sexual maturation and to influencing—but not solely determining—the level of libido; the direction, nature, and adequacy of sexual performance are controlled by psychosocial factors. Thus, the many investigations of the biology of sex deviants have failed to identify chromosomal, hormonal, or gonadal aberrations; and conversely, individuals with such biological incongruencies usually exhibit a sex-role identity conforming to sex-role assignment.

The remarkable variation in sexual behavior between societies as well as between social classes within a single society emphasizes the cultural determination of sexual behavior, given adequate biological maturation.

The ambivalence of Western society toward sexuality—manifested by the conflicts between official attitudes and private behavior, and the pervasive emphasis on sex side by side with sanctions against its expression—accounts for the difficulty, so common in adolescence, of attaining the basis for a sense of competence, freedom, and pleasure as a sexually functioning adult. Persons concerned with the development of adolescents have an important obligation to give them a clear and full explanation of biological function with emphasis on its *ethical significance* based upon a mutually meaningful relationship between human beings. Adolescents need a comprehensive knowledge of the physical and physiological differences between the sexes, of the development of sexuality, and of the appropriate stages of sexual experience en route to full maturity.

Commonly expressed fears that giving adolescents such information will lead to premature experimentation run contrary to clinical experience which indicates that ignorance and impoverishment of human relationships account for most sexual misadventures. A sense of inadequacy in sexuality not only impairs sexual function but also leads to disabilities in other adult roles and is an important source of psychological malfunction.

Origins of Delinquency

The search for identity is markedly influenced by peer groups. If these are constructive social groups which provide creative outlets for adolescent energy, the result is a sense of meaningful membership in the community and identification with its larger goals. If the peer group is a delinquent gang, with values antagonistic to those of the larger society, the result is likely to be antisocial personality organization—especially if the adolescent is a victim of discrimination for religious, ethnic, political, or economic reasons.

The experience of growing up as a member of a disadvantaged minority group, with attendant humiliation and denial of opportunity, makes it difficult for the adolescent to identify with the values of the society at large and favors, instead, hostility toward its norms and a disposition to anarchistic individualism. However, even under these circumstances, leadership and social forms which permit the disadvantaged adolescent to employ his energy in efforts to change unjust social patterns can foster his emergence into creative adulthood. If such opportunities for constructive social action are denied, the distortion of development leads to a frustrating and progressively more embittering "individual war against society" characterized by criminal activities.

Some theorists focus upon family pathology in explaining the evolution of delinquent behavior. Their thesis is based upon the finding that family psychopathology is frequent in the history of delinquents. The family is indeed an important agent in transmitting the behavior pattern and values expected of the adolescent by society. Consequently, distortions in family structure, whether idiosyncratic or socially induced, will inevitably have profound effects upon individual development. However, the family-centered viewpoint fails to recognize that family psychopathology is closely related to social structure and that the adolescent is also molded by social experiences outside the family.

The social consequences of economic disadvantage—poor health and reduced longevity, poor education, extralegal marital arrangements, inability to plan for future contingencies, necessity for exploiting children economically—themselves erode family structure and are likely to cause the victims of these social circumstances, the genesis of which they do not understand, to turn on each other in destructive ways. The unemployed, drifting father and the unmarried, deserted mother not only fail to provide their children with adequate nurture but also serve as poor identification models.

However, even though family structure be distorted, the adolescent may attain a degree of normal development *if* provided adequate education and constructive peer group experience. Unfortunately, the aggregation of disadvantaged families in decaying neighborhoods is all too likely to reinforce family psychopathology and, by exposing the adolescent to delinquent gangs and ineffective schooling, heighten his growing sense of bitterness.

Hazards and Symptoms

The sensitivity of the adolescent to the good opinion of his peers and the dependence of his sense of identity upon the attainment of competence in an adult role render him psychologically vulnerable to variation in physiological development, such as precocious or delayed growth, facial acne, obesity, enlarged mammary glands in the male, or inadequate or overabundant breast development in the female. These deviations from the expected pattern of maturation, though of no great medical significance, may, nonetheless, lead to major psychological trauma if not offset by sensitive guidance.

The adolescent with limited intellectual or physical capacity can develop a persisting and even irremedial feeling of inferiority if he is forced to compete in situations in which he experiences continual failure. The individualization of educational and vocational training for adolescents is essential, both to permit the talented individual to exploit his abilities, as well as to direct the youngster with specific limitations to activities which will develop what abilities he has.

Characteristic of adolescence is fluidity of psychological structure in the struggle to attain a new and more meaningful sense of identity. In consequence, the formation of transient symptoms, resembling many of the psychopathological syndromes of adulthood, is not uncommon during this period. The clinician must exercise great caution lest he attribute too great a significance to the turbulent but temporary maladaptive patterns manifested by the adolescent. Incorrect diagnostic formulations may lead to social consequences—for example, withdrawal from school or institutionalization—that will freeze into permanence an otherwise readily correctable deviation in the growth pattern.

It is, of course, important to recognize that schizophrenia often first appears in adolescence, as does manic-depressive psychosis. However, these are uncommon disorders and may be simulated by panic reactions in the youngster who is confronted by overwhelming internal and external stimulation. If the recent trend toward a specialty of adolescent psychiatry has any justification, it lies in the opportunity for psychiatrists to acquire particular competence in the differential diagnosis and special management of adolescents' adjustment reactions. Experience with the psychiatric problems of adolescents leads to respect for their extraordinary range of individual variability and their remarkable restorative capacity under corrective and supportive experience.

The psychological basis for a sense of individual worth as an adult rests upon the acquisition of competence in a work role during adolescence. A sense of competence is not acquired on the basis of "reassurance," but rather upon the actual experience of succeeding in a socially important task. The challenge to the educator, therefore, is to stimulate abilities to the utmost without setting standards so high that they lead to an enduring sense of defeat.

The educational accomplishment must be matched by an opportunity for the individual to exercise his competence as a worker in the economic world. The sustained motivation necessary for mastering a difficult work role is only possible when there is a real likelihood of fulfilling that role in adult life and having it respected by others. The task of providing full employment in a world in which automation is revolutionizing traditional work roles provides a challenge to the abilities of leading thinkers in all societies.

The World's Hope

No society can hope to survive that does not succeed in harnessing the constructive, searching suprapersonal and supranational drives of the adolescent. In recent world history, adolescents in underdeveloped countries have participated heroically in overthrowing the dead hand of the past and attaining the beginnings of a meaningful nationhood. The picture in the relatively developed countries is less clear and less heartening. As affluence is attained, societies tend to become frozen into traditional molds, with resultant trends toward self-preoccupation and egocentric goals that afford less challenge to adolescents. There are, fortunately, notable and inspiring exceptions to this self-preoccupation, as youngsters dedicate their energies to improving the lot of disadvantaged fellow citizens and to social betterment in underdeveloped countries far from their shores.

The capacity for engagement in meaningful social activity is clearly present in young people in every country of the world. The challenge to the behavioral scientist is to help his own country develop the forms and means to enable the adolescent to take a leading role in the struggle for the attainment of a world in which peace, freedom, and economic opportunity are omnipresent. No task is more suited to the adolescent. No task has greater potentiality for permitting the full flowering of his capacities.

Thus, the provision of an optimal framework for adolescent development is inseparable from the struggle to create a better world by helping to mold the citizens who will build it.

Selected Readings

Bloom, B. S. *Stability and change in human characteristics.* New York: Wiley, 1964.

Ebel, R. L. Cognitive development of personal potential. *National Association of Secondary School Principal's Bulletin,* 1966, **50**, 115–30.

Elkind, D. Piaget's conservative concept. *Childhood Education,* 1968, **44**, 292–300.

Erikson, E. H. Youth and the life cycle. *Children,* 1960, **7**, 2.

Flavell, J. H. Piaget's contributions to the study of cognitive development. *Merrill-Palmer Quarterly.* 1963, **9**, 245–262.

Hauighurst, R. *Developmental tasks and education.* New York: McKay, 1948, 1952.

Hunt, J. McV. Experience and the development of motivation: some reinterpretations. *Child Development,* 1960, **31**, 489–504.

Mussen, P. H., and Jones, Mary C. Late- and early-maturing boys. *Child Development,* 1957, **28**(2), 243–256.

Stennett, R. G., and Feenstra, H. J. *Late bloomers: fact or fancy. Journal of Educational Research,* 1970, **63**, 344–346.

Stodolsky, S. S., and Lesser, G. Learning patterns in the disadvantaged. *Harvard Educational Review,* 1967, **37**, 546–93.

Suppes, P. Modern learning theory and the elementary school curriculum. *American Educational Research Journal,* 1964, **1**, 79–93.

Thorndike, R. L. Intellectual status and intellectual growth; reanalysis of Harvard growth study data. *Journal of Educational Psychology,* 1966, **57**, 121–7.

CHAPTER 9

The Characteristics of Learners

9.1 Diversity of Talent[1]

Dael Wolfle

The author's theme is that diversity should be created within individuals, not only among them. Everyone cannot be "the well-rounded individual, or the broad scholar, or the man of many talents." Dr. Wolfle makes a case for the person who cannot become well rounded because he has developed some of his talents so highly that superiority evolves in these areas. Wolfle suggests that from the standpoint of society, it may be best for the individual to concentrate on what he can do best. This policy raises a number of questions to which the author gives some answers. There are implications for teaching and learning, and they relate to practices that are under the teacher's control.

A problem of continuing concern is the extent to which we are properly developing and utilizing the nation's intellectual resources. For both realistic and practical reasons it is desirable that we make better provisions than we have in the past for the full development of human talent.

SOURCE. Abridged from Dael Wolfle, "Diversity of Talent," *The American Psychologist*, **XV**, 8 (1960), pp. 535 and 539–545, by permission of the author and the American Psychological Association.

[1] The Walter Van Dyke Bingham Memorial Lecture given at Columbia University on May 10, 1960.

The more fundamental reason is that one of the basic ideals of a free society is the provision of opportunity for each person to develop to his full capacity. This ideal has been expressed in many ways, yet from time to time we need to remind ourselves that it lies at the very cornerstone of our form of society. *The Pursuit of Excellence,* the Rockefeller report on education, of which John Gardner (1958) was the principal author, phrased it this way:

"The greatness of a nation may be manifested in many ways—in its purposes, its courage, its moral responsibility, its cultural and scientific eminence, the tenor of its daily life. But ultimately the source of its greatness is in the individuals who constitute the living substance of the nation."

. . . .

"Our devotion to a free society can only be understood in terms of these values. It is the only form of society that puts at the very top of its agenda the opportunity of the individual to develop his potentialities. It is the declared enemy of every condition that stunts the intellectual, moral, and spiritual growth of the individual. No society has ever fully succeeded in living up to the stern ideals that a free people set themselves. But only a free society can even address itself to that demanding task."[2]

The idealistic reason for fostering the full development of talent is expressed in the quotation just read. There is also an urgent practical reason: the nation has an increasing need for many kinds of highly developed talent. Earlier in our history, the most critical need was for land for an expanding agriculture and then later for financial capital for an expanding industry. But now the critical need is for men and women with ideas and highly developed talents, men and women who can teach, who can roll back the boundaries of ignorance, who can manage complex organizations, who can perform the diverse and demanding tasks upon which the further development of a free, industrial society depends.

The Value of Diversity

In the selection and education of persons of ability, it is advantageous to a society to seek the greatest achievable diversity of talent: diversity within an individual, among the members of an occupational group, and among the individuals who constitute a society.

[2] From *The Pursuit of Excellence: Education and the Future of America.* Copyright © 1953 by Rockefeller Brothers Fund, Inc. Reprinted by permission of Doubleday & Co., Inc.

In speaking of diversity among individuals, I am using words in their ordinary meaning; but when I speak of diversity within an individual, the expression sounds strange. There is no customary term for the idea I am trying to express, for the adjectives with good connotations mean the opposite of what I am trying to say. I am not talking about the well-rounded individual, or the broad scholar, or the man of many talents. These are qualities we ordinarily respect; but I wish to make a case for the opposite, for the man who has developed some of his talents so highly that he cannot be well-rounded, for the one who may be called uneven or one-sided but in whom at least one side has been developed to the level of real superiority. For the sake of symmetry with the concept of diversity among individuals, I have called this kind of development diversity within an individual. If the expression still seems strange, its meaning will become clearer as we go along.

One further explanation is essential. I do not wish to maximize variance or diversity by having some persons very bright and others very dull. Obviously we want each person to reach the highest level of which he is capable. But even if we were doing as well as we know how to do in the identification and education of talented persons, the problem of optimal deployment of their various talents would still be a question of undiminished psychological and social interest. Even under these circumstances, a strong case can be made for the proposition that the value of a nation's intellectual resources—or the total achievement—would be maximized by maximizing the variety of abilities within and among individuals. This is not a new idea; but the point needs repetition and also needs analysis, for even though we agree upon the value of diversity, strong forces are constantly at work in the opposite direction. These forces tend to make us more, rather than less, alike and tend to prevent the uneven development of a talented individual.

Many of the methods that have been developed for dealing with people in groups have the effect of reducing the variability among the group members. Examples are the use of uniform lesson assignments and the use of general aptitude measures and the average grade or the rank in class as devices for selecting students for the next higher educational level. Advertising procedures, trade union policies, wage scales, and a variety of other forces also work in the direction of uniformity rather than diversity. These tendencies are supported by popular attitudes that place a premium on uniformity and conformity rather than upon diversity and individuality. Lyle Spencer quotes the mother of three bright children as saying: "I'm not interested in geniuses, all I want to do is to raise my kids to be normal, well-adjusted adults." Many parents would agree; they want their children to be like other children, and not to be different.

Teachers, too, sometimes express this attitude. De Haan and Havighurst (1957) quote a teacher as saying: "When I am finished with my class in June, the slow children are a little faster, and the fast have slowed down a bit."

Years ago, Truman Kelley protested this attitude and leveled his guns against school teachers and officials who exhibit it. He called them pedagogical plainsmen and accused them of preferring intellectual plains to intellectual hills and valleys. They were, he wrote, so obsessed with averages and norms that they devoted themselves to "the weary process of shovelling to fill valleys and steady erosion to remove mountains of human capacity."

Had Harold Benjamin not already pre-empted the title, I might have called this address "The Cultivation of Idiosyncrasy," for the major point of my argument is that the cultivation of diversity is desirable both for the individual young persons whose futures lie in our hands and for the society in which they will live and work. I cannot use Benjamin's title, but I can quote a few of his paragraphs (1955). The wit and humor with which he approached serious problems has illuminated many an educational discussion, and the fable he used in opening the Inglis lecture at Harvard in 1949 illustrates the point I want to make. The fable is the story of the school in the woods.

"All the animals had to take all the subjects. Swimming, running, jumping, and flying made up the required curriculum. . . .

"Some animals, of course, were better students than others. The squirrel, for example, got straight A's from the first in running, jumping, and climbing. He got a good passing grade, moreover, in swimming. It looked as though he would make Phi Beta Kappa in his junior year, but he had trouble with flying. Not that he was unable to fly. He could fly. He climbed to the top of tree after tree and sailed through the air to neighboring trees with ease. As he modestly observed, he was a flying squirrel by race. The teacher of flying pointed out, however, that the squirrel was always losing altitude in his gliding and insisted that he should take off in the approved fashion from the ground. Indeed, the teacher decided that the taking-off-from-the-ground unit had to be mastered first, as was logical, and so he drilled the squirrel day after day on the take-off. . . .

"The squirrel tried hard. He tried so hard he got severe Charley horses in both hind legs, and thus crippled he became incapable even of running, jumping, or climbing. He left school a failure, and died soon thereafter of starvation, being unable to gather and store nuts."

Benjamin continued the fable to relate the difficulties of the snake, the eagle, and the gopher. I shall quote only the story of the eagle.

"The eagle was a truly brilliant student. His flying was superb, his running and jumping were of the best, and he even passed the swimming test, although the teacher tried to keep him from using his wings too much. By employing his talons and beak, moreover, he could climb after a fashion and no doubt he would have been able to pass that course, too, except that he always flew to the top of the problem tree or cliff when the teacher's back was turned and sat there lazily in the sun, preening his feathers and staring arrogantly down at his fellow students climbing up the hard way. The teachers reasoned with him to no avail. He would not study climbing seriously. At first he turned aside the faculty's importunities with relatively mild wisecracks and innuendoes, but at the teachers put more pressure upon him he reacted with more and more feeling . . . [and finally quit school altogether].

I wonder how many human students have been similarly frustrated and had their talents stunted by being required to climb slowly step by step, instead of being encouraged to soar rapidly to the heights of which they were capable.

I have said that it is socially valuable to maximize diversity. Now let me try to prove the point. I should like to be able to give a rigorous proof; for, if the assertion is correct, there flow from it a number of implications for the professional work of psychologists, guidance counselors, teachers, and all who deal professionally with the identification, education, and utilization of talented persons. The proof cannot be rigorous, for we do not have adequate measures of amount of talent, or achievement, or of the social value of achievement. But it is possible to analyze these variables and to examine their interrelationships. The exercise leads convincingly to the conclusion that maximum diversity results in maximum social value.

Let us start the analysis with two points on which there is general agreement. The first is that individuals vary in the total amount of talent or ability they possess. This simple statement overlooks the whole nature-nurture problem, the effects of education, and all of the difficulties of measuring talent. Moreover, it oversimplifies the whole matter by treating ability as a trait that an individual possesses rather than as an attribute of the behavior he exhibits. Nevertheless, to say that different individuals possess different total amounts of ability is a convenient way of stating an idea that is generally accepted.

The second point is that ability is not a unitary trait but expresses itself in various forms or special abilities. We may side with L. L. Thurstone in believing that a relatively small number of more or less independent primary abilities provide a satisfactory description of human ability, or we may side with Godfrey Thompson in postulating a large number of highly specialized abilities. For our purpose, it makes little difference which of these positions one prefers. All that is essential is that we agree that ability is a many-sided affair and that an individual may be better in one kind of ability than he is in another.

Now let us suppose that an individual could distribute his ability over various kinds of performances in any way he preferred. Within limits, this is a reasonable proposition, for each individual does exercise some control. If a student neglects the academic subjects in order to practice on the piano, he will become a better pianist, and a poorer scholar. Alternatively, he can concentrate on something else and neglect the piano entirely. Students constantly make educational decisions, allocate study time, choose schools, select reading matter, or neglect their studies. All such decisions influence the extent to which one or another ability will be developed.

Now let us move from this realistic situation to its unrealistic limit, and to simplify the task let us arbitrarily assign some numbers to the situation. Suppose that a given individual has 1,000 units of ability—another individual might have more or fewer—and let us suppose that he can distribute these 1,000 units in any way he chooses over 20 different kinds of ability. If he wishes to be a completely well-rounded individual, he would assign 50 units to each of the 20 abilities. Or, he might select the 10 kinds of ability that he thinks most important and assign 100 units to each, neglecting completely the other 10 kinds of ability because they seem to him to be unimportant. Or, at the extreme, as a kind of talent gambler, he might stake his whole 1,000 units on one kind of ability and neglect the other 19 completely. Which of these ways of distributing his total talent fund would be best for the individual?

A parallel question can be asked from the point of view of society. Suppose that society rather than the individual decides how the 1,000 units will be distributed. Which would best serve society: to assign 50 units to each of 20 different kinds of ability, 100 units to each of 10 kinds, or the whole 1,000 units to a single ability?

We cannot answer these questions without considering the values involved. In real life, these values are often conflicting. The eminent young mathematician has to help care for the children, occasionally to repair the lawn mower, and take his turn in helping to run the affairs of the local Boy Scout troop. As a mathematician, he might like to concentrate all of his units of ability on mathematics. But as a human being with other interests, he has to save some of those units for other and quite nonmathematical kinds of ability and achievement. In real life, many conflicting value considerations are involved, but let us neglect them for the time being and concentrate on the problem of maximizing the social value of human talents.

The value that society places upon different levels of accomplishment does not vary directly with the amount of achievement or its underlying ability, but increases more rapidly than does the amount. A graph relating amount of talent and its social value would be a curve rather than a straight line—doubling the amount of ability more than doubles its value; doubling again the amount again more than doubles the value. The relationship can be illustrated with some arbitrary numbers: if one unit of ability is worth one dollar to society, 50 units are worth more than $50; perhaps 50 units are worth $100. Similarly for larger amounts, 100 units may be worth $500, and 1,000 units may be so valuable as to be priceless. These particular numbers are arbitrary, but that the relationship is nonlinear is clear. The salaries paid to chemists or engineers or members of other professions are not symmetrically distributed about a mean. The distributions are skewed, with a longer tail above the mean than below it. Moreover, there is general recognition that the salaries paid to the ablest people fall far short of being commensurate with their ability. On the ordinary scale of salaries for writers, physicists, and public servants, we make no effort to pay appropriate salaries to a Shakespeare, an Einstein, or a Winston Churchill.

We use other means to compensate outstanding persons whose salaries are not commensurate with their ability. We award Gold Medals to Olympic winners, Nobel Prizes to great scientists, Pulitzer Prizes to outstanding authors and editors, and we have other honors with which we recognize excellence in other fields. Partly by the amounts of money paid for different levels of ability and partly in other forms of compensation, society demonstrates that the value it places on talent increases more rapidly than does the amount of talent.

Now we can return to the question of the most valuable way of distributing talents. From the standpoint of society, the best way to distribute talent is to take maximum advantage of differences in aptitude, interest, and motivation by having each individual concentrate on the thing he can do best. Instead of having the 1,000-unit man distribute his ability 50 units on each of 20 kinds of ability or 100 units of each of 10, have him concentrate the whole 1,000 units on a single ability. In Harold Benjamin's fable, have the eagle be the best flyer in the world and forget about his ability to swim or climb, have the squirrel be the best climber in the world and stop worrying about his inability to fly. In human affairs, follow the same principle. Have one man be the best he can possibly become in one line and another the best he can possibly become in another line. Thus we would have the best physicist, the best poet, the best mathematician, and the best dramatist possible. The total value of the talents so distributed would be incomparably greater than would be the value of the same number of units of talent spread more uniformly over the different men and the different abilities involved.

Recommending that each person be helped to achieve the highest level he can reach in the area in which he has the greatest talent and interest is not the same as recommending that every scholar be a narrow specialist. Some, however, should be specialists, and some should specialize in relatively narrow fields. Physics is generally recognized as the most highly developed science. Further advances are most likely to be made by physicists who concentrate on a particular area of physics. Thus we want highly specialized physicists. But we also want physicists of wider interest and knowledge: persons who can bridge the gaps between physics and biology or physics and other sciences, persons who are interested in the practical applications of physical principles, and persons who are interested in attempting to translate physics into terms that the rest of us can try to understand. This diversity among physicists is essential if physics itself is to advance and if other fields of intellectual and practical endeavor are to benefit maximally from those advances.

From the standpoint of social value, maximum diversity would be the ideal; but like many another ideal, it is unattainable. In real life we must recognize that the best mathematician in the world must do something besides mathematics and that the best poet cannot spend all his energy on poetry. But the fact that the extreme case is unrealistic does not destroy the principle. The principle is this, and I state it now in realistic rather than imaginary terms: to the extent that we can control the distribution of talent, it is socially desirable to maximize the diversity, both within and among individuals.

This is the ideal. Before we consider methods of reaching toward that ideal, it is worthwhile briefly to look at its opposite, for then we will have set the boundaries within which we can maneuver in our educational and guidance practices.

In *Brave New World*, Aldous Huxley (1932) described a society in which most individuals were born as members of batches. Born, you will remember, is not the right word; old-fashioned human birth had been replaced by a kind of controlled embryology in which any desired number of identical individuals could be developed from a single fertilized egg. The eggs were developed in vitro, and at the proper time babies, instead of being born, were decanted. Through controlled nutrition, and through proper training and education, the members of a batch could be made to have any desired level of ability, and all the members of a batch were as alike as identical twins that had been reared together. We can dismiss

Brave New World as satirical exaggeration; but we cannot dismiss the kind of society that Huxley was satirizing, for there are forces in society that tend in the direction of homogeneity, and there are cultural values that make homogeneity seem desirable.

Between the unreality of *Brave New World* and the unreality of maximum diversity there is a wide range. Within this range we have considerable room to choose the kind of society we want ours to be. Ultimately the essential choices will be made by the nation as a whole, through the processes of democratic action. But in a more immediate sense, and on the important aspect of talent distribution, choices must be made by those persons who are professionally engaged in the development and handling of talent.

As to how far we should go in the direction of diversity, I have only two suggestions, and both must be stated in general terms. One is that we should go as far as we can. The other is that the greater the ability with which we are dealing, the greater is the amount of idiosyncrasy we can tolerate. The brief and brilliant career of the Indian mathematician Ramanujan (Newman, 1957) illustrates both principles. The name may be strange, for Ramanujan was a mathematicians' mathematician and was little known outside of mathematical circles. Yet he has been described as "quite the most extraordinary mathematician of our time." At the age of 15, he was loaned a copy of Carr's *Synopsis of Pure Mathematics*. This was all he had, and all he needed, to start him off on a strange, unorthodox, and inspired career of mathematical innovation. Working completely alone, he rediscovered much that had been developed by earlier mathematicians; he followed some false leads and made some mistakes; but in some fields of mathematics his power and originality went beyond any other mathematician in the world.

On the basis of his obvious brilliance, he was given a scholarship; but he lost it at the end of the first term because he failed his examination in English. He never did earn a university degree; but at the age of 25, after working for some years as a clerk, he was given a fellowship at Cambridge where he went to work with G. H. Hardy. Hardy faced the problem of deciding how much he should let Ramanujan go his own way, and how much he should try to correct his mistakes and make him into a more orthodox mathematician. Hardy expressed his dilemma in these words:

"It was impossible to ask such a man to submit to systematic instruction, to try to learn mathematics from the beginning once more. I was afraid too that, if I insisted unduly on matters which Rumanujan found irksome, I might destroy his confidence or break the spell of his inspiration. On the other hand there were things of which it was impossible that he should remain in ignorance. . . . It was impossible to let him go through life supposing that all the zeros of the Zeta-function were real."

The moral of the story is that, if we are dealing with a Ramanujan, we can put up with a great deal of eccentricity; if we are dealing with a lesser mind, we can insist on more conformity. Even with a Ramanujan there is a limit, but let us in all cases push that limit as far as we can.

Implications

Let me now briefly suggest some of the implications of the principle that it is socially valuable to increase the diversity of talent. Each of these implications relates to practices that are under our professional control.

The first implication is that it is desirable to make wider use of tests of special ability or aptitude to supplement our tests of general ability. De Haan and Havighurst (1957) found, in a survey of 40 school systems, that nearly all used tests of general intellectual ability as a means of appraising the potential of their students, but only 3 used tests of special aptitudes. Failure to use special tests increases the danger of overlooking students with unusually high potential in art, music, creative writing, and other abilities that are not well measured by the usual tests of general intellectual aptitude.

A second implication is that it is desirable to increase the use of separate scores for separate types of ability and to decrease the use of single scores that represent the sum or combination of several part scores. When students are being selected for awards or for admission to the next higher educational level, global measures are the easiest ones to use. Moreover, global measures are the ones that are likly to give the highest validity coefficients. Most of our usual measures of success are factorially complex and can be better predicted by factorially complex tests than by factorially simpler ones.

We pay a price, however, for the ease of use and for the higher validity of general measures of aptitude. The price we pay for using general measures is that we reduce the apparent size of the pool of talent on which we can draw. Relying solely on tests of general intellectual aptitude reduces the size of the talent pool because various kinds of ability, although usually positively correlated with one another, are by no means perfectly correlated. In the Quincy youth development study, selection of the top 10% of the children in general intellectual ability, the top 10% in leadership, and the top 2% in drawing ability included 16% of the total population. The authors estimate that, had they also included the top 10% each in music, dramatic ability, creative writing and mechanical ability, they would have brought into their talent development program 20–25% of the total child population (De Haan & Havighurst, 1957).

In Kenneth Little's study (1958) of Wisconsin high school graduates, he used the usual measures of high school grades and general intelligence. But he went beyond these measures by asking the teachers to identify those of their students who were specially gifted in any field. About 20% of the students so identified had not ranked in the upper quarter of their graduating class in either general scholastic achievement or general mental ability. Included were students whom the teachers identified as being specially gifted in art, music, science, and other fields. Clearly the use of tests of special aptitude and the use of individual grades and scores rather than averages identifies a larger number of talented young persons and thus lays the basis for the development of a larger and more diversified talent pool.

An opportunity to use the more detailed information made available by separate scores is found in the award of scholarships and fellowships. The person who is high on every score and thus high on the sum or average of his scores should, of course, be encouraged to continue his education, and such students clearly merit awards, scholarships, and fellowships. But when we drop down a step or two below the generally superior level, we still tend to base awards on the average score instead of looking for evidence of exceptionally high merit in individual fields or abilities. I would suggest that in awarding scholarships when we reach this slightly lower general level, we make some of the awards to students who have earned very high marks on individual tests or measures of ability. We will probably experience some lowering of validity coefficients, we may make awards to a few unproductive eccentrics; but we will enhance our chances of picking up a few persons so highly gifted and so intensely interested along one line that they have neglected, or rebelliously disdained, to keep pace with their fellows in other lines.

A third implication is that the patterning of abilities should be avoided in the selection or guidance of persons entering or contemplating entering a particular occupation. You may recall the long history of unsuccessful efforts to find the optimal patterns of abilities and personality traits that characterize the successful members of an occupational group. No one has stated the hope for such patterns better than Clark Hull (1928) who, thirty years ago, pointed out that vocational guidance would be easy if we had measures of the various kinds of ability and if we had carried out the analyses necessary to determine the weight with which each type of ability enters into the determination of success in each of a variety of occupations. Under the system that Hull anticipated, an applicant for vocational guidance would be given a battery of tests that measured all of the major types of ability. His scores on these tests would be fed into a computer which already contained in its storage unit the regression weights of each ability on each of a variety of occupations. The sum of the products of the ability scores and the corresponding regression weights for a given occupation would then be automatically computed and would represent the applicant's predicted standard score for success in that occupation. With a modern computer, it would be possible to determine very quickly the predicted standard scores for success in each of a large number of occupations.

In the days since Hull wrote this description, the necessary computers have reached a high stage of development; tests of different kinds of ability have been improved, although not nearly so much as the computers. But we have also learned enough about ability, vocations, and the factors that make for success to have concluded that the kind of differential prediction that Hull described is not feasible. A major reason is that relatively diverse patterns of ability are consistent with success in a single vocation. Any professional field includes opportunities for such a variety of persons—persons differing in abilities and differing in personality traits—that there is no simple or single pattern that is either essential or sufficient. Consider engineering, or medicine, or psychology, or any other field of work that demands intellectual ability. Each title covers a wide variety of tasks; each field includes opportunities for a wide variety of persons.

The search for a pattern characteristic of each profession has failed. As I have considered this failure, I have become convinced that we were on the wrong track in looking for distinctive patterns. For law, medicine, engineering, psychology, and other fields are enriched by having within their ranks a wide range of patterns of ability.

Conclusion

It would be possible to present other implications of the values of diversity, implications for the guidance and for the education of talented students. A general discussion of these fields would take far too long, and I will refrain, for now it is time to conclude. The needs of the nation for highly developed talent are growing and will continue to grow. This is an inevitable feature of the kind of complex, industrialized, specialized society in which we live. If we are to make full use of our intellectual resources, the first requisite is that we employ all the means at our command to encourage the development of talent. The second requisite is that we learn more about the social factors that aid or impede the development of talent.

I expect that these two points are noncontroversial. I am not so sure about the third point that I have advanced. Some of you may disagree with part or all of what I have said about the strategy of optimal distribution or deployment of talent. I readily grant the privilege of disagreement, for you have given me the opportunity to argue that we should go beyond personal action and beyond scientific research to consider the question of how our professional activities concerned with talent can be supported and unified by an underlying policy of talent development—a policy that seeks to maximize achievement and thus to maximize the value to society of our resources of talent.

What I have attempted to do is to state the first principles of a strategy of talent development, a strategy that provides a unifying rationale for our efforts to improve the construction and interpretation of tests, and the counseling, guidance, and education of talented young minds. The strategy is one of increasing the diversity of talent, in an individual, within an occupation, and in society. There will always be counterpressures that must be respected; but to the extent that we succeed in increasing the diversity of talent, we will have increased its value to society.

References

Benjamin, H. *The cultivation of idiosyncrasy.* Cambridge, Mass.: Harvard Univer. Press, 1955.

De Haan, R. F., & Havighurst, R. J. *Educating gifted children.* Chicago: Univer. Chicago Press, 1957.

Gardner, J. W., et al. *The pursuit of excellence: Education and the future of America.* (The "Rockefeller" report on education) Garden City, N.Y.: Doubleday, 1958.

Hull, C. L. *Aptitude testing.* Yonkers-on-Hudson, N.Y.: World Books, 1928.

Huxley, A. *Brave new world.* Garden City, N.Y.: Doubleday, Doran, 1932.

Little, J. K. A state-wide inquiry into decisions of youth about education beyond high school. University of Wisconsin, 1958.

Newman, J. R. Srinivasa Ramanujan. In, *Lives in science.* New York: Simon & Schuster, 1957. Pp. 257–269.

9.2 Intelligence: 1965 Model

J. P. Guilford

This discussion by Professor Guilford is consonant with the point of view presented by him in a previous paper. In 1959 he published his classic report on the structure of the intellect (J. P. Guilford, "Three Faces of Intellect," American Psychologist, *1959,* **14**, *469–479). He briefly reviews this work and reports further research progress. Then he presents a model for problem solving based on an epistemology derived from content and product categories in the structure of the intellect. Guilford attempts to demonstrate the difference of intellect among our pupils.*

Not all psychologists agree with the thrust of his research (See Q. McNemar, "Lost: Our Intelligence? Why?", American Psychologist, *1964,* **19**, *871–882.). McNemar argues for the use of general intelligence as opposed to multi-factor tests. He is concerned that the predictive validity of these tests is inferior to those measuring the general factor.*

The structure-of-intellect (SI) model, with its five operation categories intersecting with its four content categories, and these, in turn, intersecting with its six product categories, is the same in 1965 as it was

SOURCE. Abridged from J. P. Guilford, "Intelligence: 1965 Model," *American Psychologist,* **XXI**, 1 (1966), pp. 20–26, by permission of the author and the American Psychological Association.

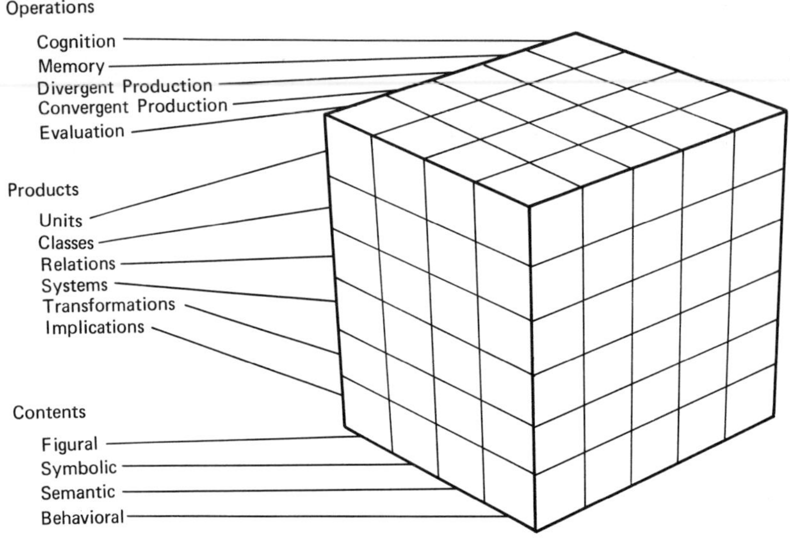

FIGURE 1. Model of the structure of intellect.

when first designed in 1958 (Guilford, 1959). To refresh your memories, a diagram of the model is given in Figure 1. In this respect there is no change or progress to report. The progress is mainly in terms of demonstration of many new intellectual abilities to occupy cells of the model, with only a very few movings of abilities within the model to give better logical fits to theory.

When efforts were first made in 1955 to organize the known intellectual abilities that had been segregated by factor analysis, 37 distinct abilities were recognized (Guilford, 1956). In 1958, there were 43 such abilities that could be placed within the model. From then on, the model has served as the heuristic source of hypotheses as to what new kinds of abilities for which to look. As of today, 80 abilities are believed to have been demonstrated and are placed within the model. Of the 120 cells of the model, five operations times four contents times six products, 75 cells are actually occupied. The discrepancy between 75 and 80 is that 3 cells have been found to contain 2 abilities each and 1 contains 3. The duplications within cells arise from distinctions among parallel visual, auditory, and kinesthetic cognitive and memory abilities. More of such duplications are to be expected when appropriate investigations are made.

To break down these figures more meaningfully, the numbers of demonstrated abilities in the various operation categories are of interest. The differences among operation categories with respect to numbers of known factors reflect the extents to which they have been investigated.

Of the 24 theoretical cognitive cells (where cognition is confined by definition simply to comprehension or induction), all 24 are now occupied, with 2 cells having 2 abilities each and 1 having 3 abilities. In the latter instance, the 3 abilities are concerned with cognition of figural systems—visual-spatial orientation, kinesthetic-spatial orientation, and auditory systems (cognition of rhythms and melodies). One cell containing two abilities pertains to cognition of units, visual on the one hand and auditory (such as radio-code signals) on the other. The other cell containing two abilities pertains to symbolic units; the cognition of printed words on the one hand and the hearing of spoken words on the other.

Of 24 projected memory abilities, 12 have been demonstrated, one cell containing 2 abilities. The latter case includes memory for visual systems and memory for auditory systems. The main difference between cognition and memory abilities can be expressed very simply. Cognitive abilities pertain to how much you do know or can know at the time of testing, whereas memory abilities pertain to how much you can remember, given a standard exposure to information. Six memory abilities are currently under investigation in the Aptitudes Research Project (ARP) at the University of Southern California, with the chance of demonstrating some new ones. By the time this paper appears in print, there may be 15 demonstrated memory factors.[1]

In the area of divergent production, which is believed to contain some of the most directly relevant intellectual abilities for creative thinking and creative production, 16 of the 24 potential abilities have been investigated and demonstrated, in both adult and ninth-grade populations; also 6 of them at the sixth-grade level. Lauritzen (1963) has demonstrated a like number at the fifth-grade level. At the present time, 6 additional hypothesized divergent-production abilities are under investigation in the behavioral-content area, by the ARP.

One of the least explored operation areas is that of convergent production. Ten of the 24 possible convergent-production abilities have been demonstrated, with 2 more of them being currently under study in an analysis of classification abilities cutting across three operation categories.

Two recently completed analyses aimed at evaluative abilities have brought the number of known factors in the evaluation category to 13, and they have added a great deal to the understanding of this particular

[1] I cannot pass by the opportunity to express a deep appreciation for liberal support to the Project from the Personnel and Training Branch, Office of Naval Research; the Cooperative Research Program, United States Office of Education; and the National Science Foundation. I should also like to pay tribute to the many graduate students who have collaborated in this effort.

class of abilities (Hoepfner, Guilford, & Merrifield, 1964; Nihira, Guilford, Hoepfner, & Merrifield, 1964).

Behavioral-cognition abilities. Of special note in recent developments is the demonstration of six cognitive abilities for dealing with behavioral information. This is the area marked off years ago by E. L. Thorndike (1920) as "social intelligence." Spearman (1927) was speaking about the same aptitude area under the heading of "psychological relations."

In the 1958 version of the SI model, an entire section involving 30 abilities was hypothesized for this area, with the belief that among the things that we can know, remember, and evaluate, and about which we can do productive thinking, is information about the behavior of other individuals and about ourselves. The major step was in bringing such areas of experience within the general concept of information. The abilities to be expected in this area were thought to be systematically parallel to abilities already found in other information areas—figural, symbolic, and semantic. There were no known abilities found by factor analysis to support such a hypothesis.

According to SI theory, there should be six abilities in the cognition column for dealing with behavioral information. In the ARP, we proceeded to build tests for each of the six hypothesized abilities, for cognition of: behavioral units, classes, relations, systems, transformations, and implications. With a decision to stay within the context of printed tests as much as possible, the cue information used was in the form of photographs and line drawings of expressions involving the face, hands, arms, head, legs, and combinations of these body parts, also cartoons and cartoon strips, and photographed scenes involving people in pairs and triplets. In three tests, vocalized sound stimuli were also used. We stayed away from tests involving verbalizations on the part of the examinee, but used verbal statements pregnant with social or behavioral meanings as item material in some tests.

With an average of four such tests for each expected factor, the factor analysis demonstrated the six predicted factors, clearly segregated from figural and semantic abilities, with most of the new tests leading on factors where expected (O'Sullivan, Guilford, & deMille, 1965). So far as basic research is concerned, it appears that the large area of social intelligence has been successfully entered. Further work is naturally needed to determine the general significance of these abilities, as measured. We are now in the process of constructing tests for a parallel analysis of abilities predicted in the operational category of divergent production where behavioral information is concerned. Such abilities should be of considerable importance where any person has special need for creative approaches in dealing with others.

Some Related Problems

Age and Differentiation of Abilities

Because of the Garrett hypothesis there is considerable interest in knowing whether as much differentiation of abilities occurs for children as for adults. Most of our own recent information has come from the testing of senior high school students, for whom the expected differentiations have always thus far appeared, when test batteries have been adequate to check on the hypothesized factors. I have mentioned the fact that ninth-grade students show the usual differentiations among the divergent-production abilities. The same kinds of differentiations are found at the same level for other categories of abilities as well. There is a little less assurance of clear separations at the sixth-grade level, but our experiences have been very limited at that level.

From other sources, it can be noted that some of the factors have been found differentiated at the age of 6 (McCartin, 1963), also at the mental ages 4 and 2, in retarded as well as in normal children (Meyers, Dingman, Orpet, Sitkei, & Watts, 1964). From still other sources (Stott & Ball, 1963), there are suggestions of a number of the SI abilities being detected for preschool and infant populations down to the age of 1. At this time it would appear that when children have reached the level of maturity at which appropriate tests for a factor can be administered and individual differences in scores can be obtained, the factors should be found differentiated. There is thus little to support the Garrett view that factors of intelligence come into being by differentiation from a single, comprehensive ability like Spearman's *g*.

This is not so strange, when we consider that the four kinds of information—figural, symbolic, semantic, and behavioral—come into the child's sphere of experience at different times, and development in coping with them progresses at different rates. Figural and behavioral information are encountered almost from birth whereas semantic information begins to come later, and symbolic information much later. The early differentiations of abilities must mean that the brain develops naturally different ways of processing the various products of information, as it develops different mechanisms for the five kinds of operations.

Predictive Validity in Mathematics

The ARP has always had a firm commitment to do basic research on the differentiable aptitudes, realizing that the number of investigators who undertake to solve such problems is exceedingly small. We have done one major study devoted to predictive validity, however, in which the criterion was achievement in ninth-grade mathematics (Guilford,

Hoepfner, & Petersen, 1965). The study was somewhat premature, since it was realized that some of the potentially relevant SI abilities had not yet been demonstrated, nor were there tests for such hypothesized abilities. But, on the basis of what factors were known, the objective was to determine how well achievement could be predicted from factor tests, singly and in combination, as compared with three traditional academic-aptitude tests and also in combination with them.

Predictions of scores from specially prepared achievement tests in general mathematics and algebra were as good from combinations of factor-test scores as those from standard aptitude tests, or better, with multiple correlations ranging from .5 to .8. The factor tests also added significantly to prediction obtainable from standard aptitude tests in the case of algebra. Discrimination between successful algebra students (above the median in achievement) and successful general-mathematics students could be made with errors of only 10%, using a weighted combination of factor tests.

Psychological Theory

The finding of differentiated abilities in the area of intelligence is largely a taxonomic exercise. The outcome is in the form of basic concepts as to kinds of ability, answering the question "What?" Further steps need to be taken in order to answer the questions "How?" and "Why?" The SI theory is a step in these directions, and inferences from that theory lead further toward the goal of general psychological theory.

Role of Information

Of the 15 categories of the structure of intellect, 10 pertain to information, indicating the relative importance of kinds of information in the economy of intellectual functioning. This has suggested the view that we should regard the organism as a processor of information. A general informational approach to psychological theory is not unique, by any means. The increasing tendency to talk about input and output in place of stimulus and response is very noticeable. It is desirable, then, that we have some systematic categories of information, if we are to have an informational psychology.

Information, of the type with which we deal in psychology, I have defined as that which the organism discriminates. Discrimination is along the lines of the content and product categories, but of course discriminations also occur within each of these categories. The emphasis upon discrimination is in line with the concept of information in the field of communication engineering, but from that point on there is considerable divergence, for by "information" the engineer means *uncertainty*, whereas the psychologist's information must be in terms of reduction of uncertainty, or in terms of probabilities approaching *certainty*. There is not time to go into these issues here.

Principle of Association

Another noteworthy innovation derived from SI theory is the proposal (Guilford, 1961) that we now interpret the ancient and respected concept of association in terms of the six products of information, giving us much more discriminative meaning and extending the possibilities for explanatory effectiveness. This suggestion will be very unpopular, for associationism has been a cornerstone for most psychological theory. The proposal is for a refinement and extension of a concept, not for complete replacement. But it does imply that what is learned and remembered is in the form of acquired products of information rather than stimulus-response connections. And it calls for the reinterpretation of habits or skills also in terms of products of information, largely systems, many of which become units.

Psychoepistemology and Psycho-logic

By his clinical-genetic approach, Piaget has demonstrated efforts working toward the goal of an epistemology empirically derived. I propose that the 24 cells derived from intersecting content and product categories in the SI model can furnish one such an epistemology. The mention of 24 categories, of course, ignores the distinct possibility that there will be more when we see how far auditory, kinesthetic, and perhaps tactual areas of information extend the number. Piaget's efforts have been directed more toward particular concepts, although generalizing somewhat in dealing with classes and relations as generic categories of information. He has by no means covered the whole range of 24 categories.

Piaget also places a great deal of emphasis upon the relation of psychology to modern logic (Inhelder & Piaget, 1964). On the one hand, he emphasizes the principle that the individual's development is in the direction of formal logic in his thinking. On the other hand, he intimates that the application of formal logic should be the goal of the theoretical psychologist and he suggests that as a step in the direction of that goal we need a psycho-logic (Piaget, 1953). The six product categories are proposed as the basis for such a psycho-logic. Although not chosen with formal logic in mind, the names of the product categories are in fairly good correspondence with concepts of formal logic. Whether formal logic is now adequate for supplying the models for theory in connection with the six products remains to be seen.

A Model for Problem Solving

My title promises a 1965 model, so here it is: an operational model for problem solving in general. Since most behavior readily involves a bit of problem-solving activity, the model could also have applications over wide areas of behavior. Although emphasizing SI concepts, the model also takes into account many of the new findings and new thinking from other sources. The model is represented in Figure 2.

The typical, traditional model for problem solving, since John Dewey (1910), has been a linear time series running through steps such as: seeing the problem, analyzing or structuring the problem, generating solutions, and judging and selecting one of the solutions. Things look more complicated now with respect to problem solving as well as with respect to intelligence. Cybernetics and the computer-simulator people have seen to that.

The occasion for a problem-solving episode begins with a certain input, mostly through the sense avenues, of course, represented at Input I in the model. The E and S stand for environmental and somatic sources of input, respectively. The somatic source may include both motivational and emotional components, from within the brain as well as from internal receptors. A filtering step determines which input goes further and has any appreciable consequences in behavior. Note that the memory storage underlies and potentially affects all steps, beginning with the filtering operation. "Filtering" is a new and more operational name for "attention." Evaluation is another operation that has to be taken into account at all steps along the way, for the organism is perpetually self-checking and self-correcting. Evaluation is not left to the final stage of problem solving, as commonly supposed in traditional models.

Awareness that a problem exists and identification or structuring of the problem are cognitive operations. During these operations there is dependence upon memory storage and there is evaluation of cognized information. In the effort to cognize the problem, there may be a seeking for new input information, as at Input II in the model. Filtering of this input also occurs, as well as evaluation.

With the problem reasonably well structured, there is a search for answers, or for information from which answers can be constructed, in memory storage, with the ubiquitous interplay with evaluation. If a solution is accepted, there is an exit from this problem-solving episode at Exit III. Exit I would be a dodging of the problem. Exit II would be a giving up or perhaps a result of distraction before the productive operation got started.

If no good solutions are found to the problem, and if there are doubts about its proper interpretation, a new major cycle begins as shown at the second cognition block. For reinterpretation of the problem, new input may be sought, with steps similar to those already outlined. A number of these major cycles may go on, in what has often been described as trial-and-error behavior. Within each major cycle there are subsidiary

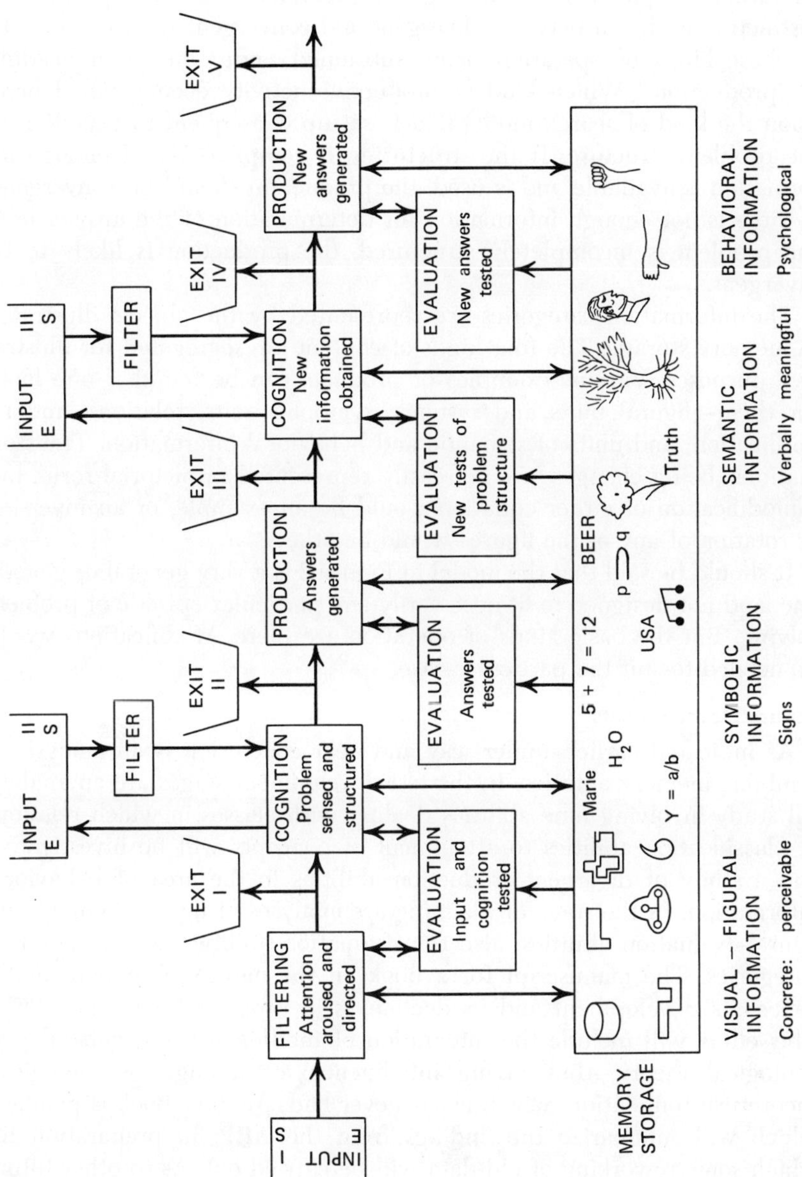

FIGURE 2. Model for problem solving.

loops in the flow of events, each of which might be followed by a number of similar loops. The looping phenomena follow cybernetic principles, with feedback information involved, and evaluation.

The relation of this model to the SI model is fairly obvious. The operation categories have been given prominent roles except that no distinction is shown between divergent and convergent production, both of these kinds of operation being subsumed under the plain heading of "production." Which kind of productive activity occurs will depend upon the kind of search model that is set up consequent to cognition of the problem structure. If the structuring is complete and if enough information is available and is used, the production should be convergent; if there is not enough information for determination of the answer or if the problem is incompletely structured, the production is likely to be divergent.

The information categories are represented by the objects illustrated in memory storage. The four kinds of content are segregated for illustrative purposes. Various examples of products can be found if one looks for them—figural units and systems; symbolic units, relations, and an implication; and units of semantic and behavioral information. Transformations, being changes, are not easily represented in pictorial form, but a modification of either equation would be an example, or an inversion or rotation of any of the figures would be others.

It should be said that the model in Figure 2 is a very general or generic one, and not designed to fit necessarily any particular episode of problem solving. But the basic kinds of operation are there. Modifications would be needed to suit the particular case.

Future Developments

As indicated earlier, under way and near conclusion is an analysis of symbolic memory abilities. In the test-development stages are an analytical study involving nine abilities dealing with classes in which relations of classification abilities to attainment of concepts will be investigated, and a study of divergent-production abilities in the area of behavioral information. In the stage of planning are analyses of figural-memory and figural-evaluation abilities, also transformation abilities across operation categories. The manuscript for a book on the nature of human intelligence, its development and its decline, is in progress (Guilford, 1967). This effort will include the integration of intelligence into general psychological theory, thus giving intelligence a thorough psychological-theoretical foundation, which it has never had. Another book is planned, which will summarize the findings from the ARP, in preparation for which some reworking of old data will be carried out. As to other future developments, these are very much in the laps of the gods.

References

Dewey, J. *How we think.* Boston: D. C. Heath, 1910.

Guilford, J. P. Les dimensions de l'intellect. In H. Laugier (Ed.), *L'analyse factorielle et ses applications.* Paris: Centre Nationale de la Recherche Scientifique, 1956. Pp. 53–74.

Guilford, J. P. Three faces of intellect. *American Psychologist,* 1959, **14**, 469–479.

Guilford, J. P. Factorial angles to psychology. *Psychological Review,* 1961, **68**, 1–20.

Guilford, J. P. *The nature of human intelligence.* New York: McGraw-Hill, 1967.

Guilford, J. P., Hoepfner, R., & Petersen, H. Predicting achievement in ninth-grade mathematics from measures of intellectual-aptitude factors. *Education and Psychological Measurement,* 1965, **25**, 659–682.

Hoepfner, R., Guilford, J. P., & Merrifield, P. R. A factor analysis of the symbolic-evaluation abilities. Report No. 33, 1964, University of Southern California, Psychological Laboratory, Los Angeles.

Inhelder, B., & Piaget, J. *The early growth of logic in the child.* New York: Harper & Row, 1964.

Lauritzen, E. S. Semantic divergent thinking factors among elementary school children. Unpublished doctoral dissertation, University of California, Los Angeles, 1963.

McCartin, Rose A. An exploration at first grade of six hypotheses in the semantic domain. Unpublished doctoral dissertation, University of Southern California, 1963.

Meyers, C. E., Dingman, H. F., Orpet, R. E., Sitkei, E. G., & Watts, C. A. Four ability-factor hypotheses at three preliterate levels in normal and retarded children. *Monographs of the Society for Research in Child Development,* 1964, **29**, No. 5.

Nihira, K., Guilford, J. P., Hoepfner, R., & Merrifield, P. R. A factor analysis of the semantic-evaluation abilities. Report No. 32, 1964, University of Southern California, Los Angeles.

O'Sullivan, Maureen, Guilford, J. P., & deMille, R. Measurements of social intelligence. Report No. 34, 1965, University of Southern California, Los Angeles.

Piaget, J. *Logic and psychology.* Manchester: Manchester Univer. Press, 1953.

Spearman, C. *Abilities of man.* New York: Macmillan, 1927.

Stott, L. H., & Ball, Rachel S. *Evaluation of infant and preschool mental tests.* Detroit: Merrill-Palmer, 1963.

Thorndike, E. L. Intelligence and its uses. *Harpers,* 1920, **140**, 227–235.

9.3 Teachers' Attitudes Toward Children's Behavior Revisited

Alexander Tolor, William L. Scarpetti, and Paul A. Lane

There is the possibility not only that teachers may fail to adjust their teaching to meet individual differences, but also that they may misinterpret and misevaluate behavior, reacting in ways that hinder rather than promote a pupil's development. There is evidence that some teachers are not able to differentiate between normal and abnormal behavior when their judgment is compared with that of psychologists. Specific kinds of behavior are listed in the discussion and disparities of evaluation emphasized.

A classic study of E. K. Wickman (1928) found a great discrepancy between the views of teachers and mental health workers toward the behavior problems of children. Although this study has been criticized on methodological grounds, its influence on American education has been profound. Several more recent investigations (Griffiths, 1952; Schrupp & Gjerde, 1953; Stouffer, 1952) suggest that while there has been considerable change in the attitudes of teachers to make them more congruent

SOURCE. Alexander Tolor, William L. Scarpetti, and Paul A. Lane, "Teachers' Attitudes Toward Children's Behavior Revisited," *Journal of Educational Psychology*, **LVIII,** 3 (1967), pp. 175–180. Reprinted by permission of Dr. Tolor and the American Psychological Association.

with those of clinicians, marked differences between the two groups continue to exist. These differences are still in the direction of teachers being more concerned with management, sexual adjustment, and adherence to authority problems whereas the mental health professionals are more sensitive to withdrawal behavior and behavior not directly related to the school routine but suggesting a deterioration of social or emotional patterns.

The purpose of this study was to explore further the relationship between the evaluations by teachers and psychologists of a wide range of child behavior patterns. More specifically, it was anticipated that by employing a comprehensive scale of unambiguous behavioral items, which can be grouped on an empirical or theoretical basis to focus on patterns of functioning, it would be possible to identify the types of behavioral patterns that teachers and psychologists perceive most differently. The effect that the teachers' experience level has on the ratings was also to be determined.

Method

The teacher respondents consisted of 90 female and 28 male elementary public school teachers randomly selected from a large urban school system. They were drawn from all grades ranging from the kindergarten to the seventh grade level, inclusively. There were 9 teachers at the kindergarten level, 13 at Grade 1, 16 at Grade 2, 15 at Grade 3, 17 at Grade 4, 16 at Grade 5, 15 at Grade 6, and 17 at Grade 7. The professional experience of the teachers encompassed the range of less than 1 year to 44 years (mean 11.0 years).

The psychologist respondents consisted of 17 males and 6 females, all of whom were functioning in clinical settings in the same state as the teachers. The highest degree held by the psychologists was the Ph.D. for 15 and the M.A. or M.S. by eight. In experience the psychologists ranged from under one year to over 30 years (mean 10.7 years).

The measuring device was the Staten Island Behavior Scale (Mandell & Silberstein, 1965) which consists of 295 items descriptive of children's behavior. The items were originally selected from published and unpublished scales used to evaluate children's adjustment and from an analysis of a large number of case records in the files of a child guidance clinic.

The items were classified for the purposes of the present study by six raters (5 advanced students and 1 Diplomate in Clinical Psychology), making independent judgments, into the following classifications: psychosomatic and physical disturbance (71 items); phobias (18 items); aggressiveness (56 items); affect expression (58 items); communication disturbance (21 items); regressive behavior (15 items); inefficiency indicators (25 items); and fantasy involvement or withdrawal (31 items).

Each item was placed into the category that represented the rating of the majority of the judges. An indication of the high degree of interrater agreement is provided by the fact that on 203 of the 295 items (69%) at least five of the raters were in complete agreement in regard to the classification of an item.

Illustrations of the different types of items are the following: For the psychosomatic and physical disturbance classification—"Is slow in his movements"; for the phobic classification—"Is afraid of being alone in a wide open space"; for aggressiveness—"Hits or attacks other child"; for affect expression—"Shows inappropriate feeling"; for communication disturbance—"Talks and talks"; for regressive behavior—"Carries blanket"; for inefficiency indicators—"Does not complete his chores"; and for fantasy involvement or withdrawal—"Doesn't join in competitive games."

The written instructions accompanying the administration of the scale are presented below:

"For each of the following items please indicate whether the behavior in question, in your opinion, indicates normal or abnormal behavior in a child falling in the age range from 1 to 16 inclusive.

"Please answer all items without omitting any, and try to check either the 'Normal' or 'Abnormal' category. In the event that you really cannot decide whether the behavior is normal or abnormal, you may check the 'Unknown' line. However, you will probably be able to arrive at a definite decision in all or nearly all instances."

The respondents were not given any time limit, but were cautioned against collaborating with anyone else in completing the scale.

The very broad age range was quite deliberately employed in the instructions since our intent was not so much to obtain reactions to a child's behavior at a specific point in time—even though we recognized that the appropriateness of behavior is age related—but more to distill from a less structured frame of reference behavior patterns that most frequently tend to be regarded as being normal or abnormal, even in the absence of a specific anchoring point.

Results and Discussion

The main findings indicated that teachers and psychologists, when their responses for each item on the questionnaire are compared by chi-square, differ significantly ($p < .05$) on 66 of the 295 items, that is, on 22.4% of the items, in regard to whether they rated the behavior to be normal or abnormal. This number of differentiating items is significantly greater than would be expected on a chance basis alone. Of the 66 critical descriptions of behavior, 7, or 11%, are in the psychosomatic and physical disturbance category, 1, or 2%, in the phobias category, 21, or 32%, in the aggressiveness category, 19, or 29%, in the affect expression category, 3, or 5%, in the communication disturbance category, 6, or 9%, in the regressive behavior category, 3, or 5%, in the inefficiency indicators category, and 6, or 9%, in the fantasy involvement or withdrawal category.

Since the categories consisted originally of unequal numbers of scale items, the percentages reported above may be somewhat misleading. Another way of analyzing the same data is to determine the proportion of items within each category that differentiates the teachers' judgments from the psychologists' ratings. Employing this approach, we note from Table 1 that the greatest disagreement occurs in the areas of regressive

Table 1
Degree of Disagreement Between Teachers and Psychologists in Specific Scale Categories

Category	Items in scale	Percentage of items disagreed upon
Physical-psychosomatic	71	10
Phobic	18	6
Aggressive	56	38
Affect	58	33
Communication	21	14
Regressive	15	40
Inefficiency	25	12
Fantasy-withdrawal	31	19

behavior, aggressiveness, and affect expression. Next in order are fantasy involvement or withdrawal, communication disturbance, and inefficiency indicators in which areas the two groups are in relatively close agreement. In regard to phobias and psychosomatic and physical disturbance, the judgments of psychologists and teachers are very much in accord, as can be seen by the negligible item disagreement.

These results indicate, therefore, that elementary school teachers in general tend to evaluate behavior that may be described as regressive, aggressive, and emotional quite differently than do psychologists. In view of the fact that nearly all of the differentiating items, that is, 61 of 66, or 92.4%, were rated predominantly normal by psychologists and abnormal by teachers, it is obvious that elementary school teachers perceive regressive, aggressive, and emotional behavior to be considerably more pathological than do mental health professionals.

Two subgroups of teachers were selected based on amounts of teaching experience. The Highs consisted of the top third in experience of the overall group of teachers. The Lows consisted of the lowest third in teaching experience. The 39 teachers in the High subgroup ranged in professional experience from 14 to 44 years with a median of 24.5 years; the 39 teachers in the Low subgroup ranged in experience from less than 1 year to 6 years with a median of 3 years.

When the attitudes toward child behavior of the Lows are compared with those of the psychologists, 83 items were rated significantly differently by the two groups. Eighty of the 83 items, or 96%, were rated normal more often by psychologists than by teachers with relatively little experience. There was disagreement primarily in regard to the significance of aggressive behavior (57% of the items in that category were rated differently), regressive behavior (33% of the items here were differently rated), and affect expressions (31% of the items were judged differently). There was no difference in the ratings of the 18 phobic items, and relatively little disparity in judgments for inefficient behavior (16%) and fantasy-withdrawal behavior (16%). Communication problems and physical-psychosomatic disturbances produced only moderate disagreements (19% and 21%).

A similar chi-square analysis was done comparing the attitudes of teachers high in experience with psychologists on each of the scale items. In this comparison only 45 behavioral descriptions significantly differentiated the groups. Moreover, the patterns of disagreements between highly experienced teachers and psychologists, on the one hand, and less experienced teachers and psychologists, on the other hand, is very different. For one thing, the more experienced teachers did not nearly as often differ from psychologists in the direction of ascribing abnormality to a description of child behavior as did the less experienced teachers. As a matter of fact, the differences between the more experienced teachers and psychologists were likely to be as often in the direction of teachers considering the behavior to be benign when psychologists regarded it as being pathological as it was to be considered pathological when the psychologists rated it as being normal. (Only 52% of the differentiating items were rated normal by psychologists more often than by highly experienced teachers.) Second, the areas in which the differences become manifest for the highly experienced teachers is very different from the Lows. More specifically, the Highs do not differ from the psychologists particularly in regard to aggressive, regressive, and affect behavior as do the Lows. The least disparity (0%), as a matter of fact, occurs in relation to regressive behavior; the greatest discrepancy (28% of the items in the category), occurs with the ratings of phobic behavior.

Finally, chi-square analyses of the item ratings for teachers high and teachers low in experience yielded the largest degree of discrepancy of all comparisons. Ninety-six, or 32.5% of the total number of behavioral descriptions, were rated significantly differently by these two subgroups. Interestingly, all 96 critical items were perceived to be normal more often by the highly experienced teachers as compared with the less experienced teachers.

Table 2

Degree of Disagreement between Highly Experienced and Relatively Inexperienced Teachers in Specific Scale Categories

Category	Items in scale	Percentage of items disagreed upon
Physical-psychosomatic	71	28
Phobic	18	67
Aggressive	56	32
Affect	58	28
Communication	21	48
Regressive	15	13
Inefficiency	25	40
Fantasy-withdrawal	31	26

Table 2 presents the percentage of items within each of the scale categories rated differently by highly experienced and relatively inexperienced teaching personnel. It will be noted that phobic behavior tends most often to be viewed differently by teachers of varying degrees of experience, and that there is considerable disagreement about behavior involving communication facility and efficiency.

Illustrative of the specific differences in ratings between the more experienced and the relatively less experienced teachers are the following items, all of which were regarded to be normal by the more experienced teachers and abnormal by the less experienced teachers:

Cries or whimpers
Plays with or fingers his mouth
Headache
At the slightest upset, coordination becomes poor
Is frightened in crowds
Is afraid of being alone in a wide open space
Child's thoughts are hard to understand
Lying

Lewis (1965), in reviewing the literature bearing on the "Continuity hypothesis," which states that ". . . emotional disturbance in a child is symptomatic of a continuing psychological process that may lead to adult mental illness [p. 465]," concluded that the acting-out child is more likely to become seriously disturbed as an adult than the timid, withdrawn child. He suggested that perhaps the judgments of teachers, as derived from the Wickman (1928) study, represented a more accurate appraisal of the pathology of children than the evaluations of clinicians, at least when adult psychiatric status is taken as the criterion. Irregardless of the validity of the perceptions of each of these groups, the study of the nature of the attitudes remains an important research problem since attitudes will influence markedly the interactions between the child and his teachers.

Beilin (1959) pointed out cogently that the attitudinal patterns of teachers and clinicians toward adjustment difficulties reflect in part their different roles, and that their roles, in turn, "influence the organization of their respective experiences [p. 22]." Since Beilin regards teachers to be essentially task-oriented, that is, concerned with the imparting of information and skills, and since mental health professionals are more concerned with preventing poor adjustment and promoting good adjustment, it is not surprising that these two groups will continue to perceive child behavior differently.

The present findings suggest that psychologists tend to be more accepting, or at least more tolerant, of a greater variety of child behavior than teachers, and tend to regard a wider range of behavior as being normal. Teachers, especially those who are relatively inexperienced, label much more behavior as being abnormal. Teachers are especially critical of categories of behavior that may be referred to as aggressive, regressive, and emotionally expressive. The fact that the greatest degree of disagreement is found between experienced and inexperienced teachers reinforces the impression that actual exposure to child behavior is an important determinant of attitudes toward pathology.

The present study also bears on the frequently voiced criticism of clinicians as being overly sensitive to the pathological aspects of others and not sufficiently sensitive to their assets. The findings indicate that this criticism is probably unjustified since the clinicians were in fact much less prone to interpret behavior as being abnormal than the teachers.

Brief reference should be made to several methodological limitations. First, a number of teachers and psychologists who were given the Staten Island Scale either did not complete the form or failed to follow instructions and had to be eliminated for that reason. Thus, of the original sample of 145 teachers, only 118 could be employed for the analysis.

Whether the respondents who cooperated differ in any essential respect from those who did not is not known. Second, although some precautions were taken against the respondents being influenced by others in making their ratings, the possibility still remains that some judgments were not made entirely independently.

Perhaps a more important problem is related to the ambiguous instructions provided the subjects. Many respondents found the task to be extremely difficult. A number took great pains to comment that since what is considered normal and abnormal is so closely related to the age level of the child, they could not arrive at a decision. Moreover, some stated that since the degree, severity, frequency, nature of onset, duration, and circumstances surrounding the appearance of the symptom remained unspecified, their confidence level in arriving at a decision was extremely low. Nevertheless, it should be noted that since both the professionals and the teachers were faced with the same need to impose structure on the scale items, there is little likelihood that the ratings reflect systematic response biases that differ for the two groups.

It is suggested that the question of whether anchoring the concept of normality versus abnormality to specific age levels affects the ratings of groups of experts and teachers merits further research attention. Also, it might be possible to investigate the effect of increased structure in the description of each item, in terms of such characteristics as frequency of the symptom, on the judgments. Other extensions of this project would concern themselves with the variance contributed to teacher ratings of such variables as their age, teaching competence, and socioeconomic status.

References

Beilin, H. Teachers' and clinician's attitudes toward the behavior problems of children: A reappraisal. *Child Development,* 1959, **30**, 9–25.

Griffiths, W. *Behavioral difficulties of children as perceived and judged by parents, teachers and children themselves.* Minneapolis: University of Minnesota Press, 1952.

Lewis, W. W. Continuity and intervention in emotional disturbance: A review. *Exceptional Children,* 1965, **31**, 465–475.

Mandel, W., & Silberstein, R. M. Children's psychopathology behavior rating scale. Paper presented at the meeting of the Eastern Psychological Association, Atlantic City, April 1965.

Schrupp, M. H., & Gjerde, C. M. Teacher growth in attitudes toward behavior problems of children. *Journal of Educational Psychology,* 1953, **44**, 203–214.

Stouffer, G. A. W., Jr. Behavior problems of children as viewed by teachers and mental hygienists. *Mental Hygiene,* 1952, **36**, 271–285.

Wickman, E. K. *Children's behavior and teachers' attitudes.* New York: Commonwealth Fund, 1928.

9.4 Alienation in the Classroom[1]

Philip W. Jackson

The author illustrates how the condition of alienation in pupils may stem from the same major "social sources" that cause alienation among adults. He believes that prevention and remediation of the condition involves first and foremost the clarification of expectations demanded of pupils and clearly stated objectives, understood not only by the teacher, but also by the pupil. Furthermore, the pupil must perceive his teachers as genuine and "unequivocal in the perception of their adult roles."

Every child experiences the pain of failure and the joy of success long before he reaches school age, but his achievements, or lack of them, do not really become official until he enters the classroom. From then on, however, a public record of his progress gradually accumulates, and as a student he must learn to adapt to the continued and pervasive spirit of evaluation that will dominate his school years. For most, the adaptation is not too difficult. Ideally, they will experience far more success than

SOURCE. Philip W. Jackson, "Allienation in the Classroom," *Psychology in the Schools*, II, 4 (1965), pp. 299–308. Reprinted by permission of Psychology Press, Inc.

[1] Revised version of a paper read at the Institute for Administrators of Pupil Personnel Services, Harvard University, summer, 1964.

failure, and will feel appropriately elated or depressed depending on the judgment their work receives. But, naturally, the ideal is not always realized. Many students do less well than they should and, more important, many—including some of the most able—do not seem to care, one way or the other, how they are doing. Although the two forms of difficulty—the academic and the motivational—are inter-related and both are serious, the apathetic student (irrespective of his achievement status) is a more disturbing example of classroom failure than is the youngster who is not doing well but who cares deeply about his lack of progress. The student who is willing but unable to do his work indicates, most frequently, the breakdown of a particular instructional sequence; but the student who no longer cares how well he does or who otherwise gives signs of being dissatisfied with school life, may signal the breakdown of social identification—a much more serious state of affairs. The remarks that follow focus chiefly on this second type of classroom failure: the student who cannot or will not respond appropriately to the values, the rewards, and the expectations, that combine to form the culture of the school.

Our understanding of social and psychological problems has been enhanced in recent years by the development of the concept of alienation. As the term was originally used by social theorists, such as Marx and Weber, alienation referred to the psychological discomfort suffered by the worker in an industrialized society. Cut off from both the means and the ends of production, the industrial worker lost the feeling of pride and commitment that had characterized the earlier craftsman. Labor, which was once a unified and intrinsically satisfying activity, had become fragmented and meaningless. The link between the product and the producer was broken, and with nothing to sell but himself, the worker began to feel curiously adrift in a world that seemed to be fashioned increasingly by and for the desires of others.

That which began as a theoretical description of the worker's plight has since been verified empirically, and as it is used today, the concept of alienation has been broadened to include not only the factory worker, but, to some extent, all who live in today's industrialized urban societies. The estrangement of modern man from himself and from others is viewed by many as the major psychological problem of our time. In the present paper ideas derived from empirical and theoretical studies of alienation will be applied to the examination of classroom problems.

Signs of Alienation in the School

As a group, educators are highly achievement-oriented. And understandably so. Not only have their own academic careers been relatively successful—indicating that typically they have embraced the school's values from the beginning—but, in addition, their professional energies are focused almost exclusively on the promotion of achievement in others. It is hardly surprising, therefore, that many teachers view scholastic success as an all-encompassing good, and have a difficult time understanding people who do not share this basic value. Normally the teacher expects the student to be delighted by high grades and deflated by low ones (as he himself was when he was a student). Even when the rewards and punishments of grades are not operating, the student is thought to be gaining personal satisfaction from the growth of his own ability (as the teacher supposedly did), and, therefore, he is expected to undertake school tasks eagerly. When these expectations are not met, the teacher may become puzzled or annoyed by what he perceives as a complete disregard for an obvious virtue. Yet as the statistics on dropouts and delinquents, and the extensive literature devoted to the topic of classroom boredom indicate, there are many students who do not share the teacher's enthusiasms.

One of the first and most important signs of disturbance in a social unit—and, hence, one of the most reliable indicators of alienation—appears when individuals or sub-groups within the unit hold fundamentally different views of either the value of the rewards dispensed to group members or the conditions under which the rewards are distributed.

It is commonly recognized that there are two major reward systems operating in the classroom: the "intrinsic," which arises naturally from the growth of ability, and the "extrinsic," which comprises the evaluations given by teachers, fellow students, and outsiders. When either of these systems begins to misfire, the danger signals of more serious difficulties have been sounded. As has been suggested, the misfiring may occur in two ways: through the devaluation of the reward system or through its misapplication (either real or fancied).[2]

The student who gets no pleasure from his own progress has devaluated the *intrinsic* reward system. Similarly, the student who doesn't care what the teacher or others think has devaluated the *extrinsic* reward system. If the student is unable to see his own progress (or sees some when there is none) the *intrinsic* reward system is being misapplied. Similarly, if the student deserves praise or punishment from others (or

[2] Rewards may also be overvalued and, thus, sought more fervently than some people think they should be. The "money-hungry" adult and the "grade-hungry" student are two examples of such overstriving. These forms of pathological motivation will not be discussed in the present paper.

thinks he does) and it is not given, the *extrinsic* reward system is being misapplied.

These two forms of malfunctioning—the devaluation and the misapplication of the school's rewards—are clearly interrelated. Indeed, in many instances there seems to be a causal relationship between the two. Devaluation (in the form of student indifference) is often a reaction to the suspicion of unfairness or illogic in the handling of rewards. The student who thinks he is being treated unfairly and who feels unable to do anything about it learns to remain detached and uninvolved. The possibility of there being this kind of causal link is important because it implies that beneath the student's bland indifference harsher feelings may lurk. These feelings may stem from a basic distrust of the classroom environment in general and of school authorities in particular.

A first step, then, in the diagnosis of alienation is to examine the degree of concordance between the objective and the subjective aspects of evaluation, between what society thinks of a person and what he thinks of himself. A lack of agreement in these matters would be interpreted as a serious danger signal. Even when there is a perfect agreement, however, and the reward system appears to be operating flawlessly, the search for symptoms of alienation cannot be abandoned. A second important diagnostic query focuses on the person's perception of the powers that give direction to his life. The important question here is how the individual believes his successes and failures come about. Who is responsible?

Basically, there are two sources of action—the self and the non-self—to which the burden of responsibility can be affixed. In extreme terms, we can believe either we are what we are bcause of our own actions or because of what others, or fate, or "Lady Luck," did to us. In the first instance, we feel in control of our life, as if we are masters of our own destiny. In the second instance, helpless and victimized, as if our destiny is in the hands of forces over which we have little or no control. The beliefs of most people are commonly somewhere between these two extremes, although one point of view may be more dominant than the other.

The student who does not accept personal responsibility for his achievement status is the educational equivalent of society's alienated man. Both his gains and his losses are a function of what others have done to him. Therefore, he cannot honestly feel pride in his achievements or shame for his failures.

Of the many manifestations of alienation, the one dealing with the assignment of responsibility has received the greatest amount of attention from researchers. An example of how this psychological condition is translated into empirical terms and used in studies of children is contained in an investigation by Crandall, Katkovsky, and Preston (1962). These researchers studied a group of forty primary grade children for whom they constructed a special test, called the Children's Intellectual Achievement Responsibility Questionnaire (abbreviated by the letters IAR). This questionnaire was designed to assess the degree to which the children believed their successes and failures to be the results of their own efforts or to be caused by what others did. The questionnaire contains descriptions of several common experiences of grade school children—some involving success and praise, others involving failure and criticism—and asks the child to tell whether these experiences, when they happen to him, are usually the result of what he does or of what others do. An example of a success item is: "Suppose you did better than usual in a subject at school. Would it probably happen (a) because you tried harder or (b) because someone helped you?" The following is a failure item: "When you make a mistake on a school assignment, is it usually (a) because the assignment the teacher gave was a particularly hard one or (b) because you were careless?" A high self-responsibility score is obtained by choosing the alternatives that imply the acceptance of personal blame or credit for failure or success.

Scores on the IAR were essentially unrelated to achievement behavior for girls, but not for boys. Indeed, the correlations between IAR scores and achievement were positive consistently for boys and were higher than similar statistics obtained with other predictor variables, including measures of need for achievement and general manifest anxiety.

An investigation of a similar phenomenon was conducted by Battle and Rotter (1963) who administered a newly designed projective test of internal-external control to a group of sixth and eighth grade students. The test consists of 29 cartoon items about which subjects are questioned concerning the assignment of responsibility for the conditions depicted (e.g., Why is she always hurting herself? Why is her mother always hollering at her?). The most important finding to come out of this study was that differences in attitudes toward internal and external control were related to social class and ethnic group. Lower class Negroes were significantly more external than were middle class Negroes or whites. Middle class children, in general, were significantly more internal than were lower class children.

A recent study by Bialer (1961) provides a third illustration of how the assignment of personal responsibility is used as a variable in research on children. Bialer developed a scale consisting of 23 questions of the following sort: "Do you really believe a kid can be whatever he wants to be?" "When nice things happen to you, is it only good luck?" "Do you often feel you get punished when you don't deserve it?" He administered this questionnaire, together with other tests, to a combined group of 89 mentally retarded and normal children selected from special classes and from regular elementary classrooms of a public school system. The tendency to perceive events as being under internal control (the opposite of being alienated) increased with age and was positively related, in particular, to the mental age of children. Bailer suggests that in the early stages of development there is no conception of the relationship between the outcome of events and one's own behavior. Consequently, he argues, young children, as a group, tend to view all of their experiences, as being controlled by the whims or fancies of fate, other people, and other external forces. Young children tend, then, to perceive events hedonistically, as merely pleasant or unpleasant, without considering whether or not their own actions might have contributed to the outcome.

The brief descriptions of these three studies give a general impression of how the concept of alienation is being used in studies of children. They also highlight the major findings with respect to the assignment of personal responsibility. They indicate that the tendency to perceive success and failure as being bestowed by outside forces (a) is more characteristic of those who fail in school than of those who succeed; (b) is likely to occur more frequently among lower class than among middle class children; (c) is associated with other types of psychological disability, such as anxiety; and (d) is particularly evident in very young and mentally immature persons.

A logical reaction to a life over which one has little control would be to withdraw or to become resigned to the inevitable. It would seem, then, that an attitude of indifference might flow as naturally from the denial of personal responsibility as from the perception of injustice in the distribution of life's rewards. This indifference—which students sometimes describe as "playing it cool"—is the most important single indicator of alienation in the classroom. Underlying it are likely to be found feelings of being mistreated or manipulated by school officials.

The Pervasiveness of Alienation

Only the surface manifestations of alienation have been treated thus far. To probe more deeply requires a consideration of how the syndrome of alienation may permeate many areas of behavior. Also, to this point, alienation has been described more as an individual psychological ailment, than as a shared mode of adaptation to some of the harsher features of social reality. In the comments that follow, the adaptive aspects of this behavioral strategy will be emphasized.

Social theory and research of the last few decades emphatically warns us not to assume that the alienated person is sick, and society well.

Indeed, many social analysts believe that the opposite is true. This being so, when the sign of alienation appears in a student it is imperative to determine to what extent the symptoms arise from a unique personal history, and to what extent they stem from the reality of present school and home conditions. Sometimes, for example, the reward system of the school does operate illogically, and sometimes teachers do exert so much control that their students no longer have a feeling of personal power. When these conditions hold it is not surprising to find indifference or apathy in the classroom. Also, many children live in homes and neighborhoods in which there is little or no support for academic values. Small wonder that such students have difficulty working up more than lukewarm enthusiasm over the tasks and the rewards of school life. The badly functioning school and the unsupportive home environment are part of the everyday experience of many children. For these youngsters the syndrome of alienation is more understandable and the steps that might be taken to eliminate it are more obvious than is true for students who do not suffer from such immediate environmental disadvantages.

As he confronts an indifferent student, then, the teacher or counselor must ask whether the signs of motivational withdrawal are situationally confined or whether they pervasively color the student's view of the world. There is a difference between the student who is apathetic during his hours in the classroom, but engrossed in other contexts, and the one who is as indifferent to life outside the classroom as he is to life inside.

Two major difficulties, however, are connected with attempts to determine whether or not alienated behavior is situationally confined. The first arises from the fact that even when the behavior seems to occur only within clearly specified limits—such as a classroom—the question of how much the present situation contributes to the student's attitude is still to be answered. Although our typical reaction might be to place blame for the condition on the immediate setting, the student's present attitudes may be almost exclusively the result of his previous experience. Consider the high school student whose poor attention in mathematics classes stems from bad experiences with arithmetic instruction during his grade school year.

A second difficulty involved in fixing the limits of alienation derives from the fact that the disorder tends to spill over from one area of behavior to another. A major assumption underlying much of the theoretical writing is that when alienation arises in connection with the performance of a person's major social roles—such as worker, or mother, or soldier—it tends to spread to the performance of other roles as well. The alienation of the factory worker, arising out of conditions of the assembly line and mass production, shows up in his home life and his leisure hours as well as in his behavior on the job. In other words, alienation, even when situationally aroused, is not like a set of dirty overalls that can be left behind when the whistle blows. Rather, it is an enduring perceptual set, which, if unchecked, may be expected to affect larger and larger portions of a person's life. Therefore, when students are identified whose total world view seems to be described appropriately as "alienated" it is unreasonable to assume that the source of this alienation is as diffuse as the symptom itself, although it might be quite difficult to identify the specific area of experience that served as the origin of the general ailment.

One way, then, of thinking about the degree or seriousness of a person's feeling of alienation is to consider the spread of the feeling in time and space; to ask, in effect, in how many different settings does he feel like this, or how many of his waking hours are tainted by these feelings? Another way is to consider the social or psychological depth, so to speak, at which the feeling seems to operate. In this regard, a helpful set of distinctions is suggested by Scott (1964), who argues that the condition of alienation may stem from four major "social sources." In order of increasing seriousness, these are: facilities, roles, norms, and values.

At the most rudimentary level, alienation consists of being unable to control facilities. Among the working class, with whom it was first identified, this feeling of powerlessness was created by the fact that the laborer no longer was able to control the speed of production (because of assembly line production) and was heightened as other major decisions concerning the means and ends of production were taken from him. At the second level, that of role, the alienated person no longer feels the need to adhere to the set of expectations society holds for him. Some of the many roles each person is expected to perform carry more status than others and, hence, are felt to be more important. The failure to accept responsibility for these "primary status-carrying roles" is naturally more serious psychologically and sociologically, than is a comparable failure with respect to more peripheral expectations.

Alienation from norms—Scott's third level—is reflected in the refusal to conform to the rules and regulations by which goals are obtained. The condition of being separated from the norms of society has received the label "anomie" from social theorists, notably Durkheim and Merton. The victim of this condition shares the values of most other men, but he cannot or will not use the normal channels for obtaining them. For such a person the usual relationship between means and ends has undergone a radical change. This change often brings with it a distrust of others, for when the means-ends relationship is altered a person can no longer believe that the motives of others are what they seem to be.

The fourth and most serious source of alienation occurs when the individual rejects, or simply fails to develop, a commitment to one or more fundamental values of his society. The person who is alienated in this sense not only rejects the means of his fellows; he rejects the ends as well. In the most extreme case he does not transfer his allegiance to a set of substitute goals but, instead, turns away from all values. When this "devaluation of valuation" begins, the victim of alienation has entered upon the final separation that threatens to cut him off from all others, and, ultimately, from himself.

There are certain important and perhaps obvious resemblances between recurring forms of student behavior and the four types of alienation suggested by Scott. It is dangerous, however, to assume that these signs of difficulty have the same meaning when observed in students as when observed in adults. It may be, for example, that the separation between the world of children and the world of adults creates strains that produce, in turn, signs of a temporary alienation that will disappear by the time the child becomes an adult. It is equally possible, of course, that the greater social dependency of the child may make it more difficult for him than for the adult to turn away from the expectations and values of other people. Consequently, the behavioral indicators of alienation may signify a much more serious condition when observed in young people than when observed in adults. A variant of the latter argument is offered by Bettelheim (1961), who points out that "with the whole pressure of school, parents, educational system, and society at large favoring success in learning, it often takes a great deal more determination on the part of the non-learner to fail than for the good learner to do well in school." The comparison between adult and juvenile forms of alienation requires much more study than it has been given to date and must, therefore, be made with caution. Nonetheless, the resemblances are there and deserve comment.

The student who is separated from the facilities of scholarship (the first level of alienation in Scott's conceptual scheme) is the one who does not know how to handle the basic tools of learning. With respect to a particular subject (and possibly to all of his work) he may feel "lost" or "at sea." This student might also be overwhelmed by the amount of work he is expected to do and may despair of ever being able to catch up with his classmates.

The classroom equivalent of the adult's separation from role would be the young person's struggles with the responsibility of being a student. It is generally overlooked that the student role involves much more than the satisfactory performance of specific academic skills. A student is expected to maintain severe restrictions on his physical movement and his speech (even in the most "progressive" classroom!); he is expected to show the proper deference to the teacher and other authorities, while demonstrating, at the same time, his growth in autonomy and independence; he is expected to become intensely absorbed in the subject of the teaching session, but he is also expected to shift his interest and his focus of concern at the sound of a bell. He is expected to compete for the approval of the teacher and other educational rewards, but he is also admonished not to be a "show-off," for the reputation he earns in the classroom has to be lived with on the playground and in the dormitory. Given these varied and, at times, conflicting demands, it is hardly surprising that some people find the role of student difficult to perform.

The goals of the school, broadly considered, have to do with learning how to become a productive member of a particular segment of society. But the school is not alone in contributing to this end. Family, friends, and other formal agencies also play a part, and, depending on the particular group in which a person is seeking acceptance, the school's contribution may be great or small compared with that from other sources. It is possible, in other words, for a person to be highly achievement-oriented (in the general sense), to have an intense desire to learn certain things, and to care very much about his status in the eyes of others, without, at the same time, viewing the school as instrumental in helping him to attain these goals. Such a person may be forced, of course, to be in school and, while there, his condition might best be described as alienation from a set of norms. For him the entire education institution, not just the role of student, is senseless. He may seek the same general goals as his classmates, but he does not perceive the classroom as a place where they may be obtained.

Separation from values, the most serious form of alienation in Scott's view, may show up in the classroom in two ways. First, some students may fail to shift from the value system of children—with its hedonistic orientation—to the value system of adults—with its emphasis on the virtues of responsibility, the control of impulse, and the like. Second, some students may fail to shift from the value system of their family and friends to the value system espoused by the school. The school, in other words, extols the virtues that characterize the mature middle class adult (or are supposed to). Students who are uninterested or unable to become either mature or middle class might exhibit signs of this fourth form of alienation. Such students need not be openly defiant, although rebellion often springs from this condition; they may, instead, behave as if the "proper" values guided their action, but their lack of commitment rarely escapes the eye of the watchful teacher.

The four levels of alienation suggested by Scott—from facilities to values—do then, seem to be crudely identifiable within the classroom. Also, although much more needs to be known about the relationship between juvenile and adult forms of alienation, the increasing seriousness as the source of the separation moves from facilities to values seems to be as applicable to students as to adults. The task remaining is to consider, even though it can only be at the level of conjecture, some of the steps the school might take to check or reverse the progress of this disorder.

The Treatment of Alienation

First, we must admit that no one really knows what to do about the alienated student. At best we can point to some of the common sources of classroom difficulty that seem to be related logically to the development of alienation and trust that improvement in these areas will have beneficial results. Second, we must recognize that the extreme forms of alienation may be too difficult for teachers to handle and may require outside help. The student who is extremely disgruntled with school life may also be disgruntled with life in general, and may need individual therapy if he is to begin to change his perceptions of himself and others.

One of the most badly needed changes in school practice is that of broadening our conventional definition of achievement. At present the assessment of achievement typically involves a normative judgment. That is, the student's work is compared with the achievement of his peers, locally and nationally, rather than with some absolute criterion or with his own previous level of performance. The normative approach is unavoidable in those school subjects where a precise statement of objectives is impossible—and there are many such subjects. But this type of evaluation often puts the student at the mercy of his classmates. If, on the one hand, he is "lucky" enough to have fellow students who do not want to work or who are not too bright, he can emerge successful from the experience. If, on the other hand, he happens to be among brilliant, hard-working students, he emerges looking a bit like a dolt. Either way, the student's evaluation is independent, to some extent, of his own efforts. Like the factory worker, he has little to do with setting the standards by which his work is judged.

If, however, some measure of growth were used or some absolute criteria set, the standards of achievement might not be as capricious as they now must seem to some students. The establishment of specific criteria of achievement is an extremely difficult job. Not enough is known about the structure of most school subjects to set anything but arbitrary standards. The use of gain scores as measures of achievement also presents problems. The interpretation of the size of gains, for instance, almost invariably reintroduces the concept of norm. Despite these difficulties, it is likely that any improvement in the variety and the logical compellingness of our achievement measures would help to reduce one of the common sources of discontent in the classroom.

Closely related to the goal of improving the assessment of achievement is the goal of clarifying academic expectations and the methods of attaining them. Students not only need to know how far they have come; they also need to know where they are headed, and precisely how to get there. Yet scholastic goals and the best methods of reaching them are anything but clear in many classrooms. The clarification of ends and means does not require necessarily that students have a hand in setting their own goals, although it is probable that in some instances student planning would increase the appeal of educational objectives. In many instructional areas, however, it is doubtful that the students are capable of establishing their own goals or of determining how best to achieve them. Clear goals, regardless of how they are set, would help to reduce some of the uncertainty that likely contributes to the development of student indifference.

Academic standards are not the only expectations that operate in the classroom. In addition, there are the requirements that have to do with performing the role of student, and, as indicated earlier, these requirements are often ambiguous and conflicting. Most of the overt disturbances in the classroom appear to result from failure to meet student role expectations rather than from failure to meet academic standards. Therefore, efforts to clarify the student role or to decrease the internal conflict among the various role expectations would almost certainly make life in the classroom easier and more attractive.

Evidence in support of the benefits of greater clarity in the definition of the student role is presented by Kounin and Gump (1958) who conducted an observational study of kindergartens. They found that when teachers made their expectations clear, defined rules precisely, and suggested positive actions the misbehaving child might take, the incidence of unruly behavior diminished. Even when it occurred under these conditions, the misbehavior did not seem to have a negative effect on the rest of the children.

The student is not alone, of course, in his discomfort. The role of the teacher contains its own peculiar stresses, which serve indirectly as an additional source of classroom difficulty. Because teaching is a moral enterprise, the teacher often is encouraged to maintain a public image that is more virtuous, more omniscient, and more altruistic than is humanly possible. When students perceive the discrepancy between what the teacher professes to be and what he truly is, they are likely to charge the teacher with being "a phony." It is not difficult to understand why the student who perceives the teacher as being a bit of a fraud might feel disillusioned and might have some difficulty remaining involved in his role. In modern fiction many of the characters of J. D. Salinger—Holden Caulfield and Franny Glass, in particular—reflect the disillusionment and disgust (harbingers of alienation) that accompany the perception of the "phony" teacher.

Contradictions between preaching and practicing are not new, and teachers are surely not the only offenders. Furthermore, in many instances the charge of phonyness is a bit too severe. As long as people strive to better themselves, a gap of some kind will exist between the real and the ideal. Failure to live constantly in accord with the ideal hardly provides grounds for applying the label "phony." Nonetheless, when students behave as if they believe such a label is appropriate, teachers must be alert enough to recognize this major sign of difficulty and to take steps to remedy it.

The classic educational solution for dealing with chronically failing students is to shower them with "success experiences." The engineering of success is certainly an important remedial strategy, but it is not the all-purpose palliative some educators believe it to be. First, if it is to be effective, the success must be in an area that is significant to the student. Success in building a doorstop or in winning a footrace is not very likely to ease the pain of failing to learn how to read, no matter how much we might believe in the benefits of compensation. The student cannot, in other words, make up for important failures by experiencing trivial successes. Second, success, if it is to have its expected therapeutic impact, must not only be perceived by the student as important, it must also be seen as resulting directly from something the student does. Success may be pre-planned, but it must not be rigged. Educational hand-outs are of doubtful value to the alienated student.

In summary, the prevention and remediation of alienation involves first and foremost the clarification of the school environment. Students need to have a clearer picture of how they are doing, they need to understand the school's expectations and they need to be shown exactly how those expectations can be fulfilled. They need help in resolving the ambiguities of the student role and they need to be surrounded by teachers and administrators who are unequivocal in the perception of their own adult roles.

Finally, a repeated word of caution. Despite the similarities that have been discussed here, the alienated student and the alienated adult are really two distinct phenomena. It would be a mistake, therefore, to exaggerate the prognostic significance of signs of alienation in young people; to imagine, for example, that every indifferent student will become an indifferent adult. Fortunately, many of our least promising students turn out to be models of self-fulfillment when they mature. Not all, however, overcome the stresses of their student days, and others show no signs of difficulty until many years after they have left the classroom. Consequently, although we should not become prophets of despair each time we encounter a student who is less enthusiastic about schooling than we are, neither should we ignore early signs of danger that might erupt into a serious form of classroom failure.

References

Battle, Esther S., & Rotter, J. B. Children's feelings of personal control as related to social class and ethnic group. *Journal of Personality,* 1963, **31**, 482–490.

Bettelheim, B. The decision to fail. *School Review,* 1961, **69**, 377–412.

Bialer, I. Conceptualization of success and failure in mentally retarded and normal children. *Journal of Personality,* 1961, **29**, 303–320.

Crandall, V. J., Katkovsky, W., & Preston, Anne. Motivational and ability determinants of young children's intellectual achievement behaviors. *Child Development,* 1962, **33**, 643–661.

Kounin, J., & Gump, P. The ripple effect in discipline. *Elementary School Journal,* 1958, **59**, 158–162.

Scott, M. B. The social sources of alienation. In I. F. Horowitz (Ed.) *The new sociology: essays in honor of C. Wright Mills.* Oxford Univer. Press, 1964. Pp. 239–252.

9.5 Educational Stimulation of Racially Disadvantaged Children

Kenneth B. Clark

When teachers do not make valid evaluations of children's characteristics, the goals they see for these children will be unrealistic and inadequate, handicapping the children for life. Kenneth Clark believes that evaluations of the characteristics of disadvantaged children made by such eminent personages as James Conant are invalid and show a lack of sophistication in the field of the social sciences. Clark argues that rather than showing a lack of potential, these children are prevented from achieving by depressed morale and lowered operations brought about by a "stigmatized, rejected, and segregated" environment.

Some Research Problems and Findings Relevant to the Education of Deprived Children

During the past year a number of books dealing directly or indirectly with the problem of the education of children in depressed urban areas have been published. Among the more significant of these books are James B. Conant's *Slums and Suburbs* (4), Frank Riessman's *The Culturally Deprived Child* (9), and Patricia Sexton's *Education and Income* (10).

SOURCE. A. Harry Passow (ed.), *Education in Depressed Areas.* (New York: Teachers College Press), 1963, pp. 145–156. Reprinted with the permission of Kenneth B. Clark and the publisher.

Dr. Sexton's analysis of the relationship between social and economic status and the quality of education provided for children in the public schools of a northern urban community is a model of objective social science and educational research. The data presented by her demonstrate conclusively that curricula, educational standards, quality of teaching, educational facilities and materials, and academic achievement of the children are directly related to the socio-economic status of the majority of children attending a particular school. Her findings add another significant dimension to the well-known and often repeated fact that academic achievement varies directly with socio-economic status. Usually this fact is interpreted as reflecting some type of selective factor wherein individuals of high intelligence attain high socio-economic status and produce more intelligent children and that higher status families provide their children with more stimulation for academic achievement. The data presented by Dr. Sexton, however, make clear, at least to this observer, the crucial role of the school in determining the level of academic achievement of the children. The traditional interpretation would continue to argue that the standards and quality of the school reflect the limitations of the home and the immediate community from which the child comes and that the school must gear its level to these limitations. This interpretation has so far not been verified through objective research although it is widely accepted as if it were.

Attempts to determine the specific role of a particular school on the average level of academic performance of the children in that school must obtain data on the general attitudes of teachers in that school towards their children—particularly if there is a marked class discrepancy between teachers and students; the expectations of these teachers and the effect of these expectations on the actual performance of their children; and the children's perspective of themselves, their teachers, and their school. It is now imperative that social scientists study with rigorous objectivity and precision the complex and interrelated problems which seem relevant to an understanding of how children from depressed backgrounds can be motivated for maximum academic achievement.

At present, the work of Allison Davis and his colleagues, which demonstrates the educationally depressing effects of the gap between working-class children and middle-class teachers, is an important starting point for future more detailed research. It is important to know, for example, not only the particular attitudinal patterns which the teacher communicates to these children but also the particular ways in which she communicates her attitudes and how these block or facilitate the academic motivation of lower-class children. The empirical data on these specific problems are sparse, and one is required to speculate on the nature of the manner in which these blockages operate. Probably a core factor in the complex inhibiting dynamics involved in the interplay between middle-class and higher-status teachers and working-class and lower-status children is the pervasive and archaic belief that children from culturally deprived backgrounds are by virtue of their deprivation of lower status position inherently uneducable.

Professor Goodwin Watson, in his introduction to Frank Reissman's book (9), has defined this problem and suggested a general solution as follows:

"In recent decades a spate of anthropological, sociological, and social-psychological studies, many of them mentioned by Professor Riessman, has revealed the appalling gap between our pretensions and our practices. We do not give the same kind of food, clothing, housing, medical care, recreation, or justice to the deprived children that we give to those in comfortably-well-off homes. We don't like to think of class distinctions in American life, so we tend to shy away from these unacceptable facts. Opportunities are far from equal.

The American public school is a curious hybrid: it is managed by a school board drawn largely from upper-class circles; it is taught by teachers who come largely from middle-class backgrounds; and it is attended mainly by children from working-class homes. These three groups do not talk the same language. They differ in their manners, power, and hierarchies of values. . . .

Under-cultured children have much to learn from education, but educators could well take some lessons from some of these youngsters. Their language may not be grammatical, but it is often more vivid and expressive than is the turgid prose of textbooks. These children face some of the "facts of life" more realistically than many of their teachers do. Even their pugnacity might be worth attention by some long-suffering, overworked, underpaid teachers. When it comes to making friends and standing by their pals, some children from under-privileged neighborhoods far outshine their priggish teachers.

The starting point is respect. Nothing else that we have to give will help very much if it is offered with a resentful, contemptuous, or patronizing attitude. We don't understand these neighborhoods, these homes, these children, because we haven't respected them enough to think them worthy of study and attention. Professor Riessman's book is likely to be the pioneer in a series of investigations that will reveal to America that we have neglected a major source of manpower and of creative talent. The stone which the builders rejected may even become the head of the corner."

One may assume that if a child is not treated with the respect which is due him as a human being, and if those who are charged with the responsibility of teaching him believe that he cannot learn, then his motivation and ability to learn may become impaired. If a teacher believes that a child is incapable of being educated, it is likely that this belief will in some way be communicated to the child in one or more of the many forms of contacts inherent in the teacher-pupil relationship.

Because of the importance of the role of teachers in the developing self-image, academic aspirations and achievements of their students, it was though desirable to conduct a preliminary study of the attitudes of teachers in ten public schools located in depressed areas of a large northern city. The children in these schools came generally from homes and communities which were so lacking in educational stimulation and other determinants of self-respect that they seemed even more dependent upon their teachers for self-esteem, encouragement, and stimulation. These children, like most deprived human beings, were hypersensitive and desperate in their desire for acceptance.

The findings of this preliminary study revealed that while there were some outstanding exceptions—individual principals and teachers who respected the human dignity and potentialities of their students—the overwhelming majority of these teachers and their supervisors rejected these children and looked upon them as inherently inferior.

For the most, the teachers indicated that they considered these children to be incapable of profiting from a normal curriculum. The children were seen as intellectually inferior and therefore not capable of learning. The qualitative flavor of this complex pattern of negative attitudes can best be communicated by the verbatim reports written by our observers:

"As soon as I entered the classroom, Mrs. X told me in front of the class, that the parents of these children are not professionals and therefore they do not have much background or interest in going ahead to college. . . . She discussed each child openly in front of the entire class and myself. . . . She spoke about the children in a belittling manner. She tried to give each child encouragement, but her over-all attitude was negative in that she did not think much of the abilities of her students. She told me in private that "heredity is what really counts," and since they didn't have a high culture in Africa and have not as yet built one in New York, they are intellectually inferior from birth."

Another teacher was described as follows:

"The teacher was a lady of about 50 who had no understanding of these children. She kept pointing to them when talking about them so that even I was slightly embarrassed. She kept repeating 'You see what I mean?', which I didn't at all. . . . She took it for granted that these children were stupid and that there was little that she could do with them."

A third description illustrates some of the subtleties of the problem:

"Mr. G. is a rather tense and nervous man. He continually played with his finger or with a pencil or tapped his fingers on the desk. What disturbed him most was the cultural deprivation that most of the students in his school suffered from. He said that often the teacher will refer to everyday facts which the children will be completely ignorant of. He says that it is most difficult if not impossible to teach them."

These and other examples clearly suggest that among many of the teachers who are required to teach children from culturally deprived backgrounds there exists a pervasive negative attitude toward these children. These teachers say repeatedly, and appear to believe, that it is not possible to teach these children. They offer, in support of their conclusion, the belief that these children cannot learn because of "poor heredity," "poor home backgrounds," "cultural deprivation," and "low IQ."

The Problem of the IQ

Probably as disturbing as these examples of rejection of these children on the part of those who are required to teach them, are the many examples of well-intentioned teachers who point to the low intelligence- and achievement-test scores of these children as the basis for their belief that these children cannot be educated. These teachers generally do not base their judgment on conscious racial bias or rejection of these children as human beings or necessarily on their "poor heredity." They point to the realities of a poor environment, cultural deprivation and lack of educational stimulation in the home as the determinants of low academic achievement of these children. They maintain that these children should not be expected to function up to the academic level of other children because the test scores clearly indicate that they cannot. Further, they state that to pressure these children for an academic achievement that they are incapable of reaching only creates frustrations and anxieties which will make even more difficult the possibility of adequate functioning on their own level. These individuals, therefore, argue that a special curriculum and a special form of education should be devised for these children from culturally deprived backgrounds who have consistently low IQs and achievement-test scores.

A disturbing aspect of this type of argument is that it does come under the guise of humanitarianism, psychology, and modern educational theory.

It becomes necessary, therefore, to look with thorough objectivity at the basis of this argument; namely, the validity of test scores as an index of the intellectual potential of children from culturally deprived backgrounds. Do these test scores indicate some immutable level of intelligence, or do they reflect primarily the obvious cultural and educational deprivations and discriminations suffered by these children?

Modern psychology findings and interpretations would seem to leave no further room for argument that test scores must be interpreted in the light of the general social and cultural milieu of a child and the specific educational opportunities to which he has been exposed. It is generally known that children from deprived educational backgrounds will score lower on available standardized tests. The pioneer work of Otto Klineberg in the 1930's clearly established the fact that intelligence test score will increase on the average as children are moved from a deprived, inferior educational situation to a more positive and stimulating one (8).

We now know that children who are not stimulated at home or in the community or in school will have low scores. Their scores and, what is even more important, their day-to-day academic performance can be improved if they are provided with adequate stimulation in one or more of these areas. When a child from a deprived background is treated as if he is uneducable because he has a low test score, he becomes uneducable and the low test score is thereby reinforced. If a child scores low on an intelligence test because he cannot read and then is not taught to read because he has a low score, then such a child is being imprisoned in an iron circle and becomes the victim of an educational self-fulfilling prophecy.

Another aspect of the problem of the meaning of the IQ, which is not generally discussed and which seems to have been lost sight of by educators and the general public, is the simple fact that the IQ is merely a score that is offered as an index of a given individual's rate of learning compared with the learning rate of others with whom he can be reasonably compared. This interpretation of the IQ is consistent with the fact that a child with a lower IQ can be expected to take longer to learn that which a child with a higher IQ will learn more rapidly. The IQ itself—at least in the normal ranges and above—does not necessarily determine how much a child will learn or for that matter even the ceiling of what he can learn. Rather it reflects the rate of his learning or the amount of effort which will be required for him to learn. In other words, it is quite conceivable that children with lower IQs, even those low IQs which more nearly reflect inherent intellectual limitations, can and do learn substantively what other children can learn. But it will take a longer time, will require more care and skill on the part of the teachers and probably more encouragement and acceptance of the child.

IQ, Snobbery, and Humiliation

Unfortunately, an objective discussion of the problem of the meaning of the IQ is made even more difficult by the fact that this problem has been contaminated by non-educational considerations such as social class status factors. This point can be illustrated by an examination of the arguments in favor of homogeneous groupings. The most persistent arguments for grouping children in homogeneous classes according to IQs are largely assertions of the convenience of such groupings for overworked teachers. The proponents of the procedure of segregating children according to intelligence for educational purposes seem to base their argument on some assumptions of special privilege, special status, special educational advantages and conspicuous recognition which are to be given to an intellectual elite. It is implied and sometimes stated that these conditions will facilitate the maximum use of the already high intelligence of the gifted children and will reduce the frustrations of those children who are not gifted. It is further suggested that if the gifted child is not given special treatment in special classes, he will somehow not fulfill his intellectual potentials—"he will be brought down to the level of the average or the dull child." So far there seems to be little empirical evidence in support of these assertions in spite of their wide acceptance by the public and by many educators.

Those who argue against this form of educational intellectual segregation must nonetheless, eventually demonstrate by empirical research that it is not the most effective educational procedure. Are children who are segregated according to IQ in the classrooms of our schools being educated in a socially realistic and democratic atmosphere? The world consists of individuals of varying levels of intellectual potential and power. Those individuals of high intelligence must be prepared to function effectively with individuals of average or below average intelligence. One important function of the schools is to train children in a socially responsible use of human intelligence. A manifestation of this social responsibility would be the ability of children of high intelligence to use their superior intelligence creatively in working with and helping children of lower intelligence to function more effectively. Children of lower intelligence could be stimulated and encouraged, in a realistic school atmosphere, by the accomplishments of other children. This would be true only if the over-all school atmosphere is one consistent with the self-respect of all children. Children who are stigmatized by being placed in classes designated as "slow" or "dull" or for "children of retarded mental ability" cannot be expected to be stimulated and motivated to improve their academic performance. Such children understandably will become burdened with resentment and humiliation and will seek to escape the humiliating school situation as quickly as possible.

Probably the chief argument against homogeneous groupings is the fact that children who are so segregated lose their individuality in the educational situation. It would seem that the development of a creative individuality would be among the high priority goals of education. Homogeneous groupings tend to require that children be seen in terms of group characteristics rather than in terms of their own individual characteristics. This would seem to be true equally for the bright children as it is for average or dull children. Furthermore, it is questionable whether it is possible to establish a homogeneous group of children on any grounds other than the arbitrary selection of some single aspect of the total complexity that is the human being.

It may be argued on the basis of evidence that even the selection of children in terms of similarity in IQ is arbitrary in that the same range of IQs may mask significant differences in intellectual abilities, patterns, interests, and propensities among children who seem similar in level of general intelligence. Any oversimplification of this fact, concretized into an educational procedure, may not be worth the human and social cost.

It is conceivable that the detrimental effects of segregation based upon intellect is similar to the known detrimental effects of schools segregated on the basis of class, nationality, or race (2). This similarity, if it is found to exist, may reflect the fact that, in general, the average intellectual level of groups of children is related to the social and racial status of their parents. The educational level and achievement of lower-status children are depressed in segregated lower-status schools for those reasons already stated, plus the fact that the morale of their teachers tend to be depressed when they are identified with low prestige schools. Furthermore, some of these teachers may accept assignments in these schools because they may be aware of the fact that the staff in these schools is generally not held to the same high professional standards which prevail in schools where it is believed that the children can learn. Teachers in more privileged schools are probably held to more strict standards of professional evaluation and supervision.

Whatever the determining factors responsible for the low educational achievement of children from lower status groups, the fact remains that up to the present, the overwhelming majority of these children attend schools that do not have a systematic educational program designed to provide the extra stimulation and encouragement which they need if they are to develop their intellectual potential. Some school officials may question whether it is the proper function of the schools to attempt to compensate for the cultural deprivations which burden these children in their homes and in the larger community. As long as this is not done by the schools or some other appropriate social institutions, the motivation and academic achievement of these deprived children will remain depressed, inferior, and socially wasteful. What is more, the schools will have failed to provide them with an effective education and thereby failed to meet a pressing contemporary need.

Mr. Conant and the Education of Culturally Disadvantaged Children

Probably the most widely discussed, if not uncritically accepted, of the recent books dealing with the problem of the education of deprived and privileged children in American cities is James B. Conant's *Slums and Suburbs* (3). In spite of the fact that Mr. Conant is by training, background and experience a chemist, college president, and statesman—and not a professional educator or social scientist—he has assumed with the aid of the Carnegie Corporation of New York, the role of educational expert and spokesman to the nation. His book was reviewed extensively—and for the most part praised—by the important education editors of newspapers throughout the nation. In discussing the complexity of educational problems found in the schools in "slum neighborhoods," Mr. Conant coined the phrase "social dynamite" which has become part of the jargon of these discussions.

Before one engages in a critical analysis of Mr. Conant's assumptions and recommendations for the improvement of the education of deprived and privileged children, it should be stated that this book presents vividly some facts which help to clarify some of the issues related to the basic problem of the inferiority of educational opportunities provided for children of the lower socio-economic classes in the public schools of the ten largest cities in our nation. For example, the book states that half of the children in deprived neighborhoods drop out of school in grades 9, 10, and 11; that the per pupil expenditure in deprived schools is less than half the per pupil expenditure in a privileged school; and that there are seventy professionals per thousand pupils in privileged schools and forty or fewer professionals per thousand pupils in deprived schools. Mr. Conant appeals to the conscience of the American public and asserts that this consistent discrepancy "jolts one's notions of the meaning of equality of opportunity."

Critical reading and analysis of this book, however, reveal that Mr. Conant's prescription for this educational disease will not cure the patient, but, on the contrary, will intensify the illness. The implicit assumptions and explicit suggestions, if accepted by American education would concretize the very discrepancies which Mr. Conant calls "social dynamite" and would lead, if not to an educational explosion to educational dry rot and social stagnation.

The basic assumptions of this book are appalling, anachronistic, and reflect the social science naiveté of its author. The unmodified theme that runs throughout the book is that there are two types of human beings—those who can be educated and those who cannot be educated. Those who can be educated live in suburbs and those who cannot be educated live in slums. And for the most part, those who live in slums are Negroes and those who live in suburbs are white. Children who live in the slums should be provided with practical, vocational—job oriented—education and children in the suburbs should be provided with that level of academic education which is appropriate to their level of intelligence.

Mr. Conant's own words are quite explicit: "The lesson is that to a considerable degree what a school should do and can do is determined by the status and ambitions of the families being served." What changes the status and ambitions of the families?

"One needs only to visit such a school (slum school) to be convinced that the nature of the community largely determines what goes on in the school. . . . The community and the school are inseparable."

Why then have schools?

"Foreign languages in Grade 7 or algebra in Grade 8 (recommendations in my Junior High School report) have little place in a school in which half the pupils in that grade read at the fourth grade level or below."

Why are these children reading at the fourth grade level or below?

Mr. Conant is most explicit in his defense of *de facto* segregated schools and in his support of the outmoded and impossible doctrine of "separate but equal" education for Negroes, and his aversion to the open enrollment program.

"In some cities, political leaders have attempted to put pressure on the school authorities to have Negro children attend essentially white schools. In my judgment the cities in which the authorities have yielded to this pressure are on the wrong track. Those which have not done so, like Chicago, are more likely to make progress in improving Negro education. It is my belief that satisfactory education can be provided in an all-Negro school through the expenditure of more money for needed staff and facilities."

It would seem as if this opinion is contradicted by the very facts which Mr. Conant presents in his book and describes as "social dynamite." Mr. Conant's lack of social science training and insights probably accounts for his belief that mere money will make a "Negro" school equal—if indeed, he does mean "equal" when he uses the word "satisfactory" in describing education in an all-Negro school. Mr. Conant obviously does not understand the role of such psychological subtleties as the depressed morale, lowered aspirations, inadequate standards of performance which seem inherent in a stigmatized, rejected, segregated situation.

The following gratuitous advice must therefore be rejected:

". . . I think it would be far better for these who are agitating for the deliberate mixing of children to accept *de facto* segregated schools as a consequence of a present housing situation and to work for the improvement of slum schools whether Negro or white."

It seems incredible that a distinguished American statesman could continue to talk about American schools in terms of the designations "Negro" and "white" as if such racial designations were compatible with the American educational imperatives in this latter part of the twentieth century. This fact merely highlights a general deficiency of this book; namely, that it discusses problems of contemporary education in terms of the static assumptions and procedures of the past rather than in terms of the dynamic imperatives of the future. This book and its recommendations might have been acceptable in the first two decades of the twentieth century. It cannot be taken seriously now when it advocates without adequate supporting evidence:

"An elementary syllabus varied according to socio-economic status of the children; ability groupings and tracks for students in grades 7 through 12; matching neighborhood needs and school services; and generally determining the nature of academic standards and expectations in terms of the 'kinds of schools one is considering.' "

Aside from the archaic educational snobbery which permeates this book—its matter-of-fact assertion of the idea that American education should gear itself to train more efficiently the "hewers of wood and the drawers of water" and provide effective academic education to an "intellectual elite" to be drawn from the socially and economically privileged groups—its author does not seem to understand the crucial role that an imaginative, creative education must play in the contemporary world. He does not understand that it is the function of contemporary American education to discover and implement techniques for uncovering every ounce of the intellectual potential in all our children without regard to their racial, national, or economic background. Creative human intelligence is an all-too-rare resource and must be trained and conserved wherever it is found. It should now be clear that it is not likely to be found in sufficient abundance in the privileged minority. The best of educational stimulation of this group will still produce an inadequate yield. It is now the obligation of our public schools to adopt those procedures, whether open enrollment, higher horizon or other forms of special stimulation and techniques for raising the aspiration of previously deprived children which are necessary to increase the yield of trained intelligence from children whose potential would be lost to a society desperately in need of their future contributions.

Equally important is the fact that Mr. Conant seems unaware of the fact that segregated schools for the privileged suburban white child provide non-adaptive and unrealistic education. He does not seem to grasp that:

Segregated education is inferior and nonadaptive for whites as well as Negroes. Put simply, no child can receive a democratic education in a nondemocratic school. A white youngster in a homogeneous, isolated, "hot house" type of school situation is not being prepared for the realities of the contemporary and future world. Such a child may have brilliant college entrance scores, be extraordinary in his mathematical ability, or read and speak a foreign language with skill and precision, but he is likely to be blocked in many circumstances in his ability to use these intellectual abilities with the poise and effectiveness essential to personal and social creativity. A racially segregated school imposes upon white children the inevitable stultifying burdens of petty provincialism, irrational fears and hatreds of people who are different, and a distorted image of themselves. Psychologically, the racial segregated school at this period of American and world history is an anachronism which our nation cannot afford. This point must be made over and over again until it is understood by those who have the power to make the decisions which control our destiny(3). . . .

9.6 Reflection-Impulsivity: The Generality and Dynamics of Conceptual Tempo[1]

Jerome Kagan

The author suggests that children differ on an impulsive-reflective continuum. There is evidence that poor achievers tend to have an impulsive cognitive tempo. In other research, Professor Kagan has reported that training children to be more reflective is possible; a change of cognitive style results. Furthermore, a reflective type of teacher causes his pupils to become more reflective.

The dramatic differences in quality of problem solving among children of the same age or among children of different ages have been attributed primarily to two categories of constructs—motivational variables and/or adequacy of conceptual skills. In effect, differences in quality of cognitive products have been explained by assuming either that one child cared

SOURCE. Jerome Kagan, "Reflection—Impulsivity: The Generality and Dynamics of Conceptual Tempo," *Journal of Abnormal Psychology*, **LXX**, 1 (1966), pp. 17–24. Reprinted by permission of the author and the American Psychological Association.

[1] This research was supported in part by research grant MH-4464 and MH-8792 from the National Institute of Mental Health, United States Public Health Service. Part of this work was conducted while the author was at the Fels Research Institute. The author is indebted to Deborah Day, William Phillips, and Barbara Lobell for their assistance in this study.

more about his performance, or that one child had more knowledge relevant to the task. However, other cognitive processes are an intimate part of problem-solving activity. One of these processes concerns the degree to which the child reflects over the adequacy of a solution hypothesis.

Some children—and adults—select and report solution hypotheses quickly with minimal consideration for their probable accuracy. Other children, of equal intelligence, take more time to decide about the validity of solutions. The former group has been called impulsive, the latter reflective. The reflection-impulsivity dimension exerts its influence at two places in the problem-solving sequence. A schematic description of the chronology of problem solving includes four phases plus a reporting phase.

Phase 1: Decoding of the problem; comprehension of the problem.

Phase 2: Selection of a likely hypothesis on which to act in order to arrive at solution.

Phase 3: Implementation of the hypothesis (e.g., carry out a relevant arithmetic operation; proliferate a series of synonyms or associates).

Phase 4: Evaluate the validity of the solution arrived at in Phase 3.

Phase 5: Report of solution to an external agent.

The reflection-impulsivity dimension is influential in Phases 2 and 4, the times when the child is selecting a hypothesis to work on mentally or when he is about to report an answer to a teacher, peer, or parent. Previous work has suggested that impulsive selection or reporting of hypotheses is associated with inaccurate performance when adequacy of the child's knowledge repertoire is controlled. Moreover, the tendency to be reflective or impulsive shows intraindividual stability over time and generality across situations involving visual recognition or matching problems (Kagan, in press; Kagan, Rosman, Day, Albert, & Phillips, 1964).

The major purpose of this paper is to explore the relation between the disposition to be reflective or impulsive, and accuracy of performance in a different kind of cognitive task. Specifically, this investigation examines the relation between impulsivity and errors of commission in a series learning task (i.e., reporting words that were never present on the original list). A preliminary study of third- and fourth-grade children revealed a positive relation between impulsivity and errors of commission and this study was a more elegant attempt at replication (Kagan, 1965).

A second purpose of this work is to inquire into the psychodynamics of the reflection-impulsivity dimension. What are some of the motives, expectancies, and sources of anxiety that make one child reflective and another impulsive? The working assumptions are listed below.

Assumption 1. The relation of reflection-impulsivity to quality of performance only obtains for problems that have response uncertainty (i.e., several response alternatives occur to the child simultaneously, or in close temporal contiguity, and the child must select the one he judges to be most valid).

Assumption 2. For problems that are difficult and have response uncertainty, the child's tendency to be reflective (i.e., have long decision times) or impulsive (short decision times) is a function of the balance between the strengths of the following two standards: produce the answer quickly versus do not make a mistake. The relation between the positive value of quick success and the anxiety generated by the possibility of committing an error determines the child's decision time (i.e., his tendency to be reflective or impulsive).

Assumption 3. If the child's anxiety over a possible error is much stronger than his desire for quick success, he will be reflective. If his anxiety over committing an error is weak in relation to his desire for quick success, he will be impulsive.

On the basis of these assumptions it was expected that situations that elicited anticipation of failure would lead to greater anxiety and greater task disruption in reflective than in impulsive children. Since psychology does not possess faithful indexes of these two constructs (i.e., desire for success, anxiety over failure), one possible strategy is to devise experimental interventions that are expected to elicit these states differentially and examine the differential effect on children previously classified as impulsive or reflective. The reader should note that *anxiety over possible failure* is psychologically distinct from *expectation of failure.* A child who has been exposed to chronic failure may enter into a problem situation with a strong anticipation of failure but minimal anxiety. Many adolescents who comprise the high school "drop out" group fit this description. They do not expect to perform with competence yet they appear to be accepting of this state of affairs. The literature on "fear of failure" has often failed to distinguish between expectancy of failure and anxiety over anticipated failure.

The Measurement of Reflection-Impulsivity

Previous research on reflection-impulsivity has used the child's performance on a visual recognition task (called MFF for Matching Familiar Figures) as the primary index of the child's position on this dimension.

In this test the children is shown a single picture of a familiar object (the standard) and six similar variants, only one of which is identical to the standard. The child is asked to select the one variant that is identical to the standard. Figure 1 illustrates two sample items from the MFF test.

The critical variables scored are response time to the child's first answer and the total number of errors across the 12-item test. Impulsive children in Grades 1–4 have a mean response time between 4 and 10 seconds and make about 15–20 errors. Reflective children have mean response times between 30 and 40 seconds and make between 2 and 6 errors.

FIGURE 1. Sample items from Matching Familiar Figures Task (MFF).

In sum, this study tested two hypotheses: (*a*) a positive association between impulsivity on the MFF test and errors of commission on a serial learning task, and (*b*) greater deterioration in serial learning performance for reflective, in contrast to impulsive, children to a communication that suggested the strong possibility of future failure.

Method

Subjects and Procedure

Third-grade subjects (*Ss*) (136 boys and 107 girls) from two public schools in neighboring Ohio communities were seen individually for a 1-hour session during which the Matching Familiar Figures and WISC vocabulary and information scales were administered. Ss were tested by either a male or female examiner.

Selection of Groups. From this pool of 243 Ss, smaller groups of reflective or impulsive children were selected. The basis of categorization of an S as reflective or impulsive included both response time and errors in the Matching Familiar Figures task. The Ss classified as reflective were above the median on MFF response time and below the median on MFF errors for their sex. Impulsive Ss were below the median on MFF response time and above the median on MFF errors. The reflective and impulsive Ss were then assigned to one of three groups—a threat group, a rejection group, and a control group. The reflective and impulsive children assigned to these groups were matched on sex and scaled score on the WISC subtests. Thus the mean and range of verbal ability were equal for the reflective and impulsive Ss across all three experimental groups. Assignment of Ss in this $2 \times 2 \times 3$ design (12 cells) yielded sample sizes varying from 13 to 24 Ss in the 12 cells. There were 53 reflective boys and 65 impulsive boys; 45 reflective girls and 40 impulsive girls.

Serial Learning Procedure. Each S was seen 3 to 4 months after the initial session by a male experimenter (*E*) for administration of the serial learning task. The detailed procedure follows:

The *E* told the child he was going to test his memory and the child was urged to do as well as he could. The exact instructions were:

"You will hear someone read some words to you on this tape recorder. Try to remember all the words you hear for I will ask you to say the words back to me. The words will be read slowly. Let's listen to a practice list of words."

The *E* allowed the *S* practice with two lists of three and four words each until the *S* understood the nature of the task. The criterion task consisted of four different lists of 12 familiar words each. The lists were recorded at a rate of 1 word every 4 seconds using the author's voice. Each S was given two trials on each list. The second trial for each list presented the words in an order that was the exact reverse of the first trial. A recall was obtained after each trial, providing two recall scores for each list. Table 1 contains the list of words.

Table 1
Lists of Words Used in Serial Learning Task

List 1	List 2	List 3	List 4
Thunder	Shoe	Plate	Chair
Dog	Water	River	Wheel
Lightning	Coat	Bread	Couch
Pencil	Rope	Pipe	Ball
Rain	Shirt	Spoon	Table
Barn	Flower	Tree	Finger
Knife	Pants	Stove	Bed
Storm	Nail	Car	Glue
Leaf	Dress	Cup	Desk
Wind	Paper	Door	Fire
Hammer	Sweater	Napkin	Lamp
	Iron	Snow	Soap

Each of the lists contained six words that belonged to a conceptual category, but each of these conceptually related words was surrounded by a word unrelated to that concept. For example, the List 1 concept included words associated with a "rainstorm" (i.e., thunder, lightning, rain, puddle, storm, wind). The List 2 concept was concerned with "articles of clothing" (i.e., shoe, coat, shirt, pants, dress, and sweater). The List 3 concept included words connected with "eating" (i.e., plate, bread, spoon, stove, cup, napkin). The List 4 concept was "furniture" (i.e., chair, couch, table, bed, desk, lamp). The six remaining words in each list were minimally related to each other or to the concept contained in that list.

All Ss were treated alike for the first two lists. The three different experimental treatments occurred following List 2.

The threat group was told:

"O.K., that was fine. These two lists we just finished were really practice lists to give you an idea of what this kind of test is like. The next two lists really count. You will have to do very well on these next two lists. They are hard and children who don't have good memories usually don't do very well, so try and concentrate."

The intent of this communication was to arouse anxiety over possible failure.

The children in the rejection group were told:

"That was poor, you are not remembering enough words. You should do better than that. You should have remembered more words than you did."

The intent of this communication was to arouse anxiety over the examiner's disapproval of the child's performance.

The children in the control group were told:

"O.K., let's take a short rest and then do some more lists."

It is acknowledged that all children may not have reacted to the instructions in the manner hypothesized, for individual differences in response to a communication are always to be expected. However, it is assumed that the majority of Ss in each group experienced thoughts and feelings appropriate to the communication, and that more Ss in the threat and rejection groups, experienced anxiety than Ss in the control group.

Following the experimental communication each S was then administered Lists 3 and 4. The major variables scored for both trials of each list were: (*a*) total number of concept words recalled, (*b*) total number of nonconcept words recalled, (*c*) number of intrusion errors, when an intrusion error was defined as the reporting of a word that was not present on the original list read to the child.

Results

Intercorrelation of Recall and Intrusion Scores

Complete intercorrelation matrices were computed for each of the recall and intrusion error scores for the sexes separately and for reflective and impulsive Ss separately for the first two lists, before the experimental interventions.

The relation between recall of concept and nonconcept words (pooling the first two lists) was high for reflective Ss but low for impulsives ($r = .36$ and .55 for reflective boys and girls, respectively; $r = .19$ and .18 for impulsive boys and girls).[2] Reflective Ss were more consistent in their recall scores for concept and nonconcept words. There was a moderate relation between Lists 1 and 2 for the recall of concept words ($r = .40$, .24 for reflective and impulsive boys; $r = .53$ and .38 for reflective and impulsive girls). For nonconcept words the corresponding coefficients were .30 and .28 for boys; .20 and .27 for girls. There was a low, positive relation between Lists 1 and 2 for intrusion errors ($r = .13$,

[2] The value of *r* for significance at .05 or better (two tailed) is .27 for reflective boys, .24 for impulsive boys, .29 for reflective girls, and .30 for impulsive girls.

.37 for boys; .24 and .10 for girls). These correlations were low because the means and standard deviation for intrusion errors were relatively low.

The relationship between recall and intrusion errors was generally negative—the higher the recall score the lower the number of intrusions. The correlations for List 1 were —.40 and —.30 for reflective and impulsive boys; .02 and —.37 for reflective and impulsive girls. For List 2, the corresponding correlation coefficients were .08 and —.40 for boys and —.25 and .07 for girls. Thus, the most consistent negative relationships between recall and intrusions for the first two lists held for impulsive boys.

Relation to WISC Scores

The relationship of WISC verbal skills to recall and intrusion scores is of interest. There was no relationship between verbal ability and intrusion errors for either sex or for reflective or impulsive Ss. The coefficients ranged from —.16 to +.12, and none of the coefficients was significant. Thus, as with response time on MFF, an impulsive attitude (in this case measured by intrusion errors) was orthogonal to verbal resources.

Verbal skills were related to recall in a complicated manner. Among boys, there was no relationship to recall of concept related words ($r = .10$ and .08); but there was a moderately positive relation with recall of nonconcept words ($r = .41$ for reflective boys and .20 for impulsive boys). Verbal skills facilitated the recall of words having no associative link among them, but had no such facilitating effect on words that were conceptually related to each other. Although this result may appear puzzling, it is not so enigmatic if one views the measure of verbal ability as reflecting, in part, motivation to master intellectual tasks. It is more difficult to recall unrelated words than related words and the greater the motivation to perform well on the learning task the higher this score should be. This increased motivation should also be reflected in higher recall scores for concept words. But the recall score for concept words was considerably higher than that of nonconcept words (a mean of 15 versus 11 for Lists 1 and 2), and it may be that all the children were performing at close to their intellectual capacity for the conceptually related words. As a result, added motivation was less facilitating for these words. It is possible that the brighter boys recall more nonconcept words because their richer verbal repertoire allowed them to create connections between the unrelated words. However, it is difficult to imagine how a third-grader might quickly connect words like dog-pencil-barn-knife-leaf-hammer as they were being read to him at a relatively fast rate.

Among girls there was no dramatic difference in the association between verbal skills and recall of concept or nonconcept words. The correlations with concept word recall were .59 and .24 for reflective and impulsive girls; the corresponding correlations for nonconcept words were .48 and .47. Thus brighter girls recall more of both classes of words. This finding is also reflected in the dramatic sex difference in degree of association between verbal skills and total recall for all words for the first two lists. The correlations were high for girls ($r = .61$ and .46 for reflectives and impulsives), but lower for boys ($r = .31$ and .18). This type of result is not unusual in our work. It is the rule rather than the exception that verbal ability is typically more highly correlated with a learning or performance measure for girls than it is for boys. Knowledge of a girl's IQ allows one to predict her performance on an intellectual task with greater accuracy than is possible from knowledge of a boy's IQ score. In sum, recall and intrusion scores displayed positive but low generality across the first two lists and recall scores were negatively related to intrusion errors.

The Superiority of Concept Recall

The superior recall of concept over nonconcept words for all Ss for the first pair of lists supports the reasonable assumption that the availability of a mediational link for a group of words facilitates recall of members of the mediationally related class. The differential recall of concept over nonconcept words was assessed for each S for the first and second pairs of lists by subtracting the latter score from the former for each S. The differences for Lists 1 and 2 were dramatic, for 75% of the boys and 80% of the girls recalled more concept than nonconcept words ($p < .001$ for each sex). The differences between concept and nonconcept recall were not as dramatic for Lists 3 and 4.

Relationship of Recall and Intrusions to Reflection-Impulsivity

The mean scores for recall and intrusions for Lists 1 and 2 are presented in Table 2 for each of the 12 groups. The maximal recall score for concept or nonconcept lists for either the first two lists or the second two lists was 24 words.

Analyses of variance were performed for each of the six major variables. In order to expedite these analyses Ss were randomly eliminated from each group containing more than 13 Ss in order to have a constant sample size of 13 for each of the 12 cells. The means and standard deviations for each of the 12 cells were proportional to the parameters derived from the slightly larger samples whose means were presented in Table 2. Summaries of these analyses of variance appear in Table 3.

Recall Data. Reflective Ss recalled more words than the impulsives,

Table 2
Mean Scores on Serial Learning Variables

	Boys						Girls					
	Reflective			Impulsive			Reflective			Impulsive		
Variable	Threat	Reject	Cont.	Threat	Reject	Cont.	Threat	Reject	Cont.	Threat	Reject	Cont.
Concept Recall Lists 1 & 2	15.1	15.8	15.6	14.0	13.6	14.0	15.4	14.8	14.7	13.9	14.4	14.6
Nonconcept Recall Lists 1 & 2	12.8	10.8	12.9	11.0	10.9	11.3	12.2	12.2	11.4	11.2	11.4	11.4
Concept Recall Lists 3 & 4	11.5	12.6	12.6	12.1	13.5	11.1	13.4	13.7	11.2	13.1	13.3	12.3
Nonconcept Recall Lists 3 & 4	11.5	12.2	12.3	10.1	11.8	10.9	12.1	11.9	11.6	10.5	12.4	10.2
Intrusions Lists 1 & 2	1.2	1.1	1.4	1.7	2.0	2.9	1.0	1.2	1.5	1.5	2.1	2.0
Intrusions Lists 3 & 4	5.8	3.2	3.1	4.3	3.9	5.2	3.2	2.3	1.6	3.6	3.3	3.1

Table 3
Analyses of Variance

Source	df	SS	MS	F	p
Concept words recalled:					
Lists 1 & 2					
Variable					
Reflection (R-I)	1	73.4	73	7.52	<.01
Sex (S)	1	0.2	0.2		
Error	153	1,485	9.70		
Nonconcept words recalled:					
Lists 1 & 2					
R-I	1	37.3	37.3	4.78	<.05
S	1	1.2	1.2		
Error	153	1,194	7.8		
Concept words recalled:					
Lists 3 & 4					
R-1	1	18	18		
S	1	15.4	15.4		
Conditions (C)	2	61.2	30.6	3.03	<.05
R × S	1	5.4	5.4		
R × C	2	6.2	3.1		
C × S	2	17.9	8.9		
R × C × S	2	15.6	7.8		
Error	144	1,459	10.1		
Nonconcept words recalled:					
Lists 3 & 4					
R	1	45.2	45.2	5.48	<.05
S	1	0.2	0.2		
C	2	57.5	28.7	3.49	<.05
R × S	1	2.1	2.1		
R × C	2	16.7	8.3		
C × S	2	2.6	1.3		
R × S × C	2	0.8	0.4		
Error	144	1,187	8.25		
Intrusion errors: Lists 1 & 2					
R	1	27.1	27.1	7.38	<.01
S	1	2.8	2.8		
Error	153	576	3.7		
Intrusion errors: Lists 3 & 4					
R	1	79.0	79.0	4.97	<.05
S	1	100.1	100.1	6.25	<.05
C	2	9.6	4.8		
R × S	1	8.8	8.8		
R × C	2	80.4	40.2		
C × S	2	18.7	9.4		
R × S × C	2	27.5	14.7		
Error	144	2,290	15.9		

especially for Lists 1 and 2. The superior recall of reflective Ss on the first two lists was significant for the nonconcept words ($t = 2.98$, $p < .01$), and also significant for the nonconcept words ($t = 2.22$, $p < .05$). The mean recall scores for Lists 3 and 4 were lower for all groups, including the controls. Thus the poorer recall scores on the second pair of lists cannot be attributed to the different experimental communications.

The superior recall of reflective Ss does not appear to be a function of either longer delays before beginning to report words or the character of the initial words reported. There was no significant difference between reflective and impulsive Ss on response latency to begin to report words after termination of the taped list. Moreover, detailed analysis of the first five words recalled by each S did not reveal a greater tendency for reporting concept words by reflective children. The initial five words reported tended to obey the laws of primacy and recency. Thus the superior recall of reflective children seems due to the fact that they persisted longer in their attempt to produce a better cognitive product, suggesting that they were more highly motivated on this task. This suggestion matches other data on reflective and impulsive children which indicates that reflective Ss persist longer with difficult intellectual tasks than their impulsive counterparts with the same verbal ability (Kagan, 1965).

The effect of conditions on recall for Lists 3 and 4 suggested a tendency for the control Ss to have lower recall scores than either the threat or rejection groups. Examination of Table 3 reveals that the "rejection" statement acted as an incentive for most of the Ss.

Intrusion Errors. A major purpose of this study was to replicate an earlier study in which impulsive children produced more intrusion errors than reflectives. These data clearly verified this association for all four lists. The analysis of variance for Lists 1 and 2 revealed a significant F ratio ($F = 7.38$, $p < .01$) for the reflection-impulsivity dimension, with impulsive Ss producing more intrusion errors than their reflective counterparts. On Lists 3 and 4, the effects of the reflection-impulsivity dimension was still present ($F = 4.97$, $p < .05$), and a sex difference occurred, with boys producing more intrusion errors than girls ($F = 6.25$, $p < .05$). This sex difference is also revealed in the results of an additional analysis. Specifically, the change in intrusion errors from List 2 to List 3 was computed for each S and a constant of 10 added to avoid negative scores. The analysis yielded only one significant F ratio ($p < .01$), with boys displaying larger increases in intrusion errors than girls.

The Effect of Threat on Reflective Ss. There was the suggestion of the predicted association between reflection and the threatening communication when the increase in intrusions from List 2 to List 3 was the score analyzed ($F = 2.56$, $p < .10$ for the interaction between reflection-impulsivity and experimental group). Specifically, reflected children following threat showed the largest increase in intrusion errors, while reflective Ss in the control group produced the smallest increase in intrusions. Moreover, the data in Table 2 reveal that the largest increase in intrusion errors, comparing Lists 3 and 4 with Lists 1 and 2, occurred among reflective boys under threat conditions. These boys showed an increase of 4.6 intrusions, compared with values of 2.1 and 1.7 for reflective boys under rejection and control conditions. A test of the significance of the difference between the threat and rejection groups (4.6 versus 2.1) yielded a t of 1.70 ($p < .10$, two tails). Furthermore, the increase in intrusion errors comparing Lists 3 and 4 with Lists 1 and 2 was greater for the reflective boys under threat than the impulsive boys under threat (4.6 versus 2.6), but this difference was not statistically significant. The frequency data indicated that 60% of the reflective boys under threat showed an increase of 3 or more intrusion errors and no reflective boy displayed a decrease. Among the impulsive boys, only 38% had an increase of 3 or more intrusions and 3 boys had fewer intrusions after threat than they did before threat. Although these differences are not statistically significant by conventional standards, they support the notion that reflective boys were more influenced by the instruction that suggested the possibility of future failure.

The differential deterioration in recall also supports these ideas. When concept and nonconcept words were pooled, the reflective boys under threat recalled 4.9 fewer words on Lists 3 and 4 than they did on Lists 1 and 2. This difference compares with a value of 2.8 for impulsive boys under threat. The recall loss of 4.9 words between the first and second pairs of lists is the largest average drop in recall displayed by any of the 12 groups (average loss of 2.0 words for remaining 11 groups). Assuming that a combination of a large increase in intrusion errors and a large decrease in recall would be most indicative of deterioration and, by inference, of anxiety, one final analysis was attempted. Subjects who showed both an increase in intrusion errors of three or more (the median value of all Ss) and a decrease in recall of four or more words were selected. Forty percent of the reflective boys under threat fulfilled this double index of deterioration in performance, in contrast to 27% among impulsive boys. Moreover, 4 of the 15 reflective boys under threat deteriorated 12 or more words comparing Lists 3 and 4 with recall in the first two lists. The largest loss in recall among the impulsives was 9 words. Although these differences missed statistical significance, they agree with the notion that telling the child that a task he was about to do was difficult—and failure a likely possibility—had a greater disruptive effect on reflective than impulsive boys.

Discussion and Conclusion

The hypothesis that children classified as impulsive on the visual matching test would make more errors of commission in the serial learning procedure was clearly supported. These data corroborate the results of an earlier investigation and add validity to the postulation of a generalized behavioral tendency to be impulsive (or reflective) in problem situations where the child should consider the validity of his answers. Impulsive children do not pause to consider the probable accuracy of their cognitive products, whether the situation involves visual matching of picture or reporting words in a recall situation.

The hypothesis that reflective Ss are anxious over possible failure received only minimal support, and primarily among boys. The largest increase in intrusion errors and largest loss in recall score occurred among the reflective boys after they were told the lists they were about to hear were difficult. This inference requires the double assumption that the "threat" instruction is likely to generate worry over quality of performance for most of the children and that the sequellae of the anxiety are poor recall and more intrusion. Since there is no independent test of intensity of anxiety this nest of assumptions may be gratuitous. This conceptual problem is pervasive in psychology and indirect inference must often be used.

This interpretation is consistent with the data and current theory but is by no means the only way to interpret the findings.

As noted earlier, anxiety over the possibility of making a mistake is to be distinguished conceptually from expectancy of failure. A child may be so accustomed to failure that he has stopped protecting himself, and as a result, is not highly anxious over possible failure. It is likely that there is a curvilinear relationship between these two variables, with maximum values for the anxiety variables associated with moderate values of expectancy of failure. Children who are maximally or minimally confident of success are apt to be minimally anxious over possible failure.

The major implication of this work is to emphasize the significance of a conceptual tempo variable for cognitive products. Investigators working with "culturally deprived" children believe that one reason for their poor intellectual performance is their impulsive orientation.

The brain-damaged child, as well as the reading-retarded child, is more prone to be impulsive than reflective and his inferior intellectual performances are more often the result of impulsivity than inadequate verbal or knowledge resources. Therapeutic regimes for these children should consider the potential value of training reflection as a specific conceptual habit, independent of the specific substantive content of the material to be mastered.

References

Kagan, J. Impulsive and reflective children. In J. Krumboltz (Ed.), *Learning and the educational process.* Chicago: Rand, McNally, 1965. Pp. 133–161.

Kagan, J., Rosman, B. C., Day, D., Albert, J., & Phillips, W. Information processing in the child, *Psychological Monographs,* 1964, **78**(1, Whole No. 578).

9.7 The Self-Picture as a Factor in the Class-Room

J. W. Staines

Evidence indicates that the self-concept is not only determined by education but is also a condition for subsequent learning. Since it is such an important characteristic, the effect of specific teacher behavior on the self-concept was investigated. Because the impact of teacher behavior was substantiated, the author emphasizes the need to recognize the presence of the self and its importance in learning. Furthermore, its development should become a major teacher objective.

The importance of the Self in psychological thinking has both empirical and theoretical foundations. Self-reference is frequent in the conversation of adults, and class-room data show that this is also true of children. Clinical records stress the importance of the Self-picture and of Self-acceptance and rejection. From such evidence it appears that the Self is empirically a matter of prime importance in that a great deal of behaviour is concerned with maintaining and enhancing the established pattern of the Self as it appears to the person, as he thinks it ought to be, and as he thinks other people believe it to be. Most psychological

SOURCE. Abridged from J. W. Staines, "Symposium: The Development of Children's Values," *British Journal of Educational Psychology*, **XXVIII**, Part II (1958), pp. 97–111, by permission of the *British Journal of Educational Psychology*.

theorists introduce the Self or a related concept in considering motivation, and writers on personality postulate the Self as the integrating factor in personality. Cattell[5] calls it the fourth factor in the economy of the personality, "the keystone of personality" integrating Id, Ego and Super-Ego into "one dynamic structure or unified sentiment." Lewin[9] sees the Self as an inner, relatively permanent structure, giving consistency to the personality. Stagner[15] believes that the Self image contributes stability to the personality, while Murphy[11] has claimed that no part of behaviour is free of the Self.

If the Self is so closely related to the empirical data of behaviour and to the theoretical aspects of personality, it is important for education and for the teacher. This is particularly so since the Self is both an outcome of education and, once it has developed, a condition of subsequent learning. Such educational relevance should lead to an investigation of the conditions under which the Self develops, the methods by which it is changed, the limitations upon change once it has developed, and the effect of a particular kind of Self-picture upon learning.

II. Theoretical Considerations

The notion of the Self is highly complex. It is primarily perceptual, "a learned perceptual system which functions as an object in the perceptual field."[12] It is built from many perceptual experiences. The child learns about his Self from his own experiences and from the behaviour of others. From the teacher who says: "John, go to the back. You're one of the big ones," the boy learns about himself and about himself-in-relation-to-others, as well as something of the social expectations centered on that aspect of his physique. He learns that he can run faster than some others, that he can read well or that he cannot sing. Gradually, the raw perceptual materials of the Self are transformed by the manufacturing processes of the mind, so that the Self also becomes conceptual. Memory images and other kinds of mental structures, notably concepts, are developed. The Self, as known to the individual, is thus both perceptual and conceptual.

One method of analysis of this complex Self-structure is to see the Self in three levels or phases, each level having a number of sectors or categories. The first level is the Cognised or Known Self which comprises all those characteristics of the individual that he recognises as part of the 'Me.' Whether or not these correspond to objective reality or to what others think about him does not matter. The Cognised Self is what the individual perceives and conceives himself to be. The second level of the Self, called the Other Self, is what the person believes others think of him: "The teacher thinks I'm no good at English." The third level is the Ideal

Self, part wish, part 'ought,' the standard to be reached: "I ought to be more careful of detail." These elements of the Self are of supreme importance for behaviour since many of the individual's actions are ordered by his constant efforts to maintain and enhance these various aspects of the Self-picture.

The categories are those aspects of the Self which individuals commonly report on. The most obvious are physical characteristics and skills of various kinds. Other appearing in conversations and in such clinical records as Roger's[13] include traits, attitudes and interests, values, wants and goals, status and role, in-groups and philosophy of life. Each of these categories appears in all three levels of the Self-picture. The individual has, for example, a picture of his physique as part of the Cognised Self, a belief that others see his physique in a certain way and a wish that it were something else.

In addition to the levels and categories, the data require the postulation of dimensions. A dimension is a direction in which people may vary, and at least nine major dimensions may be distinguished. Individuals may be placed along a continuum of Self-awareness, from the person who, through momentary pre-occupation with a task, is little aware of himself to the person who is continually and painfully self-conscious. This is the dimension of salience. Differentiation means the degree to which the person distinguishes the various levels and categories within the Self. He may have his concept of his status differentiated in great detail but his values category may be relatively undifferentiated. Potency is the sense of confidence a person develops in his own adequacy. The dimension of integration concerns the development of a hierarchy in the levels and categories so that the person can predict his behaviour, knowing that he will not be the victim of rash impulses and that he can trust himself in conflict situations. Insight is the degree to which the Self-picture corresponds to reality. Stability refers to Stagner's contention that the Self must be stable in order to give a consistent basis for personality and action. People will vary in their resistance to change and in their willingness to accommodate the Self-picture to new data. Self-acceptance is the name given to a continuum whose limiting points are an unreal overvaluation of the Self and Self-rejection. Between them lies the optimal region of Self-acceptance which occurs when the Cognised and Ideal Self are close together: "I am like this and happy to be this way." Concomitance of Cognised and Other self is also a sign of Self-acceptance: "I am like this and others think so too." When this occurs, the Ideal Self loses the tyrannical quality that Horney[6] finds in neurotics. The real dimension refers to the number of identifications which a person makes with ideas, groups, institutions and objects. Finally, people differ in the degree of certainty with which they can report on what they are like. Position on the dimension of certainty should change with age and development of the Self-picture.*

III. The First Hypothesis and Empirical Procedures.

The Self-structure develops in response to environmental stimuli. Since teachers are an important aspect of the child's environment, it is likely that they have some effect on the child's Self-picture. A number of questions arise. What part do teachers play in the development of the Self-picture? Can teachers change the child's Self-picture if they try to do so? If they can, what methods of teaching produce what kinds of Self-picture? Is it possible to distinguish between teachers in the frequency and kind of comment which they make about the child's Self? An investigation was planned to answer this last question, and to show what effects, if any, followed deliberate teaching for change in the Self-picture.

The research followed the traditions established by Lewin,[10] more fully developed by Anderson and his colleagues[2] and followed with modifications by Bales[3] and Whitall,[16] of seeing a class as a group and attempting to record and analyse data from teacher-child and child-child interaction. Their data on the educational outcomes of the interaction between personalities in the atmosphere of the classroom were sufficiently reliable to show that class-room situations are much more complex than was suspected and are producing other than orthodox lesson outcomes.

Observation of a number of teachers showed that the data of Self-reference were likely to provide a tentative answer to the investigation. Teachers made frequent comments on the child's Self: "You're better at sums than you are at spelling," "Let Rosemary come to the front—she's only small," "We expect more from you because you're older," and so on. Some teachers make such remarks more frequently than others. An hypothesis was formulated: that teachers may be reliably distinguished by the frequency of their use of words and kinds of situational management which, in the opinion of competent judges, are likely to mould the Self.

To test this hypothesis, two problems had to be solved, how to gather and how to order the data. Two pairs of teachers, one pair in the Junior and one in the Infants' school, agreed to participate in the investigation although they did not know its purpose until all the data had been collected. They permitted the investigator to copy down and classify all that was said and to interview the children at any time. The pairs of teachers were comparable in experience and were rated by their respective head

* For a full description of categories and dimensions, see: STAINES, J. W. (1954). *A Sociological and Psychological Study of the Self-Picture and Its Importance in Education.* Unpublished Ph.D. Thesis, University of London.

teachers as similar in proficiency. The classes were similar in numbers of boys and girls, in age, in intelligence, and in social class as judged from fathers' occupations. The children were mainly working class.

Table 1
Classes Used in Observation Period

Classes	Numbers		Age in Months		I.Q.	
	Boys	Girls	Mean	Range	Mean	S.D.
Junior A	15	14	129	122–134	114–4	10–4
Junior B	16	15	128	123–134	112–8	10–1
Infants C	20	24	89	84–96	No tests used in	
Infants D	26	17	87	84–100	this department.	

The times spent in observation of lessons are recorded in Table 2.

Table 2
Minutes of Observations for Various Lessons

Class	Arithmetic	English	Social Studies	Nature Study	Music	Handwork
A	100	105	30	—	—	15
B	97	87	51	—	—	15
C	86	100	30	—	20	15
D	105	100	—	30	—	15

The preponderance of Arithmetic and English in the lessons observed reflects the importance attached to these subjects in the Junior school, and the Infants' school periods were chosen to match. The children became accustomed to the presence of the observer in a preliminary period and quickly accepted him as part of the class-room set-up.

The data were classified in terms of the categories and dimensions of the Self, using a method of scoring with symbols, supplemented by the indicators, "+," "—," "n," and "ambi," "+" meant that the effect of the comment or situation was thought to be positive, "—" implied a probable negative effect and "n" stood for neutral. "Ambi" indicated that the effect was likely to be positive for some and negative for other children. The following are examples of the scoring in two of the categories:

1. *Physique*

(*a*) "Jack, you're tall. Help me with this." Score Ph.+ since the teacher values tallness and Jack sees his height as a valued possession.

(*b*) "Marie has the best complexion for Cinderella. We'll have her."

Score Ph. ambi. since Marie is chosen from a group of volunteers and the comment is positive for Marie, negative for the others.

(*c*) "You won't do for the queen—you're not tall enough." Score Ph.— because the child feels her physique is not valued.

(*d*) "You're taller than the others. You're just right for this part." Score Ph.O. since a marked comparison with others is made, and positive, negative and ambivalent judgments are included. Interview evidence showed the importance of this kind of situation.

2. *Performance*

Comments on Performance may be positive, negative or ambivalent. They may build up the child's Self-picture as able to do things, break it down or be ambivalent in their effects. Skills may bring the correct answer or performance with no comment from the teacher. The child sees himself as able by his success, or incompetent because of failure. A correct answer is scored Sk.+. Failure by silence, slowness or the wrong answer is scored Sk.—. In comments other than the routine "Yes," "You're good at . . ." "Wrong." "You don't know your . . . ," one score is given for the achievement or the failure and a second for status (St.+ or St.—). That the teacher's comments are related by the child to his status in the eyes of the class was revealed by such comments as these made in interviews: "They think I can't do it." "Everyone thinks how good you are."

A comment by the teacher is sometimes followed by a class reaction: "Good boy! Look at this everyone!" (Class approves). "Wrong. Just look what Jack's done!" (Class laughs). Each element in the situation is scored, skill, status for the teacher's comment and status for the reaction of the class. Sk. ambi. is scored when a comment makes possible a positive as well as a negative Self-picture and it is impossible to determine which occurs: "Who's right? Hands up those right." Some children are right, some wrong. Hierachy in skills is used when the teacher's comments tend to make the child see himslf as better in one skill than another, so leading to greater differentiation: "You're better at English than Arithmetic."

Similar methods of scoring were used for other dimensions and categories. The potency is the score total of all scores relating to the child's confidence in any aspect of himself. It is got by subtracting the negative from the positive Self-reference comments. The salience score is the total of all Self-ratings together with the Self-orientation total. The latter comments refer to the person as a whole rather than to any category; "You're a fine one, you are." Incisions are interruptions by the teacher in the child's own sequences of purpose and achievements, usually by way of unnecessary directions. The Self-direction category includes those comments which give the child an opportunity to see himself as a purposing, planning individual. A classification for class-room management distinguishes two modes, direct and indirect. Direct management is any routine command by the teacher. The indirect method is illustrated by co-operative relationships between the teacher and the class. It will help to form the child's concept of himself as causal. Level of aspiration is related to the Ideal Self. Task-oriented comments are those with no salience or Self-reference.

Treatment of Data. The material was rated by the writer (Judge X) and two school counsellors with three years' training in Psychology at Sydney University. When the data was divided into units by each judge, agreement on the units between Judges X and Y and X and Z was above 90 per cent and this was held to indicate sufficient accuracy. Units where agreement was not finally reached after discussion were eliminated. The remaining units were rated for categories and dimensions. After two months, a page was taken at random from the records and re-marked by Judges X and Y with a re-test reliability for X of 94 per cent. and for Y of 92 per cent.

A survey was made of the ratings for the various teachers, a total found for each teacher, and the score in each category and dimension represented as a percentage of the total. Many of the differences between the scores of the teachers were very small and are not reported here because of lack of space.* Table 3 gives the catgories where the differences are greatest or of most interest. Table 4 shows an analysis of the data for the dimensions. Many of the differences between the teachers were found by chi-squared to be significant at the 1 per cent. of 5 pr cent. level,† but because of the small numbers in many categories comparisons were made simply on the basis of observed scores.

In general, the Infants' teachers used more Self-references than the Junior teachers. B differs considerably from A, and very widely from C and D in the categories of the Self. In the dimensions, salience scores will, by definition, closely parallel the total scores, and with this sample of teachers, differentiation does also. Wide individual differences between teachers are evident in the totals for both salience and differentiation, but not in the percentages. It is in the potency dimension, however, that the most striking difference occurs. Scores in the other three dimensions show small differences, largely because of the method of scoring the data.

* For full details of methods of scoring and of results, see STAINES, J. W., *loc. cit.*

† Between A and B: 1 per cent. level, Sk.—, Status +, Status —, Self-direction, Incisions, direct Class-room Management. 5 per cent. level, Skill +, Values.

Between C and D: 1 per cent. level, Performance Total, Status —, Incisions, Self-Orientation, Traits. 5 per cent. level, Skills —, Status Total.

Table 3
Categories Showing Most Marked Differences Between Teachers

	A	B
Performance		
Skill +	107	73
Skill −	19	50
Total	141	129
Status		
Positive (+)	70	30
Negative (−)	14	48
Total	84	78
Values		
Responsibility	5	0
General	5	0
Total	11	2
Wants		
Level of Aspiration	11	7
Self-Direction	85	14
Incisions	1	14
Class-room management		
Direct	11	33

	C	D
Performance		
Skill +	64	76
Skill −	15	37
Total	79	113
Status		
Positive (+)	71	67
Negative (−)	24	63
Total	95	130
Values		
General	8	1
Total	12	5
Physique		
Total	16	1
Wants		
Level of Aspiration	15	22
Self-Direction	24	20
Incisions	8	36
Class-room management		
Direct	34	40
Traits		
Negative (−)	7	25
Self-orientation		
Total	9	35

If all positive scores are regarded as acceptance scores, and all negative scores as rejection, then the characteristics of the teachers and the class-room atmospheres are very different indeed.

IV. Discussion of Results

The Junior teachers are most alike where scores are small. In categories and dimensions where scores are large, these teachers differ widely, particularly in the performance and status categories, in the four major dimensions—areal, salience, differentiation and potency—in Self-direction and in direct class-room management, that is, in the giving of orders rather than opportunities for seeing oneself as purposive, choosing and causal.

Teacher A. The pattern is clear-cut. Teacher A is particularly strong in positive emphasis on skills and makes few negative comments. The status category shows the same pattern. He is outstanding in the opportunity he offers children for Self-determination—an important feature if,

Table 4

Scores on Dimensions of Self and on Frequency of Each Dimension as a Percentage of Total of Units

	Teachers							
	Junior A		Junior B		Infants' C		Infants' D	
Dimensions	Raw Score	% of Total	Raw Score	% of Total	Raw Score	% of Total	Raw Score	% of Total
1.—Salience	372	96.7	317	98.3	383	91.9	481	96.2
2.—Differentiation	371	96.5	313	97.0	380	90.2	475	95.0
3.—Potency +	290	75.4	130	40.3	223	53.5	217	43.4
—	54	14.0	160	49.6	93	22.3	205	41.0
4.—Integrity	1	.3	—	—	—	—	—	—
5.—Insight	5	1.3	2	.6	3	.7	1	.2
6.—Acceptance	1	.3	—	—	3	.7	1	.2
7.—Rejection	—	—	5	1.6	4	1.0	2	.4

as Murphy[11] suggests, the Self develops best where there is opportunity for Self-direction. He puts more stress on values than do two of the others. In the dimensions of salience, potency and differentiation, Teacher A's scores suggest that he is likely to make the child Self-aware—to teach him, as Kirkpatrick[7] suggests, that "It is I who am doing it." It will be a positive, Self-accepting salience. His emphasis is strongly on differentiation so that children may see their strengths and weaknesses more accurately and in greater detail, making for more adequate adjustment. A's score on the potency dimension is significant. Teachers B and D give confidence with one hand take it away with the other. Teacher A gives most (score 290) and takes least (score 54).

Teacher B. The pattern here is also clear-cut but very different. In the performance category, B makes fewer positive and many more negative comments than A. In the status category, although the totals are approximately the same as A's (A 84, B 78), the constituents are strikingly different. The pattern of the performance category is repeated in having a smaller number of positive and a greater number of negative comments. The pattern occurs again when B makes less effort than A to hold up a level of aspiration, although the difference in scores is not great. He gives very few opportunities for Self-direction. The effect of this on the Self-picture must be magnified by the repetition of incisions. The absence of Self-choice and the interference with the child's goal-directed or purposive sequences are complementary.

In the dimensions, B is widely different from the other teachers. The amount of salience is less. There is less differentiation and a tendency to use the wholistic approach with children ("You're no good . . .").

Totals for the potency dimension are widely different from those of the other teachers, as are the positive, (score 130) and negative (score 160) constituents. This teacher shows less positive development of confidence or Self-potency than the others and, at the same time, more negative effects. He gives least and takes most.

The Infants' teachers are slightly more alike than are the Junior teachers, particularly in In-group comments, values, attitudes and interests, and in the salience and differentiation dimensions.

Teacher C. This teacher comments on the physique of children more often than the other teachers, and is the only one to draw comparisons at this point. Her comments on skills are more positive than negative. She prefers positive to negative comment on status and places more emphasis on Traits than the Junior teachers, but not so much as Teacher D. She gives little opportunity for Self-direction and, as might be expected, her class-room management is largely direct. In dimensions, her outstanding score is in potency, where there is a tendency to build up the child's confidence (score 223), with only a small score for negative comments (93).

Teacher D. Teacher D stresses performance on the positive side and negative comments are less frequent than Teacher B's, and more than A's and C's. Status comments are greater than for the other three teachers, but are chiefly negative. This is also true for Traits. The opportunity that she gives for Self-direction is slight and her scores for incisions and salience are highest of all. The differentiation score is high. The potency score, got by algebraically totalling the high positive score (217) and the high negative score (205), is very low. If her effect on the Self-picture were predicted from this evidence it would seem that Teacher D tends to make children highly Self-aware in many categories, but not particularly confident in any aspect of themselves.

In summary, the teachers' comments overwhelmingly stress performance and status. It is inevitable that where the stress is on performance, it should also be on status; but the latter category is also evident independently in the verbal material, although not distinguished in the scores. The psychological significance of such emphasis on status may be argued from its numerical preponderance, but the writer feels from his experience with teachers and students that it is largely overlooked by teachers. They are, indeed, careful to avoid most of the obvious status aspects where the child's feelings are involved and are usually considerate of them. But material taken in a number of interviews with the children suggests that, much more frequently than teachers believe, the ordinary run-of-the-day comments on success and failure, and incidents where a child is casually preferred to another for what seems to the teacher an unimportant task or role, may be fraught with status possibilities and intense emotional content. While no claim is made that these unnoticed situations are always significant for all children, it is reasonable to conclude that the teachers who most frequently invoke status situations and make relevant comments are most likely to modify the child's Self-picture in this direction.

How effective is this method of distinguishing teachers? It would seem to separate them on what competent judges believe are likely to be the effects of their words and situational management on a number of categories and dimensions. These categories and dimensions are held to be central aspects of the Self and it is useful to know that teachers differ so widely in relation to them. A second obvious conclusion from the scores is that teachers do not develop to any significant degree many of the other important educational outcomes to which subject matter and teaching methods may be closely geared, and which might be drawn into the Self in order to be most effectively related to behaviour.

The point at which this method of investigation is least effective is in gauging the effect upon the child of the various verbal and situational interactions. Categorisation of what a teacher says, while indicating a prevailing classroom atmosphere, gives no clue as to how effective it really is in forming the Self-picture. Teacher D, for instance, uses reproof much more frequently than any other teacher and each reproof is rated St. –. Yet the observer could not say what effects her words had. Interviews showed that some children had a "water-off-a-duck's-back" attitude towards her but that others were much more sensitive to her flow of personal comment. In an attempt to discover whether the different teaching styles and aims would lead to changes in the Self-picture, the second part of the investigation was carried out.

V. The Second Hypothesis and Empirical Procedures

The hypothesis was formulated that teachers who differ in the frequency of their Self-referential comments would produce significantly different Self-pictures. If this were so, it would follow that class-room situations would produce educational outcomes other than the traditional skills, knowledges and appreciations.

To test this hypothesis it was decided to use the two Junior teachers previously observed, since they differed widely in certain known aspects, particularly in the opportunities they gave children for Self-direction, in their attitudes towards children's skills and their care for preserving status. Teacher A was more likely than Teacher B to produce socially desirable changes in the Self-picture as he was interested in children and their problems. Accordingly, class A was chosen as the experimental group, class B as the control. Such a design would show whether Teacher A's methods would support the hypothesis, while the results from Teacher B's class would supply additional confirmatory evidence.

The Subjects. Though the two classes were matched for age, intelligence and socio-economic class, they were not equal in attainments. The experimental group had a greater number of children whose achievement scores on standardised tests were low, although eight of them were the most intelligent children in either class. Both classes were tested with a Self-rating card test* to measure the phases and categories of the Self-picture before and after the experimental teaching period.

The Experimental Teaching Methods. The teaching period for the experiment was twelve weeks. Teacher A rated his class on the categories in the card test for each phase of the Self, and compared his ratings with the children's Self-ratings in order to decide what treatment might be given to each child. In doing so he became familiar with the general concepts used in the analysis of the Self and accepted the idea that these could be used as ends of the teaching process. He planned his methods so that situations could be arranged in which the child would be led by the teaching methods to see himself in various ways. These would include seeing himself as a planning, purposing, choosing individual, responsible and accountable, for these are basic aspects of the healthy socialised Self. The child should test his purposes by carrying them through, see himself as adequate and causal and, at the same time, differentiate his relative strengths and weaknesses. Particular attention was to be paid to preserving his status. At the same time the syllabus for entrance to grammar school was to be covered without interfering with the prospects of the candidates. For the Ideal Self, the teacher planned to hold up a suitable level of aspiration, either directly and by commendation or indirectly by allusion and suggestion. The teacher also planned to convey his judgments which make up the child's Other Self in such a way that the child would be unlikely to reject them as incongruous with the Self-picture he already had.

Provision was made for teaching methods relevant to the child's place on the dimensions of the Self. The Ideal Self for each child could be increased by identification with more objects, values, ideas and people. For the over-selfconscious child (high in salience), treatment was to include a reduction in comments referring specifically to the Self, an increase in Alper's task-involved[1] comments and in Ruger's[14] technique of the 'scientific attitude,' and care with the use of such simple situations as the public display of work. Differentiation was related to the avoidance of 'whole' comments such as 'Good' and 'You're hopeless,' and to an

* See STAINES, J. W., *loc. cit.*, for details of construction and validation.

emphasis on seeing various characteristics more accurately. Adequacy or potency was to be built up by success and appreciation and by the teacher's care for the child's status. Accepting behaviour by the teacher was thought to be the best way of teaching Self-acceptance.

The experimental period began at the end of the first month of the school term when the card test was administered for the first time. After twelve weeks, the test was re-administered and the data analysed for significant differences between the classes. To understand the results, it is necessary to make brief explanatory comments on the instructions given for the card test. In a pilot study, children were given the Self-ratings in the form of 66 cards and asked to place them in heaps or columns labelled Not True, Neither True nor Untrue, True, and Not Sure. The children asked for finer gradings. For instance, of two cards that could be placed in the 'True' column, one might be "more true than the other." Accordingly, ratings were made in Columns 1, 2, 3 for Untrue items, 4, 5, 6 for Neither True nor Untrue, 7, 8, 9 for True and 10 for Not Sure. Columns 1 (Most Untrue of Me), 5, and 9 (Most True of Me) contained items about which the children were most certain.

VI. Results

The first of two ways of considering results is to ask what differences there were between the two groups at the end of the period.

The percentage frequencies of children's rankings of various items as "Most true of me" served as the basis of the calculation. Six items of the card test showed differences between the classes at the 1 per cent level and 5 per cent level. At the 1 per cent level were "I try to see fair play," "Good at games," "Willing to have a try at things no matter how hard they are," and "Like hobbies." At the 5 per cent level were a greater willingness to admit cheating, and an item testing Self-direction. All the differences were in favour of the experimental class. Teacher A believed of the item relating to cheating that the greater freedom in his class and the rational approach led children to admit it more freely. In the item testing Self-direction ("Make up my own mind"), little change had taken place in the experimental class, but a major one had occurred in the control class. Teacher B's methods were characterised by incisions and a great deal of direction in class-room management and were likely to produce widespread uncertainty and insecurity. The effects of his methods appear in significant differences between the classes in the responses to this item. The hypothesis is thus supported in relation to a limited number of characteristics.

The second method of estimating the results of the experiment is concerned with the dimensions.

Highly significant differences were found between the initial and final scores of the experimental class and also between the final scores of the two classes in the dimensions of certainty and differentiation. For the certainty dimension, the evidence is found in the movement towards or away from the rating "Not sure" and is presented in Table 5 as the total

Table 5
Uncertainty Scores (Column 10) at the Beginning and End of the Experimental Period

	Test 1			Test 2		
	Self	Ideal Self	Other Self	Self	Ideal Self	Other Self
Experimental	123	159	385	72	34	149
Control	370	89	582	448	300	932

numbers of cards placed by each class in the "Not sure" category (column 10), for each level of the Self. That is, the 29 children in the experimental class had placed a total of 123 cards in this category in the first test and 72 in the second test. This change is interpreted as an increase in the certainty as to what the Self really was.

When the significance of the figures for the various levels of the Self is tested by chi-squared technique, Teacher A shows a significant decrease in "Not sure" scores for the Self, Ideal Self and the Other Self. The class gained significantly in certainty about the boundaries of the Self. Equally significant statistically, and numerically much greater, is the increase in scores in the "Not sure" rating in the control group. Starting with a significantly greater degree (1 per cent. level) of uncertainty than the experimental group in the Self and Other Self, after the "settling-down" period of one month, this group increased its uncertainty over its own initial score and over the experimental group in all three levels of the Self. Particularly striking are the figures for the Ideal Self and the Other Self.

Differentiation. The figures for differentiation are found by taking the scores for "Least true" and "Most true" ratings (Table 6). A movement

Table 6
Differentiation of the Self at the Beginning and End of the Experimental Period

	Test 1		Test 2	
	Most true	Least true	Most true	Least true
Experimental	621	299	522	288
Control	340	191	357	209

towards the middle ranges and away from the extreme points on the scale is differentiation. A movement towards the extremes, Columns 1 and 9, indicates a tendency to see oneself as black or white, and an inability to make moderate adjustments of the various aspects of the Self.

There is a significant decrease (1 per cent. level) for the experimental group for "Most true," and a small non-significant decrease in "Least true." The control group shows a slight non-significant increase for both columns. It is clear that the experimental group has moved significantly away from "Most true" and, to a lesser degree, from "least true." Since the numbers in "Not sure" have also decreased significantly, the movement from all three must be in the direction of the middle ranges towards greater differentiation. The control group not only failed to move away from "Most true" and "Least true," but actually increased these numbers slightly. When these two totals are added to the flight to the "Not sure" column, it can be seen to what degree the middle ranges are depleted. It indicates how little these children, compared with the experimental group, can see themselves with either certainty or moderation. If it is true that insecurity is marked by rigidity, then the scores on the differentiation dimension reinforce the conclusion drawn from the uncertainty scores. The hypothesis is thus very strongly supported.

One further line of evidence must be considered. Both classes used for the investigation were scholarship classes. Teacher A believed that, while working on the lines of the experiment, he could still secure the necessary academic results. No check was kept on Scholarship results, but standardised tests for word recognition and mechanical arithmetic were given at the beginning and end of the experimental period. The results appear in Table 7.

Table 7
Mean Scores on Standardized Tests Before and After the Experimental Period

	Test 1		Test 2	
	Vernon Word Recognition	Mechanical Arithmetic	Vernon Word Recognition	Mechanical Arithmetic
Experimental	108.4	119.8	111.8	141.1
Control	127.0	130.1	129.5	145.0

The experimental teaching can be seen to have improved attainments while achieving those changes in the Self-picture detailed above. The methods used with the control group, while securing slightly less improvement, produced the very maladjustment changes in certainty and differentiation indicated earlier. This is further support for the second hypothesis in the investigation.

VII. Discussion

These results have implications related to both teaching goals and methods, and a number of points may be briefly discussed: new light has been thrown on the variables operating in the learning situation; these are now seen to be related inevitably to adjustment; they occur in every class-room but can be controlled by appropriate teaching methods; they are the product of group situations as well as of individual attention and they can be controlled within the present examination framework.

The experiment has shown the existence of additional variables in the learning situation other than the skills, knowledges, attitudes and appreciations commonly expected as the outcomes of teaching. The measuring instrument evolved shows that changes have occurred in the Self-picture, in the Ideal Self, in the Other Self, and in the attitudes to each of these aspects. Awareness of such variables is important for learning theory and for practical teaching. Learning experiments, as well as practical teaching situations, show many conflicting results, some of which are undoubtedly due to the presence of unrecognised factors in the learning set-up. The next step in the investigation of the problems of learning is the isolation of other variables that contribute to the unpredictability of learning situations. This experiment has shown that the Self-picture is probably one such variable. Changes occur in this as an outcome of learning situations and the Self-picture must be recognised as a hitherto unnoticed factor occurring in every learning situation. Furthermore, since any learning becomes a condition of subsequent learning, the kind of Self-picture that is learnt becomes a factor to be controlled in both experimental and practical teaching situations.

The experiment has shown that good and poor adjustment are linked with the goals and teaching methods of the typical class-room. The changes that occurred in the Self-picture are usually accepted as symptoms of good and poor adjustment. Teacher A, using the free methods indicated, and stressing the aspects of the Self-picture discussed above, is able to make his pupils more sure of what they are like and more accepting of what they are, more able to differentiate themselves and to see themselves with moderation as well as with certainty, more certain of what they want to be like and more aware of what judgments they think others make of them. Such changes are accepted as the marks of good adjustment, and Teacher A clearly produces these characteristics in his children. Teacher B's data shows that typical high-pressure teaching, with vigorous personal emphasis, with great stress on correctness and on the serious consequences of failure, and with constant emphasis on the passing of examinations, can lead to significantly greater signs of insecurity. It is shown further that this insecurity spreads, not only through the items of the Self, but through the Ideal and Other Self, that is, through all the aspects of one major integrational factor of personality. Clinical evidence, of course, shows that this does happen, but the appearance and spread of insecurity in the Self have not hitherto been recorded in the ordinary class-room situation. In the light of this information, the educational significance of the Self becomes clearer and both teaching goals and teaching methods should be modified.

The educational significance of the Self is reaffirmed when it is realised that changes in the Self-picture are an inevitable part of both outcomes and conditions of learning in every class-room, whether or not the teacher is aware of them or aiming for them. They occur, as in A's class, where the teacher deliberately included them in his teaching goals and adapted his methods accordingly, and they occur in B's class where the teacher aimed at orthodox goals and was ignorant of these correlative factors. Since both classes were reasonably typical and both teachers recognised by their headmasters as competent teachers, it is reasonable to generalise and expect such factors to operate in all class-rooms.

It is also clear from the experiment that teaching methods can be adapted so that definite changes of the kind sought for will occur in the Self. The Self can be deliberately produced by suitable teaching methods. In this experiment a start has been made in the task of relating aspects of teaching methods to categories, levels and dimensions of the Self.

One of the conditions for producing the Self-picture as an outcome of education is that it is, and always will be produced in group situations. It can, of course, be produced in the special group situation of two, the teacher giving individual attention to the child, but in this experiment the normal group situation was always present. This makes the problem of obtaining the Self-picture relevant to normal class-room conditions where group situations must always hold.

Finally, the Self is relevant to class-room situations in another very important way. It was produced in this experiment in the normal conditions of teaching for examination results. Both classes were scholarship classes and it was agreed that any experimental conditions under which class A worked should not endanger the scholarship prospects of the children. On standardised tests in reading and number, Teacher A produced slightly greater mean improvement in his class. If it is objected that a teacher cannot spend his time teaching for an improved Self-picture and better adjustment because of examination pressure, here is some evidence that at least equally good academic results may be got while improving adjustment. In other words, it is possible for a teacher to conceive his educational goals in the wider terms of the Self-picture and to secure these while attaining the necessary academic standards. On the negative side, it is likely that Teacher B, conceiving his goals in academic terms and ignorant of the concomitant outcomes, laid the child open to failure in the future because he failed to strengthen the child's Self-picture. A changed emphasis thus became feasible, from subject-matter goals to goals expressed in terms of the Self, for in this way both academic and adjustment goals become attainable.

These points suggest that, because the Self is an ubiquitous factor in all learning experiences, its presence should be recognized and its importance stressed by all teachers, and its controlled development made a major teaching aim. But since the psychology of the Self has been little emphasised in courses on educational psychology and not at all by traditional practice in schools, it is certain that few teachers are aware of its importance. The implications for pre-service and in-service training are clear, but much more research must be done in the field. Two lines of investigation are likely to be fruitful. The first concerns the persistence of the pattern of the Self-picture emerging from each class. How long do such Self-pictures persist under similar conditions? What is the effect upon later learning of a child spending a second year with either A or B? Could A reverse B's pattern of Self-picture or would B, in the child's most formative years, undo A's constructive work? Do the answers differ for different 'types' of personalities? Should care be taken to prevent a child experiencing two successive teachers like B? The second line of investigation concerns the range of the curve of teachers on which A and B would be placed if the experiment were extended to include more teachers. Would B be an extreme type and A be near the norm? Or is B near the norm and A atypical? Only a wider investigation can answer such questions.

Acknowledgments.—I wish to acknowledge with gratitude the grant in 1952 of a Fellowship from the Imperial Relations Trust Fund which made this investigation possible, and to express my appreciation of the help and guidance of Dr. C. M. Fleming, Reader in Education at the University of London Institute of Education. I am grateful also to the New South Wales Department of Education which granted me leave for the period of study, and to the Education Officers, heads and teachers of public and private schools in England who allowed me to gather the data.

References

1. Alper, T. G. (1946). Task-orientation *vs.* ego-orientation in learning and retention. *Amer. J. Psychol.*, **59**, 236–248.
2. Anderson, H. H., and Brewer, J. E. (1946). Studies of teachers' class-room personalities, *II—Appl. Psychol., Monogr.*, **8**, Stanford University Press.

3. Bales, R. F. (1951): *Interaction Process Analysis: A Method for the Study of Small Groups.* Cambridge, Mass., Addison-Wesley Press.
4. Bruner, J. S. (1951). Personality, dynamics and perceiving. In Blake, J. S. and Ramsay, G. V. (ed.) *Perception, an Approach to Personality.* New York, Ronald Press.
5. Cattell, R. B. (1950). *Personality, a Systematic, Theoretical and Factual Study.* New York McGraw Hill.
6. Horney, K. (1942). *Self Analysis.* New York: Norton.
7. Kilpatrick, W. H. (1941). *Selfhood and Civilisation, a Study of the Self-Other Process.* Bureau of Publications, Teachers' College, Columbia.
8. Kluckhohn, F. R. (1953). Dominant and Variant Value Orientations. In Kluckhohn, C. and Murray, H. A. (ed.), *Personality.* London: Jonathon, 1949, Revised Edition, 1953.
9. Lewin, K. (1935). *Dynamic Theory of Personality.* New York: McGraw Hill.
10. Lewin, K., Lippitt, R., and White, R. K. (1939). Patterns of aggressive behaviour in experimentally created social climates. *J. Soc. Psychol.*, **10**, 271–300.
11. Murphy, G. (1947). *Personality, a Biosocial Approach to Origins and Structure.* New York: Harper and Bros.
12. Raimy, V. C. (1948). Self-reference in counseling interviews. *J. Consulting Psychol.* **12**, 3.
13. Rogers, C. R. (1951). *Client-Centred Therapy: Its Current Practice, Implications and Theory.* Boston: Houghton Mifflin.
14. Ruger, H. A. (1910). The psychology of efficiency. *Arch. Psychol.*, **15**, 188 pp.
15. Stagner, R. (1951). Homeostasis a unifying concept in personality theory. *Psychol. Review*, **58**, 2–17.
16. Withall, J. (1948). The development of a technique for the measurement of social-emotional climates in class-rooms. *J. Exper. Educ.*, **18**.
17. Woolf, W. (1946). *The Personality of the Pre-School Child.* New York: Grune and Stratton.

Selected Readings

Barron, F. The psychology of imagination. *Scientific American*, 1958, 2–9.

Black, M. H. Characteristics of the culturally disadvantaged child. *The Reading Teacher*, 1965, 465–470.

Gephart, W. J. Will the real Pygmalion please stand up. *American Educational Research Association.* 1970, **7**, 473–475.

Getzels, J. W., and Jackson, P. W. The meaning of "giftedness"—an examination of an expanding concept. *Phi Delta Kappan*, 1958, **40**, 75–77.

Guilford, J. P. Three faces of intellect. *American Psychologist,* 1959, **14**, 469–479.

Hurlock, E. B. American adolescents of today—a new species. *Adolescence,* 1966, 1, 7–21.

Jensen, A. R. How much can we boost I.Q. and scholastic achievement? *Harvard Educational Review,* 1969, **39**, 1–33.

Replies to the above article:

Cronbach, L. J. Heredity, environment, and educational policy. *Harvard Educational Review,* 1969, **39**, 338–347.

Crow, J. F. Genetic theories and influences: comments on the value of diversity. *Harvard Educational Review,* 1969, **39**, 301–309.

Elkind, D. Piagetian and psychometric conceptions of intelligence. *Harvard Educational Review,* 1969, **39**, 338–347.

Hunt, J. M. Has compensatory education failed? Has it been attempted? *Harvard Educational Review,* 1969, **39**, 278–300.

Kogan, J. S. Inadequate evidence and illogical conclusion. *Harvard Educational Review,* 1969, **39**, 274–277.

Jensen, A. R. Reducing the heredity–environment uncertainty: a reply. *Harvard Educational Review,* 1969, **39**, 449–483. (Jensen replies here to the above comments on his article).

Jersild, A. T. *Child psychology* (5th ed.) Englewood Cliffs, N. J.: Prentice-Hall, Inc., 1960, 116–126.

Jones, Mary C., and Mussen, P. H. Self-conceptions, motivations, and interpersonal attitudes of early-and late-maturing girls. *Child Development,* 1958, **29**, 491–501.

Kagan, J., Pearson, Leslie, and Welch, Lois. Modifiability of an impulsive tempo. *Journal of Educational Psychology,* 1966, **57**, 359–365.

Klineberg, O. Negro-white differences in intelligence test performance: a new look at the problem. *American Psychologist,* 1963, **18**, 198–203.

Lippitt, R. The learner and the classroom group. In Walter B. Waetjen (Ed.), Human variability and learning. Papers and reports for the fifth curriculum research institute, 1961, 50–61.

MacKinnon, D. W. Personality and the realization of creative potential. *American Psychologist,* 1965, **20**, 4, 273–281.

Mackworth, N. H. Originality. *American Psychologist,* 1965, **20**, 51–66.

McKeachie, W. J., Pollie, D., and Speisman, J. Relieving anxiety in classroom examinations. *Journal of Abnormal and Social Psychology,* 1955, **50**, 93–98.

McNemar, Q. Lost: our intelligence. Why? *American Psychologist,* 1964, **19**, 871–882.

Meyer, W. J., and Thompson, G. G. Sex differences in the distribution of teacher approval and disapproval among sixth-grade children. *Journal of Educational Psychology,* 1956, **47**, 385–396.

Redl, F. Our troubles with defiant youth. *Children,* 1955, **2**, 5–9.

Rogers, C. R., Kell, B. L., and McNeil, H. The role of self-understanding in the prediction of behavior. *Journal of Consulting Psychology,* 1948, **12**, 174–186.

Rosenthal, R., and Jacobson, Lenore. Teachers' expectancies: determinants of pupils' IQ gains. *Psychological Reports,* 1966, **19**, 115–118.

Tenenbaum, S. The teacher, the middle class, the lower class. *Phi Delta Kappan,* 1963, **45**, 82–86.

Thorndike, R. L. Review of Pygmalion in the classroom. *American Educational Research Journal,* 1968, **5**, 708–711.

Torrance, E. P. Individual differences in creativity among secondary school students. *The High School Journal,* 1970, **53**, 423–439.

Torrance, E. P. The creative personality and the ideal pupil. *Teachers College Record,* 1963, **65**, 220–226.

Wesman, A. G. Intelligent testing. *American Psychologist,* 1968, **23**, 267–274.

PART IV

Teaching and Learning

Emphasis in Part Four is focused on changing, maintaining, and utilizing behavior in the cognitive, affective, and psychomotor domains. The first two readings present aspects of motivation. There are a number of theories of motivation, each providing a basis for the formulation of hypotheses. Getzels reviews the historical approaches to the study of motivation and then suggests their implication for teaching. His suggestions provide a good advanced organizer for Berlyne's discussion of epistemic curiosity as an interesting theory of motivation.

Many papers could have been included in Chapter 11, "Learning the Cognitive Domain." Not only is the teacher concerned with pupils learning information, but also, good teachers guide pupils in the development of concepts, problem solving, and critical and creative thinking. In Chapter 11 Bruner, from the viewpoint of a psychologist, attempts to relate the findings for cognitive development to the problems of teaching. He points out than an individual's intellectual potential develops to the extent that culture assists him. Cultural transmission differs in a technical society from that in an indigenous one. Eisner's discussion outlines the components of critical thinking and suggests better ways for teachers to develop this important skill. Crutchfield summarizes an attempt to develop creative thinking. One of the limitations of training was its failure to generalize extensively beyond the improvement noted in the problem-solving skill for which the program was designed. In selecting any criterion task to evaluate learning, we must determine that the task provides evidence that learning will transfer.

Papers on learning in four areas of the affective domain are included in Chapter 12—attitudes, values, interests, and personal-social adjustment. Henry's paper shows that teachers often develop attitudes in children as a result of trying desperately to meet their own needs. Unfortunately, some of these attitudes prevent children from full personal development. Even teachers who try hard, are sincere, and want children to learn, may be the cause of ignorance or unconscious motivation by making the wrong hypotheses for teaching.

When pupils do not accept values that society and the schools believe are important, how does a teacher motivate his pupils to learn? Coleman found that it is indeed true that school and pupil values are in conflict. Furthermore, he does not believe that the school has been very effective in changing pupil values. He makes some suggestions for developing new values in pupils. These have yet to withstand the scrutiny of empirical research.

It is often difficult for the teacher to differentiate among attitudes, values, and interests. Getzels defines and gives examples of each. He makes suggestions for studying interests from a different vantage point.

Mental illness is a serious problem in our society today. Among the various predictions on the range of this illness is that at least one person in ten will spend some time in a mental-hospital bed. Far more attention to this problem was given in educational psychology courses a number of years ago than is true today. Yet, on one hand, high-achieving persons have been totally incapacitated by mental illness, while on the other hand, many with high capacities have been severely handicapped in school because of personal-social adjustment problems. Emotional adjustment is closely related to effective performance in the cognitive domain. Furthermore, Kubie emphasizes that learning in and of itself does not make man "wise, mature, and creative." It may prove to be "a mask for immaturity, neurosis, and lack of wisdom." Very often, he maintains, the process by which we educate children may inhibit their psychological growth.

Considerable research has been done in the armed services on improving learning in psychomotor tasks. Gagné's paper is a report of some of this research. It has direct application to the various psychomotor tasks that are learned in school—handwriting, typing, the operation of a microscope, and the like.

Loche and Bryan's study emphasizes the close relationship between the cognitive and psychomotor domains. Obviously the affective domain is also related. Attitudes, interests, and values certainly determine the effectiveness of learning psychomotor skills.

The last chapter in Part Four contains papers on retention and transfer. Teachers have always been concerned about forgetting. Various theories have suggested means to improve retention. Reynolds and Glaser found that the manipulation of spaced review had more influence on retention than did varying repetition in learning.

Ellis' paper provides an excellent summary of the research findings on transfer in addition to listing seventeen principles to improve the teaching of transfer. Knowledge that is not generalizable is of limited value.

CHAPTER 10

Motivation

10.1 Motivation Reconsidered: The Concept of Competence

Robert W. White

In his unabridged paper, the author presents an extended discussion on theories of motivation built on primary drives. There has been general disenchantment with these theories. Professor White suggests that we reconsider motivation by studying the various kinds of behavior that have to do with effective interaction with the environment in terms of competence. In other words, he suggests that competence be used to designate effective interaction with the environment. He differentiates between a competence motivation and competence in its more familiar sense. Behaviors that lead to "walking, attention and perception, language and thinking, manipulating and changing the surroundings, all . . . promote an effective—a competent—interaction with the environment." This type of behavior, competence motivation, is directed, selective, and persistent and satisfies an intrinsic need to deal with the environment.

The main theme of this paper is introduced by showing that there is widespread discontent with theories of motivation built upon primary drives. Signs of this discontent are found in realms as far apart as animal

SOURCE. Abridged from Robert W. White, "Motivation Reconsidered: The Concept of Competence," *Psychological Review*, **LXVI**, 5 (1959), pp. 297–333, by permission of the author and the American Psychological Association.

psychology and psychoanalytic ego psychology. In the former, the commonly recognized primary drives have proved to be inadequate in explaining exploratory behavior, manipulation, and general activity. In the latter, the theory of basic instincts has shown serious shortcomings when it is stretched to account for the development of the effective ego. Workers with animals have attempted to meet their problem by invoking secondary reinforcement and anxiety reduction, or by adding exploration and manipulation to the roster of primary drives. In parallel fashion, psychoanalytic workers have relied upon the concept of neutralization of instinctual energies, have seen anxiety reduction as the central motive in ego development, or have hypothesized new instincts such as mastery. It is argued here that these several explanations are not satisfactory and that a better conceptualization is possible, indeed that it has already been all but made.

In trying to form this conceptualization, it is first pointed out that many of the earlier tenets of primary drive theory have been discredited by recent experimental work. There is no longer any compelling reason to identify either pleasure or reinforcement with drive reduction, or to think of motivation as requiring a source of energy external to the nervous system. This opens the way for considering in their own right those aspects of animal and human behavior in which stimulation and contact with the environment seem to be sought and welcomed, in which raised tension and even mild excitement seem to be cherished, and in which novelty and variety seem to be enjoyed for their own sake. Several reports are cited which bear upon interest in the environment and the rewarding effects of environmental feedback. The latest contribution is that of Woodworth (1958), who makes dealing with the environment the most fundamental element in motivation.

Competence and the Play of Contented Children

A backward glance at our survey shows considerable agreement about the kinds of behavior that are left out or handled poorly by theories of motivation based wholly on organic drives. Repeatedly we find reference to the familiar series of learned skills which starts with sucking, grasping, and visual exploration and continues with crawling and walking, acts of focal attention and perception, memory, language and thinking, anticipation, the exploring of novel places and objects, effecting stimulus changes in the environment, manipulating and exploiting the surroundings, and achieving higher levels of motor and mental coordination. These aspects of behavior have long been the province of child psychology, which has attempted to measure the slow course of their development and has shown how heavily their growth depends upon learning. Collectively they are sometimes referred to as adaptive mechanisms or as ego processes, but on the whole we are not accustomed to cast a single name over the diverse feats whereby we learn to deal with the environment.

I now propose that we gather the various kinds of behavior just mentioned, all of which have to do with effective interaction with the environment, under the general heading of competence. According to Webster, competence means fitness or ability, and the suggested synonyms include capability, capacity, efficiency, proficiency, and skill. It is therefore a suitable word to describe such things as grasping and exploring, crawling and walking, attention and perception, language and thinking, manipulating and changing the surroundings, all of which promote an effective—a competent—interaction with the environment. It is true, of course, that maturation plays a part in all these developments, but this part is heavily overshadowed by learning in all the more complex accomplishments like speech or skilled manipulation. I shall argue that it is necessary to make competence a motivational concept; there is a *competence motivation* as well as competence in its more familiar sense of achieved capacity. The behavior that leads to the building up of effective grasping, handling, and letting go of objects, to take one example, is not random behavior produced by a general overflow of energy. It is directed, selective, and persistent, and it is continued not because it serves primary drives, which indeed it cannot serve until it is almost perfected, but because it satisfies an intrinsic need to deal with the environment.

No doubt it will at first seem arbitrary to propose a single motivational conception in connection with so many and such diverse kinds of behavior. What do we gain by attributing motivational unity to such a large array of activities? We could, of course, say that each developmental sequence, such as learning to grasp or to walk, has its own built-in bit of motivation—its "aliment," as Piaget (1952) has expressed it. We could go further and say that each item of behavior has its intrinsic motive—but this makes the concept of motivation redundant. On the other hand, we might follow the lead of the animal psychologists and postulate a limited number of broader motives under such names as curiosity, manipulation, and mastery. I believe that the idea of a competence motivation is more adequate than any of these alternatives and that it points to very vital common properties which have been lost from view amidst the strongly analytical tendencies that go with detailed research.

In order to make this claim more plausible, I shall now introduce some specimens of playful exploration in early childhood. I hope that these images will serve to fix and dramatize the concept of competence in the same way that other images—the hungry animal solving problems, the child putting his finger in the candle flame, the infant at the breast, the child on the toilet, and the youthful Oedipus caught in a hopeless love triangle—have become memorable focal points for other concepts. For this purpose I turn to Piaget's (1952) studies of the growth of intelligence from its earliest manifestations in his own three children. The examples come from the first year of life, before language and verbal concepts begin to be important. They therefore represent a practical kind of intelligence which may be quite similar to what is developed by the higher animals.

As early as the fourth month, the play of the gifted Piaget children began to be "centered on a result produced in the external environment," and their behavior could be described as rediscovering the movement which by chance exercised an advantageous action upon things" (1952, p. 151). Laurent, lying in his bassinet, learns to shake a suspended rattle by pulling a string that hangs from it. He discovers this result fortuitously before vision and prehension are fully coordinated. Let us now observe him a little later when he has reached the age of three months and ten days.

"I place the string, which is attached to the rattle, in his right hand, merely unrolling it a little so that he may grasp it better. For a moment nothing happens. But at the first shake due to chance movement of his hand, the reaction is immediate: Laurent starts when looking at the rattle and then violently strikes his right hand alone, as if he felt the resistance and the effect. The operation lasts fully a quarter of an hour, during which Laurent emits peals of laughter (Piaget, 1952, p. 162)."

Three days later the following behavior is observed.

"Laurent, by chance, strikes the chain while sucking his fingers. He grasps it and slowly displaces it while looking at the rattles. He then begins to swing it very gently, which produces a slight movement of the hanging rattles and an as yet sound inside them. Laurent then definitely increases by degrees his own movements. He shakes the chain more and more vigorously and laughs uproariously at the result obtained (Piaget, 1952, p. 185)."

Very soon it can be observed that procedures are used "to make interesting spectacles last." For instance, Laurent is shown a rubber monkey which he has not seen before. After a moment of surprise, and perhaps even fright, he calms down and makes movements of pulling the string, a procedure which has no effect in this case, but which previously has caused interesting things to happen. It is to be noticed that "interesting spectacles" consist of such things as new toys, a tin box upon which a drumming noise can be made, an unfolded newspaper, or sounds made by the observer such as snapping the fingers. Commonplace as they are to the adult mind, these spectacles enter the infant's experience as novel and apparently challenging events.

Moving ahead to the second half of the first year, we can observe behavior in which the child explores the properties of objects and tries out his repertory of actions upon them. This soon leads to active experimentation in which the child attempts to provoke new results. Again we look in upon Laurent, who has now reached the age of nine months. On different occasions he is shown a variety of new objects—for instance a notebook, a beaded purse, and a wooden parrot. His carefully observing father detects four stages of response: (*a*) visual exploration, passing the object from hand to hand, folding the purse, *etc.;* (*b*) tactile exploration, passing the hand all over the object, scratching, *etc.;* (*c*) slow moving of the object in space; (*d*) use of the repertory of action; shaking the object, striking it, swinging it, rubbing it against the side of the bassinet, sucking it, *etc.*, "each in turn with a sort of prudence as though studying the effect produced" (1952, p. 255).

Here the child can be described as applying familiar tactics to new situations, but in a short while he will advance to clear patterns of active experimentation. At 10 months and 10 days Laurent, who is unfamiliar with bread as a nutritive substance, is given a piece for examination. He manipulates it, drops it many times, breaks off fragments and lets them fall. He has often done this kind of thing before, but previously his attention has seemed to be centered on the act of letting go. Now "he watches with great interest the body in motion; in particular, he looks at it for a long time when it has fallen, and picks it up when he can." On the following day he resumes his research.

"He grasps in succession a celluloid swan, a box, and several other small objects, in each case stretching out his arm and letting them fall. Sometimes he stretches out his arm vertically, sometimes he holds it obliquely in front of or behind his eyes. When the object falls in a new position (for example on his pillow) he lets it fall two or three times more on the same place, as though to study the spatial relation; then he modifies the situation. At a certain moment the swan falls near his mouth; now he does not suck it (even though this object habitually serves this purpose), but drops it three times more while merely making the gesture of opening his mouth (Piaget, 1952, p. 269).

These specimens will furnish us with sufficient images of the infant's use of his spare time. Laurent, of course, was provided by his studious father with a decidedly enriched environment, but no observant parent will question the fact that babies often act this way during those periods of their waking life when hunger, erotic needs, distresses, and anxiety seem to be exerting no particular pressure. If we consider this behavior under the historic headings of psychology we shall see that few processes are missing. The child gives evidence of sensing, perceiving, attending, learning, recognizing, probably recalling, and perhaps thinking in a rudimentary way. Strong emotion is lacking, but the infant's smiles, gurgles, and occasional peals of laughter strongly suggest the presence of pleasant affect. Actions appear in an organized form, particularly in the specimens of active exploration and experimentation. Apparently the child is using with a certain coherence nearly the whole repertory of psychological processes except those that accompany stress. It would be arbitrary indeed to say that one was more important than another.

These specimens have a meaningful unity when seen as transactions between the child and his environment, the child having some influence upon the environment and the environment some influence upon the child. Laurent appears to be concerned about what he can do with the chain and rattles, what he can accomplish by his own effort to reproduce and to vary the entertaining sounds. If his father observed correctly, we must add that Laurent seems to have varied his actions systematically, as if testing the effect of different degrees of effort upon the bit of environment represented by the chain and rattles. Kittens make a similar study of parameters when delicately using their paws to push pencils and other objects ever nearer to the edge of one's desk. In all such examples it is clear that the child or animal is by no means at the mercy of transient stimulus fields. He selects for continuous treatment those aspects of his environment which he finds it possible to affect in some way. His behavior is selective, directed, persistent—in short, motivated.

Motivated toward what goal? In these terms, too, the behavior exhibits a little of everything. Laurent can be seen as appeasing a stimulus hunger, providing his sensorium with an agreeable level of stimulation by eliciting from the environment a series of interesting sounds, feels, and sights. On the other hand we might emphasize a need for activity and see him as trying to reach a pleasurable level of neuromuscular exercise. We can also see another possible goal in the behavior: the child is achieving knowledge, attaining a more differentiated cognitive map of his environment and thus satisfying an exploratory tendency or motive of curiosity. But it is equally possible to discern a theme of mastery, power, or control, perhaps even a bit of primitive self-assertion, in the child's concentration upon those aspects of the environment which respond in some way to his own activity. It looks as if we had found too many goals, and perhaps our first impulse is to search for some key to tell us which one is really important. But this, I think, is a mistake that would be fatal to understanding.

We cannot assign priority to any of these goals without pausing arbitrarily in the cycle of transaction between child and environment and saying, "This is the real point." I propose instead that the real point is the transactions as a whole. If the behavior gives satisfaction, this satisfaction is not associated with a particular moment in the cycle. It does not lie solely in sensory stimulation, in a bettering of the cognitive map, in coordinated action, in motor exercise, in a feeling of effort and of effects produced, or in the appreciation of change brought about in the sensory field. These are all simply aspects of a process which at this stage has to be conceived as a whole. The child appears to be occupied with the agreeable task of developing an effective familiarity with his environment. This involves discovering the effects he can have on the environment and the effects the environment will have on him. To the extent that these results are preserved by learning, they build up an increased competence in dealing with the environment. The child's play can thus be viewed as serious business, though to him it is merely something that is interesting and fun to do.

Bearing in mind these examples, as well as the dealings with environment pointed out by other workers, we must now attempt to describe more fully the possible nature of the motivational aspect of competence. It needs its own name, and in view of the foregoing analysis I propose that this name be *effectance.*

Effectance

The new freedom produced by two decades of research on animal drives is of great help in this undertaking. We are no longer obliged to look for a source of energy external to the nervous system, for a consummatory climax, or for a fixed connection between reinforcement and tension-reduction. Effectance motivation cannot, of course, be conceived as saving a source in tissues external to the nervous system. It is in no sense a deficit motive. We must assume it to be neurogenic, its "energies" being simply those of the living cells that make up the nervous system. External stimuli play an important part, but in terms of "energy" this part is secondary, as one can see most clearly when environmental stimulation is actively sought. Putting it picturesquely, we might say that the effectance urge represents what the neuromuscular system wants to do when it is otherwise unoccupied or is gently stimulated by the environment. Obviously there are no consummatory acts; satisfaction would appear to lie in the arousal and maintaining of activity rather than in its slow decline toward bored passivity. The motive need not be conceived as intense and powerful in the sense that hunger, pain, or fear can be powerful when aroused to high pitch. There are plenty of instances in which children refuse to leave their absorbed play in order to eat or to visit the toilet. Strongly aroused drives, pain, and anxiety, however, can be conceived as overriding the effectance urge and capturing the energies of the neuromuscular system. But effectance motivation is persistent in the sense that it regularly occupies the spare waking time between episodes of homeostatic crisis.

In speculating upon this subject we must bear in mind the continuous nature of behavior. This is easier said than done; habitually we break things down in order to understand them, and such units as the reflex arc, the stimulus-response sequence, and the single transaction with the environment seem like inevitable steps toward clarity. Yet when we apply such an analysis to playful exploration we lose the most essential aspect of the behavior. It is constantly circling from stimulus to perception to action to effect to stimulus to perception, and so on around; or, more properly, these processes are all in continuous action and continuous change. Dealing with the environment means carrying on a continuing transaction which gradually changes one's relation to the environment. Because there is no consummatory climax, satisfaction has to be seen as lying in a considerable series of transactions, in a trend of behavior rather than a goal that is achieved. It is difficult to make the word "satisfaction" have this connotation, and we shall do well to replace it by "feeling of efficacy" when attempting to indicate the subjective and affective side of effectance.

It is useful to recall the findings about novelty: the singular effectiveness of novelty in engaging interest and for a time supporting persistent behavior. We also need to consider the selective continuance of transactions in which the animal or child has a more or less pronounced effect upon the environment—in which something happens as a consequence of his activity. Interest is not aroused and sustained when the stimulus field is so familiar that it gives rise at most to reflex acts or automatized habits. It is not sustained when actions produce no effects or changes in the stimulus field. Our conception must therefore be that effectance motivation is aroused by stimulus conditions which offer, as Hebb (1949) puts it, difference-in-sameness. This leads to variability and novelty of response, and interest is best sustained when the resulting action affects the stimulus so as to produce further difference-in-sameness. Interest wanes when action begins to have less effect; effectance motivation subsides when a situation has been explored to the point that it no longer presents new possibilities.

We have to conceive further that the arousal of playful and exploratory interest means the appearance of organization involving both the cognitive and active aspects of behavior. Change in the stimulus field is not an end in itself, so to speak; it happens when one is passively moved about, and it may happen as a consequence of random movements without becoming focalized and instigating exploration. Similarly, action which has effects is not an end in itself, for if one unintentionally kicks away a branch while walking, or knocks something off a table, these effects by no means necessarily become involved in playful investigation. Schachtel's (1954) emphasis on focal attention becomes helpful at this point. The playful and exploratory behavior shown by Laurent is not random or casual. It involves focal *attention* to some object—the fixing of some aspect of the stimulus field so that it stays relatively constant—and it also involves the focalizing of *action* upon this object. As Diamond (1939) has expressed it, response under these conditions is "relevant to the stimulus," and it is change in the *focalized* stimulus that so strongly affects the level of interest. Dealing with the environment means directing focal attention to some part of it and organizing actions to have some effect on this part.

In our present state of relative ignorance about the workings of the nervous system it is impossible to form a satisfactory idea of the neural basis of effectance motivation, but it should at least be clear that the concept does not refer to any and every kind of neural action. It refers to a particular kind of activity, as inferred from particular kinds of behavior. We can say that it does not include reflexes and other kinds of automatic response. It does not include well-learned, automatized patterns, even those that are complex and highly organized. It does not include behavior in the service of effectively aroused drives. It does not even include activity that is highly random and discontinuous, though such behavior may be its most direct forerunner. The urge toward competence is inferred specifically from behavior that shows a lasting focalization and that has the characteristics of exploration and experimentation, a kind of variation within the focus. When this particular sort of activity is aroused in the nervous system, effectance motivation is being aroused, for it is characteristic of this particular sort of activity that it is selective, directed, and persistent, and that instrumental acts will be learned for the sole reward of engaging in it.

Some objection may be felt to my introducing the word *competence* in connection with behavior that is so often playful. Certainly the playing child is doing things for fun, not because of a desire to improve his competence in dealing with the stern hard world. In order to forestall misunderstanding, it should be pointed out that the usage here is parallel to what we do when we connect sex with its biological goal of reproduction. The sex drive aims for pleasure and gratification, and reproduction is a consequence that is presumably unforeseen by animals and by man at primitive levels of understanding. Effectance motivation similarly aims for the feeling of efficacy, not for the vitally important learnings that come as its consequence. If we consider the part played by competence motivation in adult human life we can observe the same parallel. Sex may now be completely and purposefully divorced from reproduction but nevertheless pursued for the pleasure it can yield. Similarly, effectance motivation may lead to continuing exploratory interests or active adventures when in fact there is no longer any gain in actual competence or any need for it in terms of survival. In both cases the motive is capable of yielding surplus satisfaction well beyond what is necessary to get the biological work done.

In infants and young children it seems to me sensible to conceive of effectance motivation as undifferentiated. Later in life it becomes profitable to distinguish various motives such as cognizance, construction, mastery, and achievement. It is my view that all such motives have a root in effectance motivation. They are differentiated from it through life experiences which emphasize one or another aspect of the cycle of transaction with environment. Of course, the motives of later childhood and of adult life are no longer simple and can almost never be referred to a single root. They can acquire loadings of anxiety, defense, and compensation, they can become fused with unconscious fantasies of a sexual, aggressive, or omnipotent character, and they can gain force because of their service in producing realistic results in the way of income and career. It is not my intention to cast effectance in the star part in adult motivation. The acquisition of motives is a complicated affair in which simple and sovereign theories grow daily more obsolete. Yet it may be that the satisfaction of effectance contributes significantly to those feelings of interest which often sustain us so well in day-to-day actions, particularly when the things we are doing have continuing elements of novelty.

The Biological Significance of Competence

The conviction was expressed at the beginning of this paper that some such concept as competence, interpreted motivationally, was essential for any biologically sound view of human nature. This necessity emerges when we consider the nature of living systems, particularly when we take a longitudinal view. When an organism does at a given moment does not always give the right clue as to what it does over a period of time. Discussing this problem, Angyal (1941) has proposed that we should look for the general pattern followed by the total organismic process over the course of time. Obviously this makes it necessary to take account of growth. Angyal defines life as "a process of self-expansion"; the living system "expands at the expense of its surroundings," assimilating parts of the environment and transforming them into functioning parts of itself. Organisms differ from other things in nature in that they are "self-governing entities" which are to some extent "autonomous." Internal processes govern them as well as external "heteronomous" forces. In the course of life there is a relative increase in the preponderance of internal over external forces. The living system expands, assimilates more of the environment, transforms its surroundings so as to bring them under greater control. "We may say," Angyal writes, "that the general dynamic trend of the organism is toward an increase of autonomy. . . . The human being has a characteristic tendency toward self-determination, that is, a tendency to resist external influences and to subordinate the heteronomous forces of the physical and social environment to its own sphere of influence." The trend toward increased autonomy is characteristic so long as growth of any kind is going on, though in the end of the living system is bound to succumb to the pressure of heteronomous forces.

Of all living creatures, it is man who takes the longest strides toward autonomy. This is not because of any unusual tendency toward bodily expansion at the expense of the environment. It is rather that man, with his mobile hands and abundantly developed brain, attains an extremely high level of competence in his transactions with his surroundings. The building of houses, roads and bridges, the making of tools and instruments, the domestication of plants and animals, all qualify as planful changes made in the environment so that it comes more or less under control and serves our purposes rather than intruding upon them. We meet the fluctuations of outdoor temperature, for example, not only with our bodily homeostatic mechanisms, which alone would be painfully unequal to the task, but also with clothing, buildings, controlled fires, and such complicated devices as self-regulating central heating and air conditioning. Man as a species has developed a tremendous power of bringing the environment into his service, and each individual member of the species must attain what is really quite an impressive level of competence if he is to take part in the life around him.

We are so accustomed to these human accomplishments that it is hard to realize how long an apprenticeship they require. At the outset the human infant is a slow learner in comparison with other animal forms. Hebb (1949) speaks of "the astonishing inefficiency of man's first learning, as far as immediate results are concerned," an inefficiency which he attributes to the large size of the association areas in the brain and the long time needed to bring them under sensory control. The human lack of precocity in learning shows itself even in comparison with one of the next of kin: as Hebb points out, "the human baby takes six months, the chimpanzee four months, before making a clear distinction between friend and enemy." Later in life the slow start will pay dividends. Once the fundamental perceptual elements, simple associations, and conceptual sequences have been established, later learning can proceed with ever increasing swiftness and complexity. In Hebb's words, "learning at maturity concerns patterns and events whose parts at least are familiar and which already have a number of other associations."

This general principle of cumulative learning, starting from slowly acquired rudiments and proceeding thence with increasing efficiency, can be illustrated by such processes as manipulation and locomotion, which may culminate in the acrobat devising new stunts or the dancer working out a new ballet. It is especially vivid in the case of language, where the early mastery of words and pronunciation seems such a far cry from spontaneous adult speech. A strong argument has been made by Hebb (1949) that the learning of visual forms proceeds over a similar course from slowly learned elements to rapidly combined patterns. Circles and squares, for example, cannot be discriminated at a glance without a slow apprenticeship involving eye movements, successive fixations, and recognition of angles. Hebb proposes that the recognition of visual patterns without eye movement "is possible only as the result of an intensive and prolonged visual training that goes on from the moment of birth, during every moment that the eyes are open, with an increase in skill evident over a period of 12 to 16 years at least."

On the motor side there is likewise a lot to be cumulatively learned. The playing, investigating child slowly finds out the relationships between what he does and what he experiences. He finds out, for instance, how hard he must push what in order to produce what effect. Here the S-R formula is particularly misleading. It would come nearer the truth to say that the child is busy learning R-S connections—the effects that are likely to follow upon his own behavior. But even in this reversed form the notion of bonds or connections would still misrepresent the situation, for it is only a rare specimen of behavior that can properly be conceived as determined by fixed neural channels and a fixed motor response. As Hebb has pointed out, discussing the phenomenon of "motor equivalence" named by Lashley (1942), a rat which has been trained to press a lever will press it with the left forepaw, the right forepaw, by climbing upon it, or by biting it; a monkey will open the lid of a food box with either hand, with a foot, or even with a stick; and we might add that a good baseball player can catch a fly ball while running in almost any direction and while in almost any posture, including leaping in the air and plunging forward to the ground. All of these feats are possible because of a history of learnings in which the main lesson has been the effects of actions upon the stimulus fields that represent the environment. What has been learned is not a fixed connection but a flexible relationship between stimulus fields and the effects that can be produced in them by various kinds of action.

One additional example, drawn this time from Piaget (1952), is particularly worth mentioning because of its importance in theories of development. Piaget points out that a great deal of mental development depends upon the idea that the world is made up of objects having substance and permanence. Without such an "object concept" it would be impossible to build up the ideas of space and causality and to arrive at the fundamental distinction between self and external world. Observation shows that the object concept, "far from being innate or ready-made in experience, is constructed little by little." Up to 7 and 8 months the Piaget children searched for vanished objects only in the sense of trying to continue the actions, such as sucking or grasping, in which the objects had played a part. When an object was really out of sight or touch, even if only because it was covered by a cloth, the infants undertook no further exploration. Only gradually, after some study of the displacement of objects by moving, swinging, and dropping them, does the child begin to make an active search for a vanished object, and only still more gradually does he learn, at 12 months or more, to make allowance for the object's sequential displacements and thus to seek it where it has gone rather than where it was last in sight. Thus it is only through cumulative learning that the child arrives at the idea of permanent substantial objects.

The infant's play is indeed serious business. If he did not while away his time pulling strings, shaking rattles, examining wooden parrots, dropping pieces of bread and celluloid swans, when would he learn to discriminate visual patterns, to catch and throw, and to build up his concept of the object? When would he acquire the many other foundation stones necessary for cumulative learning? The more closely we analyze the behavior of the human infant, the more clearly do we realize that infancy is not simply a time when the nervous system matures and the muscles grow stronger. It is a time of active and continuous learning, during which the basis is laid for all those processes, cognitive and motor, whereby the child becomes able to establish effective transactions with his environment and move toward a greater degree of autonomy. Helpless as he may seem until he begins to toddle, he has by that time already made substantial gains in the achievement of competence.

Under primitive conditions survival must depend quite heavily upon achieved competence. We should expect to find things so arranged as to favor and maximize this achievement. Particularly in the case of man, where so little is provided innately and so much has to be learned through experience, we should expect to find highly advantageous arrangements for securing a steady cumulative learning about the properties of the environment and the extent of possible transactions. Under these circumstances we might expect to find a very powerful drive operating to insure progress toward competence, just as the vital goals of nutrition and reproduction are secured by powerful drives, and it might therefore seem paradoxical that the interests of competence should be so much entrusted to times of play and leisurely exploration. There is good reason to suppose, however, that a strong drive would be precisely the wrong arrangement to secure a flexible, knowledgeable power of transaction with the environment. Strong drives cause us to learn certain lessons well, but they do not create maximum familiarity with our surroundings.

This point was demonstrated half a century ago in some experiments by Yerkes and Dodson (1908). They showed that maximum motivation did not lead to the most rapid solving of problems, especially if the problems were complex. For each problem there was an optimum level of motivation, neither the highest nor the lowest, and the optimum was lower for more complex tasks. The same problem has been discussed more recently by Tolman (1948) in his paper on cognitive maps. A cognitive map can be narrow or broad, depending upon the range of cues picked up in the course of learning. Tolman suggests that one of the conditions which tend to narrow the range of cues is a high level of motivation. In everyday terms, a man hurrying to an important business conference is likely to perceive only the cues that help him to get there faster, whereas a man taking a stroll after lunch is likely to pick up a substantial amount of casual information about his environment. The latent learning experiments with animals, and experiments such as those of Johnson (1953) in which drive level has been systematically varied in a situation permitting incidental learning, give strong support to this general idea. In a recent contribution, Bruner, Matter, and Papanek (1955) make a strong case for the concept of breadth of learning and provide additional evidence that it is favored by moderate and hampered by strong motivation. The latter "has the effect of speeding up learning at the cost of narrowing it." Attention is concentrated upon the task at hand and little that is extraneous to this task is learned for future use.

These facts enable us to see the biological appropriateness of an arrangement which uses periods of less intense motivation for the development of competence. This is not to say that the narrower but efficient learnings that go with the reduction of strong drives make no contribution to general effectiveness. They are certainly an important element in capacity to deal with the environment, but a much greater effectiveness results from having this capacity fed also from learnings that take place in quieter times. It is then that the infant can attend to matters of lesser urgency, exploring the properties of things he does not fear and does not need to eat, learning to gauge the force of his string-pulling when the only penalty for failure is silence on the part of the attached rattles, and generally accumulating for himself a broad knowledge and a broad skill in dealing with his surroundings.

The concept of competence can be most easily discussed by choosing, as we have done, examples of interaction with the inanimate environment. It applies equally well, however, to transactions with animals and with other human beings, where the child has the same problem of finding out what effects he can have upon the environment and what effects it can have upon him. The earliest interactions with members of the family may involve needs so strong that they obscure the part played by effectance motivation, but perhaps the example of the well fed baby diligently exploring the several features of his mother's face will serve as a reminder that here, too, there are less urgent moments when learning for its own sake can be given free rein.

In this closing section I have brought together several ideas which bear on the evolutionary significance of competence and of its motivation. I have sought it this way to deepen the biological roots of the concept and thus help it to attain the stature in the theory of behavior which has not been reached by similar concepts in the past. To me it seems that the most important proving ground for this concept is the effect it may have on our understanding of the development of personality. Does it assist our grasp of early object relations, the reality principle, and the first steps in the development of the ego? Can it be of service in distinguishing the kinds of defense available at different ages and in providing clues to the replacement of primitive defenses by successful adaptive maneuvers? Can it help fill the yawning gap known as the latency period, a time when the mastery of school subjects and other accomplishments claim so large a share of time and energy? Does it bear upon the self and the vicissitudes of self-esteem, and can it enlighten the origins of psychological disorder? Can it make adult motives and interests more intelligible and enable us to rescue the concept of sublimation from the difficulties which even its best friends have recognized? I believe it can be shown that existing explanations of development are not satisfactory and that the addition of the concept of competence cuts certain knots in personality theory. But this is not the subject of the present communication, where the concept is offered much more on the strength of its logical and biological probability.

References

Angyal, A. *Foundations for a science of personality.* New York: Commonwealth Fund, 1941.

Bruner, J. S., Matter, J., & Papanek, M. L. Breadth of learning as a function of drive level and mechanization. *Psychol. Rev.,* 1955, **62**, 1–10.

Diamond, S. A neglected aspect of motivation. *Sociometry,* 1939, **2**, 77–85.

Hebb, D. O. *The organization of behavior.* New York: Wiley, 1949.

Johnson, E. E. The role of motivational strength in latent learning. *J. Comp. Physiol. Psychol.,* 1953, **45**, 526–530.

Lashley, K. S. The problem of cerebral organization in vision. In H. Klüver, *Visual mechanisms.* Lancaster, Pa.: Jacques Cattell, 1942. Pp. 301–322.

Piaget, J. *The origins of intelligence in children.* (Trans. by M. Cook) New York: International University Press, 1952.

Schachtel, E. G. The development of focal attention and the emergence of reality. *Psychiatry,* 1954, **17**, 309–324.

Tolman, E. C. Cognitive maps in rats and men. *Psychol. Rev.,* 1948, **55**, 189–208.

Woodworth, R. S. *Dynamics of behavior.* New York: Holt, 1958.

Yerkes, R. M. & Dodson, J. D. The relation of strength of stimulus to rapidity of habit-formation. *J. Comp. Neurol. Psychol.,* 1908, **18**, 459–482.

10.2 Curiosity and Education[1]

D. E. Berlyne

In this paper the author argues that motivating disturbances need not be limited to visceral upheavals and external irritations, but may also arise from conflict within the subject's nervous system. A child who searches for knowledge (epistemic behavior) in the classroom may find himself in a state of conflict due to discrepant thoughts, beliefs, or attitudes.

Dr. Berlyne uses the term "epistemic curiosity" to describe the motivational condition to seek more knowledge to relieve this conflict. He examines various forms of this motivational condition and suggests how they can be induced in the classroom.

The history of the psychology of learning has taken the form of a turbulent, on-and-off, ambivalent liaison with the laws of association. The two principal laws of association, association by contiguity and association by similarity, can be traced back—a little tenuously perhaps—to the writings of Plato and Aristotle.

SOURCE. D. E. Berlyne, "Curiosity and Education." In J. D. Krumboltz (Ed.), *Learning and the Educational Process.* (Chicago: Rand McNally & Co., 1965), pp. 67–89. Reprinted by permission of Rand McNally & Co.

[1] The preparation of this paper was facilitated by Research Grant MH-06324 from the National Institute of Mental Health of the United States Public Health Service.

Have we really made very much progress or added much since, in Plato's *Phaedo,* Socrates asked: "May you not also from seeing the picture of a horse or a lyre remember a man? And from the picture of Simmias you may be led to remember Cebes? . . . or you may also be led to the recollection of Simmias himself?" Like Simmias in the dialogue, we feel bound to say: "True!" in answer to these rhetorical questions, and we have to admit that this view reflects in large measure how learning works.

Yet for centuries, there have been arguments and tussles, an inability to abandon the laws of association and yet a conviction that they are far from being enough. There have been disputes over the kinds of elements that participate in the associative relation. Are "ideas" associated with one another, or are "stimuli" associated with "responses"? Can two "stimuli" or internal correlates of stimuli ("images") be associated with each other? Can two motor acts?

There has also been a feeling that the fruits of learning must consist of more than simply a collection of associations. Surely, we often acquire not merely an association between two or more specific elements but something of more general applicability that we could properly call a "rule" or a "strategy" or a "principle." Further, it seems fairly obvious that the associations acquired through learning are organized in elaborate structures and that a great deal of their value depends on the fact that they do not exist in isolation but interact and collaborate with one another.

Association and Motivation

From our present point of view, the most glaring inadequacies of the laws of association seem, however, to lie in their neglect of motivational factors. It seems indisputable that, if something (whether it be a stimulus or a response or a central process such as an idea or image) is to participate in a learning process, it must have occurred together with something else or it must resemble something that has occurred together with something else. Nevertheless, we experience many stimultaneous pairs of events in the course of a day, and we perform many responses in the presence of particular stimulus patterns in the course of a day, but most of these contiguities produce no learning at all. And of those that produce learning, some produce much more effective learning than others. So whether or not learning will occur and, if so, how effective it will be depend not merely on conjunctions of events but also on the psychophysiological state of the learner, and especially on what we call his "motivational condition."

In the more primitive forms of learning, it makes a great difference whether or not the subject is hungry or in pain or afraid. In the more intellectual kinds of learning that are of interest to the schoolteacher, we say that it matters how "interested" the learner is. There must apparently be sufficient level of mobilization or alertness, of openness to incoming information, of "arousal" (to use a term that is enjoying a current vogue among both psychologists and neurophysiologists). Secondly, it helps if there is some correspondence between the motivational condition of the learner (what he wants at the moment) and what he is being given an opportunity to learn. A rat will be more likely to recall a means of obtaining food if it was discovered while he was hungry, and a school child will presumably remember material that belongs to a topic in which he "is interested," that contains something that he would like to know.

Moreover, it seems that, in at least some, if not all, forms of learning, it is not enough for the elements that are to be associated to occur together. There must be some additional event, which we call a source of *reinforcement*. In the classical or Pavlovian conditioning, the reinforcing event is the *unconditioned stimulus*, the biologically important stimulus (such as the appearance of food or application of an electric shock) that elicited the response in the first place. In instrumental conditioning, exemplified by the acquistion of manual or social skills, the reinforcing agent is a *reward* that closely follows the performance of the act to be learned (although some writers would also speak of a punishing consequence that weakens the response as a "negative reinforceer").

As far as human remembering and intellectual learning generally are concerned, it is still not clear how far they conform to the classical-conditioning pattern and how far to the instrumental-conditioning pattern, just as the relations between these two kinds of conditioning have not yet been fully worked out. But since some combinations of experienced events lead to remembering and some do not, it seems clear that reinforcing conditions of some kind must be playing a part. We can recognize that intellectual activities—patterns of thought—are frequently employed as means of achieving specific ends, whether practical or theoretical, and that how successful they are determines whether they will recur or whether they will be abandoned in favor of others. So there is reason to suppose that their occurrence, like that of instrumentally conditioned motor response, is governed by rewarding consequences, although the forms of reward to which they are most susceptible may well be different.

Extrinsic and Intrinsic Motivation

Psychologists began to take motivational questions seriously at the time when, under the influence of evolutionary theory, they were learning to view psychological problems in a biological perspective. They had come to see that the behavior of lower animals and of human beings consists of devices contributing to the aims of survival and health and reproduction. So it seemed reasonable to assume that the motivational conditions or drive states that impelled organisms to seek new forms of adaptive behavior and to retain them, once they had been found, would be ones in which some prerequisite of biological well-being is needed and lacking. Reinforcing conditions would, it appeared, consist of external agents that have biologically crucial effects on bodily tissues. So we find the earliest experimenters on motivation in the 1920s, the neo-behaviorists of the 1930s who were beginning to elaborate the concept of "drive," and also theorists working away from the beaten track of psychology, like Freud and McDougall, concentrating on external irritants, like pain or excessive heat, or on internal physiological disturbances, like those due to deprivation of food or to sexual arousal, as sources of motivating discomfort or "drive." At the same time, they saw anything that relieved these distresses, or, in other words, reduced drive, as a source of satisfaction or reward.

The limitations of this view became manifest as soon as motivation theorists ceased to confine their attention to standard animal learning situations and began to consider a wider range of real-life human behavior. They broadened their view of motivation enormously by invoking the laws of association in a new motivational guise. They postulated that biologically neutral or indifferent stimuli that have regularly accompanied pain or other forms of distress will become aversive in their own right and induce "secondary drive." Indifferent stimuli that happen to coincide with biological gratification or relief will, they postulated, come to function as "secondary rewards" or "secondary reinforcers." Essentially the same hypotheses underlay Freud's assertion that objects and thoughts without beneficial or harmful effects in themselves would come to occasion profound anxiety or would alternatively come to be eagerly sought after, if resemblances or contiguities between them and events of biological importance had given them the power to symbolize the latter or caused them to be "cathected."

Although there have been debates over details and wording, these hypotheses have in essence stood the tests of time and of intensive experimentation, at least in relation to the simpler kinds of human and animal learning. In recent years, however, a feeling has grown that still further additions and extensions to our motivational concepts are needed if many psychological phenomena, including activities classed as "recreational," "aesthetic," and "intellectual," are to be adequately explained. So the latest phase in the development of motivation theory has seen mounting attention paid to what are coming to be called *intrinsic* motivational conditions and *intrinsic* rewards.

The term "intrinsic motivation," which educationists have been using for some time in a kindred sense, is invoked to account for activities that are apparently performed, as we say, "for their own sake," that are "satisfying in themselves" or, as the Russians have sometimes put it, that are "self-reinforcing." These kinds of behavior have, of course, important consequences of a rewarding nature. They may well bring about changes in the perceptible external environment, and they invariably affect the subject's psychophysiological state. If these consequences fail to satisfy, the activities will cease or their form will be altered. The peculiarity of intrinsically motivated activities lies, however, in the fact that they depend for their reward-value on events in the central nervous system rather than, as in the case of food-seeking or pain-escaping behavior, on events in other tissues.

Origins of Conceptions of Intrinsic Motivation

The best way to acquire some notion of what these newly recognized motivational factors amount to and, above all, of how multifaceted they are is to review briefly some of the varied lines of research that have drawn attention to them.

1. Exploratory Behavior

During the last fifteen years, a great deal of experimentation has been devoted to the exploratory behavior of animals and human beings (Berlyne, 1960; Berlyne, 1963). Exploratory behavior is behavior aimed at receipt or intensification of stimulation with no manifest biological significance. Higher animals characteristically spend a high proportion of their time exploring their environments. This is especially so when no emergency is making overriding demands on their behavior, although curiosity will at times even take priority for a while over hunger or fear. While some exploratory behavior is aimed at stimuli bearing vital information, e.g., stimuli indicative of the whereabouts of food or of a path of escape, and can thus be termed *extrinsic* exploration, much of the exploratory behavior found in higher animals brings the organism into contact with stimuli that it subsequently does little about.

This *intrinsic* exploration presents some serious challenges to motivation theory. The strength and direction of intrinsic exploration can be affected by many factors, internal and external, but, as far as we can see, it is primarily evoked by, and aimed at, stimulus patterns that are novel, surprising, complex, incongruous, or ambiguous. The common thread tying together all these "collative" stimulus properties, as we call them, seems to be that they all mean the evocation of discrepant reactions in the nervous system when components of the pattern in question are compared with one another or with elements experienced in similar contexts in the past. They involve, in other words, *conflict*. When exploratory behavior has done its work and exposed the subject's sense organs to appropriate stimulation, a rewarding state of affairs is brought about and can evidently provide reinforcement for new learning. This can happen, apparently, either because additional stimulation brings with it additional information that resolves conflict associated with uncertainty or because the disturbance—the rise in drive or arousal—is relieved once the initial impact of the stimulus has been sustained and the nervous system recovers its equilibrium.

2. *Affective Consequences of Deviations from Expectations*

Amsel (1958) in North America and Anokhin (1955) and Sokolov (1963) in the U.S.S.R. have asserted, on the basis of experimental evidence, that, when an animal has regularly experienced a sequence of events, especially one culminating in a reward, an internal anticipatory process occurs representing what can be expected to come next. If ever the reward, or whatever else was due to ensue, fails to materialize, various signs of disturbance may appear, including manifestations of emotional upset, extinction of learned responses, exploratory behavior, refusal to eat an unexpected but otherwise acceptable food, and replacement of old by new forms of learned behavior. Bühler et al. (1928) and Hebb (1946) have observed how effectively a human infant or an ape can be scared by a stimulus pattern that deviates slightly from a familiar one—e.g., a well-known person speaking in a strange falsetto voice in the case of the baby and a model of a chimpanzee's head in the case of the ape. McClelland et al. (1953) and Fiske and Maddi (1961) have offered evidence that stimulation differing moderately from what a subject is set to receive will be judged pleasurable whereas more marked deviations will be judged adversely.

3. *Personality Theory*

Students of personality have, in recent years, been discussing dimensions like "intolerance of ambiguity" (Frenkel-Brunswik, 1949). They have devised tests whose results show that individuals differ in the extent to which they are troubled when brought face to face with something that is difficult to classify or to understand, some individuals being quite deeply discomfited. Individuals also differ in the means that they characteristically use to cope with ambiguous situations, some tending to withdraw attention from anomalous features and others to devote excessive attention to niggling details.

4. *Attitude Change*

Social psychologists have been giving more and more emphasis to "incongruity" (Osgood & Tannenbaum, 1955), "imbalance" (Abelson & Rosenberg, 1958) and "dissonance" (Festinger, 1957) as factors promoting attitude change. The attitudes that a person has built up to guide his behavior and judgment with respect to social objects are apt to interact with one another, and their interactions will sometimes be less than harmonious. Incompatibilities among attitudes may well lie dormant for quite a long time and lead to inconsistencies of behavior that fail to worry the subject or even escape his notice. There will, however, be times when he is made sensitive to points on which his attitudes are at variance with one another. The resulting discomfort can give a powerful impetus to revaluations and changes in belief, as can confrontation with unusual external conditions, e.g., those that are prevalent at times of social crisis when external reality jars painfully with what existing evaluations and beliefs lead one to expect.

5. *Child Development*

Coming somewhat nearer to the topic of immediate interest to us, we find Piaget (1957), after spending decades assiduously investigating the development of perceptual and intellectual processes in the child, voicing a rather radical conclusion. He holds that psychological development is kept moving not only by maturation and learning, as is usually believed, but also by a third and distinct factor making for change, which he calls "equilibration." This is a tendency for the child to abandon structures characterized by relative disequilibrium, which means inconsistency of judgment, uncertainty, or even, in certain conditions, inability to make a judgment at all, in favor of structures possessed of better equilibrium. According to Piaget, equilibration is the main force that conducts the child from his early complete reliance on unorganized perception, with its inherent susceptibility to illusion, to the systems of intellectual operations that make logical, mathematical, and scientific thinking possible. Although Piaget is at pains to distinguish equilibration from "learning," his conception of learning can be adjudged excessively narrow and outmoded. Equilibration fits the contemporary learning theorists' conception of learning, although it has some peculiarities which may be explained, in part at least, by its dependence on intrinsic motivation and reinforcement (Berlyne, 1965).

6. *Education*

Finally, recognition of the importance of intrinsic motivation and reward has come out of examination of the problems of education, the principal pioneer in this regard being—and this may surprise some readers—Dewey. On reading Dewey's writings, one comes across passages where he sounds very much like a spokesman of the contemporary curriculum-reform movement, which is sometimes thought of as a reaction against Dewey. He has certainly been maligned and misrepresented at times. In fact, it is hard to know whether he has suffered more wrongs at the hands of his detractors or of his followers. In the book *How We Think* (1910), he describes how thinking begins with a "felt difficulty," which commonly takes the form of a conflict "between conditions at hand and the desired or intended result, between an end and the means of reaching it." In his pedagogical writings, particularly in *Democracy and Education* (1916), he singles out the stimulation of thinking as one of the prime functions of education. The aims of education can, he claims, be achieved most effectively through "experience," which he defines as "trying to do something and having the thing perceptibly do something to one in return." Experience is particularly instructive when the child's efforts fail to have the outcome that he was anticipating or fail to achieve their goals.

The period during which North American education was dominated by Dewey's influence was one marked generally by a fear of hastening the educational process and of overstraining the child's intellectual capacities. Recent psychological research concurs with the experience of educators in other parts of the world in suggesting that the rate at which the average child, let alone the gifted child, can advance has been grossly underestimated, with unfortunate consequences. Jones and Carterette (1963) have found the reading-matter that children borrow from libraries for home reading to be distinctly more difficult, as judged by information-theoretic measures of redundancy, than the readers to which they are exposed in school. Admiral Rickover (1963) has deplored the neglect of book learning in favor of field trips and manual activities. Above all, there was a grave underestimation of the extent to which the ordinary child can find intellectual substance appetizing and intellectual effort satisfying, provided they are introduced at the right time and in the right way.

Those who have tended in these directions will find scant comfort in Dewey's writings. He made it clear that the "doing" that constituted the basis of experience could take the form of brain-work and that the "problems" to which schoolwork needs to be related may very well be theoretical problems, provided that the child experiences them as such. He condemned the misunderstanding that makes "interest" mean "merely the effect of an object upon personal advantage or disadvantage, success or failure." He denied that "to attach importance to interest means to attach some feature of seductiveness to material otherwise indifferent; to secure attention and effort by offering a bribe of pleasure." "This procedure," he writes, "is properly stigmatized as 'soft pedagogy,' as a 'soup kitchen' theory of education."

Conflict and Curiosity

The upshot of all these currents of thought, converging from vastly different starting-points, is that motivating disturbances (i.e., rises in drive or arousal that impel action and, where no effective recourse is readily available, new learning) can come not only from visceral upheavals and external irritations but also from discrepant or disharmonious relations among processes going on in the subject's nervous system or, to use the term in its most comprehensive sense, from conflict.

Conflict can be generated, by stimulus patterns possessing novelty, surprisingness, incongruity, or complexity. These, it will be recalled, are the "collative" properties that exert a preponderant influence over exploratory behavior. Every environmental feature that excites a person's sense-organs is compared with other features that accompany it, with others that might have occurred instead, with others that have been encountered in the past. More accurately, reactions called forth by the feature in question have to interact with reactions corresponding to accompanying features or previously encountered features or features whose occurrence was anticipated but did not materialize. The interacting processes may be mutually supportive and complementary, but there may alternatively be some degree of incompatibility, and therefore of mutual interference and competition, among them (i.e., conflict).

A state of conflict may be of such a kind that additional information, e.g., specification of some hidden attribute of an object or identification of some impending event, will relieve it. If this is so, the subject is beset by what both common language and the technical language of information theory call "uncertainty." It is likely that prior learning will make him resort to exploratory activity to gain access to the information whose lack is being felt. If so, the subject will be in the kind of state of heightened drive or arousal that we call "perceptual curiosity."

When a child is in a classroom, the activities, covert or overt, that are induced in him, or that we hope will be induced in him, are to a great extent aimed at the acquisition of knowledge. Knowledge is information not merely taken in through sense-organs but stored for future use in the form of systems of associations which, when appropriate circumstances are encountered in the future, will make available internal symbolic responses (thoughts) to guide behavior in conjunction with the external environment of the moment. Activities whose function is to build up knowledge constitute *epistemic* behavior, which can include thinking, rehearsing to oneself symbolic responses copied from teachers, asking questions, and observing. Epistemic curiosity, the motivational condition making for epistemic behavior, apparently results from *conceptual conflict*, which means conflict due to discrepant thoughts or beliefs or attitudes (Berlyne, 1954a; Berlyne, 1960; Berlyne, 1963; Berlyne, 1965). Epistemic behavior will be intrinsically reinforced, and the knowledge derived from it retained, when it resolves conceptual conflict or, to use Dewey's expression, "introduces a congruity" and thus relieves epistemic curiosity.

Conceptual Conflict and Discovery Methods

In recent educational practice, intrinsic motives and rewards have been used most conspicuously and deliberately in connection with so-called discovery methods. These are methods in which the child is encouraged to take steps to find the information required for the solution of a particular problem by his own efforts rather than passively registering information supplied by the teacher. Different forms of conceptual conflict are readily applicable to different educational subject matters, and it is noteworthy that those who have experimented with discovery methods have resorted to quite a wide assortment of them. So we may find it worthwhile to examine in turn some of the different ways in which epistemic curiosity can be induced through conceptual conflict and subsequently relieved to provide reinforcement for school learning.

1. Surprise

In several subject-matters, but especially in the natural sciences, it is possible to present the student with a phenomenon that violates expectations derived from his existing beliefs, a phenomenon that his prior training and experience have led him to regard as improbable or impossible. The motivational potentialities of surprise are commonly utilized in lessons using demonstrations of physical, chemical, or biological phenomena. The skills of the experimenter and the stage magician have, in fact, been fruitfully combined on many such occasions. Among recently introduced methods, Suchman's (1959) "Inquiry Training" systematically exploits the pedagogical value of surprise. The student is first shown a film sequence depicting a train of events that is unprecedented within his experience and inexplicable to him, e.g., a brass ball that is just small enough to slip through a ring sits on the ring after being heated. The student is then invited to seek an explanation by putting questions to the teacher that can be answered "yes" or "no," being encouraged especially to formulate questions that relate to the outcome of possible experiments. The conflict due to surprise is eliminated as the reality of the surprising phenomenon is established and explained.

2. *Doubt*

In subject matters like mathematics, surprise is difficult to engineer because the student will generally have insufficient previous knowledge to make firm expectations likely and, in any case, it is hard (but perhaps not always impossible) to devise a concrete situation or verbal statement to convince him of a mathematical truth that seems initially unlikely. Doubt, i.e., conflict between tendencies to believe and disbelieve, is put to good use in some of the new mathematics curricula. I once had the privilege of witnessing a sample lesson given by Dr. David L. Page under the auspices of the University of Illinois Arithmetic Project, in which third-grade children were being introduced to the fact that the difference between the squares of two adjacent integers [i.e., $(n + 1)^2 - n^2$] is always an odd number. On another occasion, I heard a lecture by Professor G. Polya, describing how, using essentially the same method as Dr. Page, he would teach Euler's theorem (that $R - E + V = 2$, where R, E, and V are, respectively, the numbers of faces, edges, and vertices of a polyhedron).

Both lessons began by showing the principle to hold true for one specific case after another. As it was confirmed with each example, the question of whether it would work for the next example was raised and the corresponding curiosity induced. Once enough examples had been given to make the universal validity of the principle seem credible, a different sort of conflict was introduced by asking whether the principle must always hold true and why. In this way, the pupils were motivationally prepared for the equivalent of a proof.

3. *Perplexity*

When students are faced with a problem and can specify a number of possible solutions but have no way of knowing which is the correct one, they are in the kind of conflict that can be called perplexity, a special case of the kind of situation to which both everyday language and information theory apply the term "uncertainty." For example, Bruner (1960) refers to an experimental geography lesson which high-school students were shown a map of the United States with only natural features such as rivers and mountains displayed on it and were required to deduce where cities would have grown up. Conflict will have stemmed from competition among tendencies to select various alternative locations and then, once a guess has been recorded, there will have been additional conflict due to doubt—wondering whether or not the guess was correct—which was relieved when the student was allowed to compare what he had deduced with a fuller map showing what was actually the case.

4. *Bafflement*

Conflict can occur when a student is confronted with a situation in which a number of apparently irreconcilable demands are made of him. Until he has found a course of action that will satisfy all of them, any response that is called to the fore by one of the requirements is inhibited, either because it seems to have consequences that violate other requirements or because, in the light of some feature of the situation it seems to be impracticable. This state of affairs may be realized when a practical task is imposed on the student but, as studies by Morozova (1955) in Russia have illustrated, it is often enough to present the problem in verbal form. For example, a student is asked to consider how he would find out where he is—what the longitude and latitude of his location are—in the middle of the desert. Younger children are told a story about a fictitious hero, with whom they can identify, who finds himself faced with this problem, but, for older children, it is enough to present the problem in an abstract form.

5. *Contradiction*

In another experiment of Morozova's (personal communication), children are first told how plants use chlorophyll to carry out the photochemical reactions on which their existence depends, and they are later told that there are plants (fungi) that lack chlorophyll and can live without sunlight. The conflict due to the apparent contradiction brings into focus the inadequacies of their picture of plant life, reinforcing the lesson that the way of life of the green plants is not the only one possible in the plant kingdom and making the children particularly attentive to the significant characteristics of vital functions in fungi. Students of mathematics can likewise be motivated to acquire new symbolic structures by their initial encounters with paradoxical inferences, such as that the number of even integers is the same as the number of odd and even integers or that the number of points in a one-inch line segment is the same as the number of points in a one-mile cube.

Programed Instruction

Techniques of programed instruction are not counted as part of the discovery-method movement, but they, likewise, make use of intrinsic motivation and reward. The early teaching machines of Pressey (1926) presented the students with multiple-choice questions and required them to press a button indicating which they took to be correct. Here, perplexity conflict is presumably at work and is relieved when the machine moves on to the next question, showing the correctness of the last choice. An experiment of mine performed some years ago (Berlyne, 1954b) showed, in fact, that retention of facts was improved by first exposing subjects to multiple-choice questions which the facts to be remembered answered. The kind of teaching machine favored by Skinner (1954) requires the student to construct and supply the answer, whereupon he is given an opportunity to compare what he has supplied with the correct answer. In this case, motivation is likely to come from doubt and reinforcement from relief of doubt as the validity of the answer given is established.

There have long been disputes over whether knowledge of results, such as teaching machines provide, acts as a reinforcing agent or simply as a source of information (e.g., Annet, 1964; Postman, 1947). If it reinforces, is this the kind of reward that can be attributed to drive reduction? Since information about the rightness or wrongness of the response causes an association to be strengthened more than it would be by contiguity alone, the information must be counted as a reinforcing agent. Although there are exceptional cases when unsought items of information are rewarding (as when one catches sight of a "Believe-it-or-not" cartoon in a newspaper), information is usually reinforcing only when the subject is in a state in which he feels the lack of it, i.e., a state of uncertainty that is also a state of raised drive or a motivational condition. Does information reduce drive? This is equivalent to asking whether the subject ceases to be in a state in which the item of information is welcome, and therefore rewarding, once the information has been received. It certainly seems that the provision of the same item of information a second or a third time will not be so powerfully rewarding as the first presentation, except when it has been forgotten between presentations. There are therefore grounds for answering this question affirmatively.

Evaluation of Discovery Methods

Ausubel (1961) has published a cautionary article, pointing out how shaky much of the evidence in favor of discovery methods is and suggesting that, in at least some circumstances, they may not be superior to more conventional methods at all. McConnell (1934), in one of the earliest relevant studies, found a discovery method of teaching arithmetical operations to produce less accuracy and speed than a drill method, although it facilitated transfer to different problems.

Anybody who has had contact with school children knows how much enthusiasm and alertness will be elicited by any departure from routine, a phenomenon well known to industrial psychologists as the "Hawthorne effect." He will be justifiably leery when he hears of zestful university professors, who have not had time to become jaded by the daily classroom grind, playing to responsive audiences for one-hour stands. But even if their novelty value were the sole reason for such success as they have, it should be remembered that novelty is one of the prime sources of intrinsic motivation and that ways of enlisting and putting it to work can surely be found by any imaginative teacher.

Another thought that readily occurs to one when witnessing exponents of discovery methods in action is that, apart from content, what they are doing is not very different from what able and zealous teachers have always done of their own accord. There must be a good deal of truth in this, but one of the aims of scientific research is surely to lay bare the workings of devices that creative individuals have arrived at through independent trial-and-error or through example and thus make them available to anyone.

The present state of knowledge calls incontrovertibly for caution in judging the potentialities of discovery methods and, above all, for intensive research on the psychological processes that they bring into play. Nevertheless, much about them is in tune with recent experimental and theoretical work on motivational problems, and it is highly significant that interest in them has sprung up simultaneously both in North America and in the Soviet Union (cf. Simon & Simon, 1963). Initial experience suggests that these new methods of instruction can substantially facilitate (1) retention of new material, (2) degree of understanding of new material, as shown by appropriate transfer and adaptation to new situations, (3) the eagerness and skill with which information is sought, (4) efficiency at solving problems by directed thinking, and (5) recognition of solutions to problems once they have been attained.

There are, in fact, indications that discovery methods can produce a qualitatively different kind of learning from traditional methods relying on rote memory and on passive absorption of facts, precepts, and habits, a kind of learning that works through "understanding," that interrelates items and builds up integrated structures of knowledge. This distinction recalls Wertheimer's (1945) distinction between "structurally sensible" learning, productive of "structural insight," and "structurally blind" learning, which works by "drill, by external associations, by external conditioning, by memorizing, by blind trial and error." It is also reminiscent of the contrast drawn by Piaget (1959), and further developed by Smedslund (1961a; 1961b), between the young child who is taught a logical mathematical or scientific truth before he is capable of understanding it and the older child who has mastered it in the normal course of development. The latter knows when to apply the principle to new situations and when not to, he defends it by appeal to deduction rather than to empirical observations that illustrate it, and he is resistant to giving it up when appearances are against it.

Discovery methods have two distinctive features. First, there is insistence that the student find solutions to problems through his own thinking or research. Secondly, there is systematic exploitation of intrinsic motivation and reward with a clearer-than-usual differentiation between an earlier phase in which the motivating conflict is induced and a later phase in which conflict is relieved by means of the response patterns that are to be acquired. These two features are, however, by no means inseparable. Independent discovery can be aimed at extrinsic or even highly mercenary goals, as in the traditional treasure hunt or in the case of the student who steals the answers to forthcoming examination questions. On the other hand, intrinsic motives can be skillfully aroused and assuaged by a writer or lecturer who wants his message to be trustfully accepted and assimilated.

The feeling that it is best for a student to search for answers by himself has derived support from at least two sources. One is the maxim, widely current among learning theorists, that, if a response is to be learned, it must be performed so that it can be followed by reinforcement. But there are by now plenty of indications that learning can occur in the absence of an overt muscular response. An internal response—a thought, a perception, an unuttered verbal statement—may be all that is elicited by a stimulus situation and retained to regulate motor activity on future occasions. Even a rat, a cat, or a dog will apparently learn its way round a maze or a room if it is carried from one point to another in a wheeled cage (see Berlyne, 1964). Human beings are evidently capable of a much wider range of "observational" or "vicarious" learning (see Bandura & Walters, 1963). Secondly, learning theory was for a long time dominated by animal experiments in which the response to be reinforced was first performed after a protracted period of trial and error. Until recently, little attention was paid to the various ways of abbreviating the search for the correct response and minimizing or eliminating random groping that are open to higher animals, especially human beings. These methods would include passive movement (e.g., guiding the hand of a child who is learning to write), imitation, verbal instruction, and reasoning. Mowrer (1950) once offered a definition of teaching (suggested by one of his students) as "the process whereby one individual enables another to learn something (solve a problem) more quickly than he would on the basis of his own trial and error behavior." It will be noted that the intervention of another individual—a teacher—is required by all of these shortcuts except the last—reasoning—and that contact with a teacher can immeasurably facilitate this one.

So while independent search may facilitate the exploitation of intrinsic motivation by bringing the subject sharply up against the latent incompatibilities within his knowledge systems and by adding the motivating contribution of frustration and surprise, it may not be essential, and it may even waste time unnecessarily. As Admiral Rickover has pointed out, it may be possible to "grasp the principle of primitive looms in half an hour from a book" instead of spending "endless hours *reinventing* such things as how to make cotton, flax, and wool cloth, how to card wool, and so on." The element of enduring value in new teaching techniques, including discovery methods and programed instruction, the secret of whatever success can be claimed for them, the real germ of a pedagogical revolution, may well turn out to lie not in independent discovery but in the attempt to pinpoint and harness the sources of epistemic curiosity.

In 1835, Herbart stressed the desirability of presenting new material in such a form that it will be easy to relate to past experience and cause the reproduction of an "apperceptive mass of ideas" as a prerequisite for attention and interest. It is a truism, amply corroborated by experiments on verbal learning, that items with "high associative value" are relatively easy to retain and to preserve from confusion with others. Herbart (1824, 1825) realized that the tendency to perceive new events in terms of old ones must make us particularly sensitive to deviation from what is expected. "How a solecism grates in the ear of the purist!" he points out. "How a false note offends the musician or a breach of etiquette the man of the world!" Perhaps a prior, motivating phase, in which the new is made to clash with the old in this way, needs to precede the phase of assimilation. The pupil is thus made sensitive to the vulnerable points in his existing knowledge structures and receptive to new information that can remedy them. In other words, a question begins to gnaw at him. Every new item of knowledge is the answer to a question and is, we may assume, most readily ingested when the question is astir within the learner.

It seems likely that the peculiarities of the intelligent kinds of learning and thinking described by Wertheimer and by Piaget are largely due to their special dependence on intrinsic motivation. Wertheimer speaks metaphorically of "stresses and strains" within thought structures as factors inducing reorganization. Some recent experiments by Smedslund (1961c; 1961d) encourage the speculation that the child is led to abandon immature ways of thinking by having their inconsistencies brought home to him and that this is what moves him on to more advanced intellectual operations that are capable of relieving the conflict. From this point of view, we can see how learning motivated primarily by conceptual conflict should be especially conducive to interrelation and integration of items of knowledge, since conceptual conflict is relieved, with consequent reinforcement, only when discrepant combinations of responses are replaced by concordant ones (Berlyne, 1965). Furthermore, the connection between the response and the reinforcement is not arbitrary, like the connection between, say, bar-pressing and the receipt of a food pellet, but inherent. Only response patterns that relieve the motivating conflict, that, in other words, solve the motivating problem and thus further understanding and integration, are amenable to reinforcement by reduction of conceptual conflict.

The experimental analysis of attention and curiosity and interest is just beginning. As Dewey (1916) put it, "No one has ever explained why children are so full of questions outside of the school (so that they pester grown-up persons if they get any encouragement), and the conspicuous absence of display of curiosity about the subject matter of school lessons." [Sic.] When research has proceeded further, this remark of Dewey's will be out of date, and the zest for action, including intellectual action, of the normal child that so often obstructs the teacher's efforts can be pressed into service as a potent ally.

References

Abelson, R. P., and Rosenberg, M. J. Symbolic psychologic: A model of attitudinal cognition. *Behav. Sci.*, 1958, **3**, 1–13.

Amsel, A. The role of frustrative nonreward in noncontinuous reward situations. *Psychol. Bull.*, 1958, **55**, 102–119.

Annet, J. The role of knowledge of results in learning: A survey. In J. P. DeCecco (Ed.), *Educational Technology.* New York: Holt, Rinehart & Winston, 1964.

Anokhin, P. K. [Peculiarities of the afferent apparatus of the conditioned reflex and its significance in psychology.] *Vop. Psikhol.*, 1955, **1**, 16–38.

Ausubel, D. P. Learning by discovery: Rationale and mystique. *Bull. nat. Ass. sec. sch. Princ.*, 1961, **45**, 18–58.

Bandura, A., & Walters, R. H. *Social learning and personality development.* New York: Holt, Rinehart & Winston, 1963.

Berlyne, D. E. A theory of human curiosity. *Brit. J. Psychol.*, 1954, **45**, 180–191. (a)

Berlyne, D. E. An experimental study of human curiosity. *Brit. J. Psychol.*, 1954, **45**, 256–265. (b)

Berlyne, D. E. *Conflict, arousal and curiosity.* New York: McGraw-Hill, 1960.

Berlyne, D. E. Exploratory and epistemic behavior. In S. Koch (Ed.), *Psychology. A study of a science.* Vol. 5. New York: McGraw-Hill, 1963.

Berlyne, D. E. Emotional aspects of learning. *Annu. Rev. Psychol.,* 1964, **15**, 115–142.

Berlyne, D. E. *Structure and direction in thinking.* New York: Wiley, 1965.

Bruner, J. S. *The process of education.* Cambridge, Mass.: Harvard Univer. Press, 1960.

Bühler, C., Hetzer, H. & Mabel, F. Die Affektwirksamkeit von Fremdheitseindrücken im ersten Lebensjahr. *Z. Psychol.,* 1928, **107**, (Abt. 1), 30–49.

Dewey, J. *How we think.* Boston: Heath, 1910.

Dewey, J. *Democracy and education.* New York: Macmillan, 1916.

Festinger, L. *A theory of cognitive dissonance.* Palo Alto, Calif.: Stanford University Press, 1957.

Fiske, D. W., & Maddi, S. R. *Functions of varied experience.* Homewood, Ill.: Dorsey Press, 1961.

Frenkel-Brunswik, E. Intolerance of ambiguity as an emotional and perceptual personality variable. *J. Pers.,* 1949, **18**, 108–143.

Hebb, D. O. On the nature of fear. *Psychol. Rev.,* 1946, **53**, 259–276.

Herbart, J. F. *Psychologie als Wissenschaft, neu gegründet auf Erfahrung, Metaphysik und Mathematik.* Königsberg: Unzer, Vol. 1, 1824; Vol. 2, 1825.

Herbart, J. K. *Umriss pädagogischer Vorlesungen.* Göttingen: Dieterich, 1835.

Jones, M. H., & Carterette, E. C. Redundancy in children's free-reading choices. *J. verb. Learn. verb. Behav.,* 1963, **2**, 489–493.

McClelland, D. C., Atkinson, J. W., Clark, R. A., & Lowell, E. L. *The achievement motive.* New York: Appleton-Century-Crofts, 1953.

McConnell, T. R. Discovery vs. authoritative identification in the learning of children. *Univer. of Iowa Stud. Educ.,* **9**, No. 5, 1934.

Morozova, N. G. [The psychological conditions for the arousal and modification of interest in children in the process of reading popular scientific literature.] *Izvestiia Akad. Pedag. Nauk. R.S.F.S.R.,* 1955, **73**, 100–149.

Mowrer, O. H. *Learning theory and personality dynamics.* New York: Ronald, 1950.

Osgood, C. E., & Tannenbaum, P.H. The principle of congruity in the prediction of attitude change. *Psychol. Rev.,* 1955, **62**, 42–55.

Piaget, J. Logique et équilibre dans les comportements du sujet. In L. Apostel, B. Mandelbrot, & J. Piaget, *Logique et équilibre* (*Etudes d'epistém génét.,* II). Paris: Presses Universitaires de France, 1957.

Piaget, J. Apprentissage et connaissance. First part in P. Gréco & J. Piaget, *Apprentissage et connaissance* (*Etudes d'epistém génét.,* VII); Second part in M. Goustard, P. Gréco, B. Matalon, & J. Piaget, *Apprentissage et connaissance* (*Etudes d'epistém. génét.*, X), Paris: Presses Universitaires de France, 1959.

Postman, L. The history and present status of the law of effect. *Psychol. Bull.*, 1947, **44**, 489–503.

Pressey, S. B. A simple apparatus which gives tests and scores—and teaches. *Sch. & Soc.*, 1926, **23**, 373–376.

Rickover, H. G. *American education—a national failure.* New York: Dutton, 1963.

Simon, B., & Simon, J. *Educational psychology in the USSR.* Palo Alto, Calif.: Stanford University Press, 1963.

Skinner, B. F. The science of learning and the art of teaching. *Harvard educ. Rev.*, 1954, **24**, 86–97.

Smedslund, J. The acquisition of conservation of substance and weight in children: II. External reinforcement of conservation of weight and of the operations of addition and subtraction. *Scand. J. Psychol.*, 1961, **2**, 71–84. (a)

Smedslund, J. The acquisition of conservation of substance and weight in dren: III. Extinction of conservation of weight acquired "normally" and by means of empirical controls on a balance. *Scand. J. Psychol.*, 1961, **2**, 85–87. (b)

Smedslund, J. The acquisition of conservation of substance and weight in children: V. Practice in conflict situations without external reinforcement. *Scand. J. Psychol.*, 1961, **2**, 156–160. (c)

Smedslund, J. The acquisition of conservation of substance and weight in children: VI Practice on continuous vs. discontinuous material in problem situations without external reinforcement. *Scand. J. Psychol.*, 1961, **2**, 203–210.

Sokolov, E. N. [The modeling process in the central nervous system of animals and man.] *Gagra Symposia*, 1963, **4**, 183–194.

Suchman, J. R. Training children in scientific inquiry. Paper read to the Society for Research in Child Development, Bethesda, Md., 1959.

Wertheimer, M. *Productive thinking.* New York & London: Harper, 1945.

Selected Readings

Arnstine, D. Curiosity. *Teachers College Record,* 1966, **67**, 595–602.

Atkinson, J. W., and Litwin, G. H. Achievement motive and test anxiety conceived as motive to approach success and motive to avoid failure. *Journal of Abnormal and Social Psychology,* 1960, **60**, 52–63.

Barker, R. G. Ecology and motivation. In R. Jones (Ed.), *Nebraska Symposium on Motivation.* Lincoln, Nebraska: The University of Nebraska Press, 1960, pp. 1–50.

Berlyne, D. E., Carey, S. T., Lazare, Sharon A., Parlow, J., and Tiberius, R. Effects of prior guessing on intentional and incidental paired-associate learning. *Journal of Verbal Learning and Verbal Behavior,* 1968, **7**, 750–759.

Coleman, J. S. Academic achievement and the structure of competition. *Harvard Educational Review,* 1959, **29**, 330–351.

Friedlander, B. Z. A psychologist's second thoughts on concepts, curiosity, and discovery in teaching and learning. *Harvard Educational Review,* 1965, **35**, 18–38.

Hunt, J. M. Experience and the development of motivation: Some reinterpretations. *Child Development,* 1960, **31**, 489–504.

Hunt, J. M. Piaget's system as a source of hypotheses concerning motivation. *Merrill-Palmer Quarterly,* 1963, **9**, 263-275.

Keisler, E. R. A descriptive approach to classroom motivation. *The Journal of Teacher Education,* 1960, **11**, 310–315.

Kolb, D. A. Achievement motivation training for under-achieving high school boys. *Journal of Personality and Social Psychology,* 1965, **2**, 783-792.

McClelland, D. C. Toward a theory of motive acquisition. *American Psychologist,* 1965, **20**, 321–333.

McKeachie, W. J., Pollie, D., and Speisman, J. Relieving anxiety in classroom examinations. *Journal of Abnormal and Social Psychology,* 1960, **60**, 52–63.

Mussen, P. H., and Jones, Mary C. The behavior-inferred motivations of late- and early-maturing boys. *Child Development,* 1958, **29**, 61–67.

Prentice, W. C. H. Some cognitive aspects of motivation. *American Psychologist,* 1961, **16**, 503–511.

Sears, P., and Hilgard, E. The teacher's role in the motivation of the learner. In E. R. Hilgard (Ed.), *Theories of learning and instruction.* Sixty-third Yearbook of the National Society of the Study of Education. Part I. Chicago: University of Chicago Press, 1964, p. 182–209.

CHAPTER 11

The Cognitive Domain

11.1 The Growth of the Mind[1]

Jerome S. Bruner

Bruner suggests that our very complex society—recent in human history—demands that the young be taught by telling out of context rather than showing in context. Knowledge and skill are converted into a more symbolical, abstract and verbal form. This practice becomes institutionalized in the school and in the teacher. It is this process of transmission that Bruner believes is not well done, and he discusses the difficulties that we face in improving the educational process.

These past several years, I have had the painful pleasure—and it has been both—of exploring two aspects of the cognitive processes that were new to me. One was cognitive development, the other pedagogy. I knew, as we all know, that the two were closely related, and it was my naive hope that, betimes, the relation would come clear to me. Indeed, 2 years ago when I first knew that in early September 1965 I would be standing here, delivering this lecture, I said to myself that I would use the occa-

SOURCE. Jerome S. Bruner, "The Growth of the Mind," *American Psychologist,* **XX**, 12 (1965), pp. 1007–1017. Reprinted by permission of the author and the American Psychological Association.

1 Address of the President to the Seventy-Third Annual Convention of the American Psychological Association, Chicago, September 4, 1965.

sion to set forth to my colleagues what I had been able to find out about this vexed subject, the relation of pedagogy and development. It seemed obvious then that in 2 years one could get to the heart of the matter.

The 2 years have gone by. I have had the privilege of addressing this distinguished audience (Bruner, 1964) on some of our findings concerning the development of cognitive processes in children, and I have similarly set forth what I hope are not entirely unreasonable ideas about pedagogy (Bruner, 1966). I am still in a very deep quandary concerning the relation of these two enterprises. The heart of the matter still eludes me, but I shall stand by my resolve. I begin on this autobiographical note so that you may know in advance why this evening is more an exercise in conjecture than a cataloguing of solid conclusions.

What is most unique about man is that his growth as an individual depends upon the history of his species—not upon a history reflected in genes and chromosomes but, rather, reflected in a culture external to man's tissue and wider in scope than is embodied in any one man's competency. Perforce, then, the growth of mind is always growth assisted from the outside. And since a culture, particularly an advanced one, transcends the bounds of individual competence, the limits for individual growth are by definition greater than what any single person has previously attained. For the limits of growth depend on how a culture assists the individual to use such intellectual potential as he may possess. It seems highly unlikely—either empirically or canonically—that we have any realistic sense of the furthest reach of such assistance to growth.

The evidence today is that the full evolution of intelligence came as a result of bipedalism and tool using. The large human brain gradually evolved as a sequel to the first use of pebble tools by early near-man. To condense the story, a near-man, or hominid, with a slightly superior brain, using a pebble tool, could make out better in the niche provided by nature than a near-man who depended not on tools but on sheer strength and formidable jaws. Natural selection favored the primitive tool user. In time, thanks to his better chance of surviving and breeding, he became more so: The ones who survived had larger brains, smaller jaws, less ferocious teeth. In place of belligerent anatomy, they developed tools and a brain that made it possible to use them. Human evolution thereafter became less a matter of having appropriate fangs or claws and more one of using and later fashioning tools to express the powers of the larger brain that was also emerging. Without tools the brain was of little use, no matter how many hundred cubic centimeters of it there might be. Let it also be said that without the original programmatic capacity for fitting tools into a sequence of acts, early hominids would never have started the epigenetic progress that brought them to their present state. And as human groups stabilized, tools became more complex and "shaped to pattern," so that it was no longer a matter of reinventing tools in order to survive, but rather of mastering the skills necessary for using them. In short, after a certain point in human evolution, the only means whereby man could fill his evolutionary niche was through the cultural transmission of the skills necessary for the use of priorly invented techniques, implements, and devices.

Two crucial parallel developments seem also to have occurred. As hominids became increasingly bipedal, with the freed hands necessary for using spontaneous pebble tools, selection also favored those with a heavier pelvic bony structure that could sustain the impacting strain of bipedal locomotion. The added strength came, of course, from a gradual closing down of the birth canal. There is an obstetrical paradox here: a creature with an increasingly larger brain but with a smaller and smaller birth canal to get through. The resolution seems to have been achieved through the immaturity of the human neonate, particularly cerebral immaturity that assures not only a smaller head, but also a longer period of transmitting the necessary skills required by human culture. During this same period, human language must have emerged, giving man not only a new and powerful way of representing reality but also increasing his power to assist the mental growth of the young to a degree beyond anything before seen in nature.

It is impossible, of course, to reconstruct the evolution in techniques of instruction in the shadow zone between hominids and man. I have tried to compensate by observing contemporary analogues of earlier forms, knowing full well that the pursuit of analogy can be dangerously misleading. I have spent many hours observing uncut films of the behavior of free-ranging baboons, films shot in East Africa by my colleague Irven DeVore with a very generous footage devoted to infants and juveniles. I have also had access to the unedited film archives of a hunting-gathering people living under roughly analogous ecological conditions, the !Kung Bushman of the Kalahari, recorded by Laurance and Lorna Marshall, brilliantly aided by their son John and daughter Elizabeth.[2] I have also worked directly but informally with the Wolof of Senegal, observing children in the bush and in French-style schools. Even more valuable than my own informal observations in Senegal were the systematic ex-

[2] I am greatly indebted to Irven DeVore and Educational Services Incorporated for the opportunity to view his films of free-ranging baboons, and to Laurance and Lorna Marshall for the opportunity to examine their incomparable archives. DeVore and the Marshalls have been generous in their counsel as well.

periments carried out later by my colleague, Patricia Marks Greenfield (1966).

Let me describe very briefly some salient differences in the free learning patterns of immature baboons and among !Kung children. Baboons have a highly developed social life in their troops, with well-organized and stable dominance patterns. They live within a territory, protecting themselves from predators by joint action of the strongly built, adult males. It is striking that the behavior of baboon juveniles is shaped principally by play with their peer group, play that provides opportunity for the spontaneous expression and practice of the component acts that, in maturity, will be orchestrated into either the behavior of the dominant male or of the infant-protective female. All this seems to be accomplished with little participation by any mature animals in the play of the juveniles. We know from the important experiments of Harlow and his colleagues (Harlow & Harlow, 1962) how devastating a disruption in development can be produced in subhuman primates by interfering with their opportunity for peer-group play and social interaction.

Among hunting-gathering humans, on the other hand, there is *constant* interaction between adult and child, or adult and adolescent, or adolescent and child. !Kung adults and children play and dance together, sit together, participate in minor hunting together, join in song and story telling together. At very frequent intervals, moreover, children are party to rituals presided over by adults—minor, as in the first haircutting, or major, as when a boy kills his first Kudu buck and goes through the proud but painful process of scarification. Children, besides, are constantly playing imitatively with the rituals, implements, tools, and weapons of the adult world. Young juvenile baboons, on the other hand, virtually never play with things or imitate directly large and significant sequences of adult behavior.

Note, though, that in tens of thousands of feet of !Kung film, one virtually never sees an instance of "teaching" taking place outside the situation where the behavior to be learned is relevant. Nobody "teaches" in our prepared sense of the word. There is nothing like school, nothing like lessons. Indeed, among the !Kung children there is very little "telling." Most of what we would call instruction is through showing. And there is no "practice" or "drill" as such save in the form of play modeled directly on adult models—play hunting, play bossing, play exchanging, play baby tending, play house making. In the end, every man in the culture knows nearly all there is to know about how to get on with life as a man, and every woman as a woman—the skills, the rituals and myths, the obligations and rights.

The change in the instruction of children in more complex societies is twofold. First of all, there is knowledge and skill in the culture far in excess of what any one individual knows. And so, increasingly, there develops an economical technique of instructing the young based heavily on *telling* out of context rather than *showing* in context. In literate societies, the practice becomes institutionalized in the school or the "teacher." Both promote this necessarily abstract way of instructing the young. The result of "teaching the culture" can, at its worst, lead to the ritual, rote nonsense that has led a generation of critics from Max Wertheimer (1945) to Mary Alice White (undated) of Teachers' College to despair. For in the detached school, what is imparted often has little to do with life as lived in the society except insofar as the demands of school are of a kind that reflect *indirectly* the demands of life in a technical society. But these indirectly imposed demands may be the most important feature of the detached school. For school is a sharp departure from indigenous practice. It takes learning, as we have noted, out of the context of immediate action just by dint of putting it into a school. This very extirpation makes learning become an act in itself, freed from the immediate ends of action, preparing the learner for the chain of reckoning remote from payoff that is needed for the formulation of complex ideas. At the same time, the school (if successful) frees the child from the pace setting of the round of daily activity. If the school succeeds in avoiding a pace-setting round of its own, it may be one of the great agents for promoting reflectiveness. Moreover, in school, one must "follow the lesson" which means one must learn to follow either the abstraction of written speech—abstract in the sense that it is divorced from the concrete situation to which the speech might originally have been related—or the abstraction of language delivered orally but out of the context of an ongoing action. Both of these are highly abstract uses of language.

It is no wonder, then, that many recent studies report large differences between "primitive" children who are in schools and their brothers who are not: differences in perception, abstraction, time perspective, and so on. I need only cite the work of Biesheuvel (1949) in South Africa, Gay and Cole (undated) in Liberia, Greenfield (1966) in Senegal, Maccoby and Modiano (1966) in rural Mexico, Reich (1966) among Alaskan Eskimos.

What a culture does to assist the development of the powers of mind of its members is, in effect, to provide amplification systems to which human beings, equipped with appropriate skills, can link themselves. There are, first, the amplifiers of action—hammers, levers, digging sticks, wheels—but more important, the programs of action into which such implements can be substituted. Second, there are amplifiers of the senses, ways of looking and noticing that can take advantage of devices ranging from smoke signals and hailers to diagrams and pictures that stop the action or microscopes that enlarge it. Finally and most powerfully, there are amplifiers of the thought processes, ways of thinking that employ language and formation of explanation, and later use such languages as mathematics and logic and even find automatic servants to crank out the consequences. A culture is, then, a deviser, a repository, and a transmitter of amplification systems and of the devices that fit into such systems. We know very little in a deep sense about the transmission function, how people are trained to get the most from their potential by use of a culture's resources.

But it is reasonably clear that there is a major difference between the mode of transmission in a technical society, with its schools, and an indigenous one, where cultural transmission is in the context of action. It is not just that an indigenous society, when its action pattern becomes disrupted falls apart—at a most terrifying rate—as in uncontrolled urbanization in some parts of Africa. Rather, it is that the institution of a school serves to convert knowledge and skill into more symbolical, more abstract, more verbal form. It is this process of transmission—admittedly very new in human history—that is so poorly understood and to which, finally, we shall return.

There are certain obvious specifications that can be stated about how a society must proceed in order to equip its young. It must convert what is to be known—whether a skill or a belief system or a connected body of knowledge—into a form capable of being mastered by a beginner. The more we know of the process of growth, the better we shall be at such conversion. The failure of modern man to understand mathematics and science may be less a matter of stunted abilities than our failure to understand how to teach such subjects. Second, given the limited amount of time available for learning, there must be a due regard for saving the learner from needless learning. There must be some emphasis placed on economy and transfer and the learning of general rules. All societies must (and virtually all do) distinguish those who are clever from those who are stupid—though few of them generalize this trait across all activities. Cleverness in a particular activity almost universally connotes strategy, economy, heuristics, highly generalized skills. A society must also place emphasis upon how one derives a course of action from what one has learned. Indeed, in an indigenous society, it is almost impossible to separate what one does from what one knows. More advanced societies often have not found a way of dealing with the separation of knowledge and action—probably a result of the emphasis they place upon "telling" in their instruction. All societies must maintain interest among the young in the learning process, a minor problem when learning is in the context of life and action, but harder when it becomes more abstracted. And finally, and perhaps most obviously, a society must assure that its necessary skills and procedures remain intact from one generation to the next —which does not always happen, as witnessed by Easter Islanders, Incas, Aztecs, and Mayas.[3]

Unfortunately, psychology has not concerned itself much with any of these five requisites of cultural transmission—or at least not much with four of them. We have too easily assumed that learning is learning is learning—that the early version of what was taught did not matter much, one thing being much like another and reducible to a pattern of association, to stimulus-response connections, or to our favorite molecular componentry. We denied there was a problem of development beyond the quantitative one of providing more experience, and with the denial, closed our eyes to the pedagogical problem of how to represent knowledge, how to sequence it, how to embody it in a form appropriate to young learners. We expended more passion on the part-whole controversy than on what whole or what part of it was to be presented first. I should except Piaget (1954), Köhler (1940), and Vygotsky (1962) from these complaints—all until recently unheeded voices.

Our neglect of the economy of learning stems, ironically, from the heritage of Ebbinghaus (1913), who was vastly interested in savings. Our nonsense syllables, our random mazes failed to take into account how we reduce complexity and strangeness to simplicity and the familiar, how we convert what we have learned into rules and procedures, how, to use Bartlett's (1932) term of over 30 years ago, we turn around on our own schemata to reorganize what we have mastered into more manageable form.

Nor have we taken naturally to the issue of knowledge and action. Its apparent mentalism has repelled us. Tolman (1951), who bravely made the distinction, was accused of leaving his organisms wrapt in thought. But he recognized the problem and if he insisted on the idea that knowledge might be organized in cognitive maps, it was in recognition (as a

[3] I have purposely left out of the discussion the problems of impulse regulation and socialization of motives, topics that have received extended treatment in the voluminous literature on culture and personality. The omission is dictated by emphasis rather than evaluation. Obviously, the shaping of character by culture is of great importance for an understanding of our topic as it bears, for example, upon culture-instilled attitudes toward the uses of mind. Since our emphasis is upon human potential and its amplification by culturally patterned instrumental skills, we mention the problem of character formation in passing and in recognition of its importance in a complete treatment of the issues under discussion.

great functionalist) that organisms go somewhere on the basis of what they have learned. I believe we are getting closer to the problem of how knowledge affects action and vice versa, and offer in testimony of my conviction the provocative book by Miller, Galanter, and Pribram (1960), *Plans and the Structure of Behavior.*

Where the maintenance of the learner's interest is concerned, I remind you of what my colleague Gordon Allport (1946) has long warned. We have been so concerned with the model of driven behavior, with drive reduction and the *vis a tergo* that, again, until recently, we have tended to overlook the question of what keeps learners interested in the activity of learning, in the achievement of competence beyond bare necessity and first payoff. The work of R. W. White (1959) on effectance motivation, of Harlow and his colleagues (Butler, 1954; Harlow, 1953) on curiosity, and of Heider (1958) and Festinger (1962) on consistency begins to redress the balance. But it is only a beginning.

The invention of antidegradation devices, guarantors that skill and knowledge will be maintained intact, is an exception to our oversight. We psychologists have been up to our ears in it. Our special contribution is the achievement test. But the achievement test has, in the main, reflected the timidity of the educational enterprise as a whole. I believe we know how to determine, though we have not yet devised tests to determine, how pupils use what they learn to think with later in life—for there is the real issue.

I have tried to examine briefly what a culture must do in passing on its amplifying skills and knowledge to a new generation and, even more briefly, how we as psychologists have dealt or failed to deal with the problems. I think the situation is fast changing—with a sharp increase in interest in the conversion problem, the problems of economy of learning, the nature of interest, the relation of knowledge and action. We are, I believe, at a major turning point where psychology will once again concern itself with the design of methods of assisting cognitive growth, be it through the invention of a rational technology of toys, of ways of enriching the environment of the crib and nursery, of organizing the activity of a school, or of devising a curriculum whereby we transmit an organized body of knowledge and skill to a new generation to amplify their powers of mind.

I commented earlier that there was strikingly little knowledge available about the "third way" of training the skills of the young: the first being the play practice of component skills in prehuman primates, the second the teaching-in-context of indigenous societies, and the third being the abstracted, detached method of the school.

Let me now become highly specific. Let me consider a particular course of study, one given in a school, one we are ourselves constructing, trying out, and in a highly qualitative way, evaluating. It is for schools of the kind that exist in Western culture. The experience we have had with this effort, now in its third year, may serve to highlight the kinds of problems and conjectures one encounters in studying how to assist the growth of intellect in this "third way."

There is a dilemma in describing a course of study. One begins by setting forth the intellectual substance of what is to be taught. Yet if such a recounting tempts one to "get across" the subject, the ingredient of pedagogy is in jeopardy. For only in a trivial sense is a course designed to "get something across," merely to impart information. There are better means to that end than teaching. Unless the learner develops his skills, disciplines his taste, deepens his view of the world, the "something" that is got across is hardly worth the effort of transmission.

The more "elementary" a course and the younger its students, the more serious must be its pedagogical aim of forming the intellectual powers of those whom it serves. It is as important to justify a good mathematics course by the intellectual discipline it provides or the honesty it promotes as by the mathematics it transmits. Indeed, neither can be accomplished without the other. The content of this particular course is man: his nature as a species, the forces that shaped and continue to shape his humanity. Three questions recur throughout:

"What is human about human beings?"
"How did they get that way?"
"How can they be made more so?"

In pursuit of our questions we explore five matters, each closely associated with the evolution of man as a species, each defining at once the distinctiveness of man and his potentiality for further evolution. The five great humanizing forces are, of course, tool making, language, social organization, the management of man's prolonged childhood, and man's urge to explain. It has been our first lesson in teaching that no pupil, however eager, can appreciate the relevance of, say, tool making or language in human evolution without first grasping the fundamental concept of a tool or what a language is. These are not self-evident matters, even to the expert. So we are involved in teaching not only the role of tools or language in the emergence of man, but, as a necessary precondition for doing so, setting forth the fundamentals of linguistics or the theory of tools. And it is as often the case as not that (as in the case of the "theory of tools") we must solve a formidable intellectual problem ourselves in order to be able to help our pupils do the same. I should have said at the outset that the "we" I employ in this context is no editorial fiction, but rather a group of anthropologists, zoologists, linguists, theoretical engineers, artists, designers, camera crews, teachers, children, and psychologists. The project is being carried out under my direction at Educational Services, Incorporated, with grants from the National Science Foundation and the Ford Foundation.

While one readily singles out five sources of man's humanization, under no circumstances can they be put into airtight compartments. Human kinship is distinctively different from primate mating patterns precisely because it is classificatory and rests on man's ability to use language. Or, if you will, tool use enhances the division of labor in a society which in turn affects kinship. So while each domain can be treated as a separate set of ideas, their teaching must make it possible for the children to have a sense of their interaction. We have leaned heavily on the use of contrast, highly controlled contrast, to help children achieve detachment from the all too familiar matrix of social life: the contrasts of man versus higher primates, man versus prehistoric man, contemporary technological man versus "primitive" man, and man versus child. The primates are principally baboons, the prehistoric materials mostly from the Olduvai Gorge and Les Eyzies, the "primitive" peoples mostly the Netsilik Eskimos of Pelly Bay and the !Kung Bushmen. The materials, collected for our purposes, are on film, in story, in ethnography, in pictures and drawings, and principally in ideas embodied in exercises.

We have high aspirations. We hope to achieve five goals:

1. To give our pupils respect for and confidence in the powers of their own minds.
2. To give them respect, moreover, for the powers of thought concerning the human condition, man's plight, and his social life.
3. To provide them with a set of workable models that make it simpler to analyze the nature of the social world in which they live and the condition in which man finds himself.
4. To impart a sense of respect for the capacities and plight of man as a species, for his origins, for his potential, for his humanity.
5. To leave the student with a sense of the unfinished business of man's evolution.

One last word about the course of study that has to do with the quality of the ideas, materials, and artistry—a matter that is at once technological and intellectual. We have felt that the making of such a curriculum deserved the best talent and technique available in the world. Whether artist, ethnographer, film maker, poet, teacher—nobody we have asked has refused us. We are obviously going to suffer in testing a Hawthorne effect of some magnitude. But then, perhaps it is as well to live in a permanent state of revolution.

Let me now try to describe some of the major problems one encounters in trying to construct a course of study. I shall not try to translate the problems into refined theoretical form, for they do not as yet merit such translation. They are more difficulties than problems. I choose them, because they are vividly typical of what one encounters in such enterprises. The course is designed for 10-year-olds in the fifth grade of elementary school, but we have been trying it out as well on the fourth and sixth grades better to bracket our difficulties.

One special point about these difficulties. They are born of trying to achieve an objective and are as much policy bound as theory bound. It is like the difference between building an economic theory about monopolistic practices and constructing policies for controlling monopoly. Let me remind you that modern economic theory has been reformulated, refined, and revived by having a season in policy. I am convinced that the psychology of assisted growth, i.e., pedagogy, will have to be forged in the policy crucible of curriculum making before it can reach its full descriptive power as theory. Economics was first through the cycle from theory to policy to theory to policy; it is happening now to psychology, anthropology, and sociology.

Now on to the difficulties. The first is what might be called *the psychology of a subject matter.* A learned discipline can be conceived as a way of thinking about certain phenomena. Mathematics is one way of thinking about order without reference to what is being ordered. The behavioral sciences provide one or perhaps several ways of thinking about man and his society—about regularities, origins, causes, effects. They are probably special (and suspect) because they permit man to look at himself from a perspective that is outside his own skin and beyond his own preferences—at least for awhile.

Underlying a discipline's "way of thought," there is a set of connected, varyingly implicit, generative propositions. In physics and mathematics, most of the underlying generative propositions like the conservation theorems, or the axioms of geometry, or the associative, distributive, and commutative rules of analysis are by now very explicit indeed. In the behavioral sciences we must be content with more implicitness. We traffic in inductive propositions: e.g., the different activities of a society are interconnected such that if you know something about the technological response of a society to an environment, you will be able to make some shrewd guesses about its myths or about the things it values, etc. We use the device of a significant contrast as in linguistics as when we describe the territoriality of a baboon troop in order to help us recognize the system of reciprocal exchange of a human group, the former somehow provoking awareness of the latter.

There is nothing more central to a discipline than its way of thinking. There is nothing more important in its teaching than to provide the child the earliest opportunity to learn that way of thinking—the forms of connection, the attitudes, hopes, jokes, and frustrations that go with it. In a word, the best introduction to a subject is the subject itself. At the very first breath, the young learner should, we think, be given the chance to solve problems, to conjecture, to quarrel as these are done at the heart of the discipline. But, you will ask, how can this be arranged?

Here again the problem of conversion. There exist ways of thinking characteristic of different stages of development. We are acquainted with Inhelder and Piaget's (1958) account of the transition from preoperational, through concrete operational, to propositional thought in the years from preschool through, say, high school. If you have an eventual pedagogical objective in mind, you can translate the way of thought of a discipline into its Piagetian (or other) equivalent appropriate to a given level of development and take the child onward from there. The Cambridge Mathematics Project of Educational Services, Incorporated, argues that if the child is to master the calculus early in his high school years, he should start work early with the idea of limits, the earliest work being manipulative, later going on to images and diagrams, and finally moving on to the more abstract notation needed for delineating the more precise idea of limits.

In "Man: A Course of Study," (Bruner, 1965) there are also versions of the subject appropriate to to a particular age that can at a later age be given a more powerful rendering. We have tried to choose topics with this in mind: The analysis of kinship that begins with children using sticks and blocks and colors and whatnot to represent their own families, goes on to the conventional kinship diagrams by a meandering but, as you can imagine, interesting path, and then can move on to more formal and powerful componential analysis. So, too, with myth. We begin with the excitement of a powerful myth (like the Netsilik Nuliajik myth), then have the children construct some myths of their own, then examine what a set of Netsilik myths have in common, which takes us finally to Lévi-Strauss's (1963) analysis of contrastive features in myth construction. A variorum text of a myth or corpus of myths put together by sixth graders can be quite an extraordinary document.

This approach to the psychology of a learned discipline turns out to illuminate another problem raised earlier: the maintenance of interest. There is, in this approach, a reward in understanding that grows from the matter itself. It is easier to engineer this satisfaction in mathematics, for understanding is so utter in a formal discipline—a balance beam balances or it does not; therefore there is an equality or there is not. In the behavioral sciences the payoff in understanding cannot be so obviously and startlingly self-revealing. Yet, one can design exercises in the understanding of man, too—as when children figure out the ways in which, given limits of ecology, skills, and materials, Bushmen hunt different animals, and then compare their predictions with the real thing on film.

Consider now a second problem: *how to stimulate thought in the setting of a school.* We know from experimental studies like those of Bloom and Broder (1950), and of Goodnow and Pettigrew (1955), that there is a striking difference in the acts of a person who thinks that the task before him represents a problem to be solved rather than being controlled by random forces. School is a particular subculture where these matters are concerned. By school age, children have come to expect quite arbitrary and, from their point of view, meaningless demands to be made upon them by adults—the result, most likely, of the fact that adults often fail to recognize the task of conversion necessary to make their questions have some intrinsic significance for the child. Children, of course, will try to solve problems if they recognize them as such. But they are not often either predisposed to or skillful in problem finding, in recognizing the hidden conjectural feature in tasks set them. But we know now that children in school can quite quickly be led to such problem finding by encouragement and instruction.

The need for this instruction and encouragement and its relatively swift success relates, I suspect, to what psychoanalysts refer to as the guilt-ridden oversuppression of primary process and its public replacement by secondary process. Children, like adults, need reassurance that it is all right to entertain and express highly subjective ideas, to treat a task as a problem where you *invent* an answer rather than *finding* one out in the book or on the blackboard. With children in elementary school, there is often a need to devise emotionally vivid special games, story-making episodes, or construction projects to reestablish in the child's mind his right not only to have his own private ideas but to express them in the public setting of a classroom.

But there is another, perhaps more serious difficulty: the interference of intrinsic problem solving by extrinsic. Young children in school expend extraordinary time and effort figuring out what it is that the teacher wants—and usually coming to the conclusion that she or he wants tidiness or remembering or to do things at a certain time in a certain way. This I refer to as extrinsic problem solving. There is a great deal of it in school.

There are several quite straightforward ways of stimulating problem solving. One is to train teachers to want it and that will come in time. But teachers can be encouraged to like it, interestingly enough, by providing them and their children with materials and lessons that *permit* legitimate problem solving and permit the teacher to recognize it. For exercises with such materials create an atmosphere by treating things as instances of what *might* have occurred rather than simply as what did occur. Let me illustrate by a concrete instance. A fifth-grade class was working on the organization of a baboon troop—on this particular day, specifically on how they might protect against predators. They saw a brief sequence of film in which six or seven adult males go forward to intimidate and hold off three cheetahs. The teacher asked what the baboons had done to keep the cheetahs off, and there ensued a lively discussion of how the dominant adult males, by showing their formidable mouthful of teeth and making threatening gestures had turned the trick. A boy raised a tentative hand and asked whether cheetahs always attacked together. Yet, though a single cheetah sometimes followed behind a moving troop and picked off an older, weakened straggler or an unwary, straying juvenile. "Well, what if there were four cheetahs and two of them attacked from behind and two from in the front. What would the baboons do then?" The question could have been answered empiracally—and the inquiry ended. Cheetahs *do no* attack that way, and so we do not know what baboons *might* do. Fortunately, it was not. For the question opens up the deep issues of what might be and why it is not. Is there a necessary relation between predators and prey that share a common ecological niche? Must their encounters have a "sporting chance" outcome? It is such conjecture, in this case quite unanswerable, that produces rational, self-consciously problem-finding behavior so crucial to the growth of intellectual power. Given the materials, given some background and encouragement, teachers like it as much as the students.

I should like to turn now to the *personalization of knowledge.* A generation ago, the progressive movement urged that knowledge be related to the child's own experience and brought out of the realm of empty abstractions. A good idea was translated into banalities about the home, when the friendly postman and trashman, then the community, and so on. It is a poor way to compete with the child's own dramas and mysteries. A decade ago, my colleague, Clyde Kluckhorn (1949) wrote a prize-winning popular book on anthropology with the entrancing title *Mirror for Man.* In some deeps way, there is extraordinary power in "that mirror which other civilizations still hold up to us to recognize and study . . . [the] image of ourselves [Lévi-Strauss, 1965]." The psychological bases of the power are not obvious. Is it as in discrimination learning, where increasing the degree of contrast helps in the learning of a discrimination, or as in studies of concept attainment where a negative instance demonstrably defines the domain of a conceptual rule? Or is it some primitive identification? All these miss one thing that seems to come up frequently in our interviews with the children. It is the experience of discovering kinship and likeness in what at first seemed bizarre, exotic, and even a little repellant.

Consider two examples, both involving film of the Netsilik. In the films, a single nuclear family, Zachary, Marta, and their 4-year-old Alexi, is followed through the year—spring sealing, summer fishing at the stone weir, fall caribou hunting, early winter fishing through the ice, winter at at the big ceremonial igloo. Children report that at first the three members of the family look weird and uncouth. In time, they look normal, and eventually, as when Marta finds sticks around which to wrap her braids, the girls speak of how pretty she is. That much is superficial—or so it seems. But consider a second episode.

It has to do with Alexi who, with his father's help, devises a snare and catches a gull. There is a scene in which he stones the gull to death. Our children watched, horror struck. One girl, Kathy, blurted out, "He's not even human, doing that to the seagull." The class was silent. Then another girl, Jeannine, said quietly: "He's got to grow up to be a hunter. His mother was smiling when he was doing that." And then an extended discussion about how people have to do things to learn and even do things to learn how to feel appropriately. "What would you do if you had to live there? Would you be as smart about getting along as they are with what they've got?" said one boy, going back to the accusation that Alexi was unhuman to stone the bird.

I am sorry it is so difficult to say it clearly. What I am trying to say is that to personalize knowledge one does not simply link it to the familiar. Rather one makes the familiar an instance of a more general case and thereby produces awareness of it. What the children were learning about was not seagulls and Eskimos, but about their own feelings and preconceptions that, up to then were too implicit to be recognizable to them.

Consider finally the problem of *self-conscious reflectiveness.* It is an epistemological mystery why traditional education has so often emphasized extensiveness and coverage over intensiveness and depth. We have already commented on the fact that memorizing was usually perceived by children as one of the high-priority tasks but rarely did children sense an emphasis upon ratiocination with a view toward redefining what had been encountered, reshaping it, reodering it. The cultivation of reflectiveness, or whatever you choose to call it, is one of the great problems one faces in devising curriculum. How lead children to discover the powers and pleasures that await the exercise of retrospection?

Let me suggest one answer that has grown from what we have done. It is the use of the "organizing conjecture." We have used three such conjectures—what is human about human beings, how they got that way, how they could become more so. They serve two functions, one of them the very obvious though important one of putting perspective back into the particulars. The second is less obvious and considerably more surprising. The questions often seemed to serve as criteria for determining where they were getting, how well they were understanding, whether anything new was emerging. Recall Kathy's cry: "He's not human doing that to the seagull." She was hard at work in her rage on the conjecture what makes human beings human.

There, in brief, are four problems that provide some sense of what a psychologist encounters when he takes a hand in assisting the growth of mind in children in the special settings of a school. The problems look quite different from those we encounter in formulating classical developmental theory with the aid of typical laboratory research. They also look very different from those that one would find in an indigenous society, describing how children picked up skills and knowledge and values in the context of action and daily life. We clearly do not have a theory of the school that is sufficient to the task of running schools—just as we have no adequate theory of toys or of readiness building or whatever the jargon is for preparing children to do a better job the next round. It only obscures the issue to urge that some day our classical theories of learning will fill the gap. They show no sign of doing so.

I hope that we shall not allow ourselves to be embarrassed by our present ignorance. It has been a long time since we have looked at what is involved in imparting knowledge through the vehicle of the school—if ever we did look at it squarely. I urge that we delay no longer.

But I am deeply convinced that the psychologist cannot alone construct a theory of how to assist cognitive development and cannot alone learn how to enrich and amplify the powers of a growing human mind. The task belongs to the whole intellectual community: the behavioral scientists and the artists, scientists, and scholars who are the custodians of skill, taste, and knowledge in our culture. Our special task as psychologists is to convert skills and knowledge to forms and exercises that fit growing minds—and it is a task ranging from how to keep children free from anxiety and how to translate physics for the very young child into a set of playground maneuvers that, later, the child can turn around upon and convert into a sense of inertia regularities.

And this in turn leads me to a final conjecture, one that has to do with the organization of our profession, a matter that has concerned me greatly during this past year during which I have had the privilege of serving as your President. Psychology is peculiarly prey to parochialism. Left to our own devices, we tend to construct models of a man who is neither a victim of history, a target of economic forces, or even a working member of a society. I am still struck by Roger Barker's (1963) ironic truism that the best way to predict the behavior of a human being is to know where he is: In a post office he behaves post office, at church he behaves church.

Psychology, and you will forgive me if the image seems a trifle frivolous, thrives on polygamy with her neighbors. Our marriage with the biological sciences has produced a cumulation of ever more powerful knowledge. So, too, our joint undertakings with anthropology and sociology. Joined together with a variety of disciplines, we have made lasting contributions to the health sciences and, I judge, will make even greater contributions now that the emphasis is shifting to the problems of alleviating stress and arranging for a community's mental health. When I find lacking is an alignment that might properly be called the growth sciences. The field of pedagogy is one participant in the growth sciences. Any field of inquiry devoted to assisting the growth of effective human beings, fully empowered with zest, with skill, with knowledge, with taste is surely a candidate for this sodality. My friend Phillip Morrison once suggested to his colleagues at Cornell that his department of physics grant a doctorate not only for work in theoretical, experimental, or applied physics, but also for work in pedagogical physics. The limits of the growth sciences remain to be drawn. They surely transcend the behavioral sciences cum pediatrics. It is plain that, if we are to achieve the effectiveness of which we as human beings are capable, there will one day have to be such a field. I hope that we psychologists can earn our way as charter members.

References

Allport, G. Effect: A secondary principle of learning. *Psychological Review*, 1946, **53**, 335–347.

Barker, R. On the nature of the environment. *Journal of Social Issues*, 1963, **19**, 17–38.

Bartlett, F. *Remembering*. Cambridge, England: Cambridge Univer. Press, 1932.

Biesheuvel, S. Psychological tests and their application to non-European peoples. *Yearbook of Education*. London: Evans, 1949. Pp. 87–126.

Bloom, B., & Broder, L. Problem solving processes of college students. *Supplementary Educational Monograph, No. 73*. Chicago: Univer. Chicago Press, 1950.

Bruner, J. The course of cognitive growth. *American Psychologist,* 1964, **19,** 1–15.

Bruner, J. Man: A course of study. *Educational Services Inc. Quarterly Report,* 1965, Spring-Summer, 3–13.

Bruner, J. *Toward a theory of instruction.* Cambridge: Harvard Univer. Press, 1966.

Butler, R. A. Incentive conditions which influence visual exploration. *Journal of Experimental Psychology,* 1954, **48**, 19–23.

Ebbinghaus, H. *Memory: A contribution to experimented Psychology.* New York: Teachers College, Columbia University, 1913.

Festinger, L. A theory of cognitive dissonance. Stanford: Stanford Univer. Press, 1962.

Gay, J., & Cole, M. Outline of general report on Kpelle mathematics project. Stanford: Stanford University, Institute for Mathematical Social Studies, undated (Mimeo)

Goodnow, Jacqueline, & Pettigrew, T. Effect of prior patterns of experience on strategies and learning sets. *Journal of Experimental Psychology,* 1955, **49**, 381–389.

Greenfield, Patricia M. Culture and conservation. In J. Bruner, Rose Olver, & Patricia M. Greenfield (Eds.), *Studies in cognitive growth.* New York: Wiley, 1966. Ch. 10.

Harlow, H., & Harlow, Margaret. Social deprivation in monkeys. *Scientific American,* 1962, November.

Harlow, H. F. Mice, monkeys, men, and motives. *Psychological Review,* 1953, **60**, 23–32.

Heider, F. *The psychology of interpersonal relations.* New York: Wiley, 1958.

Inhelder, Bärbel, & Piaget, J. *The growth of logical thinking.* New York: Basic Books, 1958.

Kluckhorn, C. *Mirror for man.* New York: Whittlesey House, 1949.

Köhler, W. *Dynamics in psychology.* New York: Liveright, 1940.

Lévi-Strauss, C. The structural study of myth. *Structural anthropology.* (Trans. by Claire Jacobson & B. Grundfest Scharpf) New York: Basic Books, 1963. Pp. 206–231.

Lévi-Strauss, C. Anthropology: Its achievements and future. Lecture presented at Bicentennial Celebration, Smithsonian Institution, Washington, D.C., September 1965.

Maccoby, M., & Modiano, Nancy. On culture and equivalence. In J. Bruner, Rose Olver, & Patricia M. Greenfield (Ed.), *Studies in cognitive growth.* New York: Wiley, 1966. Ch. 12.

Miller, G., Galanter, E., & Pribram, K. *Plans and the structure of behavior.* New York: Holt, 1950.

Piaget, J. *The construction of reality in the child.* New York: Basic Books, 1954.

Reich, Lee. On culture and grouping. In J. Bruner, Rose Olver, & Patricia M. Greenfield (Eds.), *Studies in cognitive growth.* New York: Wiley, 1966. Ch. 13.

Tolman, E. Cognitive maps in rats and men. *Collected papers in psychology.* Berkeley & Los Angeles: Univer. California Press, 1951. Pp. 241–264.

Vygotsky, L. *Thought and language.* (Ed. & trans. by Eugenia Hanfsmann & Gertrude Vakar) New York: Wiley, 1962.

Wertheimer, M. *Productive thinking.* New York & London: Harper, 1945.

White, Mary A. The child's world of learning. Teachers College, Columbia University, undated. (Mimeo)

White, R. W. Motivation reconsidered: The concept of competence. *Psychological Review,* 1959, **66**, 297–333.

11.2 Critical Thinking: Some Cognitive Components

Elliot N. Eisner

With the explosion of knowledge, the school faces the problem of equipping children with skills that will enable them to pursue independent inquiry after graduation. In his paper, Eisner discusses the components of critical thinking and emphasizes their importance in developing the kind of behavior necessary for coping with an increasingly complex environment. He is concerned that our measurement instruments do not measure this kind of behavior.

Beyond helping children learn about the most important ideas, theories, and bodies of knowledge produced in the past, educators have also been concerned with helping them develop the kinds of attitudes, interests, and cognitive skills that will enable them to pursue knowledge after they depart from school. In addition, children have been encouraged to reflect critically upon the ideas that they or others generate. Thus, schoolmen have attempted to foster a love affair between student and learning while at the same time encouraging the pupil to become critical of what he chooses to woo.

The goal of developing such abilities and interests has been couched

SOURCE. *Teachers College Record*, **LXVI**, 7 (1965), pp. 624–634. Reprinted by permission of Teachers College Record.

in a wide variety of terms. Critical thinking, reflective and independent thought, development of rational powers, educating for inquiry are only a few of the concepts that have dotted eductional literature in the past 60 years. To achieve the ends suggested by these concepts, teachers have been urged to pay attention to individual differences and to build upon the interests of the children they teach. They have been urged to avoid teaching situations in which material is learned by rote and to utilize problematic situations which by their nature provide opportunity for intelligent action on the part of the student. The problem-centered approach and project method, developed by Dewey and Kilpatrick respectively, perhaps best exemplify methods designed to achieve what were then new conceptions of education.

Towards Intelligence

Dewey's concern with the development of intelligence through inquiry can be braced to his earliest papers on education. As far back as October 31, 1896, he told (2) a group of parents attending a conference on the new children's school at the University of Chicago.

"The conception underlying the school is that of a laboratory. It bears the same relation to the work in pedagogy that a laboratory bears to biology, physics, or chemistry. Like any such laboratory it has two main purposes: 1) to exhibit, test, verify and criticize theoretical statements and principles; 2) to add to the sum of facts and principles in its special line."

What he conceived as the school's function for the education of teachers was no less true for the children who attended, for they too were treated as inquirers, seeking better ways of handling problems. This interest of Dewey's, which was continued and elaborated in *How We Think (4)* and *Democracy and Education (3)*, was almost totally devoted to articulating the process by which intelligence is most efficiently and effectively exercised. In *Logic, The Theory of Inquiry (5)*, Dewey defined inquiry as:

"The controlled or directed transformation of an indeterminate situation into one that is so determinate in its distinctions and relations as to convert the elements of the original into a unified whole."

Kilpatrick, a student of Dewey's and perhaps most influential in disseminating Dewey's ideas directly to those preparing to teach, added to this general theme. The conception of concomitant learning and the establishment of the project method as an important methodology for fostering intelligence can be traced to *The Project Method (9)*, published in 1919.

To these men and to the others who laid some of the groundwork earlier, contemporary educators and psychologists are in deep debt, for the conceptions of learning that they are constructed were not merely psychological. They were built upon a particular view of what it meant to human—that is, they were more concerned about how learning *ought* to occur rather than how it could occur. Thus, perhaps their most important contribution resided in their fresh view of man, which was, at base, a moral-ethical conception to be realized through the ages of the school.

Although American educational history since the decades of the 'twenties and 'thirties has undergone some important changes, the goal of developing independent and skilled inquirers has never been totally obscured. Today, in some quarters, this goal has ascended to an even higher position than it enjoyed 30 years ago. Interestingly enough, those whose voices has been most influential in rekindling this educational goal have not, in general, been educators. Jerome S. Bruner, for example, is a psychologist who, while long concerned with learning and thinking, has only recently directed his attention to education as it takes place in the school. In his influential *The Proccess of Education (1),* he indicates that inquiry involves not only analytic thought processes but intuition as well, that the immediate intuitive grasp of the structures of a discipline, especially for the young child, is at least as important as a careful and logical appraisal of the subject matter's elements. He also shares Dewey's view that the most realistic and educationally beneficial way to learn to think within a discipline is to cope with problems within that discipline and that a subject matter can be studied in an intellectually honest way by anybody at almost any age.

On Realizing Humanity

In his most recent book, Herbert Thelen *(17)* has also expressed concern over the process by which critical thinking or inquiry can be developed. For Thelen, inquiry is the way in which that most human is realized in man. Education, for him, is the process which is formally committed to the conscious and deliberate attempt to humanize man. Inquiry, as one way of handling stress or conflict, necessitates the use of consciousness, of diagnosis, of speculation and insight. Thelen, like Bruner, reflects the growing concern in education that the development of certain skills or certan rational capacities of man ought to be a *primary* objective of the educational enterprise.

Bruner and Thelen are not alone in this concern. Lawrence Kubie *(11)* and Gardner Murphy *(12)* have also under-scored the need for educating for inquiry—Kubie in stressing an "education for preconscious freedom" and Murphy in emphasizing the role of the teacher in freeing intelligence.

Both men have made it quite plain that as education is now generally carried on, the preconscious cannot have the freedom it needs to function creatively, nor can the teacher play the role most conducive to the development of the student's rational powers.

It is important to note that these psychologists have not only contributed to educational thought by reminding us to keep our eye upon a very important educational issue; they have also developed some intriguing conceptions of the way teaching might be carried on. This is not to imply that immediately useful theory has been developed that will aid teachers in all teaching situations; it is only to suggest that some important psychological progress has been made in the past 10 or 20 years and that this progress is represented by ideas about the human and how he learns that give us fresh vantage points with which to view the task of teaching.

For many teachers, the goal of developing "inquiry skills" "critical thinking," or "intelligence" has always been very important. Many of these teachers do whatever they can to foster these abilities. One important obstacle that they face, however, as do those who investigate this problem, is the dearth of instruments to assess critical thinking and, perhaps even more important, the lack of some clear conceptions of the specific behaviors that contribute to or constitute this cognitive act. It is to provide some conception of these behaviors that certain components of critical thought are developed here.[1] These conceptions may be useful for developing instruments capable of assessing them. It should be recognized, however, that any effort to specify and describe behaviors related to a concept as global as that of critical thinking may exclude behaviors that others believe rightfully to belong to that concept. No claim is made here for exhaustiveness. The four behaviors that will be described are considered important aspects of critical thinking, but it is recognized that others may have made other selections.

Drive and Curiosity

Two of the most seminal thinkers of the past 100 years, John Dewey and Sigmund Freud, both concerned themselves with the way in which men handle and ought to handle problems. For Dewey, man was a biological organism living *through* an environment, an organism that has the capacity to develop increasing degrees of intelligence by its perceptive assessment and resolution of problematic situations. These situations are conceived of as creating a state of disequilibrium within the organism. Intelligence is viewed by Dewey as that activity which restores equilib-

[1] I wish to thank my colleagues Francis S. Chase and Bertram Masia with whom many of the ideas in this paper were developed.

rium, in which the proper relationship between inherently good goals and the means by which they are achieved is formulated and acted upon. In this conception, the motivating force behind intelligent action is the organism's need to reattain equilibrium.

Freud's position has remarkable similarities on several major points. For one, he too conceived of man as a biological organism in a state of interaction with the environment, and he too viewed man's behavior as an effort to restore the equilibrium or homeostasis that prevailed prior to the emergence of certain threats in the environment. And it has often been stated by neo-Fredians that in one important sense the paradigm state of life, if one is to apply consistently Freud's theory in comprehending psychological man, is death. Indeed, this is alluded to in the *Ego and the Id (6)*, and is reflected in Freud's concepts of eros and thanatos. While Dewey and Freud differ markedly in their conception of the ways in which homeostasis is achieved, the conception of tension reduction and its importance in motivating human action is emphasized by both.

The function of drive or tension-reduction in man has been viewed somewhat differently in recent psychological literature. Ernest Schachtel, for example, believes that Freud's concern with tension reduction as the exclusive motivating force of human action is mistaken. Schachtel *(15)* writes.

"What he (Freud) did not see or did not emphasize in his rather negative view of childhood was that 1) the infant is not entirely helpless but shows from birth on steadily increasing capacities for active searching for satisfaction and for active discovery and exploration, and that it enjoys these active capacities; and 2) that the child in many ways shows a promise which altogether too often is betrayed by adult man and his society and by the growing child itself when it yields to those forces and aspects of culture, as transmitted by parents, teachers, and peers, which are crippling to its inherent potentialities . . . Freud's negative pleasure concept blinded him to the significance of the phenomena, so striking in the growing infant and child, of the pleasure and fulfillment found in the encounter with an expanding reality and in the development, exercise and realization of his growing capacities, skills, and powers.

The Active Quest

Thus Schachtel's position differs significantly from both Freud's and Dewey's in that he holds that man behaves not only, or even primarily, to reduce tensions, but because he inherently quests for experience and that this quest is part and parcel of the nature of the human. This quest for experience, the desire to interact with the environment, is not primarily motivated by a threatening environment, but emanates from man's need to have commerce with the world. This conception of man's need to move outward has been called *activity-affect.* Schachtel calls its counterpart *embeddedness-affect,* designating the desire to remove oneself from the world in order to enjoy the solitude of a simulated intrauterine state.

The position that Schachtel has developed, as well as those developed by White, Maslow, Rogers and others, has significance for education on two counts. First, it points out that an overriding concern with the methods by which students can be motivated may lead one to underestimate their own drive for experience; second, the question of how best to motivate is perhaps considerably less important than in finding means whereby the student's natural curiosity is not stifled.

The desirability of fostering this natural inclination of students is probably clear to anyone who values curiosity, wonder, and the disposition to pursue inquiry beyond the confines of the school. Indeed, one may strongly question the efficacy of any educational program that leads the student to cease independent inquiry after school. Yet while most of us value such a disposition and admire individuals who are able to order their own learning and establish their own goals, today's schools, by and large, do little to prepare students for this pursuit. It is the conscious and deliberate pursuit of knowledge, exemplified by the student's independently initiated search for the problematic and his disposition towards wonder, that characterizes the first component of critical thought, questing. And if it is axiomatic that all great quests commence with a question (note Harvey's wondering why blood circulates, Newton's sense of bewilderment at an apple's plunging to earth, and Freud's query, Do people really forget?), then it is important that the desire to raise seminal questions be fostered by the school. Students who were facilitated in this inclination would probably be the ones most likely to contribute to the realization of their own potentialities and the ones most likely to continue their learning.

Productive Questions

After students complete a unit of study, let's say, of the medieval period, hopefully just as many questions or more would be raised in their minds as when they began the study. If the questions are catalytic to further inquiry, and there is every reason to believe they are, then it seems that one of the teacher's tasks is to develop instructional strategies that elicit important and relevant questions as the students proceed through their individual inquiries. These newly emerging questions, combined with the data obtained through the study unit, should provide fuel for further, more sophisticated inquiries. One test of the achievement of this type of behavior might be to ask students when they complete a unit to list as many questions as they can that they think would be important for obtaining a fuller understanding of the material they have just studied. Such a list could be scored for the number and quality of the questions, quality being defined by the relevance and centrality of the questions raised.

In many classrooms, teachers themselves raise such questions. These questions, however, are not to be conceived as indications of questing because, in almost all cases, teachers have the answer to the questions they raise. Such queries whet the intellectual appetites of students and are tactical devices in teaching. But students who raise such questions are not formulating teaching tactics; rather, their questions often indicate that the study has opened rather than closed their curiosity. This does not mean that all questions raised by students in the classroom are of the questing variety. A student who asks, "Miss Jones, did you say page 237 or 247?" is clearly seeking clarification; he is *not* questing. But a student who asks, "How did the Crusaders determine their travel routes to the Holy Land?" or "Why didn't the Black Muslims become Black Buddhists?" is opening up a new domain of inquiry, one that most teachers could use quite profitably with the student and the class.

One of my colleagues, Cyril Houle, has noted that there are roughly three types of adults who are continuing learners (8). One group consists of those who are goal-oriented and who use their learning as instruments for practical rather than theoretical ends. A second group consists of those who are activity oriented; they join study and discussion groups primarily to obtain some sort of companionship or participation with others. The third group, the learning-oriented one, seeks knowledge for its own sake. Their pursuit of knowledge is generated by the love of learning. While these, Houle claims, are not pure types, "the central emphasis of each subgroup is clearly discernible." The questing student, while perhaps not solely motivated by the quest for knowledge for its own sake, is probably more closely allied to it than to the other two types. The questing student, then, is an eager, curious, questioning individual who takes pleasure in wonder and whose desire to learn and experience is motivated more by joy in this activity than by any other motive. If this type of attitude is significant in determining who will continue to inquire when the guidance of the teacher is absent, then it is an aspect of critical thinking that should be deliberately nurtured by the school.

Speculating

The inclination towards questing the problematic and the propensity towards wonder is frequently but not always followed by a second mode of behavior—one of speculation. Man possesses the wonderful capacity not only to obtain experience from his transaction with the outer world; he is also able to construct a psychological environment built upon the breezes of phantasy and imagination and removed from the conditions of the "real" world. This process can be looked upon as the ability to speculate, to formulate ideas and images of what *might* be. Speculation, as developed here, is conceived of as the ability to generate models or theories to explicate phenomena. Often these ideas are seen by the speculator as tentative, reasonable and interesting guesses about why something is or is not the case.

If we examine the cognitive behavior of students, it is not difficult to recognize that some of them display a great deal more curiosity than others; their general intellectual disposition seems to be characterized by a proclivity towards asking questions. These individuals always seem to want to know why; they are wonderers. Their type of behavior has been described as questing, and such individuals would score highly on an index of curiosity. Other students, however, while perhaps not as prone to ask as many questions, are more apt to formulate answers or offer explanations. They frequently "give you their opinions" to provide you with their point of view. They are, in short, model builders, makers of cosmologies, people who obtain great satisfaction in imaginatively constructing networks of ideas that may or may not have their base in reality but which are, nevertheless, intended to fill in or close the gaps opened by questions.

Like most typologies in the behavioral sciences, the conceptions developed here should be looked upon as tools for analysis, and few if any individuals would be defined by any one type; but if characterizations may be made, two main types of students seem to emerge.

Given a classroom discussion in history, the questing student would be the student most likely to raise the greatest number and most seminal questions. He might want to know why a particular historical figure was motivated to engage in a given act, or what effect a particular governmental statute might have had on the subsequent history of a nation. The speculator would be most likely to generate answers to such questions. He would be most prone to leap in his imagination from the stimulus of the question to develop what seemed to him an interesting and plausible answer or hypothesis. A teacher that was blessed with a large proportion of such individuals in his class would probably seldom be short on a rich and wide variety of ideas for discussion. It has been my experience that the fostering of high-level speculation in children is in large measure due to the kind of environment that is established in the class or group. If the students feel anxious or if they feel inadequate, if they feel that their remarks will suffer critical evaluation, they tend to be less able to give free rein to those processes which make this behavior possible. Osborn (*13*) has pointed out that in his brainstorming sessions a standing rule prohibits critical or evaluative comment on the part of any of the group members. His central concern at these sessions is to enable group members to get their ideas out on the table and recorded. The evaluative session comes later and often involves people other than those who originated the ideas.

Information and Risk

Speculating, however, needs more than a permissive and supportive environment if it is to occur fruitfully. In order to speculate, an individual needs some information from which he can make a speculative leap. If a problem is presented to a group of students, and if none of the students has any information that seems relevant to the problem, the likelihood of speculation is very small. The contrary informational condition also impedes speculation. If an individual is confronted with a problem, and if his informational or data resources are perceived as adequate for coping with it successfully, no speculation is likely to occur. In short, we do not need to speculate when our information is adequate, and we cannot speculate when we have no relevant information from which to move. This suggests that theoretically there ought to be some optimal informational margin, relative to a problem, which should be most conducive to productive speculation. At some point between absence and full possession of information, speculation should be most fruitfully generated.

Speculation is probably also effected by the amount of risk students are willing to take in venturing speculative propositions. Rimoldi, Haley, and Fogliatto (*14*) have constructed some exceedingly clever devices to measure the amount of data medical students need before they are willing to risk a diagnosis. Students at the sophomore level in medical school differ greatly with respect to the number of cues they need before venturing a diagnosis. As students proceed through school, variability in the number and types of cues needed decreases. Learning to make an educated guess is a necessary and useful part of the diagnostic process. By and large, however, "educated guessing" has not been strongly fostered in our schools. This is partly due to our legacy of "right answers." Frequently, speculating is looked upon as *mere* guesswork and really not appropriate for the classroom. Yet the ability to formulate perceptive speculations is the heart of hypothesis formation; without this type of cognitive act, neither philosophy nor science could have developed. Indeed, one may argue that it is the speculative leap rather than necessity that is the mother of invention in both philosophy and science because productive work in each field deals with problems for which no ready answer exists. As Whitehead (*18*) so eloquently puts it,

"Philosophy begins in wonder. And, at the end, when philosophic thought has done its best, the wonder remains. There may have been added, however, some grasp of the immensity of things, some purification of emotion by understanding."

Creative Intuition

Lawrence Kubie (*11*) has also held that if such behavior is to take place, the *preconscious* needs to be free from the highly rational and restrictive demands that permeate a great many classrooms. His identification of the preconscious as the psychological domain that gives rise to creative thought has relevance for understanding the genesis of speculation. Kubie holds that it is neither the conscious nor the unconscious that is the midwife to creativity. The conscious processes, he believes, are too rational, too restricted, and tied too tightly to reality to develop the new combinations and phantasy that are needed for creative productivity. Similarly the unconscious processes are too compulsive and chaotic to develop creative thought that is socially valuable. The preconscious, however, resides in just the right area and performs just the proper functions to foster most efficiently the phantasy and imagery necessary for creative thought. But let Kubie (*11*) speak for himself:

"In the adult who is not ham strung by conscious or unconscious fear and guilt, preconscious processes make full use of analogy and allegory, superimposing dissimilar ingredients into new preceptional and conceptual patterns, thus reshuffling experience to achieve that fantastic degree of condensation without creativity in any field of activity would be impossible."

Other researchers working in the area of creativity, J. P. Guilford (*7*) and Morris Stein (*16*) for example, have also concluded that creative thinking, of which speculating is a component, requires the ability to engage in *divergent thought* as Guilford calls it, or to be *stimulus free,* the ability to "take off" rather than to become bound to a stimulus as Stein has suggested. Indeed, creative ideation does seem to be initiated by an imaginative speculative leap into the possible; and some individuals, it seems, derive their primary satisfaction in producing such ideas. It should also be noted, however, that many individuals, once these speculations are formulated, have little desire to test them; their "kicks" come almost entirely from their fanciful, imaginative, and playful formation.

Evaluating

A third component of critical thinking is that of evaluation. Evaluation has three major dimensions. First, an idea or body of ideas in any field is evaluated for the *logic* of its propositions. Receivers of information apply gross logical criteria to the statements they read or hear. These criteria act as the first test to determine whether the reader or listener will proceed any farther with the ideas he confronts. All of us, with varying degrees of sophistication, use logic as our initial screen for whatever a statement purports to be. It is meaningless if it is in logical error.[2]

The second type of criterion is concerned with evidence. For example, an historian reading a new work on the origin of the Dead Sea scrolls not only tests it for the logic of its propositions, but also for the historical evidence that it employs in supporting them. And notwithstanding the wide range of conceptions of history, and admitting that at least some historical interpretation is highly artful, the issue of fact, of the relationship of propositions to reliable observations, is a crucial one. Even with the scientific limitations inherent in historical inquiry, specific and acknowledged criteria are still applied by historians to appraise works within their field. In some measure, all of us apply substantive criteria to propositions we encounter, for while logical consistency is a necessary criterion to be met in judging the value of propositions, it is seldom a sufficient one. Students rated high in this component of critical thought would be prone to take issue with much of what they read and would be inclined to challenge assertions they feel are unwarranted by evidence.

The third type of criterion that is applied in the evaluation of propositions is of a qualitative variety. The way in which language is organized, the types of words that are selected, the emphasis given to certain phrases, all contribute to the content and meaning of the message. Imagine three men confronted by a police officer who asks one of them if he stole the fur coat he is carrying. By changing the emphasis on each word in his response, the meaning of the man's statement is altered. He might say, "*I* didn't steal that coat" (implying that one of the others did); "I *didn't* steal that coat" (asserting emphatically that he did not steal the coat); "I didn't *steal* that coat" (implying that he obtained it some other way); "I didn't steal *that* coat" (implying that it was another coat he stole), or "I didn't steal that *coat*" (implying that he stole something else).

[2] It should be noted that I am referring exclusively to propositions which purported to be warranted or warrantable. Poetry and other forms of artistic expression need not follow any logical procedure.

While the meanings conferred upon these responses as a function of different points of emphasis are fairly easy to grasp, emphasis in literary material is often more subtle. Some authors have mastered this art so well that by their selection of key words in their written discourse, they "set one up" for acceptance of their conclusions. In fact, the denotative meaning of key words and phrases in literary works is often less important than their connotative meaning. Paradigm cases of this third mode of evaluation may be found in the evaluation procedures of those responsible for interpreting the meaning of diplomatic communiqués. But students, too, engage in this type of evaluation when they appraise the underlying meanings and biases of the material they read, the lectures they hear, and the contributions of their classmates. In the domain of the social sciences, this aspect of evaluation is much more prevalent than in the domains of physics or mathematics, where technical language is maximized and where the possibility for using language affectively is minimal.

Constructing

Constructing, a fourth component of critical thinking, is the production of relationships or parallels between seemingly unrelated concepts. It is through the construction of these relationships that the individual is able to perceive elements as part of a larger whole and in their relationships and interaction with each other. For example, a student studying the economic structure of colonial America and the Protestant ethic may recognize no relationship between the two. For him, each aspect seems independent, each is conceived as a freely swinging string on the armature of a particular historical period. Retention of unrelated concepts has been shown, as far back as Ebbinghaus, to be very short. But this is not the only issue and is not even the most important. A student hold-such a view of historical phenomena holds faulty notions about the historical period itself; in short, the conception that historical events exist in isolation provides a severely distorted picture of the past.

The student could, however, either with the help of the teacher or through his own efforts, come to formulate a relationship between Calvinistic theology and the economic practices of colonial America. Through the exercise of the appropriate type of cognition, he may construct the parallels or note the reciprocity of each of these social forces. The construction of these parallels is precisely what the theoretician does when he hypothesizes relationships among the components of a particular subject matter.

The construction of such relationships is not limited to historical events, practices, or forces existing within the same historical period. In one class in American history, the students were trying to identify the conditions that seem necessary for successful revolution. A dissatisfied public, presence of leadership in the opposition party, and a weakened leadership holding power were some of these conditions. Although the subject matter being studied was the American revolution, one student commented that similar conditions existed during the formation of the New Deal and that this, too, was a type of revolution. This type of cognition, this ability to construct relationships or parallels between events, enabled the student to use the conditions extracted from this study of the American revolution as general concepts that could be applied, in part, to other social situations. The usefulness of such activity is apparent in the type of cognitive economy it produces. While no one would argue that the two events were identical, there are some important conditions that are common, and the identification of such common components is realized through the constructive act.

Of Cues and Flashes

Now teachers of history and of other subject matters are prone to make these relationships known to students by pointing out, with various degrees of clarity, how such events are related. Teachers frequently devote specific periods deliberately to making these relationships obvious or to providing cues or raising questions that will set the student moving in the desired direction so that the relationships can be easily drawn. However, a teacher cannot point out all of the potential relationships that may be constructed within a subject matter, nor can he afford to take the time to do so. In the final analysis, the student is left to construct the relationships he can and to commit the rest to memory as isolated fact.

The construction of relationships between events and the explanation of the causes of those events are essential aspects of theory building. One task of theory is to bring together, in logical and causal (or probable) relationship, an array of diverse phenomena. Thus, we look to theory to unify, to relate, and to explain what was previously viewed as separate, unrelated, and unaccounted for. Constructing, like speculating, in a part of the theory-building task and is therefore an important ability if useful theory is to be formulated.

The process of constructing has also been discussed by Arthur Koestler (10). Koestler, however, uses the term *bisociation* and conceives of this process as the unification of what are normally considered separate mental fields. He believes that creative productivity is a function of the marriage of fields that had previously been separate and that "in a flash of insight" the creative individual finds their commonality.[3] While the construction of these relationships or the discovery of their commonality may be a product of that unexplained flash described by writers such as Blake and Chekhov and by psychologists such as Wertheimer and Köhler, the production of these conceptual bridges may also result from the careful study of the elements constituting each field. In other words, individuals may work towards the construction of theoretical links by careful and painstaking analysis and by speculating, projecting, and testing alternative ways in which such relationships may be found.

The Fault, Dear Brutus . . .

In developing these conceptions, I have tried to analyze a global concept into some constitutent parts. In turn, this analysis may prove useful in formulating educational objectives and in constructing evaluation devices. It is widely recognized that there is no scarcity of educational measures available in the market; nevertheless, the number of instruments which measure the type of behaviors I have described is quite small. The more recent achievement measures, such as the STEP test and, interestingly enough, the achievement measures developed as far back as the 'thirties by those working on the eight-year study, come closest to assessing the behaviors I have described, but they too fall short. Perhaps one reason for this scarcity is the fact that tests of this kind require a type of evaluation procedure that is very difficult to standardize; being enamored as we are with norms, national and otherwise, we have not found it expedient to develop them.

A second reason for the lack of such devices—and perhaps one that is more important—is our general tendency in education to become so intrigued with new terms that they lose almost all meaning. Terms such as critical thinking, inquiry, reflective thought, etc., can be found in almost any educational journal, but the specification of the particular behaviors that constitute them is quite another matter. The terms are often so broadly conceived as to make them functionally meaningless. Yet they are not totally devoid of meaning. Most of us using terms like critical thinking, reflective thought, or inquiry share some common conceptual threads that are important. The commonality that we intuitively share might be made explicit if we could identify their particular referents in behavior. This in turn might put us in a better position to develop such behaviors in the classroom—which is, after all, an educator's ultimate concern.

[3] An illustration of the flash is the story of the discovery by Archimedes of the relationship of fluid displacement to the volume of solids. See Koestler (*10*).

References

1. Bruner, J. S. *The Process of education.* Cambridge: Harvard Univer. Press, 1961.
2. Dewey, J. *University record.* November 6, 1896, *1,* No. 32, 417–422.
3. Dewey, J. *Democracy and education.* New York: Macmillan, 1916.
4. Dewey, J. *How we think.* Boston, New York, etc.: D. C. Health, c. 1933.
5. Dewey, J. *Logic: the theory of inquiry.* New York: Henry Holt, 1938.
6. Freud, S. *The ego and the id.* London: Hogarth Press, 1927.
7. Guilford, J. P. Basic traits in intellectual performance. In Taylor, C. (Ed.) *The second (1957) University of Utah research conference on the identification of creative scientific talent.* Salt Lake City: Univer. Utah Press, 1958.
8. Houle, C. *The inquiring mind.* Madison: Univer. Wisconsin Press, 1961.
9. Kilpatrick, W. H. *The project method.* New York: Teach. Coll. Bur. Publ., Columbia Univer., 1919.
10. Koestler, A. *Insight and outlook.* New York: MacMillan, 1949.
11. Kubie, L. *Neurotic distortions of the creative process.* Lawrence: Univer. Kansas Press, 1958.
12. Murphy, G. *Freeing intelligence through teaching.* New York: Harper, 1961.
13. Osborn, A. F. *Applied imagination: Principles and procedures of creative thinking.* New York: Scribner, 1953.
14. Rimoldi, T. J. A., Haley, J. V., & Fogliatto, H. *The test of diagnostic skills.* Psychometric Laboratory, Publ. No. 25. Chicago: Loyola Univer. Press, 1962.
15. Schachtel, E. *Metamorphosis.* New York: Basic Books, 1959.
16. Stein, M. L. A transactional approach to creativity. In Taylor, C. (Ed.) The *1955 University of Utah research conference on the identification of creative scientific talent.* Salt Lake City: Univer. Utah Press, 1956. Pp. 171–181.
17. Thelen, H. *Education and the human quest.* New York: Harper, 1960.
18. Whitehead, A. N. *Modes of thought.* New York: Macmillan, 1938.

11.3 Instructing the Individual in Creative Thinking[1]

Richard S. Crutchfield

This paper could also have been placed in Chapter 7 because it discusses the use of programmed learning. It was included here because it describes a unique method of developing creativity. Critics of the new technology have objected to the inflexibility of programming. Crutchfield's use of the medium suggests numerous possibilities for changing and developing various kinds of behavior. With the introduction of computer-assisted instruction into our schools, there are possibilities for individualized instruction not only to transmit information and develop concepts, but also to develop those skills so important for substantive achievement and creative production.

An educational dilemma facing us today is that we must meet an increasing need for individualized instruction while the continuing growth of our mass educational system makes individualization less and less pos-

SOURCE. Richard S. Crutchfield, "Instructing the Individual in Creative Thinking." In *New Approaches to Individualizing Instruction,* A Report of a Conference on May 11, 1965. Princeton, New Jersey: Educational Testing Service, 1965, pp. 13–25. Reprinted by permission of the author and Educational Testing Service.

[1] The research reported here is supported by a grant from the Carnegie Corporation of New York. Dr. Martin V. Covington has collaborated in all phases of the research.

sible. I should like first to comment briefly on three sources of the increased demand for individualized instruction—one pedagogical, one motivational, and one social.

The pedagogical reason stems from the enormous effort currently directed at educational reform. The aims of raising academic standards, of maximizing the potential of gifted students, of helping the handicapped and underprivileged, and of stimulating the underachiever, all point toward the need for improved methods of instruction in which the individual becomes the focus of attention. The widespread movements in curriculum innovation similarly involve a concern with individualization, in their explicit effort to make the developing conceptual structure of the subject matter as congruent as possible with what we are beginning to learn about the orderly developmental structure of the child's cognitive functioning. It is increasingly recognized that to make the instructional process optimal, account must be taken of the specific background, capabilities, and distinctive cognitive style of the given individual. In order that any bit of instructional information—no matter how small—be properly understood and mastered by the individual, he must be enabled to assimilate it relevantly to his own cognitive structure, to transform it according to his own preferred and distinctive cognitive style, in such a way as to "make it his own." This requires individualized instruction that is geared to the distinctive attributes, needs, and cognitions of the particular person. This does not mean, of course, that individuals must be taught singly, with different materials designed for each alone. It does require that the common instructional methods and materials have such scope and flexibility as reasonably to fit the diverse requirements of the different individuals. This is the pedagogical challenge—to make instruction sufficiently individualized while still maintaining it within the feasible limits of large-scale education.

A second major source of the demand for individualized instruction is motivational. There is acute need for ways to preserve the student's sense of individual identity in the sea of anonymity flooding the large-scale educational institutions of today. The Free Speech Movement at Berkeley is but one dramatic symptom of the widespread disenchantment of college students with the mass educational process in which the individual is drowned. Though these particular protests took the form of demonstrations for freedom of speech and political action, I believe that more basically they derive from the student's feeling of loss of identity in the impersonal educational mill, where he is processed through large lecture classes, tested by objective examinations, and recorded in symbols on computer tape. What he earnestly wants and seeks is the opportunity for learning experiences which are meaningful to *him,* in which *he* is meaningfully engaged with the teacher and the subject matter; in short, he wants individualized instruction.

A third major cause of the increased need for individualized instruction is social. It has to do with the changing nature of man's future world. The aims of educational training today must reflect the needs and purposes of tomorrow. I believe that the nature of man's tomorrow is such as to require greater and greater stress on individualized instruction today. It is a sobering thought that the children we instruct in elementary school today will be only forty years of age by the year 2000. We cannot clearly fóresee the state of the world at that time, but we can be certain that it will be vastly different from our current world. We cannot even make sensible projections from the past because the acceleration of change is so much greater now than ever before. We may confidently expect far-reaching breakthroughs of a technological nature long before the year 2000. Automation, the high-speed computer, and other technological advances will render superfluous a great part of today's routine labor and even routine skills and intelligence. Genetical engineering may by that time enable us deliberately to re-shape man's biological makeup. Physical immortality may be just around the corner. Many or most of the crucial social problems confronting us today—for example, poverty, prejudice, and over-population—may by that time have been virtually solved. The information explosion will multiply the sum total of human knowledge many-fold and will make obsolescent many of the facts and concepts of today.

In the face of all this, we cannot now pretend fully to know just what and how the child should be taught in the way of specific facts and concepts, nor even what specific skills he should acquire. What education today must therefore seek to do is to bring about the optimal development of the whole individual. He must be equipped with *generalized* intellectual and other skills, skills which will enable him to cope effectively with whatever the state of the world is as he will later encounter it, in the context of rapidly changing facts and concepts. Central among these generalized skills is the capability for creative thinking. The individual will need to be able to think creatively about the yet unforeseen problems of his society and world, in the light of facts and concepts yet to be discovered. And the individual will need to attain a greater degree of self-fulfillment of his unique creative potentialities because there will be a major shift away from preoccupation with routine work and external achievement toward preoccupation with creative experience and inner satisfaction.

These reflections about the needs for individualized instruction, especially in connection with the training of creative skills, are germane to the program of research on instructing children in creative thinking and problem solving which my associates and I have been carrying out over the past four years. We have been guided by the belief that virtually *every* child—regardless of his level of intelligence, school achievement, and socio-economic background—needs and can substantially benefit from explicit training in creative thinking, that there is, in short, an enormous gap between his usual performance on creative thinking tasks and the performance he is really capable of.

Our aim, therefore, has been to strengthen in the individual child certain cognitive skills which are central to the creative process and to encourage in him certain attitudes and dispositions which favor the use of these skills. We have sought to enhance the child's readiness and capacity for fluent generation of ideas, ideas which are unusual and imaginative, let effectively adaptive to the reality-constraints of the particular creative problem. We have sought to train the child's ability to sense problems and to grasp their essentials, to see them in fresh and insightful ways, to approach them intuitively as well as analytically. We have sought to teach him how better to bring to bear on the problem what he possesses in the way of concrete knowledge, principles, and heuristics which are germane to the solution. And, finally, we have sought to promote and strengthen in him self-confidence about his own abilities for creative thinking and to increase his motivation to engage in it.

To these ends, we have undertaken to develop special new instructional materials and procedures suitable for fifth- and sixth-grade children. Confronted with the dilemma that creativity training must be individualized as far as possible and yet that the materials and methods should be suitable for easy administration to entire classes, we have sought to resolve this dilemma by casting our training materials into what may loosely be called a programmed self-instructional form. It may seem to you paradoxical, if not downright perverse, to seek to use programmed methods for the teaching of creativity. Certainly it would seem likely that programmed instruction, if used in a rigidly orthodox fashion, might be potentially detrimental to the very creative qualities we seek to enhance. For one thing, programmed instruction may tend to produce an excessive homogeneity among the thought processes of the students commonly trained. At the end of what is allegedly a "successful" program, all individuals having been marched through the *same* set of rigidly pre-patterned steps will have arrived at the *same* way of looking at the *same* material. Such undue homogenization tends to preclude the diversity in thought processes essential to the promotion of creativity, both in the individual and in the group. For another thing, the "successful" program, by virtue of the very effortless ease of learning that it enables, may fail sufficiently to arouse and engage the individual's own activity of searching and striving after meaning, which is an essential part of creative growth. The goals of efficient learning and the goals of creative growth may thus be in intrinsic opposition. Moreover, a "successful" program through which the individual is marched in an authoritative logical lock step, may tend to inhibit the questioning and skeptical attitude that is often conducive to creativity. The locus of cognitive initiative and control is thus subtly shifted from the individual to the program; the aim becomes that of tuning the individual to the program rather than the program to the individual. Finally, one of the essentials of creativity would appear to be the ability temporarily to tolerate ambiguity, complexity, and lack of closure while progressing toward solution of the problem. Yet a cardinal aim of programmed instruction is to attain the utmost of clarity, precision, and definiteness at each step. Here, too, we see that there may be an inherent opposition between the aims of orthodox programmed instruction and those of creativity training.

But through more flexible forms and uses of programming we can avoid some of these detrimental aspects and can capitalize upon its positive potential for creativity training. Its features of self-administration and self-pacing, for example, permit the individual considerable latitude in independent regulation of his own preferred rate of work and tempo of thinking on the materials. In order to challenge the student, the size of step can be made substantially larger than it is in orthodox programming, where the monotony of repeated small steps may destroy interest. Thus, a typical frame, or page, may contain much more complex material, require more time for reflection, and call for multiform rather than single responses.

Perhaps the most crucial methodological problem in programming for creativity is how to provide appropriate feedback to the individual's ideas. In more conventional programming having to do with the straight assimilation of subject matter, what is to be reinforced is the giving of the one "correct" answer. But in creative thinking on problems, a great many *different* answers are possible and one aim of creativity training is to reinforce this diversity, uniqueness, and individuality of response. Thus we must provide a kind of "creative feedback" that will be relevant and reinforcing for all or most individuals taking the program regardless of the wide diversity in their responses. Suppose, for example, that we are stimulating the student to think of unusual uses for a particular object. An effective feedback to his responses might be to give him an illustrative set of diverse and unusual ideas that have been, or could have been, produced by others. The set would be intended to broaden the student's vision and limits of acceptance as to what constitutes unusual ideas appropriate to the problem; at the same time, it should contain some illustrative ideas not too far removed in quality from the perhaps more pedestrian ideas that he would have given. In this way his creative sights may be elevated without unduly discouraging him about his own less imperative initial creative attempts.

The auto-instructional materials that we have developed for fifth and sixth-grade children make use of these various positive features of programming. In their more recently revised form, they consist of a series of sixteen booklets, approximately 30 pages each. The booklets are worked on individually by each student at his own pace. They contain story material in a semi-cartoon presentation. On some pages the student is asked to write down his ideas on questions that are raised in the booklet; other pages are simply to be read and studied.

The booklets have a continuous story-line which follows the adventures of two school children, Jim and Lila (brother and sister), as they try to solve a series of detective problems and other mysterious and puzzling occurrences under the tutelage of their Uncle John, who is both a high school science teacher and a spare time detective.

This identification-model approach is intended to introduce the reader gradually into problem-solving activity, without threatening him with feelings of failure. By this means he can be brought vicariously to experience the vicissitudes of the creative process without himself being plunged immediately and painfully into it. Jim and Lila are school children like himself. In the early stages of the lessons they are depicted as suffering from the anxieties and ineptitudes concerning creative thinking that are all too common among school children.

As they proceed through the stories, they are depicted as gradually overcoming these handicaps—though with occasional setbacks—until at the end they reach a stage of enthusiastic interest about thinking-problems, and a strengthened sense of competence in dealing with them. The attempt is to maintain a close identification-link between them and the reader; as they move ahead, so does he, with the gap never becoming too large. Indeed, we intend that as many readers as possible will come finally to *surpass* Jim and Lila.

Uncle John is intended as a benevolent authority-figure—demi-parent, demi-teacher—who stimulates and guides Jim and Lila (and the reader) in these adventures in thinking, showing them how to think for themselves. Gradually, as the stories progress, the reader is called upon to take a more and more active role in giving his own ideas, and thus he is meant to be gradually weaned from dependence on Jim's and Lila's ideas, just as *they* are being weaned from reliance on Uncle John's.

Each lesson is a complete problem-solving episode, containing all of the principal steps and processes inherent in creative problem-solving. To begin with, Jim and Lila confront a mysterious occurrence, for example, a puzzling theft and disappearance of money on a river-boat, or strange happenings in a deserted and reputedly haunted mansion. They are encouraged to generate many ideas and to check these possibilities against the facts. With new facts coming in, they revise their hypotheses. When these fail to solve the problem, Jim and Lila are led to reformulate the problem, to sée it in a different way and thus to generate new ideas. As further incidents occur, they are led closer and closer to a solution, until finally things fall into place, and they achieve the solution. The structure of the lessons is such that the alert reader is very likely to discover the solution for himself, a step ahead of Jim and Lila. This deliberately contrived "discovery experience" is thought to be an extremely important factor in the development and reinforcement of creative thinking skills and attitudes in the student.

The lessons are constructed not only to give the reader repeated experiences in the solution of interesting problems, but also directly to instruct him in helpful strategies or heuristic procedures for creative problem-solving, by showing him how he can use them in the concrete problems. The procedures pertain to the formulation of the problem, the asking of relevant questions, the laying out of a plan of attack, the generation of many ideas, the search for uncommon ideas, the transformation of the problem in new ways, the evaluation of hypotheses, the sensitivity to odd and discrepant facts, and the opennes to metaphorical and analogical hints leading to solutions.

As we have said, the lessons are also intended to promote beneficial attitudes and motivations in the reader. Mainly the aim is to build up the child's successful experience in coping with thought problems, thus reinforcing his interest in such activity and his self-confidence in the mastery of creative thinking skills. At the same time we undertake to instill in him a variety of dispositions which favor the creative process—open-mindedness, suspension of premature criticality of ideas, readiness for the arousal of curiosity, intuitiveness, and the like.

Above all, it is indispensable that the instructional materials actively interest and involve the reader. That they clearly do so in the studies we have made of them in partly owing to the exciting nature of the mystery stories and the maintenance of suspense while on the track of the solution. As the series of lessons progresses, there is a gradual shift from the obvious drama of detective stories toward the subtler drama of more purely intellectual problems. Jim and Lila—and hopefully the reader too—thus come to discover that creative thinking is exciting, enjoyable, and personally significant.

During the past two years we have carried out two major studies of our instructional materials in 16 fifth- and sixth-grade classrooms in public schools of Berkeley and vicinity. Altogether 481 children have been studied—267 given the training materials, and the remaining 214 serving as control subjects.

First, a six-hour battery of pre-tests was given to all the children. The children in half of the classrooms were then given the series of auto-instructional lessons as part of their regular classroom work. One booklet was given each day over a three- to four-week period. Each child worked individually at his own pace, the average time taken per booklet being about 30 minutes. The control children in the other half of the classrooms, who were comparable to the trained children in intelligence, sex, racial distribution, and creative thinking proficiency, were not given the instructional materials. Some of them were given a short set of booklet materials which contained a serial adventure story in cartoon format. They were required to answer questions about the story in the booklets, but these questions had no bearing on creative thinking. The purpose was to insure a sense of task involvement in these control children and to acquaint them with work in such booklets. Others of the control children were handled in different ways; some of them were given no materials of any kind.

Following the end of the training period, all classes were given an eight-hour battery of post-tests in order to measure changes in creative thinking proficiency occurring between pre-test and post-test.

Before turning to an account of the results of the training, we should look briefly at what was included in the pre- and post-test materials. First, there were several measures of intelligence, personality, and cognitive style. Second, there were special inventories, designed by us to reveal the individual's attitudes about creative thinking and his self-evaluation as a creative thinker. Third, there were several of Torrance's tests of creative thinking in children, which have been widely used in research of this kind. Finally, and most directly relevant as criterion measures for our purposes, there were a number of tests specially constructed by us to measure creative problem-solving proficiency. Most of the available creativity tests for children, such as those of Torrance, are tests mainly of divergent thinking only. There are few available problem-solving tests of the kind we require, which entail a synthesis of both convergent and divergent thinking. Thus we undertook to develop our own set of such tests.

The test problems are presented in booklet form, each booklet constituting one entire problem that is worked through on successive pages, with ample time for thinking. The problems are ones which tend to interest children, which minimize the need for special knowledge for the solution, and which have considerable complexity and scope, requiring the child to apply a number of different thinking skills. Each problem lends itself to several alternative solutions, varying in scope and elegance, rather than to a single rigorous solution. Performances on the problems can be scored in a variety of dimensions, most importantly for number of ideas generated, for quality of ideas, and for number of solutions achieved.

Some of the problems are detective puzzles, such as the location of a jewel that has been stolen during momentary darkness at a dinner party, or the explanation of how an entire house mysteriously vanished overnight. Other puzzles are not of a detective nature, for example: how X-ray beams can be used to destroy a tumor without harming the healthy tissue that completely surrounds it, or how a man can get himself out of a deep pit with steep sides without any available tools. The problems are meant to be of general interest, not directly related to school work, though several of them do have closer curricular relevance. For example, it is alleged that an ancient city has been found buried virtually intact in the sandy desert; the problem is to think of possible causes for the apparent sudden demise of the city several thousand years ago.

Our summary account of the results of the two major studies should start with the findings on these various problem-solving tests, which were intended, of course, to be most directly suitable as post-test criteria of effectiveness of the training program. The findings are clear. The trained children showed a marked superiority in performance over the control children. This was true of every one of the test problems without exception, and for each of the main attributes of creative thinking that we measured. The trained children were able to generate about twice as many acceptable ideas as were the controls. The rated *quality* of their ideas surpassed that of the control children by an even greater margin. The trained children proved more sensitive than the controls in noticing significant clues and factual discrepancies in the problems, and were better able to benefit, from metaphorical hints to solution that were embedded in the test booklets. The largest differences of all occurred on the most important criterion, namely the achievement of actual solutions of the problems. Here the trained children surpassed the controls by margins ranging up to three to one.

It is manifest then that the auto-instructional program does succeed in improving proficiency in creative problem-solving. We also discover that the beneficial effects *generalize* to types of test materials quite different from the problems. The divergent thinking tasks adapted from Torrance show similar positive results. One of these is the Tin Can test, in which the child is asked to think of as many unusual uses of tin cans as he is able. The trained children markedly outperform the controls both on sheer volume of ideas and on the originality of their ideas, as measured by Torrance's criterion of statistical infrequency. It should be stressed that this test is quite unlike anything included in our training lessons. The same is true of the Dog Improvement test, in which the child is to suggest inventive ways in which a toy dog could be made more attractive as a toy. Here the trained children make far more suggestions than the controls and the rated quality of their ideas is even more highly superior. In the Circles test, the individual is given several pages printed with empty 1½″ circles and is asked to draw as many different objects as he can, using a circle as the integral part of each object. By being told expressly to try to draw objects "that no one else will think of," he is given a set toward production of uncommon ideas. The results are that the trained children complete a somewhat greater number of circles; what is much more important, the ideas they create are far less trite and obvious than those of the controls, as measured both by statistical infrequency of occurrence and by ratings of originality made by independent judges.

We see, therefore, that there is widespread generalization of the effects of the training lessons to the enhancement of imaginative and inventive processes in the individual. However, there are discernible limits to the generalization. For instance, in the Imaginative Story test the child is to write a short story constructed around a set of five given elements—persons and objects of a somewhat unusual nature, e.g., a "man who always smiles," a "book with black pages." In this demanding test, the trained children perform no better than do the controls. And also on several test problems of a purely *logical* nature, not requiring creative thinking, the trained children show no gain over the controls.

Turning now to the question of attitudes, we find that the training lessons did produce some modest amount of positive change in the child's attitudes toward problem-solving and creative thinking activity, but did not produce significant change in his self-confidence and evaluation of himself as a creative thinker. Clearly, the present version of the auto-instructional materials falls far short of what we had hoped to accomplish in respect to modification of these crucial attitudes, despite the marked effectiveness of the materials in strengthening creative thinking skills.

Some light on the probable persistence of the training effects is given by findings on a further follow-up testing of the children that we carried out five or six months after the end of training. The children were tested by their new teachers on several new criterion tests that we provided. The results are that the previously trained children continue to surpass the control children on some of the criterion tests, by approximately a two-to-one margin. However, it is also notable that the persistence of the original training effects is greatest for proficiency in problem-solving and is less so for performance on the divergent thinking tasks. It would thus appear that what has been most firmly established in the individual is the kind of problem-solving skill with which the training program was directly concerned and that the more generalized and by-product effects on the individual's creative thinking are not so strongly entrenched by the training.

Another issue of paramount importance, of course, is whether the lessons benefit *all* the children or only some of them. For this we must look beyond the simple statistics showing average gains of the trained children over the control children. We must ask how much the comparative gains are for children of varying levels of intelligence, of socio-economic background, and of initial levels of creative thinking proficiency. We have divided our entire sample of children into three IQ levels—those with IQ's above 115, those ranging from 100 to 115, and those below 100. The results show that for *each* of these three levels the trained children markedly surpass the controls in test performance. There is, by the way, an appreciable correlation between IQ and our criterion test scores, but it is notable that the effect of training overrides the effect of intelligence to such a degree that the low-IQ children after training actually surpass the untrained high-IQ children. A very similar result is found when we compare children of different initial levels of creative thinking proficiency.

The Negro children—predominantly from disadvantageous backgrounds—also markedly gain from the program, though only about half as much as do the white children. But note that even though on pre-tests the Negro children scored appreciably lower than the white children, subsequently the *trained* Negro children gain enough to surpass the *untrained* whites on the post-test creativity measures.

There are, of course, many remaining questions that only further research can answer. We need to know, for instance, what effect, either beneficial or detrimental, the teacher's attitudes toward and method of classroom use of these materials may have. We need to know whether such materials when expanded to full-semester or full-year length will continue to elicit the enthusiasm, interest, and involvement of the child. We need to know whether the effects we demonstrate on our test materials do significantly generalize toward improving the child's regular school performance, increasing his creativity in working on more traditional curriculum materials. And we need to know how these effects may interact with the effects produced by the new experimental curricula that are sweeping the educational system.

Though we have sought to maximize the suitability and relevance of our materials for the individual child, we have made only a short step toward the ultimate goal of individualization. We intend now to construct additional materials which will provide for a considerably larger amount of self-selection and self-guidance by the individual, and which will have greater scope and flexibility in the feedback that is provided to the responses of the individual. One of several technical approaches to this latter problem will be to adapt our methods to the use of computer-controlled feedback, such as being developed by other investigators for other purposes.

We also now intend to extend our training materials to higher and lower grade-levels and to embrace a considerably larger part of the domain of creative problem-solving. Currently we are writing new materials within the same general format which are more directly aimed at the strengthening of the child's abilities for creative understanding of complex phenomena, for inventiveness and visual imaginativeness, and for the free expression of original ideas in which the problems are themselves created by the individual.

Finally, we are undertaking a more intensive attack on the problem of modifying those attitudes which have special relevance for the encouragement and strengthening of creative drives and expressions in the individual.

Selected Readings

Anderson, Richard C. Advanced problem-solving skill at the first grade level. Can first graders learn an advanced problem-solving skill? *Journal of Educational Psychology*, 1965, **56**, 283-294.

Ausubel, D. P. A subsumption theory of meaningful verbal learning and retention. *Journal of General Psychology*, 1962, **66**, 312–324.

Ausubel, D. P. Can children learn anything that adults can—and more efficiently? *Elementary School Journal*, 1962, **2**, 270–272.

Broudy, H. S., Mastery. In Smith, B. O. and Ennis, R. O. (Eds.), *Language and Concepts in Education*. Chicago: Rand McNally, 1961, pp. 86–101.

Bruner, J. S. Learning and thinking. *Harvard Educational Review*, 1959, **29**, 184–192.

Carroll, J. B. Words, meanings, and concepts. *Harvard Educational Review*, 1964, **34** 178–202.

Christie, T. Environmental factors in creativity. *The Journal of Creative Behavior*. 1970, **4**, 13-31.

Guilford, J. P. Factors that aid and hinder creativity. *Teachers College Record*, 1962, **63**, 380–392.

Hallman, R. J. Can creativity be taught? *Educational Theory*, 1964, **14** 15–23.

Harlow, H. F., and Kuenne, Margaret. Learning to think. *Scientific American*, 1949, **181**, 36–39.

Manson, G. Classroom questions: keys to children's thinking? *Peabody Journal of Education*. 1970, **47** 302–307.

Williams, F. E. Training children to be creative may have little effect on original classroom performance. *California Journal of Educational Research*, 1966, **17**, 73–79.

CHAPTER 12

The Affective Domain

12.1 Attitude Organization in Elementary School Classrooms

Jules Henry

A teacher should be well adjusted, personally and socially, if he is to deal objectively with the needs of his pupils. Too often the teacher has such strong unmet needs of his own that he unconsciously attempts to meet them at the expense of his pupils, rather than through acceptable adult activities. As a result, he is likely to develop attitudes among his pupils that destroy defensible learning objectives and force the substitution of a compulsive desire to please the teacher. Unconscious needs in both teachers and students can force unproductive conformity.

The word *organization* in this paper is used to stand for order and determinateness as distinguished from disorder and randomness. The emotions and attitudes of prepubertal children in our culture are not, on the whole, directed toward generalized social goals, but focused rather on the peer group and parents. From the point of view of an observer who has in mind the larger social goals, like the maintenance of stable economic relations, common front against the enemy, maintenance of positive attitudes toward popular national symbols, and so

SOURCE. Jules Henry, "Attitude Organization in Elementary School Classrooms," *American Journal of Orthopsychiatry,* **XXVII**, 1 (1957), pp. 117–133. Reprinted by permission of the American Association of Orthopsychiatry.

on, the emotions and attitudes of prepubertal children in our culture may be viewed as lacking order. The adult, on the other hand, is supposed to have so organized his tendencies to respond to the environment that his emotions, attitudes, and activities subserve over-all social goals. While it is true that attitudes and feelings are bent toward social goals even from earliest infancy (1), many institutions combine to organize these attitudes and feelings so that ultimately a social steady state will be maintained. The elementary school classroom in our culture is one of the most powerful instruments in this effort, for it does not merely sustain attitudes that have been created in the home, but reinforces some, de-emphasizes others, and makes its own contribution. In this way it prepares the conditions for and contributes toward the ultimate organization of peer- and parent-directed attitudes into a dynamically interrelated attitudinal structure supportive of the culture.

This organizing process is comparable to, though not identical with, the *re*organization of attitudes and resources that takes place as a society shifts from a peacetime to a wartime footing. During a period of peace in our society, adult hostility and competitiveness may be aimed at overcoming competition in business or social mobility, while love and cooperation are directed toward family and friends, and toward achieving specific social and economic ends *within* the society. With the coming of war the instruments of government seek to direct hostility and competitiveness toward the enemy, while love and cooperation are directed toward the armed forces, civilian instruments of war (price controls, rationing, civilian officials, etc.), and national symbols. From the point of view of an observer *within the war machine,* the civilian attitudes at first seem random and unorganized. He wants to change them so that from *his point of view* they will seem organized. The situation is similar, though not identical, with respect to the child: to an observer inside the head of even some psychotic children, attitudes and behavior may seem organized. But to the observer on the outside, whose focus is on social goals, the child seems *un-* or *dis-*organized. The prime effort of the adult world is *to make child attitudes look organized to adults.* The emphasis in this paper is on the description of the process of organizing child attitudes as it can be observed in some middle-class urban American classrooms.

The Witch-Hunt Syndrome

One of the most striking characteristics of American culture since the settlement has been the phenomenon of intragroup aggression, which finds its pathological purity of expression in witch hunts (3). It comes as a frightening surprise to democratic people to find themselves suddenly in terror of their neighbors; to discover that they are surrounded by persons who carry tales about others while confessing evil of themselves; to perceive a sheeplike docility settling over those whom they considered strong and autonomous. The *witch-hunt syndrome* therefore, as constituting one of the key tragedies of democracy, is selected for the elucidation of the organization of attitudes in our culture. In this witch's brew *destructive criticism* of others is the toad's horns; *docility* the body of the worm; *feelings of vulnerability* the chicken heart; *fear of internal (intragroup) hostility* the snake's fang; *confession of evil deeds* the locust's leg; and *bordeom and emptiness* the dead man's eye. The witch-hunt syndrome is thus stated to be a dynamically interrelated system of feelings and actions made up of destructive criticism of others, docility, feelings of vulnerability, fear of internal aggression, confession of evil deeds, and boredom.

The witch-hunt syndrome in full panoply was observed in but one of the dozen classrooms in four schools studied in the research which I discuss here. Thus it seems a relatively rare phenomenon. But the question I set myself to answer is, How could it occur at all? What are the attitudes, present in the children, that were organized by this teacher into the syndrome? How could she do it? With what materials did she work? She did not create out of nothing the attitudes she manipulated in her "Vigilance Club" in this fourth-grade classroom in a middle-class American community. She had to have something to start wth. The argument of this paper will be that the feelings and tendencies to action which this teacher organized into the witch-hunt syndrome in her class are present in an *un*organized state in other classrooms. Given a certain type of teacher, he or she will be able to develop into a highly specialized, tightly integrated system in his classroom those attitudes which are present in differently organized state in the children in all classrooms. Let us now look at a meeting of the Vigilance Club.

1. In the extreme back of the room is a desk called the "isolation ward." A child has been placed there for disciplinary reasons. The Vigilance Club of the class is holding a meeting. . . . Officers are elected by the group. The purpose of the club is to teach children to be better citizens. The order of procedure is as follows: the president . . . bangs her gavel on the desk and . . . says, 'The meeting of the Vigilance Club will come to order.' Each child then takes from his or her desk a booklet whose title is *All About Me* . . . and places it on top of his desk. The vice-president calls the name of a child, gets the child's booklet, and places it on the teacher's desk. The president then calls on the child and asks, '———, have you been a good citizen this week?' The president says,

'Name some of the good things you have done,' and the child tries to recall some, like opening doors for people, running errands, etc. Next the president asks the class if it remembers any good things the child has done. Each point is written in the child's booklet by the teacher. The president then . . . says to the child, 'Name the bad things you have done. . . .' The child reports the wrongs he has committed during the week, and the class is asked to contribute information about his behavior. This too is written in the booklet by the teacher, who also reprimands the student, registers horror, scolds, etc. . . . When one child reports a misdemeanor of another the teacher asks for witnesses, and numerous children sometimes volunteer. . . . The child in the "isolation ward" reported some good deeds he had done; the children reported some more, and the isolated child was told he would soon be released. . . . [During this meeting some children showed obvious pleasure in confessing undesirable behavior. One child, by volunteering only good things of the students, seemed to be using the situation to overcome what seemed to the observer to be her unpopularity with the class.][1]"

Before analyzing this protocol for the attitudes present in it, it will be well to look at some events that occurred in this classroom on another day.

2. During the game of "spelling baseball" a child raised her hand and reported that Alice and John had been talking to each other. This occurred when neither child was 'at bat.' The teacher asked Alice if this was so, and she replied that it was, but John denied having spoken to Alice. The teacher said that John must have listened to Alice, but he denied this too. Then the teacher asked whether there had been any witnesses, and many hands were raised. Some witnesses were seated on the far side of the room, and hence could not have seen Alice and John from their location in the room. All those testifying had 'seen' Alice talking, but denied John's guilt. Alice was sent to the 'bull pen,' which meant that she had to sit on the floor behind the teacher's desk, and could no longer participate in the game. . . .

3. Mary raised her hand and said, 'It hurts me to say this. I really wish I didn't have to do it, but I saw Linda talking.' Linda was Mary's own teammate, had just spelled a word correctly, and had gone to first base. The teacher asked Linda if she had talked, and Linda said, 'No, I just drew something in the air with my finger. . . .' She was sent to the 'bull pen.'

[1] In order to prevent identification of teachers and children, the names of my student observers are not used.

In these examples we see intragroup aggression; docility of the children in conforming, with no murmur of protest, to the teacher's wishes; and confession of 'evil.' In such a situation children develop feelings of vulnerability and fear of detection. Let us now look for these phenomena in classrooms presided over by teachers who seem to represent the more normal American type, in comfortable, middle-class, white communities: teachers who are conscientious and reasonably gentle, but creatures of their culture, and humanly weak. We begin not with internal aggression as expressed in spying and talebearing, but with the milder; though closely related phenomenon of carping, destructive criticism. While this occurs throughout the sample, I give here examples only from a fifth-grade classroom in the same school system.

4. Bill has given a report on tarantulas. As usual the teacher waits for volunteers to comment on the child's report.

MIKE: The talk was well illustrated, well prepared. . . .

BOB: Bill had a piece of paper [for his notes], and teacher said he should have them on cards. . . .

Bill says he could not get any cards.

Teacher says that he should tear the paper next time if he has no cards.

BOB: He held the paper behind him. If he had had to look at it, it wouldn't have looked very nice.

5. Betty reports on Theodore Roosevelt.

A child comments that it was very good but she looked at her notices too much.

Teacher remarks that Betty had so *much* information.

BOB: She said "calvary" [instead of "calvary"].

6. Charlie reads a story he made up himself: "The Unknown Guest." One dark, dreary night . . . on a hill a house stood. This house was forbidden territory for Bill and Joe, but they were going in anyway. The door creaked, squealed, slammed. A voice warned them to go home. Spider webs, dirty furniture . . . Bill wanted to go home. They went upstairs. A stair cracked. They entered a room. A voice said they might as well stay and find out now; and their father came out. He laughed and they laughed, but they never forgot their adventure together.

TEACHER: Are there any words that give you the mood of the story? . . .

LUCY: He could have made the sentences a little better. . . .

TEACHER: Let's come back to Lucy's comment. What about his sentences?

GERT: They were too short. . . .

Charlie and Jeanne are having a discussion about the position of the word "stood."

TEACHER: Wait a minute, some people are forgetting their manners. . . .

JEFF: About the room: the boys went up the stairs and one "cracked"; then they were in the room. Did they fall through the stairs or what?

Teacher suggests Charlie make that a little clearer.

LUCY: If he feel through the step. . . .

TEACHER: We still haven't decided about the short sentences. Perhaps they make the story more spooky and mysterious.

GWYNNE: I wish he had read with more expression instead of all at one time.

RACHEL: Not enough expression.

TEACHER: Charlie, they want a little more expression from you. I guess we've given you enough suggestions for one time. (Charlie does not raise his head, which is bent over his desk as if studying a paper.) Charlie! I guess we've given you enough suggestions for one time, Charlie, haven't we? (Charlie half raises his head, seems assent grudgingly.)

The striking thing about the examples is that the teacher supports the children in their carping criticism of their fellows: Her performance in this is not, however, consistent; but even where, as in Example 6, she seems at one point to try to set herself against the tide of destruction, by calling attention to the possible artistry in Charlie's short sentences, she ends up supporting the class against him, and Charlie becomes upset. Thus the teacher, by rewarding the children's tendencies to carp, reinforces them. Teachers, however, are able to make their own contributions to this tendency. The single example given below will serve as illustration:

7. Joan reads us a poem she has written about Helen Keller . . . which concludes with the couplet:

"Helen Keller as a woman was very great;
She is really a credit to the United States."

TEACHER (amusedly): Is "states" supposed to rhyme with "great"?

When Joan murmurs that it is, the teacher says, "We'll call it poetic license."

From time to time one can see a teacher vigorously oppose tendencies in the children to tear each other to pieces. The following example is from the sixth grade:

8. The Parent-Teacher Association is sponsoring a school frolic, and the children have been asked to write jingles for the publicity. For many of the children the experience of writing a jingle seems painful. They are restless, bite their pencils, squirm around in their seats, speak to their neighbors, and from time to time pop up with questions like, "Does it

have to rhyme, Mr. Smith?" . . . At last Mr. Smith says, "All right, let's read some of the jingles now." Child after child says he "couldn't get one"; but some have succeeded. One girl has written a very long jingle, *obviously the best in the class.* However, instead of using Friday as the frolic day she used Tuesday, and several protests were heard from the children. Mr. Smith defended her. "Well, so she made a mistake. But you are too prone to criticize. If *you* could only do so well!"

It will be observed that all the examples are taken from circumstances in which the child's self-esteem is most intensely involved; where his own poetry or prose is in question, or where he has worked hard to synthesize material into a report. It is precisely at the points where the ego is most exposed that the attack is most telling. The numerous instances in the sample, where the teachers, by a word of praise or a pat on the head, play a supportive role, indicate their awareness of the vulnerability of the children. Meanwhile, as I have pointed out, the teachers often fall into the trap of triggering or supporting destructive impulses in the children.

The carping criticism of one's peers is a form of intragroup aggression, which can be quite threatening and destructive. Talebearing, however, countenanced by some teachers more than by others, can be an overwhelming threat to autonomy. While telling on others can be organized into the patrol-monitor complex (prestige through controlling and telling), useful perhaps in maintaining order in large school populations, its operation within the classroom may have serious consequences. Let us look at a couple of examples:

9. Second grade. As teacher asked the children to clear their desks one boy raised his hand, and when called on said, "Jimmy just walked by and socked me on the head."

TEACHER: Is this true?

JIMMY: He hit me first.

TEACHER: Why don't you both take seats up here (in front of the room). I'm not sure people like you belong in the second grade.

10. Sixth grade special class for bright students.

The children are working on their special nature study projects. Joseph passes where Ralph is working. Ralph (to teacher): Joseph is writing too much on his birds.

TEACHER: Joseph, you should write only a few things.

In our sample, telling on other children in the classroom is infrequent outside the class in which the Vigilance Club was formed. Destructive criticism is the preferred mode of attack in most other classrooms. The ease with which tendencies to attack peers can be organized into telling on others, however, is illustrated by the monitor-patrol complex, and by the Vigilance Club (Example 3).

Competition

Competition is an important element in the witch-hunt syndrome. Since witch hunts involve so often obtaining the attention and approval of some powerful central figure, the examples of competitiveness that I shall cite illustrate how approval and attention seeking occur as the child attempts to beat out his peers for the nod of the teacher. It would be easy to cite examples from the protocols of the merciless laughter of children at the failures or gaucheries of their classmates. I am interested, however, more in showing the all-pervading character of the phenomenon of competition, *even* in its mildest forms. The first example is from a fourth-grade music lesson:

11. The children are singing songs of Ireland and her neighbors from the book *Songs of Many Lands*. . . . Teacher plays on piano while children sing. . . . While children are singing some of them hunt in the index, find a song belonging to one of the four countries, and raise their hands before the previous song is finished in order that they may be called on to name the next song. . . .

Here singing is subordinated, in the child, to the competitive wish to have the song he has hunted up in the index chosen by the teacher. It is merely a question of who gets to the next song in the index first, gets his hand up fast, and is called on by the teacher.

The following examples also illustrate the fact that almost any situation set by the teacher can be the occasion for release of competitive impulses:

12. The observer enters the fifth-grade classroom.

TEACHER: Which one of you nice polite boys would like to take [observer's] coat and hang it up? (Observer notes: From the waving hands it would seem that all would like to claim the title.)

Teacher chooses one child . . . who takes observer's coat. . . .

TEACHER: Now children, who will tell [observer] what we have been been doing?

Usual forest of hands . . . and a girl is chosen to tell. . . .

Teacher conducted the arithmetic lesson mostly by asking, "Who would like to tell . . . the answer to the next problem?"

This question was usually followed by the appearance of a large and *agitated* forest of hands; apparently *much competition to answer.*

Thus the teacher is a powerful agent in reinforcing competition.

It has already been pointed out that carping criticism helps to settle in the child a feeling of vulnerability and threat. In this connection it is significant that *the failure of one child is repeatedly the occasion for the success of another.* I give one illustration below from the same class as the one from which I have taken Example 12.

13. Boris had trouble reducing 12/16 to lowest terms, and could get only as far as 6/8. Much excitement. Teacher asked him quietly [note how basically decent this teacher is] if that was as far as he could reduce it. She suggested he "think." Much heaving up and down from the other children, all frantic to correct him Boris pretty unhappy. Teacher, patient, quiet, ignoring others, and concentrating with look and voice on Boris. She says, "Is there a bigger number than 2 you can divide into the two parts of the fraction?" After a minute or two she becomes more urgent. No response from Boris. She then turns to the class and says, "Well, who can tell Boris what the number is?" Forest of hands. Teacher calls, Peggy. Peggy gives 4 to be divided into 12/16, numerator and denominator.

Where Boris has failed Peggy has been triumphant; *Boris's failure has made it possible for Peggy to succeed.*

This example and also Example 6 are ones in which the discomfort of the child was *visible,* and such instances may be multiplied. They illustrate how vulnerable the children feel in the presence of the attacks of the peer group in the classroom. But since these are children who face the world with serious anxiety to begin with, the classroom situation sustains it. Let us look at some stories created by these very children, and read by them to their classmates. We have already seen one, Example 6, Charlie's story of "The Unknown Guest." Here are *all* the stories read to the classmates by these children during an observation period.

14. (a) Charlotte's story: "Mistaken Identity." One day last year my family and I went to the hospital to visit somebody. When we were coming out and were walking along my father hit me. I came up behind him to hit him back, but just as I was about to do it I looked back and he was behind me! I was going to hit the wrong person!

(b) Tommy's story: "The Day Our House Was Robbed." [Observer has recorded this in the third person.] He was coming home from school one afternoon. He knew his Mom was away that afternoon. He started to go in the side door, but decided, he doesn't know why, to go round the back. He found the door open, went into the kitchen, looked into the front room where he saw a thief. Tommy "froze stiff" (chuckle of appreciation from the class), ran out, shouted, "Stop thief" as the man ran out after him. He went to a neighbor, rang the bell, called his mother at the store. The cops came, asked questions, but the man had gotten away with $99 and his mother's watch. If he had gone in the side door he would not have had a chance to see the man. Changing to the back door "may have saved my life." [Teacher's only remarks about this story were: 1) instead of having said "froze stiff," Tommy should have said, "froze stiff as something"; 2) he should have left out, the word "then" in one place; 3) he could have made the story clearer; 4) he changed from the past to the present tense.]

(c) Polly's story: "Custard the Lion." Custard the Lion was the most timid animal in Animal Town. The doctor's couldn't cure him. Then they found a new medicine. It had strange effects, but Custard wanted to try it. When he did he felt very queer. (Child gives details of queer feeling.) But he soon realized he wasn't afraid of anything. [Teacher's first remark: "You didn't let us hear the last sentence."]

(d) Dan's story: "The Boy Hero." Bill wanted to be a fireman, so he went to the firehouse. The Chief was telling him to go home when the bell clanged. While the Chief was getting into the engine, he didn't see that Bill was getting on too. (Class or teacher picks up flaw in sentence and it is reread correctly.) The Chief said O.K. as long as Bill was aboard, "But you're not to get into no mischief." (Class choruses, "Any. . . .") Everyone was out of the fire except a little girl and her doll. The firemen cannot figure out what to do, but Bill, seeing a tree near the house, climbs it over the protests of the firemen. He misses the girl on his first try, but gets her on the second. While sliding down the tree she slips and almost falls, but grabs Bill's pants and they make it to safety . . . [Children's remarks center on position of "clang, clang, clang," in the story. Teacher talks about how to use direct quotations, which, it seems, Dan had not used properly.]

(e) Bertha's story: Title not recorded. The story is about Jim who was walking home past the Smith's house one night and heard a scream. Penny Smith came out and said there was a robber in the house. When the cops came they found a parrot flying around in there, and Penny's parents told her to shut the parrot up before she read mystery stories again. [This story was followed by much carping criticism, which was terminated by the teacher's telling Bertha to change the story to suit the class.]

These stories contain elements of anxiety and even of terror. As each child finishes, the carping criticism of students and teacher then reminds him of his vulnerability. As the child sends out his cloud of fear, it returns with the leaden rain of hostility.

Docility

It comes as a somewhat shocking surprise, perhaps, to middle-class parents, to find their children described as "docile." Yet we have already seen the perfection of docility in the Vigilance Club, and we shall presently see its manifold forms in more normal classrooms.

15. First grade. The children are to act out a story called "Pig Brother," which is about an untidy boy. The teacher is telling the story. One boy said he did not like the story, so the teacher said he could leave if he did not wish to hear it again, but the boy did not leave.

16. In gym the children began to tumble, but there was much restless activity in the lines, so the teacher had all the children run around the room until they were somewhat exhausted before she continued the tumbling.

17. Second grade.
The children have been shown movies of birds. The first film ended with a picture of a baby bluebird.
TEACHER: Did the last bird ever look as if he would be blue?
The children did not seem to understand the "slant" of the question, and answered somewhat hesitantly, yes.
TEACHER: I think he looked more like a robin, didn't he?
CHILDREN, in chorus: Yes.

Item 17 is one of a large number of instances, distributed throughout all grades, in which the children exhibit their docility largely through giving the teacher what he wants. Thus in the elementary schools of the middle class the children get an intensive eight-year-long training in hunting for the right signals and giving the teacher the response wanted. The rest of the examples of docility document this assertion.

18. Fourth grade.
(a) An art lesson.
Teacher holds up a picture.
TEACHER: Isn't Bob getting a nice effect of moss and trees?
Ecstatic Ohs and Ahs from the children. . . .
The art lesson is over.
TEACHER: How many enjoyed this?
Many hands go up.
TEACHER: How many learned something?
Quite a number of hands come down.
TEACHER: How many will do better next time?
Many hands go up.

(b) Children have just finished reading the story "The Sun Moon and Stars Clock."

TEACHER: What was the highest point of interest—the climax?

The children tell what they think it is. Teacher is aiming to get from them what *she* considers the point of climax, but the children seem to give everything else but.

BOBBY: When they capture the thieves.

TEACHER: How many agree with Bobby?

Hands, hands.

19. Fifth grade.

This is a lesson on "healthy thoughts," for which the children have a special book depicting, with appropriate illustrations, specific conflictful incidents among children. The teacher is supposed to discuss each incident with the children in order to help them understand how to handle their emotions.

One of the pictures is as follows: A sibling *pair* is illustrated by *three* boys: 1) One has received a ball. 2) One is imagined to react with displeasure. 3) One is imagined to react benignly and philosophically, saying, "My brother couldn't help being given the football; we'll use it together."

TEACHER: Do you believe it's easier to deal with your thoughts if you own up to them, Betty?

BETTY: Yes it is, if you're not cross and angry.

TEACHER: Have you any experience like this in the book, Alice?

Alice tells how her brother was given a watch and she envied him and wanted one too; but her mother said she wasn't to have one until she was fifteen, but now she has one anyway.

TEACHER: How could you have helped—could you have changed your thinking? How could you have handled it? What could you do with mean feelings?

Alice seems stymied. Hems and haws.

TEACHER: What did Susie (a character in the book) do?

ALICE: She talked to her mother.

TEACHER: If you talk to someone you often then feel that "it was foolish of me to feel that way. . . ."

TOMMY: He had an experience, like that, he says. His cousin was given a bike and he envied it. But he wasn't "ugly" about it. He asked if he might ride, and his cousin let him, and then, "I got one myself; and I wasn't mean, or ugly or jealous."

Before continuing it will be well to note that since the teacher does not say Alice was wrong the children assume she was right and so copy her answer.

Two boys, the dialogue team, now come to the front of the class and dramatize the football incident.

TEACHER (to the class): Which boy do you think handled the problem in a better way?

RUPERT: Billy did, because he didn't get angry. . . . It was better to play together than to do nothing with the football.

TEACHER: That's a good answer, Rupert. Has anything similar happened to you, Joan?

Joan can think of nothing.

SYLVESTER: I had an experience. My brother got a hat with his initials on it because he belongs to a fraternity, and I wanted one like it and couldn't have one; and his was too big for me to wear, and it ended up that I asked him if he could get me some letters with my initials, and he did.

BETTY: My girl friend got a bike that was 26-inch, and mine was only 24; and I asked my sister what I should do. Then my girl friend came over and was real nice about it, and let me ride it.

Teacher approves of this, and says "Didn't it end up that they both had fun without unhappiness?"

Here we note that the teacher herself has gone astray, for on the one hand her aim is to get instances from the children in which they have been yielding, and capable of resolving their own jealousy, etc.; yet, in the instance given by Betty, it was not Betty who yielded, but her friend. The child immediately following Betty imitated her since Betty had been praised by the teacher:

MATILDE: My girl friend got a 26-inch bike and mine was only 24; but she only let me ride it once a month. But for my birthday my mother's getting me a new one, probably (proudly) at 28. (Many children rush in with the information that 28 doesn't exist.) Matilde replies that she'll probably have to raise the seat then, for she's too big for a 26.

As we go on with this lesson, we shall continue to see how the children's need for substitute gratification and their inability to accept frustration are the real issues, which even prevent them from getting the teacher's point. We shall see how, in spite of the teacher's driving insistence on her point, the children continue to inject their conflicts into the lesson, while at the same time they gropingly try to find a way to gratify the teacher. *They* cannot give the "right" answers because of their conflicts; teacher cannot handle their conflicts, even perceive them, because *her* underlying need is to be gratified by the children! The lesson goes on:

TEACHER: I notice that some of you are only happy when you get your own way. You're not thinking this through, and I want you to. Think of an experience when you didn't get what you want. Think it through.

CHARLIE: His ma was going to the movies and he wanted to go with her, and she wouldn't let him; and she went off to the movies, and he was mad; but then he went outside and there were some kids playing baseball, so he played baseball.

TEACHER: But suppose you hadn't gotten to play baseball? You would have felt hurt, because you didn't get what you wanted. We can't help feeling hurt when we are disappointed. What could you have done; how could you have handled it?

CHARLIE: So I can't go to the movies, so I can't play baseball, so I'll do something around the house.

TEACHER: Now you're beginning to think! It takes courage to take disappointments. (Turning to the class) What did we learn? The helpful way . . .

CLASS: is the healthy way!

Before entering the final section of this paper, we need to ask: Why are these children, whose fantasies contain so many hostile elements, so docile in the classroom; and why do they struggle so hard to gratify the teacher and try in so many ways to bring themselves to her attention (the "forest of hands")? We might, of course, start with the idea of the teacher as a parent figure, and the children as siblings competing for the teacher's favor. We could refer to the unresolved dependency needs of children of this age, which make them seek support in the teacher, who manipulates this seeking and their sibling rivalry to pit the children against each other. Other important factors, however, that are inherent in the classroom situation itself, and particularly in middle-class classrooms, ought to be taken into consideration. We have observed the children's tendency to destructively criticize each other, and the teachers' often unwitting repeated reinforcement of this tendency. We have taken note of the anxiety in the children as illustrated by the stories they tell, and observed that these very stories are subjected to a carping criticism, whose ultimate consequence would be anything but alleviation of that anxiety. Hence the classroom is a place in which the child's underlying anxiety may be heightened. In an effort to alleviate this he seeks the approval of the teacher, by giving right answers and by doing what teacher wants him to do under most circumstances. Finally, we cannot omit the teacher's need to be gratified by the attention-hungry behavior of the children.

A word is necessary about these classrooms as middle class. The novel *Blackboard Jungle* (2) describes schoolroom behavior lower-class children. There we see the children *against the teacher,* as representative of the middle class. But in the classes I have described we see the *children against each other,* with the teacher abetting the process. Thus, as the teacher in the middle-class schools directs the hostility of the children toward one another and away from himself, he reinforces the competitive dynamics within the middle class itself. The teacher in lower-class schools, on the other hand, appears to become the organizing stimulus for behavior that integrates the lower class, as the children unite in expressing their hostility to the teacher.

Confession

The Vigilance Club would have been impossible without confession, and the children's pleasure in confession. But, as with the other parts of the syndrome, confessing occurs in other classrooms also; it can be elicited when the proper conditions are present, and the children can be seen to enjoy it—to vie with one another in confessing. Let us follow the lesson on "healthy thoughts" a little further. We will see how confession occurs as the children seek to give teacher *precisely* what she wants.

20. Teacher asks if anyone else has had experiences like that [of two children who have just recited], where they were mean and angry.

DICK: He has a friend he plays baseball with, and sometimes they fight; but they get together again in a few minutes and apologize.

In this first example we note one of the important aspects of the confession element in the syndrome: the culprit must have given up his evil ways, and now be free of impurities.

In response to Dick's story, teacher says: You handled it just right. Now let's hear about someone who had a similar experience and didn't handle it just right.

TOM: His little brother asked for the loan of his knife, but it was lost, and he got angry with his little brother for asking. [This knife story follows a sequence of several stories about knives told by other children. The exuberance of knife stories following immediately on the teacher's approval of the first one suggests that some of them are made to order and served up piping hot for teacher's gratification.]

TEACHER: Now Tom, could you have worked it out any differently? (Observer notes that Tom seems to enjoy this confession; certainly he is not abashed or ashamed.)

TOM: Later he asked me if he could help me find it. He found it in a wastebasket, and then I let him borrow it.

HARRY: Sometimes I get angry when my friends are waiting for me and . . . (observer missed some of this) and my little sister asked if she could borrow my auto-racing set, and I hit her once or twice. (Class laughs.)

Here we see another factor so important to the flourishing of the syndrome: the audience gets pleasure through the confessor's telling about deeds the audience wishes to commit: who among Harry's listeners would not like to have hit his sister, or anyone, "once or twice"?

The teacher then goes on: What would you do now—would you hit her?

HARRY: Now I'd probably get mad at first, but let her have it later.

Thus Harry has mended his ways—in teacher-directed fantasy at least—and returned to the fold.

So far we have had confession of mean and angry thoughts and violence. We shall now see confession to unacceptable fear. In all cases the teacher says what type of confession she wishes to hear, and what the resolution should be of the unacceptable behavior; and the children vie with one another to tell commensurable tales, as they derive pleasure from the total situation—through approval of the teacher, expression of their own real or fantasied deviations, and the delight of their peers. In these situations the pleasure of the peer group is seen to derive not so much from the "happy ending" the children give their stories but rather from the content of the story itself. It is interesting that no carping criticism appears; rather the entire situation is a jolly one. It seems that within unspoken limits the children permit one another to boast of "evil" behavior because of the deep pleasure obtained from hearing it. Thus impulse expression becomes a device for role maintenance in the classroom.

The lesson proceeds:

Two children enact a little skit in which they have to go to the principal to ask him something. One of them is afraid of the principal, the other is not. The moral is that the principal is the children's friend, and that one should not be shy.

GERTRUDE: Well, anyway, the principal isn't a lion, he's your friend; he's not going to kill you.

TEACHER: That's right, the principal is a friend, he says hello and good morning to you. . . . Have you ever felt shy?

MERIAM: The first year I sold Girl Scout cookies I didn't know how to approach people; and the first house I went to I didn't know the lady; and I stuttered and stammered, and didn't sell any cookies. By the second house I had thought it all out before I rang the bell, and I sold two boxes. (Triumphantly.)

TEACHER: It helps to have self-confidence.

Ben now tells a story, with a happy ending, of being afraid of a principal. Then Paul tells a story, amid gales of laughter, about his being scared on a roller coaster. By this time there is so much excitement among the children that the teacher says: Wait a minute—manners!

JOHN: He was scared to go on the Whip-the-Wind (scornful laughter from the class); but after he went he liked it so much that he went eight times in a row. (This is well received.)

Many hands go up. Teacher waits. . . .

MICHAEL: He was at Pleasure Park on the ferris wheel (scornful Aw from the class) and a girl kept rocking it, and I started to get green (roar of laughter).

TEACHER: Now we'll have to stop.

Certain phenomena not emphasized before appear in this section. Confession is used by the authoritative figure, the teacher, to strengthen attachment to significant but potentially terrifying figures like school principals, and to polish up cultural shibboleths like "self-confidence." For the child storytellers confession becomes an opportunity for bathing in the emotional currents of the peer group, as the child stimulates the group's approval through presentation of group standards, and awakens group pleasure as the peer group responds to its own anxiety about weakness, and experiences resolution of the anxiety through the happy ending. With a perfect instinct for what is right, each child provides catharsis for his peers. By presenting himself as weak, he enables his peers to identify with him; and then, as he overcomes his weakness, he enables his companions too to feel strong.

What this lesson on healthy thoughts may have accomplished by way of creating a permanent reservoir of "healthy thoughts" is difficult to say, but that it helped create solidarity among the students, and between them and the teacher is clear from the fact that when she suddenly shifted ground to say, "Do you think you are wide enough awake for a contest in subtraction of fractions?" the children responded with a unanimous roar of "Yes," as if she had asked them whether they were ready for cookies and ice cream!

Thus in this lesson, in which all have participated more with their *unconscious* than with their conscious emotions, solidarity has been achieved. Teacher thought she was teaching the children to have healthy thoughts, but she was showing them how to gratify her. The children sensed this and struggled to gratify her, while they sought acceptance by their peers also. The essential difference between this teacher and the one who perpetrated the Vigilance Club is that though the latter tended to demolish solidarity among the children while placing the teacher in supreme command, the lesson on healthy thoughts tended to a dubious solidarity among all. *Both teachers organize some of the same elements in the children, but into different configurations, of total feeling and behavior.*

Boredom

It seems unnecessary to document the fact that children become bored in class, for much of modern thinking and curriculum arrangement is aimed at eliminating it. The shifts at 15-minute intervals from one subject to the next in the elementary school classrooms is one example of this effort. Boredom, which means emotional and intellectual separation from the environment, is an insupportable agony, particularly if the emotional vacuum created by such separation is not filled by gratifying fantasies, or if it is filled by terrifying ones. To fill this vacuum people in our culture will throw themselves into a great variety of even relatively ungratifying activities. Since in this situation, bored children attack almost any novel classroom activity with initial vigor, the witch-hunt syndrome or any modification thereof helps to overcome boredom: better to hunt than be bored. In a full and satisfying life there is no place for witch hunts. The school system that can provide a rich program for children has no need of Vigilance Clubs, nor even of lessons on "healthy thoughts."

Discussion and Conclusions

In this paper I have used suggestions from communications theory in an effort to order the data obtained from direct observation of elementary school classrooms. Information, the central concept of communications theory, refers to measurable differences in states of organization. In human behavior, as seen in the classroom under discussion, we observe *qualitative shifts in state,* for *different teachers organize the same underlying emotional characteristics of the children to achieve different organizations of the emotions.* One teacher so organizes the children's emotions as to accomplish an intensification of the fear of intragroup aggression, while she turns the children's hostility toward one another.

A different teacher may organize the emotions of the children so that a euphoria in which students and teacher are bathed in a wave of emotional gratification is achieved. The great skill in being a teacher would seem to be, therefore, a *learned* capacity to keep shifting states of order intelligently as the work demands. This does not mean the traditional classroom order, where you can hear a pin drop, but rather the kind of order in which the *emotions of the children are caught up and organized toward the achievement of a specific goal.* It is not necessary, perhaps, that even the most prominent emotions of the children, like competitiveness, for example, form part of the organized whole. Yet, on the other hand, it is difficult to see how, in the present state of our culture, competitiveness can be overlooked. It would seem, perhaps, that the important outcome to avoid is that the competitiveness should become destructive of peers, while reinforcing dependence on the teacher.

The phenomenon I have labeled "docility" occurs because of the absolute dependence for survival of the children on the teacher. That is to say success in school depends absolutely on the teacher, and self-respect, as a function of the opinion of others, in the home or among peers, is in part a function of success or failure in school. In these circumstances the child's capacity to respond automatically to the signals he gets from the teacher is bound to acquire somewhat the appearance of instinctive behavior. Although it occurs at a much higher level of integration than instinct, the child hunts for the proper signals from the teacher, and the child's responses take on instinctual quality. They *must;* otherwise, like the nestling who does not open its mouth when the mother arrives with a worm, he will never eat the ambrosia of teacher's approval, so necessary to his survival. In this situation both children and teacher easily become the instruments of their own unconscious processes, as they, like Joseph and his brethren, fall on each other's necks in a shared ecstasy of exuberant dependence. Teacher and pupil will have gratified each other, but it remains an open question whether the children will have learned what the curriculum committee planned.

We see in the organization of the components of the witch-hunt syndrome an important phase in the formation of American national character, for tendencies to docility, competitiveness, confession, intragroup aggression, and feelings of vulnerability the children may bring with them to school, are reinforced in the classroom. This means that independence and courage to challenge are observably played *down* in these classrooms. It means, on the other hand, that tendencies to own up rather than to conceal are reinforced—a development which, in proper hands, might become a useful educational instrument. It means, further, that while many teachers do stress helping others they may inadvertently develop in the children the precise opposite, and thus undermine children's feelings of security. One could come from a very secure and accepting family and yet have one's feelings of security and acceptance threatened in these classrooms. On the other hand, what seems most in evidence from the stories they make up is that the children come to school with feelings of vulnerability which are intensified in the classroom.

Meanwhile we should try to understand that all the teachers in the sample were probably trying to be good teachers,[2] and all the children were trying to be good pupils. Their unconscious needs, however, naturally dominated their behavior. The teacher who organized the Vigilance Club probably thought she was teaching her children to be upright and honest, and to perform good deeds, but her unconscious tendencies caused these worthy inclinations to seek the wrong expression. All teachers need conformity in the classroom in order that the children shall absorb a respectable amount of academic knowledge. But the teacher's (often unconscious) need for acceptance by the children, and her fear (sometimes unconscious) of her inability to control free discussion, compel her to push the children into uncritical docility at times, while they seek her approval.

The creation of stories, and their discussion by the class, are accepted principles of progressive education. But the teacher's own (at times unconscious) need to carp and criticize gets in the way of her adequately developing the creative and supportive possibilities in her charges. Thus these are not "bad," or "stupid" teachers, but human beings, who express in their classroom behavior the very weaknesses parents display in their dealings with their children. The solution to the problem of the contradiction between the requirements of a democratic education on the one hand, and the teachers' unconscious needs on the other, is not to carp at teachers, and thus repeat the schoolroom process, but to give them some insight into how they project their personal problems into the classroom situation.

References

1. Henry, Jules, and Joan Whitehorn Boggs. *Child Rearing, Culture, and the Natural World.* Psychiatry, **15**: 261–271, 1952.
2. Hunter, Evan. *The Blackboard Fungle.* Simon and Schuster, New York, 1954.
3. Starkey, Marion L. *The Devil in Massachusetts.* Knopf, New York, 1949.

[2] I am indebted to B. Bettleheim for this suggestion.

12.2 Values and Attitudes of Teenagers

James S. Coleman

What happens to academic achievement when boys value such roles as "Nationally famous Athlete" and "Jet Pilot" while girls aspire to be "popular" and to become "models"? The discrepancy between school and student values is real and presents a barrier that must be surmounted if the school is to do its job effectively. Coleman believes that it is possible to eliminate or lessen this conflict. He provides us with several ideas for doing so.

Because adolescents live so much in a world of their own, which they do not share with older people, adults remain uninformed about the way teenagers spend their time, the things that are important to them, and the things that friends have in common. Several questions which were asked in the study give a picture of their patterns of activities and interests.[1] One question asked of the boys was:

SOURCE. James S. Coleman, "Social Climates in High School." In *Cooperative Research Monography No. 4,* Office of Education, U. S. Dept. of Health, Education, and Welfare, pp. 10–34. Reprinted by permission of the author.

[1] A more complete report is given in *The Adolescent Society,* to be published by The Free Press (Glencoe, Illinois) 1961.

"If you could be any of these things you wanted, which would you want to be?"

The replies were (figures represent percent; No-answers were excluded):

Boys most wanting to be:	Fall (N = 3,892)	Spring (N = 3,746)
Jet pilot	31.6	31.3
Nationally famous athlete	37.3	36.9
Missionary	5.7	5.9
Atomic scientist	25.6	25.9

These results strikingly show the way in which the adolescent culture departs from the educational norm. The nationally famous athlete leads, the atomic scientist is a poor third after the jet pilot, and the missionary is almost neglected. The shifts over the period of the school year are little, if any. The result of course differs from school to school, but it is important to note that in *every school* the nationally famous athlete and the jet pilot were first and second in popularity. These adolescent attitudes seem to reflect the dominant mass-media themes and heroes far more than the heroes their teachers and parents would have them follow. It may be that the most impressive contracts adolescents have with the adult culture are through the distorted lens of the mass media and its "newsworthy" events, just as the most impressive contacts many adults have with adolescents are through the mass media, with their focus upon newsworthy behavior.

In response to the same question, with the following alternatives, the girls responses are slightly more in line with traditional values of service (figures represent percent):

Girls most wanting to be:	Fall (N = 4,057)	Spring (N = 3,922)
Actress or artist	18.4	19.8
Nurse	29.2	26.0
Model	32.0	33.5
Schoolteacher	20.6	20.6

Yet the glamorous model was first in popularity and schoolteachers third, with the nurse between. And over the period of the academic year, there was a slight *increase* for the glamorous model and "actresses or artist," while the nurse *decreased* and the teacher remained constant. In Chapter IV a variation in these changes in Elmtown gives some insight into the processes by which these images, somewhat counter to educational ideals, develop.

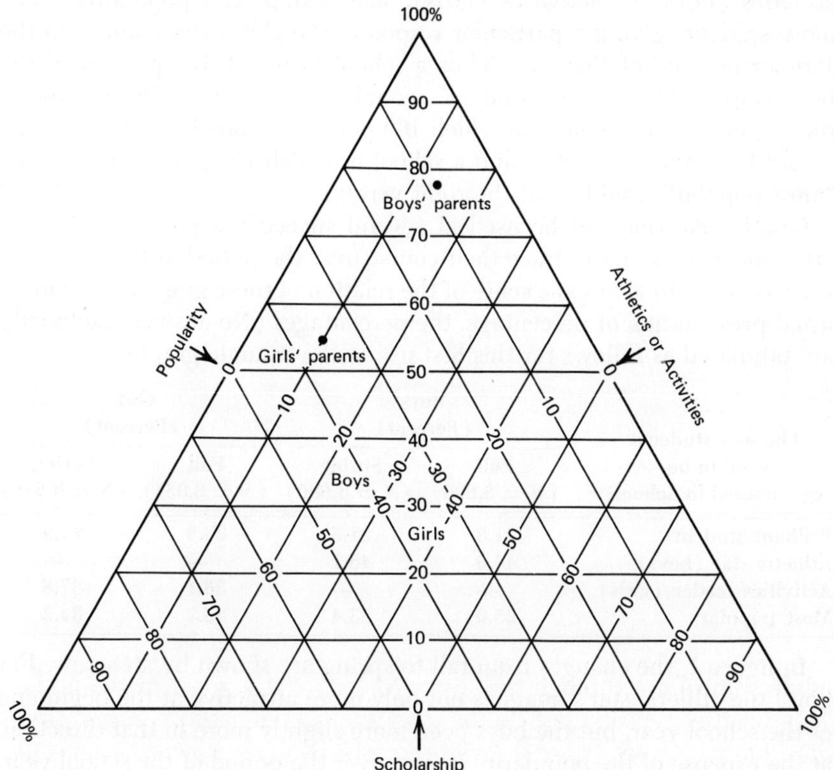

FIGURE 1. How boys and girls would like to be remembered at school, and how their parents would like them to be remembered: Relative importance of scholarship, popularity, and (for boys) athletics or (for girls) activities.

Another attitude question focused more sharply on the values current in the schools themselves. It asked a boy or girl how he or she would like most to be *remembered* in school, a matter which presumably reflects in part his own interests and in part the things that are important to his fellows. The question was:

If you could be remembered here at school for one of the three things below, which one would you want it to be?

BOYS:	Brilliant student Athletic star Most popular	GIRLS:	Brilliant student Leader in activities Most popular

The responses for the fall and spring questionnaries are shown in figure 1, for both boys and girls. The three axes of the triangle indicate athletics (boys) or activities (girls), scholarship, and popularity.[2] The more students giving a particular response, the closer the point is to the 100-percent end of that axis. Thus a school in which 100 percent of the boys responded "brilliant student" would be represented by a point at the upper vertex, a school in which 100 percent responded "athletic star" would be at the left vertex, and a school in which 100 percent responded "most popular" would be at the right vertex.

Graphs like this will be used at several succeeding points to "locate" different schools and to trace their course over the period of the academic year. In order to give some sense of the relation of these graphs to the more usual presentation of percentage, the percentages (No-answers excluded) are tabulated as follows for this first use of the triangle graphs.

The way students want to be remembered in School:	Boys (Percent)		Girls (Percent)	
	Fall (N = 3,696)	Spring (N = 3,690)	Fall (N = 3,955)	Spring (N = 3,876)
Brilliant student	31.3	31.5	28.8	27.9
Athletic star (boys)	43.6	45.1	—	—
Activities leader (girls)	—	—	36.1	37.8
Most popular	25.0	23.4	35.2	34.2

In figure 1, the changes from fall to spring are shown by an arrow. For boys, the athletic star's image is not only more attractive at the beginning of the school year, but the boys even more slightly more in that direction, at the expense of the popularity image, over the period of the school year. The girls are somewhat similar: at the beginning of the school year, the "activities leader" and "most popular" are about equally attractive images, both more popular than the brilliant student. By spring, the activities-leader image has gained slightly in attractiveness, at the expense of both the brilliant student and the most popular. These shifts are quite small, and there are differences from school to school, as later chapters will indicate. Nevertheless, the point is clear: the image of athletic star is most attractive for boys and the image of "activities leader" and "most popular" are more attractive to girls than "brilliant student."

Athletics and Activities

The importance of athletics in these cultures is striking, particularly when we realize that the school as an institution is designed to focus attention on studies, and presumably upon the brilliant student.

[2] The author wishes to thank James Davis and Jacob Feldman of the National Opinion Research Center at the University of Chicago for suggesting the use of the triangular graphs for trichotomous items.

A further view, which gives some suggestion as to why the brilliant student image is not popular, is given by a parallel question—not how would they like to be remembered, but whom would they like to *date*:

Suppose you had a chance to go out with either a cheerleader or a girl who is the best student in class, or the best looking girl in class. Which one would you rather go out with?

Cheerleader
Best student
Best looking

Suppose you had a chance to go out with either a star athlete, or a boy who is the best student in class, or the best looking boy in class. Which one would you rather go out with?

Star athlete
Best student
Best looking

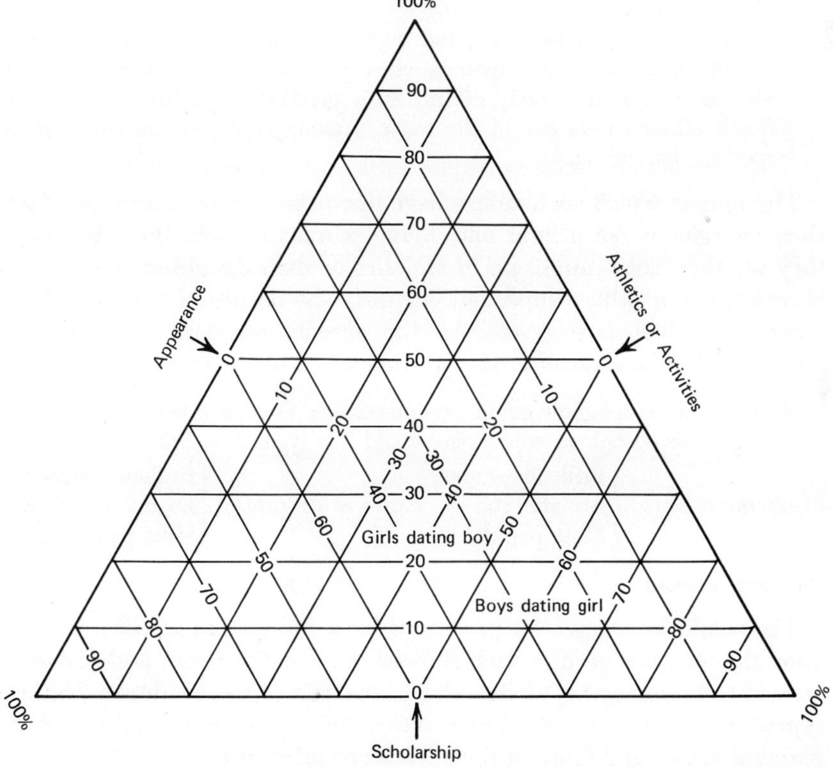

FIGURE 2. Boys' and girls' choice for a date: Relative importance of scholarship (best student), appearance (best looking), and athletics (star athlete) or activities (cheerleader).

The responses of the boys and of the girls were as indicated in figure 2. Perhaps the most striking result shown in the graph is the fact that the brilliant girl student fares so poorly as to a date for boys. Less striking, but still evident, is the poor showing of the image of brilliant boy student" as a date for girls. For both boys and girls, the movement over the school year is *away* from the brilliant student as someone to date. The best looking boy or girl gains at the expense of the best student, both for the boys and for the girls.

These values held by the adolescent community are fairly well known, at least by the adults who are in contact with teenagers. They sometimes manifest themselves strikingly, as in the following query taken from an adolescent advice column in a church magazine:

> QUESTION: If a boy isn't an athlete he isn't anything. I've been dating a girl. Last night she stood me up and went out with a footbal player. I get good grades and I have brains. That athlete is dumb. Why should he rate higher than I do?—A. G.
>
> ANSWER: Probably it isn't fair, but in high school athletes usually outrate nonathletes. Is there any sport in which you could excel? Or might you be elected to a student-body office? After graduation you'll find the really dumb athletes fade out of the scene. Among adults brains are more respected than brawn.[3]

The impact which such values have upon the way boys and girls focus their energies is not a light one. Many parents deplore these effects, as they see their sons caught up in athletics or their daughters pining to be cheerleaders or other "important" figures. The desires of these children's parents for them is suggested by the parents' responses to a question similar to the "be remembered" question asked of the students:

If your son or daughter could be outstanding in high school in one of the three things listed below, which one would you want it to be?

PARENTS OF BOYS:	Brilliant student Athletic star Most popular	PARENTS OF GIRLS:	Brilliant student Leader in activities Most popular

Parental Values

The results are shown for parents of boys and girls in figure 1, imposed upon the previous graph which showed the way their sons and daughters wanted to be remembered. The sharp constrast of these values with those expressed by the students throws into relief again the divergence of the parental values and those of the adolescent subculture.

To be sure, these values may not be the ones they express day by day

[3] *Together*, the Methodist Church Magazine, Feb. 1959, p. 45.

to their children. Indeed, the disparity between professed parental values on one hand, and the values they express in their actions, on the other, may be very great. Replies to a set of questions asked of boys and girls suggest such a discrepancy.

Bill (Ann) was doing well in biology class, because he (she) had a hobby of collecting and identifying insects. One day his (her) biology instructor asked Bill (Ann) if he (she) would act as the assistant in the class. If something like this happened to you, would it be something that would make your parents proud of you, or wouldn't they care?

	Percent of boys (N = 3,831)	Percent of girls (N = 3,956)
Both would be very proud of me	60.2	63.5
They might feel a little proud Mother would be proud, father wouldn't care Father would be proud, mother wouldn't care	31.6	30.9
They wouldn't care	5.3	4.6
No answer	2.9	1.1

What if a different situation occurred—you made the basketball team (became a cheerleader), much to your surprise. Would that make your parents proud of you, or wouldn't they care?

	Percent of boys (N = 3,831)	Percent of girls (N = 3,956)
Both would be very proud of me	68.2	77.0
They might feel a little proud Mother would be proud, father wouldn't care Father would be proud, mother wouldn't care	23.8	18.9
They wouldn't care	5.6	3.4
No answer	2.5	0.8

According to the boys' responses, their parents would be considerably more proud of them for making the basketball team than for being chosen biology assistant. The girls' responses indicate even more strongly that their parents would be prouder of them for becoming a cheerleader than for being chosen biology assistant.

These responses are at great variance with those the parents themselves gave, for the overwhelming majority of parents said they wanted their son to be a brilliant student in school, and a smaller majority, but still a majority, of parents said they wanted their danghters to be outstanding as a brilliant student.

Why this discrepancy? Is someone not being honest? Are the parents' professed values and expressed values as greatly at variance as they seem —or do boys and girls see their parents' values as they want to see them?

Perhaps neither is the case. It may be that most parents hold academic achievement as an ideal for their children in school, just as they expressed in their questionnaire, and as shown in figure 1; but parents also want their children to be successful in the things that "count" in the school, that is, the things that count in the eyes of other adolescents. And parents know what things count. Being a biology assistant counts far less in the adolscent culture than does making the basketball team for boys, or making the cheerleading squad for girls. Thus in this peculiar fashion, even the rewards a child gains from his parents may help reinforce the values of the adolescent culture—not because his parents hold those same values, but because parents want to see their children successful and looked up to by the other children at school.

The Importance of Cars

Cars are important to a teenager. Without a car, a boy must be chauffered to movies, sports events, and, most embarrassing of all, to dates. Just as cars have become more important for adults, they have become more important for their adolescent children—as the parents of adolescent children will quickly attest. Consquently, as he reaches the age when he can possess a driver's license (16 in most States, including Illinois, in which all these schools are located), a boy's pressure on parents for permission to have a car of his own becomes extremely great. Parents find it hard not to give in, at least by letting him buy a car if he can pay for it. The great jump in car owning in the sophomore and junior years is shown in figure 3, which shows in the fall (just after school had started) and in the spring, at the end of the school year, how car owning changes from the freshman to the senior years.

The increasing importance of cars is in part due to changes in the ecology of our lives with the blossoming of the surburbs. Boys who would have lived in the city, where a car is important for transportation, now live in the suburbs, where it is important. A comparison of increase in car ownership from freshmen to seniors in St. John's High, in the center of Chicago, with Newlawn, in a suburb, shows this well (fig. 3). These two schools contain boys with almost identical family backgrounds (first and second generation East European immigrants, working class, predominately Catholic); yet the car ownership increases sharply over the 4 years in Newlawn, and remains at a low level among the boys of St. John's High.

As seen in the following tabulation, there is a far greater prevalence of cars among teenagers in small town and country schools than in city or

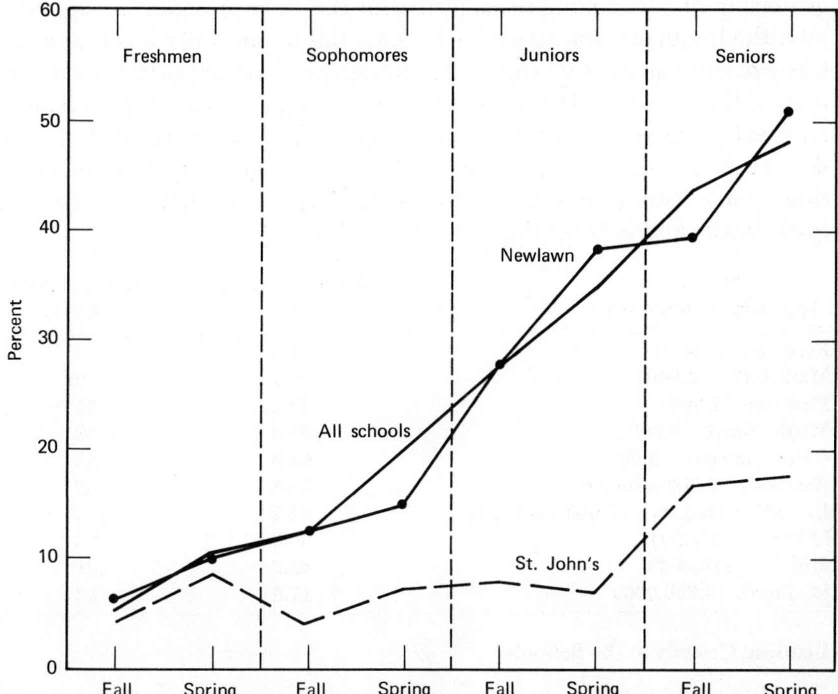

FIGURE 3. Percent of high school boys owning cars in Newlawn, St. John's, and all 10 schools of the study.

surburban schools in this study[4] When asked if most of the boys in the senior class had cars, one boy from the smallest school, Farmdale, replied that they did because many of them lived in the country, where it was a matter of necessity.

This is certainly true if they must have independence. However, necessity is not the whole answer; even the nonfarmers' sons in the small towns more often have a car than do their city and suburban counterparts, and the school buses run for the farmers' sons, who ride them in earlier grades. In small towns, a car is evidently more a part of the adolescent culture than it is in suburbs and cities. Yet in all the schools except St. John's High, in the center of the city, many of the students own cars by the end of their senior year.

The general level of economic prosperity accounts in part for the high

[4] Although schools are examined separately in a few places in this chapter, most of the differences between schools are not discussed in detail. They are examined in the full report, and thumbnail sketches of each are given.

ownership of cars among teenageers. But this only provides the opportunity; the frequency and speed with which this opportunity is seized when a boy or girl comes of driving age indicates just how important a car is to most of the teenagers. If a boy has a car or a friend with a car, then there is no great problem in dating and in going to the local hangout; but if he doesn't, he is still a child, for he is able to date a girl only with difficulty, since public transportation is poor or nonexistent in most surburbs and small towns and is becoming poorer in cities.

School (Approximate town size)	Percent owning a car	Number of boys (seniors)
Farmdale (1,000)	81.3	16
Marketville (4,000)	56.4	39
Elmtown (7,000)	42.2	45
Maple Grove (6,000)	68.4	38
Green Junction (5,000)	63.8	58
Newlawn (9,000—suburb)	50.8	59
Executive Heights (17,000—suburb)	42.2	154
Millburg (25,000)	36.6	93
Midcity (110,000)	46.2	221
St. John's (3,600,000)	17.5	102

Leading Crowds in the Schools

Just what does it take to "rate" in these schools, with one's own sex, and with the other sex? What does it take to be in the "leading crowd" in school? This question, of course, presumes something to which some might object: that there *is* a leading crowd in the school. And, to be sure, when students were asked such a question, some, particularly in the smallest school, did object to the idea that there was a leading crowd. Yet this kind of objection is in large part answered by one of the boys in another small school, Maple Grove, in a group interview, when his friend denied that there was any leading crowd at all in the school, and he responded: "You don't see it because you're in it." Another boy in the same school had this to say in an interview:

Q. What are some of the groups in school?
A. You mean like cliques? Well, there's about two cliques. There's one that's these girls and boys—let's see, there's ——— ——— ———. I'm in it, but as far as I'm concerned, I'm not crazy about being in it. I tell you, it wasn't any of my doing, because I'm not always for the underdog myself. But I'd rather be with a bunch like that, you know, than have them against me. So I just go along with them.
Q. What's the other clique?
A. Well, I don't know too much about it, it's just another clique.

Q. Kind of an underdog clique?
A. Sort of.
Q. Who are some of the kids in it?
A. Oh—I couldn't tell you. I know, but I just can't think of their names.
Q. How do you get in the top clique?
A. Well, I'll tell you, like when I came over here, I had played football over at ———. I was pretty well known by all the kids before I came over. And when I came there was ——— always picking on kids. He hit this little kid one day, and I told him that if I ever saw him do anything to another little kid that I'd bust him. So one day down in the locker room he slammed this kid against the locker, so I went over and hit him a couple of times, knocked him down. And a lot of the kids liked me for doing that, and I got on the good side of two or three teachers.
Q. What are the differences between these two cliques?
A. Well, I'll tell you, I don't like this top clique, myself. Just to be honest with you, they're all scared of me, because I won't take anything off of them, and they know it. I've had a run-in with this one girl, she really thinks she's big stuff. And I don't like her at all, we don't get along, and she knows it and I know it, and they don't say nothing. But a lot of them in the big clique, they're friends. I get along with them real good, and then I try to be real nice to the underdogs, the kids that haven't got—not quite as lucky—they haven't got as much money. They have a hard time; maybe they don't look as sharp as some of the others.
Q. What are the main interests of the top clique?
A. Just to run everything, to be the big deal.
Q. Are most of the boys in athletics?
A. Yeah—you couldn't really say that in this town, though. The really good athlete, a couple of them may be in the clique—the clique's a funny thing, it's just who they want to be in it. They don't want to have anybody in there they think might give them trouble. They want to rule the roost.
Q. Do most of them have fathers that have good jobs, are they well-to-do?
A. Most of them. They come from families that have money.
Q. Would this be the main thing that divides the top clique from the others?
A. Could be, very easily, it sure could.
Q. What does this underdog clique have in common?
A. Well, you might say they just stick together, for self-protection. And they do things together.
Q. And there are both boys and girls in the cliques?
A. Yeah.

Q. And they all go around together?
A. Um-hum.
Q. In a party, would——
A. Now there you go. The big-deal clique, that's all that's there. None of the underdogs are there at all. They won't invite————I've got some graduation pictures here now, and we can get some names from that. Now she's not in the clique.
Q. What's her name?
A. Now this girl here, she's Joyce. She's real sweet, not very sharp-looking or nothing, and I sat by her in home room. And I talked with her and stuff like that, and she really—I mean, I think she thinks a lot of me. And this is a girl who sort of sticks to herself, more or less. She's a very nice girl, but I don't think she's in the clique. And she's not in the clique and neither is———.
Q. And they aren't in the other clique either?
A. No. Well, yeah, they're probably—I'll tell you, some of them—see, the big clique rules the roost, and this underdog clique, you might say, is just there to give the other one a little competition, just to know there is another one. And a lot of them are not in it. I was automatically put in it, you might say. I didn't ask to be in it or nothing.

This account of the leading crowd in one school gives a vivid picture of how such crowds function. This is not to say of course, that the leading crowd in every school functions in just the same way. Most interviews in other schools suggested somewhat less closed circle than in this school, yet one which is not greatly different.

In every school, most students saw a leading crowd, and were willing to say what it took to get in it. This should not be surprising, for every adult community has its leading crowd, though adults are less often in such close and compelling communities. Yet laymen and educators as well are often blind to the fact that the teenagers in high school *do* constitute a community, one which *does* have a leading crowd. Consequently adult concern tends to be with questions of better ways to teach "the child" viewed as an isolated entity—whether it is the "gifted child" or the "backward child."

How to Get In

In order to see more systematically what it takes to be in the leading crowd, every student was asked in the questionnaire:

What does it take to get into the leading crowd in this school?

The major categories of response to this question about the leading crowd are shown in figure 4. Consider first the girls' responses. Most

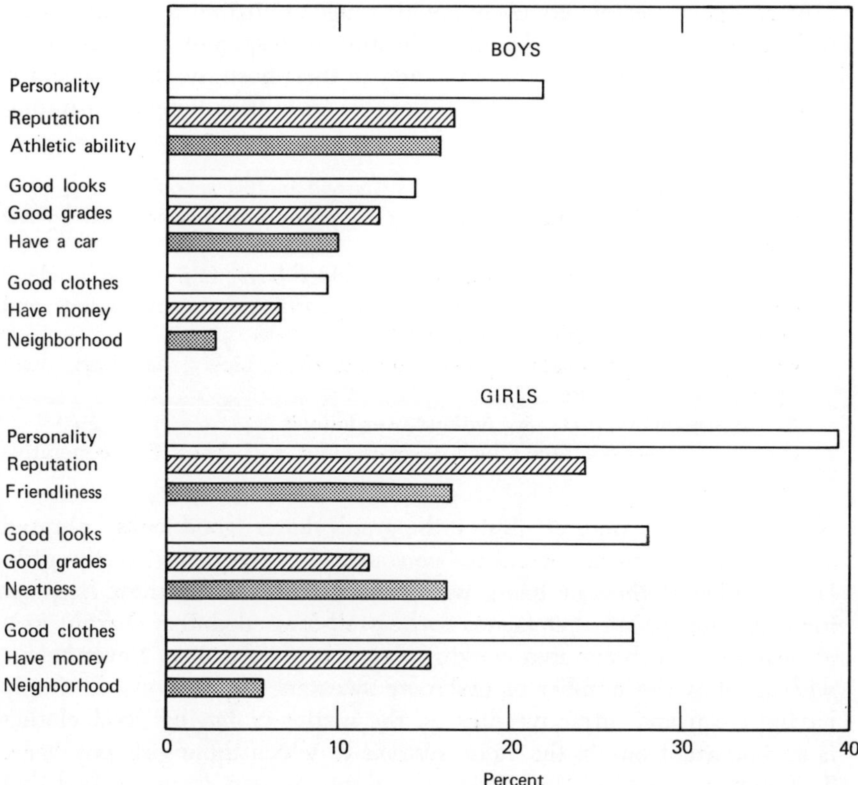

FIGURE 4. Major criteria for membership in the leading crowds of 9 schools of the study: Percent of boys and girls mentioning each.

striking is the great importance of "having a good personality." Not only is this mentioned most often in the overall study, but it is mentioned most often in seven of the nine schools.

The importance of having good personality, or, what is a little different, "being friendly" or "being nice to the other kids," in these adolescent cultures is something which adults often fail to realize. Adults often forget how person-oriented children are: they have not yet moved into the world of cold impersonality in which many adults live. This is probably due to the limits on their range of contacts; for in the limited world of grade school, a boy or girl *can* respond to his classmates as persons, with a sincerity which becomes impossible as one's range of contacts grows. One of the transitions for some children comes, in fact, as they enter high school and find that they move from classroom to classroom and have different classmates in each class.

After a good personality come a wide range of attributes and activities. A flavor of this indicated by the collection of responses listed below—some hostile to the leading crowd (and in their hostility, often seeing it as immoral), others friendly to it (and in their friendliness attributing positive virtues to it).

What does it take to get into the leading crowd in this school?

"Wear just the right things, nice hair, good grooming and have a wholesome personality."

"Money, clothes, flashy appearance, date older boys, fairly good grades."

"Be a sex fiend–dress real sharp–have own car and money—smoke and drink—go steady with a popular boy."

"Have pleasant personality, good manners, dress nicely, be clean, don't swear, be loads of fun."

"A nice personality, dress nice without overdoing it."

"Hang out at ——'s. Don't be too smart. Flirt with boys. Be cooperative on dates."

Among these various attributes, the graph shows "good looks," phrased in some fashion, to be second to "personality" in frequency for the girls. Having nice clothes, or being well-dressed, is the third most frequent item mentioned. What it means to be well-dressed differs sharply in a well-to-do surburb and in a working-class school, of course. Nevertheless, whether it is the number of cashmere sweaters a girl owns, or simply having clean and attractive dresses, the matter of having good clothes is an important one in the value systems to which these girls pay heed. This importance of clothes appears to derive in part from the fact that clothes symbolize family status. But in part, also, it appears to derive from the same source that gives importance to "good looks": these items are crucial in making a girl attractive to boys. Thus in this respect the values of the girl's culture are molded by the presence of boys—and by the fact that success with boys is itself of overriding importance.

Another element in the constellation of attributes required if one is to be in the leading crowd is indicated by the class of responses labeled "having a good reputation," which was fourth in number of times mentioned. In all these schools, this item was often mentioned, though in each school, some saw the leading crowd as composed of girls with bad reputations and immoral habits; and in some schools the leading crowd was less interested in a good reputation than in others.

A girl's reputation is crucial among adolescents. A girl is caught in a dilemma posed by the importance of good looks on the other hand, and a good reputation on the other: A girl must be popular with the boys, says the culture, but in doing so she must maintain her reputation. In some schools, the limits defining a good reputation are stricter than in others;

but in all the schools, the limits are there to define what is "good" and what is "bad." The definitions are partly based on behavior with the boys, but they also include drinking, smoking, and others less tangible matters —something about the way a girl handles herself, quite apart from what she actually *does*.

It is not such an easy matter for a girl to get and keep a good reputation, particularly if her mother is permissive in letting her date whom she likes as a freshman or sophmore. Junior and senior boys often date freshman and sophmore girls, sometimes with good intentions and sometimes not. One senior boy in Green Junction, in commenting upon the "wildness" of the leading girls in his class, explained it by saying that when his class was in the eighth grade, it was forced to go to school in the high school building because of a classroom shortage. A number of the girls in the class, he explained, had begun dating boys in the upper classes of high school. This, it seemed to him, was where the problem began.

Another criterion by which a girl gets into the leading crowd or fails to get in is expressed by a girl who said simply, "Money, fancy clothes, good house, new cars, et cetera: the best."

These qualities are all of a piece; they express the fact that being born into the right family is a great help to a girl in getting into the leading crowd. It is expressed differently in different schools and by different girls, sometimes as "parents having money," sometimes as "coming from the right neighborhood," sometimes as "expensive clothes." These qualities differ sharply from some of those discussed above, for they are not something a girl can *change*.[5] Her position in the system is ascribed according to her parents' social position, and there is nothing she can do about it. If criteria like these dominate, then we would expect the system to have a very different effect on the people in it than if other criteria, which a girl or boy could hope to achieve, were the basis of social comparison—just as in the larger society a caste system has quite different effects on individuals than does a system with a great deal of mobility between social classes.

It is evident that these family-background criteria play some part in these schools, but—at least according to these girls—not the major part. (It is true, however, that the girls who are *not* in the leading crowd more often see such criteria, which are glossed over or simply not seen by girls who are in the crowd.) Furthermore, these criteria, vary sharply in their importance in different schools.

[5] To be sure, she sometimes has a hard time changing her looks or her personality; yet these are her own personal attributes, which she can do something about, except in extreme situations.

Another criterion for being in the leading crowd is scholastic success. According to these girls, good grades, or "being smart" or "intelligent" has something to do with membership in the leading crowd. Not much, to be sure—it is mentioned less than 12 percent of the time, and far less often than the attributes of personality, good looks, clothes, and the like. Nevertheless, doing well in school apparently counts for something. It is surprising that it does not count for more, because in some situations, the "stars," heroes, and objects of adulation are those who best achieve the goals of the institution. For example, in the movie industry the leading crowd is composed of those who have achieved the top roles—they are by consensus the "stars." In a graduate school, the "leading crowd" of students ordinarily consists of the bright students who excel in their studies. Not so for these high school girls. The leading crowd seems to be defined primarily in terms of *social* success: their personality, desirability as dates, clothes—and in communities where social success is tied closely to family background, their money and family.

Different Criteria for Boys

What about boys? What were their responses to this question about criteria for the leading crowd? Figure 4 also shows the boys' responses, in somewhat the same categories used for the girls. The first difference between these and the girl's responses is the overall lower frequency. The girls sometimes set down in great detail just what is required to get in the leading crowd—but the matter seems somewhat less salient to the boys.

For the boys, a somewhat different set of attributes is important for membership in the leading crowd. The responses below give some idea of the things mentioned.

"A good athlete, pretty good looking, common sense, sense of humor."
"Money, cars and the right connections and a good personality."
"Be a good athlete. Have a good personality. Be in everything you can. Don't drink or smoke. Don't go with bad girls."
"Athletic ability sure helps."
"Prove you rebel against the police officers. Dress sharp. Go out with sharp freshman girls. Ignore senior girls."
"Good in athletics; 'wheel' type; not too intelligent."

By categories of response, figure 4 shows that a good personality is important for the boys, but less strikingly so than it is for the girls. Being good looking, having good clothes, and having a good reputation are similarly of less importance. Good clothes in particular are less important for the boys than for the girls. Similarly, the items which have to do with parents' social position—having money, coming from the right neighborhood, and the like, are less frequently mentioned by boys.

What then are the criteria which are more important for boys than for girls? The most obvious is, as the graph indicates, athletics. Of the things that a boy can *do,* of the things he can *achieve,* athletic success seems the clearest and most direct way to gain membership in the leading crowd.

Having good grades, or doing well academically, appears to be a less sure path to the leading crowd than is athletics (and sometimes it is a path away, as the final quotation listed above suggests). It does, however, sometimes constitute a path, according to these responses. The path is apparently stronger for boys (where scholastic achievement is fifth in frequency) than for the girls (where it is eighth in frequency). This result is a little puzzling, for it is well known that girls work harder in school and get better grades than boys do. The ambivalence of the culture concerning high achievement among girls will be examined in some detail later. At this point, it is sufficient to note that such achievement is apparently less helpful to a girl for getting into the leading crowd than it is for a boy.

An item which is of considerable importance for the boys, as indicated on the bar graph, is a *car*— just having any car, according to some boys, or having a *nice* car, according to others—but which-ever it is, a car appears to be of considerable importance in being part of the "inner circle" in these schools. In four of the five small-town schools—but in none of the larger schools—a car was mentioned more often than academic achievement. When this fact is coupled with the fact that the reresponses included not only juniors and seniors, but also freshmen and sophomores, who were too young to drive, the place of cars in these adolescent looms even larger.

As a whole, how do the criteria for the leading crowd among boys differ from the criteria for girls? Several sharp differences are evident. Family background seems to matter less for boys; it is apparently considerably easier for a boy than a girl from the wrong side of the tracks to break into the crowd. Clothes, money, and being from the right neighborhood hold a considerably higher place for the girls.

The same appears to be true for personal attributes such as personality, reputation, good looks—all of the things which define what a person *is.* In contrast, the criteria for boys include a much larger component of what a person *does,* whether in athletics or in academic matters. Such a distinction can be overdrawn, for a girl's reputation and her personality are certainly determined by what she does. Yet these are not clear-cut dimensions of achievement in which a person can actively do something; they are far less tangible. Furthermore, they are pliable in the hands of the leading crowd itself, whose members can define what constitutes a good reputation or a good personality but cannot ignore football touchdowns or scholastic honors. Numerous examples of the way the leading crowd can shape reputations were evident in these schools. For example, a girl reported:

"It is rumored that if you are in with either ——— or ——— that you've got it made. But they are both my friends. You've got to be popular, considerate, have a good reputation. One girl came this year with a rumor started about her. She was ruined in no time by ——— especially."

The girl who had been "ruined" was a top student and a leader in school activities, but neither of these things was enough to give her a place in the leading crowd. At the end of the school year she was just as far out of things as she was at the beginning, despite her achievements in school.

The matter is different for boys. There are fewer solid barriers, such as family background, and fewer criteria which can be twisted at the whim of the in-group, than there are for girls. To be sure, achievement must be in the right area—and athletics is by far the area which is more right than any other—but achievement *can in* most of these schools bring a boy into the leading crowd, which is more than it can do in many instances for girls.

Again there is the suggestion that the girls' culture is in some fashion derived from the boys: The girl's role is to sit there and look pretty, waiting for the athletic star to come for her. A girl must cultivate her looks, be vivacious and attractive, wear the right clothes, but then wait—until a football player, whose status is determined by specific achievements, comes along to choose her. This is, of course, only part of the matter, for in a community where the leading crowd largely reflects the "right families" in town, or in a school where "activities" are quite important, the girls have more independent power. Also, the fact that girls give the parties and determine who is invited puts a tool in their hands which the boys do not have.

It is as if the adolescent culture were a Coney Island mirror, throwing back a reflection of the adult society, distorted but recognizable. And just as there are variations in different places in the adult society, there are variations in different schools in the adolescent society. Their existence should be kept in mind, in order not to make the serious mistake of seeing the "adolescent culture" as all of a piece, as a single invariant entity.

Popularity with Own or Opposite Sex

In the questionnaire, boys were asked what it takes to be popular with other boys, and then, in a separate question, what it takes to be popular with girls. Girls were asked a similar pair of questions about popularity with their own sex and popularity with the opposite sex.

A comparison of the pair of questions shows an interesting result: "good grades," or doing well in school counts for something with one's *own* sex, but for very little in popularity with the opposite sex. In contrast, out-of-school activities and attributes (a boy's having a car, or a girl's having good clothes) count for much more in popularity with the opposite sex. The differences are especially great for a girl's popularity. Doing well in school is of some value in making a girl popular with other girls, but it has little or no value in her popularity with boys.

Perhaps these results are to be expected. Yet their implications are not so obvious. Let us suppose that the girls in a school valued good grades more than the boys did. One might naively expect this to mean that the presence of these girls would be an influence on the boys toward a higher evaluation of studies. Yet these data say that is *not* the case; they say that a boy's popularity with girls is based less on doing well in school, more on such attributes as a car, than in his popularity with other boys. Similarly for girls—their popularity with boys is based much less on academic studies than is their popularity among members of their own sex.

The standards men and women use to judge each other have always included a large component of physical attractiveness and a smaller component of the more austere criteria they use in judging members of their own sex. Yet adults seem to ignore that this is just as true in high schools as it is in business offices, and that its cumulative effect may be to deemphasize education in schools far more than they realize. In the normal activities of a high school, the relations between boys and girls tend to increase the importance of physical attractiveness, cars, and clothes, and to decrease the importance of achievement in school activities. Whether this *must* be true is another question; it may be that the school itself can shape these relations so that they will have a positive effect rather than a negative one on the school's goals.

The general research question is this: What kinds of interaction among boys and girls could lead each sex to evaluate the other less on grounds of physical attraction, and more on grounds which are not so superficial? It seems likely, for example, that in some private schools such as the Putney School, the kinds of common work activities of boys and girls lead to different bases for evaluating the opposite sex than do the usual activities surrounding a public high school. The question of practical policy, once such a research question has been answered, is even more difficult: What can a school do to foster the kinds of interactions and activities which lead the judgments of the opposite sex to be made on grounds which implement the school's goals?

It is commonly assumed, both by educators and by laymen, that it is "better" for boys and girls to be in school together during adolescence —if not better for their academic performance, then at least better for their social development and adjustment. But this may be not at all true —the benefits may depend wholly upon the kind of activities within which their association takes place. Coeducation in some high schools may be inimical to *both* academic achievement *and* social adjustment. Again, we should emphasize that the dichotomy often forced between "life-adjustment" and "academic emphasis" is a false one, for it forgets that most of the teenager's energy is not directed toward either of these goals. The relevant dichotomy is instead cars, clothes, and the cruel jungle of rating and dating versus school activities, whether of the academic or life-adjustment variety.

Perhaps this is where the emphasis *should* be among girls: on making themselves into desirable objects for boys. Perhaps physical beauty, nice clothes, and an enticing manner are the attributes which should be most important among adolescent girls. Yet in none of the roles in adult life that most girls will occupy are physical beauty, an enticing manner, and nice clothes as important for performing successfully as they are in high school. Even receptionists and secretaries, for whom personal attractiveness is a valuable attribute, must carry out their jobs well, or they cannot survive. Comparable performance is far less important in the status system of the high school. A girl can survive much longer on personal attractiveness, an enticing manner, and nice clothes.

The adult activities of women in which such attributes *are* most important are of a different order from those of wives, citizens, mothers, career women, secretaries: they are the activities of chorus girls, models, movie and television actresses. In all these activities, women serve as *objects of attention* for men, and even more, objects to *attract* men's attention. These attractions are quite different from the attributes of a good wife, which involve less superficial qualities. If we want our high schools to inculcate the attributes which make girls successful as objects to attract men's attention, then these values of good looks and nice clothes discussed above are just right; if not, then the values are quite inappropriate.

A second answer to the question, "What is wrong with these values?" is this: Nothing is wrong with such values, so long as they do not completely pervade the atmosphere. The values are all right, as long as there are also *other* ways a girl can become popular and successful in the eyes of her peers. And there are other ways, as indicated by the emphasis on "a nice personality" in the questions discussed above. Yet these two questions suggest that in adolescent cultures, these superficial, external attributes of clothes and good looks do pervade the atmosphere to the extent that girls come to feel that this is the only basis or the most important basis on which to excel.

Effect on Girls of Emphasis on Attractivness

There are several sets of responses in the questionnaire which indicate that girls do feel that the attributes of attractiveness are most important. One is the response to the question in which more girls checked "model" as the occupation they would like than any of the other three: "nurse," "schoolteacher," or "actress or artist." As suggested before, a model is one of the few occupations which most embodies the attributes of beauty and superficial attractiveness to men.

Further consequences of this emphasis in high school on being attractive to boys are indicated by responses to a set of sentence-completion questions. Comparing the boys' responses and the girls' will give some indication of the degree to which the high school culture impresses these matters upon girls. Table 1 shows the proportion responding in terms of popularity or relations with the opposite sex. These questions were asked in a supplementary questionnaire, filled out by the 6,289 students in the nine schools who completed the basic fall questionnaire early.

Table 1
Sentence-Completion Responses Related to Popularity

	Boys (percent)	Girls (percent)
More than anything else, I'd like to:		
Responses involving popularity with opposite sex	5.4	10.8
Responses involving popularity, unspecified	5.3	11.4
Total codable responses	(2,343)	(2,776)
The best thing that could happen to me this year at school would be:		
Responses involving relations with opposite sex	4.5	20.7
Responses involving relations with others, unspecified	3.2	9.0
Total codable responses	(2,222)	(2,702)
The most important thing in life is:		
Responses involving popularity with opposite sex	6.3	7.4
Responses involving popularity, unspecified	4.6	7.9
Total codable responses	(2,151)	(2,737)
I worry most about:		
Responses involving popularity with opposite sex	9.2	13.9
Responses involving personal attributes related to popularity (weight, hair, figure, etc.)	2.7	8.6
Total codable responses	(2,201)	(2,803)

To each one of these sentence-completion questions, girls gave far more responses involving popularity with the opposite sex than the boys did. The responses suggest that the emphasis of these cultures on a girl's being an object of attention for boys has powerful consequences for the girl's attitudes toward life and toward herself. A further indication that success with boys is tied to rather superficial external qualities is shown by the greater proportion of girls who say they worry most about some personal characteristic (most often an external attribute such as weight or figure or hair or skin, but also including such attributes as shyness).

One might suggest, however, that girls' concern with popularity with boys, and with physical attributes which help make them popular, would be just as strong in the absence of the adolescent culture. A simple comparison of these four sentence-completion questions suggests that this is not so. The question in which girls *most* often give responses involving relations with the opposite sex is the one which refers directly to the school life: "The best thing that could happen to me this year at school would be. * * *" When the question refers to life in general (The most important thing in life is * * *), then the boy-girl differential is sharply reduced. This suggests that it is the system itself, the social system of adolescents, which makes relations with boys, and physical attractiveness, so important to girls.

These values which feature a girl as an object of a boy's attention have other effects on the girls, of which we have only the barest knowledge. One of the effects is on her self-conception. One would expect that if a girl found herself in a situation where she was not successful in "the things that count," she would be less happy with herself, and would want to change, to be someone different; on the other hand, the more successful she was in the things that counted, the more she would be satisfied with herself.

We have no measure of the objective beauty of girls, and we are not able to single out those who are particularly unattractive in dress or beauty, to see the impact that these values have upon their conceptions of themselves. However, it is possible to pick out the girls who are, in the eyes of their classmates, the best-dressed girls, to allow an indirect test of the effect of the emphasis on clothes and on being attractive to boys. In the questionnaire, every girl was asked:

"Of all the girls in your grade, who is the best dressed?"

The girls who were named most often by their classmates were at one end of the continuum—better dressed than their classmates. Thus, if this is an important attribute to have, these girls should feel considerably better about themselves than do their classmates. The following tabulation shows that they did, and that those named most often felt best about themselves.

"If I could trade, I would be someone different from myself":

	Percent	Number
All girls who agreed	21.2	3,782
Girls named 2–6 times as best dressed	17.0	282
Girls named 7 or more times as best dressed	11.2	98

The effect of being thought of as "best dressed" by her classmates was striking, reducing by half the likelihood of a girls wanting to be someone different. Or to put it differently, the effect of *not* being thought of as "best dressed" by her classmates more than doubled a girl's likelihood of wanting to be someone different.

To see the strength of this effect, relative to the effect of competing values, it is possible to compare these responses with those of girls who were highly thought of by their classmates, but in other ways. The following questions were asked along with the "best-dressed" question:

"Of all the girls in your grade, who
—is the best student?
—do boys go for most?"

The girls who were named most often by their classmates on these two questions and the previous one can be thought of as "successful" in each of these areas—studies, relations with boys, and dress. Insofar as these things count, they should make the girls feel happier about themselves—and conversely, make the girls who are not successful less happy about themselves.

The degree to which these three values count in making a girl happy or unhappy about herself can be seen in figure 5. It is apparent that all have some effect. Being successful with boys apparently has most effect, being thought of as best dressed (which seems to be important in large part because it contributes to being successful with boys) is somewhat less effective, and being thought of as best student is apparently the least effective of the thre. The results of the companion questions for boys are shown along with those for the girls, to indicate that this result is not simply due to the personality of those popular with the opposite sex. For boys, it is athletics which is apparently most effective, more so than popularity with girls.

Summary

It appears that the role of girls as objects of attention for boys is one emphasized by the adolescent values in these schools. Its consequences are multifarious, and we have only touched upon them; but

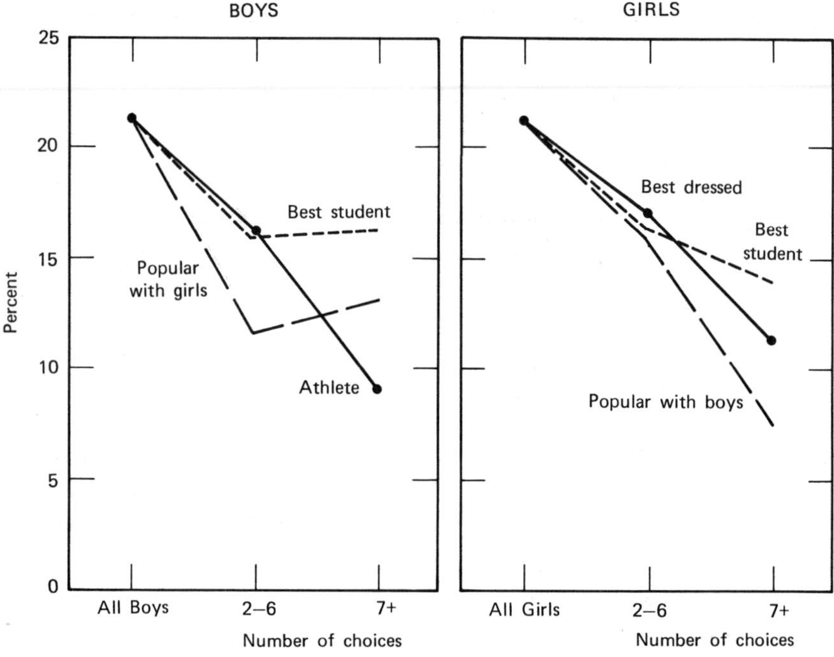

FIGURE 5. Percent wanting to be someone else among all boys or girls and those chosen as outstanding on three criteria.

one point is clear: just "putting together" boys and girls in the same school is not necessarily the "normal, healthy" thing to do. It does not necessarily promote adjustment to life; it may promote, as indicated by these data, adjustment to values appropriate to the life of a model or chorus girl or movie actress. It may, in other words, promote *mal*adjustment to the kind of life that these girls will be expected to lead after school.

Common sense is not enough in these matters. It is not enough to put boys and girls in a school and expect that they will be a "healthy influence" on one another. Serious research is required to learn the kind of activities and the kind of situations which will allow them to be such, rather than emphasizing the superficial values of a hedonistic culture.

To show fully the way in which such interactions can affect the value system which pervades a school, one of two supplementary schools in the study, school 10, can be of aid.[6] This private school, with students

[6] This school and another were added to the study to learn more about the causes of the puzzling lack of respect for academic achievement in Executive Heights. Examination of these cases is carried out in the larger report, *op. cit.*

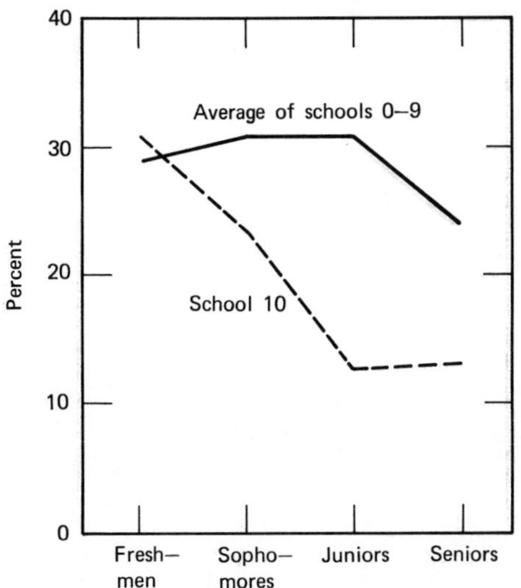

FIGURE 6. Percent of girls in each class naming "good looks" as a necessary attribute for membership in the leading crowd in 9 schools of the study and in a supplementary school (No. 10).

of upper middle class backgrounds similar to those of students in Executive Heights, but in a very serious-minded university setting. Figure 6 shows the importance during the 4 years of "good looks" as an attribute for membership in the leading crowd, in school 10 and on the average in the nine schools of the study. The contrast is striking: They start out at almost the same point in the freshman year, but in school 10, the importance of good looks goes *down* sharply over the 4 years; in nine schools of the study, the average even *rises* slightly as dating begins in earnest in the sophomore and junior years, before dropping off somewhat in the senior year. This graph gives only the faintest hint of the different experiences these two school situations would present for a girl. In the one, she would be competing on the basis of good looks; in the other, on different grounds.

This is not to suggest that all the schools of the nine in the study showed this same pattern; some did not. Marketville, in particular, showed a continual decline similar to that of school 10, while others showed a sharp rise in the importance of good looks in the sophomore and junior years, then a decrease among the seniors. The results indicate that the importance of attractiveness to the opposite sex is not fixed and invariant in the adolescent community but depends on activities in the particular community.

12.3 The Problem of Interests: A Reconsideration

J. W. Getzels

Although this paper is a summary of an address about interest as it relates to reading, the substance is generalizable to all subject areas. The contribution of this paper lies in Getzel's suggestion that teachers should assume that children are interested. If they are not, the following question should be asked: "Why isn't this child interested?" In the course of his remarks, Getzel clarifies his position with illustrations concerning disadvantaged children.

I began my paper of ten years ago by saying that my area of specialized competence, if any, was not in the field of reading. This remains the same today—perhaps even more so. I went on to say that from my limited point of vantage, work on reading interests seemed peculiarly deficient in three important respects: precision of definition, rigor of theory, and depth of analysis. I do not know whether there has been any marked alteration in this over the period. But today I would add to my initial list a fourth item—exactness of observation—which at the time seemed

SOURCE: J. W. Getzels, "The Problem of Interests: A Reconsideration." In H. Alan Robinson (Ed.), *Reading: Seventy-five Years of Progress.* (Chicago: University of Chicago Press, 1966), pp. 97–106. Reprinted by permission of the authors and the University of Chicago Press.

to me so self-evident that I neglected to mention it, an omission for which I have since been taken to task and which I would now rectify.

I then proceeded in my original paper to a formal examination of the concept of *interest* by placing it in the context of motivation theory and differentiating it from other motivational concepts like *preference, attitude,* and *drive,* with which it is often used interchangeably. Is an interest psychologically the same as a preference? an attitude? a drive? or is it in some significant way distinguishable from these?

I took the position that not only are interests, preferences, attitudes, and drives distinguishable as motives but that they *must* be distinguished if we are to understand the unique function of interests in the psychic economy of the human being. By way of illustration, I distinguished between an interest and a preference. We have a preference for broccoli over asparagus, but we may have absolutely no interest in either. We would not expend a minuscule effort to learn more about one than the other. The child faced with a choice of subjects already available in school may admit to a *preference* for one subject over another. But he may have no *interest* in either. A preference is a disposition to *receive* one object as against another; it does not induce one to seek out the particular object for acquisition or study. In contrast, the basic nature of an interest is that it does induce us to *seek out* particular objects and activities.

Similarly, I argued that there is a significant distinction between an interest and merely a positive attitude, although the two are often used synonymously. We may, for example, have a positive attitude toward the Eskimo and yet have no particular interest in them. By contrast, we may have a decidedly negative attitude toward the Soviets but have a very keen interest in them. An attitude is a disposition to react in a particular direction with regard to a given object or event. We do not ordinarily speak of being driven by an attitude; we are necessarily driven by our interests.

Finally, I distinguished between a drive and an interest. A drive has its source in a specific physiological disequilibrium, and the individual seeks conditions that will reduce the drive. An interest has its source in experience and challenges us to exert ourselves even though there is no necessity in any biological sense. Technically speaking, we may say a drive is a function largely of our *instinctual* processes, an interest largely of our *ego* processes. Against this background, I attempted to formulate a working definition of interest. An interest, I said, is a characteristic disposition, organized through experience, which impels an individual to seek out particular objects, activities, understandings, skills, or goals for attention or acquisition.

It is a punishing experience to reexamine what one has perpetrated in the past, especially what one has had the temerity to put in writing—in the present case, to observe the now self-evident omissions, to say nothing of the shoddy thought and awkward rhetoric. I am, for example, chagrined to discover that I neglected to distinguish between an interest and two other important types of motives, that is, *needs* and *values.* I can also rectify this now. A need is a disposition or force within a person which impels him consistently toward one type of activity as against another. Thus we may speak of an individual as having a high or a low need for achievement or for affiliation. Insofar as a need is not necessarily biological but may have its source in experience, it is distinct from a drive; insofar as it disposes the individual toward a general type of activity rather than toward a specific object or goal, it is distinct from an interest. The need for achievement may, for example, find expression in the school situation in the arts, sciences, athletics, or extracurricular activities. The need is the same; the interests are different. An interest may also be distinguished from a value. A value is a conception of the *desirable*—that is, of what ought to be desired, not what is actually desired—which influences the selection of behavior. Thus, it is possible for an interest and a value to be quite incompatible; an interest disposes us toward what we *want* to do, a value toward what we believe we *ought* to do. And in fact, we have not paid sufficient attention to the discrepancies between our values and our interests and, more especially, between *our* values and *children's* interests.

Despite these and other omissions, I would maintain that *within the assumptions about human behavior I made at the time* there is not much I would change in the original paper. The definition of *interest* I gave is tenable, and the determinants of interest which I cited are not unreasonable. But if we *alter the assumptions about human behavior*, then a number of the formulations about interests must also be altered. It is my contention that the basic assumptions about human behavior have undergone change during the past decade, and therefore we must rethink our prior conceptions of motivation and the nature of interests. Or rather I should say more carefully, my own assumptions have undergone change, and accordingly my conception of motivation and of interests has also undergone alteration. It is the nature of these transformations and their consequences for thinking about education that I should like to consider in this paper.

I.

Stated most simply, my basic assumption a decade ago was that human activity could best be explained in terms of a combination of the homeostatic model of self-maintenance and the drive-or-tension-reduction theory of behavior.[1] According to this theory, the organism's optimum state is held to be one of rest and equilibrium, and the organism is said to act in such a way as always to return to the optimum state of rest and equilibrium. Hunger raises the organism's level of tension and drives it to seek food; the organism ceases to seek food when it has eaten, that is, when the tension produced by the hunger has been reduced. Fear raises the organism's level of tension and drives it to seek cover; the organism ceases to seek cover when the danger is over, that is, when the tension produced by the fear has been reduced. And so on. With respect specifically to learning (or thinking, problem-solving, and other forms of intellectual activity including reading), the organism is said similarly to be driven or stimulated (we call it "motivated" in education) as it is into any other behavior. As Ernest R. Hilgard in his famous book *Theories of Learning* states Hull's position, "Without drives the organism does not behave and hence does not learn."[2] Learning always involves the reduction of a drive state, a decrease in tension. In these terms, an interest could also be conceived as a tension-producing state which impels the individual to action and stimulates him to behavior that reduces the tension raised by the interest.

During the past decade there has been a growing discontent with this homeostatic model of the human being and the drive-or-tension-reduction theory of behavior, at least as they are applied to the problem of learning and other forms of intellectual activity. It is felt that learning, thinking, and problem-solving may indeed be means of reducing certain drives but that they are not only that. They may also be ends in themselves, the organism acting to *increase* stimulation as well as to *decrease* stimulation. The optimum state of the human being may not be *passivity* but *activity;* and although he may be threatened by what is unfamiliar, by what he does not know, by what he has yet to learn, he is often challenged by what is new, intrigued by what is strange, and will go out of the way to encounter, explore, and master it. He seems to be *interested,* if I may put it this way, even when there seems to be no apparent drive or specific tension that is being reduced. The organism is said to act not only to *avoid* stimulation as previously assumed but also to *seek* stimula-

[1] Parts of this section are based on J. W. Getzels, "New Conceptions of the Learner: Some Implications for the Classroom," in *Reading and Emerging Cultural Values,* Twenty-eighth Yearbook of the Claremont Reading Conference, edited by Malcolm P. Douglass (Claremont, Calif.: Claremont Graduate School and University Center, 1964), pp. 10–21.

[2] Hilgard, *Theories of Learning* (New York: Appleton-Century-Crofts, 1948), p. 78.

tion. That is, the human being is not only a *stimulus-reducing* organism but also a *stimulus-seeking* organism.

Once pointed out, the evidence of this comes from so many sources that it is surprising this view is not more firmly established in academic psychology and in education. One of the most obvious features of the behavior of animals, for example, is the tendency to explore the environment, that is, to be "interested" in their whereabouts. As Robert W. White has put it, "Cats are reputedly killed by curiosity, dogs characteristically make a thorough search of their surroundings, and monkeys and chimpanzees have always impressed observers as ceaseless investigators."[3] Indeed, in a series of beautifully executed experiments, Harry F. Harlow and his associates at Wisconsin have shown that monkeys who are viscerogenically sated—that is, are not hungry, thirsty, or otherwise driven, at least by any unrecognizable drive—will explore apparently just for the sake of exploring and will learn to unassemble a puzzle of some complexity with no other motive than, as Harlow has said, "the privilege of unassembling it."[4]

We who are humanistically inclined may be quite skeptical about the relevance of animal experiments, and more especially about the direct applicability of animal learning experiments, for human education. And in fact, the model of the hungry rat as the prototype of human learning and behavior has done harm enough. But at least for animals, the homeostatic drive-reduction model of behavior is being put to severe question. As Harlow points out, the learning behavior of the animals in his experiments reduced no recognizable primary drive, decreased no identifiable tension or stimulation. Indeed, far from trying to reduce tension or stimulation, the animals seemed to be seeking it.

Discontent with the orthodox concepts of motivation and behavior has not been restricted to the animal laboratory, as White shows. It is increasingly being argued that the central motive in the growth of children is not food satisfaction or thirst satisfaction or some other so-called primary-drive satisfaction but effective interaction with the environment as exemplified by the child's curiosity and exploratory activity. Consider, for example, as White suggests, the readily observable play of contented children. A child all of whose bodily needs have been satisfied does not, as the stimulus-reduction theory of human motivation and behavior would

[3] White, "Motivation Reconsidered: The Concept of Competence," *Psychological Review*, LXVI (1959), 298.

[4] Harlow, "Motivational Forces Underlying Learning," in Kentucky Symposium, *Learning Theory, Personality Theory, and Clinical Research*, (New York: John Wiley & Sons, 1954), pp. 36-53.

suggest, remain at rest. On the contrary, it is just then that his play is most active; it is just then that he seems most *interested*. Careful observations by Piaget and others show that as early as the first year of life the child gives evidence of curiosity, exploration, and even experimentation. He has the capacity for being interested. And, of course, later it is almost impossible to keep up with the normal child's incessant questioning. Why is this, how is that, he wants to know. If I may put it this way—and this, I think, is the crux of our changing conception—there seem to be not only the familiar viscerogenic drives such as hunger and thirst to be satisfied by *satiation* but also neurogenic needs to be gratified by *stimulation*, that is, needs for excitement, novelty, and the opportunity to deal with the problematic.

There are numerous lines of evidence for this more recent conception of the human being as a stimulus-seeking and not only a stimulus-reducing organism. Donald O. Hebb, of McGill University, for example, directs our attention to such common human interests as mystery or adventure stories, skin-diving, exploring caves, climbing dangerous mountains, traveling to strange places—all of which seem to provide pleasure by raising the level of tension and stimulation rather than by reducing it.[5]

In order to examine this apparent human need for stimulation systematically, Hebb instituted a series of experiments on the effect of "stimulus deprivation." He asked the question, What would happen if we provided the human being with everything he needed—food, water, shelter, bodily comfort, and so on—that is, if we satisfied all his primary drives, but deprived him of varied environmental stimulation, that is, deprived him of the opportunity to be interested.

To cite only one of the studies, Bexton, Heron, and Scott paid subjects more than they could otherwise earn just to do nothing.[6] The subjects were well fed and comfortably housed—all they had to do was to remain in bed. But there was one experimental condition: stimulation was minimized. The arrangements were such that they could not see, hear, touch, or communicate with anyone. At first nothing happened; quite sensibly, the subjects merely slept. But soon they could not sleep, became restless, and displayed constant random behavior. They would sing, whistle, and talk to themselves. Their thinking and problem-solving abilities deteriorated, so that they could not answer questions which they had had no trouble answering before the experiment started. The experience became

[5] Hebb, *The Organization of Behavior* (New York: John Wiley & Sons, 1949), pp. 227–34.

[6] W. Harold Bexton, Woodburn Heron, and Thomas H. Scott, "Effects of Decreased Variation in the Sensory Environment," *Canadian Journal of Psychology*, VIII (1954), 70–76.

so unpleasant that, despite the high pay for presumably doing nothing, it was difficult to keep the subjects in the experiment for more than two or three days, and some subjects left even sooner. More than this, upon leaving and for some hours afterward, the subjects reported feelings of confusion, headaches, mild nausea, intellectual lethargy, and physical fatigue.

As Hebb and his colleagues argue, the maintenance of normal, intelligent, interested behavior requires a continually varied sensory input to cope with. It is well known that the organism may become disorganized through too much stimulation—we call it *frustration.* But the organism can also become disorganized through too little stimulation—we call it *boredom.* And it is said people have "died" of it, or at least they can be permanently crippled, intellectually and emotionally, by such a condition. Indeed, is not the effect of prolonged solitary confinement often just this? From this point of view, if we may use an analogue for the sake of brevity, the human being is not, as the preceding dominant concepts would have it, like a calculating or information-processing machine that may lie idle indefinitely and respond only when the electric motor is triggered, so to speak, by some drive or stimulus; he is more like a machine that is perpetually in motion and must be permitted to keep working—in fact, he must be given something to work on—if he is to function effectively and remain in good repair.

In these terms, interests may be seen as serving a vital function beyond those usually attributed to them: they assure that the organism will seek or at least remain open to the continuous sensory input needed for optimum functioning over and above the input required by the primary bodily drives like hunger and thirst.

II.

Recent studies of culturally deprived and segregated children show that a crucial characteristic of these children is just this; their capacity to be interested has been impaired.[7] These studies have a theoretical and practical significance beyond the children themselves, significant as they are, of course. For just as we learned a great deal about the nature and development of mental health by studying its loss, so can we learn a great deal about the nature and development of interests by studying the loss of interests. Lower-class status places the child in an inferior position physically, intellectually, and emotionally. Physical surroundings are dispiriting, intellectual stimulation is lacking, and family life is un-

[7] See J. W. Getzels, "Pre-School Education," in *Contemporary Issues in American Education* (U.S. Office of Education, Bulletin No. 3 [1966]; Washington, D.C.: Government Printing Office, 1966), pp. 105–14.

stable. Empirical evidence shows that the motives and interests of lower-class children do in fact reflect these experiences. They tend to have lower need-achievement than middle-class children;[8] their educational and occupational aspirations tend to be depressed;[9] they respond more to material than to non-material rewards as incentives for learning, whereas the reverse is true for middle-class children;[10] their time-orientation is shorter,[11] and they are less willing to defer gratification than are middle-class children.[12] That is, their interests are focused on the present rather than on the future.

If we take the extreme case of cultural deprivation as represented by the segregated status of the Negro, the conditions become extremely adverse: well over 50 per cent of Negro families live at the very lowest level of the lower-class standard.[13] But segregation has implications for emotional and mental development going well beyond the conditions of lower-class membership. The segregated child perceives himself as socially rejected by the prestigeful elements of society and develops a sense of his own *worthlessness*. Others may hope to escape and surmount their surroundings, even if the hope is often illusory; but the stigma of segregation is seen as inescapable and insurmountable. Under these circumstances, what does it mean to be interested—interested in what and for what?

As Ralph Ellison writes for the Negro, "I am an invisible man. No, I am not a spook like those who haunted Edgar Allen Poe, nor am I one of your Hollywood-movie ectoplasms. I am a man of substance, of flesh and bone, fiber and liquids—and I might even be said to possess a mind. I am invisible, understand, simply because people refuse to see me.

[8] Bernard C. Rosen, "The Achievement Syndrome: A Psychocultural Dimension of Social Stratification," *American Sociological Review*, XXI (1956), 203–11; "Race, Ethnicity, and the Achievement Syndrome," *American Sociological Review*, XXIV (1959), 47–60.

[9] William H. Sewell, Archie O. Haller, and Murray A. Straus, "Social Status and Educational and Occupational Aspirations," *American Sociological Review*, XXII (1937), 67–73.

[10] Glenn Terrel, Jr., Kathryn Durkin, and Melvin Wiesley, "Social Class and the Nature of the Incentive in Discrimination Learning," *Journal of Abnormal and Social Psychology*, LIX (1959), 270–72.

[11] Lawrence L. Leshan, "Time Orientation and Social Class," *Journal of Abnormal and Social Psychology*, XLVII (1952), 589–92.

[12] Louis Schneider and Sverre Lysgaard, "The Deferred Gratification Pattern: A Preliminary Study," *American Sociological Review*, XVIII (1953), 142–49.

[13] David P. Ausubel and Pearl Ausubel, "Ego Development among Segregated Negro Children," in *Education in Depressed Areas*, edited by A. Harry Passow (New York: Bureau of Publications, Teachers College, Columbia University, 1963), pp. 109–41.

. . . When they approach me they see only my surroundings, themselves, figments of their imagination—indeed, everything and anything except me."[14]

What, then, do children growing up in these conditions tell us about interests? Unfavorable socialization experiences, dispiriting physical surroundings, unequal school opportunities, manifest occupational discrimination, a sense of personal worthlessness, all conspire to depress not only the range of interests but the *capacity* to be interested, and especially to be interested in what we are likely to value. In this regard, these children are not unlike the subjects in the experiment who were deprived of stimulation or, perhaps better, like the children in Wayne Dennis' study of the Teheran orphanages, where stimulus variation was minimal, who despite good physical health were retarded in other respects.[15] The condition of cultural deprivation or segregation like the condition of minimum stimulus variation or stimulus deprivation prohibits the effective functioning of the organism by impairing the capacity to be interested. The etiology of this impairment was suggested by Piaget: "The more a child has seen and heard, the more he wants to see and hear."[16] We have already indicated that an interest is a disposition organized through experience, that is, through seeing and hearing, and that the capacity for interests is retained through stimulation, that is, through continued seeing and hearing. Cultural deprivation, segregation, minimal stimulus variation, stimulus deprivation, all act to restrict the child's opportunity to see and hear and thereby not only limit the range of interests he can acquire but may damage the capacity for interests itself.

The central pedagogic question raised in my paper and in the entire conference of a decade ago was: How can pupil interests be fostered? The assumption was that the teacher could not expect children to be interested; he had to instill interests in them. Classroom strategy was based on this assumption. Lesson plans, no matter what the nature of the lesson, often automatically began with a statement of the steps the teacher would take, the devices he would use, and the rewards and punishments he would mete out in order to motivate, that is, to interest, the pupils.

[14] Ellison, *Invisible Man* (New York: Modern Library, 1952), p. 3.

[15] Dennis, "Causes of Retardation among Institutional Children: Iran," *Journal of Genetic Psychology*, XCVI (1960), 47–59.

[16] See J. McVicker Hunt, "The Psychological Basis for Using Pre-School Enrichment as an Antidote for Cultural Deprivation," *Merrill-Palmer Quarterly*, X (July, 1964), 226; and J. Piaget, *The Origins of Intelligence in Children*, trans. Margaret Cook (New York: International Universities Press, 1952 [originally published, 1936]), pp. 276 f.

All this was founded on the conception of the human being as exclusively a stimulus-reducing organism. That is, the child would not be interested if the teacher did not take steps to interest him. But if we now add the conception of the human being as also a stimulus-seeking organism, then instead of posing the question as we did formerly, How can we interest children? we may now begin with the more fruitful question, Why is *this* child not interested?

The altered conception of the human being and the consequent transformation in our basic pedagogic question changes the anticipated teacher-pupil relationship in a crucial way: from a relationship in which the teacher expects pupils not to be interested to one in which she expects them to be interested. To be sure, many children are not interested, and no amount of expectation is by itself going to create interest. But our conceptual reformulation has two important practical results. First, if there is anything that may be said about human beings with any certainty at all, it is that they ordinarily try to live up to the expectations of others who are significant to them. Although the expectation that children will be interested may not make them interested, the teacher's expectation that they will not be interested surely creates the likelihood of a self-fulfilling prophecy: the pupils will live up to her expectation not to be interested. The reformulation mitigates against the possibility of this type of self-fulfilling prophecy. Second, and more important, the change in the basic question from how we can instill interests in children to why this child is not interested leads us to look at the individual child rather than children in the mass, to focus on causes rather than on symptoms, and to think of ways to prevent the loss of interest rather than to deal with the lack of interest as if lack of interest were the child's natural state. This is a signal gain not only theoretically but practically, for in the long run it may be easier to head off the loss of capacity to be interested than to try to instill interests after the capacity for interests has been damaged.

I have purposely said very little about reading. I am not a reading specialist or a reading teacher, and I do not pretend to be one. I am not sure what the implications of what I have been saying about the human being and his interests are for materials and methods of instruction in reading—if any. Nonetheless, I wonder whether current materials and methods are immutable, whether they are "givens of the natural order," so to speak. My own inclination is to believe that some radical transformations must be made in the light of our changing conceptions of the human being and his interests, at least for the disadvantaged child, if not for all children. I wonder, for example, whether the first activity of a school in a disadvantaged area cannot be, say, breakfast in small family-type groups rather than a garbled recitation of the pledge of allegiance—and this not because the children may be hungry but because it is a situation which many children have learned the uses of responsible give-and-take ("please pass the salt"), gained insight into the nature of quantity ("how many cups in a quart"), and perhaps even acquired an interest in the idea of reading ("from colorful cereal boxes"). More than this, since the critical characteristic of some children is not only that they do not have an "interest in reading" but that their "capacity to be interested" at all has been damaged, I wonder whether the early portion of their school experience might not be directed more imaginatively at repairing the damaged capacity to be interested than at drilling so-called reading readiness skills in conventional workbooks.

These suggestions are naïve in the extreme and are intended to prime the pump for useful ideas rather than to be useful in themselves. But in view of the results with current materials and methods, there seems to me so pitifully little to lose in trying something else that almost anything reasonable is worth the risk. I cannot help recalling that, despite seventy-five years of progress, I was recently told that in one urban junior college the average student who comes to them from a disadvantaged school reads at the fifth- or, at best, sixth-grade level.

These children tell us something about the need for reconsidering what we have been doing or, perhaps more exactly, what we have not been doing. And it seems to me that what they are telling us is that this is a time for boldness—boldness in conceptualization and boldness in practice.

12.4 Educating for Maturity

Lawrence S. Kubie, M. D.[1]

Dr. Kubie is in disagreement with those who believe that critical and creative thinking can be taught. He believes that the failure to develop these important abilities is the result of neurotogenic rigidity and he holds the school, among other institutions, responsible for this malady. Everyone will not agree that it is possible for a teacher with many pupils to accomplish what appears to demand a one-to-one clinical relationship. However, the importance of good personal-social adjustment for effective learning will not be denied.

I am impatient with educators and psychiatrists, with scientists and artists—with all of us in fact—for our failure to implement criticism of education by an experimental search for new ways.

My central thesis here is that we do not need to be taught to *think;*

SOURCE. Abridged from Lawrence S. Kubie, M.D., "Are We Educating for Maturity?" *National Education Association Journal,* **XLVIII**, 1 (1959), pp. 58-63, by permission of the author and the National Education Association.

[1] Dr. Kubie is Clinical Professor of Psychiatry in the Department of Psychiatry of the School of Medicine of the University of Maryland. He is also affiliated with the Sheppard and Enoch Pratt Hospital at Towson, Maryland as Consultant in Research Training.

indeed that thinking is something that cannot be taught. Memorizing (i.e., the recording and recalling of factual data) and also creative thinking (i.e., the assembling of such data in new combinations) are automatic, swift, and spontaneous processes, if these are allowed to proceed undisturbed by other influences.

Under ideal circumstances, memory and thinking are carried on neither consciously nor unconsciously but in the preconscious stream of automatic mentation, which proceeds at phenomenal speed. Of this swift stream, conscious processes provide us with tentative summaries and fragmentary samples; but conscious and, even more, unconscious processes combine to distort and delay and impede and sometimes wholly to block the processes of conscious summary and sampling by which the data from the preconscious stream can be put to work in human affairs.

For this, there is abundant clinical and experimental evidence, the crucial implications of which have been largely neglected by educators. What we need is to learn how to avoid interfering with this inherent preconscious capacity of the human mind.

This concept of a preconscious core of all human mentation is essential to my thesis. It implies that there is an incessant current of thought and feeling which is incredibly swift, which is neither conscious nor unconscious, which can learn, record, recall, and respond appropriately and also creatively, and all this without conscious awareness of any one of these steps.

We need also to be helped to improve the tools of conscious sampling and communication: i.e., how to read and listen to words, how to speak and write them. Yet even this is only one component in the complex art of communication, since here again the imperative need is to learn how not to let unconscious conflicts, affects, and defenses distort the work of even the fully educated eye and ear and tongue and hand.

Eventually, education must accept the full implications of the fact that the free creative velocity of our thinking apparatus is continually being braked and driven off course by the play of unconscious forces. As long as educational procedures refuse to recognize this, they will continue to increase this interference from masked and unrecognized neurotogenic processes. This happens in school today from the first grade through the highest echelons of postgraduate study.

It has long been known that in early years children have extraordinarily inventive imaginations, and use delightful and original figures of speech and allegory. What happens to this poetic gift when it is exposed to formal education? Or to rephrase the question: What happens to the free play of preconscious (spontaneous, "intuitive") functions in the course of conventional education?

It has been the assumption of education that learning would make man wise, mature, and creative. It is my unhappy conviction that learning alone achieves none of these goals, but more frequently is a mask for immaturity, neurosis, and a lack of wisdom. Furthermore, much of the learning which has traditionally been looked upon as an essential attribute of the educated man has no necessary relevance either to creativity or to maturity. Instead many ingredients in the very process by which men become learned tend actively to prevent psychological growth. It is not learning or the learning process which matures men; it is maturity, however won, which makes it possible for men to learn and to be creative with their learning.

I must warn that I am not going to prescribe remedies for this state of affairs, or to describe preventive measures. We must diagnose before we can cure or prevent; and educators must first acknowledge that something is amiss, before they will even tolerate a search for remedies.

I will be content if I am able to convince even a few that there is something quite basically wrong with our approach to education, and then to define what is wrong in terms of the crippling influence on the creative process of much of what now occurs in school. Only at the end will I suggest a few directions in which it is reasonable to seek for corrective or preventive techniques.

This is as far as I will presume to go; but I hope that experienced educators, with their more intimate knowledge of the details of educational procedures, may be able to offer more definitive remedies. Indeed, some educators and certain special schools have begun to attack the problems that I will describe. But I must leave this to them. My function is to challenge, not to offer panaceas.

The premises from which I start are not happy ones. Nor are they pessimistic, since they carry the implication that if we face these problems, we can solve them and that if we solve them, we will open a new era in human culture. Let me then state my premises.

The great cultural institutions of human society, including art and literature, science, education in general, the humanities and religion, have three essential missions; namely, to enable human nature itself to change; to enable each generation to transmit to the next whatever wisdom it has gained about living; to free the enormous untapped creative potential which is latent in varying degrees in all men.

It is my belief that in all of these respects our great cultural efforts and institutions have failed, and will continue to fail until new techniques of education are developed.

Evidence for this is found in the fact that our knowledge of the external world and our ability to represent the world as it is or as we would like it to be has grown enormously, while our ability to meet wisely the challenge of how to be human beings has not developed. Everyone acknowledges this intellectually; yet few have accepted the full implications which this failure entails for education itself as an instrument of human growth.

The failure of education to make it possible for man to change is due to a specific component in human nature; to wit, that psychological rigidity which is the basic and universal expression of the neurotic process. Indeed, this neurotogenic rigidity is so universal that it is frequently accepted as normal (even among some psychiatrists), as though the mere fact that everybody is rigid in one or more aspects of his personality means that rigidity is normal.

Since all that I will say is predicated upon what I regard as this basic failure of human culture, I will list the indices of this failure:

1. There is the universality of the neurotic process itself, which is manifested with minor variations in every culture about which we know anything.
2. There is the resulting failure of the race as a whole, and of men as individuals, to evolve and change psychologically.
3. There is the failure of all traditional methods to impart to successive generations that wisdom about living which a few individuals in each generation slowly acquire. Specifically, the kinds of behavioral conventions which protect the association of men into livable societies are well known. We call these ethical principles. Yet we do not know how to perpetuate and inculcate such ethical principles, nor how to seat them firmly in the saddle of human affairs.

These are basic gaps in our knowledge of how to transmit the fruits of experience from one generation to the next. The consequence is that in forms which change only in detail, country after country and generation after generation repeat the errors of their predecessors.

These manifestations of the failure of culture signify that the universal masked neurotic component in "normal" human nature is the major obstacle to progress. No system of education which fails to accept this challenge can educate in any meaningful sense. Therefore, we must ask ourselves whether the educational process as we know it increases or decreases in the student the sway of hidden neurotic forces in his life. It is my contention that education as it is increases the power of the neurotic processes in our culture, and that this need not be true.

Every adult bears the imprint of the child. The unconscious projection of the years of childhood onto the screen of adult years anchors us to the past. Consequently, the educator who is interested in making education assist the individual to move toward maturity must study how such projections from the past influence education, and whether the educational process tends to perpetuate their influence.

First of all, we face the obvious fact that the schoolroom and school as a whole confront the child with substitute parents and siblings. This provides an opportunity to resolve the fateful and destructive conflicts of the nursery. Yet the opportunity is not utilized. Instead, the child in school merely relives and buries even deeper the hates and loves and fears and rivalries which had their origins in his home.

The schoolroom may partially balance or neutralize these conflict-laden feelings; but it fails utterly to render them less fixed and less rigid *by bringing them within the reach of conscious selection, direction, and control.* Self-control, as it is taught, is almost invariably concentrated on control of the secondary consequences of such conflicts, rather than focusing on the elimination of their inner sources.

One could choose at random a number of illustrations of the consequences of this. There is the child who in his struggle with authority becomes an obsessional dawdler. This will have begun in the nursery in dawdling about eating, washing, or dressing. Unless this neurotic deviation has been effectively resolved in the home before the youngster reaches school, it will warp his every activity in this new setting.

At the opposite pole from the obsessional dawdler is the compulsive rusher, the youngster who has to plunge headlong from one half-finished task to another, afraid to tarry long enough to complete anything lest he be overtaken by some nameless fate, some dreaded exposure. These two oppositely paced obligatory patterns may alternate in the same individual, and may arise out of almost identical unconscious conflicts.

The relevant and disconcerting point is that both of these opposing neurotic patterns (as well as others) tend to be reinforced and not lessened by the pressure of our formal educational processes. Yet instead of giving the child insight into and freedom from this reaction to authority, the school usually increases its paralyzing influence. Consequently, it persists to plague the lifework of potentially brilliant and creative adults.

Many such adults are seduced by the illusory freedom of a blind automatic rejection of all external authority. Yet because the road to external freedom is never found by submitting to irresponsible internal compulsion, these obligatory rebels pay for this in the stereotyped and repetitive quality of their pseudo-rebellious productions, whether these are in literature, art, music, politics, or science.

In considering how to deal with these difficult and ubiquitous problems, we do not need to conjure up a Utopian school in which no nursery battles would be re-enacted. Whether the immediate and remote effects of such conflicts upon each child and adult are creative or destructive will depend not upon the mere fact that such struggles occur, but upon the *level on which they are waged,* i.e., whether this level is preponderantly conscious, preconscious, or unconscious.

Therefore the schools face the challenge to see what they can do to make sure that these battles will be fought out on conscious and preconscious levels. It would seem that an essential aspect of any truly educational experience would be to enable each child to face in himself those painful conflicts from which he shrinks, but which shape his character.

Neither traditional disciplinary education nor progressive education solves the technical problems which this goal involves. Disciplinary techniques alone, even when seemingly successful, give the child a sense that he must control *something,* but fail to make clear what there is inside that needs controlling or redirecting.

In its early years, progressive education encouraged the child to act out his problems, but failed to realize that acting-out will not alone bring any increase in self-understanding or in self-mastery. Indeed, like blind discipline, blind acting-out can distort and block insight—as it does in the case of the psychopath.

In addition to its failure to accept the challenge of buried neutrotogenic processes, even at its current best, the educative process tends to reinforce the neurotic process through the misuse of the techniques of repetitive drill.

In the tangled interweaving of the processes of learning and the neurotic process, repetition plays a major role. By imperceptible gradations, the repetitive drills of the learning process shade over into the automatic involuntary repetitions of the neurosis. This intensification of the neurotic process through repetitive drill mars our educational system from primary grades through professional and graduate levels.

Limitless repetition without the guidance of insight is not merely self-defeating; it does deeper damage by hampering spontaneous, "intuitive," i.e., preconscious, functions.

Nevertheless, in the acquisition of skills, many teachers continue to place major emphasis on repetitive drill; and this in spite of the well-known and repeatedly demonstrated fact that the most efficient learning is essentially effortless and almost instantaneous.

For example, under hypnosis enormous amounts of material can be recorded effortlessly, almost as on a photographic plate. Here drill and repetition play no role, and their introduction would merely interfere with automatic recording and recall. In general, the degree to which learning depends upon repetitive drill is a measure of the degree to which guilt, anxiety, anger—whether conscious or unconscious—are blocking the assimilative component of education.

For a number of reasons, therefore, we are forced to conclude that there is a continuous conflict rather than a happy alliance between erudition and maturity. This conflict begins in the primary grades and continues unabated to and through postgraduate education.

Every educator knows scholars who lack the least quality of human maturity and wisdom, yet who are technical masters of their own fields, whether this field is the humanities, art, music, philosophy, religion, law, science, the history of ideas, or the languages by which men communicate ideas. The measure of our wisdom about living is determined neither by the breadth of the area of our knowledge nor by the sharpness of our specialization.

It might shed some light on the elusive relationship between formal education and maturation to consider what happens to medical students when they are brought into contact with the sufferings of patients. This is a moment which forces them to accept some measure of responsibility for human suffering other than their own. For each student, this is an experience which precipitates a powerful, if masked, external struggle among conflicting impulses.

Shall he cling to the unrecognized prerogative of childhood to shut out the suffering of others or even secretly to exult in it? Or shall he yield to those simultaneous, powerful internal and external pressures of medical tradition to accept the challenge of human needs other than his own? Will it extricate him from the cocoon of his childhood to identify with other individuals through ministering to them?

This may give us a clue to other basic defects in our educational process. Perhaps above anything else, the adolescent needs not only to be exposed to human suffering, but also to be given the responsibility of ministering to it. Yet instead of this, the educational years cultivate in each student a maximal concentration on himself. Moreover, we know that the essence of maturity can come only through the insight which arises out of the interaction between living and blundering, and then of studying and dissecting our blunders. Neither living without self-study nor study without living is enough.

One obvious implication runs through everything I have said; namely, that if education is to become a matter not only of the mind but of the spirit, and if it is ever to facilitate the maturing process instead of limiting and distorting it, then it must deal with the universal, masked, neurotic ingredient in human nature. Clearly then, self-knowledge in depth is essential for any solution.

It is my conviction that education without this understanding can never mean wisdom or maturity; and that self-knowledge in depth is a process which, like education itself, is never complete. It is a process which goes on throughout life. Like the fight for external freedom, the fight for this inner freedom from the internal tyranny of unconscious processes demands eternal vigilance and continuous struggle.

This is because in every one of us, from the beginning of life until its end, active forces are at work which tend repeatedly to confuse and obscure our images of ourselves. Consequently, those who do not struggle continuously throughout life to attain and then to retain self-knowledge in depth, cannot be creative. Without such knowledge, society has no adults, but only aging children, armed with words and paint and clay and atomic weapons, none of which they understand.

And since self-knowledge has been a neglected aspect of our educational system, and indeed of human culture in general, most scholars have been only erudite rather than wise. Wisdom when it has graced any one of us has come not by design but as a happy accident. This challenges us to have the courage to face this failure of education as we have always known it, with a determination to do something effective about it.

Even if we do not already possess the technique by which to implement fully our determination, we can at least formulate our goals.

The increasing duration of the process of formal education tends to imprison the student for many decades in an adolescence of limited responsibility in which he lives on a dole from an adult world toward which—whether or not he manifests it openly—he harbors much unconscious hostility. Thus we obstruct the very processes of maturation for which we are striving.

I take it for granted that our educational processes must continue to last longer and longer. This means, however, that unless the student is exposed concurrently to maturing experiences, he will continue to end up as an erudite adolescent. The need to achieve the fullest degree of intellectual preparation without emotional stunting challenges us to find ways in which without limiting education we can facilitate those aspects of emotional maturity which emanate only from the direct experience of living and from carrying a sobering responsibility for others.

Yet the amount of data which every educated man must master is enormous already and is constantly increasing. Moreover, we know that if we hold him at the student level too long, the process of emotional maturation which is so essential an ingredient of education is in danger of being stunted. Obviously, then, some means must be found to remake the life of the student, so that in itself it will become a maturing experience. Alternatively, periods of study must be interspersed with periods devoted to other types of experiences, or techniques of psychotherapy must be adapted to the educational scene to supplement formal education in the service of greater emotional maturity.

When we meet the currently popular and all too easy assumption that the humanities will solve our problems, we should remind the optimist that the humanities have never served us that well in the past.

We cannot be wise, yet remain immature. Maturity requires the capacity to change, to become different, to react in varied and unanticipated ways. The emotional and intellectual maturity which the returning veteran brought to his studies after World War II, the subtle birth of maturity in the medical student as he first experiences the suffering of others and participates in its alleviation, what we have learned about the imprisoning of the human spirit by the neurotic process—all these indicate the directions toward which we must move as we seek solutions to these fundamental problems of how education for the first time in human history can enable the human spirit to grow and change. Progress will not come just from sitting back and hoping. It will come only as a reward for an uncompromising defense of the creative value of doubt, and from an unsparingly critical reexamination of every educational premise.

Selected Readings

Allport, G. W. Values and our youth. *Teachers College Record*, 1961, **63**, 211–219.

Almy, Millie. Intellectual mastery and mental health. *Teachers College Record*, 1962, **63**, 468–75.

Ausubel, D. P. Personality disorder is disease. *American Psychologist*, 1961, **16**, 69–74.

Bandura, A. Social learning through imitation. In M. R. Jones, *Nebraska Symposium on Motivation.* Lincoln, Nebraska: The University of Nebraska Press, 1962, Pp. 211–269.

Baurenfeind, R. H. What to look for in a review of an interest inventory. *Personnel and Guidance Journal*, 1964, **42**, 925–927.

Bronfenbrenner, U. Soviet method of character education: some implications for research. *American psychologist*, 1962, **17**, 550–564.

Bronfenbrenner, U. The changing American child—a speculative analysis. *Journal of Social Issues*, 1961, **1**, 6–18.

Crites, J. O. Interests. In R. L. Ebel (Ed.), *Encyclopedia of educational research* (4th ed.). London: Macmillan, 1969, pp. 678–686.

Murphy, G. New vistas in personality research. *Personnel and Guidance Journal*, 1961, **40**, 114–12.

Hovland, C. I., Janis, I. L., and Kelley, H. *Communication and persuasion.* New Haven: Yale University Press, 1953, pp. 73–83.

Jackson, P. W., and Getzels, J. W. Psychological health and classroom functioning; a study of dissatisfaction with school among adolescents. *Journal of Educational Psychology*, 1959, **50**, 295–300.

Mowrer, O. H. Sin, the lesser of two evils. *The American Psychologist*, 1960, **15**, 301–304.

Rogers, C. R. Toward a modern approach to values: the valuing process in the mature person. *Journal of Abnormal and Social Psychology*, 1964, **68**, 160–167.

Scott, W. A. Attitude change by response reinforcement. *Sociometry*, 1959, **22**, 328–335.

Warner, R. W., Jr. Alienated youth: the counselor's task. *The Personnel and Guidance Journal.* 1970, **48**, 443–448.

White, Mary Alice. Little red schoolhouse and little white clinic. *Teachers College Record*, Columbia University, 1965, **61**, 188–199.

CHAPTER 13

Learning in the Psychomotor Domain

13.1 Principles of Learning in the Psychomotor Domain[1]

Robert M. Gagné

The author reviews principles of learning, such as giving reinforcement and providing knowledge of results, and finds them wanting in teaching psychomotor skills. He then suggests principles related to the variables of task analysis, intratask transfer, component task achievement and sequencing, which he believes to be of great importance. Now that the new principles have been stated, they must be tested empirically.

Suppose that I were a learning psychologist, fresh out of an academic laboratory, who was to take a new job in charge of a program of research on some type of military training. What principles of learning would I look for to bring to bear on training problems? What kinds of generalizations from laboratory studies of learning would I search for

SOURCE. Abridged from Robert M. Gagné, "Military Training and Principles of Learning," *American Psychologist,* **XVII,** 2 (1962), by permission of the author and the American Psychological Association.

[1] Presidential address delivered at the annual meeting of the Division of Military Psychology, 69th Annual Convention of the American Psychological Association, New York, N. Y., September 5, 1961. [This research was] supported in part by Contract AF 49(638)–975, with the Office of Scientific Research, U. S. Air Force. The opinions expressed are those of the author.

and attempt to make use of in training situations? The answers I shall suggest for these questions require first a consideration of what kinds of principles have been tried, and how they have fared.

Some Representative Military Tasks

First, we need to have in mind certain representative military tasks for which training either is or has been given in order that we can consider in detail the kinds of learning principles that are applicable. Here are three which will serve well as examples: (1) flexible gunnery; (2) putting a radar set into operation; (3) finding malfunctions in an electronic system.

Flexible-Gunnery. The gunner of a now obsolete type of bomber aircraft was typically located in the waist or the tail of the plane, and aimed and fired a gun at fighter aircraft attacking on what was called a "pursuit course." To do this he looked at the attacking fighter through a reticle containing a central dot, which he lined up with the target by rotating his gunsight horizontally and vertically. At the same time, he had to "frame" the aircraft within a set of dots arranged in a circle whose circumference could be varied by rotating the round hand-grip by means of which he grasped the gunsight. This is the kind of task the psychologist calls "tracking," on which a great many laboratory studies have been carried out. It was, of course, tracking simultaneously in the three dimensions of azimuth, elevation, and range. To perform this task, the individual had to learn a motor skill.

Putting a Radar set in Operation. This kind of task is typically what is called a "fixed procedure." That is, the individual is required to push buttons, turn switches, and so on, in a particular sequence. Here, for example, is a set of steps in a procedure used by radar operators to check the transmitter power and frequency of an airborne radar (Briggs & Morrison, 1956):

1. Turn the radar set to "Stand-by" operation.
2. Connect power cord of the TS-147.
3. Turn power switch on.
4. Turn the test switch to transmit position.
5. Turn DBM dial fully counter-clockwise.
6. Connect on RF cable to the RF jack on the TS-147.

There are 14 more steps in this procedure. Notice that each of the steps by itself is easy enough; the individual is quite capable of turning a switch or connecting a cable. What he must learn to do, however, is to perform each step in the proper sequence. The sequence is important, and doing step 5 before step 4 may not be only an error, it may be dangerous. What must be learned, then, is a sequence of acts in the proper order.

Finding Malfunctions in Complex Equipment. This is in many respects a most complex kind of behavior. There are of course some very simple kinds of equipment in which this activity can be reduced to a procedure; and when this is true, the task is one that can be learned from that point of view. But the major job, for complex equipment, is one of troubleshooting, a problem-solving activity that has considerable formal resemblance to medical as well as other kinds of diagnosis. Suppose this is a radar set, again, and that the initial difficulty (symptom) is that no "range sweep" appears on the oscilloscope tube face. Beginning at this point, the troubleshooter must track down a malfunctioning component. He does this first by making a decision as to how he will check the operation of subordinate parts of the system, next by carrying out the check and noting this information it yields, next by making another decision about a next check, and so on through a whole series of stages until he finds the malfunctioning unit. In each of these stages, he presumably must be formulating hypotheses which affect his actions at the next stage, in the typical and classically described manner of problem solving. What does the individual have to learn in order to solve such problems? This is indeed a difficult question to answer, but the best guess seems to be that he must acquire concepts, principles, rules, or something of that nature which he can arouse within himself at the proper moment and which guide his behavior in diagnosing malfunctions.

Here are, then, three types of activities that are not untypical of military jobs, and which are aimed at in military training: a motor skill like flexible gunnery; a procedure like putting a radar set into operation; and troubleshooting, the diagnosing of malfunctions in complex electronic equipment. Each one of these tasks has been examined more or less intensively by military psychologists and learning specialists. Among other things, each of these tasks can be shown to be not entirely unique, but to represent a rather broad class of tasks, in its formal characteristics, which cuts across particular content or occupational areas. For example, flexible gunnery is a tracking skill, which formally resembles many others, like maneuvering an airplane, sewing a seam on a sewing machine, hovering a helicopter, and many others. As for procedures, these are common indeed, and may be found in jobs such as that of a clerk in filling in or filling forms, a cook preparing food, or a pilot prefighting an airplane. Diagnosing difficulties is certainly a widely occurring kind of activity, which may be engaged in by the leader of a group who detects this symptom of low morale, as well as by a variety of mechanics who "fix" equipment of all sorts. Accordingly, one should probably not consider these particular examples as peculiar ones; instead, they appear to be representative of a wide variety of human activities.

Learning

How are these three kinds of tasks learned? What is it that the learning psychologist can say about them which will enable anyone (the teacher, the curriculum builder, the training manager) to undertake to arrange the external conditions in such a way that the desired performances will be acquired with the minimal expediture of time, money, and wasted effort?

Suppose that you were, in fact, a psychologist who had studied learning, both animal and human, from the standpoint of experiment and theory, and that you were faced with this problem. How can scientific knowledge of learning be used to improve the process of training? Notice how I have stated this question. I am not asking, how can a scientific approach be applied to the study of training? Nor am I asking, how can experimental methodology be applied to the study of training? There are certainly answers to these questions, which have been provided by several people, notably Crawford (1962). The question is, rather, how can what you know about learning *as an event,* or *as a process,* be put to use in designing training so that it will be maximally effective?

The psychologist who is confronted with this question is likely to appeal, first, to a basic point of view towards learning which is so highly ingrained it may be called an *assumption.* Beyond this, and secondly, he looks for certain *principles* which have been well established by experiment. These are principles which relate certain variables in the learning situation, like time intervals between trials, sequence of trials, kind of feedback after each trial, and so on, to such dependent variables as rate of learning or goodness of performance. Let us try to see what can be done both with the basic assumption and with some of the more important of the principles.

The Assumption. The assumption that many learning psychologists would bring to the problem of designing training is something like this: "The best way to learn a performance is to practice that performance." I should like to show, later on, that this assumption is by no means a good one. But before I do that, I want to consider the question, where does this assumption come from, anyhow? First, it seems to have a cultural basis, by derivation from the writings of John Dewey, preserved in the educational catch-phrase "learning by doing." Second, it appears to come by unwarranted generalization from laboratory prototypes of learning such as the conditioned response. In conditioning, classical or otherwise, one observes learning only *after* the animal has made the first *response.* Thus, performance comes first, and learning is often considered to result from practice of this performance. Third, the assumption comes from theory which deals with conditioning, and which conceives of what is learned as either a response or an association terminating in a response, in either case established by *practicing the response* (with reinforcement). Without going into the matter further at the moment, the basic reason that generalization of this notion to the learning of the human tasks I have mentioned seems questionable is simply that the responses required (turning switches, inserting plugs, moving handles) do not have to be learned at all—they are already there in the human's repertoire.

Principles

Beyond this assumption that learning comes about when performances are practiced, what *principles* can the learning psychologist depend on? What kinds of conditions have been found to affect the rate of learning? What findings can he bring to bear on the problem of designing training to be maximally effective?

Let me mention some of the best-known of these principles not necessarily all of them, using various sources. In part, I shall depend on an excellent article by Underwood (1959). First of all, there is *reinforcement,* the principle that learning will be more rapid the greater the amount of reinforcement given during practice. Other principles include *distribution of practice, meaningfulness,* increasing the *distinctiveness* of the elements of a task, and *response availability.*

These principles would appear to provide the learning psychologist with a fairly adequate bag of tricks with which he can approach the job of designing effective training. There is much evidence in the experimental literature that one can in fact alter the rate of learning by manipulating these variables in the learning situation, whether one is working with single conditioned responses or with verbal material having a somewhat more complex organization. Each of these variables, so far as is known, can be manipulated to make a dependable difference on learning, if the direction of increased as well as decreased effectiveness.

Using these Assumptions and Principles in Training Design

How does one fare if he seriously attempts to use this basic assumption and these principles to design effective training situations? *Not particularly well.* The assumption that the most effective learning is provided by practice on the final task leads one astray on many occasions. As for the principles, sometimes they can clearly not be applied, that is, there is no way to manipulate the training situation in the manner suggested by the principle. In other instances, the evidence simply fails to support the principle. When this happens, there may be good theoretical reasons for the event, but this still does not restore one's faith in the usefulness of the principle.

It will be possible here only to give a few examples of military training situations in which these assumptions and principles failed to work, but I have chosen them to be as representative as possible. Let me emphasize again that I do not maintain that these examples demonstrate that the principles are invalid. I simply want to show that they are strikingly inadequate to handle the job of designing effective training situations.

Motor skill. First let's consider what is perhaps the most difficult case, the learning of a motor skill like gunnery. What happens if we try to employ the assumption that the best way to learn gunnery is to practice gunnery? Using the kind of task required of a flexible gunner, a number of studies were made of the conditions of learning for this performance. One of the earliest ones, during World War II, reported by Melton (1947), showed that different amounts of practice in firing at sleeve targets during one through ten gun-camera missions made no significant difference in the measured proficiency of gunners. A number of other studies of gunnery also indicate the very small and often insignificant effects of practice continued beyond the first three trials or so (Rittenhouse & Goldstein, 1954). Furthermore, several such studies confirm the finding that the major improvement in this performance comes as a result of informing the learners of the correct picture to be achieved in ranging (i.e., so that the dots just touch the wing tips of the target aircraft) (Goldstein & Ellis, 1956). In other words, to summarize the finding very briefly, the evidence is that simple practice on the gunnery task is not a particularly effective training method; instructions about the correct sighting picture for ranging is much more effective in bringing about improved performance. Perhaps there are good theoretical reasons for this. But the fact remains that practicing the performance is *not* the best way to learn.

What about the principles of learning? Well, let's consider the one which a learning psychologist might be inclined to think of first—reinforcement, or the introduction of knowledge of results during practice. Translated into a form applicable to motor skills learning, the more adequate are the knowledge of results, the more rapid the learning. This variable, too, has been tried out in a number of studies. Typically what was done was to augment the knowledge of results that come to the gunner through his observing his own tracking performance on a screen, by providing an extra cue, such as a buzzer, which sounded whenever the gunner was exactly on target in all three dimensions. The effect of this extra cue, it was found, was to improve the performance during learning. But did this mean that the learning itself was more effective, or simply that the buzzer "propped up" the performance? One seeks the answer to this question by comparing the performance of buzzer-trained and non-buzzer-trained groups on a standard criterion task without the buzzer. When this was done, the findings in several studies were negative (cf. Goldstein & Ellis, 1956), and one (Goldstein & Rittenhouse 1954) actually showed that learners who had the advantage of augmented knowledge of results (reinforcement) exhibited a lower performance on a second gunnery task.

Other learning principles were unconfirmed in training situations. For example, a carefully executed study could find no evidence for changes in learning as a result of alterations in conditions of practice and rest periods (Rittenhouse & Goldstein, 1954). Still other variables simply cannot be used in the training situation. For example, the meaningfulness of the task is set by the task itself, and cannot be altered by changing the conditions of training. Similarly, the internal similarity of the elements of the task are fixed by the task; one cannot, for example, change the degree of resemblance of the aircraft or of the tracks they follow by simply re-designing the training, without setting about to change the nature of the task itself. (I omit here a discussion of the transfer effects of training with an easy discrimination to performance on a hard discrimination, and vice versa. This is a different principle than the one under discussion, and the evidence about it is not clear-cut.) What about response availability or familiarity? From the evidence on practice previously cited, as well as studies on part-training (cf. Goldstein & Ellis, 1956) it seems fairly clear that the responses in this task (turning knobs, moving the gunsight up and down with a handle) were highly familiar in the first place. No one, so far as I know, ever seriously proposed that they were not.

Perhaps these examples are sufficient to at least raise doubts about the usefulness of the learning psychologist's assumptions and principles, when he attempts to apply them to the practical job of designing training for motor skills. On the whole, it may fairly be said, I think, that the assumption was often wrong and the principles were seldom useful in bringing about training improvement. I caution you again that I am not saying the learning psychologist was unsuccessful in improving training. In many instances, he was very successful. What I am trying to answer is the question, when he was successful, what knowledge or set of principles was he using?

Procedures. There are not many analytical studies of the learning of procedures. Perhaps the reason for this is that learning procedures is relatively such an easy matter, and the methods used to train them seem relatively so obvious, that little work was done on them. Consequently, I shall have to base my arguments primarily on these obvious features, rather than on a great deal of experimental evidence.

Suppose one is faced with the task of training someone to "turn on" a radar set by turning and pushing a series of fifteen switches in a particular sequence. (This is taken to be a simplified version of a representative procedural task.) How does one go about it? If one proposes to conduct training simply by "practicing the task" it becomes obvious almost immediately that this is an inefficient method to use. What is usually done is this: the learner is provided with a *list*, which states, in effect, "First, turn on power switch; second, depress voltage switch; third, set voltage knob to reading 10; etc." (e.g., Briggs & Morrison, 1956). Now the individual may be required to commit the list to memory first, and then proceed to the task; or, he may be allowed to use the list while he practices going through the sequence. The important thing is, however, that it is the *learning of the list* that contributes most to the performance of the task, not the practice of the switch-pressing responses, another example contrary to the principle that the best way to learn is to practice the required performance. I do not say that the performance should never be practiced, simply that something other than direct practice of the final task is more effective for learning procedures, just as is true for motor skills in the example previously described.

Learning principles applied to the training of procedures do not fare very well, either, although again I must note the absense of experimental evidence. One cannot alter meaningfulness, and in most cases the responses required are highly familiar. When they are not, as may be the case when a single step requires the use of an unfamiliar tool, this principle may actually have some limited usefulness. Sometimes the principle of increasing the distinctiveness of the elements of the task can be used, and one would indeed expect it to work. For example, one could put distinctive cues or labels on each of the switches in the 15-switch procedure, and this might be expected to speed up the rate of learning. However, it may be noted that this becomes a matter of changing the task (i.e., the equipment), rather than of changing the conditions of learning. From evidence on the learning of nonsense-syllable lists, one would not expect a variable like distribution of practice to make much difference as a training variable, as Underwood (1959) has noted. Again a review of learning assumptions and principles has indicated limited usefulness.

Diagnosing Malfunctions. When we turn to a consideration of troubleshooting complex equipment, even the most theoretically-dedicated learning psychologist is forced to recognize, almost from the start, that the idea of learning to troubleshoot by simply practicing troubleshooting verges on the ridiculous. The most obvious reason is that one cannot identify a single *task* to be practiced. The troubleshooter is faced with a great variety of initial problem situations, each of which may have a great variety of causes. He cannot possibly practice solving all of them. In fact, it is clear that he must learn not a single task, but a *class of tasks*, or perhaps even several classes of tasks. Yet people do learn to do them, quite successfully, without ever doing anything that can legitimately be called "practicing the final performance."

What they do learn, among other things, is an elaborate set of rules pertaining to the flow of signals through a complex circuit. To a large extent, they learn these rules by looking at and responding to a circuit diagram which is a representation of the equipment rather than the equipment itself. And they use the rules in thinking about the signal flow, that is to say, in making successive decisions leading to a solution of the problem (finding the malfunction).

Since, as I have said, it is impossible to define a single task to be practiced in learning troubleshooting, it is just about equally difficult to apply the principles of reinforcement, meaningfulness, internal differentation, and so on, to the design of training. If one accepts the task of "learning the rules" as what must be done, it is of course possible to ask the question as to whether such learning variables would apply to that task. This is a job that may some day be done by those interested in research on "learning programing." But it has not been done as yet. The evidence to date (such as it is) has not indicated strong effects, or even significant ones, for the variable of reinforcement in connection with learning programs (Goldbeck & Briggs, 1960). Other variables have not yet been investigated in relation to the learning of rules and principles.

What is Applicable to the Design of Training?

Does this mean that the psychologist has virtually nothing to offer the problem of designing effective training? Have the results of psychologists' efforts to improve training been entirely negative? Quite to the contrary, it seems to me that efforts can be identified which were quite effective in producing significant improvements in training, and which led to some demonstrably useful designs for training. But the principles which were found to be effective for such purposes were not those that have been mentioned.

Here are the psychological principles that seem to me to be useful in training:

1. Any human task may be analyzed into a set of component tasks which are quite distinct from each other in terms of the experimental operations needed to produce them.
2. These task components are mediators of the final task performance; that is, their presence insures positive transfer to a final performance, and their absence reduces such transfer to near zero.

3. The basic principles of training design consist of: (*a*) identifying the component tasks of a final performance; (*b*) insuring that each of these component tasks is fully achieved; and (*c*) arranging the total learning situation in a sequence which will insure optimal mediational effects from one component to another.

These statements certainly imply a set of principles which would have very different names from those we are now most familiar with. They are concerned with such things as *task analysis, intra task transfer, component task achievement,* and *sequencing* as important variables in learning, and consequently in training. These principles are not set in opposition to the traditional principles of learning, such as reinforcement, differentiation of task elements, familiarity, and so on, and do not deny their relevance, only their *relative importance.* They are, however, in complete opposition to the previously mentioned assumption "the best way to learn a task is to practice the task."

It should also be pointed out here that I am unable to refer to any well-organized body of experimental evidence for these newly proposed principles. They come instead by inference and generalization from a wide variety of instances of learning and military training. I do not claim more for them than this. But they have to be stated before any systematic experimental work can be done on them.

Let me try now to illustrate a definite meaning for these principles with some examples. Consider first the procedure task described previously. "1. Turn radar set to 'standby' operation; 2. Connect power cord of the TS-147; 3. Turn power switch on; 4. Turn test switch to transmit position; etc." The first step to be undertaken here is to analyze this task; and (with certain minor assumptions on our part), this is seen to be, first, the learning of an order series of responses to things; and second and subordinate to this, the locating of these things. These two *component tasks* have a hierarchical relationship to each other, and immediately suggest the proper *sequencing* for the arrangement of the learning (or training) situation. That is to say, what must first be undertaken is that the learner learn what and where the "things" are (the "standby operation" switch, the "TS-147," the power switch, the test switch, and so forth). This is a matter of identification learning, which has considerable resemblance to the paired-associate learning of the psychological laboratory. Having achieved this subordinate task, it is then possible for the learner to undertake the second, or "serial order of things" task. According to the principle proposed here, maximal positive transfer to this task would be predicted following completely adequate performance on the subordinate task of identifying the "things."

Laboratory experiments which have undertaken to test such a hypothesis seem to be scarce. It is possible, however, to make reference to two studies (Primoff, 1938; Young, 1959) which have some suggestive findings. Generally, speaking, when one learns a set of paired associates first, and then undertakes the learning of these units serially, there is high positive transfer; but when one learns units serially first, the amount of transfer to paired associate learning is very low indeed. These results strongly suggest that there is a *more efficient* and a *less efficient* sequence which can be arranged for the learning of a procedural task, and that this sequence involves learning one subtask before the total task is undertaken. A procedure is a task that can be analyzed into at least two component tasks, one of indentification, and the other of serial ordering. The first is subordinate to the second in the sense that it mediates positive transfer to the second, provided it is first completely mastered.

Can this kind of analysis be applied to a more complex task like troubleshooting? Indeed it can, and those psychologists who thought about the problem of training troubleshooting came close to the kind of analysis I have suggested. Generally speaking, they recognized that troubleshooting some particular equipment as a final performance was supported by two broad classes of subordinate tasks. First, there was knowledge of the rules of signal flow in the system, and second, the proper use of test instruments in making checks. The rules of signal flow themselves constitute an elaborate hierarchy of subordinate tasks, if one wants to look at it that way. For example, if the signal with which the mechanic is concerned is the output of an amplifier, then it may be necessary that he know some of the rules about data flow through an amplifier. Thus the task may be progressively analyzed into subordinate components which support each other in the sense that they are predicted to mediate positive transfer.

The task of using test instruments in making checks provides an even clearer example, perhaps. Obviously, one subordinate task is "choosing the proper check to make" (presumably a matter of knowing some "rules"); another is "selecting the proper test instrument" (an identification task); still another is "setting up the test instrument" (a procedural task, which in its turn has components like those previously described); and another is "interpreting the instrument reading" (another task involving a "rule"). Even identifying these component tasks brings to troubleshooting a vast clarification of the requirements for training. If one is able to take another step of arranging the proper sequencing of these tasks in a training program, the difference which results is remarkable. This is the interpretation I should be inclined to make of the studies which have demonstrated significant improvements in troubleshooting training, such as those of Briggs and Besnard (1956); of Highland, Newman and Waller (1956); and of French, Crowder, and Tucker (1956). In providing training which was demonstrably successful, these investigators were giving instruction on a carefully analyzed set of subordinate tasks, arranged in a sequence which, so far as they could tell, would best insure positive transfer to the variety of problem situations encountered in troubleshooting. It was *the identification of these tasks and this sequence* which I believe was the key to training improvement.

A good deal of other work also proceeded along these lines, although not always with a terminal phase of measured training effectiveness. For example, a whole series of studies by Miller and Folley, and their associates, were concerned with what was called *task analysis*. They had such titles as these: Line maintenance of the A-3A fire control system: III. Training characteristics (Folley & Miller, 1955); Job anticipation procedures applied to the K-1 system (Miller, Folley, & Smith, 1953); A comparison of job requirements for the line maintenance of two sets of electronic equipment (Miller, Folley, & Smith, 1954). What was all this talk about task analysis? Did it have anything to do with training? My answer is that it had to do with training more than with anything else. These were thoroughgoing and highly successful attempts to identify the variety of tasks contained in a job, and the variety of subtasks which contributed to each task. There was in fact explicit recognition of the idea that successful final performance must be a matter of attaining competence on these subtasks. So here again was the notion that effective training somehow depended on the identification of these subordinate tasks, as well as on their arrangement into a suitable sequence to insure positive transfer to the final performance.

A third source of these ideas in military training research should be mentioned. This was the development of training devices applicable to such jobs as electronic maintenance. It came to be recognized that these devices were in some respects very different from the traditional trainers such as those for developing skill in aircraft maneuvers. They were called "concept trainers", and this, as Briggs' (1959) discussion of them implies, was another name for "teaching machines." As such, they were developed independently of Skinner's ideas, and they were in fact based upon an entirely different set of principles, as is clear from the accounts provided by Briggs (1956), Crowder (1957), and French (1956). Each of these training devices (or teaching machines), aside from its hardware engineering, was developed on the basis of a painstaking task analysis, which identified the subordinate tasks involved in a total task like troubleshooting a particular electronic system. The subordinate tasks thus identified were then incorporated into a sequence designed to insure maximal positive transfer to the final task. There were certainly some programing principles, but they bore little resemblance to those which are most frequently mentioned in recent literature; in my opinion, they were much more important than these.

Still a fourth area of effort in training research was related to these ideas. This was the development of techniques to provide behavioral guides, or "jobs aids" in support of performance in various technical jobs (Hoehn, Newman, Saltz, & Wulff, 1957). In order to do this, it was found necessary to distinguish between those kinds of capabilities which could best be established by thorough training, and those kinds which could be established by minimal training plus the provision of a check list or handbook. Obviously, here again there had to be a detailed task analysis. Subordinate tasks had to be identified which would mediate transfer either to the kind of performance required without a handbook, or the kind required with a handbook. Besides the initial task analysis, it is again evident that this line of work was making use of ideas about component task achievement and intratask transfer.

Summary

Now that I have conveyed the message, my summary can be quite brief. If I were faced with the problem of improving training, I should not look for much help from the well-known learning principles like reinforcement, distribution of practice, response familiarity, and so on. I should look instead at the technique of task analysis, and at the principles of component task achievement, intratask transfer, and the sequencing of subtask learning to find those ideas of greatest usefulness in the design of effective training. Someday, I hope, even the laboratory learning psychologist will know more about these principles.

References

Briggs, L. J. A troubleshooting trainer for the E-4 Fire Control System. *USAF Personnel Train. Res. Cent. tech. Note*, 1956, No. 56–94.

Briggs, L. J. Teaching machines for training of military personnel in maintenance of electronic equipment. In E. Galanter (Ed.), *Automatic teaching: The state of the art.* New York: Wiley, 1959. Ch. 12.

Briggs, L. J., & Besnard, G. G. Experimental procedures for increasing reinforced practice in training Air Force mechanics for an electronic system. In G. Finch & F. Cameron (Eds.), *Research symposium on Air Force human engineering, personnel, and training research.* Washington, D.C.: National Academy of Sciences-National Research Council, 1956. Pp. 48–58.

Briggs, L. J., & Morrison, E. J. An assessment of the performance capabilities of fire control system mechanics. *USAF Personnel Train. Res. Cent. tech. Memo.*, 1956, No. ML-56-19.

Crawford, M. P. Concepts of training. In R. M. Gagné (Ed.), *Psychological principles in system development.* New York: Holt, Rinehart, & Winston, 1962. Ch. 9.

Crowder, N. A. A part-task trainer for troubleshooting. *USAF Personnel Train. Res. Cent. tech. Note.* 1957, No. 57–71.

Folley, J. D., Jr., & Miller, R. B. Line maintenance of the A-3A Fire control system: III. Training characteristics. *USAF Personnel Train. Res. Cent. tech. Memo.*, 1955, No. 55–5.

French, R. S. The K-System MAC-1 troubleshooting trainer: I. Development, design, and use. *USAF Personnel Train. Res. Cent. tech. Note*, 1956, No. 56–119.

French, R. S., Crowder, N. A., & Tucker, J. A., Jr. The K-System MAC-1 troubleshooting trainer: II. Effectiveness in an experimental training course. *USAF Personnel Train. Res. Cent. tech. Note*, 1956, No. 56–120.

Goldbeck, R. A., & Briggs, L. J. An analysis of response mode and feedback factors in automated instruction. Santa Barbara, Calif.: American Institute for Research, 1960. (AIR tech. Rep. No. 2)

Goldstein, M., & Rittenhouse, C. H. Knowledge of results in the acquisition and transfer of a gunnery skill. *J. exp. Psychol.*, 1954, **48**, 187–196.

Goldstein, M., & Ellis, D. S. Pedestal sight gunnery skills: A review of research. *USAF Personnel Train. Res. Cent. tech. Note*, 1956, No. 56–31.

Highland, R. W., Newman, S. E., & Waller, H. S. A descriptive study of electronic troubleshooting. In G. Finch & F. Cameron (Eds.), *Research symposium on Air Force human engineering, personnel, and training research.* Washington, D. C.: National Academy of Sciences-National Research Council, 1956. Pp. 48–58.

Hoehn, A. J., Newman, S. E., Saltz, E., & Wulff, J. J. A program for providing maintenance capability. *USAF Personnel Train. Res. Cent. tech Memo.*, 1957, No. ML-57-10.

Melton, A. W. (Ed.) Apparatus tests. *USAAF Aviat. Psychol. Program Res. Rep.*, 1947, No. 4, pp. 917–921.

Miller, R. B., Folley, J. D., Jr., & Smith, P. R. Job anticipation procedures applied to the K-1 system. *USAF Hum. Resources Res. Cent. tech Rep.*, 1953, No. 53–20.

Miller, R. B., Folley, J. D. Jr., & Smith, P. R. A comparison of job requirements for line maintenance of two sets of electronics equipment. *USAF Personnel Train. Res. Cent. tech. Rep.*, 1954, No. 54–83.

Primoff, E. Backward and forward association as an organizing act in serial and in paired associate learning. *J. Psychol.*, 1938, **5**, 375–395.

Rittenhouse, C. H., & Goldstein, M. The role of practice schedule in pedestal sight gunnery performance. *USAF Personnel Train. Res. Cent. tech. Rep.*, 1954, No. 54–97.

Underwood, B. J. Verbal learning in the educative processes. *Harvard Educ. Rev.*, 1959, **29**, 107–117.

Young, R. K. A comparison of two methods of learning serial associations. *Amer. J. Psychol.*, 1959, **72**, 554–559.

13.2 Cognitive Aspects of Psychomotor Performance[1]

Edwin A. Locke and Judith F. Bryan

The formulation of standards was more effective in improving the psychomotor performance of the subjects than in exhorting them to do their best. Evidence from other kinds of learning indicates that the clarification of goals improves performance. The difficulty of goals must be adjusted between the production of boredom and of frustration if they are to present a challenge.

A previous experiment by Mace (1935) on the effects of performance standards on level of performance found that subjects (Ss) given specific scores or standards of performance to beat on each trial (based on their initial ability) improved much faster on a mathematical computation task than Ss told simply to "do their best." The major purpose of the present experiment was to replicate this finding with a complex *motor*

SOURCES. Edwin A. Locke and Judith F. Bryan, "Cognitive Aspects of Psychomotor Performance: The Effects of Performance Goals on Level of Performance," *Journal of Applied Psychology*, L, 4 (1966), pp. 286-291. Reprinted by permission of Dr. Locke and the American Psychological Association.

[1] This research was supported by Contract No. Nonr 4792(00) between the Office of Naval Research and the American Institutes for Research. The opinions expressed are not necessarily those of the Department of the Navy.

task. The task was the Complex Coordination task described previously by Melton (1947) and Fleishman and Hempel (1954).

However, there were a number of intentional differences in procedure between the Mace experiment and the present one. First, Mace did not report just how hard the standards were for the groups with specific standards. The present investigator (Locke, 1966) has shown that the difficulty of reaching the intended level of performance (i.e., the actual *level* of the standard) has a significant effect on performance: the higher the standard the higher the performance. The standards in these previous experiments ranged in difficulty from 93% (the percentage of trials on which Ss were able to beat them) to 4%; in other words, from "very easy" to "very hard." In the present experiment the standards were set at a moderately hard difficulty level, in this case such that Ss were able to beat them less than 30% of the time. Second, as Mace (1935, p. 20) suggests, Ss told to "do their best" could, if given their scores after each trial, set standards for themselves even though they are not told to do so. In fact, in the present investigator's experience it is very difficult to *stop* experimental Ss from doing this especially where the "demand characteristics" (Orne, 1962) of the situation are high. Usually an S not instructed to set goals (but given knowledge of his score) will set himself a goal of "constant improvement" or a specific score to beat that is considerably above his initial performance (i.e., a "long term" goal). In order to prevent this in the present experiment, Ss who were not given standards were also not given their total scores for each trial, though they were given knowledge of the *correctness* of their response sequences (see task description below). It is true that this group therefore lacked specific "knowledge of total score" which the group with standards had. However, this knowledge was not knowledge about the *correctness* of individual responses or responses sequences (this was given in the task itself), but knowledge about the *number* of correct responses made. The latter information could not give the Ss knowledge of how to perform the task better; it could only give them knowledge with which they could regulate their level of effort. Payne and Hauty (1955) made this same distinction between these different kinds of knowledge in a previous study. Mace (1935) has suggested that the motivational effects of knowledge of results are entirely a consequence of giving the Ss information with which to set themselves performance standards. Thus, it is argued in the present case that knowledge of total score and standards affect Ss cognitively in the same way, namely, by giving them information which they can use only to regulate their level of effort. Standards were introduced to insure that all Ss used their knowledge in the same way, thus the "confounding" of the two is not considered relevant to the primary purpose of the study which was to examine the effects of standards.

Of secondary interest in the present study were the effects of a specific learning plan or strategy on Complex Coordination performance. Previous research by Fleishman and Hempel (1954) had found Discrimination Reaction Time to be an important ability at the early stages of practice in this task and Simple Reaction Time to be important at the later stages. However, one pilot S who worked at the task for 5 hours indicated that he had eventually tried to learn to memorize and thus anticipate which pattern was coming. This S attained a very high level of performance. It was not known, however, how soon Ss could begin to memorize the pattern sequence successfully nor if all Ss could do it at all. It was thought that 1 hour's practice was a minimum prerequisite for any attempt to memorize the patterns. The interest here was in whether trying to memorize the patterns would improve performance.

Method

Task. The Complex Coordination apparatus consists of two pairs of adjacent rows of horizontal lights separated by a pair of adjacent vertical rows of lights (so that the display looks like an H on its side). One row of each adjacent pair of rows consists of red lights and one of green lights. One red light in each row is illuminated at any given time to form a pattern (consisting of three red lights). The S's task is to move a set of controls in order to illuminate a pattern of green lights to match the pattern of illuminated red lights. The controls consist of foot pedals that control the illumination of the bottom horizontal row of green lights and a "joy stick" which moves laterally and forward and back to control the illumination of the top horizontal and the vertical rows of green lights, respectively. When the S "matches" the red-light pattern with a green-light pattern, the pattern of red lights automatically changes to a new pattern. There are 13 different patterns given in sequence. Actually the apparatus is programed so that after every 3 repetitions of the 13 patterns (in the same order), Pattern No. 11 comes on before the cycle begins again. Thus, for all intents and purposes, it is a 13-cycle pattern "with complications." Thus, feedback about the *correctness* of his movement sequences is given to S automatically, since the red-light pattern changes when it has been correctly matched. However, information as to the total number of matches made during a given time period could be withheld from the S as necessary. The Ss without standards or knowledge of scores could still get some idea of how well they were doing by the relative frequency with which the red-light patterns changed (with which they made successful matches). One S who was in the No Standard group actually counted the number of matches he made on his last trial. Another counted the number of matches on two different trials.

Subjects. The Ss were 29 University of Maryland, paid, male volunteers who responded to an advertisement in the college newspaper. (One S was dropped from the analysis; see Results section.)

Conditions. The design was a 2 × 2 fixed model with 7 Ss in each cell. (*a*) "Standard" condition—half the Ss were given specific performance goals or standards to beat on each trial. The standards for each coming trial were determined by adding a fixed increment to the S's best previous score after each trial. The increment was 15 (matches) if the S's 10-minute trial score was below 100, 10 if it was over 100 but under 130, and 5 if the previous best score was over 130 (the reduced increments being due to the fact that improvement was more difficult as S's score became higher). The Ss were told that beating these standards constituted "what we considered to be successful performance on the task on the basis of our experience with the task." The Ss were told that the standards represented "above the average performance for college students." The Ss without standards were told at the beginning of the first experimental trial to "do their best" on every trial, and were not given their total scores nor any standards. (*b*) Plan condition—at the end of the halfway point in the experiment (i.e., after 1 hour's practice), half the Ss were told to "try and memorize the number and sequence of the red light patterns." They were told that this would improve their performance since they would be able to anticipate which patterns were coming, and, therefore, to respond faster. They were reminded on each subsequent trial to continue to try and memorize the patterns.

Procedure. The experiment was introduced as a study of the way in which motor skills develop and relate to each other. After preliminary testing on the Jump and Discrimination Reaction Time tests found by Fleishman and Hempel (1954) to predict performance on this task at the late and early stages, respectively, the functioning of the Complex Coordination task was explained to the Ss, and then all Ss were given a 2-minute practice trial during which they were told to "do their best." After this it was decided what condition to put each S in. In each case, this was decided only on the basis of the practice score and so as to equalize the practice scores of the 4 experimental groups as much as possible. The Ss were told they would have 12 trials of 10 minutes each, separated by a 2-minute rest period. At this point, the method of goal setting was explained to the groups with standards (the goal for Trial 1 was 5 × the practice score plus 15) and the remaining Ss were told to "do their best." Nothing was said to the Plan groups at this point. After each trial the Ss with standards were given their score on that trial and their standard for the next trial. (Between trials all Ss made some ratings and described "what they were thinking about" but these data are not of relevance to the present experiment.)

After Trial 6 all Ss were told that Trial 7 was to be an experimental trial during which they should "experiment with new ways of doing the task." The Plan Ss, however, were told explicitly to use this trial to begin to memorize the red-light patterns. The No Plan Ss were told to do as they pleased. The Ss with standards were told no scores or standards would be given on this trial.

Before Trial 8 the Standard Ss were given their new goal based on their best performance before Trial 7. The Plan Ss were told to continue trying to memorize the patterns.

At the end of the experiment Ss were given a questionnaire asking them (*a*) whether they tried to reach the goals or not (if applicable) and, if not, what goals they were trying for, and (*b*) how many of the patterns they had been able to memorize. This was checked by an actual recall test in which Ss had to reproduce as many of the red-light patterns (by marking Xs on a paper design) as they could.

Results

Success of Experimental Manipulations. Since the true independent variables in this study were conceived of as "cognitive" rather than "situational," it was necessary to determine whether or not the Ss followed instructions about the goals they were asked to pursue. It was found that one S in the Standard-Plan condition was not doing so at all, so he was dropped from the condition and replaced with another S. The decision to drop this S was not based on this answer alone. There were other pieces of evidence, that is, his response to another written question; specific questions put to him by the experimenter (*E*) after the experiment; the S's spontaneous comments during the experiment (e.g., claiming he was falling asleep and asking for stimulants); observations of the S's behavior during the experiment (bowing his head and almost falling asleep); and comments made by the S on a dictaphone between trials about his "thoughts during the trial." It was only because all these pieces of evidence completely substantiated his questionnaire response that it was felt justifiable to drop him from the analysis. In the case of other Ss who indicated that they were not *fully* following instructions, such "convergence of evidence" was lacking, thus they were retained.

All remaining Ss in the Standard-Plan condition claimed to have tried to beat the standards. Three of the seven Standard-No Plan Ss claimed they were not trying to reach the goals set by the *E*. However, one replaced these goals with his own goals which were of equivalent difficulty; another said he tried not to beat the standards by too much since he did not want them to go too high and tire him out; a third said he followed the goals at first, but did not later. It was felt that these Ss were trying for the goals (or equivalent goals) at least to some degree so that removing them was not justified.

Nine of the 11 No Standard Ss who responded to the question about goals indicated they were trying to "do their best" or something similar. One claimed he was trying for gradual improvement and another's answer was not interpretable. Three Ss did not respond to the question. (This was probably due to ambiguous instructions on the questionnaire.)

All the Plan Ss indicated they had tried to memorize some aspect of the patterns, but 2 indicated they emphasized recognition over anticipation, 4 said they tried mainly to memorize the bottom red-light (matched with the foot pedal) sequence and one the top red-light (matched with lateral stick) sequence. However, 9 of the 14 Plan Ss said that memorizing was too difficult and/or that it did not help them and (in some cases) actually hurt their performance. This suggests that the memorizing plan might have been introduced too soon in the learning process.

In terms of the actual difficulty of the goals, the Ss in the goal condition were able to reach or exceed their standards on only 29% of the trials, suggesting that the standards were quite difficult. In Locke's (1966) experiment Ss who were given standards this hard or harder attained the highest output of any group.

Effects of Standards and Plans. First, it should be noted that the four experimental groups were successfully matched on the basis of initial ability, as measured by scores on the practice trial ($F_{\text{bet}} = < 1$). The groups were also matched successfully on the Discrimination Reaction Time and Jump Reaction Time tests found previously by Fleishman and Hempel (1954) to predict performance at the early and late stages of practice on this task, respectively.

The linear slope of the performance scores from the practice trial (multiplied by 5) to Trial 12 (omitting Trial 7) was calculated for each S, and the individual slope scores were subjected to an F test. The effect of standards was highly significant $F = 17.75$ ($p < .001$). The actual performance means of the Standard and No Standard conditions are plotted by trial in Figure 1. It is evident that the effect of the standards was immediate and that the difference between the groups increased continually during the 12 trials. The mean total number of matches over all trials (excluding 7) was also significantly greater for the Standard group ($t = 2.78$; $p < .01$).

There was no significant effect of Plans on the linear slopes ($F = 1.44$;

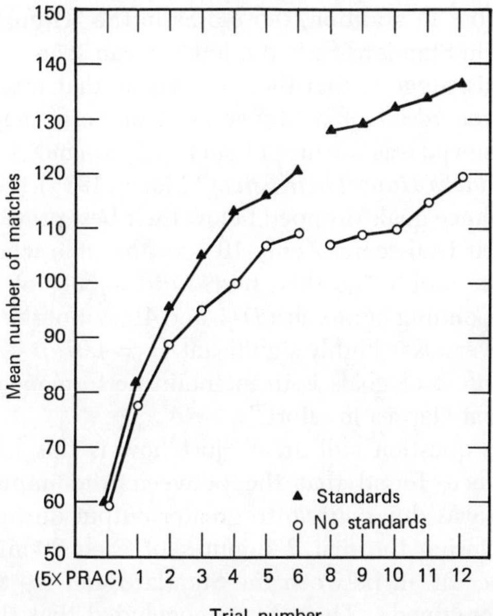

FIGURE 1. Mean number of matches by subjects with and without standards (by trial).

$p > .05$) and no interaction effect ($F = 3.28$; $p > .05$). Since the Plan instructions were introduced only after Trial 6, the linear slopes were recalculated on the basis of performance from Trial 6 to 12 only (omitting Trial 7), but again the Plan effect was not significant ($F = 1.20$; $p > .05$). The responses to the post-experimental questionnaire indicated that most Ss were not able to make much headway at memorizing in the 2 hours allowed. Most could reproduce only three patterns or less and these were not exact nor were they recalled in order. (The Ss were considered to have "reproduced" a pattern if they could reproduce its "essential shape"; they did not have to name which pattern they were trying to reproduce.)

However, as it turned out several Ss in the Plan condition were not able to reproduce any patterns. On the other hand, several Ss in the No Plan condition were able to reproduce several of the patterns, indicating that they had memorized some of the patterns even though they were not instructed to do so. When all Ss were reclassified according to the number of patterns they were able to reproduce (dividing the Ss at the median), the "High Memory" group made significantly more matches on Trials 8–12 than the "Low Memory" group ($t = 2.12$; $p < .05$). However, this reclassification put 9 of the 14 Standard Ss into the "High Memory condition; in addition, those 5 Ss in the "High Memory" condition who were No Standard Ss had a lower mean score than that of the 9 Standard Ss. This suggests that the memorizing that was done may have been as much the *result* of a higher level of performance (which the Standard Ss achieved) as a cause of such performance.

How do Standards Have Their Effect? Mace (1935) found that Ss with specific performance goals dropped below their best previous performance (in terms of their trial scores) only 10% of the time whereas Ss without such goals (those told to "do their best") did so 50% of the time. In this study the corresponding figures are 21% and 41%. But the mean difference in number of reversals is highly significant ($t = 4.07$; $p < .001$). This suggests that one effect of goals is to maintain performance between trials, that is, to prevent "lapses in effort."

However, the question still arises, just how is this level maintained? Mace, for instance, found that the between trial improvement of the Standard group was due *entirely* to greater output during the *latter* part of each trial. During the first 2 minutes of each 20-minute trial there was no difference at all between the Standard and No Standard groups (for all trials combined). Thus, Mace concluded that the effects of the standards were to *prolong* effort during the work period rather than to *intensify* effort at all stages of the trial.

The appropriate data from the present study are shown in Figure 2.

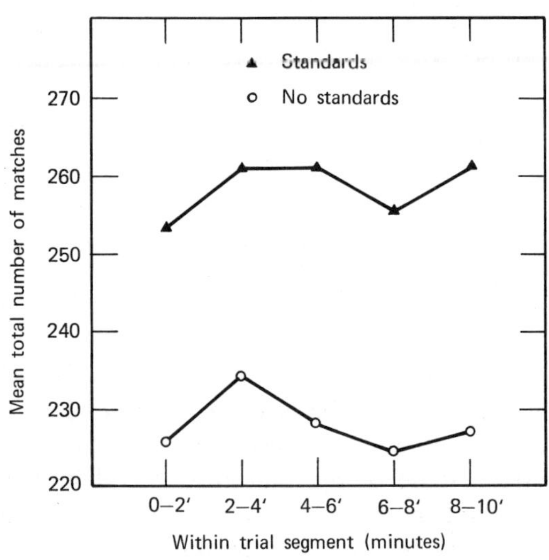

FIGURE 2. Mean total number of matches by subjects with and without standards (by within trial segments).

These are the mean performance scores of the Standard and No Standard groups for each 2-minute segment of the 10-minute trials summed over all trials (excluding Trial 7, and, of course, the 2-minute practice trial). It is evident that in the present study the difference between the Standard and No Standard groups is substantial for *all* the 2-minute segments. The t values for the mean differences for each 2-minute segment total are, respectively, 2.44, 2.60, 2.81, 2.71, and 3.01, all of which are significant at $p < .05$ or better. The difference in the mean within trial (linear) slopes of the Standard and No Standard groups, however, is not significant ($t = 1.42$; $p > .05$) though it is in the right direction. However, there is a significant difference between the Standard-Plan group and the No Standard-Plan group ($t = 2.24$; $p < .05$) in mean within trial slopes. Apparently, the major effect of the goals in the present case was to improve performance between trials at every stage of the trial, though there was some difference within trials as well.

One of the reasons for the difference of the two studies might have been that Mace's trials were 20 minutes long while they were only 10 minutes long in the present study. The longer the trials, the more likely the Ss without specific goals should be expected to lag near the end of the period (as fatigue increases). However, it appears that standards can *intensify* effort at all points in the trial as well as to *prolong* effort (as in Mace's study) during the work period.

Discussion

The findings of Mace (1935) using an arithmetic computation task were clearly replicated with a psychomotor task, indicating that the principle that performance goals influence level of performance has some generality over tasks. A recent experiment by Church and Camp (1965) yielded a similar finding using a reaction time task (though the theoretical interpretation of these investigators' results is at variance with our own). Although a previous study by Locke (1966) found a strong relationship between the level of the performance goal (level of intended achievement) and level of actual performance, the present findings (along with those of Mace) may have greater practical implications as in the latter two cases, Ss with specific goals performed better than those told to "do their best." The latter is a typical instruction in most industrial, military, and educational training situations, but the present results indicate that such instructions (or goals) may not result in the highest possible level of performance.

A second finding of interest in the present study was that performance goals were shown to influence the *intensity* of the effort per unit time, whereas previously (Mace, 1935) they had been shown only to *prolong* effort better over the work period. The fact that performance goals can have both effects argues for the general importance of such goals.

Finally the present findings are of theoretical interest in that they emphasize the effects of cognitive (intentional) aspects of motivation. Ryan[2] (1958) and Ryan and Smith (1954), for instance, have argued that the "task" or "intention" be taken as the fundamental unit in motivation and that intentions are the direct cause of most human behavior. The present study, in addition to demonstrating how such notions can be put to a test, supports the validity of this approach.

References

Church, R. M., & Camp, D. S. Change in reaction time as a function of knowledge of results. *American Journal of Psychology*, 1965, **78**, 102–106.

Fleishman, E. A., & Hempel, W. E. Changes in factor structure of a complex psychomotor test as a function of practice. *Psychometrika*, 1954, **19**, 239–252.

Locke, E. A. The relationship of intentions to level of performance. *Journal of Applied Psychology*, 1966, **50**, 60–66.

Mace, C. A. Incentives: Some experimental studies. Industrial Health Research Board (Great Britain), 1935, Report No. 72.

Melton, A. W. (Ed.) *Apparatus Tests. AAF* Aviation Psychology Program Research Report No. **4**, 1947.

Orne, M. T. On the social psychology of the psychological experiment with particular reference to demand characteristics. *American Psychologist*, 1962, **17**, 776–783.

Payne, R. B., & Hauty, G. T. Effect of psychological feedback upon work decrement. *Journal of Experimental Psychology*, 1955, **50**, 343–351.

Ryan, T. A. Drives, tasks, and the initiation of behavior. *American Journal of Psychology*, 1958, **71**, 74–93.

Ryan, T. A., & Smith, P. C. *Principles of industrial psychology*. New York: Ronald, 1954.

Selected Readings

Bilodeau, E. A. (Ed.). *Acquisition of skill*. New York: Academic Press Inc., 1966.

[2] Unpublished mimeos, 1964. Chapter I: Explaining behavior; Chapter II: Explanatory concepts; Chapter V: Experiments on intention, task, and set; Chapter VI: Intentional learning; Chapter VII: Unintentional learning. Cornell University, Department of Psychology.

Colville, F. M. The learning of motor skills as influenced by knowledge of mechanical principles. *Journal of Educational Psychology*, 1957, **48**, 321–327.

Fitts, P. M. Factors in complex skill training. In R. Glaser (Ed.), *Training research and education.* New York: John Wiley and Sons, 1965, pp. 177–197.

Guilford, J. P. A system of the psychomotor abilities. *American Journal of Psychology*, 1958, **7**, 164–174.

CHAPTER 14

Retention and Transfer of Learning

14.1 Effects of Repetition and Spaced Review Upon Retention of a Complex Learning Task[1]

James H. Reynolds and Robert Glaser

The use of programmed instructional techniques enables researchers to reexamine evidence formerly obtained through experimental designs unable to cope with the control of some variables. The relative importance of two variables related to retention was explored in this paper. Spaced review was found to be far more effective in improving retention than variations of repetition. Teachers will find the information significant for organizing reviews.

Laboratory investigations of overlearning (Krueger, 1929; Postman, 1961) and retroactive inhibition (e.g., Briggs, 1957) have generally shown that retention of paired-associate lists is positively related to degree of original learning. These findings are consonant with most existing learning theories, which assume that the strength of learning—and therefore

SOURCE. James H. Reynolds and Robert Glaser, "Effects of Repetition and Spaced Review Upon Retention of a Complex Learning Task," *Journal of Educational Psychology*, LV, 5 (1964), pp. 297–308. Reprinted by permission of the authors and the American Psychological Association.

[1] The research was supported through the Cooperative Research Program of the Office of Education, United States Department of Health, Education, and Welfare, Project No. 1343.

resistance to forgetting—varies as a function of the number of practice repetitions. In contrast, several early investigations reviewed by Welborn and English (1937) have indicated that retention of meaningful material tends to remain constant regardless of amount of repetition during original learning. Most of these investigations employing meaningful tasks, however, are subject to certain criticisms regarding methodology, primarily with respect to the inadequate control procedures used in presentation of the experimental material and other proactive and retroactive material which might affect retention. Because of such methodological problems, the validity of past results indicating that repetition has little effect upon retention of meaningful tasks has been questioned (e.g., Slamecka & Ceraso, 1960).

One purpose of the research reported here was to evaluate the effect of repetition upon retention of a complex and meaningful learning task using programed instruction as an apparatus for controlling the relevant presentation variables assumed to be related to retention. Through the use of various program sequences, the amount of repetition and the order of presentation of both experimental and interpolated material could be manipulated with considerable precision. At the same time, the programing technique permitted presentation of the learning task in an environment similar to that in which complex learning often takes place, i.e., in the classroom. Thus the technique provided for evaluation of repetition effects upon retention of meaningful materials learned under classroom conditions, but controlled with respect to relevant presentation variables.

A second problem investigated, using the same programed materials, was the effect of spaced review upon retention of meaningful material. Although periodic review of material previously learned is a prevalent teaching method, little attention has been given to systematic evaluation of its effect upon retention. Distribution of practice studies using lists of paired-associate materials has indicated that temporal factors in presentation have varying and complicated effects upon learning (Underwood, 1961). Typically, however, the designs used in such investigations are not analogous to spacing procedures which are used in reviewing meaningful material, so generalizations from the laboratory to the classroom are difficult to make.

In the present research, an attempt was made to replicate the use of review as employed in the classroom by inserting review sequences into an instructional program at various points following original learning. The retention of groups receiving spaced review was compared with the retention of other program groups which received no spaced review after learning the same tasks. Because the variable studied was one which interacted with the length of the retention interval, comparisons of review and nonreview treatments were made under two conditions: (*a*) retention at equivalent times following the end of original learning, and (*b*) retention when the amount of time following last exposure to the experimental material was equivalent for the review and nonreview groups. Results for the first condition, and for the investigation of repetition and spaced review effects upon retention, are described in Experiment I. The second condition under which spaced review effects were further evaluated is presented in Experiment II.

Experiment I

Method

Materials. Programs. A 1,280-frame program, covering the 10 topics in biology outlined in Table 1, was used. Within this program the sixth topic, a 115-frame sequence on mitosis, was selected for experimental variation. The topic introduced 11 new technical terms—mitosis, interphase, prophase, methaphase, anaphase, telophase, spindles, cell plate, indentation, equaltor, chromosomes—and required the subject to learn their meanings and usage in describing the mitosis process. Using the original 115-frame sequence as a standard, two new sequences were written which taught the same material, but differed from the original and from each other in the frequency with which the technical terms were repeated. To construct the new sequences, the number of stimulus and response repeti-

Table 1
Title and Order of Biology Topics Presented to Three Massed Repetition Groups and Two Spaced Review Groups

Order of Topics	A Massed Repetition Groups (M-.5, M-1.0, M-1.5)[a]	B Spaced Review Groups (R-1.0, R-1.5)
1	Cells	Cells
2	Protozoa	Protozoa
3	Tissues	Tissues
4	Organs and Systems	Organs and Systems
5	Green Plants	Green Plants
6	Mitosis (.5 or 1.0 or 1.5)	Mitosis (.5 or 1.0)
7	Plant Reproduction (107 frames)	Plant Reproduction (107 frames)
(Review)	—	Review Mitosis (28 frames)
8	Animal Reproduction (217 frames)	Animal Reproduction (217 frames)
(Review)	—	Review Mitosis (22 frames)
9	Classification (165 frames)	Classification (165 frames)
10	Heredity (95 frames)	Heredity (95 frames)

[a] The numbers .5, 1.0, and 1.5 indicate the relative amounts of repetition used in the different experimental versions.

tions of each of the 11 critical terms in the original sequence (hereafter designated as the 1.0 sequence) were first tabulated. Then a second sequence of frames, similar in content to the 1.0 sequence, but containing just half as many stimulus and response repetitions of each term, was written. Finally a third sequence, also similar to 1.0, but containing 50% more stimulus-response repetitions of each term, was constructed. These new sequences, designated .5 and 1.5, respectively, were 75 frames and 175 frames in length.

By inserting any one of the three experimental sequences (.5, 1.0, 1.5) into the larger program as Topic 6, amount of repetition of the experimental material could be varied while keeping presentation of both prior and subsequent learning materials constant. Column A of Table 1 illustrates the three repetition conditions thus formed. These conditions were designated M-.5, M-1.0, and M-1.5, indicating that the three repetition levels were presented intact as massed (M) practice.

The .5 and 1.0 sequences were also used in constructing two spaced review (R) conditions. To provide for spaced review, two short sections were written; these sequences were 22 and 28 frames in length and together contained the same number of repetitions of the 11 terms as the .5 sequence. As shown in Column B of Table 1, the review sections were inserted after Topic 7 and Topic 8 (Plant and Animal Reproduction). Thus one review condition (R-1.0), consisting of the .5 sequence and the two review sections, contained the same number of repetitions of the 11 terms as condition M-1.0, but spaced them out over several topics rather than presenting them intact. A second review condition (R-1.5), consisting of the 1.0 sequence plus the review sections, was equivalent in number of repetitions to M-1.5, but they were also distributed over topics rather than massed.

Tests. Measures of unaided recall, aided recall, and recognition of the 11 mitosis terms were used to assess retention. The Unaided Recall Test (22 points) required the subject to describe and illustrate the mitosis process without the aid of external cues. The Aided Recall Test contained 15 incomplete sentences which required the use of the experimental terms as fill-ins. The Recognition Test was an 18-item multiple-choice measure. Two additional tests, evaluating aided recall and recognition of material from three nonexperimental topics (Cells, Plant Reproduction, and Animal Reproduction), were employed as control measures.

Subjects. A total of 75 junior-high-school students participated in the experiment. Scholastic aptitudes, as measured by the Otis Quick-Scoring Mental Ability Test (Beta), ranged from 100 to 134, with a median IQ of 117. At the time of the experiment, all subjects belonged to one of three classes taking a general science course. None of the subjects had taken previous courses in biology, and none had had previous experience with programed instruction.

Design and Procedure. Prior to the experiment, the subjects with equivalent intelligence were assigned to one of five groups by a randomized blocks method (Edwards, 1960, Ch. 11). Each group received one of the five experimental conditions. The programs were administered with Min-Max II teaching machines to all groups in 20 consecutive classroom science periods, each period lasting 40 minutes. At the beginning of every period the teacher, who served as the experimenter for all groups, assigned to each group the number of frames that were to be completed in that session. The subjects finishing an assignment early were permitted to use the remainder of the session as a study period, provided they did not study biology. Since the programs contained slightly different number of frames because of the experimental variations, daily work assignments to the groups varied from session to session, ranging from assignments of 50 frames to a maximum assignment of 80 frames for any single 40-minute session. By regulating the daily assignments, all of the five groups completed the experimental mitosis section during Sessions 10 and 11, and completed the entire program in the twentieth session.

Before beginning the program, the subjects were given the Recognition Test as a pretest to determine the equivalence of the five groups on prelearning knowledge of mitosis. The first retention testing (T_1) was administered on the 2 days immediately following completion of the program. In T_1, Aided Recall Tests were given first for both the experimental and control material. These measures were followed by the experimental and control Recognition Tests. After a 3-week interval, during which the subjects were not exposed to any of the material learned in the programs, a second retention testing (T_2) was administered. T_2 was composed of four separate tests, presented in order of decreasing difficulty. First the Unaided Recall test was administered, which had not been given at T_1, but was used in T_2 both as a warm-up task and as an additional retention measure; then the Aided Recall (completion) and the Recognition (multiple-choice) tests of mitosis, and finally the Recognition test for the control materials, were given. The subjects were unaware that this T_2 battery was to be administered, and all four tests were given in a single session to prevent the possibility of reviewing.

Results

Table 2 summarizes the means and standard deviations of all groups on the pretest and the various measures obtained during T_1 and T_2. Analyses of variance, employing the randomized-blocks technique (Ed-

Table 2
Summary of Means and Standard Deviations for All Groups on Pretest and Retention Tests Administered at T_1 and T_2

Test	Total Possible Score	Statistic	Group: Massed Repetition M-.5	M-1.0	M-1.5	Spaced Review R-1.0	R-1.5
Pretest							
Recognition (Mitosis)	18	X	3.62	2.92	2.54	3.92	2.92
($N = 13$)		s	1.66	1.98	1.76	2.43	2.22
Immediate retention (T_1)							
Aided Recall ($N = 14$)							
Mitosis	15	X	3.79	5.21	7.57	10.00	9.79
		s	3.49	4.59	5.67	4.76	4.69
Control	39	X	18.57	17.50	17.79	22.14	19.36
		s	9.15	7.05	9.25	9.85	7.37
Recognition ($N = 13$)							
Mitosis	18	X	6.00	7.08	8.54	10.00	8.92
		s	4.26	5.22	4.79	5.93	3.66
Control	13	X	11.31	12.77	12.69	13.08	12.38
		s	3.55	4.17	3.61	3.25	2.47
Delayed retention (T_2)							
Unaided Recall ($N = 14$)							
Mitosis	22	X	2.93	4.29	3.14	6.57	6.14
		s	3.60	4.92	3.80	4.90	4.87
Aided Recall ($N = 14$)							
Mitosis	15	X	4.86	6.14	6.71	9.50	10.07
		s	4.45	5.19	5.40	4.77	4.75
Recognition ($N = 14$)							
Mitosis	18	X	6.79	7.71	8.29	10.50	10.93
		s	4.21	5.92	5.72	6.35	6.08
Control	20	X	12.29	12.86	12.86	15.00	13.93
		s	3.77	3.51	3.57	2.83	2.62

wards, 1960, Ch. 11), were used to compare the groups on each of these measures. Several subjects were absent at various times during the series of testings. Each absence required that the entire block with which the absent subject was matched be eliminated from the analyses, reducing the size of all groups by one. Fortunately, the absences were distributed over the testing periods in a way that necessitated removal of only one or two blocks of subjects from each of the analyses made. However, it was necessary to remove different blocks on different analyses, so that the group *N*s of 13 or 14 that were used in the various analyses did not always represent the same subjects in each analysis.

As can be seen in Table 2, mean scores among the five groups on the pretest ranged from 2.54 to 3.62. An analysis of variance showed that the pretest differences among groups were not significant ($F = 1.22$, $df = 4/64$, $p > .05$). A series of correlated t tests, made for each group on the differences between the Recognition pretest scores and the T_1 Recognition scores, yielded significant t values ranging from 2.34 to 3.84, indicating that the higher mean scores for each group at the time of T_1 were due to the effect of the program treatments rather than chance.

Repetition Effects. The M-.5, M-1.0, and M-1.5 groups received the experimental T_1 measures of Aided Recall and Recognition on the tenth day following original learning of mitosis. A simple analysis of variance showed no significant differences among the groups on the T_1 Recognition Test ($F = .98$, $df = 2/24$, $p > .05$). For the T_1 Aided Recall Test, however, a significant difference among means was indicated ($F = 4.50$, $df = 2/26$, $p < .025$). Further analysis of the Aided Recall results showed that the M-.5 group mean was significantly lower than the mean for the M-1.5 group ($t = 3.12$, $df = 13$, $p < .01$); but, although there is a regular trend of higher performance with increased repetition, all other mean differences were within chance limits. The results of analyses of variance performed for the T_1 control measures were not significant ($F < 1.00$ and $F = 1.17$ for Aided Recall and Recognition control tests, respectively), implying that the reliable difference obtained for the experimental Aided Recall Test was due to the varying repetition levels received and not to extraexperimental differences among the groups.

The Unaided Recall, Aided Recall, and the experimental and control Recognition Tests were administered at T_2, 21 days following T_1. Analyses of variance comparing the M-.5, M-1.0, and M-1.5 groups on all four T_2 measures yielded F values below 1.00, indicating no significant differences among the repetition levels in retention of either the experimental or the control materials. The significant difference obtained for Aided Recall at time T_1 apparently dissipated between T_1 and T_2, leaving retention equivalent for all three massed repetition groups three weeks after termination of the program.

Effects of Spaced Review. Table 2 shows that the performance of the R-1.0 and R-1.5 groups was generally higher than the M groups on all retention tests administered at T_1 and T_2. Since the R-1.0 and R-1.5 groups received the same T_1 and T_2 measures as were obtained for Groups M-1.0 and M-1.5, these four groups could be compared on all measures in a series of 2×2 analyses of variance to evaluate statistically the effects of two levels of repetition (1.0 and 1.5), two levels of review (R and M), and their interaction.

Results of the factorial analyses of the two experimental and the two control tests administered at T_1 showed that neither the repetition effect nor the interaction between repetition and review was significant for any measure, indicating that the two levels of repetition used had neither a general nor a differential effect upon retention of the M and R groups.

In comparing the two levels of review, a significant F value of 13.17 ($df = 1/55$, $p < .01$) obtained for the experimental Aided Recall Test indicated that recall of the mitosis material was reliably greater for the R treatment than for M. The difference between M and R treatments on the other experimental test, Recognition, was not significant ($F = 2.31$, $df = 1/51$). On the control Recognition Test, also, no difference between M and R was found ($F < 1.00$); however, a significant difference between the M and R treatments was obtained for the control Aided Recall Test ($F = 4.22$, $df = 1/55$, $p < .05$). This latter finding of a reliable difference on one of the control measures implies that the superior aided recall of the experimental material demonstrated by the R groups at T_1 may have been due to some effect other than the experimental treatment alone.

Turning to the analyses of the data obtained from the M-1.0, M-1.5, R-1.0, and R-1.5 groups at T_2, there were again no significant differences for the repetition effect or the Repetition $\times$ Review interaction on any of the four T_2 tests administered. At this time, performance of the R groups was superior to M on all three of the retention tests of the experimental material; with $df = 1/59$, the F values for the review effect were 7.76 ($p < .01$), 13.15 ($p < .01$), and 4.54 ($p < .05$) for the Unaided Recall, Aided Recall, and Recognition Tests, respectively. As at time T_1, however, R performance was also significantly higher than M on the control test ($F = 5.56$, $df = 1/55$, $p < .05$). Again the control data indicate that the superior retention demonstrated by the R groups on the experimental material may not have been due to the experimental treatment alone.

Delayed Retention. The Aided Recall and Recognition Tests of mitosis, and the control Recognition Test, were administered to all groups at both T_1 and T_2. Table 2 indicates that many of the T_2 means were slightly higher than the T_1 means obtained for the same group on the same test. Individual t tests between T_1 and T_2 means failed to reveal significant changes over time for any group in either direction. These comparisons, which suggest that no forgetting occurred during the 3-week intertest interval, will be discussed further after the results of the second experiment have been presented.

Discussion

The results from the T_1 and T_2 testings of the M-.5, M-1.0, and M-1.5 repetition groups indicate that stimulus-response repetition differences as large as 200% had only a limited effect upon retention of programed materials after a period of interpolated learning, and that even this limited effect disappeared over a relatively short period of time. Although the general failure to obtain significant repetition effects is contradictory to findings from investigations employing paired-associate lists in transfer designs (e.g., Briggs, 1957), it supports earlier research in retention of meaningful material as a function of repetition (Welborn & English, 1937).

Slamecka and Ceraso (1960, p. 459), in a comprehensive review of research on proactive and retroactive inhibition, have criticized much of the previous research in retention of meaningful material. They list such control problems as whole presentation, unlimited recall times, and group testing and presentation procedures as reasons for the discrepancies found among studies of retention of meaningful and nonmeaningful material. To demonstrate the effects of such design problems, these reviewers cite one study using meaningful rote material under controlled laboratory conditions which indicated that when appropriate control measures are taken the retention of meaningful material can be shown to vary with repetition in the same way as does retention of unconnected materials. In the present study, group testing and presentation procedures were used intentionally in an effort to replicate the classroom learning environment. However, the use of the programing instrument permitted sequential presentation of the learning task to each subject individually and also controlled the quantity of stimulus presentation and response evocation for all of the materials learned. The partial and transitory effect of repetition obtained under these conditions suggests that, while a relationship between number of stimulus-response repetitions and retention of meaningful material may be demonstrable in the laboratory, the relevance of this relationship in more complex learning situations is limited.

Comparisons of the M and R treatments at T_1 and T_2 indicate that retention was generally superior for the R treatment on both the experimental and the control materials. Since all groups were equivalent in intelligence and pretest knowledge of the experimental material, there is some basis for assuming that spaced review had facilitating effects upon retention of both experimental and control topics. The alternative possibility exists, however, that the groups receiving the R treatment were superior in general knowledge of biology prior to the experiment—or at least in prior knowledge of the control materials, which was not evaluated in the pretest. Such a difference would account for the difference in retention of the control topics and even suggests that the R groups may have had some advantage in retaining the experimental material simply because the other tasks presented were already familiar. This possible influence of pre-experimental differences in general knowledge of the total learning task was evaluated further in the second experiment.

A second problem in interpreting the spaced review results is the discrepancy in length of the interpolated interval elapsing between the last practice frames of the experimental mitosis topic and the retention tests. All subjects receiving the M treatment finished instruction in mitosis at the end of Day 11, while those in the R groups did not receive final review of this material until Day 15. Since retention testings were administered to all groups at the same time relative to the end of the program, the retention intervals for the R treatment were consistently 4 days shorter than for M. This discrepancy was unavoidable, since no single experiment can vary spacing while simultaneously controlling both prior learning and total learning. Therefore, a second experiment evaluating the effect of spaced review was performed, this time controlling amount of prior learning and length of interval between last practice and test, but permitting the total amount of learning material presented to vary.

Experiment II

The design of Experiment II differed from that of Experiment I in several major respects. First, although groups received either the M or the R treatment in the same manner as previously described, only one level of repetition (1.5) was used. Second, a pretest and additional retention tests of the control materials were administered to evaluate more precisely the effect of spaced review upon retention of the control topics. Third, the R group did not receive a T_1 testing immediately following completion of the program, but instead received other interpolated tasks before being given T_1. Although this procedure necessarily resulted in the R group receiving more interpolated (and possibly interfering) material than group M, it permitted an equating of the M and R groups with regard to the length of the retention interval elapsing between the last frame of the mitosis material and administration of the retention measures. These changes in design, and several other procedural variations, are described in more detail below.

Method

Subjects. Two intact eighth-grade science classes were selected to participate in the experiment on the basis of the following criteria: neither had been exposed to biology instruction during the school year, neither had had previous familiarity with programed instruction, and the mean IQs of the two groups were equivalent. The classes chosen were from different schools and had different science teachers.

Materials. Prior to Experiment II certain modifications were made in the first five sections of the original biology program in order to make it a more effective instructional tool. Modifications consisted of making minor changes in the wording of certain frames, and adding new frames in some cases to clarify difficult sections. The resulting program differed from that used in Experiment I in that it was 64 frames longer (totaling 1,344 frames) and was divided into 14 sections rather than 10. Table 3 summarizes the newer revision, giving the names, order, and sizes of each topic. Since the changes occurred only in control topics, their possible effects upon the data of Experiment II were equivalent for the experimental treatments compared. All programs were administered with Min-Max II teaching machines. The experimental mitosis sequences inserted into the revised program were the same sequences used in Experiment I, and the retention tests were also identical to those previously described.

Design and Procedure. A massed-learning group (M) received the M-1.5 program described in the first experiment, followed by a T_1 retention test at the end of the program. Because of the increased length of the revised program, the time taken to complete it was 1 day longer than in Experiment I. Consequently, the length of the interpolated learning interval between the last trial of the mitosis topic and T_1 was 10 school days for Group M. An R group was administered the same treatment as described previously for the R-1.5 group, except that the T_1 testing was not given immediately following completion of the program. Instead, Group R received five science periods of teacher instruction in astronomy after finishing the program, and received the T_1 test in the sixth science period. These interpolated astronomy periods extended the Group R interval between the last review trial of mitosis and T_1 to 10

Table 3
Description of Biology Program Presented to All Groups in Experiment II

Unit	Topic	Number of Frames
1	Introduction to Cell Structure	150
2	The Plastids	74
3	The Nucleus	43
4	The Cytoplasm	74
5	Animal and Plant Cells	31
6	Protozoa	39
7	Tissues, Organs, and Systems	50
8	Green Plants	183
9	Mitosis	115
10	Reproduction of Seed Plants	107
11	Animal Reproduction	217
12	Men in Biology	39
13	Classification of Plants and Animals	123
14	Heredity	99
	Total frames	1344

school days, making it equivalent to the interpolated learning interval of Group M. As in Experiment I, a T_2 retention test was administered to both groups 3 weeks following T_1.

Testing procedures varied slightly from those used in Experiment I so that more information concerning prior knowledge and learning of the control materials could be obtained. The pretests consisted of the Recognition measures for both experimental and control materials, providing an assessment of equivalence of the groups in general knowledge of biology as well as knowledge of mitosis. At both T_1 and T_2 the Aided Recall and the Recognition Tests for the experimental and control topics were administered. As in the first experiment, the Unaided Recall Test of mitosis was given only at T_2, as a warm-up task and an additional retention measure.

Daily administration of the program was accomplished as described for Experiment I. All tests at T_1 and T_2 were administered in one session, without prior warning from the experimenter that they would be given. In the interval between T_1 and T_2 both groups received instruction in science topics unrelated to biology, minimizing the probability of systematic practice and review during the 3-week forgetting period.

Results

Two subjects in Group R and six subjects in Group M failed to complete the entire program and all retention tests because of absence, and were eliminated from the final data. The results for the remaining subjects are summarized in Table 4, including the measures taken for the R and M groups prior to administration of the program, and also at the retention testing intervals which occurred 10 days (T_1) and 31 days (T_2) following the last review trial of the mitosis material. Differences between the group means for each measure were evaluated by independent two-tailed t tests, and the resulting t values are also included in Table 4.

There were no significant differences between group means on any of the pretest measures, indicating that the groups were equivalent in intelligence and also in preprogram knowledge of the experimental and control materials. The means on the Recognition pretest of mitosis are no higher than would be expected from guessing on an 18-item 5-choice multiple-choice test, suggesting that neither group had any knowledge of the mitosis topic prior to taking the program. Control-item means for the Recognition pretest were above chance limits of guessing, however, reflecting some degree of preprogram knowledge of the control materials.

As shown in Table 4, no significant differences between Group M and Group R were found for any of the control tests at either T_1 or T_2. The two groups, equivalent in pretest performance on the control material

Table 4
Means and Standard Deviations of R and M Groups on All Tests and Results of *t* Tests for Differences Between Means

	Spaced Review (R) ($N = 23$)		Massed Repetition (M) ($N = 35$)		
Test	X	s	X	s	t
Pretests					
IQ	118.74	6.81	119.17	9.98	1.18
Recognition					
Mitosis	2.87	1.49	3.37	1.93	1.05
Control	10.30	2.28	11.31	2.52	1.55
Immediate retention (T_1)					
Aided Recall					
Mitosis	11.00	3.44	8.14	4.41	2.62[a]
Control	20.30	7.55	20.37	6.39	.04
Recognition					
Mitosis	12.22	4.00	9.23	4.73	2.50[a]
Control	13.96	2.79	14.91	2.28	1.42
Delayed retention (T_2)					
Unaided Recall					
Mitosis	11.74	4.21	7.00	3.49	4.58[c]
Aided Recall					
Mitosis	11.13	3.40	8.17	4.71	2.60[a]
Control	21.52	8.08	21.66	6.09	.75
Recognition					
Mitosis	12.83	4.18	9.34	4.44	3.00[b]
Control	14.09	2.25	14.17	2.72	.12

Note.—$23 + 35 - 2 = 56$ *df*.
[a] $p < .02$.
[b] $p < .01$.
[c] $p < .001$.

and given equivalent presentations of that material during learning, retained their learning to the same degree. On the experimental mitosis materials, however, significant differences were found between the groups on all tests administered at T_1 and T_2. All differences were in the same direction, with Group R demonstrating higher retention performance than Group M regardless of the type of retention tested or the length of the retention interval.

The same Aided Recall and Recognition Tests were administered to both groups at both T_1 and T_2. Inspection of the means shows that for each group the T_2 performance is nearly the same, and in all but one case slightly higher, than performance on the same test at T_1. As in Experiment I, none of the changes are significant in either direction, indicating that neither forgetting nor significant improvement in retention occurred during the T_1–T_2 interval.

Discussion

The consistent superiority of Group R over M in retention of the experimental material, even with length of the forgetting interval between last practice and testing equated, confirms the previously tentative finding that the spacing of review sequences has a facilitating effect upon retention of material learned in a programed sequence. The fact that Group R was exposed to more new material (i.e., the additional astronomy topic presented by the teacher) between the end of the program and T_1 does not detract from the results, since this material, if it had any effect at all upon retention, would presumably serve as additional interference rather than as an aid in retaining the experimental material.

In contrast to Experiment I, no differences between the M and R conditions in retention of control materials were obtained in Experiment II. Two explanations must be considered in accounting for this discrepancy. First, it is possible that the extension of the retention interval in Experiment II to 5 days following the end of the program for the R group caused additional forgetting of the control topics, masking a superior retention of this material that may have existed at a point immediately following the end of the program. An alternative explanation, however, is that the findings obtained for the control material in Experiment I were due simply to unmeasured differences between groups in prior knowledge of the control topics, and that neither the R treatment itself nor the change in retention intervals in Experiment II had any reliable effect upon this material.

Although the present data cannot rule out either of these interpretations, the latter one appears to be more likely. The changes in retention interval did not affect results for the experimental task, so there is little reason to expect that the same change would, in itself, have a significant effect upon the control material. Also, the Experiment II pretest indicated equivalence of groups in prior knowledge of the control topics, and a subsequent equivalence in retention of these topics. These aspects of the data suggest that the spaced review treatment, while producing a significant facilitation in retention of the material that was spaced, had no differential effect upon retention of the accompanying material that was not spaced.

In both experiments, comparisons of the means obtained on the same tests given at the two retention intervals showed no significant forgetting, and in most cases a slight but nonsignificant improvement in performance, over the 3-week interval separating the two retention testings. Two aspects of the testing procedures used may explain the failure to obtain the expected decrease in retention over time. First, it is noted that the initial testing (T_1) occurred several days after the last experimental and control materials were presented for learning, the interim days being used to present other biology topics which were not included in the tests used (e.g., Men in Biology, Classification, Heredity). These interpolated topics may have interfered with an initially high level of learning of the experimental and control topics, causing rapid forgetting to a moderate, but stable, level of retention. Hovland (1951, p. 646) has presented evidence that retention of meaningful material dissipates rapidily following learning, soon reaching a level which is maintained without further retention loss over long periods of time. If such a stable level of retention had already been reached at the time of initial testing, it would be expected that (*a*) performance would not be at ceiling, and (*b*) little further forgetting would occur over the next several weeks. These expectations are substantiated by the data from both experiments. Second, it has been shown that, when identical tests are used at two retention intervals, practice effects tend to carry over from the first testing and elevate performance artificially on the second test (Ammons & Irion, 1954). Either of these explanations, or both, may account for the failure to obtain a decrease in retention performance over the 3-week period separating the two testings.

The combined results of the two experiments have implications for several areas of learning research which may warrant further investigation. Regarding programed instruction, the findings suggest that the often-criticized monotony of repetition found in many early programs may in fact be of little value in enhancing retention and may be profitably replaced by a series of short instructional sequences in several related topics, each interspersed with short reviews of the preceding material. Further research would be required to determine optimal spacing procedures when a number of topics are being taught simultaneously. A second consideration is the extent to which the present findings are generalizable to classroom instructional procedures other than programing. Systematic evalution of the effects of spaced review under a variety of instructional conditions may indicate that retention is optimized not so much by instructional procedures per se as by temporal conditions employed in their presentation. Finally, the present studies illustrate the utility of programed instruction as a research tool for investigation of learning variables in complex learning situations. By controlling presentation variables systematically, while allowing environmental factors to vary in ways that are often present in complex learning situations, the programing instrument can be useful in investigating variables which may be relevant in the context of meaningful learning environments but have received little attention in the controlled environment of the laboratory.

References

Ammons, A., & Irion, A. L. A note on the Ballard reminiscence phenomenon *J. exp. Psychol.*, 1954, **48**, 184–186.

Briggs, G. E. Retroactive inhibition as a function of degree of original and interpolated learning. *J. exp. Psychol.*, 1957, **53**, 60–67.

Edwards, A. L. *Experimental design in psychological research.* (Rev. ed.) New York: Holt, Rinehart, & Winston, 1960.

Hovland, C. I. Human learning and retention. In S. S. Stevens (Ed.), *Handbook of experimental psychology.* New York: Wiley, 1951. Pp. 613–689.

Krueger, W. C. F. The effect of overlearning upon retention. *J. exp. Psychol.*, 1929, **12**, 71–78.

Postman, L. Retention as a function of degree of overlearning. *Science*, 1961, **135**, 666–667.

Slamecka, N. J., & Ceraso, J. Retroactive and proactive inhibition of verbal learning. *Psychol. Bull.*, 1960, **57**, 449–475.

Underwood, B. J. Ten years of massed practice on distributed practice. *Psychol. Rev.*, 1961, **68**, 229–247.

Welborn, E. L., & English, H. Logical learning and retention: A general review of experiments with meaningful verbal materials. *Psychol. Bull.*, 1937, **34**, 1–20.

14.2 Transfer and the Educational Process

Henry C. Ellis

This chapter from Ellis' excellent little volume summarizes the information on transfer pertinent to the educational process. Unfortunately, teaching methods in the modern classroom often reflect a belief in the old theories of formal discipline and mental faculties. In this reading, Ellis gives teachers the basic information necessary for making decisions to increase transfer. Teaching for transfer is the sine qua non of all effective teaching.

So far we have described a number of conditions known to influence transfer of learning and indicated several theoretical problems of transfer. We now turn our attention to the role of transfer in the educational process and examine those factors which are relevant and applicable to classroom learning activities. At this point, it is significant to note that early studies of transfer of learning, indeed much of human learning, were first conducted in the classroom as distinct from the laboratory in an attempt to better understand the teaching-learning process; in addi-

SOURCE. Henry C. Ellis, *The Transfer of Learning*. New York: The Macmillan Co., pp. 61–75.

tion, many of these studies were orientated towards examining conceptions of transfer which had direct relevance to educational practices.

Later, around 1930, increasing effort was placed upon laboratory studies of learning that had as one of their main goals the attempt to develop *laws* of behavior. It was felt that a science of human behavior could be best developed through carefully controlled laboratory studies of the learning process. Certainly, classroom studies of learning are important, but it was argued that the complexity of the classroom environment made it difficult to discover fundamental laws of learning.

Although the necessity for carefully-controlled and systematic studies of learning process has never been doubted by most psychologists (for example, Spence, 1956), rumblings were heard which suggested that all was not well. A number of educators and training specialists began to ask psychologists for help in problems associated with learning. Increasingly, psychologists faced the question: "What is there in the psychology of learning which is useful and applicable to educational problems?" It was possible for psychologists to take at least three rather distinct positions on this issue: (1) one alternative was to reject the plea of the educator by either showing little interest in his problems or by arguing that psychology was not ready to help because it didn't have adequately-developed laws of behavior; (2) a second approach of the psychologist was to take stock of his facts, principles, and theories and to make recommendations, in some cases quite tentative, about applying principles of learning to educational problems and to make suggestions about potentially fruitful areas for further research; (3) a third alternative was for the psychologist to tackle directly the problems of education by becoming an educator himself.

This chapter reflects the view that, for the present, the second option appears most fruitful. Here the role of the psychologist is to help clarify what is known about the learning process and to make suggestions about specific practices based on his knowledge of this process. This position implies that some psychologists will serve the function of translating knowledge of learning into useful principles for educational practice; in other words, an important task for at least *some* learning psychologists is to bridge the gap between the events of the laboratory and those of educational practice. A more detailed account of points of view on the relationship between learning theory and educational practice may be seen in a recent symposium by Spence, Melton, and Underwood (1959).

Early Theories of Transfer and Education

A prominent and long-held view by many educators was the doctrine of *formal discipline*. This view contended that the "mind" was composed of several faculties such as reasoning, memory, judgment, and attention, and that these faculties could be trained, improved, and strengthened through the steady of certain kinds of subject matter. An important objective of education was the study of specific subjects in order that such study would "discipline" the "mind." Studies such as mathematics and Latin were regarded as extremely important because they strengthened reasoning and memory. Geometry was regarded as an especially good subject for improving logical reasoning and ancient languages as important because they sharpened the students memory ability.

Around the turn of the century this doctrine came under experimental attack. An early study by Thorndike and Woodworth (1901) critically examined the notion of formal discipline and failed to find any substantial evidence in support of it. For about twenty-five years following their classic study, a number of investigations were conducted with little or no support for the doctrine resulting. As a result, educators gradually abandoned this viewpoint and, in turn, modified some of their teaching goals. For example, students were no longer taught mathematics because of presumed strengthening of reasoning ability, but were taught mathematics because it was an important subject matter in its own right.

The theory of formal discipline tended to assume that transfer was widespread and fairly automatic. As a result of attack upon it, however, a new view emerged that regarded transfer as much more limited in scope. As indicated, the challenge to formal discipline came from Thorndike and Woodworth (1901) who, on the basis of their investigations, concluded that transfer of training was limited to those situations in which the two tasks contained "identical elements." The theory of *identical elements* contended that training in one kind of activity would transfer to another as long as certain features such as aims, methods, and approaches were identical in the two tasks. Whereas formal discipline argued that transfer was very general and widespread, the theory of identical elements viewed transfer as more restricted in scope. Thus, hope for widespread transfer decreased and more emphasis was placed upon direct training of desired educational objectives.

Critics of the identical elements theory appeared and argued that it was too specific, and that transfer was not limited to situations containing identical elements. The concept of element itself was also under attack with some arguing that complex experiences could not be reduced to simple elements. There is reason to think, however, that Thorndike and Woodworth had a much broader conception of "elements" than some of their critics assumed. For example, these elements included such things as general principles and attitudes as well as more specific aspects of the tasks.

In addition, the identical elements theory came under attack as a result of studies by Judd (1908) and his colleagues. Judd argued that the important condition for transfer was that the student be able to abstract general rules or principles for himself. He called this a *theory of generalization,* which meant that a student was able to "generalize" his experiences from one situation and apply them to another. Thus, in order to teach for transfer, emphasis should be placed on getting the student to think about those features of the problem that might be generalized to new situations. The generalization theory had the advantage of at least recognizing that transfer was not an automatic process, and that, if one wanted students to transfer, they must be given practice in transfer. Unfortunately, as Schulz (1960) has noted, it is not enough to exhort a teacher to "teach for transfer." Clearly, in order to teach for transfer we must have a fairly explicit understanding of the criterion behaviors to be exhibited by students and the kinds of conditions which will insure the development of these behaviors. In other words, we must have a fairly explicit understanding of the *variables* known to influence transfer before a technology of application can develop.

A Contemporary Approach to Transfer

These existing theories of transfer, perhaps better described as *points of view* rather than theories in the more formal sense, serve as focal points for viewing educational issues. The theories are all stated in rather general language, thus making them somewhat difficult to test in a rigorous fashion. Indeed, for this reason, Osgood (1953) has indicated that one cannot be sure that the old doctrine of formal discipline is invalid. Quite conceivably, there is some validity to all of these points of view and that the issue is to determine the conditions under which each might be useful. Nevertheless, the author contends that it is more fruitful for education to take stock of the known variables which do influence transfer rather than to debate more speculative points of view. This approach is neither antitheoretical nor atheoretical as such but contends that in order to apply principles of transfer in the classroom, the teacher should have a good understanding of the basic factors which do influence transfer. So far, we have examined a number of important factors in transfer and this chapter will examine several additional factors which have been studied in the context of classroom teaching.

Learner Characteristics and Transfer

Several learner characteristics are also known to influence transfer. These characteristics include such factors as intelligence of the learner and motivational factors including anxiety. In general, it is difficult to make over-all generalizations about many of these factors, partly because not enough information is known about them and partly because these factors appear to be important in some learning situations and not in others.

It would be quite surprising if the intelligent student were not the more successful in transferring his knowledge and skills to new situations. Many studies which have investigated the role of intelligence do find that the more intelligent students show greater transfer (for example, Craig, 1953, Werner, 1930); however, this generalization has not been tested over a wide variety of tasks and school subjects. A typical finding is that of Werner (1930), who found that students above average in intelligence were able to profit from foreign language studies when tested on their ability in English whereas students of average intelligence were not. A reasonable interpretation of this and similar findings is that brighter students tend to seek out relationships and are more likely to have a set for transfer than do the less bright students.

To the extent that motivational variables influence learning, they are also likely to influence transfer. If a student is poorly motivated he will tend to learn less, thus reducing the chance of transfer to new learning situations. One motivational variable, anxiety, has been extensively studied in recent years (Spence, 1964), and some fairly reliable generalizations about its effect on learning are evident. One generalization which has significant implications for classroom teaching is that anxiety appears to facilitate performance in relatively simple types of learning, such as conditioning, but interferes with performance in more complex learning tasks. Certainly, it is reasonable to assume that anxiety will interfere with most classroom learning which generally consists of tasks of a fairly complex nature.

In the studies of Spence (1964) and his colleagues, anxiety is viewed as a motivational variable that increases the probability of various responses being made in a learning situation. If there is only one or at best a few responses which are possible, then anxiety tends to increase the likehood of a correct response. This will occur simply because there are so few response alternatives. On the oher hand, if many responses are possible, which is the case with more complex learning tasks, then anxiety tends to increase the likelihood of one or more incorrect or competing responses. This theoretical conception of anxiety has been shown to handle the laboratory studies of learning quite well and appears to be applicable to a study of clasroom learning reported by Gaier (1952).

Specifically, Gaier was interested in finding out the effects of anxiety on thinking and on subsequent test performance of students in a social science course. In this study he distinguished between two kinds of tests: those requiring primarily the factual recall of material and those emphasizing more complex behaviors such as analysis, synthesis, and application of principles. In general, his findings were in agreement with those of the latter laboratory studies regarding the interaction between anxiety and task complexity. For example, he found that students of high anxiety performed somewhat better than those of low anxiety on tests emphasizing memory for facts. In contrast, students of low anxiety performed significantly better on tests that required more complex behaviors such as synthesis and application. An interesting finding about the students' thought processes in class was that the anxious students spent significantly more time in thinking about concrete objects in the class such as the instructor's dress or a crack in the wall than on aspects of the lecture. Gaier's findings, in general, are consistent with the notion that heightened anxiety lowers the threshold for additional responses which are irrelevant to and compete with the desirable intellectual responses necessary for adequate classroom performance.

Transfer and Problem Solving

One of the significant objectives of education is that of teaching students effective ways of solving problems. Sometimes this objective is cast in the form of teaching students to "think" or to "reason for themselves." Regardless of the manner in which this objective is stated, it clearly implies that the conditions under which a student learns will govern to some extent his subsequent skill in solving problems. The methods, approaches, and attitudes that are present during learning will affect in some way the student's later performance, that is, these conditions have the potentiality of producing transfer of some magnitude and direction.

Traditionally, the topic of problem solving has been treated separately from that of transfer (Duncan, 1959). A recent analysis, however, has shown that many studies of problem solving can, in fact, be treated as studies of transfer (Schulz, 1960). Generally, studies of problem solving involve two phases: some type of preliminary activity in which the learner practices a task under specified conditions and a subsequent criterion task which is related to the preliminary activity. Usually, the criterion task is high on the discovery dimension; that is, the learner has to discover appropriate responses for solving the problem. In addition, the preliminary task is frequently designed so that it will interfere with efficient problem solving activity. Thus, the usual study of problem solving takes the form of a negative transfer design although there is nothing about problem solving *per se* which requires this feature.

Both Duncan (1959) and Marx (1958) have made the plea that problem solving especially needs research orientated toward determining functional relationships between antecedent conditions, such as conditions of practice, and various measures of performance. This view is quite consistent with that expressed at the beginning of this chapter. At present, the field of problem solving is poorly integrated and with the exception of a few areas (for example, Maltzman, 1955), it lacks systematic and intensive investigations of a long-term nature. Nevertheless, there are several important generalizations which can be made about transfer effects in problem solving and these will be described in this section. This discussion is naturally selective and we will confine ourselves to three types of factors studied: (1) variations in the mode of problem solving—that is, meaningful versus "rote" approaches; (2) the effects of group participation; and (3) the variety of tasks experienced during training. These factors were selected because of their relevance to classroom practices.

The effect of different methods of first-task practice on transfer to a second task has been studied by Hilgard, Irvine, and Whipple (1953). College students were first required to learn solutions to card trick problems in which they had to arrange a deck of cards so that when dealt the cards would appear in a certain order. One group was shown a formula by which the ordering could be reasoned out or "understood," and a comparable group simply memorized the solutions. Although the "understanding" group took more time to learn the solutions, they performed significantly better when they were required to learn new but related problems. In other words, transfer to the new task was superior when the students understood the principle involved.

Another problem of concern to education is the issue of transfer effects from group participation. Although a number of investigations have shown that group problem solving activity is superior to that of individual activity (for example, Taylor and Faust, 1952), the assumption that skills acquired in group activity will necessarily transfer to the individual situation is unwarranted. In a recent study, Hudgins (1960) addressed himself to this problem by noting that this assumption appeared to be widely accepted despite the fact that little evidence on the issue was available. Using fifth-grade students, Hudgins first gave them three consecutive days of practice in solving arithmetic problems, half working in groups of four students and half working alone. During this phase, he found that the students working in groups solved consistently more problems than did those working as individuals. On the second or transfer phase, all students continued to solve arithmetic problems, but on an individual basis. Here he found no difference in performance between those who had earlier worked as members of a group and those who had worked as individuals. In other words, there was no evidence for any transfer as a function of working with a group despite the fact that groups were superior in the original task.

Hudgins' findings do not, of course, mean that there are no possible advantages from group activity. Conceivably, desirable social skills and other behaviors are acquired and do transfer to new situations. His findings do indicate that considerably more research on this factor needs to be made before general conclusions are drawn about the transfer effects of group activity. Perhaps three days of practice was not sufficient to provide opportunity for group experiences to transfer. On theoretical grounds, it would appear that the effect of working with a group might transfer to an individual situation, provided that students were reinforced for group activity as such. In other words, the benefits of mutual exchange of information and skills could conceivably transfer if direct emphasis were placed upon these kinds of events. This might involve instructing students to assist each other in solving problems in a rather definite fashion.

The third factor to be considered concerns the role of task variety on the transfer of problem-solving skills. We noted in Chapter V that there was evidence to indicate that greater task variety led to enhanced positive transfer in studies that involved paired-associate learning tasks. The evidence suggests that a similar relationship holds with problem-solving tasks as well. In a relatively simple study, Morrisett and Hovland (1959) have demonstrated the importance of task variety in human problem solving. The most significant finding of their study was that preliminary training that gives the learner opportunity to both fully learn a particular type of problem as well as experience several types of problems yields maximum transfer. A high degree of original learning is important in order to strengthen the correct response tendencies, and practice with a variety of tasks provides the learner with opportunity to discriminate between relevant and irrelevant cues.

Transfer and Programed Instruction

A development of considerable interest in recent years is that of programed instruction and teaching machines. Briefly, programed instruction is a procedure for teaching various topics by requiring students to respond to well-developed sequences of problems that have been organized on the basis of learner responses. The student reads a statement and is usually required to answer some question about the statement. The material is developed in a logical and orderly fashion so that the student gradually acquires understanding of more complex concepts. The chief features of programed instruction are as follows: (1) the learner responds in an active fashion to the material; (2) the learner receives immediate confirmation of the correctness of his response; (3) the learner proceeds at his own pace; and (4) the learner studies a program that has been carefully designed and tested in order to insure maximum learning. It is not our purpose to describe the considerable details of programed instruction because numerous accounts of this educational technology have been given (for example, Lumsdaine and Glaser, 1960, Skinner, 1958, Stolurow, 1961). Rather, our purpose is to note some implications of programed instruction for transfer.

An interesting feature about programed instruction is that programs are generally developed with the purpose of maximizing student achievement, usually defined in terms of performance on some test given upon completion of the program, or in terms of the difference between pretest and posttest scores (Ellis, 1964). In other words, the success of the program is largely defined by the amount of achievement it produces. This approach is certainly not unreasonable and does have the advantage of establishing relatively objective criteria for evaluating programs. Nevertheless, this emphasis tends either to ignore or to leave unanswered the issue of transfer of knowledge and skills that presumably result from practice with programed instructional materials. Indeed, with the exception of a few studies (for example, Gagné and Dick, 1962, Taber and Glaser, 1962), research in programed instruction has largely ignored the issue of transfer.

What appears to be especially desirable are studies that yield evidence that not only does the program teach, but that students can transfer their learning beyond the immediate context of the program. Such studies would be directed toward discovering features of programs that produce considerable transfer. At present, Stolurow (1963) and his colleagues are engaged in intensive investigations of this type in which they are studying the form, sequence and size of step, where step refers to a unit of material in the program, as possible factors influencing transfer with the objective of being able to specify guide line for writers of programs.

Teaching for Transfer

We are now ready to specify a few guidelines for teaching so that what is taught is more likely to transfer to new learning situations. We have examined a large number of factors influencing transfer and will now illustrate how several of these might be applied to classroom teaching. Undoubtedly, any attempt to make an exhaustive list of illustrations would leave us with an unwieldy list, so the present list is to be regarded as only suggestive of a number of possibilities.

1. *Maximize the similarity between teaching and the ultimate testing*

situation. A teacher who hopes to induce much transfer must attempt to teach under conditions which are at least somewhat similar to the ultimate testing situation. The attempt to maximize similarity can be made in several ways, although it should be realized that this is an idealized goal and many events may make it difficult to achieve. A good way to begin to apply this principle is to first ask yourself what it is that you want your students to know—that is, what you think is important—and to begin by both teaching and testing for these consequences. Obviously, to teach for one thing and test for another is to invite difficulty.

Ways of implementing this principle are numerous. For example, in teaching students to solve arithmetic problems, direct practice in solving "word problems" can be given rather than simply expecting students to solve word problems when they first face them. Similarly, students can be familiarized with various aspects of a complex task by viewing it as it exists in a "real" situation via educational films or television. Also, if a typist is likely to work in a pool of typists, then somewhere during her training she should be given practice in typing among other typists in order to experience conditions of noise and interruption as well as other conditions. In general, the application of this principle requires that somewhere during the student's educational sequence, he be given practice in an environment which contains many of those factors which will exist in the ultimate working environment.

2. *Provide adequate experience with the original task.* We have seen that extensive practice on the original task increases the likelihood of positive transfer to a subsequent task, whereas more limited practice may yield no transfer or even negative transfer. Related to this point is the work of Harlow (1949), which implies that very thorough practice should be given in the early stage of developing new skills and concepts. Later on, such thoroughness may not be required. It is difficult, of course, in a given learning situation to specify precisely how much practice is desirable on a specific task; nevertheless, a good rule of thumb would be to have students receive as much practice as is feasible considering the restraints imposed by the various activities in a modern classroom. In addition, the teacher is somewhat free to be selective in the degree of emphasis placed on various topics. Perhaps greater emphasis could be placed on those topics that are known to be necessary for the mastery of subsequent course work. For example, if a student is to pursue additional work in mathematics, it is necessary that he understand the more elementary aspects of the subject. Other subject matter, in contrast, which does not have this sequential dependency, may not require as much practice.

3. *Provide for a variety of examples when teaching concepts and principles.* Studies in concept formation and in problem solving indicate that

stimulus variety is an important factor leading to positive transfer. Several examples of concept serve to strengthen the student's understanding so that he is more likely to see the applicability of a concept in a new situation. In addition, the students should be given examples of instances which do not represent the concept, particularly examples which are likely to be confused by the student. Distinctions, particularly among vague concepts, are more likely to be clarified with many examples.

4. *Label or identify important features of a task.* We have seen in studies of stimulus predifferentiation that the labeling of important features of a task aids in our subsequent learning of the task. Labeling helps us to distinguish important features of a task, although we are not entirely sure whether this is due merely to increased attention given to these features or whether it is due to the label itself. An illustration of this principle can be seen in teaching of young children to distinguish between the letters *b* and *d*, a fairly common source of difficulty. One way of helping them is to show them similar words such as *big* and *dig* and help them to identify the crucial difference between the two words.

5. *Make sure that general principles are understood before expecting much transfer.* If we expect students to show much transfer in course work that involves general principles, we must be reasonably sure that the principles are thoroughly understood. In the course of teaching a particular concept or principle, such as how to solve quadratic equations, the teacher can check periodically to discover if students do understand certain operations. In addition, the problem can be presented several ways and students may be required to discover errors in solutions and correct them. Sometimes the teacher can check for the students' understanding by presenting a problem in a novel context, such as using new symbols in the same formula.

Some Principles of Transfer

It is appropriate at the end of this chapter to summarize some of the major empirical principles of transfer. The principles are stated in rather general fashion and detailed qualifications have been largely avoided for purposes of simplicity. The statements can serve as general guidelines for educational practice and as a point of departure for future research.

1. *Over-all task similarity.* Transfer of training is greatest when the training conditions are highly similar to those of the ultimate testing conditions.

2. *Stimulus similarity.* When a task requires the learner to make the same response to new but similar stimuli, positive transfer increases with increasing stimulus similarity.

3. *Response similarity.* When a task requires the learner to make a

new or different response to the same stimuli, transfer tends to be negative and increases as the responses become less similar.

(a) Under conditions of high response similarity, this condition can produce positive transfer.

(b) Also, it is usually more difficult under this condition to obtain negative transfer in verbal learning than it is in motor skills learning.

4. *Joint stimulus-response variation.* If the repsonses in the transfer task are different from those in the original task, then the greater the similarity of stimuli, the less the positive transfer.

5. *Learning-to-learn.* Cumulative practice in learning a series of related tasks or problems leads to increased facility in learning how to learn.

6. *Early-task learning.* Transfer is maximized if greater effort is spent in mastering the early of a series of related tasks.

7. *Insight.* Insight, defined behaviorally as the rapid solution of problems, appears to develop as a result of extensive practice in solving similar or related classes of problems.

8. *Warm-up.* Warm-up is the pronounced but temporary facilitating effect resulting from practice in some activity prior to learning the transfer task.

9. *Time interval between tasks.* Performance on the second task is minimally determined by the time elapsing between original and transfer tasks, as long as the transfer task involves little memory for specific aspects of the original task.

10. *Mediated transfer.* Transfer can occur as a result of mediation due to the network of associative linkages between tasks.

11. *Bilateral transfer.* Positive transfer can be obtained as a result of practice with one limb to its analogous limb.

12. *Task or stimulus variety.* In general, variety of tasks, or of their stimulus components, during original learning increases the amount of positive transfer obtained.

13. *Amount of practice on the original task.* The greater the amount of practice on the original task, the greater the likelihood of positive transfer; negative transfer is likely to occur following only limited practice on the original task.

14. *Task characteristics.* No clear-cut generalizations about the role of task characteristics such as difficulty or complexity appear evident.

15. *Stimulus predifferentiation.* Relevant S pretraining leads to positive transfer when the transfer task involves learning; evidence for relevant S effects on perceptual tasks is negative or at best dubious.

16. *Understanding and transfer.* Transfer is greater if the learner understands the general rules or principles which are appropriate in solving new problems.

17. *Group learning.* There is no evidence for the automatic transfer of problem solving skills from a group to an individual situation.

References

Craig, R. C. *The transfer value of guided learning.* New York: Teachers College, Columbia University, 1953.

Duncan, C. P. Recent research on human problem solving. *Psychol. Bull.*, 1959, **56**, 397–429.

Ellis, H. C., Bessemer, D. W., Devine, J. V., and Trafton, C. L. Recognition of random tactual shapes following predifferentiation training. *Percept. Mot. Skills,* 1962, **10**, 99–102.

Gagne, R. M., and Dick, W. Learning measures in a self-instructional program in solving equations. *Psychol. Rep.*, 1962, **10**, 131–146.

Gaier, E. L. The relationship between selected personality variables and the thinking of students in discussion classes. *Sch. Rev.*, 1952, **40**, 404-411.

Harlow, H. F. The formation of learning sets. *Psychol. Rev.*, 1949, **56**, 51–65.

Hilgard, E. R., Irvine, R. P., and Whipple, J. E. Rote memorization, understanding, and transfer: An extension of Katona's card-trick experiments. *J. Exp. Psychol.*, 1953, **46**, 288–292.

Hudgins, B. B. Effects of group experience on individual problem solving, *J. Educ. Psychol.*, 1960, **51**, 37–42.

Judd, C. H. The relation of special training and general intelligence. *Educ. Rev.*, 1908, **36**, 42–48.

Lumsdaine, A. A., and Glaser, R. *Teaching machines and programmed learning.* Washington, D. C. National Education Association, 1960.

Marx, M. H. Some suggestions for the conceptual and theoretical analysis of complex intervening variables in problem-solving behavior. *J. Gen. Psychol.*, 1958, **58**, 115–128.

Morrisett, L. J., and Hovland, C. I. A comparison of three varieties of training in human problem solving. *J. Exp. Psychol.*, 1959, **58**, 52–55.

Osgood, C. E. *Method and theory in experimental psychology.* New York: Oxford, 1953.

Schulz, R. W. Problem solving behavior and transfer. *Harvard Educ. Rev.*, 1960, **30**, 61–77.

Skinner, B. F. Teaching machines. *Science,* 1958, **128**, 969–977.

Spence, K. W. *Behavior theory and conditioning.* New Haven: Yale University Press, 1956.

Spence, K. W., Melton, A. W., Underwood, B. J. A symposium: Can the laws of learning be applied in the classroom? *Harvard Education Review,* 1959, **29**, 83–107.

Spence, K. W. Anxiety (drive) level and performance in eyelid conditioning. *Psychol. Bull.,* 1964, **61**, 129–139.

Stolurow, L. M. *Teaching by machine.* Cooperative Research Monograph No. 6, Washington, D. C., U. S. Government Printing Office, 1961.

Stolurow, L. M. Comparative studies of principles for programming mathematics in automated instruction. *Semi-Annual Report,* Educational Media Branch, U. S. Office of Education, Project No. 711/51.01, 1963.

Taber, J. I., and Glaser, R. An exploratory evaluation of a discriminative transfer learning program using literal prompts. *J. Educ. Res.,* 1962, **55**, 508–512.

Taylor, D. W., and Faust, W. L. Twenty questions: Efficiency in problem solving as a function of size of group. *J. Exp. Psychol.,* 1952, **44**, 360–368.

Thorndike, E. L., and Woodworth, R. S. I. The influence of improvement in one mental function upon the efficiency of other functions; II. The estimation of magnitudes; III. Functions involving attention, observation and discrimination. *Psychol. Rev.,* 1911, **8**, 247–261, 384–395, 553–564.

Underwood, B. J. An evaluation of the Gibson theory of verbal learning. In C. N. Cofer (Ed.), *Verbal learning and verbal behavior,* pp. 197–217. New York: McGraw-Hill, 1961.

Werner, O. H. The influence of the study of modern foreign language on the development of desirable abilities in English. *Stud. in Mod. Lang. Teach.,* 1930, **17**, 97–145.

Selected Readings

Berlyne, D. E. Conditions of prequestioning and retention of meaningful materials. *Journal of Educational Psychology,* 1966, **57**, 128–132.

Dorsey, M. F., and Hopkins, T. The influence of instruction upon transfer. *Journal of Educational Psychology,* 1930, **21**, 410–417.

Fitzgerald, D., and Ausubel, D. P. Cognitive versus affective factors in the learning and retention of controversial materials. *Journal of Educational Psychology,* 1963, **54**, 73–84.

Gagné, R. M., and Wiegand, Virginia K. Some factors in children's learning and retention of concrete rules. *Journal of Educational Psychology,* 1968, **59**, 355–361.

Harlow, H. F. The formation of learning sets. *Psychological Review,* 1949, **56**, 51–65.

Humphreys, L. G. Transfer of training in general education. *Journal of General Education,* 1951, **5**, 210–16.

Klausmeier, H. J., and Check, J. Retention and transfer of low, average, and high intelligence. *Journal of Educational Research,* 1962, **55**, 319–322.

Philbrick, J. L., and O'Donnell, P. I. Precision in grading practices: panacea or problems? *Journal of Educational Research,* 1968, **62**, 173–176.

Slamecka, N. J. Studies of retention of connected discourse. *The American Journal of Psychology*, 1959, **72**, 409–416.

Underwood, B. J. Forgetting. *Scientific American,* 1964, **210**, 91–99.

PART V

Measurement and Evaluation Needs of the Future

Measurement and evaluation have earned a solid place in educational psychology. However, there is so much information in this area that is basic to a good teaching-learning situation that the author has been able to include only a few papers discussing issues of genuine importance for the teacher.

Although an old problem, there has been a revival of interest in ascertaining the validity of test items. Criticism of the limitations of objective tests, in particular, have focused attention on the relationship beween teaching objectives and test instruments. Nelson's article in Chapter 15 illustrates how items can be constructed to measure complex behavior. Fishman makes it clear that no matter how well a test instrument is constructed for middle-class children, it may not produce valid results for children who have been at a cultural or social disadvantage. He discusses three critical issues that must be considered in testing these disadvantaged groups.

After we measure behavioral change, we must then interpret these changes in the light of the goals we have specified. Did achievement occur? Was it adequate? The feedback that we get through measurement helps us to evaluate progress and aids us in determining the effective aspects of teaching and what remains to be done. Glock and Millman call attention to errors in procedure and suggest methodology for doing one kind of evaluation—the giving of grades.

Chapter 16 should help the reader to become aware of the public's concern with testing. Test results exert a powerful influence over our lives today. To a large extent they determine school progress, admission to quality institutions, and the jobs we are able to obtain and progress in after graduation. This places a heavy obligation on those who use tests. Strengths and weaknesses of these instruments must be carefully considered. Anastasi's and Ebel's papers clarify the issues.

The last chapter of the volume emphasizes the need to use criterion-referenced tests with the new technology and for determining the status of educational achievement in the nation. This type of measurement is unlike that described by Glock and Millman for the typical grading situation. They suggest the use of norm-referenced tests, which enable one to relate an individual's performance to that of others on the same test. On the other hand, criterion-referenced tests are used for comparing an individual's performance with respect to some criterion, such as an established performance standard. They enable us to determine what the pupil can do, rather than how he compares with others. Test specialists are not agreed on the advantages of using the criterion-referenced tests suggested by Glaser and Tyler. They have presented arguments both pro and con.

CHAPTER 15

Measuring and Evaluating Objectives

15.1 Evaluating of Objectives of Science Teaching

Clarence H. Nelson

In Chapter 3 Krathwohl discussed the taxonomies and their importance in curriculum building. In this reading Nelson gives us a number of examples of test items that measure science objectives within certain categories of the Cognitive Domain. The ideas offered, however, could easily be applied to disciplines outside the sciences. Nelson makes a plea for developing test sophistication so that we can do a better job of measuring important educational objectives.

Those who teach science courses at the college and university level have perhaps been even less objectives-conscious than their secondary and elementary school counterparts. This seeming apathy has no doubt been due in part, at least to the chaotic and confused status of higher education objectives. A committee of university and college examiners has in recent years undertaken to bring some order out of the prevailing chaos by organizing and classifying various objectives under carefully conceived headings in the hierarchy listed in the following taxonomy:

SOURCE. Abridged from Clarence H. Nelson, "Evaluation of Objectives of Science Teaching," *Science Education,* **XLIII**, 1 (1959), pp. 20–27, by permission of *Science Education.*

Taxonomy of Educational Objectives

By A Committee of University and College Examiners

Benjamin S. Bloom, Editor

Max D. Engelhart — Walker H. Hill
Edward J. Furst — David R. Krathwohl
Pub. by Longmans, Green & Co. — New York

Cognitive Domain

1.00 Knowledge.
  1.10 Knowledge of specifics.
    1.11 Knowledge of terminology.
    1.12 Knowledge of specific facts.
  1.20 Knowledge of ways and means of dealing with specifics.
    1.21 Knowledge of conventions.
    1.22 Knowledge of trends and sequences.
    1.23 Knowledge of classifications and categories.
    1.24 Knowledge of criteria.
    1.25 Knowledge of methodology.
  1.30 Knowledge of the universals and abstractions in a field.
    1.31 Knowledge of principles and generalizations.
    1.32 Knowledge of theories and structures.

Intellectual Abilities and Skills

2.00 Comprehension—ability to make use of materials or ideas.
  2.10 Translation.
  2.20 Interpretation.
  2.30 Extrapolation.
3.00 Application—The use of abstractions in particular and concrete situations.
4.00 Analysis—Making clear the relative hierarchy of ideas in a communication.
  4.10 Analysis of elements.
  4.20 Analysis of relationships.
  4.30 Analysis of organizational principles.
5.00 Synthesis—The putting together of elements and parts so as to form a whole.
  5.10 Production of a unique communication.
  5.20 Production of a plan, or proposed set of operations.
  5.30 Derivation of a set of abstract relations.
6.00 Evaluation.
  6.10 Judgments in terms of internal evidence.
  6.20 Judgments in terms of external criteria.

Table 1
Two-Axis Chart of Specifications for Nat. Sci. 181 Examination, Fall Term, 1955

Course Content / Course Objectives	1.00 Knowledge of Terminology, Facts, Conventions, Trends, Sequences, Categories, etc.	2.00 Comprehension (Translation, Interpretation, Extrapolation)	3.00 Application	4.00 Analysis	5.00 Synthesis Production of a Unique Communication	6.00 Evaluation—Satisfying Criteria, Ability to Indicate Logical Fallacies in Arguments
I. Perception, symbolization, and methods of science	3, 7, 8	1, 2, 6, 11	4, 9, 10		(No items for these two categories of objectives were included in this particular objective test. Attainment of ability in synthesis and evaluation can better be demonstrated in non-structured, free-response testing situations in which the students create their own answers.)	
II. The cell—structure and functions; cell principle	12, 13, 15, 16, 17–19	14		20–27		
III. Spontaneous generation—Biogenesis			46			
IV. Sexual reproduction in animals and plants; human production and sex hormones	28–31 32–35		5			
V. Cellular reproduction—mitosis	41–43					
VI. Meiosis—chromosomes and genes	36–40, 47, 89, 90	48–52	44, 45			
VII. Single-factor cross		55–57	53			
VIII. Two-factor cross			58–62, 69–72, 63–68			
IX. Blood group inheritance; heredity in man		73–82	54			
X. Linkage and crossing-over	87	83, 85, 88	84, 86			
XI. Sex determination Sex linkage			91–94	95–100		

The above outline is the summary of a 192-page volume which contains extensive discussions as to the meaning of each objective and its sub-headings. In addition to the explanatory material, test items are included which illustrate how the attainment of each objective could be measured.

Table 1, a two-axis chart of specifications for a Natural Science Examination, lists the major objectives on the horizontal axis (across the top) and the subject-matter content topics on the vertical axis at the left. Each number in the columns under the objectives is the number of an item in this examination which embodies the objective listed above it as well as the subject-matter topic listed to its left. Thus each item in the examination is keyed to a specific objective as well as to a specific topic of course content.

While limitation of space forbids reprinting the entire examination, one set of items to illustrate each objective is presented herewith as follows:

1.00 Knowledge of terminology, facts, convention, trends, sequences, categories, etc.

Items 36–40 involve a comparison of mitosis and meiosis. For each item select from the Key the most appropriate response.

Key: 1. Meiosis.
2. Mitosis.
3. Both mitosis and meiosis.
4. Neither mitosis nor meiosis.

36. A sperm and an egg unite by ....
37. The nuclear membrane disappears in ....
38. Haploid cells are formed by ....
39. Diploid cells are formed by ....
40. The zygote undergoes ....

2.00 Comprehension—Translation, Interpretation, Extrapolation.

Items 48–52 are concerned with the life cycle of a typical plant (corn). Study the diagram carefully before you begin to answer these items.

48. Meiosis takes place between Stages.
1. A and B. 2. B and C. 3. C and D.
4. C and E. 5. D and E.
49. If the polar or endosperm nuclei of Stage C fuse, how many chromosomes will there be altogether within the embryo sac?
1. 160 2. 90 3. 80 4. 50 5. 20
50. The total number of chromosomes in all the microspores and all

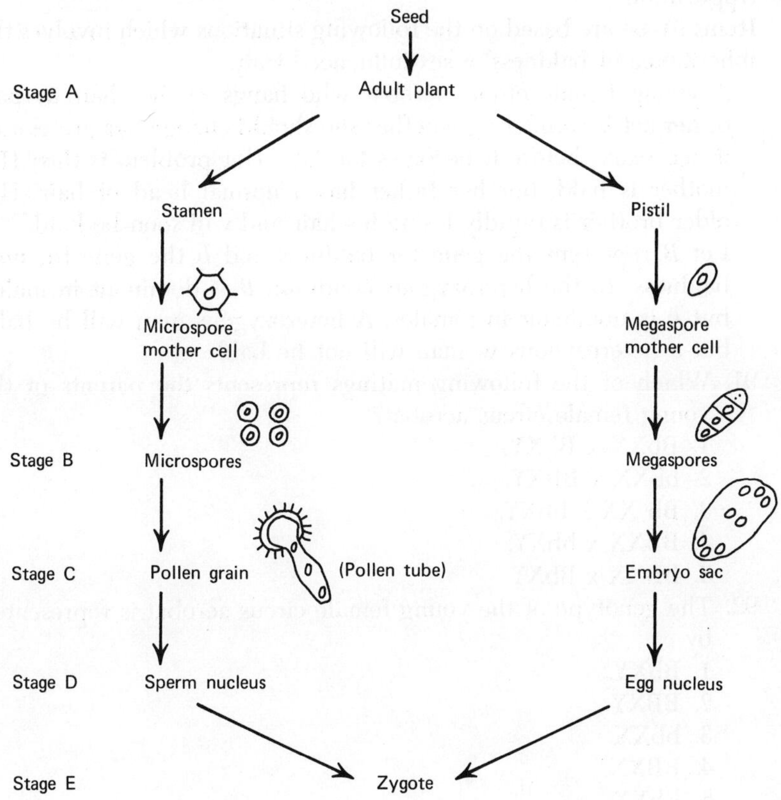

FIGURE 1. The life history of corn, a plant in which the diploid number of chromosomes is 20. Black dots represent nuclei.

the megaspores shown in Stage B—all added together—would be
1. 10 2. 20 3. 30 4. 40 5. 80

51. How many chromosomes are there altogether in all the nuclei shown in the pollen grain plus all the nuclei shown in the embryo sac in Stage C?
1. 220 2. 110 3. 40 4. 30 5. 20

52. The number of chromosomes in the nucleus of the microspore mother cell plus the number of chromosomes in the nucleus of the megaspore mother cell will total
1. 10 2. 20 3. 30 4. 40 5. 80

* * * * * * * *

3.00 Application

Items 91–94 are based on the following situations which involves the inheritance of baldness, a sex-influenced trait.

A young female circus acrobat who hangs by her hair as part of her act is wondering whether she should change her profession, if necessary, before it becomes too late. Her problem is this: Her mother is bald, but her father has a normal head of hair. Her older brother is rapidly losing his hair and will soon be bald.

Let *B* represent the gene for baldness and *b* the gene for non-baldness. In the heterozygous condition *B* is dominant in males, but *b* is dominant in females. A heterozygous man will be bald, but a heterozygous woman will not be bald.

91. Which of the following matings represents the parents of the young female circus acrobat?
    1. BbXX x BbXY.
    2. bbXX x BBXY.
    3. Bb XX x bbXY.
    4. BBXX x bbXY.
    5. BBXX x BbXY.
92. The genotype of the young female circus acrobat is represented by
    1. BbXY.
    2. BBXY.
    3. bbXX.
    4. BBXX.
    5. BbXX.
93. The genotype of the older brother of the young female circus acrobat is represented by
    1. BbXY.
    2. bbXY.
    3. BbXX.
    4. BBXY.
    5. BBXX.
94. On the basis of the data, which of the following suggestions to the young female circus acrobat would be most justifiable?
    1. You need not change your profession—according to the genetic evidence there is no likelihood at all that you will become bald.
    2. The chances are 1 in 4 that you will become bald.
    3. The chances are 3 in 4 that you will become bald.
    4. There is a 50 per cent chance that you will become bald.

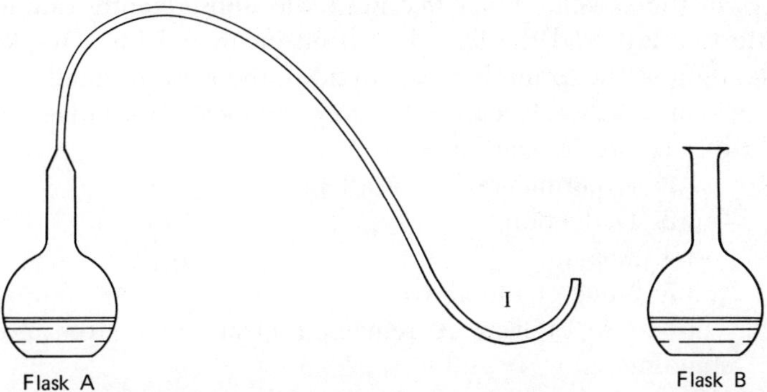

5. Change your profession—according to the genetic evidence you are almost certain to become bald.

4.00 Analysis.

Items 20–27 are based upon the following passage which describes some of Pasteur's later experimental work on spontaneous generation.

After some preliminary experimentation Pasteur developed a refinement in his method which was designed to meet various objectives raised by his critics. This time he boiled the sugared yeast water in a swan-neck flash like flask A below.

Pasteur's swan-neck flask (A) and open-top flask (B). The sugared yeast water in both flasks was boiled, then allowed to cool and stand for several weeks. Air could enter flask A via the long bent tube. The contents of flask B were exposed to the air through its open top. A dense clouding soon appeared in flask B, but none developed in flask A.

Pasteur allowed the contents of flask A to cool very slowly. This time the end of the stem was not sealed. Any air entering the swan-neck was believed to have lost its load of dust, microorganisms, and other suspended debris when it began ascending the long uphill part of the swan-neck. In all likelihood only air free of microorganisms came into contact with the sugared yeast water inside the swan-neck flask. No clouding appeared in flask A, even after months of standing.

Pasteur believed that any microorganisms borne by the air entering the swan-neck tube may have lodged in the lowermost curve near the entrance of the tube. To find out if this were indeed true, he tilted the flask in such a way as to allow some of the fluid within the flask to run down into the portion of the curve designated by "X" in the sketch. When this fluid was subsequently drained back into the flask and the flask had been incubated for a week longer, clouding of the formerly clear liquid in the flask gradually occurred.

For items 20–24 select from the Key the most appropriate category.

Key: 1. Generalization.
2. Experimental observation.
3. Deduction.
4. Analogy.
5. None of the above.

20. The liquid is flask A remained clear even after months of standing.
21. Whenever sugared yeast water is kept sterile it remains clear but whenever microorganism-laden air comes into contact with sugared yeast water, the liquid becomes clouded.
22. Since clouding occurred in flask A after fluid had been drained back into the flask from point "X" of the swan-neck tube, microorganisms must have been present in the tube in the vicinity of point "X."
23. Since the liquid in flask A showed no growth of microorganisms, the air which entered the body of the flask must have been sterile.
24. Since the liquid in flask A remained clear, it contained no growth of microorganisms.

* * * * * * * *

25. Pasteur allowed the contents of flask A to cool very slowly in order to
    1. give himself time to make observations while the contents of the flask were cooling.
    2. prevent the flask from cracking and spilling its contents.
    3. avoid the danger of an explosion inside the flask.
    4. prevent an inrush of air and microorganisms.
    5. avoid shock to the microorganisms by sudden temperature change.
26. No critic could rightfully say of Pasteur's swan-neck flask experiment that
    1. Pasteur deserved the prize offered by the French Academy.
    2. air entering the flask had been deprived of its vegetative force or vital spirit by heating or treatment with harsh acids.
    3. microorganisms would have appeared had he used mutton broth instead of sugared yeast water as culture medium.

4. Pasteur's success was due in part to a fortunate choice of culture medium.
5. the question of spontaneous generation of microorganisms was any nearer settlement now than it had been prior to Pasteur's experimentation.

27. By this experiment Pasteur
    1. obtained conclusive evidence that sterile sugared yeast water in contact with germ-free air does not engender microorganisms.
    2. proved that spontaneous generation has never occurred on the earth.
    3. proved that microorganisms arise by spontaneous generation in a culture medium if the experimenter is careless but they do not arise if he is careful.
    4. demonstrated that no culture medium, if it has been boiled, will become contaminated with microorganisms even if germ-free air comes into contact with the fluid inside the flask.
    5. went down to defeat from which he never recovered.

Those who are acquainted with objective testing only in its worst manifestations vociferously maintain that (1) objective tests can measure only the attainment of minute, disjointed factual information, and (2) the only means by which one can measure the student's understanding of a somewhat extended and involved concept, theory, or principle is to give the student an essay test; it is impossible to measure understanding of an organized sequence of ideas by using objective test items. The following set of 21 objective test items pursue one major idea, disposing first of prevailing misconceptions, then presenting hypotheses which evidence tends to support, until a chain of proof has been established. The student must work through the items and accept or reject each of the four hypotheses in turn, then select the best single conclusion that can be drawn from the data. (Answers are indicated in parentheses following each item.)

Problem. What role do the sex chromosomes play is determining sex in Drosophila?

Hypothesis I. Maleness in Drosophila can be attributed to the presence of Y chromosome in the genotype.

Data. Occasionally, during gamete formation in the female, the two X chromosomes do *not* separate. Instead, both go to a single gamete, and the corresponding gamete receives no X chromosome. In such cases the mating with a normal male would be as follows:

The results of such a mating show 50 per cent males and 50 per cent

♀ / ♂	XX	—
X	XXX	X—
Y	XXY	Y—

females, but the number of offspring is only one-half the usual number obtained. A cytological examination of the chromosomes showed that there were only XXY and X— individuals among the offspring. For reasons as yet unknown, XXX individuals and Y— individuals died before birth; these combinations are apparently lethal. Among the offspring that survived, however, *females* were XXY and males were X—.

For items 80–85 mark space

1–if the item is true according to the data and tends to support Hypothesis I;
2–if the item is true according to the data but tends to refute Hypothesis I;
3–if the item is false according to the data, but if true, would tend to support Hypothesis I;
4–if the item is false according to the data, but if true, would tend to refute Hypothesis I;
5–if the item is irrelevant to Hypothesis I, regardless of its truth or falsity according to the data.

Suggestion. It will be easier if you decide first whether each statement is true or false according to the data.

80. The presence of a Y chromosome in the genotype inevitably produces a male individual.(3)
81. An individual that inherits a Y chromosome cannot be a female.(3)
82. The presence of a lone Y chromosome in the genotype is lethal.(2)
83. An individual that lacks a Y chromosome cannot be a male.(3)
84. The presence of three X chromosomes in the genotype is lethal. (5)

* * * * * * * *

85. What is the status of Hypothesis I at this point?
    1. It is established as true beyond doubt.
    2. It is probably true—the evidence tends to support it.
    3. It is probably false—the evidence tends to refute it.
    4. It is definitely false without any doubt.
    5. It remains as much unsettled as at the outset.(3)

Hypothesis II. Maleness in Drosophila can be attributed to the presence of one X chromosome and the lack of a second X chromosome in the genotype.

For items 86–88 mark space

1–if the item is true according to the data and tends to support Hypothesis II;

2–if the item is true according to the data but tends to refute Hypothesis II;

3–if the item is false according to the data, but if true, would tend to support Hypothesis II;

4–if the item is false according to the data, but if true, would tend to refute Hypothesis II;

5–if the item is irrelevant to Hypothesis II, regardless of its truth or falsity according to the data.

86. An individual with a lone X chromosome in its genotype is a male.(1)
87. The presence of three X chromosomes in the genotype is lethal.(5)
88. An individual with two X chromosomes and one Y chromosome in its genotype is not a male.(1)

* * * * * * * *

89. What is the status of Hypothesis II at this point?
    1. It is established as true beyond doubt.
    2. It is probably true—the evidence tends to support it.
    3. It is probably false—the evidence tends to refute it.
    4. It is definitely false without any doubt.
    5. It remains as much unsettled as at the outset.(2)

Hypothesis III. Femality in Drosophila can be attributed to the absence of a Y chromosome in the genotype.

For items 90–93 mark space

1–if the item is true according to the data and tends to support Hypothesis III;

2–if the item is true according to the data but tends to refute Hypothesis III;

3–if the item is false according to the data, but if true, would tend to support Hypothesis III;

4–if the item is false according to the data, but if true, would tend to refute Hypothesis III;

5–if the item is irrelevant to Hypothesis III, regardless of its truth or falsity according to the data.

90. An individual with two X chromosomes and one Y chromosome in its genotype is a female.(2)

91. An individual with a lone X chromosome in its genotype is not a female.(2)
92. The presence of three X chromosomes in the genotype is lethal.(5)
93. The presence of a lone Y chromosome in the genotype is lethal.(5)
94. What is the status of Hypothesis III at this point?
    1. It is established as true beyond doubt.
    2. It is probably true—the evidence tends to support it.
    3. It is probably false—the evidence tends to refute it.
    4. It is definitely false without any doubt.
    5. It remains as much unsettled as at the outset.(3)

Hypothesis IV. Femality in Drosophila can be attributed to the presence of two X chromosomes in the genotype.

For items 95–98 mark space

1–if the item is true according to the data and tends to support Hypothesis IV;

2–if the item is true according to the data but tends to refute Hypothesis IV;

3–if the item is false according to the data, but if true, would tend to support Hypothesis IV;

4–if the item is false according to the data, but if true, would tend to refute Hypothesis IV;

5–if the item is irrelevant to Hypothesis IV, regardless of its truth or falsity according to the data.

95. An individual with two X chromosomes and one Y chromosome in its genotype is a female.(1)
96. The presence of three X chromosomes in the genotype is lethal.(5)
97. An individual with a lone X chromosome in its genotype is not a female.(1)
98. The presence of a lone Y chromosome in the genotype is lethal.(5)

* * * * * * * *

99. What is the status of Hypothesis IV at this point?
    1. It is established as true beyond doubt.
    2. It is probably true—the evidence tends to support it.
    3. It is probably false—the evidence tends to refute it.
    4. It is definitely false without any doubt.
    5. It remains as much unsettled as at the outset.(2)
100. On the basis of the foregoing data and its analysis in the preceding 20 items, which one of the following is the best single conclusion that can be drawn?
    1. Maleness is due to the presence of a Y chromosome in the genotype and femaleness is due to its absence.

2. No individual that bears a Y chromosome in its genotype can be female and no individual lacking a Y chromosome can be a male.
3. An individual with more than two X chromosomes is a super female and an individual with two X chromosomes and one Y chromosome is a super male.
4. Femaleness in Drosophila is due to the presence of a second X chromosome in the genotype, and maleness is due to its absence.
5. None of the above conclusions fit the data.(4)

In evaluating the outcomes of science teaching we have not begun to exhaust the potentialities of the measuring devices that we have known for years. Testing in many quarters persists at the most primitive and slip-shod levels. To raise the level of testing and evaluation would require a re-study of objectives and teaching methods in an attempt to implement the objectives in the teaching. This is largely a matter of establishing an atmosphere in the classroom that is appropriate to science teaching—an atmosphere in which inquiry, exploration and discovery are encouraged. With adequate planning well in advance of examination time, the teacher who can create the appropriate teaching situation should also be imaginative enough to be able to develop adequate measuring devices. If the semester examination were planned and begun the first week of school and an average of two questions per day were to be written while the material is fresh in mind, by the end of the semester it should be possible to have a creditable final examination ready for use. An excellent reference for aid in test construction is the book entitled *Educational Measurement,* edited by E. F. Lindquist and published by American Council on Education, Washington, D. C. Attention is especially called to Chapter 7 which is entitled, "Writing the Test Item." Recent extensive bibliographies on educational and psychological testing may be found in *Review of Educational Research,* Vol. 26(1), Feb. 1956. With these aids any resourceful teacher should be able to develop achievement tests that will adequately evaluate the degree of attainment of the objectives of science teaching.

15.2 Guidelines for Testing Minority Group Children*

Joshua A. Fishman et al.

As the need to improve the educational opportunities of disadvantaged youth, whether in urban or rual areas, receives more attention, it is important for us to look carefully at the selection and application of educational tools. The authors emphasize that psychological tests are the most popular and helpful tools in the schools, but they require intelligent and responsible use. When used properly as a means of understanding these minority-group children, they can generate effectual means of helping to overcome early social and cultural disadvantages.

Introduction

American educators have long recognized that they can best guide the development of intellect and character of the children in their charge if they take the time to understand these children thoroughly and sympathetically. This is particularly true with respect to the socially and culturally disadvantaged child.

SOURCE. *Journal of Social Issues*, **XX**, 2 (1964), pp. 129–144. Reprinted by permission of Society for the Psychological Study of Social Issues.

* Prepared by a Work Group of the Society for the Psychological Study of Social Issues (Division 9 of the American Psychological Association), Martin Deutsch, Joshua A. Fishman, *Chairman*, Leonard Kogan, Robert North, and Martin Whiteman.

Educators must realize that they hold positions of considerable responsibility and power. If they apply their services and skills wisely they can help minority group children to overcome their early disadvantages, to live more constructively, and to contribute more fully to American society.

Educational and psychological tests may help in the attainment of these goals if they are used carefully and intelligently. Persons who have a genuine commitment to democratic processes and who have a deep respect for the individual, will certainly seek to use educational and psychological tests with minority group children in ways that will enable these children to attain the full promise that America holds out to all its children.

Educational and psychological tests are among the most widely used and most useful tools of teachers, educational supervisors, school administrators, guidance workers, and counselors. As is the case with many professional tools, however, special training and diagnostic sensitivity are required for the intelligent and responsible use of these instruments. That is why most colleges and universities offer courses in educational and psychological testing. It is also the reason for the growing number of books and brochures designed to acquaint educators and their associates with the principles and procedures of proper test selection, use and interpretation.[1]

Responsible educational authorities recognize that it is as unwise to put tests in the hands of untrained and unskilled personnel as it is to permit the automobile or any highly technical and powerful tool to be handled by individuals who are untrained in its use and unaware of the damage that it can cause if improperly used.

The necessity for caution is doubly merited when educational and psychological tests are administered to members of minority groups. Unfortunately, there is no single and readily available reference source to which test users can turn in order to become more fully acquainted with the requirements and cautions to be observed in such cases. The purpose of this committee's effort is to provide an introduction to the many considerations germane to selection, use and interpretation of educational and psychological tests with minority group children, as well as to refer educators and their associates to other more technical discussions of various aspects of the same topic.

The term "minority group" as we are using it here is not primarily a quantitative designation. Rather it is a status designation referring to cultural or social disadvantage. Since many Negro, Indian, lower-class

[1] See, for example, Katz (1958), Froelich and Hoyt (1959), Cronbach (1960), Anastasi (1961), Thorndike and Hagen (1961).

white, and immigrant children have not had most of the usual middle-class opportunities to grow up in home, neighborhood, and school environments that might enable them to utilize their ability and personality potentials fully, they are at a disadvantage in school, and in after-school and out-of-school situations as well. It is because of these disadvantages, reflecting environmental deprivations and experiential atypicalities, that certain children may be referred to as minority group children.

The following discussion is based in part on some of the technical recommendations developed for various kinds of tests by committees of the American Psychological Association, the American Educational Research Association, and the National Council on Measurement in Education (1954, 1955). Our contribution is directed toward specifying the particular considerations that must be kept in mind when professional educators and those who work with them use educational and psychological tests with minority group children.

Critical Issues in Testing Minority Groups

Standardized tests currently in use present three principal difficulties when they are used with disadvantaged minority groups: (1) they may not provide reliable differentiation in the range of the minority group's scores, (2) their predictive validity for minority groups may be quite different from that for the standardization and validation groups and (3) the validity of their interpretation is strongly dependent upon an adequate understanding of the social and cultural background of the group in question.

I. Reliability of Differentiation

In the literature of educational and psychological testing, relatively little attention has been given to the possible dependence of test reliability upon subcultural differences. It is considered essential for a test publisher to describe the reliability sample (the reference group upon which reliability statements are based) in terms of factors such as age, sex, and grade level composition, and there is a growing tendency on the part of test publishers to report subgroup reliabilities. But to the best of our knowledge, none of the test manuals for the widely used tests give separate reliability data for specific minority groups. Institutions that use tests regularly and routinely for particular minority groups would do well to make their own reliability studies in order to determine whether the tests are reliable enough when used with these groups.

Reliability Affected by Spread of Scores. In addition to being dependent on test length and the specific procedure used for estimating reliability (e.g., split-half or retest), the reliability coefficient for a particular test is strongly affected by the spread of test scores in the group for which the reliability is established. In general, the greater the spread of scores in the reliability sample, the higher the reliability coefficient. Consequently, if the tester attempts to make differentiations within a group which is more homogeneous than the reference or norm group for which reliability is reported, the actual effectiveness of the test will be found to be lower than the reported reliability coefficient appears to promise. For many tests, there is abundant evidence that children from the lower socio-economic levels commonly associated with minority group status tend to have a smaller spread of scores than do children from the lower socio-economic levels commonly associated with minority group status tend to have a smaller spread of scores than do children from middle-income families, and such restriction in the distribution of scores tends to lower reliability so far as differentiation of measurement with such groups is concerned.[2]

Characteristics of Minority Group Children that Affect Test Performance. Most of the evidence relating to the contention that the majority of educational and psychological tests tend to to be more unreliable, i.e., more characterized by what is technically called "error variance," for minority group children, is indirect, being based on studies of social class and socio-economic differences rather than on minority group performance *per se.* Nevertheless, the particular kinds of minority groups that we have in mind are closely associated with the lower levels of socio-economic status. The results of studies by Warner, Davis, Deutsch, Deutsch and Brown, Havighurst, Hollingshead, Sears, Maccoby, and many others are cases in point. Many of these studies are discussed by Anastasi (1958), Tyler (1956) and Deutsch (1960).

For children who come from lower socio-economic levels, what characteristics may be expected to affect test performance in general, and the accuracy or precision of test results in particular? The list of reported characteristics is long, and it is not always consistent from one investigation to another. But, at least, it may be hypothesized that in contrast to the middle-class child the lower-class child will tend to be less verbal, more fearful of strangers, less self-confident, less motivated toward scholastic and academic achievement, less competitive in the intellectual realm, more "irritable," less conforming to middle-class norms of behavior and conduct, more apt to be bilingual, less exposed to intellectually stimulating materials in the home, less varied in recreational outlets, less knowledgeable about the world outside his immediate neighborhood, and more likely to attend inferior schools.

Some Examples. Can it be doubted that such characteristics—even if

[2] See Anastasi (1958) and Tyler (1956).

only some of them apply to each "deprived" minority group—will indeed be reflected in test-taking and test performance? Obviously, the primary effect will be shown in terms of test validity for such children. In many cases, however, the lowering of test validity may be indirectly a result of lowered test reliability. This would be particularly true if such characteristics interfere with the consistency of performance from test to retest for a single examiner, or for different examiners. Consider the following examples and probable results:

Example. A Negro child has had little contact with white adults other than as distant and punitive authority figures. *Probable Result:* Such a child might have difficulty in gaining rapport with a white examiner or reacting without emotional upset to his close presence. Even in an individual testing situation, he might not respond other than with monosyllables, failing to give adequate answers even when he knows them. The examiner, reacting in terms of his own stereotypes, might also lower the reliability and validity of the test results by assuming that the child's performance will naturally be inferior, and by revealing this attitude to the child.

Example. Children from a particular minority group are given little reason to believe that doing well in the school situation will affect their chance for attaining better jobs and higher income later in life. *Probable Result:* Such children will see little purpose in schooling, dislike school, and will reject anything associated with school. In taking tests, their primary objective is to get through as rapidly as possible and escape from what for them might be an uncomfortable situation. Their test performance might, therefore, be characterized by a much greater amount of guessing, skipping, and random responses than is shown by the middle-class child who never doubts the importance of the test, wants to please his teacher and parents, and tries his best.

Special Norms Often Needed. When the national norms do not provide adequate differentiation at the lower end of the aptitude or ability scale, special norms, established locally, are often useful. For instance, if a substantial number of underprivileged or foreign-background pupils in a school or school district rank in the lowest five per cent on the national norms, local norms might serve to provide a special scale within this range. If the score distribution with the first few percentiles of the national norms is mainly a function of chance factors, however, a lower level of the test or an easier type of test is needed for accurate measurement of the low-scoring children.

Responsibilities of Test Users. The sensitive test user should be alert to reliability considerations in regard to the particular group involved and the intended use of the tests. In assessing reports on test reliability provided by test manuals and other sources, he will not be satisfied with high reliability coefficients alone. He will consider not only the size of the reliability samples, but also the nature and composition of the samples and the procedures used to estimate reliability. He will try to determine whether the standard error of measurement varies with score levels, and whether his testing conditions are similar to those of the reliability samples. He will ask whether the evidence on reliability is relevant to the persons and purposes with which he is concerned. He will know that high reliability does not guarantee validity of the measures for the purpose in hand, but he will realize that low reliability may destroy validity.

The examiner should be well aware that test results are characteristically influenced by cultural and subcultural differentials and that the performance of under-privileged minority group children is often handicapped by what should be test-extraneous preconditions and response patterns. He should not necessarily assume that the child from a minority group family will be as test-sophisticated and motivated to do his best as are the majority of environment-rich middle-class children.

If the examiner finds—and this will be typical—that the reliability sample does not provide him with information about the reliability of the test for the kind of children he is testing, he should urge that the test results not be taken at face value in connection with critical decisions concerning the children. Very often, careful examination of responses to individual test items will indicate to him that the apparent performance of the child is not adequately reflecting the child's actual competence or personality because of certain subcultural group factors.

II. *Predictive Validity*

Of course, if an individual's test scores were to be used only to describe his relative standing with respect to a specified norm group, the fact that the individual had a minority-group background would not be important. It is when an explanation of his standing is attempted, or when long-range predictions enter the picture (as they usually do), that background factors become important.

For example, no inequity is necessarily involved if a culturally disadvantaged child is simply reported to have an IQ of 84 and a percentile rank of 16 on the national norms for a certain intelligence test. However, if this is interpreted as meaning that the child ranks or will rank no higher in learning ability than does a middle-class, native born American child of the same IQ, the interpretation might well be erroneous.

Factors Impairing Test Validity. Three kinds of factors may impair a test's predictive validity. First, there are test-related factors—factors or conditions that affect the test scores but which may have relatively little relation to the criterion. Such factors may include test-taking skills, anxiety, motivation, speed, understanding of test instructions, degree of item or format novelty, examiner-examinee rapport, and other general or specific abilities that underlie test performance but which are irrelevant to the criterion. Examples of the operation of such factors are found in the literature describing the problems of white examiners testing Negro children (Dreger and Miller, 1960), of American Indian children taking unfamiliar, timed tests (Klineberg, 1935), and of children of certain disadvantaged groups being exposed for the first time to test-taking procedures (Haggard, 1954).

It should be noted that some test-related factors may not be prejudicial to disadvantaged groups. For example, test-taking anxiety of a disruptive nature (Sarason et al., 1960) may be more prevalent in some middle-class groups than in lower-class groups. In general, however, the bias attributable to test-related factors accrues to the detriment of the culturally disadvantaged groups.

The problem of making valid predictions for minority group children is faced by the Boys' Club of New York in its Educational Program,[3] which is designed to give promising boys from tenement districts opportunities to overcome their environmental handicaps through scholarships to outstanding schools and colleges. Although the majority of the boys currently enrolled in this program had mediocre aptitude and achievement test scores up to the time they were given scholarships, practically all of the boys have achieved creditable academic success at challenging secondary boarding schools and colleges. In this program, normative scores on the Otis Quick-Scoring Mental Ability Test and the Stanford Achievement Test are used for screening purposes, but they are regarded as minimal estimates of the boys' abilities. The Wechsler Intelligence Scale for Children (WISC) is frequently used in this program to supplement the group tests. The boys typically score 5 to 10 points higher on the WISC than on the Otis, probably because the WISC gives less weight to educational and language factors.

Interest and Personality Inventory Scores. When standardized interest inventories are used, special caution should be observed in making normative interpretations of the scores of culturally disadvantaged individuals. When a child has not had opportunities to gain satisfaction or rewards from certain pursuits, he is not likely to show interest in these areas. For example, adolescent children in a particular slum neighborhood might rank consistently low in scientific, literary, musical, and artis-

[3] Information about this program is obtainable from The Boys Club of New York, 287 East 10th Street, New York, N.Y.

tic interests on the Kuder Preference Record if their home and school environments fail to stimulate them in these areas. With improved cultural opportunities, these children might rapidly develop interests in vocations or avocations related to these areas.

Scores on personality inventories may also have very different significance for minority group members than for the population in general (Auld, 1952). Whenever the inventory items tap areas such as home or social adjustment, motivation. religious beliefs, or social customs, the appropriateness of the national norms for minority groups should be questioned. Local norms for the various minority groups involved might again be very much in order here.

Predicting Complex Criteria. A second class of factors contributing to low predictive validity is associated with the complexity of criteria. Criteria generally represent "real life" indices of adjustment or achievement and therefore they commonly sample more complex and more variegated behaviors than do the tests. An obvious example is the criterion of school grades. Grades are likely to reflect motivation, classroom behavior, personal appearance, and study habits, as well as intelligence and achievement. Even if a test measured scholastic aptitude sensitively and accurately, its validity for predicting school marks would be attenuated because of the contribution of many other factors to the criterion. It is important, therefore, to recognize the influence of other factors, not measured by the tests, which may contribute to criterion success. Since disadvantaged groups tend to fare poorly on ability and achievement tests (Anastasi, 1958; Tyler, 1956; Masland, Sarason, and Gladwin, 1958; Eels et al., 1951; Haggard, 1954), there is particular merit in exploring the background, personality, and motivation of members of such groups for compensatory factors, untapped by the tests, which may be related to criterion performance.

In some instances, such as in making scholarship awards on a statewide or national basis, test scores are used rigidly for screening or cut-off purposes to satisfy demands for objectivity and "impartiality." The culturally disadvantaged child (quite possibly a "diamond-in-the-rough") is often the victim of this automatic and autocratic system. Recourse lies in providing opportunities where the hurdles are less standardized and where a more individualized evaluation of his qualifications for meeting the criterion may prove to be fairer for him.

For example, the following characteristics that may be typical of minority group children who have above-average ability or talent are among those cited by DeHaan and Kough (1956), who have been working with the North Central Association Project on Guidance and Motivation of Superior and Talented Secondary School Students:

They learn rapidly, but not necessarily those lessons assigned in school.

They reason soundly, think clearly, recognize relationships, comprehend meanings, and may or may not come to conclusions expected by the teacher.

They are able to influence others to work toward desirable or undesirable goals.

Effects of Intervening Events on Predictions. A third set of contributors to low criterion validity is related to the nature of intervening events and contingencies. This class of conditions is particularly important when the criterion measure is obtained considerably later than the testing—when predictive rather than concurrent validity is at stake. If the time interval between the test administration and the criterial assessment is lengthy, a host of situational, motivational, and maturational changes may occur in the interim. An illness, an inspiring teacher, a shift in aspiration level or in direction of interest, remedial training, an economic misfortune, an emotional crisis, a growth spurt or retrogression in the abilities sampled by the test—any of these changes intervening between the testing and the point or points of criterion assessment may decrease the predictive power of the test.

One of the more consistent findings in research with disadvantaged children is the decline in academic aptitude and achievement test scores of such children with time (Masland, Sarason, and Gladwin, 1958). The decline is, of course, in relation to the performance of advantaged groups or of the general population. It is plausible to assume that this decline represents the cumulative effects of diminished opportunities and decreasing motivation for acquiring academic knowledge and skills. When such cumulative effects are not taken into consideration, the predictive power of academic aptitude and achievement tests is impaired. If it were known in advance that certain individuals or groups would be exposed to deleterious environmental conditions, and if allowances could be made for such contingencies in connection with predictions, the test's criterion validity could be improved.

Looking in another direction, the normative interpretation of the test results cannot reveal how much the status of underprivileged individuals might be changed if their environmental opportunities and incentives for learning and acquiring skills were to be improved significantly. In the case of the Boy's Club boys mentioned above, estimates of academic growth potential are made on the basis of knowledge of the educational and cultural limitations of the boys' home and neighborhood environment, observational appraisals of the boys' behavior in club activities, and knowledge of the enhanced educational and motivational opportunities that can be offered to the boys in selected college preparatory schools. With this information available, the normative interpretation of the boys' scores on standardized tests can be tempered with experienced judgment, and better estimates of the boys' academic potential can thus be made.

In situations where minority group members are likely to have to continue competing with others under much the same cultural handicaps that they have faced in the past, normative interpretation of their aptitude and achievement test scores will probably yield a fairly dependable basis for short-term predictive purposes. When special guidance or training is offered to help such individuals overcome their handicaps, however, achievement beyond the normative expectancies may well be obtained, and predictions should be based on expectancies derived specifically from the local situation. In this connection, it should be recognized that attempts to appraise human "potential" without defining the milieu in which it will be given an opportunity to materialize are as futile as attempts to specify the horsepower of an engine without knowing how it will be energized.

"Culture Fair" and "Unfair"—in the Test and in Society. The fact that a test differentiates between culturally disadvantaged and advantaged groups does not necessarily mean that the test is invalid. "Culturally unfair" tests may be valid predictors of culturally unfair but nevertheless highly important criteria. Educational attainment, to the degree that it reflects social inequities rather than intrinsic merit, might be considered culturally unfair. However, a test must share this bias to qualify as a valid predictor. Making a test culture-fair may decrease its bias, but may also eliminate its criterion validity. The remedy may lie in the elimination of unequal learning opportunities, which may remove the bias in the criterion as well as in the test. This becomes more a matter of social policy and amelioration rather than a psychometric problem, however.

The situation is quite different for a test that differentiates between disadvantaged and advantaged groups even *more* sharply than does the criterion. The extreme case would be a test that discriminated between disadvantaged and advantaged groups but did not have any validity for the desired criterion. An example of this would be an academic aptitude test that called for the identification of objects, where this task would be particularly difficult for disadvantaged children but would not be a valid predictor of academic achievement. Here, one could justifiably speak of a true "test bias." The test would be spuriously responsive to factors associated with cultural disadvantage but unrelated to the criterion. Such a test would not only be useless for predicting academic achievement, but would be stigmatizing as well.

While certain aptitude and ability tests may have excellent criterion validity for some purposes, even the best of them are unlikely to reflect the true *capacity for development* of underprivileged children. For, to the extent that these tests measure factors that are related to academic success, they must tap abilities that have been molded by the cultural setting. Furthermore, the test content, the mode of communication involved in responding to test items, and the motivation needed for making the responses are intrinsically dependent upon the cultural context.

Elixir of "Culture-Fair" Tests. The elixir of the "culture-fair" or "culture-free" test has been pursued through attempts to minimize the educational loading of test content and to reduce the premium on speed of response. However, the efforts have usually resulted in tests that have low validities for academic prediction purposes and little power to uncover hidden potentialities of children who do poorly on the common run of academic aptitude and achievement tests.

In spite of their typical cultural bias, standardized tests should not be sold short as a means for making objective assessments of the traits of minority-group children. Many bright, non-conforming pupils, with backgrounds different from those of their teachers, make favorable showings on achievement tests, in contrast to their low classroom marks. These are very often children whose cultural handicaps are most evident in their overt social and interpersonal behavior. Without the intervention of standardized tests, many such children would be stigmatized by the adverse subjective ratings of teachers who tend to reward conformist behavior of middle-class character.

III. The Validity of Test Interpretation

The most important consideration of all is one that applies to the use of tests in general—namely, that test results should be interpreted by competently trained and knowledgeable persons wherever important issues or decisions are at stake. Here, an analogy may be drawn from medical case history information that is entered on a child's record. Certain features of this record, such as the contagious-disease history, constitute factual data that are easily understood by school staff members who have not had medical training. But other aspects of the medical record, as well as the constellation of factors that contribute to the child's general state of health, are not readily interpretable by persons outside the medical profession. Consequently, the judgment of a doctor is customarily sought when an overall evaluation of the child's physical condition is needed for important diagnostic or predictive purposes. So, too, the psychological and educational test records of children should be interpreted by competently trained professional personnel when the test results are to be used as a basis for decisions that are likely to have a major influence on the child's future.

There are several sources of error in test interpretation stemming from a lack of recognition of the special features of culturally disadvantaged groups. One of these may be called the "deviation error." By this is meant the tendency to infer maladjustment or personality difficulty from responses which are deviant from the viewpoint of a majority culture, but which may be typical of a minority group. The results of a test might accurately reflect a child's performance or quality of ideation, but still the results should be interpreted in the light of the child's particular circumstance in life and the range of his experiences. For example, a minister's son whose test responses indicate that he sees all women as prostitutes and a prostitute's son whose test responses give the same indication may both be accurately characterized in one sense by the test. The two boys may or may not be equally disturbed, however. Clinically, a safer inference might be that the minister's son is the one who is more likely to be seriously disturbed by fantasies involving sex and women.

There is evidence to indicate that members of a tribe that has experienced periodic famines would be likely to give an inordinate number of food responses on the Rorschach. So too might dieting Palm Beach matrons, but their underlying anxiety patterns would be quite different than those of the tribesmen. Or, to take still another example, the verbalized self-concept of the son of an unemployed immigrant might have to be interpreted very differently from that of a similar verbalization of a boy from a comfortable, middle-class, native-American home.

A performance IQ that is high in relation to the individual's verbal IQ on the Wechsler scales *may* signify psychopathic tendencies but it also may signify a poverty of educational experience. Perceiving drunken males beating up women on the Thematic Apperception Test may imply a projection of idiosyncratic fantasy or wish, but it may also imply a background of rather realistic observation and experience common to some minority group children.

For children in certain situations, test responses indicating a low degree of motivation or an over-submissive self-image are realistic reflections of their life conditions. If these children were to give responses more typical of the general population, they might well be regarded as sub-group deviants. In short, whether test responses reflect secondary defenses against anxiety or are the direct result of a socialization process has profound diagnostic import so that knowledge of the social and cultural background of the individual becomes quite significant.

What Does the Test Really Measure? A second type of error, from the viewpoint of construct and content validity,[4] might be called the "simple determinant error." The error consists in thinking of the test content as reflecting some absolute or pure trait, process, factor, or construct, irrespective of the conditions of measurement or of the population being studied. Thus, a fifth-grade achievement test may measure arithmetical knowledge in a middle-class neighborhood where most children are reading up to grade level, but the same test, with the same content, may be strongly affected by a reading comprehension factor in a lower-class school and therefore may be measuring something quite different than what appears to be indicated by the test scores.

Generally, the test-taking motivation present in a middle-class group allows the responses to test content to reflect the differences in intelligence, achievement, or whatever the test is designed to measure. On the other hand in a population where test success has much less reward-value and where degree of test-taking effort is much more variable from individual to individual, the test content may tap motivation as well as the trait purportedly being measured.

Caution and knowledge are necessary for understanding and taking into account testing conditions and test-taking behavior when test results are being interpreted for children from varying backgrounds. A child coming from a particular cultural subgroup might have very little motivation to do well in most test situations, but under certain conditions or with special kinds of materials he might have a relatively high level of motivation. As a result, considerable variability might be evident in his test scores from one situation to another, and his scores might be difficult to reconcile and interpret.

How a question is asked is undoubtedly another important factor to consider in interpreting test results. A child might be able to recognize an object, but not be able to name it. Or, he might be able to identitfy a geometric figure, but not be able to reproduce it. Thus, different results might be obtained in a test depending upon whether the child is asked to point to the triangle in a set of geometric figures or whether he is required to draw a triangle.

Response Sets May Affect Test Results. In attitude or personality questionnaires, response sets[5] such as the tendency to agree indiscriminately with items, or to give socially desirable responses, may contribute error variance from the viewpoint of the content or behavior it is desired to

[4] For a discussion of various types of test validity, see Anastasi (1961), Cronbach (1960), Guilford (1954), Thorndike and Hagen (1961), Lindquist (1950).

[5] For a discussion of this and related concepts, see Anastasi (1961), Cronbach (1960).

sample. To the extent that such sets discriminate between socially advantaged and disadvantaged groups, the target content area may be confounded by specific test format. Thus, a scale of authoritarianism may be found to differentiate among social classes, but if the scale is so keyed that a high score on authoritarianism is obtained from agreement with items, the social class differences may be more reflective of an agreement set rather than an authoritarian tendency. If authoritarian content is logically distinct from agreement content, these two sources of test variance should be kept distinct either through statistical control, by a change in the item format, or by having more than one approach to measurement of the trait in question.

From the standpoint of content validity, there is a third type of error. This may be termed the "incompleteness of content coverage" error. This refers to a circumscribed sampling of the content areas in a particular domain. In the area of intelligence, for instance, Guilford (1954) has identified many factors besides the "primary mental abilities" of Thurstone and certainly more than is implied in the unitary concept of intelligence reflected by a single IQ score. As Dreger and Miller (1960) point out, differences in intellectual functioning among various groups cannot be clearly defined or understood until all components of a particular content area have been systematically measured.

Familiarity with the cultural and social background of minority-group children not only helps to avoid under-evaluating the test performance of some children, but also helps to prevent over-evaluating the performance of others. For example, children who have been trained in certain religious observances involving particular vocabularies and objects, or those who have been encouraged to develop particular skills because of their cultural orientations, might conceivably score "spuriously" high on some tests or on particular items. In other words, any special overlap between the subgroup value-system of the child and the performances tapped by the test is likely to be an important determinant of the outcome of the test.

Failure Barriers May Be Encountered. Failure inducing barriers are often set up for the minority-group child in a testing situation by requiring him to solve problems with unfamiliar tools, or by asking him to use tools in a manner that is too advanced for him. To draw an analogy, if a medical student were handed a scalpel to lance a wound, and if the student were to do the lancing properly but were to fail to sterilize the instrument first, how should he be scored for his accomplishment? If he had never heard of sterilization, should his skillful performance with the instrument nevertheless be given a "zero" score? Similarly, if a child from a disadvantaged social group shows a considerable degree of verbal facility in oral communication with his peers but does very poorly on tests that stress academic vocabulary, can he justifiably be ranked low in verbal aptitude?

In a broad sense, most intelligence test items tap abilities involving language and symbol systems, although opportunities for developing these abilities vary considerably from one social group to another. One might reasonably expect that a child living in a community that minimizes language skills—or, as depicted by Bernstein (1960), a community that uses a language form that is highly concrete—will earn a score that has a meaning very different from that of the score of a child in a community where language skills are highly developed and replete with abstract symbolism. It is important, therefore, to interpret test results in relation to the range of situations and behaviors found in the environments of specific minority groups.

Some Suggested Remedies. While this analysis of the problems involved in the use and interpretation of tests for minority group children may lead to considerable uneasiness and skepticism about the value of the results for such children, it also points up potential ways of improving the situation. For example, one of these ways might consist of measuring separate skills first, gradually building up to more and more complex items and tests which require the exercise of more than one basic skill at a time. With enough effort and ingenuity, a sizable universe of items might be developed by this procedure. Special attention should also be given to the selection or development of items and tests that maximize criterial differentiations and minimize irrelevant discriminations. If a test is likely to be biased against certain types of minority groups, or if its validity for minority groups has not been ascertained, a distinct *caveat* to that effect should appear in the manual for the test.

Furthermore, we should depart from too narrow a conception of the purpose and function of testing. We should re-emphasize the concept of the test as an integral component of teaching and training whereby a floor of communication and understanding is established and *learning* capabilities are measured in repeated and cyclical fashion.

Finally, we should think in terms of making more use of everyday behavior as evidence of the coping abilities and competence of children who do not come from the cultural mainstream. Conventional tests may be fair predictors of academic success in a narrow sense, but when children are being selected for special aid programs or when academic prediction is not the primary concern, other kinds of behavioral evidence are commonly needed to modulate the results and implications of standardized tests.

Conclusion

Tests are among the most important evaluative and prognostic tools that educators have at their disposal. How unfortunate, then, that these tools are often used so routinely and mechanically that some educators have stopped *thinking* about their limitations and their benefits. Since the minority group child is so often handicapped in many ways his test scores may have meanings different from those of non-minority children, even when they are numerically the same. The task of the conscientious educator is to ponder what lies behind the test scores. Rather than accepting test scores and indicating fixed levels of either performance or potential, educators should plan remedial activities which will free the child from as many of his handicaps as possible. Good schools will employ well qualified persons to use good tests as one means of accomplishing this task.

In testing the minority group child it is sometimes appropriate to compare his performance with that of advantaged children to determine the magnitude of the deprivation to be overcome. At other times it is appropriate to compare his test performance with that of other disadvantaged children—to determine his relative deprivation in comparison with others who have also been denied good homes, good neighborhoods, good diets, good schools and good teachers. In most instances it is especially appropriate to compare the child's test performance with his previous test performance. Utilizing the individual child as his own control and using the test norms principally as "bench marks," we are best able to gauge the success of our efforts to move the minority group child forward on the long, hard road of overcoming the deficiencies which have been forced upon him. Many comparisons depend upon tests, but they also depend upon *our* intelligence, our good will, and our sense of responsibility to make the proper comparison at the proper time and to undertake proper remedial and compensatory action as a result. The misuse of tests with minority group children, or in any situation, is a serious breach of professional ethics. Their proper use is a sign of professional and personal maturity.

References

American Educational Research Association and National Committee on Measurements Used in Education. *Technical recommendations for achievement tests.* Washington, D.C., National Education Association, 1955.

American Psychological Association. Technical recommendations for psychological tests and diagnostic techniques. *Psychol. Bull.,* 1954, **51**, No. **2**.

Anastasi, A. *Psychological testing.* (2nd Ed.) New York: Macmillan, 1961.

Anastasi, A. *Different psychology.* (3rd Ed.) New York: Macmillan, 1953.

Auld, F., Jr. Influence of social class on personality test responses. *Psychol. Bull.*, 1952, **49**, 318–332.

Bernstein, B. Aspects of language and learning in the genesis of the social process, *J. child Psychol. Psychiat.*, 1961, **1**, 313–324.

Bernstein, B. Language and social class. *Brit. J. Sociol.*, 1960, **11**, 271–276.

Cronbach, L. *Essentials of psychological testing.* (2nd Ed.) New York: Harper, 1960.

DeHaan, R., and Kough, J. Teacher's guidance handbook: Identifying students with special needs (Vol. I Secondary School Edition). Chicago: Science Research Associates, 1956.

Deutsch, M. *Minority group and class status as related to social and personality factors in scholastic achievement.* (Monograph No. 2) Ithaca, New York: The Society for Applied Anthropology, 1960.

Deutsch, M. The disadvantaged child and the learning process: some social, psychological and developmental considerations. In H. Passow (Ed.), *Education in depressed areas.* New York: Teachers College Press, 1963.

Deutsch, M., and Brown, B. Some data on social influences in Negro-white intelligence differences. *J. Social Issues,* XX, No. **2**, 24–35.

Dreger, R., and Miller, K. Comparative psychological studies of Negroes and Whites in the United States. *Psychol. Bull.*, 1960, **57**, 361–402.

Eells, K., et al. *Intelligence and cultural differences.* Chicago: University of Chicago Press, 1951.

Fishman, J. A., and Clifford, P. I. What can mass testing programs do for-and-to the pursuit of excellence in American Education? *Harvard Educ. Rev.,* 1964, **34**, 63–79.

Froehlich, C., and Hoyt, K. *Guidance testing.* (3rd Ed.). Chicago: Science Research Associates, 1959.

Guilford, J. *Psychometric methods* (2nd Ed.). New York: McGraw-Hill, 1954.

Haggard, E. Social status and intelligence: an experimental study of certain cultural determinants of measured intelligence. *Genet. Psychol. Monogr.,* 1954, **49**, 141–186.

Klineberg, O. *Race differences.* New York: Harper, 1935.

Katz, M. *Selecting an achievement test: Principles and procedures.* Princeton: Educational Testing Service, 1958.

Lindquist, E. (Ed.) *Educational Measurement.* Washington: American Council of Education, 1950.

Masland, R., Sarason, S., and Gladwin, T. *Mental subnormality.* New York: Basic Books, 1958.

Sarason, S. et al. *Anxiety in elementary school children.* New York: Wiley, 1960.

Thorndike, R., and Hagen, E. *Measurement and evaluation in psychology and education.* (2nd ed.). New York: Wiley, 1961.

Tyler, L. *The psychology of individual differences* (2nd Ed.). New York: Appleton-Century-Crofts, 1956.

15.3 The Assignment of School Marks

M. D. Glock and J. Millman

The typical grade earned by a pupil is likely to represent his relative achievement in the class. No matter what teachers say, they tend to give easy or hard tests to make adjustments so as to get the "correct" distribution of scores. The authors make suggestions for improving the validity of marks. They present a method of analyzing test scores that is easy to use and avoids some of the pitfalls in evaluating pupils' achievement. They suggest the use of norm-referenced criteria, in which each pupil's performance is compared with others for purposes of grading.

A teacher has a three-fold responsibility: he must decide what he wants to accomplish with a class (state his objectives); he must provide the experiences that will help his pupils attain those objectives; and he must determine whether the objectives have been achieved.

In determining achievement, the teacher makes a value judgment based on measures such as tests, grades on projects, and ratings on laboratory performances. Once the measures have been obtained, it is necessary to to convert them into a final grade. The purpose of this bulletin is to discuss the conversion procedure.

SOURCE. M. D. Glock and J. Millman, "The Assignment of School Marks," *State of New York Bulletin*, 1963. Reprinted by permission of the authors.

A Basic Concept

When a student correctly answers seven of 10 questions about the Civil War, it does not mean that he knows 70 percent of the facts about the War. If the questions were easier or harder, the student could get 0 percent or 100 percent on the test. To illustrate, consider tests A and B which were given to the same group of students. No one did better on test A than on test B; several students received 100 percent on test B and 0 percent on test A. Our judgment of how much a student knows about world geography and maps could vary greatly depending upon which test he took.

Test A

1. Give a rank of 1 to the continent with the largest area; a rank of 3 to the continent with the smallest area.
   _____ Antarctica
   _____ Europe
   _____ South America
2. What is the name of a map projection that represents a "true picture" projection of any given half of the earth?
3. Lake Geneva is really a part of the
   _____ (a) Rhine River
   _____ (b) Rhone River
   _____ (c) Seine River
   _____ (d) Volga River

Test B

1. Give a rank of 1 to the continent with the largest area; a rank of 3 to the continent with the smallest area.
   _____ Africa
   _____ Asia
   _____ Australia
2. Which of the following types of map projections has the longitude and latitude lines at right angles to each other?
   _____ (a) Conic projection
   _____ (b) Mercator projection
   _____ (c) Polar projection
   _____ (d) Sinusoidal projection
3. A famous river valley in China is the
   _____ (a) Amazon
   _____ (b) Po
   _____ (c) Rhine
   _____ (d) Yangtze

The actual score on a test does not tell us how well a student has mastered the material for which we are testing. To convert test scores directly to grades is meaningless, but test scores do permit us to make *relative judgments* about the students who took the tests. To arrive at a final grade, we need some idea of how Henry's test scores and other measures of performance compare with those for other students being graded. To provide a basis for making comparisons, it is necessary to combine the component measures into a composite value or score.

Determining a Composite Score

When combining scores on informal quizzes, reports, class participation, final examinations, and so forth, one must decide what each component shall be given. There is no consensus on the exact emphasis or weight various measures should have, but it is agreed that measurements reflecting pupils' progress in the more important course objectives should be given greater weight than those reflecting progress toward less important objectives. For example, if a French teacher feels that the ability to carry on a conversation in French is more important than knowledge of French history, her measures of students' conversational skill should have more weight than a test score in French history.

A Necessary Precaution

A precaution must be taken in determining a composite mark, however, no matter what weight is chosen. Applying a weight to test scores is insufficient because of distortion from inequalities in score variability. Variability is the degree of spread or dispersion of a set of test scores along the score range. The more variable component score will receive greater weight than desired. This can be illustrated by a simple example in which a teacher wishes to weight two test scores equally. Bill received the highest score in the class on test 1 and the lowest score in the class on class 2; Mary had the lowest score in the class on test 1 and the highest score in the class on test 2. Their scores and the tests' range (varability) are shown below:

	Test 1	Test 2	Composite Score
Bill	90	50	140
Mary	70	80	150
Test Range	20	30	

Because both Bill and Mary had one top score and one bottom score, and because each test was to be weighted equally, each student should receive the *same* composite score. Mary's composite score was higher because her better performance was on the test with the greater variability.

Making the average of each test the same is not the solution because test 1, which has the higher average, exerts less influence. Changing the test scores to percentages is not the solution either, because these scores could as well have been percentage scores. The scores must be converted in such a way that each test has the same variability. Because the original scores provide us with relative judgments, the converted scores should not disturb the ranking of the students.

Stanines

To control the variability of test scores, test makers frequently change the original test scores to standard scores. For example, College Board test scores are reported by a type of standard score. Conversion of the obtained scores of all the component measures to any one of the many types of standard scores will equalize the variability of the several component scores. Stanines, a type of standard score rapidly growing in popularity, have been selected for illustration because no calculation is necessary to convert obtained scores to stanines.

Stanines are a STAndard NINE-point scale in which 1 represents the lowest scale value and 9 the highest scale value. To convert a set of obtained measures into stanines, it is necessary to rank the measures. The table on the next page indicates how many students should receive each stanine value. For example, if 33 measures were being ranked, one student would receive a stanine of 1; two students a stanine of 2; four students a stanine of 3; six students a stanine of 4 and so forth.

To illustrate, a teacher has ranked 15 papers with scores as follows:

30 28 27 27 25 25 25 23 23 21 20 20 7 5 0

The teacher might next place a slanted line between the scores to separate them into stanine groups according to the breakdown in the preceding table.

30/ 28/ 27 27/ 25 25/ 25 23 23/ 21 20/ 20 7/ 5/ 0

The two top scores will receive stanines of 9 and 8 respectively and the two scores tied at 27 will, of course, both receive a 7. At this point the teacher needs to be careful to give the three scores tied at 25 the same stanine value. Because the majority of the 25's are in the 6th stanine level, assigning all a 6 results in the least distortion. The next problem involves the two scores tied at 20. Because the 20 is more nearly a 21 than a 7, converting both 20's to a stanine of 4 is the least distorting procedure.

There are no hard and fast rules for assigning stanine values to tied scores that span more than one stanine level. Common sense will be your best guide, and a shift of one stanine level makes little difference. The original scores, with their stanine equivalents, are shown below:

30/ 28/ 27 27/ 25 25/ 25 23 23/ 21 20/ 20 7/ 5/ 0
9 8 7 7 6 6 *6* 5 5 4 4 *4* 3 2 1

By converting test scores and other measures into stanines, most students' progress in comparison to others in a class can be easily noted during a year. An exception, of course, is the student who does best (stanine = 9) on one measure and cannot be higher on another. A very low scoring student may actually improve his achievement, but if the other members of the class improve as well he may remain in the bottom stanine level. In addition, differences of less than three stanine levels on two measures probably do not represent statistically significant changes because of the low reliability of most teacher-made tests.

Stanines also provide a basis for comparing intelligence and achievement scores which can be converted into stanines according to the procedure described above. All things being equal, a pupil should be achieving at the stanine level of his scholastic aptitude. We would probably consider Johnny an underachiever if his intelligence score were at the ninth stanine and his achievement at the fifth, although a difference of less than three stanine levels between these two measures is not significant.

The Composite Average

Because distributions of stanine scores all have the same variability, the desired weight can be assigned to component scores being combined into a composite by applying the following formula:

$$C = \frac{(W_1 x S_1) + (W_2 x S_2) + (W_3 x S_3) + \ldots}{W_1 + W_2 + W_3 + \ldots}$$

C is the composite average; W_1 is the weight and S_1 is the stanine level on the first component measure; W_8 and S_2 are the weight and stanine level on the second component measure, and so forth.

To illustrate, suppose that a student has the stanine scores on four component measures to be weighted as indicated in Table 1.

Composite Measure	Weight	Stanine
Unit Test #1	1	3
Unit Test #2	1	2
Reports	1	4
Final Examination	2	6

His composite average would be:

$$C = \frac{(1x3) + (1x2) + (1x4) + (2x6)}{1 + 1 + 1 + 2} = \frac{21}{5} = 4.2$$

If the student were absent for the first unit test, his composite average would be:

$$C = \frac{(1x2) + (1x4) + (2x6)}{1 + 1 + 2} = \frac{18}{4} = 4.5$$

In the earlier example of Bill and Mary, each student received a top and a bottom score on two tests of equal weight. In each case their composite average would be:

$$C = \frac{(1x9) + (1x1)}{1 + 1} = \frac{10}{2} = 5.0$$

Table 1

Number of Students Receiving Each Normalized Stanine Score[a]

Number Being Measured	Stanine Score 1	2	3	4	5	6	7	8	9	Number Being Measured	Stanine Score 1	2	3	4	5	6	7	8	9
	Number of Students Receiving Score										Number of Students Receiving Score								
15	1	1	2	2	3	2	2	1	1	45	2	3	5	8	9	8	5	3	2
16	1	1	2	3	2	3	2	1	1	46	2	3	5	8	10	8	5	3	2
17	1	1	2	3	3	3	2	1	1	47	2	3	6	8	9	8	6	3	2
18	1	1	2	3	4	3	2	1	1	48	2	3	6	8	10	8	6	3	2
19	1	1	2	3	5	3	2	1	1	49	2	4	6	8	9	8	6	4	2
20	1	1	2	4	4	4	2	1	1	50	2	3	6	9	10	9	6	3	2
21	1	1	2	4	5	4	2	1	1	51	2	3	6	9	11	9	6	3	2
22	1	2	2	4	4	4	2	2	1	52	2	4	6	9	10	9	6	4	2
23	1	2	2	4	5	4	2	2	1	53	2	4	6	9	11	9	6	4	2
24	1	2	3	4	4	4	3	2	1	54	2	4	7	9	10	9	7	4	2
25	1	2	3	4	5	4	3	2	1	55	2	4	7	9	11	9	7	4	2
26	1	2	3	4	6	4	3	2	1	56	2	4	7	9	12	9	7	4	2
27	1	2	3	5	5	5	3	2	1	57	2	4	7	10	11	10	7	4	2
28	1	2	3	5	6	5	3	2	1	58	2	4	7	10	12	10	7	4	2
29	1	2	4	5	5	5	4	2	1	59	3	4	7	10	11	10	7	4	3
30	1	2	4	5	6	5	4	2	1	60	3	4	7	10	12	10	7	4	3
31	1	2	4	5	7	5	4	2	1	61	3	4	7	10	13	10	7	4	3
32	1	2	4	6	6	6	4	2	1	62	3	4	7	11	12	11	7	4	3
33	1	2	4	6	7	6	4	2	1	63	3	4	7	11	13	11	7	4	3
34	1	3	4	6	6	6	4	3	1	64	3	4	8	11	12	11	8	4	3
35	1	3	4	6	7	6	4	3	1	65	3	4	8	11	13	11	8	4	3
36	1	3	4	6	8	6	4	3	1	66	3	4	8	11	14	11	8	4	3
37	2	3	4	6	7	6	4	3	2	67	3	5	8	11	13	11	8	5	3
38	1	3	5	6	8	6	5	3	1	68	3	5	8	11	14	11	8	5	3
39	1	3	5	7	7	7	5	3	1	69	3	5	8	12	13	12	8	5	3
40	1	3	5	7	8	7	5	3	1	70	3	5	8	12	14	12	8	5	3
41	1	3	5	7	9	7	5	3	1	71	3	5	8	12	15	12	8	5	3
42	2	3	5	7	8	7	5	3	2	72	3	5	9	12	14	12	9	5	3
43	2	3	5	7	9	7	5	3	2	73	3	5	9	12	15	12	9	5	3
44	2	3	5	8	8	8	5	3	2	74	3	5	9	13	14	13	9	5	3

[a] This procedure should probably not be used for classes of less than 15. If more than 74 students are being measured, the distribution of stanines may be determined by adding together two or more rows. For example, if 77 students are being measured, add together such rows as "37" and "40". If this is done, then 2+1 or 3 of the 77 students should receive a stanine of one; 3+3 or 6 students should receive a stanine of two; and so forth.

Although composite averages are not stanines, they do provide a means for ranking students which reflects the desired relative weight for several measures. On the basis of this distribution, the teacher may assign final marks.

Assigning a Final Grade

Once a composite score is computed for each student, and the composite scores ranked, final grades can be assigned. In absolute terms, a composite score tells little about how much a student knows, but it has meaning in comparison to composite scores of others in a class. Because test scores have no absolute zero, all scores indicate relative judgments. Standardized tests that measure objectives in which the school is interested can give an idea of the degree to which standards are being met. A school that requires a percentage score of 75 to pass need not have higher standards than a school in which 65 percent is passing. Tests can be made easier or harder at the whim of the teacher. Teachers who convert percentage scores directly into school marks are constantly adjusting by having make-up tests, raising marks by some mysterious formula, making the next test easier, altering their grading standards, or some other device. Whether they wish to admit it or not, many teachers decide in advance what the frequency of each grade they are going to give will be, and adjust their composite measures accordingly.

How Many A's?

The distribution of final grade involves an arbitrary decision. It may depend upon school policy, the ability or vocational plans of the students, the presence of gaps in the distribution of composite scores, and so forth. Oddly enough, most schools do not consider a C an average grade. Most schools give more A's and B's than D's or E's, so the typical grade is nearer a B than a C.

Giving Grades Meaning

Regardless of the marking system (number grades, letters grades, graphs) it is important that school grades present a clear and uniform meaning to all who use them. Because grades should reflect a student's achievement in a particular subject, effort, neatness, punctuality, and other non-achievement component measures should not enter into the final calculation. If it is desirable to indicate these traits, a separate grade should be given.

School personnel should agree on the criteria for determining the percentage of pupils in a class to be assigned a given grade. Classes in the same subject with students of similar ability should receive the same grade distribution. It may be desirable to give a higher percentage of students a top grade in certain subjects (physical education), in honors sections, and at the elementary school level, but these decisions should be made by the school personnel.

To illustrate how grades may be assigned unfairly, consider Tom, Dick, and Harry who each have an achievement in history comparable to that of the average college-bound student. Tom is in a college-bound class where the teacher gives only 40 percent A's and B's; and Tom gets a C. Dick is also in a college-bound class, but his teacher gives 60 percent A's and B's, and he receives a B in history. Harry, equal in achievement to Tom and Dick, is in a history class for students in a general curriculum. In this class, Harry is one of the best students and he receives an A. Despite their equal achievement in history, Tom, Dick, and Harry receive grades of C, B, and A respectively because they are in different classes.

Adjusting for Differences in Ability of Classes in the Same Subject

One way to rectify the inequality in the case of Tom, Dick, and Harry is to obtain some common and relevant measure by which the three history classes could be compared. Scores from a scholastic aptitude test, a standardized history test, or a common examination could be used. To see how this would work, suppose it is decided that 18 percent of the 150 students taking history shall receive a grade of A. When the students are ranked according to the common measure, suppose that 10 of the top 27 (18 percent x 150 = 27) scores are made by students in an honors section. Consequently, the teacher of the honors class will give A's to the 10 students with the highest composition averages, although they need not be the 10 who scored highest on the common measure. It is possible that a class would have no pupils who received one of the top 27 scores. Therefore, no A's would be given in that class.

Grades for other subjects would be distributed in a similar manner. The principle would be the same, although the percentages of each grade may differ.

Summary

Measures of achievement can provide only a relative judgment about a student. They do not represent an absolute percentage of mastery in a course. A defensible procedure in assigning grades is to determine a pupil's composite score in a subject, giving careful consideration to weight. To prevent a bias in weighting, it is helpful to convert raw scores into standard scores such as stanines.

After composite scores are determined and ranked, grades may be assigned. Assignment of grades involves an arbitrary decision about the percentage of each grade to be awarded. Percentages will differ on the basis of subject matter, ability grouping, and vocational goals. When there is more than one class in a subject area, it is wise to consider a procedure providing for a fair distribution of grades.

References

Ahmann, J. Stanley and Marvin D. Glock. *Evaluating Pupil Growth* (4th ed.). Boston: Allyn and Bacon, 1971.

Durost, Walter N. "The Characteristics, Use and Computation of Stanines." *Test Service Notebook #23*, Harcourt, Brace & World, Inc., Tarrytown, New York. 1961.

Johnson, Mauritz. "Solving 'the Mess in Marks'," *New York State Education*, **49**, 1961, 12–13, 30.

Thorndike, Robert L. and Elizabeth Hagen. *Measurement and Evaluation in Psychology and Education*. New York: John Wiley & Sons, Inc. 1961. (Chapter 17)

Selected Readings

Alexander, E. D. The marking system and poor achievement. *The Teachers College Journal*, 1964, **36**, 110–113.

Anderson, R. H., and Ritsher, C. Pupil progress. In R. L. Ebel (Ed.), *Encyclopedia of educational research* (4th ed.). London: Macmillan, 1969, pp. 1050–1060.

Carter, R. S. How invalid are marks assigned by teachers? *Journal of Educational Psychology*, 1962, **43**, 218–228.

Cummins, P. De-escalate grades. *Journal of Secondary Education*, 1970, **45**, 158–162.

Davis, F. B. The role of testing in reading instruction. In Helen Robinson (Ed.), *Reading: seventy-five years of progress*. 1966, **96**, 178–189.

Ebel, R. L. Improving the competence of teachers in educational measurement. *Clearing House*, 1961, **36**, 67–71.

Ebel, R. L., and Suehr, J. H. The continuing debate: to mark or not to mark? *Michigan Journal of Secondary Education*, 1964, **6**, 12–30.

Ebel, R. L. Measurement and the teacher. *Educational Leadership*, 1962, **20**, 20–43.

Godshalk, F. I., Swineford, F., and Coffman, W. E. The measurement of writing ability. Princeton: College Entrance Examination Board, 1966.

Jarrett, C. D. Marking and reporting practices in the American secondary school. *Peabody Journal of Education*, 1963, **41**, 36–48.

Millman, J. Reporting student progress: a case for a criterion-referenced marking system. Unpublished paper, March, 1970.

Ricks, J. R. On telling parents about test results. Test Service Bulletin No. 54. New York: *The Psychological Corporation,* 1959.

Simon, S. B. Grades must go. *School Review.* 1970, **78**, 397–402.

Thorndike, R. L. Marks and marking systems. In R. L. Ebel (Ed.), *Encyclopedia of educational research* (4th ed.). London: Macmillan, 1969, pp. 759–766.

Thorndike, R. L. The measurement of creativity. *Teachers College Record,* 1963, **64**, 422–424.

Tyler, R. What is evaluation? In Helen Robinson (Ed.), *Reading: seventy-five years of progress,* 1966, **96**, 190–198.

CHAPTER **16**

Social Implications of Testing

16.1 Psychology, Psychologists and Psychological Testing[1]

Anne Anastasi

The author discusses seven categories of objections to the use of tests. She points out that these objections arise in part because of popular misinformation about current testing practices; nevertheless, she emphasizes that psychologists themselves are partly to blame because the development of refinements of test construction have surpassed their understanding of the behavior they are measuring. She expresses concern about the lag between the information used in building a test and current psychological data. It takes time and effort to build a test, and the investment often results in infrequent revisions. Another reason for the gap between psychological science and testing is the misuse of tests in attempting to give answers to unsolvable problems on popular demand. Developments within various areas of psychology are discussed when relevant to the improvement of testing.

SOURCE. Anne Anastasi, "Psychology, Psychologists, and Psychological Testing," *American Psychologist*, XXII, No. 4 (1967), pp. 297–306. Reprinted by permission of the author and the American Psychological Association.

1 Address of the President, Division of Evaluation and Measurement, American Psychological Association, September 5, 1966.

It is the main thesis of this paper that psychological testing is becoming dissociated from the mainstream of contemporary psychology. Those psychologists specializing in psychometrics have been devoting more and more of their efforts to refining the techniques of test construction, while losing sight of the behavior they set out to measure. Psychological testing today places too much emphasis on testing and too little on psychology. As a result, outdated interpretations of test performance may remain insulated from the impact of subsequent behavior research. It is my contention that the isolation of psychometrics from other relevant areas of psychology is one of the conditions that have led to the prevalent public hostility toward testing.

The Antitest Revolt

Without question the antitest revolt has many causes and calls for a diversity of remedies. No one solution could adequately meet its multiplicity of problems. These problems have been repeatedly and thoroughly discussed from several angles.[2] For the present purpose, therefore, a brief overview of the principal objections will suffice.

The one that has undoubtedly received the greatest amount of attention, including Congressional investigations, is the objection that psychological tests may represent an invasion of privacy. Although this problem has generally been considered in reference to personality tests, it can logically apply to any type of test. When elderly illiterates are approached for testing, even with a nonverbal test, it is amazing how many have mislaid or broken their glasses that very morning. This mild little subterfuge is their protection against the risk of being asked to read and the resulting embarrassment of admitting illiteracy. Nor is the problem limited to tests. Any observation of an individual's behavior or any conversation with him may, of course, provide information about him that he would prefer to conceal and that he may reveal unwittingly.

For this problem—as for all other problems pertaining to testing—there is no simple or universal solution. Rather, the solution must be worked out in individual cases in terms of two major considerations. The first is the purpose for which the testing is conducted—whether for individual counseling, institutional decisions regarding selection and classification, or research. In the use of tests for research, preserving the subjects'

[2] See, e.g., Carter, Brim, Stalnaker, and Messick (1965), Ebel (1964), Hathaway (1964), Ruebhausen and Brim (1966), Testimony (1966), Testing and Public Policy (1965), Westin (1967), Wolfle (1963). For a survey of the use of tests and the opinions held about them, see the series of questionnaire studies conducted by the Russell Sage Foundation in elementary schools, high schools, and a representative adult sample (Brim, Goslin, Glass, & Goldberg, 1965; Brim, Neulinger, & Glass, 1965; Goslin, Epstein, & Hallock, 1965).

anonymity substantially reduces but does not eliminate the problem. The second consideration is the relevance of the information sought to the specific testing purpose. For example, the demonstrated validity of a particular type of information as a predictor of performance on the job in question would be an important factor in justifying its ascertainment. The interpretation given to scores on a particular test is also relevant. An individual is less likely to consider his privacy to have been invaded by a test assessing his readiness for a specific course of study than by a test allegedly measuring his "innate intelligence."

A second and somewhat related problem is that of confidentiality. Basically, this problem concerns the communication of test information. It is a two-pronged problem, however, because the implications of transmitting test information to the individual himself and to other persons are recognizably different. With regard to the transmittal of information to other persons—such as parents, teachers, supervisors, or prospective employers—professional ethics requires that this be done only when the individual is told at the outset what use is to be made of test results. Any subsequent change in the use of such results could then be introduced only with the individual's consent.

There is another difficulty, however, in the communication of test results, which is common to both prongs of the problem. Whether the information is transmitted to the examinee himself or to others, the likelihood of misinterpretation is a serious concern. The questions of how much information is communicated, in what form, and under what circumstances are of basic importance (Berdie, 1960, 1965; Brown, 1961; Goslin, 1963). Certainly there is no justification for reporting answers to specific questions on a personality inventory, as some laymen apparently fear will be done (see, e.g., Testing and Public Policy, 1965, p. 978). Nevertheless, even total scores, duly referred to appropriate norms and accompanied by a suitable margin of error, can be misleading when perceived in terms of prevalent misconceptions about the nature of certain tests.

There has been considerable concern about the impact that a knowledge of test scores might have upon the individual and his associates; and the need for more research to gauge such impact has been recognized (Berdie, 1965; Goslin, 1963, Ch. 8). Some suggestive evidence is already available indicating that teachers' knowledge of children's intelligence test scores significantly affects the children's subsequent intellectual development (Rosenthal & Jacobson, 1968). The mechanism of this "self-fulfilling prophecy," as it affects the individual's self-concept and the behavior of his associates toward him, is of course well known. With regard to test scores, however, detrimental effects are most likely to result from misconceptions about tests. Suppose, for example, that an IQ is regarded as a broad indicator of the individual's total intelligence, which is fixed and unchanging and of genetic origin. Under these circumstances, releasing the IQs of individuals, to teachers, parents, the individuals themselves, or anyone else is likely to have a deleterious effect on the subsequent development of many children.

A third major category of test criticism has centered on test content. It is a common reaction among laymen, for example, to ask what a specific test item is supposed to show. What does it *mean* if you cross the street to avoid meeting someone you know? If the psychologist falls into the trap of trying to answer the question on the layman's own terms, he will soon find himself in the untenable position of claiming high validity and reliability for a single item. Moreover, he may try to defend the item in terms of its factual or veridical content, which can be challenged on many grounds. In this sort of evaluation, the critics not only ignore the objective processes of item selection and test validation, but they also overgeneralize from a relatively small number of selected items.

In the same vein, some critics make much of the fact that multiple-choice items are sometimes misunderstood and that they may occasionally penalize the brilliant and erudite student who perceives unusual implications in the answers (see Dunnette, 1964; Educational Testing Service, 1963). Granted that this is possible, the obvious conclusion is that the tests are not perfect. A realistic evaluation, however, requires that such tests be compared with alternative assessment procedures. How do the tests compare with grades, essay examinations, interviewing procedures, application forms, ratings, and other predictors whose utilization is practicable in specific situations? An even more appropriate question pertains to how much the introduction of a test improves predictions made with other available assessment procedures.

Attention should be called, however, to a few sophisticated critiques of certain item forms, which provide constructive and imaginative suggestions for improvements in test development (e.g., Feifel, 1949; LaFave, 1966; Sigel, 1963). This approach includes thorough logical analyses of the limitations of such existing item forms as analogies, similarities, classification, and vocabulary, together with some ingenious proposals for the analysis of errors, qualitative grading of responses, and the development of items to identify styles of categorization. In contrast to the superficial critiques of the popular writers, these analyses merit serious consideration.

A fourth type of criticism blames the tests for any objectionable features of the criteria they are designed to predict. Thus it has been argued that objective tests of scholastic aptitude tend to select unimaginative college students, or that personality tests tend to select executives who are conformists and lack individuality. Insofar as these criticisms may be true, they are an indictment not of the tests but of the criteria against which selection tests must be validated. If we were to ignore the criteria and choose less valid tests, the persons thus selected would merely fail more often in college, on the job, and in other situations for which they were selected. Predictors cannot be used as instruments of criterion reform. Improvements must begin at the criterion level.

It should be noted, however, that criteria do change over time. The nature and personnel requirements of jobs change in industry, government, and the armed services. Educational objectives and curricula change. It is therefore imperative to conduct periodic job analyses or task analyses in these various contexts. Such analyses may themselves suggest that some of the tests in use as predictors may be outdated in a particular context. Periodic revalidation of instruments against current criteria provides a more definitive safeguard against the retention of instruments that may have become irrelevant.

A fifth type of criticism asserts that psychological tests are unfair to culturally disadvantaged groups (Anastasi, 1961; Deutsch, Fishman, Kogan, North, & Whiteman, 1964). To criticize tests because they reveal cultural influences is to miss the essential nature of tests. Every psychological test measures a sample of behavior. Insofar as culture affects behavior, its influence will and should be reflected in the test. Moreover, if we were to rule out cultural differentials from a test, we might thereby lower its validity against the criterion we are trying to predict. The same cultural differentials that impair an individual's test performance are likely to handicap him in school work, job performance, or whatever other subsequent achievement we are trying to predict.

Tests are designed to show what an individual can do at a given point in time. They cannot tell us *why* he performs as he does. To answer that question we need to investigate his background, motivations, and other pertinent circumstances. No test score can be properly interpreted in a vacuum—whether obtained by a culturally disadvantaged person or by anyone else.

If we want to use test scores to predict outcome in some future situation, such as an applicant's performance in college, we need tests with high predictive validity against the specific criterion. This requirement is commonly overlooked in the development and application of so-called culture-free tests. In the effort to include in such tests only activities and information common to many cultures, we may end up with content having little relevance to any criterion we wish to predict (Anastasi, 1950). A better solution is to choose test content in terms of its criterion relevance and then investigate the effect of moderator variables. Validity coefficients, regression weights, and cutoff scores may vary as a function of certain background conditions of the subjects (Hewer, 1965). For example, the same scholastic aptitude score may be predictive of college failure when obtained by an upper-middle-class student, but predictive of moderate success when obtained by a lower-class student. In addition, we need to consider the interaction of initial test score and available differential treatments (Cronbach, 1957). Given a certain score obtained by Individual A with a particular cultural background what will be his predicted college achievement following a specified remedial training program?

The inclusion of both moderator variables and differential treatments in the prediction process requires far more empirical data than are now available. Efforts should certainly be made to gather such data. In the meantime, an awareness of the operation of these variables will at least introduce some needed cautions in the interpretation of test scores. Finally, it is apparent that the use of objective selection procedures, such as appropriate tests, should serve to reduce the operation of bias and discrimination against individuals for irrelevant reasons.

A sixth objection to tests is that they foster a rigid, inflexible, and permanent classification of individuals. This objection has been directed particularly against "intelligence tests," and has aroused the greatest concern when such tests are applied to culturally disadvantaged children. It is largely because implications of permanent status have become attached to the IQ that the use of group intelligence tests has been discontinued in New York City public schools (Gilbert, 1966; Loretan, 1966). That it proved necessary to discard the tests in order to eliminate the misconceptions about the fixity of the IQ is a revealing commentary on the tenacity of the misconceptions. Insofar as these misconceptions do prevail, of course, information about a child's IQ would undoubtedly initiate the self-fulfilling prophecy cited earlier. It can be seen that this objection to tests has much in common with questions already discussed in connection with confidentiality and with the testing of culturally disadvantaged groups.

Underlying the popular notion of the fixity of the IQ is the assumption that intelligence tests are designed to measure some mysterious entity known as "innate capacity." In the light of this assumption, the tests are then criticized for their susceptibility to environmental differences. The critics fail to see that it is these very differences in environment that are largely responsible for individual differences in qualifications or readiness for job performance, job training, and educational programs. If these differences in present developed abilities are ignored or obscured by any assessment procedure, the individual will be assigned to a job in which he will fail or be exposed to an educational program from which he will not profit. Under these conditions, he will simply fall farther and farther behind in those abilities in which he is now deficient. A recognition of his present deficiencies, on the other hand, permits the application of suitable and effective training procedures.

A seventh and final type of objection has again been directed chiefly against intelligence tests. It has been argued that, because of their limited coverage of intellectual functions, intelligence tests tend to perpetuate a narrow conception of ability. It is certainly true that the limited sample of cognitive functions included in standard intelligence tests is inconsistent with the global connotations of the test names. This is but one more reason for discarding the label "intelligence test," as some psychologists have been advocating for several decades. To be sure, all test labels are likely to imply more generality than the test possesses. A clerical aptitude test does not cover all the traits required of an office clerk, nor does a mechanical aptitude test cover all aspects of mechanical tasks. A test title that tried to provide a precise operational definition of its content would be unwieldy and impracticable. Hence the layman's tendency to judge a test by its label is always likely to mislead him. Nevertheless, the difficulty is augmented by the use of such a term as "intelligence." Not only is "intelligence" an unusually broad concept, but it has also acquired an impressive array of erroneous connotations.

Dissociation of Psychological Testing from Psychological Science

It is apparent that all seven classes of objections to psychological testing arise at least in part from popular misinformation about current testing practices, about the nature of available tests, and about the meaning of tests scores. Nevertheless, psychologists themselves are to some extent responsible for such misinformation. Nor is inadequate communication with laymen and members of other professions the only reason for such prevalent misinformation. It is my contention that psychologists have contributed directly to the misinformation by actively perpetuating certain misconceptions about tests.

Heretofore, discussions of the current antitest revolt have considered the problems chiefly from a professional point of view. Examining the same problems from the viewpoint of the science of psychology may throw fresh light on them. To be sure, some of the problems—notably invasion of privacy and confidentiality of test results—pertain in large part to questions of professional ethics and responsible professional practice. Even these problems, however, involve substantive considerations stemming from the science of psychology. In the other five types of criticisms outlined, substantive matters are of central importance.

Although the very essence of psychological testing is the measurement of behavior, testing today is not adequately assimilating relevant developments from the science of behavior. The refinements of test construction have far outstripped the tester's understanding of the behavior the tests are designed to measure. I do not mean to belittle the value of these technical advances. Rather I would urge that the understanding of the behavior to be measured keep pace with the development of quantification techniques.

It is noteworthy that the term "test theory" generally refers to the mechanics of test construction, such as the nature of the score scale and the procedures for assessing reliability and validity. The term does not customarily refer to psychological theory about the behavior under consideration. Psychometricians appear to shed much of their psychological knowledge as they concentrate upon the minutiae of elegant statistical techniques. Moreover, when other types of psychologists use standardized tests in their work, they too show a tendency to slip down several notches in psychological sophistication.

A common enough example is encountered when an experimenter sets out to assemble two groups of children to serve as experimental and control subjects. He first decides to equate the groups in such obvious variables as age, sex, parental education, and parental occupational level. As he looks around for other handy variables to hold constant, he thinks, "Ah, of course, the children themselves ought to be equated in IQ." Very likely there are some IQs conveniently available in the children's cumulative school records. They may not all be derived from the same test, but they will provide a good enough approximation for the experimenter's purpose. After all, he wants only a rough estimate of each child's *IQ*.

What does the experimenter really want to equate the children in? Does his experimental variable utilize verbal material, so that vocabulary should be held constant? Is facility in numerical computation relevant to the experiment? Or perhaps perceptual speed and accuracy or spatial visualization are appropriate. Is overall scholastic attitude his chief concern? Would a reading achievement test serve his purposes better? What does he believe he is ruling out when he equates the groups in IQ? Perhaps the IQ merely provides a sufficiently obscure label to conceal the fuzziness of his thinking.

We shall probably always have misconceptions with us. But to hold fast to old misconceptions after they have been recognized as such seems to be needlessly conservative. Yet psychometricians themselves have contributed to the perpetuation of the IQ label, with its vast appendage of misleading connotations. Even when the original ratio IQ proved too crude and was generally supplanted by standard scores, the IQ label was retained. The standard score simply became a deviation IQ. Psychologists have even begun to adopt the popular term "IQ test." The IQ is accepted as a property of the organism, and the "IQ test" measures it, of course.

The confusion engendered by this sort of thinking is illustrated by a statement appearing within the past 2 years in a bulletin about testing issued by a government agency. The statement reads:

"Because of the misunderstandings which have arisen over the meaning and use of the IQ, many schools are currently administering scholastic aptitude tests rather than IQ or intelligence tests. Results cannot be reported in terms of an IQ. The report of a scholastic aptitude test is most often in terms of a percentile rank [McLaughlin, 1964, p. 11]."

This statement tends to encourage the prevalent confusion between a type of score and a type of test. There is the further and rather startling implication that scholastic aptitude tests do not measure intelligence and intelligence tests do not measure scholastic aptitude. Let me hasten to add that this statement was not chosen as a particularly horrible example, but rather because it appeared in an otherwise sophisticated and carefully written discussion of testing. In the rest of the bulletin, the author reveals considerable familiarity with the technical aspects of test construction.

Some reference should also be made to the strange notion of "innate intelligence." Every psychologist would undoubtedly agree that what the individual inherits is not intelligence in any sense, but certain chemical substances which, after innumerable interactions with each other and with environmental factors, lead eventually to different degrees of intelligent behavior. To identify "intelligence" with any one of the many conditions that contribute to its development appears quite illogical. Nevertheless, one still hears the request for a test of innate intelligence, of potential for intellectual development, of hereditary intellectual capacity. And what is meant is not a biochemical test but a behavioral test. It should be obvious that the relation between the intellectual quality of the individual's behavior at any one time and his heredity is extremely indirect and remote. The traditional multiplicative model of the interaction of heredity and environment is a gross oversimplification of this relationship. The product of each interaction between specific hereditary and environmental factors itself determines subsequent interactions. This cumulative effect leads to a rapid and ever-widening divergence of paths that may have started at the same point with regard to heredity.

All the illustrations cited so far concern intelligence tests. It is about intelligence tests that misconceptions are most prevalent. It is also in reference to intelligence tests that popular objections to testing are most closely bound with substantive matters in which psychologists themselves are involved. But let us take a brief look at personality testing in this light. Because personality testing is a more recent development than intelligence testing, misconceptions are less deeply rooted in this area. Personality testing today is characterized not so much by entrenched misconceptions as by confusion and inconsistencies. For example, there is the inconsistency—I might almost say conflict—between what clinical psychology students learn about personality tests in their psychometrically oriented testing courses and what they often learn to do with the same tests in practicum training. The same discrepancies can be found between the reviews of many personality tests in the *Mental Measurements Yearbooks* and the uses to which the tests are put in professional practice.

The examples mentioned serve to illustrate a growing dissociation between psychological testing and other psychological specialties. One reason for this dissociation is the increasing specialization of psychology itself. The psychometrician is subject to the same isolation that characterizes other specialists. He may become so deeply engrossed in the technical refinements of his specialty that he loses touch with relevant developments in other psychological specialties. Yet these developments may basically alter the meaning of the very tests he is busy elaborating and refining.

A second reason is to be found in the built-in inertia of tests. Because it takes several years to develop a test, gather adequate norms, and obtain a reasonable minimum of validity data, there is an inevitable lag between the original conception of the test and its availability for professional use. Moreover, the effectiveness of a test is likely to increase markedly as more and more data accumulate from long-term longitudinal studies and other research conducted with the test. Consequently, some of our best tests are fairly old tests. Even when they are revised, the original conception of the tests is embedded in the psychology of an earlier period. These long-lived tests are among our most valuable measurement tools. But the test user needs to be aware of intervening changes in the science of behavior and to update his interpretation of test scores.

A third reason for the widening gap between testing and psychological science is an undue willingness on the part of psychologists to accede to the layman's requests. Psychologists feel a strong social obligation to put their findings and techniques to work. In their eagerness to apply their science, they sometimes capitulate to unrealistic and unsound popular demands. The public wants shortcuts and magic. Some test constructors and users have tried to give them just that. It is an important function of the applied psychologist to help laymen reformulate problems in ways that permit a sound solution. It is not their role to provide ready-made solutions for insoluble problems. It might be salutary if testing gave less heed to the pull of practical needs and more to the thrust of behavioral science.

When tests are used by members of other professions, such as educators, sociologists, or psychiatrists, the gap between testing and psychological science is likely to be even wider. In addition to the reasons already mentioned, there is a further lag in communicating substantive advances to persons in other fields. It is a curious fact that members of these related fields tend to find out about new tests sooner than they find out about developments pertaining to interpretive background.

Psychology and the Interpretation of Test Scores

One way to meet the outside pressures that threaten to undermine psychological testing is to make improvements from within. Improvements are needed, not so much in the construction of tests, as in the interpretation of scores and the orientation of test users. Existing tests need not be summarily replaced with new kinds of tests; they sample important behavior and provide an accumulation of normative and validation data that should not be lightly dismissed. It would require many years to gather a comparable amount of information about newly developed instruments.

How, then, can the utilization of available psychological tests be improved in the light of modern psychological knowledge? Let us consider a few examples. First, in the assessment of individual differences, attention should be focused on *change*. Tests do not provide a technique for the rigid and static classification of individuals; on the contrary, they are instruments for facilitating change in desired directions. Not only do they permit the measurement of change as it occurs under different experiential conditions, but they also provide essential information about the individual's initial status, prior to the introduction of any intervention procedures. Any program for effecting behavioral change, whether it be school instruction, job training, or psychotherapy, requires a knowledge of the individual's present condition. Readiness for a particular stage or course of academic instruction, for instance, implies the presence of prerequisite intellectual skills and knowledge. How well the individual has acquired these intellectual prerequisites is what the various ability tests tell us—whether they be called intelligence tests, multiple-aptitude batteries, special aptitude tests, or achievement tests. At different stages and in different testing contexts, one of these types of ability tests may be more appropriate than another; there is a place for all of them in the total testing enterprise. But we should not lose sight of the fact—so often stated and so often forgotten—that all these tests measure current developed abilities and that their scores should be interpreted accordingly.

A second example pertains to the *nature of intelligence,* that human characteristic which so many tests endeavor to measure in one way or another (McNemar, 1964). If we consider intelligence to be the overall effectiveness of the individual's adaptive behavior (Baldwin, 1958), it is evident that the nature and composition of intelligence must vary with time and place. Factor analysis has been employed chiefly to provide detailed descriptions of the composition of intelligence for specific populations and in specific cultural contexts (see, e.g., Guilford, 1959, 1966). Even under these restricted conditions, the resulting factorial picture is not absolute. Whether the description is formulated in terms of a few broad factors or a much larger number of narrower factors depends upon the objectives of the study (Humphreys, 1962; Vernon, 1965). Different levels of fractionation of abilities may fit the data equally well.

Although factor analysis itself is a descriptive technique, it can be employed in experimental designs that help to clarify the nature of intelligence. Factor-analytic research over time or across cultures, for example, can contribute to an understanding of how traits develop and how abilities become organized. There is a growing body of research that utilizes factor analysis in this dynamic fashion. Some investigators have compared the organization of intellectual functions in different cultural milieus, including national cultures, socioeconomic levels, and types of school curricula (Burnett, 1955; Dockrell, 1966; Filella, 1960; Guthrie, 1963; Vernon, 1965). Others have studied changes in factorial composition of intelligence over time. This approach is illustrated by investigations of age changes in the number, nature, and interrelations of factors (Burt, 1954; Garrett, 1946; Hofstaetter, 1954; Lienert & Crott, 1964; Smart, 1965). It should be noted, however, that attempts to subsume all such age changes under the single principle of either differentiation or generalization of ability represent an oversimplification. It would seem more realistic to expect some functions to become more differentiated, others less so, with time, depending upon the nature of intervening experiences in a particular cultural context. Comparative studies of age changes in trait organization among persons in different occupations, for example, would be very informative.

While covering a shorter time span than the age-difference studies, research on the role of learning in trait organization provides more direct information on the conditions that bring about change. These investigations have demonstrated that the factorial composition of the same objective tasks alters systematically in the course of practice or after relevant instruction (Anastasi, 1958, pp. 357–366; Ferguson, 1956; Fleishman & Hempel, 1954, 1955). Another promising application of this approach is illustrated by an ongoing longitudinal study of management performance, which involves repeated factor analyses of various criterion and organizational variables at 6-month intervals (MacKinney, in press).

Among the possible reasons for observed changes over time as well as population differences in factor patterns is the use of different work methods by different individuals in carrying out a given task. In support of this hypothesis is the finding that the factorial composition of the same test differs between groups of subjects classified according to their typical problem-solving styles (French, 1965).

At the theoretical level, there have been some ingenious attempts to link intelligence with learning, motivation, and other psychological functions. Of particular interest are the discussions of how factors may develop through the establishment of learning sets and transfer of training (Carroll, 1962; Ferguson, 1954, 1956; Hunt, 1961; Whiteman, 1964). The breadth of the transfer effect would determine whether the resulting factor is a broad one, like verbal comprehension, or a narrow one, like a particular motor skill. Traditional "intelligence tests" cover intellectual skills that transfer very widely to tasks in our culture. This may be one of the reasons why they can predict performance in so many contexts. Another reason may be that any given criterion task can be performed by different persons through the use of different work methods which require different patterns of ability. The characteristic heterogeneity of function which contributes to a global intelligence test score may thus fit criterion situations in which a deficiency in one ability can be compensated by superiority in another alternative ability.

From a different point of view, intelligence has been linked with motivation through the strength of certain "experience-producing drives" (Hayes, 1962). Recognizing that intelligence is acquired by learning, this theory maintains that the individual's motivational makeup influences the kind and amount of learning that occurs. Although the theory proposes that the experience-producing drives constitute the hereditary component of intelligence, the basic relationship still holds if the drives themselves are determined or modified by environmental conditions. Regardless of the origin of the experience-producing drives, the individual's emotional and motivational status at any one time in his development influences the extent and direction of his subsequent intellectual development. It might be added that longitudinal studies of intelligence test performance have provided some empirical support for this proposition

(Sontag, Baker, & Nelson, 1958; Haan, 1963). It would thus seem that adding a measure of a child's motivational status to tests of developed abilities at any one age should improve the prediction of his subsequent intellectual development.

Personality testing itself provides a third area in which to illustrate the role of psychology in the interpretation of test scores. The hypothesis just discussed suggests one important point to bear in mind, namely, that the separation between abilities and personality traits is artificial and the two domains need to be rejoined in interpreting an individual's test scores. It is now widely recognized that an individual's performance on an aptitude test, in school, on the job, or in any other context is significantly influenced by his achievement drive, his self-concept, his persistence and goal orientation, his value system, his freedom from handicapping emotional problems, and every other aspect of his so-called personality. Even more important, however, is the cumulative effect of these personality characteristics upon the direction and extent of his intellectual development (see, e.g., Combs, 1952). Conversely, the success the individual attains in the development and use of cognitive functions is bound to affect his self-concept, emotional adjustment, interpersonal relations, and other "personality traits." To evaluate either ability or personality traits without reference to the other, because of limited testing or compartmentalized thinking, is likely to prove misleading.

Apart from the need for a comprehensive consideration of the individual's behavior, the user of personality tests must keep abreast of a rapidly growing body of relevant research in personality theory, clinical psychology, and social psychology—to name only the most obvious fields. To continue to use personality tests without keeping in close touch with developments in psychological research is especially unwise, since personality tests represent tentative gropings in promising directions, rather than established techniques. A case in point is the self-report inventory, which began as a canned psychiatric interview, with veridical interpretation of the subject's responses. Gradually these inventories are being metamorphosed into more sophisticated measuring instruments, particularly in the light of research on self-concepts (Loevinger, 1959) and response styles (Jackson & Messick, 1958).

As a fourth and final illustration we may consider the *assessment of environment.* The individual does not behave in a vacuum. He responds in a particular environmental context, which in part determines the nature of his responses. It has been suggested that the prediction of criterion behavior from test scores or from earlier criterion performance could be improved by taking situational factors into account (MacKinney, 1967). Given an individual with a certain level of developed abilities and certain personality characteristics at Time A, how will he react in a specified criterion situation at Time B?

Even more important for prediction purposes is information about the environment to which the individual will be exposed in the interval between Time A and Time B. There is some suggestive evidence that correlations approaching unity can be obtained in predicting intelligence test performance or academic achievement when environmental variables are included along with initial test scores as predictors (Bloom, 1964, Ch. 6).

Despite the general recognition of the importance of environmental variables, little progress has been made in the measurement of such variables. The available scales for evaluating home environment, for example, are crude and the choice of items is usually quite subjective. Moreover, environments cannot be ordered along a single continuum from "favorable" to "unfavorable." An environment that is quite favorable for the development, let us say, of independence and self-reliance may differ in significant details from an environment that is favorable for the development of social conformity or abstract thinking. In this connection, a promising beginning has been made in the empirical development of home environment scales against criteria of intelligence test performance and academic achievement (Wolf, 1965).

Summary

In conclusion, it was the thesis of this paper that psychological testing should be brought into closer contact with other areas of psychology. Increasing specialization has led to a concentration upon the techniques of test construction without sufficient consideration of the implications of psychological research for the interpretation of test scores. Some of the relevant developments within psychology have been illustrated under the headings of behavioral change, the nature of intelligence, personality testing, and the measurement of environment. Strengthening psychological testing from within, by incorporating appropriate findings from other areas of psychology, is proposed as one way to meet the popular criticisms of the current antitest revolt.

References

Anastasi, A. Some implications of cultural factors for test construction. *Proceedings of the 1949 Invitational Conference on Testing Problems, Educational Testing Service*, 1950, 13–17.

Anastasi, A. *Differential psychology* (3rd ed.). New York: Macmillan, 1968.

Anastasi, A. Psychological tests: Uses and abuses. *Teachers College Record*, 1961, **62**, 389–393.

Baldwin, A. L. The role of an "ability" construct in a theory of behavior. In D. C. McClelland, A. L. Baldwin, U. Bronfenbrenner, & F. L. Strodtbeck, *Talent and society*. Princeton, N.J.: Van Nostrand, 1958. Pp. 195–233.

Berdie, R. F. Policies regarding the release of information about clients. *Journal of Counseling Psychology*, 1960, **7**, 149–150.

Berdie, R. F. The ad hoc Committee on Social Impact of Psychological Assessment. *American Psychologist*, 1965, **20**, 143–146.

Bloom, B. S. *Stability and change in human characteristics*. New York: Wiley, 1964.

Brim, O. G., Jr., Goslin, D. A., Glass, D. C., & Goldberg, I. The use of standardized ability tests in American secondary schools and their impact on students, teachers, and administrators. Technical Report No. 3, 1965, Russell Sage Foundation.

Brim, O. G., Jr., Neulinger, J., & Glass, D. C. Experiences and attitudes of American adults concerning standardized intelligence tests. Technical Report No. 1, 1965, Russell Sage Foundation.

Brown, D. W. Interpreting the college student to prospective employers, government agencies, and graduate schools. *Personnel and Guidance Journal*, 1961, **39**, 576–582.

Burnett, A. Assessment of intelligence in a restricted environment. Unpublished doctoral dissertation, McGill University, 1955.

Burt, C. The differentiation of intellectual ability. *British Journal of Educational Psychology*, 1954, **24**, 76–90.

Carroll, J. B. Factors of verbal achievement. *Proceedings of the 1961 Invitational Conference on Testing Problems, Educational Testing Service*, 1962, 11–18.

Carter, L. F., Brim, O. G., Stalnaker, J. M., & Messick, S. Psychological tests and public responsibility. *American Psychologist*, 1965, **20**, 123–142.

Combs, A. W. Intelligence from a perceptual point of view. *Journal of Abnormal and Social Psychology*, 1952, **47**, 662–673.

Cronbach, L. J. The two disciplines of scientific psychology. *American Psychologist*, 1957, **12**, 671–684.

Deutsch, M., Fishman, J. A., Kogan, L., North, R., & Whiteman, M. Guidelines for testing minority group children. *Journal of Social Issues*, 1964, **22**, 127–145.

Dockrell, W. B. Cultural and educational influences on the differentiation of abilities. *Proceedings of the 73rd Annual Convention, American Psychological Association*, 1966, 317–318.

Dunnette, M. D. Critics of psychological tests: Basic assumptions: How good? *Psychology in the Schools*, 1964, **1**, 63–69.

Ebel, R. L. The social consequences of educational testing. *Proceedings of the*

1963 Invitational Conference on Testing Problems, Educational Testing Service, 1964, 130–143.

Educational Testing Service. *Multiple-choice questions: A close look.* Princeton, N.J.: ETS, 1963.

Feifel, H. Qualitative differences in the vocabulary responses of normals and abnormals. *Genetic Psychology Monographs*, 1949, **39**, 151–204.

Ferguson, G. A. On learning and human ability. *Canadian Journal of Psychology*, 1954, **8**, 95–112.

Ferguson, G. A. On transfer and the abilities of man. *Canadian Journal of Psychology*, 1956, **10**, 121–131.

Filella, J. F. Educational and sex differences in the organization of abilities in technical and academic students in Colombia, South America. *Genetic Psychology Monographs*, 1960, **61**, 115–163.

Fleishman, E. A., & Hempel, W. E., Jr. Changes in factor structure of a complex psychomotor test as a function of practice. *Psychometrika*, 1954, **19**, 239–252.

Fleishman, E. A., & Hempel, W. E., Jr. The relation between abilities and improvement with practice in a visual discrimination task. *Journal of Experimental Psychology*, 1955, **49**, 301–312.

French, J. W. The relationship of problem-solving styles to the factor composition of tests. *Educational and Psychological Measurement*, 1965, **25**, 9–23.

Garrett, H. E. A developmental theory of intelligence. *American Psychologist*, 1946, **1**, 372–378.

Gilbert, H. B. On the IQ ban. *Teachers College Record*, 1966, **67**, 282–285.

Goslin, D. A. *The search for ability: Standardized testing in social perspective.* New York: Russell Sage Foundation, 1963.

Goslin, D. A. The social consequences of predictive testing in education. In H. M. Clements & J. B. McDonald (Eds.), *Moral dilemmas in schooling.* Columbus, Ohio: Charles Merrill, in press.

Goslin, D. A., Epstein, R. R., & Hallock, B. A. The use of standardized tests in elementary schools. Technical Report No. 2, 1965, Russell Sage Foundation.

Guilford, J. P. Three faces of intellect. *American Psychologist*, 1959, **14**, 469–479.

Guilford, J. P. Intelligence: 1965 model. *American Psychologist*, 1966, **21**, 20–26.

Guthrie, G. M. Structure of abilities in a nonwestern culture. *Journal of Educational Psychology*, 1963, **54**, 94–103.

Haan, N. Proposed model of ego functioning: Coping and defense mechanisms in relationship to IQ change. *Psychological Monographs*, 1963, **77** (8, Whole No. 571).

Hathaway, S. R. MMPI: Professional use by professional people. *American Psychologist*, 1964, **19**, 204–210.

Hayes, K. J. Genes, drives, and intellect. *Psychological Reports*, 1962, **10**, 299–342.

Hewer, V. H. Are tests fair to college students from homes with low socio-economic status? *Personnel and Guidance Journal*, 1965, **43**, 764–769.

Hofstaetter, P. R. The changing composition of "intelligence"; A study in T-technique. *Journal of Genetic Psychology*, 1954, **85**, 159–164.

Humphreys, L. G. The organization of human abilities. *American Psychologist*, 1962, **17**, 475–483.

Hunt, J. McV. *Intelligence and experience.* New York: Ronald Press, 1961.

Jackson, D. N., & Messick, S. Content and style in personality assessment. *Psychological Bulletin*, 1958, **55**, 243–252.

La Fave, L. Essay vs. multiple-choice: Which test is preferable? *Psychology in the Schools*, 1966, **3**, 65–69.

Lienert, G. A., & Crott, H. W. Studies in the factor structure of intelligence in children, adolescents, and adults. *Vita Humana*, 1964, **7**, 147–163.

Loevinger, J. A theory of test response. *Proceedings of the 1958 Invitational Conference on Testing Problems, Educational Testing Service*, 1959, 36–47.

Loretan, J. O. Alternatives to intelligence testing. *Proceedings of the 1965 Invitational Conference on Testing Problems, Educational Testing Service*, 1966, 19–30.

MacKinney, A. C. The assessment of performance change: An inductive example. *Organizational Behavior and Human Performance*, 1967.

McLaughlin, K. F. Interpretation of test results. OE-25038 Bulletin, 1964, No. 7.

McNemar, Q. Lost: Our intelligence? Why? *American Psychologist*, 1964, **19**, 871–882.

Rosenthal, R., & Jacobson, L. Self-fulfilling prophecies in the classroom: Teachers' expectations as unintended determinants of pupils' intellectual competence. In M. Deutsch, A. R. Jensen, & I. Katz (Eds.), *Race, social class, and psychological development.* New York: Holt, Rinehart & Winston, 1968.

Ruebhausen, O. M., & Brim, O. G., Jr. Privacy and behavioral research. *American Psychologist*, 1966, **21**, 423–437.

Sigel, I. E. How intelligence tests limit understanding of intelligence. *Merrill-Palmer Quarterly*, 1963, **9**, 39–56.

Smart, R. C. The changing composition of "intelligence": A replication of a factor analysis. *Journal of Genetic Psychology*, 1965, **107**, 111–116.

Sontag, L. W., Baker, C. T., & Nelson, V. L. Mental growth and personality development. *Monographs of the Society for Research in Child Development*, 1958, **23**, No. 2.

Testimony before House Special Subcommittee on Invasion of Privacy of the

Committee on Government Operations. *America Psychologist,* 1966, **21,** 404–422.

Testing and public policy. (Special issue) *American Psychologist,* 1965, **20,** 857–992.

Vernon, P. E. Ability factors and environmental influences. *American Psychologist,* 1965, **20,** 723–733.

Westin, A. F. *Privacy and freedom.* New York: Atheneum, 1967.

Whiteman, M. Intelligence and learning. *Merrill-Palmer Quarterly,* 1964, **10,** 297–309.

Wolf, R. The measurement of environments. *Proceedings of the 1964 Invitational Conference on Testing Problems, Educational Testing Service,* 1965, 93–106.

Wolfle, D. Educational tests. *Science,* 1963, **142,** 1529.

16.2 The Social Consequences of Educational Testing

Robert L. Ebel

The author lists four common arguments of critics of testing and then discusses these criticisms in the light of popular misunderstandings and the role that test specialists can play in eliminating these misunderstandings. He concludes his paper with a discussion of the possible consequences of not testing. Nevertheless, he stresses that it is of vital importance for the future of tests that they be used with wisdom and care.

Tests have been used increasingly in recent years to make educational assessments. The reasons for this are not hard to discover. Educational tests of aptitude and achievement greatly improve the precision, objectivity, and efficiency of the observations on which educational assessments rest. Tests are not alternatives to observations. At best they represent no more than refined and systematized processes of observation.

But the increasing use of tests has been accompanied by an increasing flow of critical comment. Again the reasons are easy to see. Tests vary in

SOURCE. Abridged from Robert L. Ebel, "The Social Consequences of Educational Testing," in *Proceedings of the 1963 Invitational Conference on Testing Problems.* Princeton, New Jersey: Educational Testing Service, 1964, pp. 130–134, by permission of the author and the college entrance examination board. (By special arrangement with the American Council on Education.)

quality. None is perfect and some may be quite imperfect. Test scores are sometimes misused. And even if they were flawless and used with the greatest skill, they would probably still be unpopular among those who have reason to fear an impartial assessment of some of their competencies.

Many of the popular articles critical of educational testing that have appeared in recent years do not reflect a very adequate understanding of educational testing, or a very thoughtful, unbiased consideration of its social consequences. Most of them are obvious potboilers for their authors, and sensational reader-bait in the eyes of the editors of the journals in which they appear. The writers of some of these articles have paid courteous visits to our offices. They have listened respectfully to our recitals of fact and opinion. They have drunk coffee with us and then taken their leave, presumably to reflect on what they have been told, but in any event, to write. What appears in print often seems to be only an elaboration and documentation of their initial prejudices and preconceptions, supported by atypical anecdotes and purposefully selected quotations. Educational testing has not fared very well in their hands.

Need for Research Cited

Among the charges of malfeasance and misfeasance that these critics have leveled against the test makers there is one of nonfeasance. Specifically, we are charged with having shown lack of proper concern for the social consequences of our educational testing. These harmful consequences, they have suggested, may be numerous and serious. The more radical among them imply that, because of what they suspect about the serious social consequences of educational testing, the whole testing movement ought to be suppressed. The more moderate critics claim that they do not know much about these social consequences. But they also suggest that the test makers don't either, and that it is the test makers who ought to be doing substantial research to find out.

If we were forced to choose between the two alternatives offered by the critics, either the suppression of educational testing or extensive research on its social consequences, we probably would choose the latter without much hesitation. But it is by no means clear that what testing needs most at this point is a large program of research.

Before proceeding further, let us mention specifically a few of the harmful things that critics have suggested educational testing may do.

1. It may place an indelible stamp of intellectual status—superior, mediocre, or inferior—on a child, and thus predetermine his social status as an adult, and possibly also do irreparable harm to his self-esteem and his educational motivation.
2. It may lead to a narrow conception of ability, encourage pursuit of

this single goal, and thus tend to reduce the diversity of talent available to society.

3. It may place the testers in a position to control education and determine the destinies of individual human beings, while, incidentally, making the testers themselves rich in the process.
4. It may encourage impersonal, inflexible, mechanistic processes of evaluation and determination, so that essential human freedoms are limited or lost altogether.

Harmful Consequences Listed

These are four of the most frequent and serious tentative indictments. There have been, of course, many other suggestions of possible harmful social consequences of educational testing. It may emphasize individual competition and success, rather than social cooperation, and thus conflict with the cultivation of democratic ideals of human equality. It may foster conformity rather than creativity. It may involve cultural bias. It may neglect important intangibles. It may, particularly in the case of personality testing, involve unwarranted and offensive invasions of privacy. It may do serious injustice in particular individual cases. It may reward specious test-taking skill, or penalize the lack of it.

Consider first, then, the danger that educational testing may place an indelible stamp of inferiority on a child, ruin his self-esteem and educational motivation, and determine his social status as an adult. The kind of educational testing most likely to have these consequences would involve tests purporting to measure a person's permanent general capacity for learning. These are the intelligence tests, and the presumed measures of general capacity for learning they provide are popularly known as IQ's.

Most of us here assembled are well aware of the fact that there is no direct, unequivocal means for measuring permanent general capacity for learning. It is not even clear to many of us that, in the state of our current understanding of mental functions and the learning process, any precise and useful meaning can be given to the concept of "permanent general capacity for learning." We know that all intelligence tests now available are direct measures only of achievement in learning, including learning how to learn, and that inferences from scores on those tests to some native capacity for learning are fraught with many hazards and uncertainties.

But many people who are interested in education do not know this. Many of them believe that native intelligence has been clearly identified and is well understood by expert psychologists. They believe that a person's IQ is one of his basic, permanent attributes, and that any good intelligence test will measure it with a high degree of precision. They do not regard an IQ simply as another test score, a score that may vary considerably depending on the particular test used and the particular time when the person was tested.

Patterns Usually Consistent

Whether or not a person's learning is significantly influenced by his predetermined capacity for learning, there is no denying the obvious fact that individual achievements in learning exhibit considerable consistency over time and across tasks. The superior elementary school pupil may become a mediocre secondary school pupil and an inferior college student, but the odds are against it. Early promise is not always fulfilled, but it is more often than not. The "A" student in mathematics is a better bet than the "C" student to be an "A" student in English literature as well, or in social psychology.

On the other hand, early promise is not always followed by late fulfillment. Ordinary students do blossom sometimes into outstanding scholars. And special talents can be cultivated. There is enough variety in the work of the world so that almost anyone can discover some line of endeavor in which he can develop more skill than most of his fellow men.

In a free society that purports to recognize the dignity and worth of every individual, it is better to emphasize the opportunity for choice and the importance of effort than to stress genetic determinism of status and success. It is better to emphasize the diversity of talents and tasks than to stress general excellence or inferiority. It is important to recognize and to reinforce what John Gardner has called "the principle of multiple chances," not only across time but also across tasks.

IQ Concept Overgeneralized

The concept of fixed general intelligence, or capacity for learning, is a hypothetical concept. At this stage in the development of our understanding of human learning, it is not a necessary hypothesis. Socially, it is not now a useful hypothesis. One of the important things test specialists can do to improve the social consequences of educational testing is to discredit the popular conception of the IQ. Wilhelm Stern, the German psychologist who suggested the concept originally, saw how it was being overgeneralized and charged one of his students coming to America to "kill the IQ." Perhaps we would be well advised, even at this late date, to renew our efforts to carry out his wishes.

Recent emphasis on the early identification of academic talent involves similar risks of oversimplifying the concept of talent and overemphasizing its predetermined components. If we think of talent mainly as something that is genetically given, we will run our schools quite differently than if we think of it mainly as something that can be developed through the educational process.

If human experience, or that specialized branch of human experience we call scientific research, should ever make it quite clear that differences among men in achievement are largely due to genetically determined differences in talent, then we ought to accept the finding and restructure our society and social customs in accord with it. But that is by no means clear yet, and the structure and customs of our society are not consistent with such a basic assumption. For the present, it will be more consistent with the facts as we know them, and more constructive for the society in which we live, to think of talent, not as a natural resource like gold or uranium to be discovered, extracted, and refined, but as a synthetic product like fiber glass or DDT—something that, with skill, effort, and luck, can be created and produced out of generally available raw materials to suit our particular needs or fancies.

This means, among other things, that we should judge the value of the tests we use not in terms of how accurately they enable us to *predict* later achievement, but rather in terms of how much help they give us to *increase* achievement by motivating and directing the efforts of students and teachers. From this point of view, those concerned with professional education who have resisted schemes for very long-range predictions of aptitude for, or success in, their professions have acted wisely. Not only is there likely to be much more of dangerous error than of useful truth in such long-range predictions, but also there is implicit in the whole enterprise a deterministic conception of achievement that is not wholly consistent with the educational facts as we know them, and with the basic assumptions of a democratic, free society.

Whenever I try to point out that prediction is not the exclusive, nor even the principal purpose of educational measurement, some of my best and most intelligent friends demur firmly, or smile politely to communicate that they will never accept such heretical nonsense. When I imply that they use the term "prediction" too loosely, they reply that I conceive it too narrowly. Let me try once more to achieve a meeting of the minds.

I agree that prediction has to do with the future, and that the future ought to be of greater concern to us than the past. I agree, too, that a measurement must be related to some other measurements in order to be useful, and that these relationships provide the basis for, and are tested by, predictions. But these relationships also provide a basis, in many educational endeavors, for managing outcomes—for making happen what we want to happen. And I cannot agree that precision in language or clarity of thought is well served by referring to this process of controlling outcomes as just another instance of prediction. The etymology and common usage of the word "prediction" imply to me the process of foretelling, not of controlling.

Descriptive Use Important

The direct, exclusive, immediate purpose of measurement is always description, not either prediction or control. If we know with reasonable accuracy how things now stand (descriptions), and if we also know with reasonable accuracy what leads to what (functional relations), we are in a position to foretell what will happen if we keep hands off (prediction) or to manipulate the variables we can get our hands on to make happen what we want to happen (control). Of course, our powers of control are often limited and uncertain, just as our powers of prediction are. But I have not been able to see what useful purpose is served by referring to both the hands-off and the hands-on operations as prediction, as if there were no important difference between them. It is in the light of these semantic considerations that I suggest that tests should be used less as bases for prediction of achievement, and more as means to increase achievement. I think there is a difference, and that it is important educationally.

Consider next the danger that a single, widely used test or test battery for selective admission or scholarship awards may foster an undesirably narrow conception of ability and thus tend to reduce diversity in the talents available to a school or to society.

Here again, it seems, the danger is not wholly imaginary. Basic as verbal and quantitative skills are to many phases of educational achievement, they do not encompass all phases of achievement. The application of a common yardstick of aptitude or achievement to all pupils is operationally much simpler than the use of a diversity of yardsticks, designed to measure different aspects of achievement. But overemphasis on a common test could lead educators to neglect those students whose special talents lie outside the common core.

Those who manage programs for the testing of scholastic aptitude always insist, and properly so, that scores on these tests should not be the sole consideration when decisions are made on admission or the award of scholarships. But the question of whether the testing itself should not be varied from person to person remains. The use of optional tests of achievement permits some variation. Perhaps the range of available options should be made much wider than it is at present to accommodate greater diversity of talents.

The problem of encouraging the development of various kinds of ability is, of course, much broader than the problem of testing. Widespread commitment to general education, with the requirement that all students study identical courses for a substantial part of their programs, may be a much greater deterrent of specialized diversity in the educational product. Perhaps these requirements should be restudied too.

What of the concern that the growth of educational testing may increase the influence of the test makers until they are in a position to control educational curriculums and determine the destinies of students?

Student's Destiny Unaffected

Those who know well how tests are made and used in American education know that the tests more often lag than lead curricular change, and that while tests may affect particular episodes in a student's experience, they can hardly ever be said to determine a student's destiny. American education is, after all, a manifold, decentralized, loosely organized enterprise. Whether it restricts student freedom too much or too little is a subject for lively debate. But it does not even come close to determining any student's destiny, not nearly as close as the examination systems in some other countries, ancient and modern.

But test makers have, I fear, sometimes given the general public reason to fear that we may be up to no good. I refer to our sometime reluctance to take the layman fully into our confidence, to share fully with him all our information about his test scores, the tests from which they were derived, and our interpretations of what they mean.

Secrecy concerning educational tests and test scores has been justified on several grounds. One is that the information is simply too complex for untrained minds to grasp. Now it is true that some pretty elaborate theories can be built around our testing processes. It is also true that we can perform some very fancy statistical manipulations with the scores they yield. But the essential information revealed by the scores on most educational tests is not particularly complex. If we understand it ourselves, we can communicate it clearly to most laymen, without serious difficulty. To be quite candid, we are not all that much brighter than they are, much as we may sometimes need the reassurance of thinking so.

Another justification for secrecy is that laymen will misuse test scores. Mothers may compare scores over the back fences. The one whose child scores high spreads the word around. The one whose child scores low may keep the secret, but seek other grounds for urging changes in the teaching staff or in the educational program. Scores of limited meaning may be treated with undue respect and used to repair or to injure the student's self-esteem rather than to contribute to his learning.

Again it is true that test scores can be misused. They have been in the past and they will be in the future. But does this justify secrecy? Can we minimize abuses due to ignorance by withholding knowledge? We do not flatter our fellow citizens when we tell them, in effect, that they are too ignorant, or too lacking in character to be trusted with the knowledge of their children, or of themselves, that we possess.

Revealing Results Helpful

Seldom acknowledged, but very persuasive as a practical reason for secrecy regarding test scores, is that it spares those who use the scores from having to explain and justify the decisions they make. Preference is not, and should not, always be given to the person whose test score is the higher. But if score information is withheld, the disappointed applicant will assume that it was because of his low score, not because of some other factor. He will not trouble officials with demands for justification of a decision that, in some cases, might be hard to justify. But, all things considered, more is likely to be gained in the long run by revealing the objective evidence used in reaching a decision. Should the other, subjective considerations prove too difficult to justify, perhaps they ought not to be used as part of the basis for decision.

If specialists in educational measurement want to be properly understood and trusted by the public they serve, they will do well to shun secrecy and to share with the public as much as it is interested in knowing about the methods they use, the knowledge they gain, and the interpretations they make. This is clearly the trend of opinion in examining boards and public education authorities. Let us do what we can to reinforce the trend. Whatever mental measurements are so esoteric or so dangerous socially that they must be shrouded in secrecy probably should not be made in the first place.

The testers do not control education or the destinies of individual students. By the avoidance of mystery and secrecy, they can help to create better public understanding and support.

Finally, let us consider briefly the possibility that testing may encourage mechanical decision-making, at the expense of essential human freedoms of choice and action.

Those who work with mental tests often say that the purpose of all measurement is prediction. They use regression equations to predict grade-point averages, or contingency tables to predict the chances of various degrees of success. Their procedures may seem to imply not only that human behavior is part of a deterministic system in which the number of relevant variables is manageably small, but also that the proper goals of human behavior are clearly known and universally accepted.

Danger Inherent in System

In these circumstances, there is some danger that we may forget our own inadequacies and attempt to play God with the lives of other human beings. We may find it convenient to overlook the gross inaccuracies that plague our measurements, and the great uncertainties that bedevil our predictions. Betrayed by overconfidence in our own wisdom and virtue, we may project our particular value systems into a pattern of ideal behavior for all men.

If these limitations on our ability to mold human behavior and to direct its development did not exist, we would need to face the issue debated by B. F. Skinner and Carl Rogers before the American Psychological Association some years ago. Shall our knowledge of human behavior be used to design an ideal culture and condition individuals to live happily in it, at whatever necessary cost to their own freedom of choice and action?

But the aforementioned limitations do exist. If we ignore them and undertake to manage the lives of others so that those others will qualify as worthy citizens in our own particular vision of Utopia, we do justify the concern that one harmful social consequence of educational testing may be mechanistic decision-making and the loss of essential human freedoms.

A large proportion of the decisions affecting the welfare and destiny of a person must be made in the midst of overwhelming uncertainties concerning the outcomes to be desired and the best means of achieving such outcomes. That many mistakes will be made seems inevitable. One of the cornerstones of a free society is the belief that in most cases it is better for the person most concerned to make the decision, right or wrong, and to take the responsibility for its consequences, good or bad.

The implications of this for educational testing are clear. Tests should be used as little as possible to *impose* decisions and courses of action on others. They should be used as much as possible to provide a sounder basis of *choice* in individual decision-making. Tests can be used and ought to be used to support rather than to limit human freedom and responsibility.

In summary, we have suggested here today that those who make and use educational tests might do four things to alleviate public concern over their possibly adverse social consequences:

1. We could emphasize the use of tests to improve status, and deemphasize their use to determine status.
2. We could broaden the base of achievements tested to recognize and develop the wide variety of talents needed in our society.

3. We could share openly with the persons most directly concerned all that tests have revealed to us about their abilities and prospects.
4. We could decrease the use of tests to impose decisions on others, and instead increase their use as a basis for better personal decision-making.

When Paul Dressel read a draft of this paper, he chided me gently on what he considered to be a serious omission. I had failed to discuss the social consequences of *not* testing. What are some of these consequences?

If the use of educational tests were abandoned, the distinctions between competence and incompetence would become more difficult to discern. Dr. Nathan Womack, former president of the National Board of Medical Examiners, has pointed out that only to the degree to which educational institutions can define what they mean by competence, and determine the extent to which it has been achieved, can they discharge their obligation to deliver competence to the society they serve.

Not Testing More Harmful

If the use of educational tests were abandoned, the encouragement and reward of individual efforts to learn would be made more difficult. Excellence in programs of education would become less tangible as a goal and less demonstrable as an attainment. Educational opportunities would be extended less on the basis of aptitude and merit and more on the basis of ancestry and influence, and social class barriers would become less permeable. Decisions on important issues of curriculum and method would be made less on the basis of solid evidence and more on the basis of prejudice or caprice.

These are some of the social consequences of *not* testing. In our judgment, they are potentially far more harmful than any possible adverse consequences of testing. But it is also our judgment, and has been the theme of this paper, that we can do much to minimize even these possibilities of harmful consequences. Let us, then, use educational tests for the powerful tools they are with energy and skill, but also with wisdom and care.

Selected Readings

Brayfield, A. H. (Ed.). *American Psychologist*, 1965, **20** (entire issue).

Brim, O. G., Jr. Intelligent testing. *American Psychologist*, 1968, **23**, 267–274.

Dunnette, M. D. Critics of psychological tests: basic assumptions, how good? *Psychology in the Schools*, 1963, **1**, 63–69.

Dyer, H. L. Is testing a menace to education? *New York State Education*, 1961, **49**, 16–19.

Hoffman, B. Toward less emphasis on multiple-choice tests. *Teachers College Record*, 1963, **64**, 183–189.

Messick, S. Personality measurement and the ethics of assessment. *American Psychologist*, 1965, **20**, 136–142.

Multiple questions: a close look. Princeton, N.J.: Educational Testing Service, 1963.

CHAPTER 17

A New Look at Measurement

17.1 Instructional Technology and the Measurement of Learning Outcomes: Some Questions[1]

Robert Glaser

Teachers have tended to use test scores to give grades representing students' relative achievement. That is, an A signifies higher achievement than a B. However, A or B work does not typically define an absolute standard of quality. We do not necessarily know what the A student has achieved, or his degree of competency relative to the subject matter he has studied. In this reading the author suggests a need in measurement to identify levels of proficiency and to describe the tasks that pupils should be able to perform. He refers to this kind of measurement as being criterion-referenced. The use of this kind of data for reporting, provides evidence for a different purpose than do the methods recommended by Glock and Millman (Reading 15.3), who suggest the use of norm-referenced measurement for purposes of grading.

SOURCE. Robert Glaser, "Instructional Technology and the Measurement of Learning Outcomes: Some Questions," *American Psychologist,* **XVIII,** 8 (1963), pp. 519–521. Reprinted by permission of the author and the American Psychological Association.

[1] Symposium address presented at meetings of American Educational Research Association, Chicago, February 1963. This paper is concerned with student educational achievement; however, similar notions have been expressed with respect to the human component in man-machine systems in R. Glaser and D. J. Klaus (1962).

Evaluation of the effectiveness of teaching machines and programed learning, and of broadly conceived instructional systems, has raised into prominence a number of questions concerning the nature and properties of measures of student achievement. In the evaluation of instructional systems, the attainment of subject matter knowledge and skill as well as other behavioral outcomes must, of course, be considered, but the remarks in this paper will be restricted primarily to the measurement of subject matter proficiency, as it may be defined by recognized subject matter scholars.

Achievement measurement can be defined as the assessment of terminal or criterion behavior; this involves the determination of the characteristics of student performance with respect to specified standards. Achievement measurement is distinguished from aptitude measurement in that the instruments used to assess achievement are specifically concerned with the characteristics and properties of present performance, with emphasis on the meaningfulness of its content. In contrast, aptitude measures derive their meaning from a demonstrated relationship between present performance and the future attainment of specified knowledge and skill. In certain circumstances, of course, this contrast is not quite so clear, for example, when achievement measures are used as predictor variables.

The scores obtained from an achievement test provide primarily two kinds of information. One is the degree to which the student has attained criterion performance, for example, whether he can satisfactorily prepare an experimental report, or solve certain kinds of word problems in arithmetic. The second type of information that an achievement test score provides is the relative ordering of individuals with respect to their test performance, for example, whether Student A can solve his problems more quickly than Student B. The principal difference between these two kinds of information lies in the standard used as a reference. What I shall call criterion-referenced measures depend upon an absolute standard of quality, while what I term norm-referenced measures depend upon a relative standard. Distinctions between these two kinds of measures have been made previously by others (Flanagan, 1951; Ebel, 1962).

Criterion-Referenced Measures

Underlying the concept of achievement measurement is the notion of a continuum of knowledge acquisition ranging from no proficiency at all to perfect performance. An individual's achievement level falls at some point on this continuum as indicated by the behaviors he displays during testing. The degree to which his achievement resembles desired performance at any specified level is assessed by criterion-referenced measures of achievement or proficiency. The standard against which a student's performance is compared when measured in this manner is the behavior which defines each point along the achievement continuum. The term "criterion," when used in this way, does not necessarily refer to final end-of-course behavior. Criterion levels can be established at any point in instruction where it is necessary to obtain information as to the adequacy of an individual's performance. The point is that the specific behaviors implied at each level of proficiency can be identified and used to describe the specific tasks a student must be capable of performing before he achieves one of these knowledge levels. It is in this sense that measures of proficiency can be criterion-referenced.

Along such a continuum of attainment, a student's score on a criterion-referenced measure provides explicit information as to what the individual can or cannot do. Criterion-referenced measures indicate the content of the behavioral repertory, and the correspondence between what an individual does and the underlying continuum of achievement. Measures which assess student achievement in terms of a criterion standard thus provide information as to the degree of competence attained by a particular student which is independent of reference to the performance of others.

Norm-Referenced Measures

On the other hand, achievement measures also convey information about the capability of a student compared with the capability of other students. In instances where a student's *relative* standing along the continuum of attainment is the primary purpose of measurement, reference need not be made to criterion behavior. Educational achievement examinations, for example, are administered frequently for the purpose of ordering students in a class or school, rather than for assessing their attainment of specified curriculum objectives. When such norm-referenced measures are used, a particular student's achievement is evaluated in terms of a comparison between his performance and the performance of other members of the group. Such measures need provide little or no information about the degree of proficiency exhibited by the tested behaviors in terms of what the individual can do. They tell that one student is more or less proficient than another, but do not tell how proficient either of them is with respect to the subject matter tasks involved.

In large part, achievement measures currently employed in education are norm referenced. This emphasis upon norm-referenced measures has been brought about by the preoccupation of test theory with aptitude, and with selection and prediction problems; norm-referenced measures are useful for this kind of work in correlational analysis. However, the imposition of this kind of thinking on the purposes of achievement measurement raises some question, and concern with instructional technology is forcing us toward the kind of information made available by the use of criterion-referenced measures. We need to behaviorally specify minimum levels of performance that describe the last amount of end-of-course competence the student is expected to attain, or that he needs in order to go on to the next course in a sequence. The specification of the characteristics of maximum or optimum achievement after a student has been exposed to the course of instruction poses more difficult problems of criterion delineation.

The Uses of Achievement Measurement

Consider a further point. In the context of the evaluation of instructional systems, achievement tests can be used for two principal purposes. First, performance can be assessed to provide information about the characteristics of an individual's present behavior. Second, achievement can be assessed to provide information about the conditions or instructional treatments which produce that behavior. The primary emphasis of the first use is to discriminate among individuals. Used in the second way, achievement tests are employed to discriminate among treatments, that is, among different instructional procedures by an analysis of *group* differences.

Achievement tests used to provide information about *individual* differences are constructed so as to maximize the discriminations made among people having specified backgrounds and experience. Such tests include items which maximize the likelihood of observing individual differences in performance along various task dimensions; this maximizes the variability of the distribution of scores that are obtained. In practical test construction, the variability of test scores is increased by manipulating the difficulty levels and content of the test items.

On the other hand, achievement tests used primarily to provide information about differences in treatments need to be constructed so as to maximize the discriminations made between *groups* treated differently and to minimize the differences between the individuals in any one group. Such a test will be sensitive to the differences produced by instructional conditions. For example, a test designed to demonstrate the effectiveness of instruction would be constructed so that it was generally difficult for those taking it before training and generally easy after training. The content of the test used to differentiate treatments should be maximally sensitive to the performance changes anticipated from the instructional treatments. In essence, the distinction between achievement tests used to maximize individual differences and tests used to maximize treatment or group differences is established during the selection of test items.

In constructing an achievement test to differentiate among *individuals* at the end of training, it would be possible to begin by obtaining data on a large sample of items relating to curriculum objectives. Item analysis would indicate that some test items were responded to correctly only by some of the individuals in the group, while other items were answered correctly by all members of the group. These latter 1.00 difficulty level items, since they failed to differentiate among individuals, would be eliminated because their only effect would be to add a constant to every score. The items remaining would serve to discriminate among individuals and thus yield a distribution of scores that was as large as possible, considering the number and type of items used.

On the other hand, if this test were constructed for the purpose of observing *group* instead of individual differences, the selection of items would follow a different course. For example, where instruction was the treatment variable involved, it would be desirable to retain test items which were responded to correctly by all members of the post-training group, but which were answered incorrectly by students who had not yet been trained. In a test constructed for the purpose of differentiating groups, items which indicated substantial variability within either the pre- or posttraining group would be undesirable because of the likelihood that they would cloud the effects which might be attributable to the treatment variable.

In brief, items most suitable for measuring individual differences in achievement are those which will differentiate among individuals all exposed to the same treatment variable, while items most suitable for distinguishing between groups are those which are most likely to indicate that a given amount or kind of some instructional treatment was effective. In either case, samples of test items are drawn from a population of items indicating the content of performance; the particular item samples that are drawn, however, are those most useful for the purpose of the kind of measurement being carried out. Hammock (1960) has previously discussed such a difference.

The points indicated above reflect the achievement measurement concerns that have arisen in my own work with instructional technology. There is one further point which must be mentioned, and that is the use of diagnostic achievement tests prior to an instructional course. It appears that, with the necessity for specifying the entering behavior that is required by a student prior to a programed instructional sequence, diagnostic assessment of subject matter competence must take on a more precise function. This raises the problem of developing an improved methodology for diagnostic achievement testing. In this regard, researchers using programed instructional sequences to study learning variables point out that prior testing influences learning, and that this effect must be controlled for in determining the specific contribution of programing variables. In an instructional sense, however, the influence and use of pretesting is an important variable for study since it is not the terminal criterion behavior alone which dictates required instructional manipulations, but the differences between entering and terminal behavior. Furthermore, pretesting of a special kind may contribute to "motivation" by enhancing the value of future responses; there is some indication that this may be brought about by prior familiarity with future response terms (Berlyne, 1960, pp. 296–301) or by permitting some early aided performance of the terminal behavior eventually to be engaged in (Taber, Glaser, & Schaefer, 1963, Ch. 3).

In conclusion, the general point is this. Test development has been dominated by the particular requirements of predictive, correlational aptitude test "theory." Achievement and criterion measurement has attempted frequently to cast itself in this framework. However, many of us are beginning to recognize that the problems of assessing existing levels of competence and achievement and the conditions that produce them require some additional considerations.

References

Berlyne, D. E. *Conflict, arousal, and curiosity.* New York: McGraw-Hill, 1960.

Ebel, R. L. Contest standard test scores. *Educ. psychol. Measmt.*, 1962, **22**, 15–25.

Flanagan, J. C. Units, scores, and norms. In E. T. Lindquist (Ed.), *Educational measurement.* Washington, D.C.: American Council on Education, 1951. Pp. 695–763.

Glaser, R., & Klaus, D. J. Proficiency measurement: Assessing human performance. In R. Gagné (Ed.), *Psychological principles in system development.* New York: Holt, Rinehart & Winston, 1962. Pp. 421–427.

Hammock, J. Criterion measures: Instruction vs. selection research. *Amer. Psychologist*, 1960, **15**, 435. (Abstract)

Taber, J. I., Glaser, R., & Schaffer, H. H. *A Guide to the preparation of programmed instructional materials.* Reading, Mass.: Addison-Wesley, in press.

17.2 On National Assessment

Ralph Tyler

The National Assessment program will use the criterion-referenced measures discussed by Dr. Glaser in the previous reading. The author distinguishes among the various common uses of evaluation and differentiates their purposes from the different goals of this new program. Various census data are available to help us cope with national problems such as health, employment, and natural resources. Because one of our greatest problems is to utilize human potential to its fullest, it is important for us to know the status of educational achievement, nationwide. The author describes the procedures for collecting the data and illustrates how they will be reported. Testing is now underway in this national program. Current releases about its progress may be obtained from National Assessment of Educational Progress, 201A Huron Towers, 2222 Fuller Road, Ann Arbor, Michigan 48105.

The student should be aware that the program is not without its critics. Among their opposing arguments are that "it would provide very inadequate, limited evaluations of our educational product," "knowledge

SOURCE. Abridged from Ralph W. Tyler, "A Program of National Assessment," in *American Association of School Administrators—Official Report 1965–1966*, Washington, D.C.: American Association of School Administrators, 1966, pp. 8–17, by permission of the American Association of School Administrators.

to be acquired through this project is so likely to be misleading," and "it would divert the schools from their efforts to attain other significant educational goals that we accept as basic to adequate education for boys and girls." Objectives are "certain to be attacked by the left, the right or the just plain different." The program also "ignores the planning of educational programs for specific pupils."

You will want to read such articles as Katzman's and Saylor's to help you understand the issues raised by this expensive and important project. (See Selected Readings pp. 719, 720)

Because a national assessment differs so markedly from kinds of educational evaluation in current use, it may be helpful to relate assessment, as we are using the term in this project, to the range of evaluation purposes and procedures. One common use of evaluation is to appraise the achievement of individual students. I think most of us are most familiar with this. This is usually done with several purposes in mind. It may furnish a further incentive for students to study because they know they will be tested. It may be used as one of the factors in promoting students. It provides information that can be used by the student and counselor in planning for further education, and it often furnishes one of the bases for awarding scholarships.

A second use of evaluation is to diagnose the learning difficulties of an individual student or an entire class to provide information helpful in planning subsequent teaching.

A third use of evaluation is to appraise the educational effectiveness of a curriculum or part of a curriculum, of instructional materials and procedures, and of administrative and organizational arrangements, using evaluation to see how well students are learning as an indication of the effectiveness of these things.

Each of these kinds of evaluation is an essential part of the processes of teaching and of administration. Teachers and administrators are using evaluation of one sort or another as one of their normal procedures. The information gained from these appraisals is focused upon individual student's efforts, class performance, or the effectiveness of the plans, materials, and procedures used by the teacher, the school, or the school system.

These are common uses of evaluation. And I want to distinguish them from a fourth use of evaluation which we are concentrating on this afternoon. This is to assess the educational progress of larger populations in order to provide the public with dependable information to help in the understanding of educational problems and needs and to guide in efforts to develop sound public policy regarding education. This type of assessment is not focused upon individual students; it is not focused on particular classrooms. But it furnishes over-all information about the educational attainments of large numbers of people. We know, for example, in what age groups heart disease is most likely to occur. We know it is more common with certain occupational groups than others. We know it is more common in the Midwest and the Mountain States than it is in the East. These kinds of knowledge the public has about health, which help us in planning public policy about research in medicine, about support of medical efforts, hospitalization, and so on.

The distinction may be illuminated perhaps by comparing the situation in education and the situation in the field of health. The public has information about the incidence of heart disease, cancer, and other diseases for different age and occupational groups and for different geographic regions. This information is useful in developing public understanding of the progress and problems in the field of health where greatest effort and support may be needed. At the same time that the public has this kind of general information about incidence, physicians have evaluative procedures to diagnose illnesses. The way in which a physician determines whether you or I have heart disease is not the kind of statistical data that the public at large uses. The physician has evaluative procedures to diagnose disease, to appraise the progress patients are making, and to evaluate the effectiveness of treatments. The physician's evaluative techniques are devised to serve his purposes, and the public health assessments are designed to serve the public by providing helpful information. One type does not take the place of the other.

This is a rough parallel to the difference in education between the tools needed and used by teachers and administrators and those needed to gain information helpful for the guidance of responsible citizens. Heretofore, little attention has been given in education to the assessment problem, because the need for wide public understanding of educational progress and problems was not generally recognized. Now it is.

Because education has become the servant of all our purposes, its effectiveness is now of general and public concern.

You will notice that the President in his messages refers to education more frequently than to any other topic. Governors typically do. Newspapers are filled with it because education is the means by which practically all of our people will be able to find effective ways to participate in a modern technological society. The educational tasks now faced require many more resources than have thus far been available, and they must be wisely used to produce maximum results. To make wise decisions, dependable information about the progress of education is essential, otherwise we scatter our efforts too widely and fail to achieve our goals. Yet we do not now have the necessary comprehensive and dependable data. We have reports on numbers of schools, buildings, teachers, and pupils, and about the moneys expended, but we do not have sound and adequate information on educational results. Because dependable data are not available—and I emphasize this—we depend now on personal views, distorted reports, journalistic impressions. These are the sources of public opinion. And the schools are frequently attacked and frequently defended without having neccessary evidence to support either claim. This situation will be corrected only by a careful, consistent effort to obtain valid data to provide the facts about the progress of American education.

Because the purpose of the assessment is to provide helpful information about the progress of education that can be understood and accepted by public-spirited lay citizens, some new procedures are being developed. In each field, scholars, teachers, and curriculum specialists have formulated statements of the objectives which they believe faithfully reflect the contributions of that field and which the schools are seriously seeking to attain. For each of these major objectives, prototype exercises have been constructed which, in the opinion of scholars and teachers, give students an opportunity to demonstrate the behavior implied by the objective, for example, exercises illustrating what is meant by the youngsters' being able to get the plain sense meaning of a newspaper paragraph. These lists of objectives and the prototype exercises which help to define them have been reviewed by a series of panels of public-spirited citizens living in various parts of the country—in cities, towns, and villages.

Actually, there were twelve panels for four geographic regions, and in each of these regions, a panel representing large-city residents, another panel representing suburban residents, and another panel representing smaller town and rural areas, because of the possibility that the views of what was important in education might differ among these different types of communities as well as for the different regions of the country.

Each panel spent two days reviewing the material and making a judgment about each objective in terms of the questions: "Is this something important for people to learn today? Is is something I would like to have my children learn?"

This process resulted in some revisions of the original listing of objectives and some eliminations. However, the procedure was designed to insure that every objective being assessed is (1) considered important by scholars, (2) accepted as an educational task by the school, and (3) deemed desirable by leading lay citizens. This should help to eliminate the criticism frequently encountered with current tests in which some item is attacked by the scholar as representing shoddy scholarship or criticized by school people as something not in the curriculum or by prominent laymen as being unimportant or technical trivia.

A national assessment to identify kinds of progress being made in education and problems and difficulties arising will not be very meaningful unless separate measures are obtained for populations within the total country which vary among themselves and thus present different degrees and kinds of progress and different problems to be solved. The particular populations that need to be treated separately may change over the years ahead, but for some time ago, sex, socio-economic status, geographic location, and rural-urban-suburban differences will probably be significant. Hence, the present plan is to assess a probability sample for each of 192 populations defined by the following subdivisions: boys and girls, four geographic regions (Northeast, Southeast, Middle West, and Far West), four age groups (9, 13, 17, and adult), three divisions by urban, suburban, rural classifications, and two socioeconomic levels.

Of course, some of the differences that may be found will be found in the differences inherent in these population groups. It is likely, for example, that boys will be making more progress than girls in such fields as science, and girls will usually be making more progress than boys in fields like reading and fine arts. It is probably true that there will be differences among city, suburban, and rural groups; some differences among socioeconomic levels; and certainly a good deal of difference among the age groups.

The fact that populations are to be assessed and not individuals makes it possible to extend the sampling of exercises far beyond that of an individual test in which each person takes it all. It may be that a comprehensive assessment would require so many exercises that if they were to be taken by one person he would need 10 hours or more to complete them. With a population sample, 20 persons, each spending 30 minutes, would together take all the exercises. (We are familiar with this, of course, in public-opinion sampling.) In this case, a population of 10,000 persons would furnish a sample of 500 for each of the assessment exercises, and one would have given more than 30 minutes of his time. Assuming that an assessment would be made every 3 to 5 years in order to ascertain the kinds of progress taking place, it is very unlikely that many of those individuals who participated in the earlier assessments would be involved in any of the subsequent ones. Assuming a sample, say, of 17-year-old boys in the Southeast lower socioeconomic status, the boys in the sample of 1967 would not be in the sample of 1970.

Hence, from the point of view of the child, or adult, no serious demand would be made on his time. Furthermore, it is unlikely that the children taking exercises in later years would be drawn from the same classrooms as the earlier ones. Samples will probably be drawn by identifying blocks or sections or other geographic areas, so that they will take all the 9-year-olds in such-and-such blocks in a city. There, of course, will be some in public schools, some in private schools some in parochial schools; some may not be in school at all.

Therefore, the demands made upon a teacher in releasing a child for half an hour will be minimal. The assessment, though costly, should be feasible and involve little or no inconvenience to individuals or to schools.

Since the assessment does not require that all participants be in classes, the exercises to be used are not limited to the usual test items. Interviews and observational procedures are also to be employed to furnish information about interests, habits, and practices that have been learned. Because school objectives commonly include these areas, it is necessary to see that some assessment is made of the levels of attainment.

The assessment exercises will differ from current achievement tests in another important respect. I want to point this out very strongly, because many school people are under the impression that because they are using current achievement tests, they do have information of the sort that we are talking about. An achievement test seeks to measure individual differences among pupils taking the test. Hence, the items of the test are concentrated on those which differentiate among the children. Exercises which all or nearly all can do, as well as those which only a very few can do, are eliminated because these do not give much discrimination. Therefore, when we looked over the date available in 100 sample school systems, we found no information about what practically all children can do, only information about what children have been able to do with this narrow a range of achievement tests, which was from the 40-percent level of difficulty to the 60-percent level. But, for the purposes of assessing the progress of education, we need to know what all or almost all of the children are learning and what the most advanced are learning, as well as what is being learned by the middle or "average" children. To get exercises of this sort is a new venture for test constructors. They are required, by the terms of our specifications and the contract with them, to develop exercises at each age level in which approximately one-third represent achievements characteristic of most of those at that age level, one-third represent achievements characteristic of about half of those at that age level, and one-third which represent the achievements characteristic of the most advanced, that is, the top 10 percent, of that age level.

To summarize the educational attainments of these several populations, it is not necessary to compute test scores, because we are not trying to find out whether Sally Jones made a higher score than Mary Smith. Instead, the following sorts of things would be reported:

In a sample of 17-year-old boys of higher socioeconomic status from rural and small-town areas of the Midwest region—just trying to define one of these 192 populations—it was found that

- 93 percent could read a typical newspaper paragraph like the following (and then an example to show the public what we mean by a typical newspaper paragraph).
- 76 percent could write an acceptable letter ordering several items from a store like the following (and then an example).
- 52 percent took a responsible part in working with other youth in playground and community activities like the following (and then describe the kinds of cooperative endeavors in which under the heading of citizenship these youngsters have been engaged).
- 24 percent had occupational skills required for initial employment.

It is anticipated that the assessment would be in charge of a commission of highly respected citizens. We have here, for example, the precedent of the thirties, when the depression hit so heavily and youth were unable to get jobs and many of them were out of school and uncertain about what to do: Several foundations together appointed the American Youth Commission, headed by Owen D. Young, who was then the chairman of the Board of the General Electric Corporation, and other prominent American citizens from industry, labor, agriculture, education, and the professions. Under this commission a series of studies was made. Those of you who were mature in the depression years—I fear not many of you were —may recall a series called "How Fare American Youth?" in which we had brought before us these kinds of problems: What are our youth doing? How many of them are employed? How many are unable to get food? How many seek education? and so on—the kind of information that was very important in trying to help the schools develop new programs during the depression period to meet the unexpected change in our situation.

We think of a somewhat similiar sort of thing for this commission: we think that a commission might be appointed by a collection of foundations or some other groups with no axe to grind, a commission made up of highly respected citizens who individually are respected and collectively come from various backgrounds. The commission and its staff would prepare reports of the findings of the assessment, much as we now obtain reports of the findings every 10 years of the decennial census. These reports would be available to all people interested in education, providing them with significant and helpful information on what has been learned by each of the 192 populations. In subsequent years, the progress made by each of these populations since the preceding assessment would also be reported.

I think we ought to get a clear understanding of what the project is. It is being confused with a nationwide, individual testing program, and several common fears are expressed by those who make this confusion. They note that tests used in a school influence the direction and amount of effort of pupils and teachers. In this way, if national tests do not reflect the local educational objectives, pupils and teachers are deflected from the work. This criticism does not apply to the assessment project because no individual student or teacher can make a showing. No student will take more than a small fraction of the exercises. No scores will be obtained on his performance. He will not be assessed at any later time and can gain no desired end, such as admission to college or a scholarship.

A second fear is that such an assessment enables the federal government to control the curriculum. This is also a misunderstanding. The objectives to be assessed are not those that have been suggested by a federal group or any group outside the schools, but they are those that are accepted by teachers and curriculum specialists as goals toward which they work. They have been reviewed by lay leaders throughout the country so as to include only aims deemed important by public-spirited citizens. This project will report on the extent to when children and youth and adults are learning things considered important now by both professional school people and the informed public. It is not a means by which you can get changes in the curriculum through pressure for new objectives that schools are not now aiming to attain.

A third fear is sometimes raised that this project would stultify the curriculum by not allowing changes over the years in instructional methods and educational goals. It should be made clear that the project, so far as methods are concerned, will assess what children, youth, and adults have learned, not how they have learned it. Hence, the assessment is not dependent upon any particular instructional methods. For example, we shall report the percentage of 13-year-olds who can comprehend the plain sense of a typical newspaper paragraph. We will not be reporting the methods of reading instruction that are used in various schools. Or, as another illustration, we shall report on the percentage of adults who participate regularly in civic affairs but not on the methods used in teaching high school civics.

The matter of changing educational goals is a relevant question, because the objectives determine what will be assessed. Our plan calls for a review one year in advance of each assessment of the objectives of each field in order to identify changes and to include the new objectives in the assessment.

Through the various conferences with school people and interested laymen, the Committee has been able to identify concerns and problems that such an assessment must deal with. As the plans are shaping up it appears to be possible to conduct the project in a way that will not injure our schools but will help them by providing greatly needed information.

The need for data on progress has been recognized in other spheres of American life. During the depression, the lack of dependable information about the progress of the economy was a serious handicap in focusing efforts and in assessing them. Out of this need grew an index of production, the gross national product, which has been of great value in guiding economic development. Correspondingly, the consumer price index was constructed as a useful measure of the changes in cost of living and inflation. Mortality and morbidity indices are important bases for indicating needed public health measures. Facing the need for massive efforts to extend and improve education, the demand for valid information to support the requests and to guide the allocation of resources must be met. The assessment of the progress of education should make an important and constructive contribution to this purpose.

Selected Readings

Anderson, A. C. The national assessment of educational progress: Some technical deficiencies. *School and Society*, 1967, **95**, 48–50.

Beymer, L. The pros and cons of the national assessment project. *Clearing House*, 1966, **40**, 540–543.

Campbell, V. N., and Nichols, D. G. National assessment of citizenship education. *Social Education,* 1968, **32**, 279–281.

The Committee on Assessing the Progress of Education. Demonstration packages of the national assessment program. Forms for age 9, 13, 17. Ann Arbor, Michigan.

Hand, H. C. National assessment viewed as the camel's nose. *Phi Delta Kappan*, 1965, **47**, 8–13.

Higgins, M. J., and Merwin, J. C. Assessing the progress of education. *Phi Delta Kappan*, 1967, **48**, 378–380.

Hoffman, B. National educational assessment—will it give us a true picture? *NEA Journal*, 1966, **55**, 25–26.

Katzman, M. T. The science and politics of national assessment, *Teachers College Record,* 1970, **71**, 571–586.

Keppel, F. National assessment, we badly need it. *NEA Journal*, 1966, **55**, 24, 26.

National Assessment of Educational Progress. *Writing objectives,* Ann Arbor, Michigan: Committee on Assessing the Progress of Education, 1969, (there will be other statements of objectives available, e.g.: science, reading, etc.).

Page, E. B. Grading essays by computer. *Phi Delta Kappan,* 1966, **47**, 238–243.

Popham, W. J., and Husek, T. R. Implications of criterion-referenced measurement. *Journal of Educational Measurement,* 1969, **6**, 1–9.

Saylor, G. National assessment: pro and con. *Teachers College Record,* 1970, **71**, 588–597.

Sizer, T. Pressing problems and national assessment. *PTA Magazine*, 1966, **61**, 18–22.

Free Materials on Testing

Items. Princeton: Cooperative Test Division, Educational Testing Service.

Miscellaneous publications. Los Angeles: California Test Bureau.

Normline. New York: Harcourt, Brace & World, Inc.

Tests and Measurements Kit. Princeton: Educational Testing Service.

Test Service Notebook (Series). New York: Harcourt, Brace & World, Inc.

Test Service Bulletin. New York: Harcourt, Brace & World, Inc.

Test Service Bulletins. New York: The Psychological Corporation.

PART VI

The Subject of Educational Psychology

You are now familiar with a number of the important issues in educational psychology. Furthermore, you know what the substance of educational psychology is about. The field has experienced a revival this past decade stimulating mature researchers in new directions and attracting able talent. Critical appraisal of past research and concern for future direction has occupied many of the leaders.

Three nationally prominent authors in the field have been chosen to state what content and methodology they believe should represent educational psychology. All agree that educational psychology is not the application of principles of psychology to classroom teaching and learning. All would recommend that research in educational psychology be done in the complex setting of the classroom with pupils rather than with infrahuman subjects, and all would agree that the new rigor in educational psychology research is timely. Furthermore, they insist that research questions must be chosen that yield answers of a generalizable nature for the improvement of teaching and learning. Typically, research studies of the type designed to determine whether teaching Method A is better than Method B have too often produced equivocal results. There tended to be no theoretical base from which the research evolved. Furthermore, there was likely to be a lack of design rigor. Variables were not carefully controlled and analyses were often inadequate.

With new methods of design and analysis, with a realization that research settings must be relevant to the classroom, and with the formulation of pertinent questions, educational psychology is likely to make a greater impact on learning in the next decade.

CHAPTER 18

The Method and Content of Educational Psychology

18.1 The Place of Educational Psychology in the Study of Education

John B. Carroll

Carroll suggests four criteria for identifying a discipline:

1. *A specifiable scope of inquiry.*
2. *The possession of structured subject matter.*
3. *A recognized set of procedures for gaining new knowledge (including criteria for stating the validity of new knowledge), and a set of procedures for ordering new knowledge.*
4. *Accepted techniques and tools for applying knowledge in specific cases to specified practical ends.*

He then proceeds to show that educational psychology meets these criteria and has to be classified as a discipline. Furthermore, Carroll believes that educational psychology has a great deal to say to the teacher. He would be more comfortable, however, if there were research to provide unequivocal evidence that educational psychology courses promoted skill and competence in teaching.

SOURCE. John B. Carroll, The Place of Educational Psychology in the Study of Education. John Walton and James Keuthe, Eds. In *The Discipline of Education*. Madison: University of Wisconsin Press, 1963, pp. 105–119. Reprinted by permission of The University of Wisconsin Press.

1. *The scope and aims of educational psychology.* The question of the scope of educational psychology is an extremely important one. We shall be more inclined to view educational psychology as a discipline if we can define scope. As a practical matter, the way we define this scope will influence our decisions respecting the training of educational psychologists and the training of teachers in educational psychology.

The scope of educational psychology as an applied science might be regarded as practically coterminous with that of psychology itself. This is true for at least two reasons. There is hardly any aspect of the whole field of psychology which could not conceivably be brought into play in some educational problem, because the enterprise of education is concerned with many kinds of people—of different ages, degrees of ability and drive, and kinds of personality—as well as with many kinds of subject matter and skills. The description, analysis, and prediction of such diverse forms of behavior as may be encountered in education could demand findings, principles, and techniques from almost any phase of psychological science. Secondly, it can be claimed that the concept which unifies all psychology, and which is its central concern, is *learning.* Obviously, learning is the concern of education.

Educational psychologists would hardly care to bargain for all the trouble psychologists have had in defining the science of psychology. If psychologists try to identify *behavior* as the object of their concern, they must be prepared to differentiate their interest from that of the economist, who studies economic behavior; the lawyer, who is concerned with legal behavior; or even the mathematician, who might be said to study mathematical behavior. And there has long been a question as to the degree to which the psychologist interested in sense perception is poaching on the territory of the sensory psychologist. Nevertheless, psychologists have been able to come to terms with the problem of defining their science by constructing definitions which refer to the generalized properties of organismic behavior in relation to the characteristics of the organism itself and to the environment. Educational psychologists can rest content with these definitions as far as psychology proper is concerned. Educational psychology is the study of the behavioral properties of human organisms which may have to be taken into account in the management of learning and other behavior in educational seetings if certain specified objectives are to be attained. In pursuing this study, the educational psychologist may draw upon techniques and results from any branch of psychology, including, for example, comparative psychology. Education ordinarily concerns only certain standard techniques for modifying behavior, such as the use of verbal and graphic communication, but the educational psychologist may wish to take cognizance of abnormal ways of modifying behavior, such as hypnosis and brainwashing, either to consider their possible usefulness or to provide protection against them.

From the fact that educational psychology may reach into almost any field of general psychology, it does not follow that every scientific problem in psychology is necessarily of interest to educational psychology. The *Journal of Educational Psychology* could hardly open its pages to contributions from *any* phase at all of psychology. The criterion of immediate or potential significance for the conduct of education would have to be applied. For example, a study of visual acuity would not normally be admissible, but other things being equal, if it included a study of the perception of typefaces by school children, it might be highly relevant to the choice or design of textbooks for the school and could be accepted for publication. There is a continuous spectrum of scientific concerns ranging from those which are highly general and of little specific interest to education to those which are centrally positioned in the area of educational psychology.

Still, there are problems in selecting and treating material for educational psychology textbooks. To what extent should one include, in an ideal textbook or treatise on educational psychology, the topics on sensory psychology, perception, reaction time, emotion, and mental mechanisms which are standard fare in general psychology texts? Educational psychology texts tend to exclude consideration of these matters; a casual search has disclosed only one contemporary educational psychological textbook[1] which attempts to cover general principles of psychology including the topics mentioned here. But most educational psychology texts are written for teachers and prospective teachers, rather than for prospective educational psychologists; because it may be difficult to convince teachers of the relevance of certain materials from experimental psychology, these materials are omitted. Yet I would claim that a specialist in educational psychology should have a substantial acquaintance with various branches of experimental psychology, because the learner's behavior is dependent upon many characteristics of stimuli both seen and heard. The educational psychologist must know something about these characteristics—how they affect behavior and how they can be studied. Similar arguments can be made to support the proposition that the educational psychologist should be well acquainted with methods, theories, and findings in social, abnormal, and clinical psychology. Indeed, he must be as much of a generalist as he can afford to be, but he will have to go

[1] William C. Morse and G. Max Wingo, *Psychology and Teaching* (Chicago: Scott, Foresman and Co., 1955).

far beyond the current textbooks in order to become one. There is need for truly professional textbooks in this field which will interpret the total range of material in psychology for its educational implications.

In seeking to expand the usual concept of the scope of educational psychology, I take it for granted that human learning and human development in all of their phases are of central concern. The modern study of learning developed, in the hands of E. L. Thorndike, in an educational setting. Apart from their value in pure science, findings, about learning, if they are to have any application at all, have their principal application *in education,* and it is of significance that many psychologists who are in the forefront in the study of learning—for example, Guthrie, Hilgard, Skinner, and Bruner—have indeed worked on problems of education.

Despite the great overlap between the subject matter of educational psychology and that of psychology in general, it will keep matters straight to distinguish the two fields—psychology as a pure science of behavior with no obligation to concern itself with practical applications, and educational psychology as an applied science of behavior in educational settings which possesses the moral imperative to produce knowledge and technology that will be useful in those settings. The distinction is in large measure only theoretical. It is pointless to concern oneself with the degree to which the day-to-day work of the psychologist, pure or applied, is oriented toward pure science or toward application. Attempts to apply theories in practical settings often lead to useful extensions or modifications of those theories, and even the purest of theories may suddenly be seen to have some unexpected practical utility.

A statement of the scope of educational psychology should also mention its aims. Two kinds of objectives can be spelled out for this science. First, it aims to be useful in providing part of the research background which is needed to formulate educational policy, educational policy being understood to concern itself with such questions as who should be educated, when and at what ages the various parts of the curriculum should be presented, and what kinds of education should be provided for different groups of potential students. Secondly, educational psychology can provide knowledge and tools that are of value in the practice of education. The tools and techniques of measurement and diagnosis developed in educational psychology have obviously had a widespread acceptance and influence. There is reason to hope that generalizations and principles derived from the study of learning, perception, and cognition will have an increasing impact upon the preparation of learning materials, upon the training of teachers, and upon the conduct of the classroom.

2. *The structure of the subject matter of educational psychology.* To what extent does the content of educational psychology present itself as structured, ordered, and lawful? In approaching this question, as with the previous question, we find that we must answer not only for educational psychology but also for the broader field of psychology. And there we find a puzzling, though somewhat hopeful picture—puzzling because of the fact that resolution has by no means been found among the many systematic positions that have been proposed and hopeful because of the success that has thus far been achieved in developing and testing postulational systems. Hull's system remains an unfinished monument to its shaper. The mathematical learning theories of Bush, Mosteller, Estes, and others[2] are as yet too limited in scope to be regarded as general postulational systems. Skinner's efforts towards building a comprehensive description of behavior[3] are buttressed at least as much by *a priori* speculation as by experimental data. There are certain bright spots within the field of psychometrics where a set of postulates can carry us a decent way along the road to a complete theory of the limited set of behavior we call test-item responses, for example, Thurstone's development of test theory,[4] and Lord's more recent development of a theory of test scores.[5] In the main, however, psychology continues to be an aggregation of small-scale, limited-focus theories, plus a multitude of loosely related empirical facts. It is not yet possible to write a treatise in psychology with the operational rigor and sequence of subject like physics. Even if it were, one doubts that a highly quantified psychological system would be of any help to teachers, although it might indeed be useful to educational psychologists in formulating experiments or planning educational programs.

What we have in psychology today is a useful set of concepts and a series of reasonably well-attested empirical laws. For example, Hilgard has presented a list of fourteen "statements" or generalizations about learning about which he thinks there would be general agreement among learning theorists.[6] Most of these statements may be seen to have ready application in the management of the school learning process. For example, No. 4, "Learning under the control of reward is usually pre-

[2] Ernest R. Hilgard, *Theories of Learning*, 2d ed. (New York: Appleton-Century-Crofts, 1956).

[3] B. F. Skinner, *The Behavior of Organisms* (New York: Appleton-Century, 1938), and *Science and Human Behavior* (New York: Macmillan Co., 1953).

[4] L. L. Thurstone, *The Reliability and Validity of Tests* (Ann Arbor, Michigan: Edwards Bros., 1931).

[5] Frederic M. Lord, A Theory of Test Scores, *Psychometric Monographs*, No. 7, 1952.

[6] Hilgard, *Theories of Learning*, pp. 485–87.

ferable to learning under the control of punishment," constitutes a major part of the scientific basis for "programmed instruction" and the teaching machine.

What is still unavailable is a series of mathematically expressed statements or formulas which would systematize the relations between individual differences and learning rates under various conditions. Elsewhere I have attempted to sketch the outines of a system which would describe the degree of learning as a function of five generalized variables: individual aptitude (stated in terms of time required to achieve criterion performance on a task under optimal learning conditions), individual general intelligence (conceived as the individual's ability to comprehend instruction), perseverance (time engaged in active learning), the quality of instruction, and opportunity (time afforded for learning).[7] Thus far, this remains merely a conceptual model. Much research would be required to confirm or modify the proposed functional relations and to supply the necessary parametric information. Nevertheless, we have available the techniques for securing this kind of information, and thus it looks as if the development of a parametric system for describing learning and individual differences is possible. Presumably that system could be refined to such an extent that it would be possible to make accurate predictions of the course of learning for given individuals under given conditions. If this could be done, educational psychology would acquire a structural coherence that would enhance its stature as a discipline.

3. *The methodology of educational psychology.* Of the four criteria of a discipline that we are considering, the one referring to methodology is the one that is most clearly met by educational psychology. Indeed, it can be said that methods in educational psychology have proliferated while effective applications of these methods have been much less frequent. There exist extensive rationales and prescriptions for developing measuring instruments, for sampling behavior, for designing experiments, and for analyzing and summarizing data. Given the time, facilities, research talent, and necessary cooperation on the part of school authorities, we are prepared to set up an efficient design to test nearly any hypothesis that might be reasonably proposed. Furthermore, we have the tools and techniques for implementing the program of research which I sketched out just above—the program to discover the parameters of school learning in relation to aptitude, intelligence, motivation, and other variables.

Only one caution may be noted, but it is a large caution. A heuristic

[7] John B. Carroll, "A Model of School Learning," *Teachers College Record*, LXIV (1963), 723–33.

method for obtaining new knowledge ought to contain a procedure for leading the researcher to ask the right questions. Educational psychology is deficient in theories which can generate useful research questions. For example, it has been pointed out by several research workers that fifty years or more of research on the problem of teacher competence have yielded very little of practical use; they suggest that this may mean that research workers have failed to ask the right questions in this area. The very promising results on teacher competence which are issuing from the work of Washburne and his collaborators at Brooklyn College[8] would on the other hand exemplify a kind of research which has been guided by detailed and well-considered theories. Theories with heuristic value in educational psychology will apparently have to be rather complex theories, appealing to several levels of interaction between variables.

It will remain true, of course, that the development of good theories requires ingenuity and not merely the ability to see gaps in a pre-existing structure.

4. *Tools and techniques for practical application.* In respect to this criterion also, educational psychology measures up to our requirements. One can identify many kinds of tools and techniques which are sufficiently well developed and standardized to be used confidently in practical situations. The bulk of these tools are what we call *tests*—tests of ability, personality, interest, attitude, and achievement. Tests vary widely in quality, and even the best of them could stand improvement in some respects, but the very fact that criteria exist by which we can identify the better tests is another stone in building the edifice of a discipline. The tools and techniques of educational psychology also include teaching devices, such as reading pacers, and teaching machines and techniques of programming.

One could wish, however, for a closer nexus between educational and psychological theory, on the one hand, and the tools and techniques, on the other. Tools and techniques get most closely identified with their discoverers or developers, rather than with broad principles or theories. For example, in the field of intelligence testing it should now be possible to set up standardized procedures for measuring each of a series of ability factors, named in terms of the kind of behavior or achievement involved in each case. One could then abandon the practice of associating names with particular assemblages of test materials, such as Binet, Otis, Terman, and Thurstone. In some branches of science it is quite appropriate to name certain objects or procedures after their discoverers—the fissure

8 Carleton Washburne and Louis M. Heil, "What Characteristics of Teachers Affect Children's Growth?" *School Review*, LXVIII (1960), 420–28.

of Rolando, the Van Allen radiation belts, Babinski's test and so on—but in such cases the object or procedure identified is something that would not have changed its character had it been discovered by another. It is unlikely, however, that various psychological tests would have been developed in the same way had they been developed by persons other than their originators. Furthermore, psychological techniques must be constantly refined and modified to keep pace with the development of psychology. Ideally, they should be constructed according to rules independent of the predilections of any given set of investigators, deriving only from relevant psychological theory. This process of the standardization of the techniques of educational psychology *by reference to theory* would further increase the stature of educational psychology as a discipline and incidentally increase the comparability of research findings from different laboratories.

It would be easy to be iconoclastic about the view of educational psychology as a discipline which I have presented here. Perhaps educational psychology is a discipline, but a relatively empty, futile, and useless one. It has sometimes been claimed that educational psychology is nothing more than "putting what everybody knows in language which nobody can understand."[9] In a dissertation completed at Yale University in 1950, W. W. Lynch showed that freshmen in teachers colleges, even before taking any courses in educational psychology, were able to answer questions on certain parts of the content of these courses quite accurately, and at any rate as well as seniors who had taken three years of educational psychology courses.[10]

Scrutiny reveals, however, that the test questions on which freshmen did as well as seniors were the vaguest of generalizations, like the following:

(T or F) Teaching may improve methods of reasoning.
(T or F) Readiness for learning may be suggested by pupil interest.
(T or F) Periodic reports to parents from the school should include only the data on children's subject matter achievement.

Those items of content where seniors showed significant achievements in knowledge over the freshmen tended to have to do with matters of special terminology, names of tests, and other technical details. Lynch even reported that in some cases seniors had a greater amount of mis-

[9] Walter S. Monroe, *Teaching-Learning Theory and Teacher Education 1890–1950* (Urbana: University of Illinois Press, 1952), p. 379.

[10] W. W. Lynch, Jr., "The Development of Proficiency in Educational Psychology," (Unpublished Ph.D. Dissertation, Yale University, 1950).

information than freshmen as a result of taking educational measurement courses; for example, 96 per cent of the freshmen accepted the proposition that "drill facilitates learning" whereas only 76 per cent of seniors recognized the "correctness" of the proposition. It is possible, of course, that Lynch was wrong in thinking this statement correct, and that the 24 per cent of seniors who marked it incorrect were at least correct in recognizing it as too easy a generalization.

Let us not be too hasty, however, in drawing the conclusion that educational psychology is a recitation of the obvious. Lynch's results are principally a commentary on the relatively poor quality of the test items he had to use, or perhaps on the lack of intellectual starch in the teachers college courses in educational psychology that were involved in his study. They do not necessarily imply a condemnation of all educational psychology courses or deny the possibility that educational psychology is a discipline. They should put us on notice, however, that the content of educational psychology that we present students must be scrutinized for its informativeness, and also for its relevance to the solution of educational problems which cannot be adequately solved on the basis of so-called common sense alone.

The question that will be asked at this point is this: Does educational psychology have anything to say, anywhere in the spectrum of educational problems, that teachers dare not at their peril, so to speak, overlook? Bridge builders dare not neglect physical laws and information about the strength of physical materials. Are there similar matters which teachers ought not to neglect? It might be thought risky for a speaker to set forth such a challenge for himself. It is particularly risky when occasion provides opportunity to answer only in general terms, or with an unsatisfying set of instances.

My general answer is, Yes, there are many findings and principles in the discipline of educational psychology that teachers ought not to neglect. Facts about learning, about personality development, about types of reaction to frustration, about kinds of learned abilities, about teaching for transfer, about the construction and use of tests, and many other aspects of psychology can, I believe, be presented in sufficient richness of detail to be informative and effective in furthering better teaching. Teachers ought not to neglect these facts, but they *do*—partly because they often lack time to consider or plan their actions in the light of these principles, or because in education there are not the kinds of controls on teachers which insure that they take account of findings from educational psychology. There are few controls, for example, which insure that teachers always determine the readiness of children to receive a given level of instruction, always present new information in such a way that the student can constantly check the correctness of his learning, always give properly designed achievement tests, or always take into account the possibility that aggression is a reaction to frustration.

If we cannot insure that teachers will take adequate account of the technology of instruction which comes from the discipline of educational psychology, it is conceivable that at least some of this technology can be built into the materials and media of instruction. The research on the readability of prose has had a significant effect on the writing of textbooks, even though some would say that the effect has not been uniformly beneficial. There is much to be learned about the presentation of verbal material. Recently a thesis at Harvard by David Purpel demonstrated that the most profitable way of using time in the presentation of social studies case material at the junior high school level is *not* to repeat every statement in its original or a reworded form, but to give concrete illustrations of generalizations wherever possible. We are learning that in the teaching of many subjects—arithmetic, physics, and so on—the use of concrete models like the Cuisenaire rods or the ripple tank can make an enormous difference between good and bad teaching. The teaching machine is offered as a physical embodiment of a science of learning.

These developments point to a generalization which probably applies in every instance in which uses of basic science are sought in practical action: the basic science itself grows and is fed by the efforts to put it to practical use. Countless examples could be given of important developments in psychology which have stemmed from practical educational needs—the development of mental tests, the development of learning theory, and now the development of teaching machines. Psychology, especially educational psychology, has at least as much to learn from the practice of education as it has to teach it.

We have mentioned some of the difficulties in applying educational psychology to practical problems. In many instances, the difficulty lies in a lack of adequate research information. Most educational researchers would concede that upon such important topics as the selection and training of teachers and the evaluation of their success, the programming of instruction, and the diagnosis of children's learning difficulties, there is still a near-dearth of solid research information. Sometimes what is needed is an interpretation of research which will be intelligible to the potential user. It has often seemed to me that writers of test manuals address themselves more to their professional colleagues than to the ultimate consumer of such tests.

We also frequently meet the argument that specific educational problems are too complex, with too many interacting variables, to be soluble by the application of scientific knowledge. If this is so, it means that educational research must pay increasingly greater attention to interactions between variables. But even if knowledge becomes more precise, there will always remain cases to which no formula can be applied. Clinical psychologists do not let this fact deter them in their efforts to build and test complex hypotheses to help them in the understanding of individual cases. Meehl, of course, has demonstrated that actuarial prediction—by formula, as it were—is usually as good as, if not better than, clinical prediction.[11] But in the absence of the information which is needed to yield actuarial prediction, the judgment of the practitioner will be aided when he is steeped in the "sensitizing" concepts of educational psychology. For example, a teacher faced with the problem of how to help a minority-group child adjust and respond to what appears to be discriminatory attitudes on the part of other children, will possibly be better able to cope with this problem if he or she is aware of such concepts as scape-goat mechanisms, peer group status needs, and so on. Educational psychology does not inform the teacher exactly how to use these concepts in a particular case; it merely suggests that these concepts are relevant. As far as the training of teachers is concerned, there is the clear implication that not only do the concepts need to be learned as abstractions, but they also need to be illustrated in a variety of practical contexts so that teachers will be more likely to perceive their relevance to new situations. The application of scientific knowledge in actual situations by practitioners is clearly a problem of "transfer of learning"; much that can be said about transfer of learning in general can also be said about this particular situation, and when we teach educational psychology we must teach for transfer, with a vengeance.

In conducting such a complex and multi-dimensional enterprise as education, and in "applying" knowledge from other disciplines, one is never quite sure as to the source of the knowledge one is seeking to apply. Indeed, one is seldom conscious of the process of application: *application* (and likewise the word *transfer*, in transfer of training) is a word in a metalanguage of analysis, not a word corresponding to any separate event or process. Thus, if I devise a lesson in English grammar, it is difficult to identify the actual steps in which I "apply" my knowledge of educational psychology, or my knowledge of structural linguistics, or of logical analysis. Conscious attention to this kind of application would possibly inhibit me in the preparation of the lesson, but I believe I will produce a better lesson if I have a knowledge of certain aspects of educational psychology and of stuctural linguistics. For example, I

[11] Paul E. Meehl, *Clinical* versus *Statistical Prediction* (Minneapolis: University of Minnesota Press, 1954).

would begin in the lesson by informing the student what he is going to learn and why it is important; I would proceed to present simple, systematic variations in the material so that the student would perceive the basis for the concept he is to form; I would attempt to elicit responses from the student which would indicate his attainment of the concept; and I would be careful to arrange that he is informed of the correctness or incorrectness of his responses.

18.2 Focus on Educational Psychology

M. Wittrock

Wittrock's concern is to build an organized body of knowledge to aid us in controlling and understanding instruction. He differentiates between research and development and suggests that the contributions of both must be utilized to improve teaching. But he is even more concerned with the improvement of the methodology of conducting research and development, and he suggests five practices to effect this improvement. In the final analysis, he believes that research will contribute more to instruction than will development.

Research in educational psychology has not progressed far toward the development of an organized body of knowledge relevant to the understanding and the control of instruction and teaching. Infrequently have we designed our studies to build sequentially upon earlier findings or to produce useful knowledge about the cause and effect relations between instruction and individual differences, on the one hand, and the multiple outcomes of instruction and teaching, on the other hand. We

SOURCE. M. C. Wittrock, "Focus on Educational Psychology," *The Educational Psychologist*, IV, 7 (1967), pp. 17–20. Reprinted by permission of the author and *The Educational Psychologist.*

need to discuss ways to make the next fifty years of work build results sequentially into knowledge useful in instruction and teaching.

In this article, two ways to improve our research and developmental activities are suggested: (1) a liberal conceptualization of the field of educational psychology; and (2) increased emphasis on methodologically rigorous, theory-oriented research aimed at understanding *and* control of instruction and teaching.

Research or Development is one choice offered to educational psychologists concerned with using their time and resources to effect differences in what we know and do about education. The more immediate and tangible rewards of development, teaching, and dissemination are attracting many educational psychologists, so called "product-oriented" researchers, into writing instructional programs or into developing teaching apparatus. Both of these developmental activities are important for improving instruction. But they are aimed at control *without* understanding. With attention to theory and methodology, they could contribute much to the development of useful, transferable concepts in educational psychology.

While our developmental activities have usually emphasized control without understanding, our research on learning and teaching has often emphasized understanding without control. Our studies tend to be descriptive, correlational, but not manipulative or theory oriented. With a few notable exceptions, educational psychologists interested in learning, teaching, and instruction have depended upon other psychologists to do basic research on learning. Far too little rigorously controlled research in school settings aimed at fundamental understanding *and* the control of learning, instruction, and teaching has been performed by educational psychologists in the last 50 years. It is this error of omission which, in large part, has produced, as Cronbach describes it, such a small gap between what we know and what we do about teaching and instruction. If the field is to grow cumulatively as a science, we need a liberal definition of research and development appropriate for the study of educational psychology.

Both research and development contribute to improvements in classroom practices. We seem not to have realized that research and development have products of different natures. Instead, developers, e.g., product-oriented researchers, seem to have been misled into believing that if they were only patient long enough, surely basic research would produce instructional materials and teaching apparatus—products to the product researchers. But these types of products haven't been forthcoming from basic research. They won't be. Disappointed, the product researchers seem to have concluded there are no products to research. They have set about the construction of materials and apparatus, explicitly using principles from basic psychological research, e.g., reinforcement and contiguity, while at the same time claiming that no useful products come out of research on learning. Logically, this is an untenable position to maintain. On the other hand, the researchers seem to have felt that surely their clear-cut, statistically significant findings, even if they said little about control, would be applied, by others of course, to the ready solution of problems of classroom teaching.

Research and development each has its own distinctive functions and products. The fundamental issues involved in improving knowledge in educational psychology are not choices between research and development, or even between basic research and applied research. We need not make either/or choices such as these. Instead, the fundamental issues include (1) our conceptualization of educational psychology, and (2) our formal methods for learning and transferring results from our research and development activities. To improve knowledge about learning, teaching, and instruction, I believe we must change our archaic conceptualization of educational psychology: and we must introduce new methods into research and development studies to obtain both understanding *and* control.

First let us consider conceptualizations of educational psychology. It is time for us to conceive of educational psychology in a liberal, less restrictive sense to include activities ranging from basic research to dissemination.

Educational psychology goes beyond the archaic conceptualization that it is "the application of psychological principles to education." It is time for us to practice a liberal conceptualization of educational psychology as the scientific study of human behavior in educational settings. As scientists, we should attempt to describe, understand, predict, and control behavior in education. That is, educational psychology should invest most of its resources into its most important activity—basic research aimed at control and understanding of the problems and phenomena of instruction in schools. Research explicitly aimed at the production of useful knowledge is an activity defensible in its own right, with its own important *products*—functional relations, generalizations, and theories.

What uses does this conceptualization offer to educational psychologists? First, it makes us responsible not only for developmental work in applying research findings, but primarily and most importantly for basic research on understanding and controlling the phenomena and situations that comprise our subject matter. Educational psychologists should do more than collect and apply principles developed by other psychologists.

We should be free to use our mentalities in a variety of endeavors, especially in basic research.

Some readers may advance arguments against conducting fundamental research on the understanding and control of learning, teaching, and instruction. Common arguments are: (1) basic research is time-consuming and costly; (2) carefully controlled presentation of stimuli and recording of responses of individuals are not possible; (3) subjects are not readily accessible to us for long periods of time; (4) we do not have the methodological tools or the theories to design and analyze change in behavior as a function of instructional variables interacting with individual differences; (5) to improve learning, instruction, and teaching, one should do developmental work, e.g., write instructional materials and build apparatus, but not bother with basic research aimed at developing knowledge or generalizations, because research doesn't develop "products"; and (6) educational psychology is the application of psychological principles to educational problems, and as such it is not responsible for the development of an organized body of useful knowledge.

I believe these six arguments are no longer defensible. The first four arguments have lost much of their impact because of extramural support, advances in research equipment, improvements in relationships with many local school districts, and advances in knowledge about experimental designs and multivariate analyses. The fifth and sixth arguments are questioned throughout this article.

The second major point of this article relates to the methods of conducting research and developmental activities to contribute both to understanding and to control. Most of our basic research has been conducted with subjects and situations different from those found in schools. I strongly support laboratory research: but we do need to complement it with a new type of basic research—long-term, rigorously conducted, theory-oriented research with the subjects and problems common in school settings. Our developmental work usually does use the problems and the subjects of instruction in school; but unfortunately "cut-and-try" methodologies and crude data contribute little to the understanding and the control of phenomena of instruction and teaching.

To achieve the combined goals of understanding and control, I suggest that in our methodology we emphasize the following practices: (1) use as laboratories for research those situations and subjects which sample the phenomena we strive to study; (2) use sophisticated apparatus to control carefully the presentation of stimuli and the recording of responses; (3) use designs and analyses that will evidence interactions among treatments and groups of individuals; (4) in "true experiments," obtain data about treatments which differ from one another conceptually; and (5) test theoretical approaches to instruction. We can use sophisticated designs, analyses, and apparatus to obtain results which will transfer to related events, situations, and phenomena. We can also insure that the tremendous financial resources and talent now committed to developmental activities in educational psychology are used in sound methodological approaches appropriate for producing an organized body of useful knowledge.

The two suggestions of this paper lead us to ask important questions about how we choose to organize and use our time and resources to learn the most we can from them. To the researcher, the suggestions imply the following type of question about transfer and savings: To what extent will my work advance knowledge about human behavior, including individual differences, useful in the understanding and control of significant problems of educational psychology? To the developer of instructional materials, a related type of question about transfer and savings is implied: As a result of writing the last program, to what extent have I, as a scientist, provided the means to learn how to write other, related programs?

In my opinion, the conduct of basic research, an activity largely avoided by educational psychologists to date, offers far greater potential for contributing to educational psychology, teaching, and instruction than does developmental work. Most of our time, talent, and other resources should be committed to research, especially basic research.

Whether we choose to do research or development, we should be liberal enough in our thinking to value the different contributions of basic research, applied research, and development to educational psychology. Development has its marketable products. Basic research has its useful products, too: functional relations, rules, generalizations—maybe even a good theory. If knowledge about teaching, learning, and instruction is to develop systematically, we should design and rigorously control our research and development to interact with each other and to contribute both to understanding and control of psychological phenomena in education.

18.3 The Educational Psychology of American Teachers

N. L. Gage

Gage focuses attention directly on the content matter of educational psychology as it is taught in the colleges for the purposes of teacher preparation. In substance, he contends that educational psychology should focus as much on the process of teaching as it does on the process of learning.

Let me turn now to the ways in which I would like to see the course change so as to provide more adequately the kind of help that prospective teachers have a right to expect from educational psychology. My first point is that educational psychology has not had enough to say about teaching. Our courses are full of ideas about how learners learn, grow, and mature; about how we should measure our learners' achievements, abilities, interests and adjustments; about factors affecting the mental health of learners. But when it comes to teaching, educational psychologists have had too little to say. Our courses have implied to the student, "Wait until you get to your methods course; then you will be told how to teach."

SOURCE. N. L. Gage, "The Educational Psychology of American Teachers." In R. H. Beck, Ed., *Society and the Schools: Challenge to Education and Social Work.* New York: National Association of Social Workers, 1965, pp. 86–103. Reprinted by permission of the author.

I do not want to belittle the importance of knowing about learners and learning. But the need for discourse on teaching stems from the insufficiency in principle of theories of learning and understanding of the learner. Changes in education must depend in large part upon what the teacher does. That is, changes in how learners go about their business of learning will occur in response to changes in the behavior of their teachers. Much of our knowledge about learning can be put into practice in the first instance only by teachers. Practical applications have not been gleaned sufficiently from the study of learning because that study has not been translated into specific implications for the behavior of teachers. In training teachers, we often seem to rely on mere inference from knowledge about learning to the practice of teaching. But much of what teachers must know about teaching does not directly follow from a knowledge of the learning process; it must be acquired explicitly rather than by inference. Farmers need to know more than how plants grow. Mechanics need to know more than how a machine works. Physicians need to know more than how the body functions. Similarly, teachers need to know more than how a pupil learns. Teachers must know how to manipulate the independent variables, especially their own behaviors, that influence learning. To explain, control, and improve the teaching act requires a science and technology of teaching in its own right.

It seems to me that this kind of orientation is well served by the *Handbook of Research on Teaching*. Research on teaching should give educational psychologists more to say about teaching by increasing our knowledge and understanding of the teaching process, of the ways in which teachers behave, and the causes and effects of different kinds of teacher behavior.

At this point, then, I see a need for more content about the theory and practice of teaching in our educational psychologies. One way to conceive of such content is to say that every major heading that we now apply to learners ought to be turned around, or stood on its head, and applied to teachers. Hence, our textbooks would be concerned with the motivations of teachers, with the perceptions and cognitions of teachers, with the actions and behaviors of teachers, and with the knowledge of results, or rewards and punishments, that teachers can acquire. If we have a chapter on transfer as it applies to the learners in our classrooms, we ought perhaps to have a chapter on transfer as it applies to the work of the teacher—his transfer of his training to his practice in the classroom. If we have a treatment of the growth and development of pupils, perhaps we ought to have one on the growth and development of teachers. In general, chapters on the learning behavior of students ought to be parallelled by treatments of the teaching behavior of teachers.

My second point deals with the sources of much of the content of educational psychology. Some of our textbooks seem to be oriented toward the mental hygiene movement, others toward the child study movement, others toward the psychology of individual differences, and others seem to draw their main sustenance from theory and research on learning. None of the books in educational psychology, so far as I know, has yet drawn heavily enough on the vast practical literature to be found in the journals and books that deal with teaching methods in the various grade levels and subject matter fields. A huge gap seems to exist between educational psychologists and the specialists in teaching methods in our colleges for teacher education. The teaching methodologists have accumulated a storehouse of practical wisdom and lore on how to teach, say, the number of facts, the skills of writing, the theory of chemical bonds, and the meaning of the Bill of Rights. So far as I know, educational psychologists have not yet fed upon this storehouse. And I am optimistic about what would happen if the ideas of the teaching methods people were processed through the cognitive structures of the educational psychologists.

My third point is that the content of our educational psychologies should be restricted much more to the research and literature on classroom learning and teaching and much less to that which deals with learning and development outside the school, in the neighborhood, in human laboratory situations, or in animal laboratories. One effective way to reduce the overlap between educational psychology and general psychology, and to provide greater assurance of the relevance of educational psychology to classroom teaching, would be to see how far one could go in excluding everything from the course that did not deal explicitly with teachers and learners in classrooms. Then the adults that would be discussed would be adults in the role of classroom teachers—not parents, not group leaders, not psychologists, but teachers. And children would be discussed in their role as pupils in classrooms—not sons and daughters, not residents of a neighborhood, not members of a youth group, not denizens of a summer camp, but pupils. Let us see how far we can go without having to extrapolate from nonclassroom situations and research into the classroom. This orientation would mean, for example, that we would deal with teachers who suffer all the limitations of time and opportunity that real teachers must live with. We would not then discuss the high school teacher's role as if he had the time and opportunity to do sociometric research, act as a clinical psychologist, or provide private tutoring, as if he had only a few pupils all day, instead of about 100 different students every day for fifty minutes only. It might also mean that we should deal with such altogether neglected matters as classroom lecturing, or making of oral explanations, the conduct of classroom discussions, the proper organization of classroom discourse—activities which are actually performed by most teachers but are almost altogether neglected in our educational psychologies.

As a corollary of this approach we would pay much greater attention to differentiating the discussion in educational psychologies according to the subject matter and grade level of the teacher being addressed. Just as Dr. Conant makes such distinctions in finding present-day educational psychology much more suitable for elementary school teachers than for those in secondary schools, so should educational psychologists differentiate according to whether they are addressing a teacher of English, or science, or social studies. We should not imply that all these kinds of teachers have the same kinds of problems and should handle them in the same way. Such differentiation cannot be carried very far, of course, within the scope of a single book or course. But it ought not to be neglected so completely as is now the case.

Summary

My dicta as to change were that the course ought to be (1) as much concerned with teaching and the teacher as with learning and the learner, (2) drawn much more from the literature on teaching methods, (3) restricted much more to adults and children in their classroom roles rather than their roles in the family, neighborhood, or psychological laboratory, (4) differentiated more according to grade level and subject matter.

Selected Readings

Ausubel, D. P. Is there a discipline of educational psychology? *Educational Psychologist,* 1968, **5**, 1–9.

Ausubel, D. P., and Robinson, F. G. *School learning: an introduction to educational psychology.* New York: Holt, Rinehart and Winston, Inc., 1969, Chapt. 1.

Bernard, H. W. *Psychology of learning* (2nd ed.). New York: McGraw-Hill Book Co., 1965, Chap. 1.

Biehler, R. F. *Psychology applied to the art of teaching.* Boston: Houghton Mifflin Co., 1971, Chap. 1.

Bigge, M. L., and Hunt, M. P. *Psychological foundations of education.* New York: Harper and Row, 1968, epilogue.

Blair, G. M., Jones, R. S., and Simpson, R. H. *Educational psychology* (3rd ed.). New York: Macmillan Co., 1968, Chap. 1.

Cronbach, L. J. *Educational psychology* (2nd ed.). New York: Harcourt, Brace & World, Inc., 1963, Chap. 1.

DeCecco, J. P. *The psychology of learning and instruction: educational psychology.* Englewood Cliffs, New Jersey: Prentice-Hall, Inc., 1968, Chap. 16.

DiVesta, F. J., and Thompson, G. G. *Educational psychology: instruction and behavioral change.* New York: Appleton-Century-Crofts, Meredith Corporation, 1970, Chaps. 1 and 2.

Edwards, A. J., and Scannell, D. P. *Educational psychology.* Scranton, Pa.: International Text Book Co., 1968, Introduction.

Eson, M. E. *Psychological foundations of education.* New York: Holt, Rinehart and Winston, Inc., 1964, Chap. 1.

Hill, W. F. *Does learning theory apply to education?* Unpublished paper.

Kolesnik, W. B. *Educational psychology* (2nd ed.). New York: McGraw-Hill Book Co., 1970, Chap. 1.

Lindgren, H. C. *Educational psychology in the classroom* (3rd ed.). New York: John Wiley & Sons, Inc., 1967, Chap. 1.

Mathis, B. C., Cotton, J. W., and Sechrest, L. *Psychological foundations of education.* New York: Academic Press, 1970, Chap. 1.

Mouly, G. J. *Psychology for effective teaching* (2nd ed.). New York: Holt, Rinehart and Winston, Inc., 1968, Chap. 1.

Sawrey, J. M., and Telford, C. W. *Educational psychology* (3rd ed.). Boston: Allyn and Bacon, Inc., 1968, Chap. 1.

Smith, L. M., and Hudgins, B. B. *Educational psychology.* New York: Alfred A. Knopf, 1970, Chap. 1.

Travers, J. F. *Fundamentals of educational psychology.* Scranton, Pa.: International Textbook Co., 1970, Chap. 1.

Watson, G. What psychology can we feel sure about? *Teachers College Record,* 1960, **61**, 253–57.

Weiss, T. M., Hoover, K. H., Belok, M., and Mills, D. F. *Psychological foundations of education.* Dubuque, Iowa: Wm. C. Brown Co., Pub., 1963, Chap. 1.

Cross-Reference Chart to Textbooks in Educational Psychology

Chapter Numbers	1	2	3	4	5	6	7	8	9	10	11	12	13	14	15	16	17	18
Ausubel (1968)				XIII	IX	XII XIV	VII	V XI	VI	X	II XV XVI	XI	V	III IV VIII	XVII	XVII		I
Ausubel & Robinson (1969)		XVIII	II	XV		X XI XIV XVI	XI	VII	VIII IX XIII	XII	III IV XVII			V VI	XIX			I
Bernard (1965)				XXI		VI XVII	XVIII	VIII XV	IX X XII XIII	XI	IV XI	XIX		III	XX	IX		I
Biehler (1971)		II		XI		V XV	V	III	IV X XII XIII	IX	VI	VIII XIII XIV	VIII	VII	XI	XII		I
Blair, Jones, & Simpson (1968)				XXI XXII		XI XIV	VI	II III IV	VI XVI XVII	VII	III XI	VIII XIII XV		X	XVII XIX			I
Cronbach (1963)		II	XIV		XII	XV	XII	IV	V VI VII VIII	VI	XI	XIII XVII	IX	X	XVI			I
DeCecco (1968)		I	II		XIII		XII	IV	III IV	V	IX X XI		VIII		VI XIV			
DiVesta & Thompson (1970)			VI	IV		VI VIII XX		III	V XV XIX	VII	XI XII XIII	VIII XIV XV XVI XVII		IX X	XVIII			I II
Edwards & Scannell (1968)							XII		II III IV	V VI VII	XIII	XIV		X XI	XVI XVII		XII	I
Eson (1964)			XVI			VII VIII XV	VII		II X XI		IV	VI	XII	III V	IX			I
Klausmeier & Goodwin (1966)		III	II	V		VI	XV		IV XIV	XII	VII VIII	X XI	IX	XIII	XVII			I
Kolesnik (1970)				II		VIII XV		III IV	V VI VII XVI	XIII	XI XII	XVII		IX X	XIV			I

Lindgren (1966)		VIII				V X XI XII	XII	III	II XIV		IX	VI IX			XIII XVI	I
Mathis, Cotton, & Sechrist (1970)				II		III XVI	IV	IX X	VIII XIII XIV XVII	XI XII	III VI	XIII	IX	III V	XV	I
McDonald (1965)		II	III			XIII	III	XII	XI	IV	V VI VII	VIII IX	X	XV XVI		I
Morse & Wingo (1969)	II	I VII		I	I VI VII IX XI	VIII	III	IV V X	X	VIII	VIII XII	VIII	XIII	XIV		
Mouly (1968)						XII	XII Appen- dix	V IX	IV X	III XII	IV IX XII XV XVIII	VII		XIV XVI		I
Sawrey & Telford (1968)						XVI	I	II	IX XIII XIV	VIII	IV	X		VI VII	XII XVII	I
Smith & Hudgins (1970)		X	X			VII IX	XV		VIII		XII XIV	XIV	XIII		II	
Sorenson (1964)				V			VIII	I III	II VI VII VIII	XIV		XI XII		XV XVI	II	
Stephens (1965)		I	I	XVI	X	I V XII	I V	II	XV	IV	VI VII	XIII XIV		VIII	III	
Strom (1969)				III		II III	IV		I VII		IV V	VII		IV	VI	
Travers, J. F. (1970)		II		II XI XV		II X	IX	III IV V VI	XI XIV	VII	VIII	IX XI XII		VII	XIII	I
Travers, R. M. W. (1967)						I III XII	XVI	IX	XV	VI	IV V XI	IV XIII XIV	IV XV	VIII X		
Wilson, Robeck, & Michael (1969)		I	XXI	XIX		IV XVII		VIII IX X XI	XII XIII XIV	III XVI	V VI	XV XVIII XX			XXII XXIII	

Author Index

Subject Index